Cardinal
Herbert Vaughan

HIS EMINENCE CARDINAL HERBERT VAUGHAN
Archbishop of Westminster

From a photo by Barraud which appeared in a Supplement to *The Tablet* to
commemorate Vaughan's death, on 27 June 1903

Cardinal
Herbert Vaughan

Archbishop of Westminster
Bishop of Salford
Founder of the Mill Hill Missionaries

ROBERT O'NEIL, M.H.M.

With a Foreword by
MAURICE McGILL, M.H.M.
Superior General, St Joseph's Missionary Society

Burns & Oates

A Crossroad Herder Book
The Crossroad Publishing Company
New York

First published in Great Britain 1995 by
BURNS & OATES
Wellwood, North Farm Road
Tunbridge Wells, Kent TN2 3DR

First published in the U.S.A. 1997 by
THE CROSSROAD PUBLISHING COMPANY
370 Lexington Avenue
New York, NY 10017

Reprinted (with revisions) 1997

ISBN 0 86012 262 X (UK)
ISBN 0-8245-1717-2 (USA)

Library of Congress Catalog Card Number: 97-67265

Typeset by Search Press Limited
Printed and bound by Biddles Limited, Guildford and King's Lynn

Contents

ILLUSTRATIONS

Frontispiece

    Cardinal Herbert Vaughan, Archbishop of Westminster

Between pages 248 and 249

1. Eliza Vaughan, 1810–53, Herbert Vaughan's mother
2. John Francis Vaughan, 1808–80, Herbert Vaughan's father
3. John Snead-Cox, 1855–1939, Vaughan's cousin and biographer
4. Cardinal Nicholas Wiseman, 1802–65, first archbishop of Westminster after the restoration of the hierarchy in 1850
5. Herbert Vaughan at St Edmund's, Ware, aged twenty-four
6. Vaughan receiving a letter of introduction for his missionary project from Cardinal Wiseman, 1863
7. Archbishop, later Cardinal Henry Edward Manning, 1808–92, in 1868
8. William George Ward, 1812–82
9. Austin Oates, Vaughan's secretary, 1859–1912
10. Canon Peter Benoit, 1820–92
11. Herbert Vaughan as rector of St Joseph's Missionary College, 1868
12. Canon James Moyes, 1851–1927
13. Wilfrid Ward, 1856–1915
14. Rt Revd Louis Casartelli, 1852–1925, fourth bishop of Salford
15. Revd John R. Slattery, 1851–1926
16. Alice Ingham, Mother Mary Francis, 1830–90
17. Madeleine-Marie Justine Dupont, Mother Mary of Jesus, 1851–1942
18. The Mill Hill chapter of 1884
19. John Francis Bentley, 1839–1902, architect of Westminster Cathedral
20. Bishop John Cuthbert Hedley, 1837–1915
21. Lady Mary Elizabeth Herbert of Lea, 1822–1911, at Wilton in 1902; with (inset) Lady Herbert, from a portrait at Mill Hill, made shortly after her marriage to Sidney Herbert in 1846
22. Cardinal Vaughan and the bishops of England and Wales, 1897

Sources: Front.: Westminster Diocesan Archives; 15: Josephite Archives; 21: The British Picture Library. All others: the author/Mill Hill Archives

Foreword

"We are hewn out of a mighty rock and the memory of those who have gone before inspires us to a sense of duty and unyielding courage in the face of all difficulties." These words of Fr Thomas McLaughlin, D.D., fifth superior general of St Joseph's Missionary Society (1947-61), used as a Foreword to *The Story of Courtfield* (the ancestral home of the Vaughan family) encapsulate the reasons for a new biography of Cardinal Vaughan. The immediate reason for the writing of this book was the acceptance by St Joseph's Missionary Society of candidates from the areas where the first members worked: India, Uganda, Kenya, Cameroon, the Philippines; along with their European and American confrères, there was need for them to be able to reflect on the life of the man whose vision they wish to share.

The list of Herbert Vaughan's achievements is formidable; the foundation of his life and work is summed up in his episcopal motto, *"Amare et servire"* (to love and to serve): conscious of the unbounded and unconditional love of God for him, he was drawn to serve others with similar individual, self-sacrificing and generous love. In tracing the life of this man of action from his home in Courtfield to his resting-place at Mill Hill, Fr Robert O'Neil has succeeded in conveying to the reader the restless energy, the demanding schedule, the deep faith and zeal that compelled him.

Fr O'Neil is well qualified to write on Herbert Vaughan. A native of Connecticut, Robert completed his studies at Mill Hill and was ordained in 1965. He then spent fifteen years as a missionary in English-speaking Cameroon, before going on to doctoral studies in History at the universities of Fordham and Columbia in his home country. In Cameroon he taught in secondary schools and ministered to the diverse peoples of the grassland hills and steamy valleys of the North-West Province.

In the 1991 Encyclical Letter *Redemptoris Missio*, Pope John Paul II writes, "I wish to invite the Church to renew her missionary commitment.... For missionary activity renews the Church, revitalizes faith and Christian identity, and offers fresh enthusiasm and new incentive" (no. 2). This is the biography of a man who worked tirelessly for the Church in England: in so doing, he never lost sight of the wider horizons—of a world awaiting the message of Christ. May his life be an inspiration for all of us in our work for the local and universal Church.

MAURICE MCGILL, M.H.M.
Superior General, St Joseph's Missionary Society
Mill Hill, September 1995

vii

ACKNOWLEDGMENTS

I have been a member of Herbert Vaughan's St Joseph's Missionary Society of Mill Hill for more than thirty years. In 1990 the general council of the society asked for a new biography of the Cardinal. At the time I had returned from working in Cameroon and was on a sabbatical at Gonzaga University in Spokane, Washington. Frs Hans Stampfer and William Tollan explained that the council wanted the membership, especially younger members and candidates, to know the founder better and thought that his story should be retold. Therefore the society has sponsored the writing of this book.

Many people have helped over the past five years. Some of them must be mentioned here. Fr Peter Logue of Mount St Bernard's Monastery in Leicester is a friend from the Cameroon mission who has never failed to support me with his honesty and cheerfulness. Fr Ian Dickie, the archivist of Westminster Diocese, has been an intelligent and enthusiastic colleague, host and friend. Mrs Emily Salzberg of New York City devoted many days of her 1995 summer holiday to editing the manuscript. Mrs Jane Gallichio of the Mill Hill office in Yonkers has read and corrected early manuscripts and cared for my correspondence throughout.

The archivist of Salford Diocese, Fr David Lannon, has been helpful at Oldham more than once. Fr Peter Hogan of the Josephites in Baltimore and Sister Mary of St Philip of the Carmelites at Notting Hill in London have helped in similar ways. A few have read and commented on sections of the manuscript. They are: John Olin, Richard Cunningham, Vincent Alan McClelland, and Sheridan Gilley.

Some others who have helped are: Fr John Ball, Sister Mary Joanna Callender, Mrs Elsie Allen, Mr John Cleary, Fr Jeremiah Doona, Fr Peter Dirven, Prof. David Hugh Farmer, Sister Moira Geary, Fr Noel Hanrahan, Fr Gerard Heuthorst, Fr Geoffrey Holt, SJ, Fr Michael Hurley, Fr Philip Jebb, OSB, Sr Judith, SVP, Fr John Klaver, Fr James Lloyd, the Sisters of St Mary's Abbey, Mrs Mary McInally, Fr William Mol, Fr Austin Monaghan, Fr Terence O'Farrell, Fr Henry Palhuber, Sister Mary Paul Reynolds, Mr Jonathan Spain, Mr Oliver Stoney, Fr Frederick Turner, SJ, Mr and Mrs Oliver Vaughan, Mrs Sarah Vaughan, Mr Michael Walsh, and Fr Almiro Werle. In Spain: Fr Valeriano Ordoñez, SJ, Prof. and Mrs Pedro Caldentey, Mr and Mrs Eduardo Sánchez Junco. In the United States: Sister Marguerita Smith, Sister Ann Curry, Mgr Francis Weber, Fr Richard Doheny, Fr Edmund Hayburn, Mr Charles Lamb and Fr Robert McNamara. I made use of the library resources at St Joseph's Seminary at Dunwoodie in the archdiocese of New York and am grateful for the privilege. For their kindness and hospitality: Brother Theodore Tolboom in New York and Brother Edmund Ladstatter in London; the Sisters of St Joseph of Peace in Nottingham and the Sisters of St Francis in Hastings-on-the-Hudson.

I am grateful to Mr Paul Burns, Editor of Burns & Oates, for his constructive comments during the months of work on a final manuscript.

ROBERT O'NEIL
Sept 4, 1995

Introduction

Erasmus wrote in his life of St Jerome: "Truth has its own power, matched by no artifice."[1] Herbert Vaughan's biographer and cousin, John Snead-Cox, aimed at this ideal in his 1910 study. He wanted to correct a general impression that Cardinal Herbert Vaughan was a hard, unsympathetic, and rather narrow-minded man, whose career had been rescued from mediocrity by a remarkable energy. In his preface he explained that he intended to give a more balanced view of Vaughan, and in doing so "to write an absolutely candid book, without reserves and without suppressions, describing the man as he was, in his strength and in his weakness, with his gifts and his limitations."[2]

Vaughan had won the affection and loyalty of men and women who knew him best. One was Snead-Cox, who had the opportunity to write a two-volume biography. Another was John Cuthbert Hedley, Bishop of Newport and Menevia, who, when speaking at Vaughan's funeral, responded to criticism that he had been harsh and uncharitable in religious controversy. But those "who really knew the man appreciated how foreign to his character was the least thought of unkindness." Some weeks later at the Vaughan family home he spoke of Vaughan's qualities of mind and heart, and urged: "Let his friends and the clergy of this country never forget him." In Salford, Bishop Louis Casartelli called him a "missionary in his Master's vineyard" who began as a missionary and ended as one. More than one admitted that Vaughan was scarcely popular, but those who knew him well spoke of being touched by his benevolence and what one referred to as his "transparent simplicity."

In writing this biography I have found a Herbert Vaughan who could be both grim and inspiring at the same time.

Summer 1887

On a summer evening in 1887, Herbert Vaughan was nearing the height of his public career when he visited his family home, at Courtfield near Ross-on-Wye, and went for a walk with a relative.

From across the Wye River valley a local farmer watched the two men stroll along the river bank on a path towards the Welsh-Bicknor church. The Wye River is about thirty yards across at that point and slowly forms a horse-shoe bend peninsula. Flat fields near the river meet a gradual slope up to a wooded

1

crest and Georgian manor house. "They must be guests at Courtfield Manor," he thought, and turned back to his work.

They continued walking for nearly an hour until they approached Symonds Yat. The river and its surroundings were more beautiful than they could remember. The taller of the two men was Herbert Alfred Vaughan. He was considered handsome, with blue eyes and grey thinning hair. His voice was strong, with what close friends considered a slight American accent that remained with him after three trips to the United States. He was by right the squire of the manor, a gentleman who, as eldest son, inherited the family estate. The lands were still extensive, though far from the estimated fifty thousand acres of the early eighteenth century.

The younger man was John Snead-Cox—Johnny to his family and friends—a journalist, editor of *The Tablet* and cousin of Herbert Vaughan.[3] More than twenty years later he was to become Vaughan's biographer.

Herbert Vaughan was fifty-five years old on that beautiful evening in 1887. The area of Courtfield where they strolled, then part of Herefordshire, had long been associated with Monmouth and what was referred to as the Welsh Marches, the borderlands between England and Celtic Wales. However, it was no longer Vaughan's home. On the death of his father, Colonel John Francis Vaughan, in 1880, Herbert handed over his inheritance to a younger brother, Francis.

In his youth Herbert had chosen the Catholic priesthood instead of a possible army commission and the life of a country gentleman for which his father had hoped. In 1866 he had founded a missionary society, which by 1887 had members working in the United States, India, Borneo and New Zealand. In 1872 he was consecrated bishop of Salford.

During his years in Lancashire in England's north-west, he was to Protestants "Herbert Salford," the very incarnation of "Romish Sacerdotalism" for what they considered his constant use of the pomp and splendour of a Roman bishop's office.[4] Even some of his fellow Catholics did not like him for the cold manner in which he related to others. For this he was often labelled as being proud and arrogant. He admitted that he was often impatient and tactless in dealing with others. He was not subtle and often chose to be direct and straightforward rather than diplomatic. His unpopular—some considered narrow-minded—positions on issues such as Irish Home Rule and the idea of corporate reunion with the Church of England are well known, as were his disagreements with Cardinal Manning's views on temperance and social radicalism.

In 1887 he still had fifteen years to live, including ten as cardinal archbishop of Westminster. They were to be years filled with projects and controversy.

Despite his appearance, Herbert Vaughan lived a life of great austerity.

Although he was unpopular as a public figure with others both inside and outside his Church, he had many devoted friends and supporters. At Salford he chose to live in an apartment attached to St Bede's Commercial College, opposite Alexandra Park. When he was with the staff and students of St Bede's, some recognized in him, contrary to the impression he made, great benevolence and transparent simplicity.

On his death in 1903 one newspaper commented that although Vaughan was not as gifted as his predecessor Manning as a leader of men, "it may be doubted whether, in the less brilliant but eminently useful capacity for organization, his work has been surpassed by any of his predecessors."[5]

Vaughan was a single-minded and relentless worker who was fortified by an extraordinary energy and faith. He was also known for his disarming sincerity, romanticism and a detachment from personal gain.[6]

Evangelization, both overseas and at home in Engand and Wales, was a key idea for Vaughan. In 1879 he wrote an article titled "The Evangelization of Africa." He asked: "Where, then, is the Catholic who refuses light and help to these millions of his brethren? How long shall we remain deaf, stone-deaf, to their claim on our souls? The God who made us dependent upon those who preached the Gospel of salvation to our souls has made them dependent upon us." His great work for the evangelization of the world is St Joseph's Missionary Society.

At home—one historian of Salford diocese said he ran Salford like a small missionary diocese—he was always searching for ways in which to evangelize.[6] His mission was the conversion of England. That was his motive, for example, in using the press. He owned *The Tablet* and later the *Dublin Review*. He also supported James Britten when he restarted the Catholic Truth Society. At Westminster he began the Catholic Missionary Society.

He was bishop of Salford from 1872 to 1892. While at Salford he opened many new parishes, founded St Bede's College—where he lived and dined with the students and staff for twelve years—and started the Rescue Society, recruiting religious communities and more than two thousand volunteers.

In 1892 he was chosen to succeed Cardinal Manning. Despite disagreements over issues such as temperance, and, in Manning's later years, the Cardinal's social concerns, they remained friends. All the years that Manning was at Westminster, Vaughan had a small room at Archbishop's House and was near him, saying Mass, when he died.

In Vaughan's eleven years at Westminster he built Westminster Cathedral, started the Crusade of Rescue, the Catholic Social Guild, the Ladies of Charity, among other achievements. He was also a great friend and supporter of religious communities in the diocese. One group that still remembers his kindness is the Carmelite community of Notting Hill.

He was involved in controversy: over Irish Home Rule, voluntary schools and the Education Bills, his views of the papacy, the questioning of the

Church by intellectuals, and so on. Vaughan had a habit of saying the wrong thing, forgetting names and faces, and was often cold, aggressive and impulsive, on first meeting. Some thought he was a zealous but blundering romantic, and one called him a holy villain. He never made many friends in his youth during the controversies between Wiseman and Manning against the Westminster Chapter and many Old Catholics. Nor did he win friends with his abrasive style during the debates over papal infallibility in *The Tablet*.

But he had many who loved him and recognized a person with a deep spiritual life who was truly humble despite the "swaggering ostentation" which others, who did not know him well, sometimes complained of. His whole life was dedicated to the gospel and the Roman Catholic Church. Cardinal Manning once told him to relax and do some light reading, for he was too grim and only came alive when speaking of building material or similar things. But Herbert Vaughan was not a man of amusements and light reading. He was relentless and rigorous with himself, and often with those around him.

Those who wish to learn more of Vaughan's motivation and ideals can turn to two books published after his death in 1903.[7] In his final months he completed a series of conferences that became a book titled *The Young Priest*. The source of much of the material can be found in the many pastorals he wrote in his years at Salford and Westminster. He felt he was, as a bishop, a debtor to "Christ for Whom he acts" and to the "priests he has ordained." He wished to assist them to be apostolic men and he dedicated the book to all the missionaries he had ordained and "sent forth for a life into the midst of the heathen populations of the world." He also wrote for those he had ordained "*ad titulum missionis*," an oath taken binding the priest to serve on the English Mission, to work for the conversion of England. One reviewer thought the book had a special meaning since it came "from the deathbed of a venerable and wise guide of the clergy."

The other book, one he translated from the Italian, is *Humility of Heart* by Cajetan da Bergamo. In the Introduction Herbert Vaughan writes: "I have the strongest possible conviction that our Lord desires to be served, especially in a country like England, where we are 'the little flock,' by a great development of religious activity among the laity.... But I am equally convinced that unless these new workers are formed on the humility of heart which our Lord told all of us to learn of Him they and their overtures will be rejected by God and man."

One of his last messages was a note to the students of a small missionary seminary near Liverpool. He encouraged them to have a devotion to the Holy Will of God, and that they should not look for a long life or an easy life but rather for a "long life and a hard working life."

There is an effigy of Herbert Vaughan in a chantry of Westminster Cathedral, but he is buried elsewhere, at his missionary college in Mill Hill.

Vaughan's achievements on behalf of the newly restored Roman Catholic hierarchy in England and the revival of the Roman Catholic community were partly due to the application of an extraordinary personal energy. The practical skills of organizing and fund-raising were for all to see. His goodness was not always clearly, nor easily, seen or appreciated. But in his spiritual life Vaughan found his greatest resource. He had an awareness of a spiritual world that was more real to him than the material. For him to die was like going into the next room. However, on his death-bed, his view of the world was tested. He was attacked and tormented by the thought, a whisper that his faith were but a dream, and all its truths pious imaginings, that there was no God, no hereafter.[8]

There was also a sadness about Herbert Vaughan. To understand his melancholy and an attitude towards death and suffering that one friend thought was "chilling," one must look to his memories of a happy childhood and an affectionate mother who died young. Vaughan's thoughts often dwelled on the passing away of all things. They were reinforced by the sudden death of his mother in January 1853. From that time onward he saw nothing else of value for him in life but "to work for God and his glory." The emptiness and restlessness he experienced at home the summer after his mother's death confirmed his decision to choose, not the inheritance and family estates, but the Catholic priesthood, and perhaps the life of a foreign missionary.

The two men began to walk back towards the manor, continuing a light conversation about the Church, politics and Bishop Vaughan's projects at Salford. Fish broke the surface of river pools and wild birds were everywhere. Rabbits ran for safety and the calls of pheasant carried across the fields. They came to a gate and for a few moments Herbert Vaughan leaned against it, taking in the beauty of the surroundings. Breaking the silence, John Snead-Cox remarked to his cousin that returning to the home where he had played as a boy must be a pleasure. He was surprised by the sharpness of Vaughan's reply: "Why should it be a pleasure to come here? The whole place is peopled with the dead; there is a ghost at every turn; it is like coming back to a land of tombs, every field, every lane, every tree reminds me of those who have gone before." He was expressing the feelings experienced thirty-four years earlier. They were full of sadness, and yet in the pain of disappointment and loss was something of the driving force of his adult life.

They resumed their walk. Herbert Vaughan, half smiling at the sudden harshness of his reply, began to speak of his childhood but soon became quiet and they passed the rest of the way in total silence. The next morning the two cousins left for London by train from Ross Station.

Notes

1. James Brady and John Olin, editors, *The Collected Works of Erasmus*, 61, Toronto, Toronto University Press, 1992, p.23.

2. John Snead-Cox, *The Life of Cardinal Vaughan*, London, Burns & Oates, 1911, 2 volumes, Preface.

3. John George Snead-Cox was born in 1855. He was the son of Colonel Richard Snead-Cox, who was High Sheriff for Hereford in 1858, and Mary Theresa, daughter of George Weld and a niece of Cardinal Weld. He was related to Herbert Vaughan through his mother. He studied at Stonyhurst and then law at the Inner Circle. He turned to journalism and began writing for *The Tablet*—the weekly owned by Vaughan, assisting G. E. Rankin in editing. He became editor in 1884 and remained in that position for thirty-six years. In 1891 he married Mary, the daughter of George Porteous of New Orleans in the United States and became the father of four sons. See: *The Tablet*, 16 April 1920, p.480; *The Tablet*, 6 January 1940, pp.20-1. Michael Walsh, *The Tablet, 1840-1990*, London, 1990, p.20. He was "Johnny Cox" in family correspondence. See: Vaughan Family Archives (VFA). The stroll along the Wye is remembered by Snead-Cox in his biography, 1, pp.21-23.

4. VFA. Scrapbooks.

5. *ibid*.

6. W. S. Lilly, "Cardinal Vaughan," *Nineteenth Century*, August 1910, p.284.

7. Herbert, Cardinal Vaughan, *The Young Priest*, Burns & Oates, London, 1904; Cajetan Mary da Bergamo, *Humility of Heart*, translated with an introduction by Herbert Cardinal Vaughan, TAN, Rockford, 1978.

8. Snead-Cox, 2, p.484.

PART ONE

ANTECEDENTS

CHAPTER I

Courtfield and the Vaughan Family

In 1995 the manor at Courtfield and some of its former estate lands were owned by the missionary society Herbert Vaughan founded at Mill Hill in London in 1866. Direct descendants of the Vaughans live close by and continue to own most of the estate property while dividing their time between Herefordshire and London homes. Game is still plentiful and the views of the river are as lovely as they were in the nineteenth century.[1] But today the silence can be broken by heavy lorries passing between Monmouth, Ross and Gloucester on the road across the valley, or the sudden roar of the jet engines of RAF fighter aircraft practising low-level approaches to targets miles out to sea.

In the early 1980s, Thomas Francis Vaughan, a great-grand-nephew of Herbert Alfred Vaughan, walked to the London offices of "Juliana Discotheques," an international entertainment business he and two of his brothers were associated with. Nearly all his forbears, he thought, "had turned to the music of a rather different calling."[2] As he passed Westminster Cathedral, built by his ancestor Herbert Vaughan, it became for him "an awesome reminder of the zeal with which many earlier members of the family had thrown themselves body and soul into the calling of the Roman Catholic church."[3]

More than 130 years earlier, one of those zealous members, Thomas' great-great-grandfather, the father of Herbert, was championing both Church and pope at a Monmouthshire County meeting at Usk. The high sheriff, chief executive of the Crown, was chairman. John Vaughan stood and addressed the meeting at a time when there was much public agitation about the restoration of Roman Catholic dioceses in England—the "hot days of papal aggression:"[4] "I am happy and proud to take my stand today by my friend Mr. Herbert, of Llanarth. We belong to two of the few Roman Catholic families in this neighbourhood who have survived 300 years of persecution." During the introduction the meeting broke into shouts of "claptrap" and "nonsense," and every other sentence was greeted with "yells, hooting and confusion." In spite of the noisy reception, Colonel John Vaughan stood his ground and completed the speech, according to the report, in "good humour and amicably."[5]

In 1850 John Francis Vaughan and his wife Louisa Elizabeth Rolls were the parents of twelve children and owners of Courtfield Manor and its estate. Their home was six miles from Ross, on the Welsh-Bicknor peninsula formed by a horse-shoe bend of the Wye River in the southwest corner of Hereford-shire. The parish of Welsh-Bicknor had been part of Monmouthshire until it was transferred to Herefordshire in 1845.[6]

A History of Courtfield

Courtfield was originally called Greenfield until Harry of Monmouth, the future Henry V—"remembered and revered in this part of the country as our great national hero"—was nursed there. After his birth at Monmouth on 9 August 1387 he was brought to the manor.[7] His father, Henry IV, at that time Earl of Hereford, Lancaster and Derby, learned of his son's birth while crossing the Wye at the Goodrich ferry on his return to Monmouth. The child "being of a weak and sickly habit"[8] was brought to the manor then owned by John Montague and his wife Margaret. The lady who nursed the infant Prince Harry was Joan Vaughan.[9]

The manor, from that time called Courtfield, remained in the possession of the Montague family—except for a period when it was confiscated by the government—until it was forfeited for high treason in 1539, when Margaret, daughter of the Duke of Clarence and wife of Sir Richard Pole, was executed. In 1540 it was leased to George Baynham, then to Thomas Reve and George Cotton, and finally sold for £800 to John Gwillym. Gwillym was the father of Sybil, who married James Vaughan from Llanrothal-Veibronavel. James was the eldest son of Thomas and Anne Vaughan, "a family of ancient Welsh lineage."[10] Their eldest son John was born in 1575 and he inherited Courtfield. The Vaughans remained at Courtfield from that time.

The estate was not limited to the immediate surroundings. In later years it included properties on both sides of the Welsh border, and from its begin-nings there were holdings in Ruardean and Gloucester. It became difficult to assess the acreage, but in the early eighteenth century there were thousands of acres.[11]

In 1799, the mayor of Monmouth described the manor as "running to disorder" but still retaining the "remains of ancient grandeur." When he visited, the approach to the old house was along what is now a back road and the entrance was at the rear of the present manor. The mayor thought that the interior was a disappointment. Part of the manor had been rented to a farm tenant with ten children. One of the rooms was set aside as a chapel where Mass was offered regularly each month; neighbouring Catholics were free to attend.

The mayor visited Courtfield again and found that part of the old manor had been taken down and on its site a very handsome mansion, "compatible with the comforts of modern life," had been erected. It commanded a prominent place on a slope falling to the edge of the Wye. William Vaughan erected the new house in 1805. His architect, Mr Maddox of Monmouth, planned the house in the pseudo-classical style of the later Georgian era. The entrance was changed and a new carriage road made through the deer park, destroying the old gardens. This was the manor house familiar to Herbert Vaughan.[12]

The approach to Courtfield is from the small village of Goodrich; in Goodrich there is a twelfth-century border castle. The approach is by a little winding road on the left flank of Coppit Hill. The first turn gives a beautiful view of Kerne bridge, built in 1845. On the Courtfield side of the bridge is the ruin of Franeford Augustinian priory, founded in 1346 at a time when Goodrich castle was an important fortress, and a ford existed on the river.[13]

The Vaughan Family

The Vaughan family is a branch of the Herbert clan. The surname "Vaughan" is an anglicization of "Fychan," a mutation of "bychan," or little.[14] It is used in Welsh genealogies for a son who had the same Christian name as his father. In Herbert Vaughan's family it refers to the younger of two brothers. They were the sons of Howel ap Thomas ap Gwillym of Perthir in Rockfield, Monmouthshire, who was in turn the fourth son of Gwillym ap Jenkin, lord of Wern Ddn near Abergavenny in the middle of the fourteenth century. The Vaughans of Courtfield are one of the families of the Welsh border who maintained the old faith and loyalty to Rome. Their record of fines, imprisonment and double land-tax for their fidelity to the old faith is a remarkable one.[15]

The Vaughans were also part of a much larger distinctive group of British families, many of ancient lineage, who suffered for their belief during the centuries following the Reformation. On account of their religion they tended to intermarry, and to become almost like one extended family.[16]

For at least two centuries members of the Vaughan family featured regularly in the list of recusants, popish malignants—supporters of Charles I— and convicts. Courtfield, by its situation in the remote parish of Welsh-Bicknor, became a favourite hiding place for priests who were known to be seeking sanctuary in the woods and quarries and disused kilns on the estate. The priests were cared for by the Vaughans at risk to themselves.

The Vaughans were often helped by neighbours and friends, who were not necessarily Catholics, who leased their land and acted on their behalf. Without the help of Protestant neighbours they could not have survived at all.[17]

Monmouthshire, and the area of Courtfield, were regarded early in the Reformation as a centre of recusancy, that is, of people who refused to attend the newly established Church of England, or submit to its authority, or comply with its regulations. In 1609 it was stated that few cases arise in the shire which do not involve a "question between protestant and recusant."[18]

Monmouthshire was also first in the land with the number of convicted recusant householders: 117 per 1000.[19] In the opinion of solicitor and Monmouthshire archivist, John Hobson Matthews, the north-eastern half of the shire was "remarkable for the fidelity with which its inhabitants clung to the Catholic Church throughout the penal times." The Protestant movements of the late eighteenth and early nineteenth centuries "left almost untouched the Cambro-British or Silurian population of Gwent and the Celtic part of Herefordshire."[20]

For a greater part of the seventeenth century, the headquarters of the Jesuits at Cwm, in the parish of Llanrothal, was a rallying point for persecuted Catholics of the South Wales missions. Persecution under the Penal Laws had failed to weaken the recusant families who strengthened their position by intermarriage with other Catholic families and remained opposed to the established Church. They were part of civil war and resistance until in the late eighteenth century when the administration of acts against Catholics was relaxed.[21]

In the Vaughan family archives at Courtfield there is a record of the contributions made by the family to support the old faith during Penal days.[22] The earliest recorded act of resistance by the Vaughan family took place not at Courtfield but in Hereford in 1605, when a number of people were prosecuted for hearing Mass at the Darren on the Herefordshire slope of the Monnow valley.[23] The parish church of Llanrothal, near the Vaughan's Hereford home, was, according to tradition, the last church in that part of the country where Mass was offered after the Reformation began. A branch of the family, as we have seen, moved to Courtfield with the marriage of James Vaughan and Sybil Gwillym. The second son of this marriage, William of Clifford, married Jane Clarke of Wellington in Hereford and inherited the Welsh-Bicknor manor of Courtfield in 1577.[24]

John, the son of William and Jane Vaughan, became executor of the family estates on his father's death in 1601. He is often referred to as the first Vaughan of Courtfield, probably because he was the first to settle at the manor. In state papers and recusant rolls he is called "a royalist and popish recusant," that is, loyal to the monarchy of Charles and the Church of Rome. For his refusal to submit to the English government he was forced to sell a large portion of his estate to satisfy fines imposed by the government.

In 1639, John and Jane's son, Richard, succeeded his father. Richard Vaughan married twice, first to a Wigmore of Lucton,[25] whose family were recusants like the Vaughans, and then Agatha Berington of Little Malvern Court, Worcestershire. The marriages linked the Vaughans with two other families loyal to the old faith. Richard inherited Courtfield at the age of thirty-eight and held it until his death at ninety-seven in 1697.

Richard Vaughan's home provided hospitality for priests and was a rallying point for Catholics. Therefore the estate was targeted by agents on the lookout for hidden priests and "mass stuff." On one occasion a mob of "priest finders" broke into the house at night, tied up Richard, and plundered the manor when they did not find the Jesuit, Fr James Richardson.[26]

Despite the severity of the laws, Richard Vaughan was not reduced to poverty. Trustees who were reliable Protestant friends and relatives helped him to survive. The names of Protestants frequently appear in papers connected with estate transactions. Among the leases of property during Richard's lifetime there is frequent mention of a secret proviso that the property be held only for the use and benefit of the grantor.

In the 1640s, during the civil war in Herefordshire, Richard Vaughan took up arms on behalf of Charles II. Two Vaughans are listed as being at Goodrich Castle when it surrendered to Colonel Birch on 31 July 1646.[27]

Richard's son John became the third squire of Courtfield in 1697. In 1721 he also inherited estates at Ruardean, in Gloucestershire, and Clyro, in Radnorshire. John was a Royalist and refused to take the Oath of Allegiance to George I in 1715. In 1717 his name appears on a list of convicted popish recusants.

Richard and William, two of John's sons of a second marriage in 1705 to a relative, Elizabeth Jones—of the Herbert family—daughter of Philip Jones of Llanarth Court, Monmouthshire, became "the most romantic members of this quixotic family."[28] They were both Jacobites who supported the Stuart cause. Richard—born about 1708— became involved with the Stuarts and made frequent journeys between Madrid, Rome, and Paris, where his brother William—born about 1716—joined him prior to the rebellion of 1745. The uprising aimed at regaining the throne for the Stuarts and Prince Charles Edward.

There is a Vaughan tradition that the Fords of Munster, exiled to Spain from Ireland after the Battle of the Boyne in 1690, had been well known to the family. In each generation at least one of the Vaughan sons stayed with the Fords in Spain. One of them, Richard, visited the home of General Fuord (Ford) in 1736 and fell in love with his daughter, Doña Francisca Fuord y Magueire (Maguire). They married and went to stay at Courtfield. The marriage at first alarmed Richard's parents because of its connection with one of the exiled "wild geese" families of Ireland. Their stay at Courtfield was brief, and, in 1737, they returned to Spain.

In 1745 Richard and William joined the army of Charles, Prince of Wales, after the prince had landed in Scotland. William left Monmouthshire for the north with David Morgan—who was later executed for high treason on 30 July 1746—and joined Prince Charles' army at Preston on 27 November 1845. He was first attached to the prince's life-guards but later served as a Lieutenant-Colonel in the Manchester Regiment. Richard joined the Duke of Perth's division. With other Jacobites in the cause of Charles Edward Stuart, they were defeated at Culloden in 1745. The two Vaughans followed Charles into exile in Spain, were outlawed at home, and their property seized. In 1847 they were expressly excluded from a general pardon.[29]

Both made their home in Madrid and joined the armies of the king of Spain. William served in the Hibernia regiment for twenty-nine years. He became a brigadier in December 1773 and on 26 October 1777 he was promoted to major-general. In 1788 he joined an expedition at Cadiz bound for Argentina to help the Spanish viceroy prevent the Portuguese from invading the country and taking Buenos Aires. He is last mentioned in records as appointed to serve under Don Vitoria de Navia. It is thought that William died on the expedition to Buenos Aires. Richard, Herbert Vaughan's great-great-grandfather, died and was buried at Barcelona in 1795.[30]

Richard's only surviving son, also named William, was born on 23 September 1738. At a young age he returned from Spain and married Frances Turner of Hampstead in 1767. He never saw his mother, sister and Spain again.[31] His uncle, John, had not been involved in the rebellion and was still living at Courtfield on his return. William took possession of Courtfield as heir to his uncle but he lived mostly at Cornwall House on Monnow St in Monmouth. Most of the Courtfield estate was rented to a farmer, John Jackson. William Vaughan occupied part of the manor. John Jackson farmed much of the land and was church warden of the Welsh-Bicknor Protestant church.

William Michael Vaughan and Theresa Weld

The first child of William and Frances Vaughan was a girl, Frances, who was sent to Louvain, Belgium, for her education in about 1783.[32] Their only son, William Michael, was born on 25 September 1781. He was fifteen years old when his father died suddenly in 1796. William Michael Vaughan was the grandfather of Herbert Alfred Vaughan.

The under-age William Michael Vaughan was entrusted to the care of Charles Bodenham of Rotherwas and John Jones of Llanarth Court. He was educated at Gloucester by the Revd M. R. Greenway. When he inherited Courtfield he began to restore the manor and estates which had fallen into serious disrepair—mentioned in Mayor Heath's observations made during a 1797 visit.

William built a late Georgian-style house which is the front section of the present manor and has a southern view overlooking the river Wye on the site of the original gardens. He began building soon after his marriage to Theresa Maria Weld, daughter of Thomas Weld of Lulworth Castle, Dorset, and a sister of Thomas, later Cardinal, Weld.[33]

William and Theresa Vaughan had eight children—five sons and three daughters—of whom five chose religious vocations; two daughters became nuns and three sons were ordained priests. Both the Vaughans and the Welds were families known for their religious conviction and zeal. The atmosphere of their upbringing, the emotional religiosity of the age and the almost mystical veneration of their mother, Theresa, may have contributed to many of the children going "into the church."[34]

John Francis was their only son to marry. A daughter, Teresa, married Thomas Weld-Blundell of Ince, Lancashire, in 1839.[35] Of the other sons, William became Bishop of Plymouth, Richard a Jesuit, and Edmund a Redemptorist. The daughters, Frances and Mary, became Visitation nuns.

The return of William to Courtfield and the rebuilding of the manor by his son William Michael became possible, in part, due to the relaxation of laws against Catholics.[36]

In 1778 King George III and Queen Charlotte visited the Catholic Lord and Lady Petre, and set the seal on the allegiance of the Catholic families to the house of Hanover. Jacobitism was dead.[37] There were other landmarks: the Second Catholic Relief Act of 1791 and finally the granting of Catholic emancipation in 1829. The 1829 Act opened parliament to the members of all Christian denominations. Catholics, at least of the middle and upper classes, were able to aspire for a share of political power and hold public office. The French Revolution and Napoleonic Wars had already forced expatriate English religious communities to leave France for home. The wars also gave some Catholics their first opportunity to fight for King George as officers in the army.[38]

In Wales and Monmouthshire, among the few Catholic families that survived the struggle for more than two hundred years were the Mostyns, the Vaughans of Courtfield and the Joneses of Llanarth.[39]

John Francis Vaughan

John Francis, Herbert Vaughan's father, the eldest surviving son of William Vaughan and Theresa Weld, was born on 2 July 1808; an elder brother, William, died on Palm Sunday 1809. John spent his early childhood at Courtfield. According to his eulogist, Bishop Hedley, writing in 1881, young John had, at the age of seven, an experience that impressed him that only God was to be feared. "Here he learned the fear of God, here he learned the history of his race. Here he began to fear God, and it was here as a child of seven, in the gloom of dark nights among these graves and glades, that he first realized the temper of his nature to be so fine that he never knew what fear was of any other thing but God."[40] The manor house had a library, a room used for a chapel and at times a resident priest. John remained within the manor at Courtfield until he was eleven years old.[41]

At eleven John went away to the Jesuit school at Stonyhurst where he met Fr James Brownbill, a man for whom he had a lifelong esteem and affection.[42] Stonyhurst College is in the Ribble valley, four miles from Whalley in Lancashire. John Vaughan later told his children that he had never known a man more devoted, more full of self-sacrifice, or more thoroughly self-disciplined than Father Brownbill. At Stonyhurst John joined the Sodality of Our Lady and began saying the little office of the Blessed Virgin, a practice he continued for the rest of his life. John Vaughan wrote of his youth in a notebook during a trip to France in 1836.[43]

He thought that he had acquired almost all his classical knowledge—which was considerable for a boy of seventeen—at the Lancashire school, although his last eight months at the Jesuit school were not happy. For protecting his brother William,[44] who was six years younger than John, he endured "persecutions and dishonourable treatments." But he felt it taught him among other things a healthy pride and self-confidence. "Thus did my little misfortunes under the kind hand of Providence turn to my future good."

On 20 April 1825, when he was sixteen years of age, John left Stonyhurst and was enrolled at the Jesuit school of St Acheul, at Amiens in France.

After St Acheul, John returned to Courtfield, where he remained for about a month, gathering "more rust than polish." He began to argue with his father, challenging his opinions and considering him "imperious and over-bearing." On the other hand, John always had a great affection for his mother Theresa. Towards her, he wrote, he was always "gentle and submissive."

After a short stay at Courtfield, father and son agreed that John should apply for a commission in the army. He made up his mind to enlist, but for some unnamed difficulty the idea of a military career was abandoned.

Instead, John Vaughan went to Paris[45] to study under "Père" Joseph Emmanuel Bailly. Bailly was a lay-person, the owner of a printing business and a newspaper correspondent, and "Père" was an affectionate nickname.[46] Bailly's home near the Sorbonne at 7 Rue du Petit Bourbon and later a hall in Place de l'Estrapade, were the centres of the Catholic revival in France. In his home were founded the newspapers L'Avenir and Tribune Catholique, and the Society of St Vincent de Paul. There, John saw and heard Hugo Felicité Robert de Lamennais, Henri Dominique Lacordaire, Alphonse Gratry, Frédéric Ozanam and other Catholic leaders and thinkers of the time.[47] Vaughan returned to France and Bailly's house, probably late in 1827, when he was nineteen years old. Looking back he saw it as an important time when his restless mind was disciplined by intense study. In Paris he studied philosophy, literature, French, Latin, and English, and, unlike his earlier schooling, where he felt restrained by the threat of punishment, he was introduced to the honour system. "This is an important lesson," John Vaughan wrote in 1836, "and one which for Herbert's sake, I must keep before my eyes."[48]

On a visit to Courtfield in the summer of 1828, he was more confident and found himself more mature. He writes that he was even allowed by his father to hold an opinion of his own and was treated with courtesy. While at home he "took to the gun with all the enthusiasm of nineteen" and soon became an excellent shot.

John returned to Paris again after the holidays and stayed first in Rue Grenoble and later Rue de l'Université, where he joined with "Thomas Weld, Rigby and others."[49] In the summer of 1829 he finally left Paris for Courtfield. Once at home he was more attracted to a country life than the study of philosophy, which had interested him so much in Paris. And so he exchanged town life for the life of a country gentleman. He especially enjoyed hunting, and liked the straightforward, honest values he found in the country. He also began to look for a suitable wife,[50] and he quoted Friedrich von Schlegel "that the being of man is incomplete until united with woman." John Vaughan was convinced that Providence was directing him to married life. He wrote, six years after he was married, that "every step has been on the road of happiness," from the time he made his choice. When he returned from Paris in 1829, he fell in love with Eliza Rolls of The Hendre, an estate about twelve miles from Courtfield.

Bishop Hedley remembered John Vaughan as a handsome, gallant figure, with a "noble head," curly hair and "resonant far-reaching voice." His Jesuit teachers in France had cultivated a natural talent for public speaking. In speech, his confidence, ease and grace combined with a memory of a "thousand passages." In adult life, he became more reserved, well known for his cheerfulness and at times caustic humour.[51]

According to John Snead-Cox, Herbert Vaughan's father was a man of strong and marked personality, "very frank, energetic, with perhaps little comprehension for weakness of any sort." He was also a model of sincerity and directness.[52]

Eliza Rolls

The young woman John Vaughan set his sights on was not a Catholic. She became one after they married and developed a great love for Catholic devotion and practice. Her prayer life was remembered, by those who knew her, as extraordinary. To a few who have read about her, and of her prayer on behalf of her children, she has seemed eccentric. The figure of a young woman praying an hour each day that her children follow a calling to the Church has been misleading. What emerges from her correspondence is the figure of an active mother of a large family, a person with a remarkable prayer life who was at the same time filled with love and affection for her husband and children, her family and friends.[53]

Louisa Elizabeth Rolls was born into a family of "earnest Evangelicals,"[54] dissenters within the established Church of England. They originally came from Penrose in Monmouthshire and were described as yeoman farmers in 1732.[55] John Rolls, 1735-1801, the son of Aaron Rolls, took his inheritance and went up to London "with the intention of bettering himself."

He bought farm land south of the Thames, in Surrey—freeholds and

leaseholds, on both sides of today's Old Kent Road, including Little Tyburn—
and did well selling livestock to a demanding urban London market. John
married Sarah Coysh in 1767. Sarah's father was a distinguished London
physician, Thomas Coysh of Camberwell,[56] and her uncle was Henry Allen of
Bath. The marriage increased John Rolls' London holdings in Bermondsey,
Camberwell, Newington and Southwark.

With the help of her money, John made a fortune "from building on
agricultural land as the demand for housing in south London grew rapidly."[57]
He built houses for London's gentry and later for its growing artisan population. He continued to raise livestock and was often termed "cowkeeper" in
legal documents.[58] He also bought large estates in Monmouthshire, where he
was appointed high sheriff in 1794.

One property at Bermondsey, Surrey, was purchased by John Rolls in
1790. It consisted of "premises, stables, farm yard, coach houses, at Grange
Road, Westside." The seller was "William Golightly and others."[59] The
country house and farm buildings were on the site of "St Thomas a Waterings,"
the place where pilgrims rested on their way to the shrine of Thomas à Becket
at Canterbury.[60] In the eleventh century, Cluniac monks had built two large
monastic houses on what was low-lying marshland south of the Thames
River. The monastery was called Holy Saviour and gave hospitality to pilgrims.[61]

The Rolls' home was called Grange House after the grange of the monastery.[62] Gordon Bruce writes that in the late 1700s the area was known as Rolls'
Marshes and that the "elegant Palladian mansion" he built was on a site on
today's Old Kent Road between Dunton Road and Cooper's Road. The Rolls'
tomb in the churchyard of the Anglican St Mary Magdalene's at Bermondsey
is inscribed with names of family members beginning with Mrs Elizabeth
Rolls, wife of Aaron, who died on 21 June 1780, and John Rolls, who died on
8 September 1801.[63] John Rolls was Eliza's grandfather.

John, the father of Eliza Rolls, was born in 1776. He was the eldest
surviving son, and it was he who completed Grange House. According to the
Gwent County records in Wales, he reportedly lost a very large sum of money
in 1803. Over the next three years he nearly destroyed the family fortune by
gambling. A newspaper reported that a "dashing cow-keeper's son in the
Kent Road had, during the past summer, been pigeoned of nearly 60,000L."
John's friend, the architect Michael Searles, thought that the loss was closer
to eighty thousand.[64]

On 27 January 1804, John married Martha Barnet at St Mary Magdalene's,
Bermondsey. The minister was Edward Waloby, DD, and one of the wit-
nesses was Felix Whitmore, a brother-in-law. Martha was also from
Bermondsey.[65] Their first son died in 1806. A second son, John Etherington
Rolls, was born in 1807, followed by Alexander in 1808, a daughter, Martha
Sarah, and a daughter, Jesse, in 1809. The youngest, Elizabeth Louisa—

Eliza—was born at Grange House in Bermondsey on 8 October 1810. Due to his gambling debts, and probably connected with the depression that followed the Napoleonic Wars, Eliza's father lost the house. In 1812 it was demolished and all the materials sold.[66] Records show that land and premises at Grange Road were finally sold by "Felix Whitmore and John Hosier together with John Rolls to Richard Phillips" in 1815.[67]

After losing Grange House, John Rolls and his family made their residence at 50 Harley Street in London between 1811 and 1815. In 1816 they moved to Swansea and settled at the Burrows, Britton Ferry. They remained there until 1820 but continued to spend long periods of time in London. In his diary for 1820, John Rolls made notations between February and May of his activities in London. For example: On Sunday, 6 February 1820, Eliza was sick. John Rolls went to St James Church and was impressed by a beautiful sermon given by a Mr Andrews. On another Sunday, he and his family could not get seats in St James Church and so went to a chapel where they heard a "grand sermon by Mr. Rawlings."[68]

In another diary, Rolls describes the family move to France, where they remained till 1826.[69]

While Michael Searles was left to care for John Rolls' financial affairs [70] the family left Britton Ferry at 10.30 p.m. on Monday 9 October 1820 aboard the ship *Sybil*, for Ostend. The Rollses settled in France—at least for the time recorded in the diary—at St Omer.

It was while living in France that young Eliza received lessons in drawing, painting, singing and music and was able later to "recite, or sing her own songs or hymns about heaven as she accompanied herself on the harp."[71] During the years the family lived on the Continent, when she was between ten and sixteen years of age, Eliza also came into close contact with Roman Catholicism.[72]

On Sundays the family attended an Anabaptist chapel. But on occasion they went to Catholic ceremonies, processions and other services. For example, on Wednesday 14 March 1821, Mrs Rolls "went to the convent with Patti, Miss Husard and Eliza to see a young woman take her veil."[73] There is a story recorded by Bence-Jones that after her engagement to John Francis Vaughan, Eliza had announced, to her fiancé's dismay, that she wished to become a nun.[74] It is speculation, but one can wonder what impression the ceremony made on the ten-year-old girl that March Sunday in 1821.

The Rolls family returned from France in 1826. From 1827 to 1837 they kept a residence at 3 Bryanston Square in London, and, from about 1830, the country estate—a farmhouse and shooting-box—called The Hendre. "Hendre" is a frequent Welsh place name meaning the wain or winter dwelling. Under Eliza's brother, John Etherington Rolls, it became "one of the finest and largest Monmouthshire estates."[75]

It is unclear where John Vaughan first met Eliza Rolls. It may have been at

The Hendre, or in London. His first impression of her he extravagantly described as a "mystic attraction" that told him she was to be his "guardian angel upon earth."[76] His love increased each time he met her.

Of the courtship, Eliza's mother, Martha Rolls, simply noted six times in her diary for 1830 that John Vaughan came to their home at Bryanston Square in London between Sunday 14 March and Friday 28 May.[77] John and Eliza often attended Mass together.

During the time of engagement, arrangements were made by the two families for the marriage. Mutual proposals were made by William Vaughan and John Rolls for the settlement of Eliza Rolls' dowry. Central to the dowry arrangement was a sum that would pay a fixed amount—William Vaughan proposed eight thousand pounds—and an annuity of between four hundred pounds and six hundred pounds. The final settlement is not recorded.[78] Eliza's parents made their home in London at Bryanston Square and only visited Monmouth occasionally. It was only on the death of Eliza's father, John Rolls, in 1837, that the family seat was removed to The Hendre.[79] John Etherington Welch Rolls, Eliza's brother, settled there, probably when he married in 1833. He made it the family seat in 1837, built a mansion and improved their Monmouthshire estates.

The marriage of John Vaughan to Eliza Rolls was set for July 1830. On 3 June Eliza's personal maid arrived at Bryanston Square. On 12 July 1830, at St Mary's Anglican church in Bryanston Square, a short walk from Marble Arch, John Francis Vaughan married Louisa Elizabeth Rolls. John gave as his residence an address in St George's Parish, Hanover Square. The bride's sister, Martha Rolls, was a witness. Others signing the marriage document were Sarah Rolls, William Vaughan, Mr Powell, Mr Blount and William Rolls. The civil law in 1830 still required all marriages to take place in the established Church. The minister signed himself, B. Luyard, Rector of Uffington.[80] Soon afterwards they took up residence at Courtfield. John's father and mother, William and Theresa Vaughan, left Courtfield to live at the Waterloo Villa in Gloucester—now known as the Spa Hotel.[81]

Eliza was conditionally baptized a Roman Catholic at Courtfield, on 31 October 1830, by the chaplain, Francis Joseph Daniel.[82] She was confirmed more than ten years later, on 18 September 1842, by Bishop Thomas Joseph Brown. Her confirmation name was Ellen.[83]

In his memoir, John Vaughan addressed his children and especially Herbert—then four years old—"who per chance will ponder this page" about his love for their mother.

> Then will Herbert perhaps on the eve of his marriage wonder how his father loved—what feelings his mother enshrined and breath of hope that his union should be blest as theirs had been. You should know it all my children if e'er you read this page and may God bless you with happiness as true as that which we have found.[84]

Eliza's mother-in-law, Theresa, died in 1832. In a book of meditations and prayers,[85] William Vaughan had noted the deaths of his father in 1796, his mother in 1807, and, finally: "my dearly beloved wife Theresa Mary calmly expired with her crucifix in her hand on Saturday June 30th 1832 about 20 minutes after one, aged 49." Eliza would join her in death twenty years later.

Notes

1. A daughter, Mary, Sister Clare Magdalene, wrote to her father on 14 Jan. 1870 that she remembered Courtfield in the summer and could see "the hills and Wye in perfection and sit under the dear old Beech trees with all the enchanting birds ... but what are hills and water when we have our dear Lord always to go to." VFA.
2. Thomas Vaughan, *No Ordinary Experience*, London, Severn House, 1986, p.2.
3. *ibid*.
4. "Loyal in Life and Death," a discourse preached at the funeral of J. F. Vaughan, Courtfield, 11 Jan. 1881 by Bishop Hedley, OSB, London, Burns & Oates, 1881, p.8ff.
5. "Papal Aggression" by Colonel J. F. Vaughan, 18 Dec 1850. VFA.
6. The name is Saxon for "a Welsh place" and has been applied to the site from at least 1150 A.D. See: Mary Vaughan, *Courtfield and the Vaughans*, London, Quiller, 1989, p.7: "Though the Welsh language died out in Welsh Bicknor quite 150 years ago, the natives are Cambrian by race, as their physique and (in many cases) their patronymics testify." See: John Hobson Matthews, *The Hundred of Wormlow*, Hereford, 1915, p.40.
7. Mary Vaughan, p.4: The future King Henry V, victor of Agincourt on 25 Oct. 1415, died on 31 Aug. 1422 and was buried at Westminister Abbey.
8. C. Heath, *Historical and Descriptive Accounts of Monmouthshire and its Neighbourhood*, 1804, p.37.
9. Matthews, *Wormlow*, p.12; about Joan Vaughan: Mary Vaughan refers to her as "Joanna Waring." See: Mary Vaughan, p.1.
10. Mary Vaughan, p.2.
11. Snead-Cox, 1, pp.1-3; Riley, Kate, *More Tales of Old Ross*, Ross, 1927, p.77.
12. C. Heath, *Excursion Down the Wye*, 1799.
13. Goodrich castle dates from Norman times. See: Robert Gibbings, *Coming Down the Wye*, London, Dent, 1942, p.107.
14. An historian of Wales, Gwynfor Evans, uses the example of one Vaughan family to illustrate "the devastating effect of Britishness on the life of Wales" in the seventeenth century, and criticizes landowners such as the Vaughans of Courtfield. Evans continues: "When one sees how servile its aristocracy had become one realises how much of a miracle the survival of this nation is. It was serving England that gave a purpose to the squirearchy of Wales, and which brought wealth and fame to their families." Gwynfor Evans, *Land of My Fathers*, Talybont, Y Lolfa Cyf., 1992, pp. 316-8.
15. See: T. R. Davies, *Book of Welsh Names*, London, Shepherd, 1952; John Hobson Matthews, "Records of Catholics in the South Wales Marches," Catholic Record Society; Dom J. L. Caesar, "The Recusants of Wales," in *The Clergy Review*, October 1947, vol.viii, pp.245-9.
16. Mark Bence-Jones, *The Catholic Families*, London, Constable, 1992.
17. Mary Vaughan, p.15.
18. J. Bossey, *The English Catholic Community, 1570-1850*, London, 1975, p.97.
19. Brian Magee, *The English Recusants*, 1938, p.201.
20. John Hobson Matthews, "The Catholic Registers of Perthir in the County of Monmouth,

1758-1818," Catholic Record Society, 1, London, Art and Book, 1904–5, pp.271-2: "It is necessary to add that since the date of Catholic Emancipation, the Church has greatly lost ground in this her ancient stronghold. The loss is due to the extinction of the old Catholic families of gentry, to the submersion of the yeoman and, still more, to the enormous emigration of the original peasantry, consequent upon the decay of agriculture. Truth compels one to say that apathy and the failure of the old missionary spirit have largely contributed to the 'leakage.' Perhaps, also, man values less a treasure of which no one seeks to forcibly deprive him, than one the possession whereof is perilous to his liberty and life." Monmouth, 15 Nov. 1904.

21. "Monmouth Recusants, 1584-1626," South Wales and Monmouth Record Society, no.4, pp.59-69. See also: D'Ambrose Jones, *A History of the Church in Wales*, Carmarthen, Spurrell, 1926, p.148: In a religious census made in 1676 as many as 541 Roman Catholics belonged to Monmouthshire and no less than 416 were in the Protestant deanery of Abergavenny alone. In 1679 the Jesuit College at Cwm was discovered and a number of "Welsh Popish books lately printed were found on the premises."

22. B. G. Owens, "The Courtfield Deeds and Documents," The National Library of Wales, *Journal*, pp.258-68.

23. Catholic Record Society Transactions, 2, p.293.

24. *ibid.*: Jane was among a group prosecuted in 1603 for hearing Mass at the house of John Ireland in Hereford. Her father and uncle were among "lay gentlemen" seen to be on the side of the Jesuits and against the King in 1605; See also: H. R. Foley, SJ, *Records of the English Province of the Society of Jesus*, IV, 1878, p.371.

25. Her father, John, had three brothers who became Jesuit priests, and a sister who was a Benedictine nun at Boulogne. See: Foley, pp.420-8.

26. Snead-Cox, 1, p.5; Comtesse de Courson, *The Condition of Catholics under Charles II*, 1899, p.195.

27. John Hobson Matthews, "Papers from the Courtfield Muniments," Catholic Record Society, London, Ballantyne, 1913, pp.150-1: Matthews was "examining and calendaring the large number of family documents at Courtfield"; Revd T. D. Fosbroke, *Gilpin on the Wye*, 1826, p.132.

28. Mary Vaughan, p.26.

29. After 1715, Jacobite support among Catholic families diminished. Apart from a few Lancashire gentlemen like Francis Townley, executed for commanding the Manchester Regiment ... and the two younger brothers of John Vaughan at Courtfield, English and Welsh families stayed aloof from the 1745 uprising, however much support it may have had among the Catholics of Scotland: Bence-Jones, p.25. See also: Riley, *Old Ross*, p.77; Sidney Lee, ed., *Dictionary of National Biography*, viii, New York, Macmillan, 1899, p.187.

30. Mary Vaughan, p.30; See also an article about Kenelm Vaughan, Herbert's brother, in the *Records of the American Catholic Historical Society of Philadelphia*, xv, 1904, "The Catholic Church and Popular Feeling in South America" by James J. Walsh, p.173: The President of the Argentine Republic gave a donation to Fr Kenelm for a chapel in Westminster Cathedral and added a tribute to the Vaughans and William Vaughan in particular.

31. *ibid.*, p.31.

32. Up to 1778 Catholic schools were illegal. Sons of Catholic families wealthy enough were sent to be educated at colleges run by the expatriate English religious communities on the Continent. Daughters were sent to convent schools such as those of the Benedictine nuns at Cambrai and of the "Blue Nuns" and Augustinian Canonesses in Paris. Bence-Jones,p.77; See also: A. C. F. Beales, *Education Under Penalty*, London, Athlone, 1963, Preface.

33. Mary Vaughan, p.37; Bence-Jones, p.34: The family fortunes of the Welds were founded by Sir Humphrey Weld, lord mayor of London in the reign of James I, though the family had been of some consequence since the end of the fourteenth century.

34. Mary Vaughan, p.42.

35. Bence-Jones, pp.139, 236.

36. *ibid.*, p.27: In 1778 the first Catholic Relief Act made life easier for Catholics while still leaving them shut out of the political and official life of the nation.

37. *ibid.*, pp.1,23,25: The Catholic Relief Act ... struck the general prejudice against them to its centre. See also: Charles Butler, *The Struggle for Catholic Emancipation, 1750-1829*, London, 1928.

38. See: R. K. Webb, *Modern England*, New York, Harper and Row, 1968; Bence-Jones, p.27.

39. *ibid.*, p.33: In addition to their Catholicism almost all the families had one thing in common, namely their antiquity.

40. On one occasion John met Pius IX and the Pope wrote in the front of his prayer book: "Initium sapientiae timor Domini." VFA.

41. John Hobson Matthews, *The Vaughans of Courtfield*, London, Sands, 1912, p.43. The present chapel was built only in the 1860s: Snead-Cox, 1, p.2; Heath describes the chapel in 1797 as being up a flight of stairs. There were two unpleasant-looking figures of dead religious in the old chapel. Mass was regularly offered once a month for neighbouring Catholics.

42. Father James Brownbill was born on 31 July 1798. He became a Jesuit in 1815 and was sent back to Stonyhurst after his novitiate to teach. He was ordained in 1829 and became rector in 1836. Between 1841 and 1854 he was the priest-in-charge of the Jesuit house in London, first at 25 Bolton St, Piccadilly, and later at 9 Hill St, the first presbytery of the new Farm St church. While he was in London he received many converts, including Cardinal Manning. Manning and his friend James Hope were received separately on the same day, Passion Sunday, 6 Apr 1851. See: *The Tablet*, 27 Jan 1880, p.83; Harold Roper, *Farm Street Church*, London, Salesian, 1960, pp.1-7. On Stonyhurst, see: Arthur McCormack, *Cardinal Vaughan*, London, Burns & Oates, 1966, p. 17, n. 2; *New Catholic Encyclopedia*, 13, p.726: the Jesuit College in Lancashire is a lineal descendant of the college founded by Father Persons at St Omer in north-eastern France in 1593. It moved first to Bruges in 1762 and to Liège in 1773. During the French Revolution, in 1894, it moved to Lancashire and the Stonyhurst mansion offered by Thomas Weld of Lulworth. It existed precariously until January 1829 when Pope Leo XII definitively interpreted the Bull of Restoration (1814) to apply to England as elsewhere. The roll of 120 boys in 1829 grew to 300 in 1884: Bence-Jones, pp.48, 80; *New Catholic Encyclopedia*, 13, p.726; T. E. Muir, *Stonyhurst College, 1593-1993*, London, James, 1992, p.9: "Continental in origin, English in character, tenacious in purpose but innovative in method, Stonyhurst presents a startling tension of opposites." "From 1773 to 1829 the college had been the main link between the suppression and restoration of the English Jesuits, then from its re-establishment at Stonyhurst until the opening of Farm Street in 1849, it was the *de facto* headquarters of the English province."

43. VFA. "A Sketch of My Life," Memoir by John F. Vaughan, Boulogne, 1836. About James Brownbill at Stonyhurst, *The Tablet* wrote: "... in his character as teacher and prefect he was characterised as meek and gentle and just, and devoted to the promotion of the bodily and spiritual wants of every individual committed to his charge. Hundreds of persons, differing in character, position, abilities, and habits, were during several years placed under his care; but by all, notwithstanding the waywardness of youth, he was esteemed as a paternally kind Superior, who had their interests sincerely at heart." *The Tablet*, 27 Jan. 1880.

44. William was born in London on 14 Feb. 1814 and died 25 Oct. 1902. When he was nine years old he was sent to Stonyhurst where he remained for twelve months; he was withdrawn and sent to St Mary's, Oscott. See *The Tablet*, 1 Nov. 1902.

45. English Catholics did not have their own university and most families declined to send their sons to the English Protestant universities.

46. See: John Derum, *Apostle in a Top Hat, the Life of Frédéric Ozanam*, New York, Hanover, 1960, p.59: "Monsieur Joseph Emmanuel Bailly de Surcy ... students of the University in the neighbourhood called him "Père." He founded La Société des Bonnes Etudes and was pub-

lisher and editor of *La Tribune Catholique*. See also: G. Hourdin, *New Catholic Encyclopedia*, 2, p.17: Joseph Bailly's father had preserved the manuscripts of St Vincent de Paul during the French Revolution and his brother brought the saint's body to Paris. Joseph, with Frédéric Ozanam, was one of the founders of the conferences of St Vincent de Paul in 1833 and "operated a boarding house for students in Paris and was active in all religious movements"; Kathleen O'Meara *Frédéric Ozanam*, London, Kegan Paul, 1878.

47. Hedley, Loyal.

48. VFA. Memoir.

49. *ibid.*

50. *ibid.*

51. "Well-known for his cheerfulness and at times caustic humour." Hedley, Loyal.

52. Snead-Cox, 1, p.9.

53. MHA. Correspondence concerning the possible promotion of a cause for the beatification of Eliza Vaughan in the 1960s: Charles Davis, editor, *Clergy Review*, 9 Nov. 1966: Davis expresses one view that "She seems to have been a remarkable woman, though I find her prayer that all her children should be priests or nuns eccentric. This particular feature of her outlook does not seem to me to be suitable as a model for Catholic mothers today, but a person must always be understood in his or her historical context and the beatification of a wife and mother would in itself be helpful."

54. "Anglican Evangelicalism was a distinct movement, with its own marked characteristics, which have continued to be the characteristics of the Evangelical wing of the Church of England till the present day.... Evangelicals in the Church of England have never been a party. They have always been obstinate individualists (who) ... regarded the parish as the place where the work of the Lord was primarily to be carried out." They were people who took seriously what they read in the Bible and Prayer Book. See: Stephen Neill, *Anglicanism*, London, Penguin, 1965, pp.190-3; David Newsome studied the various influences at work within the Anglican Church during the first half of the nineteenth century in *The Parting of Friends*. Introduction: To see the strength of early nineteenth-century Evangelicalism one "must look rather to the extraordinary proliferation of philanthropic and missionary societies; to the mounting circulation of the cheap repository tracts; to the astounding demonstration of pertinacity, solidarity and inspired leadership afforded by the successful campaign for the abolition of the slave trade; and, finally, to the influence of a small number of remarkable men. Of these William Wilberforce was perhaps the most important."

55. J. C. E. Harding-Rolls, *The Family of John Rolls*, 1963; Gordon Bruce, *Charlie Rolls—Pioneer Aviator*, Derby, Rolls-Royce Heritage Trust, 1990, pp.9-10; *Correspondence*, Mrs Sarah (Rolls) Vaughan; Mary Vaughan, p.44.

56. Mary Vaughan, p.44.

57. Southwark Local Studies Library; Gwent Public Record Office (GPRO).

58. GPRO. Records exist for properties in Southwark and Whitechapel purchased by John Rolls in the 1780s.

59. GPRO: This was most likely The Grange, home of the Rolls family at Bermondsey. Harding-Rolls puts the date earlier, in the 1770s.

60. Harding-Rolls, p.9.

61. John Adair, *The Pilgrims Way*, New York, Thomas and Hudson, 1978, p.43.

62. Surrey Archives; On a walk through Bermondsey, now a part of London, I found only street names to recall the Rolls' home: Grange Rd, Grange Walk, The Grange, Grange Mews: Author, 20 Mar. 1992.

63. The inscriptions on the cemetery monuments have been washed away. The church of St Mary Magdalene is still active. On the afternoon the author visited, Christ Believers Fellowship International, led by Prophet Kingsley Adu-Afriye, was holding a service to which he was welcomed.

64. GPRO. The report is of John Rolls losing £80,000 at the gambling table. Bruce's source places it in 1806. See: pp.9-10.

65. Greater London Records Office (GLRO), St Marylebone, 1803, p.415, no.1243. The second witness was Alexander (illegible), possibly "Higginson."

66. A family story is that the fixtures were sold off the walls of the home and the building demolished. Also: Bruce, *Rolls*, p.9.

67. GPRO.

68. "Albermarle Chapel."

69. GPRO.

70. Michael Searles was to manage the sale of Rolls' properties on 3 Oct.

71. Snead-Cox, l, p.28: Bernard Vaughan to Snead-Cox.

72. John Rolls, diary. GPRO.

73. John Rolls, diary. GPRO.

74. Bence-Jones, p.148.

75. Mary Vaughan, p.44.

76. VFA. John Vaughan, Memoir.

77. Mrs Rolls, diary. GPRO.

78. "Settlement of the fortune of his daughter Miss Eliza Rolls on her marriage with John Francis Vaughan, Esq., Williams, Brooks, Powell and Broderip, Lincoln's Inn." GPRO. There is a story that two public houses were included in Eliza's dowry.

79. His wife, Martha, died at Cheltenham in 1858.

80. For notes on the law, see L. C. B. Seaman, *Victorian England*, London, Routledge, 1973, p.180. In 1837 civil marriages before a registrar were legalized; Also: Webb, *England*, p.187: The obligation to pay church rates to the Anglican Church, inability to be married by anyone but an Anglican minister, burial difficulties, exclusion from Oxford and Cambridge, etc.

81. VFA. William Vaughan to John Vaughan, 3 Nov. 1831: "probable . . . never disturb you in the occupancy of Courtfield."

82. He was chaplain until 1834.

83. VFA.

84. VFA. Memoir.

85. The book was: Abbé De La Hogue, *Journée du Chrétien*, London, 1813.

CHAPTER II

John Francis and Louisa Elizabeth Vaughan at Courtfield

Courtfield

The newlyweds, John and Eliza, came to live at Courtfield "in the pedemented house among woods overhanging the River Wye."[1] John's father, William, began to divide his time between Courtfield, Waterloo Villa in Gloucester and later Portman Square in London. His departure from Courtfield was hastened by the death of his wife, Theresa, on 30 June 1832.[2] Her lingering illness and death distracted the family from the birth of John and Eliza's first son, Herbert Alfred, on 15 April 1832. William could not bring himself to return to Courtfield. "God knows when I shall have the courage to even visit the dear spot where we passed our early years."[3] In 1835 William married Mary Anne, widow of Sir Thomas Gage; she died in 1840.

Despite the sadness of his mother's death in 1832, Eliza's father's death in 1837, and the loss of a newborn son in 1837, the young couple appear to have been very happy. In 1836 John wrote in his notebook that Eliza's "simple faith, exquisite purity, fervid devotedness to virtue" endeared her "more to me than all her other charms." After eighteen years of marriage, he could still write to his wife affectionately once, and sometimes twice, a day while travelling in Ireland.[4]

John travelled through Waterford, Cork and Kerry, looking for property to buy and develop. He finally purchased some land near Mulranny in County Mayo. The property included land, hunting and fishing rights on Achill Island, and a promontory overlooking Clew Bay, with some offshore islands. At Rosturk, on the site overlooking the bay, with a view of Croagh Patrick in the distance, he built a replica of a fortified Norman keep, with turrets and a walled garden. The Victorian building still stands and is known as Rosturk Castle. Vaughan worked the property until the early 1870s when it was sold to the Stoney family.[5]

The achievements of her children, and their devotion to her memory, have made it difficult to present a balanced picture of Eliza. She was remarkable for her goodness, but her prayer life seemed too unusual to promote her as a

27

model for others.[6] Eliza was to be mentioned in Ripley's "Believe it or not" series and Mary Vaughan thought Eliza "would be surprised, and maybe horrified to see herself so immortalised!" on an Anglo-American chewing gum packet: "The fabulous Mother—Louise Elizabeth Vaughan of Courtfield, England, was the mother of a cardinal, two bishops, three priests, and five nuns. For twenty years she spent an hour in prayer every day that all her sons should become priests. She was the mother of eight sons and five daughters.... This record is unequalled in the entire history of the Church (*sic*)."[7]

John and Eliza took their two children, Herbert and Roger, to Bruges, Belgium, in 1836 for the winter. From Bruges, Eliza wrote to her husband, who had returned to England on business: "You precious old man.[8] How I long to see your sparkling eyes again! One long week more and then I shall embrace you." Later she writes[9] that she is near despair having to wait a few days more to see him. "Patience and resignation are virtues which are very useful for me in the absence of the husband of my soul ... what are the joys and sufferings of nuns in comparison to those of married women."[10]

Each of her letters flows with expressions of cheerfulness and affection. This tenderness also extended to others in the family. In a letter to a niece, the daughter of John Rolls, she thanked her for "two bottles of wine you sent me. I am half tipsy so I musn't write much to you today," and for the enjoyable visit she and her children had at The Hendre: "I too rejoiced to be at our dear lovely home again."[11]

By her own admission, Eliza was quick tempered.[12] Her opinions were enthusiastic and impetuous. There were—at least in her own mind—scenes of irritability, impatience and bad temper between her and her husband. "I am sorry for the scandal I must have often given you," she wrote him. In the care of her personal things, she could be disorderly, according to her brother-in-law, Richard, a Jesuit priest. He once compared her quarters to a "lumber room."[13]

Her husband, with all his noble qualities, was also remembered for his sternness. One of his children wrote that his training "was somewhat drastic but it was fine counter-part to that of the ever-tender mother."[14]

The ever-tender, attractive and energetic Eliza, with all her liveliness, had another side to her character, one that profoundly influenced her and in turn her family; an active spiritual life.

Eliza's experience of Roman Catholicism in France and Belgium had made a lasting impression. Little is known of her six years on the Continent, between 1820 and 1826. With her parents she witnessed expressions of Catholic life, for example, in processions and in the "clothing" of nuns. We do know more about her experiences after her marriage and reception into the Catholic church in 1830. She wrote to John from Bruges in 1837: "Really, the more I see of the churches, of the piety, the ceremonies of this town, the more edified I am.... Last night we went to Benediction at Notre Dame and we both agreed that we had never felt such devotion—the lights, the incense, the dear devout women in their mysterious black cloaks, some with arms extended in silent adoration, all conspired to elevate one's heart above this world." She dreamed of a visit to Rome in 1838: "Oh it must really be heaven" she wrote her husband.[15]

Not only was Eliza's mind filled with impressions of Catholic life experienced through travel and acquaintances, but at Courtfield she also had the family's tradition laid open in the library. Today only remnants of the Vaughan library—well established by William and added to by John—are found at Courtfield.[16] Eliza had access to the library, and also used to buy every book she heard about on the subject of prayer,[17] spiritual direction and the saints. Her son Herbert often saw her with two books, *The Spirit of Prayer* by St Alphonsus and *Pensées Pieuses*.[18]

Eliza Vaughan also read the lives of saints. Among them was a series produced by Puseyites—after Edward Bouverie Pusey of the Oxford Movement.[19] Snead-Cox quotes a "curious passage" from a letter she wrote to her friend "Madame Rio" in November 1846. Madame Rio was most likely Appolonia Jones (Herbert) of Llanarth, sister of John Vaughan's close friend, and wife of Alexis François Rio, a French academician and author of *L'Art Chrétien*.[20] Eliza wrote: "Have you ever read any of the Puseyite Lives? The life of St. Stephen will quite delight you."[21] The small book she refers to was the first of a series called *Lives of the English Saints* partly edited by John Henry Newman at Littlemore in January 1844. Saint Stephen is Stephen Harding, one of the founders of the Cistercian Order.[22] It was in this book that she found a special inspiration: "Ever since I read the account of St.Bernard and his four brothers leaving the world and retiring into a monastery I have prayed that all of my sons may follow their example." Of Herbert, who was then fourteen years old, she was "confident Herbert will become a priest." Anyone who reads about St Bernard's mother, Elizabeth of Montbard, and her six sons and one daughter in eleventh-century France must be impressed by the number of similarities between the family at Fontaines and the one at Courtfield.

Each day for nearly twenty years Eliza Vaughan spent an hour, between 5 and 6 p.m., at prayer before the Blessed Sacrament in the old manor-house chapel.[23] At some point she began to add the prayer of Elizabeth, wife of Tecelin of Fontaines, that some of her children would be called to serve God.[24] In answer to Eliza's prayer all of her five daughters became nuns and six of her eight sons became priests.

At Courtfield there is a copy of the *Life of St Bernard* by Abbé Marie Theodore Ratisbonne. It is in French and from the old Vaughan library. There is also an English translation with a preface by Henry Manning.[25] A prayer card in another book belonging to Eliza commemorates the appearance of the Blessed Virgin to the author's brother, Alphonsus Ratisbonne, in the

Church of St Andrew della Fratti in Rome, on 20 January 1842. He saw his conversion to be a result of saying St Bernard's prayer, the *Memorare*.[26] Theodore Ratisbonne begins his story of St Bernard: "Blessed is the man whose infancy has been watched-over, kindled, penetrated by the eye of a tender and holy mother." He continues that her "glance has a magical power over the soul of the child." St Bernard had this "inestimable blessing."[27]

Bernard was Elizabeth's third eldest, born in 1090. She had offered her first two sons to the Lord at the moment of birth "but she consecrated Bernard to him in a more especial manner." She wished that all of her children would be called to serve God, in "the high vocation which in her youth, she believed, she had herself received."[28]

Eliza Vaughan was advised by her sister-in-law, Sister Frances Angela. She helped to refine the development of Eliza's spiritual life and to define her hopes. Sister Frances Angela was born on 22 April 1805 and became a Visitation nun, along with her sister, Mary Chantal, who was five years younger. Eliza visited Frances Angela at her convent in Bristol around Christmas 1837. In their conversation Eliza discussed some difficulties she was experiencing in her spiritual life and asked for her sister-in-law's help.[29]

Sometime in 1838 Eliza wrote to Sister Frances Angela about questions that continued to trouble her. She had been a Catholic and in the Courtfield environment for eight years. "Look upon me therefore my beloved sister as one indeed truly devoted to your spiritual interests," Frances Angela replied in a long letter found in the Vaughan family archives. The confusion Eliza Vaughan complained about had upset her peace of mind. It was caused, according to Frances Angela, partly by her indiscriminate reading habits. She had been reading a wide selection of spiritual books since her conversion, without any guidance. Frances Angela suggested that Eliza become more discerning and rely more on prayer and personal direction than what she read in books. She thought that she should have as a goal a union with God using a peaceful, simple and direct road led by the Holy Spirit. Suspecting that she was too hard on herself, and motivated more by fear and hope than love, Frances Angela urged her to do all for love.

In a postscript, Sister Frances Angela suggested that Eliza do something with her children that her own mother had done at Courtfield when she was a child. "On the Feast of the Presentation [21 November] will you take your three little children [Herbert, Roger and Gwladys] to the foot of the altar and present them to the Eternal Father? Herbert and Roger are old enough to understand." She described what her mother, Theresa Weld Vaughan, had done: "She used to carry the youngest in her arms and make us all kneel round the rails ... while she made the offering of us to God ..." Frances Angela and Mary Chantal Vaughan, Eliza's sisters-in-law, were "often presented at those very rails and perhaps were indebted to that early consecration for ... having left all things and followed Christ."[30]

Snead-Cox thought that Eliza's gentle and protecting influence at Courtfield sheltered everyone and tempered the hardness that sometimes marked her husband's dealing with the children.[31] Herbert and Roger remembered her great love of the Blessed Sacrament and how a chaplain who "was nearly mad, and otherwise disagreeable"[32] was liked by their mother because he often visited the chapel.[33]

Eliza was also an example to her children in her works of charity, especially in the kindness she showed to the poor. Her husband encouraged her in this.[34] Courtfield accounts for the year 1849 show that "In charity and clergy donations including chaplains salary" John Vaughan paid out £272.12.6.[35] In addition, another one hundred pounds was set aside for a poor school on the estate; the ruins of the school can be seen in the brush and trees at the Glen Wye road junction.[36]

Eliza Vaughan's goodness extended beyond the confines of the Courtfield estates. One who fell under her influence was George Lawrence Bernard Burder, second Abbot of Mt St Bernard's Cistercian Monastery near Leicester from 1853 to 1858. Bernard Burder was an Anglican curate at Ruardean across the Wye River from Courtfield, and a friend of the Vaughan family. He is said to have become a Roman Catholic through the influence of Mrs Vaughan.[37] The vicar of Ruardean was Henry Formby who is buried near Herbert Vaughan in the cemetery of St Joseph's College, Mill Hill. Formby and Burder were both received into the Church on the same day, 24 January 1846.[38]

Eliza Vaughan had fourteen pregnancies in less than twenty-three years of married life. One child, Kenelm, died soon after his birth in 1837. There was often concern over Mrs Vaughan's health: "I am truly glad to hear that dear Eliza is recovering her health," Sister Frances Angela wrote to her brother John, on 29 April 1841. In addition, her children were often ill and her husband was frequently away. It was not easy for Eliza to keep to the "simple and direct road" to God suggested by Sister Frances Angela.

Eliza's use of leisure time was criticized, including one of her hobbies, drawing and painting. At Courtfield there is a ten-inch by ten-inch hardcover artist's book containing caricatures in watercolour and sketches of nineteenth-century personalities. With a few exceptions, all of the faces have been carefully cut out. One explanation given is that Eliza had been told by a priest in confession that such drawings and watercolours were vain and unkind. A relative has described Eliza as a skilful and sometimes derisive caricaturist. After the priest's correction, she defaced her work.[39]

Eliza Vaughan's eldest son, Herbert Alfred, kept by him a tiny picture of his mother until shortly before his death in 1903. About her, his brother Bernard said once, Herbert was unable to speak without emotion.[40]

Notes

1. Bence-Jones, p.148: "where John Vaughan and his beautiful wife Eliza lived a life of conjugal bliss and Catholic piety."
2. Mary Vaughan, p.47. She was forty-nine years old.
3. VFA. His daughter Frances Angela, a Visitation nun at a Bristol convent, wrote him on 16 April 1832: "That you suffer much at Courtfield I can indeed well believe but where, my beloved father, in this vale of tears will you be without the Cross or some drop at least of the bitter chalice of our loving Saviour."
4. VFA. John Vaughan, Memoir:"Tho I wrote to you, my dear Eliza, not many hours ago, yet to follow up the thread of my narrative ... I sit down before going to bed to give you a sketch of my days work since I dispatched my letter this morning."
5. VFA. Waterford, 19 November 1848; The Vaughan name is found in Ireland. The surname MAHON—O'Mochai'n in Irish and properly Mohan—in English, spread into Munster where it was usually anglicised as VAUGHAN. Though Vaughan is of course a common Welsh name most of our Irish Vaughans are in fact of this Gaelic stock. See: Edward Mac Lysaght, *Irish Families*, New York, Crown,1972. pp.218 and xix-xx. An 1848 chart of Clew Bay has no buildings marked at Rosturk except for a coast guard lookout—watching for wrecker's fires along the bay. In the nineteenth century it was one of the most remote and underdeveloped areas of Ireland. The inhabitants grew oats and potatoes on small plots barely able to support the population. Fisherman hunted the basking shark. Money sent back from emigrants helped. See: Brendan Lehane, *The Companion Guide to Ireland*, London, Collins, 1985, p.369; At Dugot, on the north coast of Achill, there was a colony of Protestants who settled in 1834. See: J. Burrows, *Tour Round Ireland*, 1835; Over the main door of Rosturk Castle is written: "Christe casa intra mecum. Donec caelos intrem tecum." John Vaughan finally sold Rosturk during the land troubles. According to one story, the agent for the Gibbing's estate, near Rosturk, was shot at during a dispute over turf rights. On one of Vaughan's small islands, a herdsman named Kane was also fired upon during a land dispute. John Vaughan sold the property to Robert Vesey Stoney, who was a railway engineer in India. According to *Owners of Land in Ireland, 1876* and Major Stoney, *Some old Annals of the Stoney Family*, London, Maclure, 1879, Stoney owned Rosturk Castle and 6,757 acres. The Stoney family kept Rosturk until the 1980s when the house and one hundred and twenty acres were sold to John Healy, a Dublin surgeon. There was a friendly connection with a Vaughan by the last owner, Mr Oliver Stoney, of Loughcrew, Co Meath. His grandmother knew the Vaughans. He had met a niece of Herbert Vaughan at the Royal Marine Hotel in 1952. Conversation with Oliver Stoney, Meath, 30th March 1992.
6. MHA. Davis, 1966.
7. VFA. Scrapbook. Obituary: Herbert Vaughan, *The Standard*. "His mother was a Miss Rolls of Hendre, Monmouthshire, and as we have recently said of Wesley, of Shakespeare and Goethe, and might say of most of the great ones of all time, the qualities of the family were largely traceable to the mother. Originally a Protestant, she became a convert to her husband's faith, and a most devout one.... Mrs Vaughan was a handsome woman, her sons and daughters inherited her good looks and not less distinctive, her stately and dignified charm of manner, and with these qualities, a certain element of decision of character." The obituary of Herbert Vaughan in *The Hereford Times* referred to her as "a lady distinguished for her remarkable beauty and charm ... also for her piety, and this quality—indeed her combination of gifts—gave her a wonderful influence over her children."
8. VFA.
9. VFA.
10. VFA. Mrs Eliza Vaughan: "I have learned a number of guitar songs for you.... I am quite determined to make you (you little devil) compose some verses for Mrs S on the birth of her son ... so in your leisure moments think of it ... my dearest Pip. How I long to see you..." The

following year she wrote: "Come back soon my darling. I am dying for you" and sent her love to her brother John Rolls, at The Hendre, and his children, "the little monsters." She remembered the pet dog and added: "Kiss the little spaniel's nose for me."

11. VFA.

12. Lady Lovat, *Clare Vaughan*, London, Burns & Oates, 1887: "All Clare's likes and dislikes which were enthusiastic, vehement—as it was in her nature to be about everything—were learned at her mother's knee." Mary Elizabeth Barbara Vaughan, or Sr Clare Magdalene as she was known, "had a brilliant sense of satire ... inherited from her mother, herself an expert caricaturist till she renounced this dangerous amusement;" MHA. Box 25, file b, Book 2, p. 6: "Her observations and judgements were very sharp. She indulged at times in refined derision and possessed great skill at caricatures... (she was) extremely beautiful with charming manners ... (to) easily win the affection of people, fascinate them and influence them."

13. Snead-Cox, 1, p.28; Mary Vaughan, p.41.

14. Snead-Cox, 1, p.26: "I do not wish any of my boys to indulge in fancies about food; fancies are the privilege of your sisters;" C. C. Martindale, SJ, *Bernard Vaughan, S.J.*, London, Longmans, London, 1924, pp.5-7.

15. VFA; Wilfrid Ward, "Cardinal Vaughan," *Dublin Review*, July 1910: "Mother ... in childhood a strong evangelical. Becoming a Catholic she had all the intense piety of a devout convert. To their Spanish ancestry and their descent from one with antecedents so different from those of the old Roman Catholic families of England ... their taste for romance and adventure, their immense energy and love of the heroic and daring enterprise."

16. MHA. *Wales Daily News*, 12 October, 1912: "Courtfield is a house famous for its books, in fact there are books in every room;" *The Ross Gazette*, August 1913, Welsh Country Homes, CXLVII, Courtfield: "Loyalty to ideals is not the monopoly of any religious body and wherever it is manifest it is worthy not only of respect but of admiration ... notable among the treasures of Courtfield is its collection of documents...in point of antiquity and completeness ... it has been my good fortune to examine;" See: Matthews, Vaughans, p.192.

17. Snead-Cox, 1, pp.12-13.

18. The Courtfield library has one of her books: Herbert Vaughan gave his mother a copy of *Visits to the Blessed Sacrament* by St Alphonsus Liguori on 1 November 1849.

19. Edward Bouverie Pusey was born in 1800, and was a fellow of Oriel College, Oxford, in 1823. He became Regius professor of Hebrew and Canon of Christ Church. At the end of 1833 he joined the Tractarians and became their leader. See: Owen Chadwick, *The Spirit of the Oxford Movement*, Cambridge, Cambridge University Press, 1990, p.135: The first general name for the people of the Oxford Movement was Tractites: Chadwick, *Victorian Church*, p.168: By the end of 1837 everyone knew the group as Puseyites. The sound was smooth and comic and disrespectful; see also: R. W. Church, *The Oxford Movement*, London, Macmillan, 1891, p.104: The Tracts were short papers, in many cases mere short notes, on the great questions, which had suddenly sprung into such interest.

20. See: W. G. Roe, *Lammenais and England*, Oxford, OUP, 1966, p.88, fn.1; See also: "Rio's Memoirs on Christian Art," *Dublin Review*, October 1872, p.448ff.

21. Snead-Cox, 1, pp.20-1, n.1.

22. *Lives of the English Saints*, projected and partly edited by the V. Rev J. H. Newman, and others of the Oxford school, originally published by M. Toovey, London; John Henry Newman, *St Stephen Harding, The Cistercian Saints of England*, London, James Toovey, 1844.

23. Snead-Cox, 1, p.14; Lady Herbert, "Gwladys Vaughan," London, Wyman, n.d.: Little Gwladys used to follow her and once asked: "But why do you shut your eyes so that you can see nothing?" "My darling," she answered, pointing to the tabernacle, "Jesus is there." Mary, later Mother Clare Magdalene of the Augustinian Canonesses of the Lateran, had such a "passionate love for the Blessed Sacrament and her contagious enthusiasm in its service" that perpetual adoration was established by her community. *The Month*, April 1936, CLXVII, no. 862, p.354.

24. See: A. J. Luddy, *The Life and Teaching of St Bernard*, Dublin, Gill, 1927, p.vii: The National Library in Paris possesses more than sixty biographies of Bernard by different authors.

25. Translated from the French, New York, Sadler, 1884. The first Sadler edition was in 1855. It was reissued in 1991 by TAN Books, Rockford, Ill.

26. Henry Manning wrote the introduction to the English translation of Ratisbonne book: "One has written his life, another through using a prayer composed by him, was converted to Christianity ..."; Bernard Vaughan visited the brother, Abbé Marie, in Paris in 1866, when on his way to begin his Jesuit novitiate. Bernard Vaughan, p.25.

27. The story which inspired Eliza was about Elizabeth, or Aleth, a daughter of Count Bernard de Montbar, who married Tecelin, lord of a feudal castle at Fontaines, north-west of Dijon, in Burgundy. Elizabeth was fifteen and had wanted to become a nun but was encouraged by her father to marry Tecelin. She accepted, taking it to be the will of God. Her husband had a deep respect and love for his wife. "He was a noble knight, of gentle manners, and full of the fear of God ... and distinguished himself on all occasions by his valour, his uprightness, and his probity." Her husband left the education of his children to his wife. He hoped that all of his sons would follow him into a military life. Meanwhile, Elizabeth "sought to inspire them with a deep love of God in and with sentiments of mutual esteem and charity." She was an example to them, visiting the sick and poor, sweeping out their rooms and feeding them. Bernard's brothers followed their father into the service of the Duke of Burgundy, while he, because of poor health, was sent to school. When Elizabeth was forty years old, on the feast of St Ambrose, patron of the church at Fontaines, 1 September, 1110, she died after a brief illness. "Bernard remained like one stunned by so heavy and unforeseen a stroke." He was undecided what to do: "Whenever the world smiled on him, the memory of his mother recalled him to the reality of life." He felt attracted to the Benedictine Monastery of Cîteaux, founded fifteen years earlier about sixteen miles from Dijon by Robert of Molesme, Alberic, and Stephen Harding. One day while praying at a wayside shrine for guidance concerning his future, he heard a voice within his heart: "Come to me all you that labour and are heavy laden, and I will refresh you; take my yoke upon you, and you shall find rest for your souls." All doubt left him and he resolved to enter Cîteaux. Within a few weeks he had convinced thirty-one Burgundian nobles to go with him. Among those who followed Bernard were all but one of his brothers, Nivard. They arrived at Cîteaux around Easter of 1112. See: Joseph Vann, OFM, Editor, *Lives of the Saints*, New York, Crawley, 1954, pp.194-5.

28. Luddy, pp.19-34.

29. Correspondence, Visitation Convent, Waldron, Sussex, 23 January 1993: "As to Visitation nuns, we had two, Mary Francis who became Sister Frances Angela and was elected Superior in 1846 and her sister Mary Teresa who took the name Sister Teresa Chantal—both of these were aunts of Cardinal Vaughan.... This community has had a Weld—Sister Mary Weld, daughter of Thomas Weld of Lulworth entered—and there is one sitting by me as I write!" Concerning the Visitation convent see: John Nicholas Murphy, *Terra Incognita or Convents of the United Kingdom*, London, Longmans, 1873, p.367: Visitation nuns were founded by St Francis de Sales and St Jane Frances de Chantal at Annecy in Savoy in 1610. They are contemplative but at the time had boarding schools attached to their convents. One was at Westbury-on-Trym, near Bristol.

30. Sister Frances Angela wrote letters full of information about the family, comments about books, devotions, travel, daily prayer and enquiries about her brother, John, and the Vaughan family. Her letter to Eliza begins: "I received your letter at the end of my retreat.... Blessed Lord ... employ me as his feeble instrument in the service of your precious soul.... Look upon me therefore my beloved sister as one indeed truly devoted to your spiritual interests.... I will begin by exposing to you my dear Eliza the idea I have formed in the presence of God of the actual state and disposition of your soul."

31. At John Vaughan's funeral Bishop Hedley said that Vaughan "was reserved with his

children." Snead–Cox concluded that there was "no doubt that the preacher's estimate was the right one, and that Col. Vaughan was what would be usually described as a stern man. But . . . whatever was tenderest in him had always gone out to his eldest son, Herbert."

32. From a record-book in Courtfield manor: Some of the chaplains at Courtfield were: 1830, Daniel; 1834, Reeve; 1843, Dawson; 1847, Neary; 1849, Farant; 1853, Muldoone; 1853, Madden.

33. Snead–Cox, 1, p.14.

34. C. C. Martindale, SJ, *Bernard Vaughan*, London, Longmans, 1924, pp.5-9; A Mill Hill Father, *Remembered in Blessing*, Glasgow, Sands, 1955, p.28.

35. Bernard Kelly, *English Catholic Missions*, London, Kegan Paul, 1907: "In 1836 when J. Reeve was chaplain, the chapel of Hatherop was dependent on Courtfield for a monthly Mass."

36. VFA.

37. Brother Jonathan, Archivist, St Bernard's Abbey, Coalville, Leicester: The story of Burder's conversion "does reveal something of his mother's missionary zeal;" George Burder was born in 1814 and educated at Magdalene Hall, Oxford. He was curate at Babbacombe in Devon and then at Ruardean with Henry Formby. When he was Abbot of Mt St Bernard's he was of the first to subscribe to an association which promoted Christian unity. See: E. B. Stuart, "Roman Catholic Involvement in the A.P.C.U.," JEH, vol 41, January 1990, no.1, p.49; Abbot Burder also took up the work of a Catholic reformatory founded at Mt St Bernard's by the Cistercians in 1856. Cardinal Wiseman, who had supported the work, was appointed to look into a dispute within the order over the reformatory. He discovered that there were serious management problems. Abbot Burder resigned in 1858. See: Richard Schiefen, *Nicholas Wiseman and the Transformation of English Catholicism*, Shepherdstown, Patmos, 1984, pp.264-5; The *Catholic Directory* for 1879 lists Burder as living at St Charles, Ogle St, Fitzroy Square, London. He died about 1881.

38. The Oxford Movement, John Henry Newman, and a dispute Formby had with the government over the division of his parish, in which his bishop did not support him, contributed to Formby's conversion. Henry Formby was born in 1816 at Formby in Lancashire. He attended Charterhouse School and went to Brasenose College, Oxford, where he graduated with an MA. He was vicar of Ruardean until he resigned in the autumn of 1845. He was ordained at Oscott in September 1847. For many years he was editor of *Rosary* magazine. One of his popular books was *The Book of the Most Holy Rosary*. For the last twenty-six years of his life he lived at St Peter's Priory, Hinckley. He died in 1884 and was buried at Calvary in the grounds of St Joseph's College, Mill Hill. See: *The Tablet*, 22 Mar. 1884, pp.473-4.

39. Among the figures are: Miss Dumesnet, an actress, Mme de Lafayette, Madame Dacier and Jane Seymour.

40. *Remembered in Blessing*, p.31.

PART TWO

CHILDHOOD AND FORMATIVE YEARS

CHAPTER III

Herbert Alfred Vaughan

Herbert Alfred Vaughan, the first child of John and Louisa Elizabeth Vaughan, was born on Sunday 15 April 1832 at Beaufort Buildings in Gloucester. His parents were visiting his grandfather, William, who had moved from Courtfield due to his wife's poor health; she required constant medical attention. Three days later Herbert was baptised without ceremonies by Father Joseph Daniel. On the 27th of June the baptismal ceremonies took place at Courtfield. His sponsors were Joseph Weld, a great-uncle, who was a brother of Cardinal Weld and proprietor of Lulworth Castle, and Maria Teresa Vaughan, his aunt.[1]

Herbert was born to a life of privilege at Courtfield. The setting on the Welsh–Bicknor peninsula along the river Wye was beautiful. As the scion of the Vaughan estate and with good and loving parents, he had many material advantages. At home he became the leader of his brothers and sisters and played in the fields and woods where rabbits and pheasant are still abundant. He had his ponies, dogs and fishing rods, and later hunting guns. He was happy carrying his gun wherever he went, and however occupied, his thoughts would wander to the brush and woods of Courtfield. He also became an excellent horseman and even learned to tame wild Welsh ponies from the hills.[2] The family was not alone on the property. There were household and estate workers,[3] among them a Mrs Barker who was the nurse.[4] She was replaced by a new governess, Miss Duval, in 1838.[5]

John Vaughan thought his son Herbert would become his successor and squire of Courtfield. Perhaps the boy would pursue the army career that was denied to his father when he left Stonyhurst.[6] There is little doubt that John Vaughan took the upbringing of his first son very seriously.

Herbert's mother prayed that God had other plans for him and his brothers and sisters. As a little boy he had been impressed by her devotion to the Blessed Sacrament. He often watched her from the gravel path in the garden; the chapel was in what is now the sacristy and its tall windows opened into the garden.[7]

Herbert's brother, Roger, was two years younger. The boys were close companions until their activities parted them, due to Roger's poor health and lack of interest in sports, except fishing. Roger and Herbert used to follow their mother around the manor. Imitating what they saw in the chapel, they began "playing at saying Mass" and at anything "ecclesiastical."[8] The children travelled with their parents, and so, when the Vaughans spent the winter on the continent, they went along. Sometimes they stayed with the Welds of Ince Blundell, who had a home at Bruges. Mrs Weld, the former Maria Teresa Vaughan, was Herbert's aunt and godmother.[9] Roger and Herbert did not enjoy life with the Welds. The governess once reported to Mrs Vaughan that the "little boys cannot bear Teresa" and one said that "I hope Mama will soon send Aunt Teresa away if not their cousins." On another occasion, his mother wrote that Herbert was a very talkative child: "Poor dear little Herbert ... I was obliged to consent on condition that he would not again be such a chatterer ... so he has been quiet and good ever since."[10]

School at Monmouth

Herbert's first formal schooling took place at St Mary's mission, Monmouth. The mission church was a small, plain meeting house hidden behind homes on St Mary's Street. It had been built in 1793 and his great-grandfather William was a member of the committee which arranged for the chapel's construction.[11] His teacher was Thomas Burgess Abbot, nephew of the parish priest, Thomas Burgess. Abbot was born in 1820 in the Fylde of Lancashire. He joined the Benedictines at Ampleforth and was sent to Prior Park Seminary, where he was the first student to enter Bishop Baines' school. Soon afterwards he accompanied his uncle, Thomas Burgess, to Monmouth where he helped in the work of the mission and taught in a school started by Burgess. At the same time Abbot studied for the priesthood. Thomas Abbot was ordained in 1845, and, when he retired in the 1890s, had spent fifty-eight years at Monmouth. He outlived Herbert Vaughan, dying as the oldest priest in the diocese of Newport, on Thursday, 18 February 1904.[12] In a letter to Lady Herbert of Lea in 1897 Father Abbot wrote: "In 1836 at the request of the Vicar Apostolic of the Western District ... a Catholic school was commenced at Monmouth by the late Bishop Burgess of Clifton who was then the missioner at that town. I think in 1838-9, Mr Vaughan of Courtfield brought his two young sons Herbert and Roger to us."[13]

We know little of the lessons given by the young Thomas Abbot except that the boys were taught Latin,[14] and, according to Roger's biographer, that they were "developing habits of goodness, gentleness, truth and piety."[15] Abbot's uncle, Thomas Burgess, was also a Benedictine who came from an old Lancashire Catholic family at Clayton Green, near Chorley. When he was sent to Monmouth, St Mary's was a parish of "one hundred and sixty souls and ninety-six communicants." In 1851 Burgess became the second Bishop of Clifton.[16] Monmouth is not far from Courtfield and so Roger and Herbert were at home often.

Stonyhurst College

Herbert's lessons at Monmouth came to an end in 1841 when he was enrolled at the Jesuit school, Stonyhurst, which his grandfather, father and uncles had attended.[17] At the beginning of April 1841, two weeks before his ninth birthday, his parents took Herbert to Birmingham. While Mrs Vaughan remained at Birmingham, John Vaughan took their son to the school. Herbert entered the Stonyhurst Preparatory School at Hodder Place. He was to remain at Hodder Place for fifteen months and during his second year he is recorded as being "Next in Merit" for a class prize. There was only one class at Hodder Place, according to the Stonyhurst archivist, Fr Turner. For a boy of nine, leaving home for school far away in the Ribble valley could not have been a happy experience.[18] A letter from Stonyhurst, dated 6 May 1841, mentions that he received his First Communion on Easter Sunday, and a birthday gift, a half-sovereign, from his grandfather.[19]

Like his father before him, Herbert became a member of the Sodality of Our Lady. Almost sixty years later, he wrote: "I was solemnly consecrated to our Blessed Lady when I was thirteen years of age and later became her slave." The Sodality was dedicated to the Immaculate Conception and directed by one of the Jesuit priests. He also learned a type of cricket played at the school, and became a "hard-hitting batsman."[20]

During the holidays at Courtfield he improved his horsemanship and often spent the whole day riding over the countryside. His companion was his uncle, Edmund Vaughan, five years his senior, who became a Redemptorist priest. Uncle Edmund recalled that Herbert was always generous in sharing his pocket money with his younger brothers and not only became a good horseman but also learned to shoot. Soon Herbert seemed to care for nothing else: "His gun was his delight."

Herbert was withdrawn from Stonyhurst on 12 July 1845 after a difference of opinion between his father and the rector, Henry Walmesley. It was an unsettled period at Stonyhurst. Muir refers to it as a time of "riotous behaviour" which the authorities seemed helpless to control. One of Herbert's contemporaries was also withdrawn because the boy's mother was convinced that "the college was in the greatest disorder" and her son was sure to be ruined.[21]

Herbert was very young when he entered Stonyhurst and left when he was only fourteen, so it is not surprising that there is little in school records except that "his fees were always paid exactly on time." In one register containing class results for 1845 his name appears in Grammar class once as being twenty-first and twice as twenty-fifth out of thirty-three. Fr Turner thought this probably represented his academic level at Stonyhurst.[22] On leaving Stonyhurst he was immediately enrolled at another Jesuit school at Brugelette in Belgium. It was near Ath, twenty-seven miles west of Bruxelles; later it was transferred to the Rue Vaugirard in Paris. Brugelette was a school of three hundred boys. For an English public schoolboy, Brugelette was a strange experience. Sports had no place on the curriculum, and, according to Snead-Cox, the only game was a kind of prisoner's base played with hoops. Herbert thought the system of constant supervision a type of espionage, and disliked his French counterparts.[23] No doubt they felt likewise for he was nicknamed "Milord Roastbeef," his cricket bat was confiscated on arrival, and, he admitted years later, he had to use his "English fists" on occasion. Young Lord Roastbeef moved among a crowd of unsympathetic French boys as a serious and solitary teenager. He had no liking for games of "rolling hoops" but threw himself into his studies with the energy and concentration of a person with purpose. He wrote years later to his father that despite his criticism of the school, he had studied and learnt more during his three years at Brugelette than he had ever done before. Despite his unhappiness with other aspects of the school: "I always thought the tone and spirit of the college were very high and raised one after the ordeal of an English school."[24]

During the summer holidays of 1848 Herbert was in London, where he was present at the opening of St George's Cathedral in Southwark. On Tuesday 4 July 1848, the vicar-apostolic of the London district, Bishop Nicholas Wiseman, celebrated the Mass and gave the homily. Among the Mass servers at St George's were the future Archbishop Stonor and Herbert Vaughan.[25]

It is unclear why, but Herbert was at home near the end of 1848. He had returned to Brugelette and then left again on 16 August,[26] possibly due to the trouble caused by the revolutions of 1848 and the fall of Louis Philippe in France. He was still at Courtfield in November. In a letter written from Ireland by John Vaughan to his wife on 22 November 1848, he reminds her to "please tell Herbert that I trust too that the fat cattle get hay."[27] It was while he was at home that he went on a retreat, and, at sixteen years of age, decided to become a priest and devote himself to the Welsh Mission. His mother was not surprised. She had already confided to her friend Madame Rio in 1846 that she prayed that all her sons follow the example of St Bernard and his brothers and was "confident Herbert will become a priest."[28] His father was probably aware of Herbert's intentions in November when he travelled in Ireland. He visited a school at Cork run by a Dr Sullivan on 23 November, 1848, and wrote to Eliza: "a nice sensible man and he took me over his establishment this morning. It might suit either Roger or Herbert—about half of the one hundred and twenty boys are for the Church."[29]

Roger had spent four or five years at home in Courtfield after leaving Father Abbot's school in Monmouth.[30] He was withrawn because "it was thought that he was suffering from a disease of the heart." In the winter of 1848 Roger was with his parents on the island of Jersey. There, he too informed his mother that he was determined to become a priest and a Jesuit. However, Roger's health was still too poor for him to leave home.

The news about Herbert's intention to become a priest was a great disappointment to his father. At the end of his life John Vaughan wrote to Herbert that he had wanted him "to have a good career as a soldier—for which I thought you were well adapted—and looked forward to you succeeding me at Courtfield."[31] Snead-Cox described the news as "humanly speaking, a bad and bitter disappointment. He was beginning to live his life over again in the person of his son." Yet he was too good to oppose such a vocation and said simply: "Well, if Herbert goes, all the others may go too;" which they all nearly did.[32]

Missionary to Wales

Along with a determination to become a priest came the first thoughts of a missionary life. "My idea was to become a missionary up and down Wales." Like his Uncle William, Herbert may have been inspired by Thomas Vaughan, who was ordained priest in 1627 and "devoted himself to labour for souls in South Wales at a time when it was exposing himself to be hanged, drawn and quartered."[33] Herbert proposed to his father and Bishop Thomas Joseph Brown, OSB, the vicar apostolic of the Welsh District, that he go to Brecon and learn the language under a Welsh-speaking priest "in preparation for a ministry to Wales. The Bishop did not agree,[34] and, although the idea of becoming a missionary to Wales was not abandoned, Herbert later regretted not having learned the Welsh language.[35]

The Welsh-speaking priest under whom Herbert Vaughan hoped to study was most probably Fr Lewis Havard (1774-1858) or his nephew, also Lewis, who succeeded his uncle, at Brecon in 1845. The younger Havard studied for the priesthood at Lisbon where he and two Kavanaughs, all three "natives of Wales," were reported by the president, Edward Winstanley, to be studying Welsh: "They are made to practise with one another the Welsh language and to read books—the same." The Havards were an example of the kind of missionary priest Herbert hoped to become.[36]

While Herbert Vaughan dreamed of learning Welsh, Wales, according to Gwynfor Evans, had reached "a fateful turning point" in her history. Central to the story of the language and nationality of Wales was the report of a Government commission published in 1847. The aim was to anglicize Wales through education: "to kill the Welsh language; and it had to be killed—for the sake of the people." The success of the English in the nineteenth century, according to Evans, was to sow the seeds of modern Welsh nationalism.[37]

According to John Davies, the claim that two-thirds of the inhabitants of Wales spoke Welsh in the 1840s is "probably correct;" that is, about 750,000 people out of a total population of 1,163,139. This, based on the census of 1851, included an estimated 10 per cent born in England, twenty thousand people born in Ireland.

By the 1850s the majority no longer earned their living through agriculture, though this was still the most important single industry; about 35 per cent of the male labour force were employed in agriculture and 10 per cent in the coal industry, the second largest source of employment. Therefore, not only was anglicization promoted by education but "industrialization and urbanization, and the new mentality which developed in their wake, were the root causes" of the transformation of Wales.[38]

The influx of poor Catholic migrants from Ireland—most of them from the south-west—aroused anti-Catholic hostility. "But as the Welsh had a long anti-Catholic tradition, the Irish among them had to suffer indignities far greater than those suffered by the Nonconformists at the hands of the Anglicans." In addition, Protestants were alarmed at the spread of Catholic churches; "twenty-one of them were recorded in Wales in 1851."[39]

During this time of change, Wales in the mid-nineteenth century was reawakening culturally . There was Welsh scholarship and a popular, and profitable, Welsh language press.[40] The young Herbert Vaughan was influenced not only by his heritage as a Vaughan but also by an attraction to a revival in Wales that seemed to make a return to the old faith a possibility—provided he took the step to learn the language and become a missionary.

Downside

It is likely that Herbert returned to Brugelette at the beginning of 1849 but it is not certain how long he remained; probably till April of 1850.[41] In the summer of 1850 Bishop Brown and Mr Vaughan arranged for Herbert to enter St Gregory's, Downside, the Benedictine school near Bath that originated at Douai in 1605.[42] J. W. Richards, OSB, a contemporary of Herbert at St Gregory's, wrote a letter to the *Downside Review* in 1911 concerning the Snead-Cox biography of Herbert Vaughan and "an error as to the date of his coming" to Downside.[43] Fr Richards wrote that Herbert Vaughan came to the college in the summer of 1850 after three years at Brugelette and remained until the summer of 1851.[44] Herbert was a "parlour boarder," that is, one who lived with the monastic community. He was not like the ordinary parlour boarder because he dressed in cassock, Roman collar and biretta, just as those studying for the priesthood at Ushaw and Oscott. He had not gone to Downside to become a Benedictine, as his brother Roger would a short time later, but did join in choir for the daily office. Herbert's one purpose in attending Downside, according to Fr Richards, was to join the classes of young monks who were studying theology under Fr Sweeney, who taught dogma, and Fr Hall, who taught moral theology. Both professors had been trained by Bishop Joseph Brown, who was a theologian and a former prior of Downside.

Health

A battle with poor health was to trouble Herbert Vaughan throughout his life. There has been speculation that the state of his health influenced his decision to become a priest. There is even a tradition in the Vaughan family that Herbert's "thoughts were first turned towards the priesthood as the result of a medical examination for the army revealing a weakness of the heart which would unfit him for the field."[45] Snead-Cox rejected the story, reasoning that, as Herbert made his decision when he was sixteen, he would have been too young for an army examination.[46] However, he did not have to take an army physical to realize that his health was not as good as his appearance led others to believe. Heart problems were not unknown to the family; his brother Roger had been withdrawn from school because of a suspected weak heart. At Downside the students learned that the eighteen-year-old Herbert Vaughan, "though of splendid athletic build ... had a weak heart." Because he was a parlour boarder, he mixed with both monks and elder students. He never joined in football, recalled Fr Richards, but played cricket with a substitute running for him because of his weak heart. This enabled Herbert "to achieve that reputation as a slogger which has been handed down even to our days." Despite the heart problem, Richards remembered that he did enter into one sport with "amazing spirit and with occasional recklessness." He once joined Herbert Vaughan, Fr Placid Hall, the moral theology professor, and others, along the banks of the Lucum Brook as far as Charlton. The test was to leap from one bank to the other using long jumping-poles—and sometimes without the poles. "I have seen both the theologian and the future Cardinal, in attempting an almost impossible jump, shot backward from the opposite bank into the stream...."

Richards continued to reflect on his days at Downside sixty years earlier. The elder boys Herbert Vaughan came into contact with were impressed by the strong personality of such a forceful and earnest young man. Although Herbert was naturally reserved, the barrier came down as soon as he saw some way to be of help to others. For example, he personally invited the first twelve boys in the school to meet him in the old palace and from that meeting came the "first Downside Debating and Literary Society, the earliest work of organization of a man whose life was the unfolding of one of the greatest organizing geniuses of the times." Herbert was its chairman and wrote an address to the "Priors and Professors of the College," in which he set out the aims of the Society. In addition to regular debates, literary contributions were welcomed. "We shall receive," Vaughan wrote, "articles on all subjects, from the light novelist or the grave historian, from the anxious politician or the mysterious letters of ghosts and goblins, from the kind and sportive essayist or thoughtful and ponderous philosopher, from the sprightly poet or the severe sarcastic critic—nor shall we even spurn the attic salt of the saucy punster."[47]

During the first six months of 1851, meetings were held every two weeks. At one meeting he chaired, on 12 February 1851, his brother Roger was present and seconded a resolution during a discussion of the relative merits of Napoleon and Wellington: "Napoleon, throughout his military career proved himself the most distinguished general of his time." Herbert also took part in the Society debates. "His speeches were more noted for their vigour than their eloquence ... he brought to bear on an opponent in debate those weapons of irony and sarcasm which were characteristic of the powerful speeches with which his father, Colonel Vaughan, thrilled the Catholics of two generations ago."[48] So thoroughly did Herbert endow the Society with his own vitality that "after sixty years" it still lived on.

Fr Richards had in his possession a serial story in Herbert's handwriting entitled "Life and Adventures of William Pilton by X"—his first, and probably his last, essay in the realms of fiction.[49]

Another contemporary, Fr Alphonsus Morrall, recalled that Herbert went to see Placid Hall about becoming a Benedictine monk at Downside. Fr Placid cautioned Vaughan: "Young man! You will want more elbow room than you would find here!" Fr Richards concluded his reminiscences with the comment that "Cardinal Vaughan's life's work was the finding or making of more elbow room." In the summer of 1851 Herbert Vaughan left St Gregory's, Downside, and the Benedictines, to begin his studies for the secular priesthood in Rome.

Leaving Courtfield for Rome

In the fall of 1851 Herbert prepared to leave for Rome. At Courtfield in October, Thomas Brown, who had been ordained bishop of Menevia and Newport on 29 September 1850, gave Herbert the cleric's tonsure and minor orders.

It was the same year in which the Russell government passed the Ecclesiastical Titles Bill which imposed a fine on any bishop of a church other than the Anglican Church who took on a territorial title. This was a reaction to the decision of Pope Pius IX in 1850 to restore the hierarchy of the English Roman Catholic Church. The structure of dioceses and bishops had been lost since the Reformation. Instead of vicars apostolic and districts there were now, once more, bishops and dioceses. For example, Nicholas Wiseman became the first Archbishop of Westminster rather than Vicar Apostolic for the London District. "The plan was moderate and practical but the language by which it was advanced, especially in Wiseman's 'From the Flaminian Gate' was extravagant, and so it was interpreted as papal aggression."[50]

Herbert's mother wrote a note in her missal: "Our beloved child Herbert left us on Monday 13th October 1851 and crossed to Boulogne on his way to the eternal city on 23rd October."[51]

Notes

1. The *Gloucester Journal* of that weekend reported a cholera epidemic in Paris, the House of Lords' debate of the Reform Bill and the charging of a local seventeen-year-old "loutish lad" with the murder of a gamekeeper. *Gloucester Journal*, Saturday 14 April, 1832; His full baptismal name was Herbert Alfred Henry Joseph Thomas. John Francis Vaughan and Louisa Elizabeth Rolls were to deliver fourteen children: Herbert, Roger, Kenelm (died soon after birth), Gwladys, Helen, Kenelm, Joseph, Clare, Mary, Francis, Bernard, Reginald, Margaret and John.
2. Snead-Cox, 1, p.17.
3. There is an old photograph at Courtfield showing a carriage and the household staff in front of the new chapel, probably taken in the 1880s.
4. When he learned she was dying, Herbert wrote to her from school in 1842: "Dear Old Barker ... You must remember me in heaven for I have loved you on earth." Snead-Cox, 1, p.15-6.
5. VFA. Eliza to her niece, no date, at The Hendre: "Hope nothing will prevent their visit to the Hendre—Miss Duval, the new governess will accompany them ... I am sick to death of the Iron Duke—I am no great admirer of him—I am not fond of hard hearts." She refers to Wellington.
6. VFA. John Vaughan, Memoir: "Enquiries about a commission were made and my mind was made up. However some difficulty arose."
7. Snead-Cox, 1, p.14.
8. Henry Norbert Birt, OSB, *Benedictine Pioneers in Australia*, 2 vols, London, Herbert and Daniel, 1911, 2, p.405.
9. Bence-Jones, pp.236-7: Thomas and Teresa had five sons and seven daughters. Ince-Blundell became a second home to Bishop Herbert when he became Bishop of Salford.
10. VFA. Eliza at Bruges, to John at Courtfield (no date).
11. See: John Hobson Matthews, "The Catholic Mission of Monmouth," *Catholic Record Society*, vol ix, London, Aberdeen University Press, 1911, pp.131ff: After the first Catholic Relief Act, in 1778, until about 1825, "the Monmouth Mission was united with Holywell, Flintshire, both chapels sharing the same endowments, which included certain farms in cos (*sic*) Monmouth and Flint."
12. Obituary, "The Rev. Thomas Abbot," *The Tablet*, 27 February, 1904, pp.342-3: "He succeeded his uncle, afterwards Bishop of Clifton (Dr Thomas Burgess), at Monmouth in 1856, and was incumbent of that mission up to 1894, when he retired. He was buried at St Peter's, Lancaster, on Tuesday, February 23.... He combined in a marked degree the seriousness and depths of the priestly office with child-like light-heartedness that was all his own.... He had passed 58 years of his life at Monmouth. He was a part of that ancient town. Always at his post, seldom away from home, he was familiar to Catholic and non-Catholic, to young and old." After he took charge of the mission in 1856 he improved the church with the help of the people and Catholic soldiers in Colonel John Vaughan's Royal Monmouthshire Militia. Father Abbot was, the article continues: "A priest who is always at home and at work comes to obtain a strong hold on his people, and it is quite remarkable how many of the young people who had left continued to keep up communication with him."
13. Referred to as "Catholic Seminary, St Mary's."
14. Snead-Cox, 1, p.15.
15. Birt, *Australia*, 2, p.401: Roger "... at age six he was sent with his brother to a boarding school at Monmouth under the management of Rev. Dr. Burgess ... and Thomas Abbot (who died but a few years ago)...remained about three years ... health soon began to be so delicate ... taken home because it was thought that he was suffering from a disease of the heart and spent the next four or five years at Courtfield."
16. See: *Arundel to Zabi*, by Brian Plumb: Burgess was sent to Monmouth when St Augustine's,

Bath, was closed in 1841.

17. About Stonyhurst: See: T. E. Muir, *Stonyhurst College*, 1593-1993, London, James & James, 1992.

18. Snead-Cox, 1, p.15; MHA, Eliza Vaughan, diary "extract": In May the family left for the continent. Eliza was expecting Joseph, born September 24th 1841. They visited Bruges, Ghent, Brussels, Liège, Aix-la-Chapelle, Cologne, Bonn, Coblenz, Wiesbaden, Frankfurt and other places.

19. Snead-Cox, 1, p.16.

20. *Bernard Vaughan*, p.12; Carmel Archives, Notting Hill (CANH). Vaughan to Mother Mary of Jesus, 8 Dec. 1899: "Just after coming up from my prayer of thanks and gratitude to our Lady for having allowed me to be solemnly consecrated to her on this day 55 years ago;" Muir, *Stonyhurst*, p. 99: "The most vigorous transplants were Stonyhurst cricket and Stonyhurst Football. The former was probably derived from 'Cat.'" Herbert's house-master was Father Zanetti, SJ. They met again when Herbert was at St Edmund's, Old Hall, and Zanetti was associated with a poor school at Westminster.

21. Muir, *Stonyhurst*, pp.91-2: The late 1840s were also a period of indiscipline due to outside influences, matriculation at London University, the rapid spread of railways, and also a growing number of books, periodicals and newspapers to be censored. "Numerous petty restrictions combined with the harsh rigour of Stonyhurst life to give endless opportunities for challenge." In 1845, trouble came to a head with the arrival of "a number of insubordinate and tumultuous spirits who about this time came to the College." They brought a kind of "Land League insolence and wantonness and were soon defying all authority". As the quotation implies, the Irish were at the centre of many a disturbance.

22. Stonyhurst College Archives. The Archivist, Fr F. J. Turner, wrote that although Snead-Cox says Vaughan left the College in July 1847, in fact, he left two years earlier, during July 1845. "He was not therefore by that time likely to have gained any position of distinction." Fr Turner adds: "If you have worked on this kind of schoolboy record, up to the early years of this century, you will have noticed that boys entered and left much earlier than we should now expect. This may be misleading. The Register marks the boy as present in the school, for, say five years. But investigation may show that the boy entered at nine, and left at fourteen, so that it is not surprising that there was not much to record. An accurate record was kept of fees— Herbert Vaughan's fees were always paid exactly on time. But unless a boy was clever, and his name occurs in Prize Lists, the record has not much to say, and Herbert Vaughan was certainly not academically interested at this period. His outside interests were shooting and riding, and even today, the school record might have little to say about them. With Herbert Vaughan we must bear in mind, how young he was when he first came to Stonyhurst—and that was to the Preparatory department—and how young he was when he left." Correspondence with the author, 24 Sept. 1993.

23. Snead-Cox, 1, p.19; A Hewitson, *Stonyhurst College, Present and Past*, Preston, Chronicle, 1878, 2nd ed, p.279: Shortly after Herbert Vaughan became bishop of Salford in 1872, he visited Stonyhurst, which was in his diocese, and "in a public speech, alluded, with much feeling, to his having sat on the benches of the college when he was one of its students."

24. *ibid.*, Snead-Cox.

25. Bernard Ward, *The Sequel to Catholic Emancipation*, 2, New York, Longmans, 1915, p. 185, n. 1; Bernard Bogan, *The Great Link, A History of St George's, Southwark*, London, Burns & Oates, 1948, pp.128-9: "A little after eleven, the procession began to move from the Sacristy, down the 'cloister' and outside the church to the grand entrance, and the great congregation rose up as the head of the procession entered the western door ... the organ 'rolled forth its billows of sound', and the psalm 'Quam dilecta tabernacula' was chanted ... ;" Fifty years later Cardinal Vaughan preached at the jubilee celebrations of St George's. Since Bishop Wiseman stood on the same spot fifty years earlier, he said, "Most assuredly the grace of God had been abundantly

poured out on their country."

26. MHA: "Having left Brugelette, Aug 16th."

27. VFA.

28. Snead-Cox, 1, pp.20–21fn.

29. VFA.

30. Birt, *Australia*, 2, p.401.

31. VFA. 22 July 1880: "How blind were my wishes! And how superabundantly my little sacrifice has been rewarded. Your saintly mother who has drawn so many blessings on all of us expressed her conviction (a few days before her death) that I should give myself entirely to God before I died. May her prayers and the prayers of my sons obtain for me that happiness…."

32. Snead-Cox, 1, p.23.

33. WDA.; *The Tablet*, 23 April, 1898, p.657: His ancestor, Father Thomas Vaughan, worked in Wales for twenty years before he was imprisoned on a hulk where he died. Herbert's uncle, William, became Bishop of Plymouth.

34. MHA. Notes of Fr Thonnen; *The Tablet*, 17 April, 1880, p. 498: "Death of the Right Rev. Thomas Joseph Brown, O.S.B., Bishop of Newport and Menevia." Brown was born at Bath on 2 May, 1798. He was educated by the English Benedictine monks at Acton Burnell, Shropshire, where the monks had set up a shelter after being expelled from Douai during the French Revolution. On 19 April 1813 he was admitted to the Benedictines. The following year he went with the community to Downside near Bath and made his religious profession on 28 October 1814. In 1834 he was elected prior of Downside. On 28 October 1840 he was appointed to the apostolic vicariate of Wales with the title of Bishop of Appolonia *in partibus*. On 29 September 1850, with the restoration of the hierarchy, he became bishop of Newport and Menevia, caring for South Wales. He was considered a "zealous and exemplary a pastor" and an "earnest, straightforward, and single-minded a friend."

35. Snead-Cox, 1, p.20: He quotes from a diary entry for 19 January 1853.

36. John Cleary of Wrexham, Clwyd, discovered the identity of the "Brecon priest." Mr Cleary writes: "Lewis Havard was an indigene: Welsh as they come, his name so utterly Welsh— animals; the single family; isolation; the wind and the rain." Brecon was the Big City. There was a single Welsh-speaking Franciscan down at Abergavenny—David Powell, and in Brecon town, Fr John Morgan Williams." It was in 1816-17 that the senior Lewis Havard was sent to Brecon. Bishop Collingridge stressed that Havard was "the only priest in England possessed of a knowledge of Welsh required for the mission of Brecon."Correspondence, John Cleary, 23 Jan. 1994; See also: Michael R. Lewis, *From Darkness to Light, The Catholics of Breconshire, 1536-1851*, Old Bakehouse Publications; Abbot Charles Fitzgerald-Lombard, *English and Welsh Priests, 1801-1914*, Bath, Downside, 1993.

37. Evans, *Land of My Fathers*, pp.366ff: "The 1847 report was very clear about this. It saw to it that people would associate the national language with ignorance and barbarity, with immorality and material failure.

38. John Davies, *A History of Wales*, London, Penguin, 1994, pp.398-9.

39. *ibid.*, pp.385.

40. *ibid.*, pp.416-7; see also pp.421ff, concerning the "interweaving of Welshness and religion."

41. MHA. Fr Thoonen says that Herbert entered Downside in January 1849. Fr John Thoonen died in 1981. He was archivist at Mill Hill for many years. He gathered much of the material for Arthur McCormack's *Cardinal Vaughan*. Fr Arthur McCormack worked in Cameroon and later became a demographer and writer. He was a professor at Mill Hill during the Vatican Council, a man of enthusiasm, energy and wit. I often benefited from his generous spirit. He prepared his *Cardinal Vaughan* for the Society centenary in 1966. He died in 1992.

42. The school began at Douai in France in 1607. Englishmen unable to become monks in England joined Benedictine houses in Spain and then moved to Douai in what was then the Spanish Netherlands, where they tried to start a community and work among English Catho-

lics. The community was called after St Gregory and the first prior was Augustine Bradshaw. A school for boys was founded between 1614 and 1618 and continued up to the French Revolution. In 1793, the revolutionary government closed St Gregory's and monks and students escaped to England in 1794. There they were joined by others who had been imprisoned in Picardy for several months. They stayed at Acton Burnell in Shropshire on the estate of an alumnus, Sir Edward Smythe, until they purchased Mt Pleasant at Downside in 1814. Brown, Ullathorne and other pioneer missionaries were Downside students; See: *National Catholic Encyclopedia*, 4, p.1028; H. E. Ford, *First Abbot of Downside*, London, 1947; McCormack, p.19, n.1.

43. J. W. Richards, OSB, Correspondence, Cardinal Vaughan and Downside, *The Downside Review*, pp.133-6, no.88, vol XXX, 21 Mar. 1911.

44. His brother Roger entered on 12 Sept. 1850. Birt, *Australia*, p.402.

45. Snead-Cox, 1, p.20.

46. Was Herbert Vaughan "gazetted," as one article in the United States stated? The author found no evidence to support this.

47. Richards, Downside, p.135: "He formulated its rules, was chosen its first Chairman and penned in Volume I of its minutes, which lies before me, the Address to the Prior and Professors of the College. I select a passage. He writes: 'We, few in number, have formed ourselves into a Society for the attainment of that part of the education of a gentleman, which is of the first importance to him, which leaves its indelible impress on the mind and materially affects the whole of his future career: we mean the cultivation of oratory and literature. The younger the mind the more susceptible of impressions, and he who has early acquired a taste for oratory and literature will carry it with him through life, daily reaping from it abundant advantages to himself, whilst he becomes the muscle of the cause which he espouses and the ornament of the sphere in which he moves.'" Downside Abbey Archives. Correspondence with the author, Fr William Jebb, Archivist, 3 Oct. 1993. Minutes of the Society are at Downside. Fr Jebb sent the author extracts.

48. *ibid*: His brother Roger succeeded Herbert and wielded the "same oratorical weapons with even greater adroitness and effect."

49. *ibid*., p.136: The scene is in a Lancashire village. The main characters are Pilton and Son, operators of a cotton factory; "no romance about them ... nor much piety." Downside Abbey Archives: An extract from the handwritten text: "Edward Pilton, the father of our hero was brought into the world about the middle of the last century in the picturesque little parish of B—in Lancashire ... he was really an original. About 5ft.6in. in height, he was of very meagre proportions, with long sinewy arms, dark hair, thin drawn face, receding forehead, small nose directed towards heaven, a peculiar cast of the eyes, and to set off all this, an immense mouth through which projected two or three large teeth.... But unfortunately one grand blemish in his character rendered him the subject of constant railleries: from a boy at the village school he had gone by the name of "stingy Ned": and to such an extent was he avaricious, that even as a man, he was the sport of the village children, and the subject of sneer for his fellow workmen ... probably the future Mrs Pilton was the only person who ever loved poor Edward unless perchance his mother had loved him when he was a baby;" New York Public Library (NYPL): Did Welsh writer Morgan Vaughan know Herbert? There are even similarities in writing style. Morgan Vaughan used the pseudonym "Herbert Vaughan" to write a short story about "Polly Darlington" the "Cambridge Grisette" in 1862: "At the time of which I write, Polly was beyond all comparison, the prettiest girl in Cambridge." See: *The Cambridge Grisette*, by Herbert (Morgan) Vaughan, London, Tinsley, 1862. Also *Poems and Plays by Morgan Vaughan*, Abertillery, *South Wales Gazette*, 1917.

50. Webb, *Modern England*, p.301; J. Bossy, *The English Catholic Community, 1570- 1850*, London, Darton, Longman & Todd, 1976, pp.296-7; René Kollar, *Westminster Cathedral from Dream to Reality*, Edinburgh, Faith and Life, 1987, p.24: The actual timing of the restoration

was tragic, according to Kollar. "Many Anglicans believed that restoration of the hierarchy constituted nothing less than a frontal attack on the established Church." In September 1850 Pius IX established thirteen sees in England and, shortly afterwards, Nicholas Wiseman as Cardinal Archbishop of Westminster."
51. Mary Vaughan, p.64.

CHAPTER IV

Rome and Priesthood

Journey to Rome

Herbert Vaughan left England with his cousin, William Clifford—who became Bishop of Clifton in 1857—and Mr Maskell, a convert and former chaplain to the Anglican Bishop of Exeter. Maskell kept a journal which Snead-Cox used in his biography.[1] They travelled in stages by horse-drawn coach through Paris, Avignon, Marseilles, Genoa, Pisa and Florence. When they reached Siena, Maskell and Clifford were exhausted but Vaughan was still full of energy and "kept singing any random song that came to his head." His companions wondered how he could be singing when they were tired and had no food left. Herbert's answer was that he was very happy and "above all earthly things," and so he continued to sing songs of "six pence and pockets full of rye."

On 15 November 1851 they reached Rome, and Herbert began at once to enquire about attending lectures at the *Collegio Romano*. In the meantime he stayed for a few days at the Hotel l'Angleterre. Afterwards some rooms were found over a stable; they reminded Maskell of a place they had stayed during their journey with "its fearful stench." Occasionally Herbert visited his relatives for a meal; Snead-Cox mentions a visit to the Vavasours.

Herbert Vaughan continued to think of an apostolate to Wales. In his diary he wrote: "Wales calls with saddened and, as it were, a dying voice for someone to help her." He prayed that the Lord let him be "a house which is lighted up for those poor souls whom you have redeemed . . . ." His sentiments are in the spirit of the many Welshmen who kept alive a love for the old faith.[2] He recalled visiting an old man one night near Courtfield. Returning, he crossed the river and followed the winding road along the ridge to the manor: "It seemed as though the stars had eyes all intent to count the steps of his servant. Oh, how cheerful and glad must be the heart of the missioner be when all is cheerless and sad around him!"

In Rome he found a room in a house near the Piazza della Minerva, where he was to remain for most of his first year in the city. After living there for some months, a compatriot, Aubrey de Vere, who had been received into the Church at Avignon by Manning, who was on his journey to Rome in 1851,[3] knocked at his door to ask if he might share his "excellent sitting room" with another student. "Avanti," Herbert called out, and the poet de Vere entered to meet him for the first time. De Vere was impressed by the handsome twenty-year-old Vaughan, and wondered: "What must your sister be?" De Vere and Vaughan shared rooms and became friends. De Vere wrote that he liked his companion "better every day … handsome and refined and as innocent as a child." During 1852, while at home in England, de Vere visited Courtfield and met the Vaughan family: "such simply noble, generous, devout and humble people with a beautiful mother of twelve." De Vere makes no mention of Vaughan's sisters, but Wilfrid Ward, in his life of de Vere, says that the poet "wrote constantly" to Vaughan's mother and one of his sisters.[4]

The tall, fair Herbert Vaughan, "stern of figure with fearless blue eyes, aquiline nose and firm-set mouth" was a handsome man. In temperament, he was impulsive, warm-hearted and humble, and, despite the austerities he practised throughout his life, along with a piercing sense of his personal unworthiness, he had an excellent sense of humour.[5]

Roman College

Vaughan returned to Rome at the end of the summer in 1852. His travelling companions were the former archdeacon, Henry Edward Manning, Robert Whitty, who became Cardinal Wiseman's vicar-general, and William Lockhart. Manning had been received into the Catholic Church by James Brownbill, the Jesuit admired by Herbert Vaughan's father. Herbert was impatient with the "grave and solemn convert parson" and joked about Manning's excessive concern in trying to prevent his silk hat from being crushed in the carriage. At Lyons, Vaughan said to Whitty: "I can stand this old parson no longer. Let us go straight on and leave him to follow as long after as he likes."[6]

After arriving at Rome he transferred to the *Pontifica Accademia dei Nobili Ecclesiastici*, a house for the sons of aristocratic families, nicknamed the "Nursery of Cardinals." At the academy he became friends with Henry Manning, whom he could not tolerate at Lyons. Manning wrote nearly thirty years later that Herbert served his Mass at 6 a.m. nearly all the time he was there. "We became very intimate and our affection has lasted and grown till this day." That friendship, according to John Snead-Cox, "proved strong enough to survive the many divergencies of view which separated the two men before the close of Manning's life."[7]

Herbert lived at the Pontifical Academy and attended lectures at the Roman College. The Jesuit school was the forerunner of the Gregorian University. It had been founded by St Ignatius in 1551, lost during the French Revolution, and restored again to the Jesuits in 1824. One of Herbert's close friends during his student days at the Academy was William Eyre. Eyre had a sense of humour which "made him the most genial of companions," and a certain "Falstaffian quality in his wit which never showed to more advantage than when he was hard pressed by an opponent worthy of his steel. Many of his *mots* were long remembered by his friends." Educated at Prior Park, Ushaw and Oscott before going to Rome, Eyre was ordained in 1853 and shortly afterwards became a Jesuit.

William Eyre spent many years at St Beuno's in Wales, at Stonyhurst and at Farm Street. In 1869 Vaughan stopped at St Beuno's on a trip back from Dublin to see him. He wrote to Elizabeth Herbert that Eyre had been "the most intimate of friends. Now we are separated, each busy with different careers, both serving the same Master, and carrying out to some extent the resolve" they had talked over "in the woods about Tivoli and riding through the Abruzzi."[8]

Herbert Vaughan kept a diary from 1 January 1853, soon after moving to the academy.[9] The first entry concerns a visit to Father Carlo Passaglia who was his director of studies and professor of dogmatic theology at the Roman College.[10] Noel Hanrahan thought that Vaughan's knowledge and love of the Fathers of the Church were very likely due to the influence of Passaglia, one of the pioneers of the modern revival in patristic studies.[11] "I called yesterday upon Father Passaglia," Herbert wrote on 1 January:

> He was as usual kind and magnificent. I told him I had counted seventy-two English ecclesiastics in and about Rome preparing for the vineyard. He hoped they were getting a good course, but could not believe it of those who did not frequent the Roman College. I told him that many were too old and their minds too formed by habit to understand his lectures so as to profit by them. Passaglia replied that those who could not get sufficient knowledge of theology should take to some other state of life and not become a drag and a disgrace to our religion in England by their ignorance.[12]

Among the other professors at the Roman College were Ballerini, who taught moral theology, Schrader for scriptural exegesis, and Giovanni Perrone for dogma.[13]

Wales and Daniel Rock

The next evening, Sunday, 2 January, Vaughan visited Dr Daniel Rock, an historian and "antiquary" of the Church; Daniel Rock was staying at the Scotch College. His great work was *The Church of Our Fathers*, published in four books of three volumes between 1849-53. One critic wrote that: "Dr Rock has at last brought to a conclusion this valuable and erudite work; one particularly interesting to ecclesiologists of every Church, but more especially to Englishmen, as containing the fullest and most complete account which we possess of the religious observances of our forefathers...."[14] In his conversation with Rock, Herbert brought up the idea of a mission apostolate to Wales, which included a special seminary for the training of missionaries for Wales.

He wrote that, on a drive to see St Calista's, St Pancrazia's and other Roman churches, Rock "spoke with interest on Wales, (and) agreed with me that a college for Welsh priests is absolutely necessary...."

Herbert Vaughan's interest in the missions had grown over the two previous years. In 1851 at Courtfield his father and Bishop Brown had disapproved of his idea to learn Welsh and directed him rather to study theology at Rome. He wrote in his diary: "Later on the thought of the great want of zealous missionary priests turned my mind to think of a seminary for Wales in order to supply such missionaries. This then became my uppermost thought, a Seminary for Wales."[15] The idea struck Rock's sense of history, and he continued to comment on the subject: "The Welsh are a most religious people (and it was) not their fault that they are not now Catholics. The priesthood died out among them. They are as obstinate now against the truth as they were formerly obstinate and resolute in its defence." He advised Herbert to learn Welsh early and if he should go to England during the summer, not to return to Rome but to pick up the Welsh language and finish his theology in England or Wales. Rock thought that theology could be learned as well in England as in Rome; "It is a question of method," he said. Vaughan's diary entry concluded with the question: "When shall I begin?".[16]

Vaughan wandered around Rome, one of the many English "seen everywhere," he wrote. An Italian told him that "wherever you go you are sure to see English from the top of St Peter's to the least interesting sight." He made notes on homilies and conversation, and described the rubrics of religious services such as those of an Armenian Mass he witnessed at St Andrea's. One evening he joined some relatives and English people for dinner with Lord Clifford. There he met "Doyle, Albert Petre, Sir Trevillion and some ten others."[17]

More Poor Health

Despite the energy evident in his diary entries for early 1853, life was not going well for Vaughan at Rome. From Snead-Cox, and his sources, another Herbert Vaughan emerges, one who was not accustomed to the studies and self-discipline required of students at the Academy and the Roman College. "I must now accustom myself to the crosses of the student—crosses of sickness, of irritation, disgust; it is well with him who has borne the yoke from youth. But, alas!"

So far, no records have been found to indicate his aptitude for studies in Rome. The young man who sang songs travelling from England in 1851 seems to have disappeared. This introspective Vaughan is impatient with himself for not suffering in silence the feelings of mental weariness and lack of interest in his studies, and of being overcome by fatigue, "headache and indigestion." "I complain to whomsoever may ask me how I feel." He began to miss lectures, and there was a possibility that he might abandon his studies in Rome. Feeling ill and depressed, he later decided to admit to others only that "the climate does not agree with him."[18]

Herbert Vaughan had a weak heart while at Downside. Were his health problems at Rome related to that problem? Periodically, throughout his life, he experienced the effects of heart disease; he mentions a heart attack at Ware, another in 1897, and then his final illness, dropsy, was a complication resulting from heart-failure. So serious did his deteriorating health become—whatever its cause—at the beginning of 1853, that "even outsiders became convinced of what Herbert Vaughan feared, that he might not live to the canonical age required for reception of Holy Orders."[19] His determination and goals were challenged; his body was betraying him. This may have contributed to his difficulties with his life as a Roman student and been a cause of his depression and introspection.

Death of His Mother

At the beginning of February 1853 a new trial was added when news reached him from Courtfield that his mother had died. For Herbert Vaughan it was the most painful, and, at the same time, perhaps the most important event of his life. In his final days, when he gathered together his notes for his book *The Young Priest*, he wrote: "How often those who are crushed by grief, who are wild in their despair, who are suddenly stunned by the feeling that now they stand alone in the world for the first time, that all that they loved and trusted has been snatched away from them forever—how often such as these may be calmed, consoled, and finally sanctified by the discovery that after all and above all God Himself is their Father, and Heaven is their Home."[20]

On 19 January 1853 Sr Angela wrote to Eliza Vaughan enquiring about her first son's health: "I am particularly anxious to hear how dear Herbert is going on at Rome and if his health is better."[21] Early in the month, violent storms had done a great deal of damage throughout England. They were a prelude to a storm that brought to an end the happiness of the Vaughans at Courtfield, an event that is a key to any attempt to understand the subsequent lives of the Vaughan children.[22]

Mrs Vaughan was at Courtfield preparing to deliver her fourteenth child. She wrote to her sister-in-law, Sr Frances Angela, then at the Visitation Convent in Westbury-on-Trym, asking for her prayers for a safe delivery. Angela replied on 19 January: "I received your few lines yesterday and hasten to assure you that we will indeed pray for you and confidently trust that all will go well with you and that the blessings of Heaven will attend you, as it has ever hither done." She included the relic of a saint and a memorial card of the Immaculate Conception, recommending that Eliza pray to the Lord's mother: "My beloved Mamma always believed that she owed to our holy mother the grace of having all her children baptised."[23]

Elizabeth Louisa Rolls Vaughan was forty-two years old. Twelve of the thirteen children she was to deliver in less than twenty-two years of marriage to John Vaughan survived. She was often ill and often carrying a child. For example, she delivered Kenelm in August 1840 and, in April 1841, Angela wrote: "Truly glad to hear that dear Eliza is recovering her health."[24] By September 1841, another baby, Joseph, was born. When she delivered her fourteenth child, John, in January 1853, and lost her life, her youngest daughter, Margaret, was only seventeen months old.[25]

The Vaughan children looked upon their days with their mother at Courtfield as a "golden age." Clare found her "greatest happiness was to talk of those wonderful days ... and her saintly mother."[26] Their mother was the central figure of the happy group of Vaughans. One daughter, Gwladys, used to follow her mother around the manor. To her she was "the mainspring of the faith and love which ... characterized the whole of the thirteen children." For Gwladys, to recall "her mother's tender watchfulness over her ... made her realize more than anything else the watchful love of Jesus."[27]

One person, described as a close friend, and who may have been Mrs Vaughan's confessor, remembered that he had seen her "visibly increasing in sanctity during the final months of 1852." He wondered later why he did not suspect "what was at hand" on a wintry 24 January 1853. During the day the Vaughan children were told that they had a new brother; he was John, who later became a priest and bishop.[28] As they had done in the past they "flocked in to their mother's rooms as happy and noisy as usual." Their mother, Eliza, talked and listened to them for a while but then "complained of fatigue." The children were sent away. In the evening Mrs Vaughan tried with a "faithful friend" who was with her to say the prayers of Vespers and Compline. After a time she began to experience more and more pain which warned those with her that she was in danger. Soon it was clear that she was dying and "all hope had vanished." After a few hours, conscious and "praying fervently to the last, her beautiful soul went home." She had gone to her eternal home, but for some she had left behind, "earth could never more be but a place of exile. Their home was with her...."[29]

As soon as his wife died, John Vaughan, "almost beside himself with agony," went into the school room where his children were gathered together praying and told them that they no longer had a mother. They were suddenly called upon "to practise heroic virtue, which till then they only knew in name."[30] For the whole family the death of Eliza was a catastrophe. Bernard Vaughan remembered going down to the library where the blinds were drawn and all were in black. His father's face was "grief-stricken" and all the children were sobbing. Colonel Vaughan called the eldest daughter, Gwladys, and placed on her wrist their mother's "simple silver bracelet, with crucifix and medal attached." He told the children that their mother "had gone to

Heaven" and that Gwladys was to take her place. Bernard did not remember what else his father said that day, thinking to himself: "If mother had gone to Heaven, she would somehow be back soon."[31]

In his register, the chaplain, Thomas Muldoone, noted for 1853: "Died 24th January at Welsh-Bicknor, Eliza Vaughan."[32] On Saturday, 29 January, the *Monmountshire Beacon* contained the following obituary: "January 29th at Courtfield near Monmouth, very suddenly, Eliza Louisa, the beloved wife of John Francis Vaughan, Esq, and sister of John E. W. Rolls, Esq, of Hendre and Alexander Rolls, Esq, of Croftbilla." On 5 February the *Gloucestershire Chronicle* reported: "Deaths: January 24th in childbirth Eliza Louisa the beloved wife of John F. Vaughan, Esq., of Courtfield."[33] John Vaughan's brother William offered the Mass and "performed the funeral service and addressed a few words to the people." A friend of Eliza Vaughan, Madame de Le Portme, wrote to Sr Frances Angela: "All feel that she is in heaven and can look up to her as saints in glory."[34]

The evening before the funeral, Eliza's body was brought to the chapel, where it remained overnight. William Vaughan described what took place in a letter to his sister, Sr Frances Angela. He came down about 3 a.m. to see about his brother, John, who was sitting by the body. "I made him sit by the fire and he seems to have been wonderfully fortified in his prayer in the Garden." Colonel Vaughan's brother gave him his own prayer-book for the office of the day and John said: "I now feel I have an angel ... we are united more closely than in life." When John Vaughan's own death approached in 1880 he was to write of all the blessings the family had received from his late wife. William Vaughan continued his letter to his sister, saying that he had no anxiety for their brother John: "He is a Christian hero—intense depth of feeling united with intense sense of religion.... We may rejoice in having such a brother."[35]

John Vaughan's friend, J. Steinmetz, wrote from Bruges on 29 January. He referred to a letter he had just received that reported: "Vaughan bears his calamity like a man—and like a Christian." He had advised his friend to throw the whole weight of his troubles upon "Him who is our only strength and consolation.... It is one of the most precious privileges of Christian Friendship to weep with those who weep. I have nothing to say to you on this occasion that has not been already suggested by your own piety or by the kind friends who surround you."[36]

Unaware of the sad events at Courtfield, Herbert Vaughan continued to investigate the antiquities of Rome. On Sunday 23 January, he went to visit the catacombs of St Calistus with "Lord Shrewsbury, Dr Rock, Dr Grant and Garside." On the day of his mother's death he visited the "Convent of St Bonaventure in the Forum or rather built of the remains of the palace of the Caesars." On the 29th, his diary entry referred to the last few days spent "learning and judging the state of Rome," a conversation with a Father

Franco, and the admonition that "truthfulness in God is a virtue peculiarly necessary to a missionary." The final entry is on 2 February when he "had a conversation with a convert." Then, until 25th February, there are no further entries.[37]

On 4 February 1853 Herbert received the news of his mother's death. His father wrote: "Your sainted mother is in Heaven. She died soon after her confinement."[38] Herbert could not weep. "Tears refused their aid and the sorrow is heavy on my heart ... now and then the idea has come to me that I must be all my life unhappy, and I felt that my energy for the mission is gone; but, my God, these are only passing thoughts." He urged himself not to be too sorrowful: "Grieve not as those who have no hope, says St Paul." Herbert wrote to his father that same day: "We are now closer bound to God than ever, since my dear mother is with Him; earthly ties are joined to heavenly ones."[39]

A few days later, when Herbert was ill again, another letter arrived from his father. Herbert wrote at once: "The school of sorrow is the school of the heart of Christ—and happy we if it be ours." He often thought of his mother, talking "to her now and I am sure she hears me; she answers me in whispers and spreads over my soul a great calm.... I invoke her as a saint; whenever I call upon one Mother, I call upon the other."[40]

Care of the Vaughan Family

At Courtfield Colonel Vaughan began to arrange for the care of his family. For a governess, his brother William recommended a Miss Pole who was at Clifton. Mrs Henry Robinson gave a character reference and William suggested that John see her before she left Clifton.[41] She was employed and became Miss "North Pole" to the children. Miss Pole "practically ruled the house with an iron rod" but was "as good as she was rigid" according to Bernard Vaughan.[42]

On 10 March 1853, the newborn child was baptised by Father Edmund Madden at Courtfield and given the name John.[43]

Among the Vaughan children, Roger was a student at St Gregory's, Downside. He had thought of becoming a priest when a boy, but he was not strong enough, and soon forgot about the idea. It returned with great force after the death of his mother. "The love of home seemed to have been extinguished in him and its charm to have departed and he made up his mind to become a Benedictine." Roger received the Benedictine habit on 12 September 1853 from Prior Peter Wilson.[44]

Clare Vaughan, according to her biographer and relative, Lady Lovat, "never nursed her grief but it was present to her to the last day of her life as a loss which she could never get over, as a love which she could never replace but this was not from habit but because her mother really was everything to her—humanly speaking. It was the one earthly tie she clung to the last ... it was the sober truth, the keynote to her life. The raison d'être of a great deal which otherwise might appear exaggerated and unreal."[45]

Shortly after his mother's death, another son, Joseph William, who was twelve years old, was sent by his father to the Benedictines at Downside. He was to become a priest in 1867.[46]

Lady Mary Elizabeth Herbert wrote a short biography of Gwladys, the sickly child so loved by Sr Frances Angela. Gwladys used to follow her mother into the chapel "often without her knowledge." Gwladys, the child born at Bruges in 1838, experienced a "terrible blow and an irreparable loss" at the death of her "devoted mother." She later became a Visitation nun, joining a community at Marqueta in France.[47]

In the spring of 1853, Colonel John Vaughan prepared to take his family away from Courtfield and its memories of a "home more happy, more full of good merriment" than he could ever hope for again.[48] In Italy, on Holy Thursday, 24th March 1853, Herbert left Rome for Courtfield. Early on the same day that Herbert began his journey across Europe, John Vaughan sat in the manor chapel and thought of his late wife. He was meditating on the sufferings of Jesus when he was being bound to the pillar for the scourging, "when I saw in my imagination within the sanctuary on my left hand, Eliza kneeling and bending forward in adoration.... She was in pure white, but her face was radiant and calm and joyous.... I bowed my head and heart and my tears began to flow." The next day he returned but the experience did not happen again. He concluded that "I no longer think of her as the human being, the gentle, tender wife; she is more lovely, more attractive to me, as the sweet guardian spirit, the beauteous angel."[49]

Herbert remained at Courtfield for only a brief time, before returning to Rome to prepare to become a sub-deacon. On 22 April he began a retreat in preparation for minor orders; they were to be given on 1 May. In his diary he continued a theme of self-criticism: "I am closed up in myself—I am simply Herbert Vaughan."

In June he returned again to Courtfield and wrote of his family: "How much I love them!" He did not feel well. Bad health and an inability to study and a lack of "something to stimulate, to occupy, to engross, to urge me on" was missing. For three weeks he felt "tired of everything, so dry and wanting in devotion ... in the energy of virtue that I become nearly dispirited."[50] Herbert Vaughan saw himself as a young, ardent and enthusiastic man, ready and anxious to work on behalf of the Catholic Church, and being prevented "by miserable and crippling ill-health." He reflected on his temperament: his impetuosity, his natural arrogance, his inclination to force his way, and tendency to impose his own will on others. He began to see his ill-health as a means to root out his bad habits, as he saw them: his hastiness, sweeping condemnations, assertiveness, being opinionated, seldom giving way to others, and obstinacy. He complained that he always ran instead of walked: "How often in the streets do I put my hand up to a horse's head to let myself pass by before him." His impatience, hurrying and "love of the object to be attained and of recklessness as to the means" were sources of anxiety throughout his adult life.

Herbert Vaughan thought that he often blundered because he did not have patience with the feelings of others. His lack of interest in his own comfort led him to be "hasty and rash." He determined to put a stop to his "impetuosity," a tendency to "uncharitable criticism" and "unpunctuality." "If I live for over fifty years and by that time have learnt never to criticise, to become quieter and gentler in manner, I shall have done something." Concerning his introspection and resolutions, his father advised him to be careful not to break the powers of nature, but to master them and use them for what is good: "Great energy is too valuable a quality to be killed."[51]

At the beginning of 1854 Herbert was so ill that his friends thought he was going to die.[52] His diary gives little indication of the seriousness of his condition. On 5 March he refers for the first time to Cardinal Wiseman's ideas to form the Oblates of St Charles in Westminster. He knew Wiseman's vicar-general, Dr Robert Whitty, and during a conversation the topic of the training of priests was raised. "Some time ago," Vaughan wrote, "I received the following papers from Dr Whitty after we had been talking on the subject of Ecclesiastical Education and training." They were proposals drawn up by Father Faber in response to a paper from Cardinal Wiseman titled: "Suggestions for the improvement of College and the promotion of Theological studies." The proposal included a "voluntary association of ecclesiastics under the patronage of St Charles Borromeo for the preservation and diffusion of the Ecclesiastical spirit in England...." Soon after his ordination Herbert Vaughan was to become the second recruit—after Henry Manning—of Wiseman's Oblates.[53]

To recover his health, Vaughan left Rome on 1 April for the sea at Fiumicino. At the end of April he travelled to the hills near Florence where he stayed with his uncle, Thomas Weld-Blundell. He admired his Uncle Thomas for his patience with his children. He thought his Aunt Teresa was affectionate "to a fault; impetuosity and earnestness which speaks out everything with such simple-mindedness."[54]

The Weld-Blundells had another home near Boulogne. It was to Boulogne that John Vaughan had moved his family after leaving Courtfield. The children were to live there for nearly three years: "Three dreary years, a monotonous round of school-room duties ... daily constitutional on the ramparts or an occasional excursion into the neighbouring country." Aunt Teresa helped to care for the children while John Vaughan continued to be distracted by Eliza's death. War was to help relieve his sorrow.[55]

When war broke out in the Crimea, Colonel Vaughan volunteered to join the regular army. His militia regiment, the Royal Monmouthshire, was called up and placed on garrison duty in Pembroke dockyard. "During the first winter of the war about four hundred of his men volunteered to join the 23rd Welsh Fusiliers, the line regiment of the country." The Colonel was invited by the army to take out his "little Welsh-men" to the war front. In the Crimea he remained, during the winter of 1854-5, at the headquarters of the Light Division until the war was over.[56]

At Rome, Mgr George Talbot petitioned the Vatican for a special dispensation that would enable Herbert to receive Holy Orders eighteen months earlier than laid down in Church law. Herbert wondered whether he would live to see the priesthood and prayed: "My God, give me five talents, I pray Thee ... and the grace to double them.... I hope indeed that I may live to be a priest. Yet God's will be done." Herbert resolved to devote all his energies to God: "But I am dull and an ass and do nothing but support badly and impatiently ill-health, irritable feelings, weariness and disgust and the ordinary trials of a student's life."[57]

Ordination

In September 1854 he left Florence and travelled to a Passionist monastery, "Il Ritiro dell'Angelo" in Lucca, for a retreat in preparation for the diaconate on 23 September. On 19 October he began another retreat, this time at the Franciscan Convent of Bargo near Lucca to prepare for his ordination to the priesthood on Saturday 28 October 1854. Lucca is at the base of the Tuscan Apennines, twenty-six miles from the Mediterranean. There had been an English colony in the city since the thirteenth century. In the nineteenth, wealthy English people had homes at Bagni di Lucca, a place known for its curative waters and peacefulness. [58] "Ordained priest at Lucca ..." is the simple entry in his diary. He was twenty-two years old. The Archbishop of Lucca, Giulio Arrigoni, ordained him.[59] His father could not attend the ordination: Colonel Vaughan was on his way to the Crimea.[60]

Herbert Vaughan's academic preparation for the priesthood was interrupted frequently; it was finally cut short by his early ordination. Although later he was referred to as a "Doctor of Divinity," he explained to readers of *The Tablet* some years later that his degree was an honorary one, "only *honoris causa*, and so carried no presumption of ecclesiastical attainments."[61] Following his ordination he went in the evening to Pistoia, where he slept the night, and on Sunday morning he reached Florence, staying at the Arno Hotel. The next morning he offered his first Mass at the altar of the Blessed Virgin Mary of the Annunciation. He had some problems with the sacristan "who was not satisfied with my papers." A number of Herbert's English friends attended; Charles Plowden, who served his Mass, and Lady Lothian, the Ladies Kerr, the Scott-Murrays, Mrs Davison, Mrs Anstice and her daughter, and Miss Buckle "besides other English were kind enough to come and hear my first

Mass" at 8.30 a.m.[62]

At noon, he began a solitary journey to Vallombrosa, where he stayed the night at a monastery, noting that there was "an air of aristocracy" about the whole place, evidence to him that the rule was not of the "severest," and the monks were "comfortable." He left the next morning on foot to Mt Alverno. He said his second Mass at Mt Alverno, where St Francis of Assisi received the stigmata.

On 4 November he went with Lady Lothian and her two daughters to Monte San Savino to visit Domenichina Baragli, a women well known locally for her holiness. She stayed in a small cottage and greeted them from a bed so high "her face was parallel to mine." Vaughan had continued to think of a missionary career but had also been approached by Cardinal Wiseman through his vicar general and provost of the Westminster Chapter, Dr Whitty, asking him to go to St Edmund's College, Old Hall, Ware. And so, when each visitor asked Domenichina Baragli to remember their intentions "so that she might speak with God about them during Mass," Herbert made his for: "Mrs Scott-Murry's brother in the East, a soldier in the Crimean Army—and that I should be enlightened to know whether I ought to accept an invitation to go to Old Hall College, or go on the Mission in my own destitute Diocese." After some time "without preface" she said "that I should go to the College ... in England and occupy [myself] in the education of ecclesiastics." She called Vaughan back, and repeated again: "finish your studies and go to the College and accept whatever austerity God may place in your hands ..." for the good of the Church and people he would be able to influence.[63]

Herbert Vaughan continued to wander about the Italian countryside until he was interrupted by a request that he be present at Rome for the proclamation by Pope Pius IX of the Dogma of the Immaculate Conception on 8 December 1854.[64]

Notes

1. Snead-Cox, 1, p.31; William Joseph Hugh Clifford was born in 1823 and died in 1893. He was the second son of the seventh earl Clifford. He studied at Prior Park seminary and at the Accademia dei Nobili Ecclesiastici in Rome. He served Newman's first Mass in 1847 and was ordained in 1850.

2. Snead-Cox, 1, p.33; One of the noblest and most attractive of the Welsh martyrs was schoolmaster B. Richard Gwynn of Wrexham who wrote from prison: "Should it be asked who sang this, one under the warrant of Jesus, desiring of God every day, To bring the faith to Wales." From J. L. Caesar, OSB, "The Recusants of Wales," *The Clergy Review*, October 1947, p.249, vol xxviii, no 4; John Hobson Matthews was quoted in a *Tablet* article on devotion to Our Lady in Wales: "The Wales of old was second to no country in her devotion to the Blessed Virgin; and the intensity of the popular love for Our Lady is attested by the prevalence of prayers, hymns and practices which linger on in spite even of the bitter Puritanism of the Wales of today." See: "Our Lady in Wales," *The Tablet*, 7 May, 1904, pp.738-9.

3. McCormack, p.20; See: Wilfrid Ward's book on the Irish poet Aubrey de Vere.

4. Snead-Cox, 2, pp.370-1; See: James Broderick, Introduction, p.xix, in *Letters of Herbert Cardinal Vaughan to Lady Herbert of Lea*, by Shane Leslie, London, Burns & Oates, 1942.

5. McCormack, p.21.

6. Snead-Cox, 1, pp.454-5. McCormack mistakenly places the meeting of Vaughan with Manning during his first journey to Rome in 1851. See: McCormack, p.21. Manning's first trip was in the October following his ordination in 1851. He went to the Accademia on 4 December. See: Edmund Purcell, *Life of Cardinal Manning*, London, Macmillan, 1896, 2, pp.18-19: quoting from Manning's journal. In the summer of 1852, Manning had been in England and gave a series of lectures in St George's Cathedral, Southwark, before returning to Rome. See: James Pereiro, "'Truth Before Peace': Manning and Infallibility," *Recusant History*, 21, no 2, October 1992, p.238.

7. Snead-Cox, 1, p.38; Purcell, *Manning*, p.20, fn.2: "The intimacy between Manning and Herbert Vaughan... lasted over forty years.... Such an intimacy does not, however, imply that these two zealous fellow-workers in the cause of the Church at home and abroad were always, or on every point, even in grave matters of policy, of one mind."

8. Leslie, *Vaughan Letters*, p.140: Chester Station, 27 January 1869; Archivist, St Beuno's, Obituary of Fr Eyre: Father Eyre was nine years older than Herbert, the youngest son of Count Eyre. He was born near Petergate in York. Of four brothers three became priests; one the archbishop of Glasgow. His father had hoped he would study law, but while staying with his family at London, he decided on the priesthood. He went first to Ushaw and then to Oscott. In 1847 he left England to continue his studies at Rome, and, until 1853, when he was ordained, he studied at the Roman College; See also: Obituary, *The Tablet*, Saturday 12 March 1898, p.420.

9. WDA. Vaughan Diary .

10. Carlo Passaglia—1812-1887—joined the Jesuits aged fifteen and studied under Perrone. He left the Jesuits in 1857 and became a leader of the liberal clergy. In 1867 Bishop Clifford tried to have him reconciled to the Church. See notes on Passaglia in the NCE, p.1051.

11. Noel Hanrahan, "Cardinal Vaughan," *Clergy Review*, Dec. 1961, p.729; Passaglia was perhaps the first Catholic theologian to have developed a detailed conception of the Church as the Mystical Body of Christ. His book *De Ecclesia Christi*, prepared with Professor Schrader, was published in 1853-4. See: Pereiro, *Truth Before Peace*, p.237.

12. WDA. Vaughan Diary; Henry Manning had Passaglia as his main director of studies. The public lectures didn't suit Manning—"I found myself at forty-two among youths, and a stranger among foreigners"—and so he started to read at home under the direction of some of the professors. Passaglia, for example, guided him in the study of Thomas Aquinas' *Summa Theologica*.

13. Wilfrid Ward, *The Tablet*, Dec. 1892; Pereiro, *Truth Before Peace*, p.237. Father Perrone, SJ, was appointed rector of the Collegio Romano in 1853. Giovanni Perrone was born in 1794 and died in 1876. He was a teacher of "positive theology." During the revolution of 1848 he went into exile at St Beuno's. He returned to Rome after three years.

14. See: Bernard W. Kelly, "The Life of the Very Rev Daniel Rock," DD, in *The Church of Our Fathers by Daniel Rock*, 1, London, John Murray, 1905, pp.xvi-xxvi; Also: *Catholic Encyclopedia*, p.105: Daniel Rock was born at Liverpool on 31 August 1799. He died at Kensington on 28 November 1871. He studied at St Edmund's College, Old Hall, from April 1813 to December 1818. Rock came under the influence of Louis Havard and was a close friend of the future historian Mark A. Tierney. He was among the first students sent to reopen the English College at Rome where he received his Doctor of Divinity in 1825. He was ordained on 13 March 1824, and returned to England. In 1840 he became chaplain to Sir Robert Throckmorton of Buckland in Berkshire. There he wrote his great work *The Church of Our Fathers* in which he studied the Sarum rite and other medieval liturgies. Due to this book he was recognized as the leading authority on the study of the liturgy. The first two volumes were published in 1849, and the

second two soon after Herbert Vaughan met him at Rome, in 1853-4. In the 1840s he was a prominent member of an association of London priests called Adelphi; they were working for the restoration of the hierarchy. In 1852 he was chosen as one of the first canons of Southwark. He retired from parish work soon afterwards and he was a resident near Lewes in Sussex and Brook Green, Hammersmith, and finally in South Kensington, near the museum he was very interested in. For many years he was honorary President of the Old Brotherhood of the English Secular Clergy.

15. WDA. Vaughan Diary. See also: WDA, "Notes on the development of the idea of foreign missions"; The idea of a seminary to train Welsh-speaking clergy was not new to Wales. Anglican Bishop Thomas Burgess founded St David's at Lampeter in 1822. He thought that the success of Methodism in Wales was due to the prevalence of the Welsh language and his policy was to anglicise the Welsh church. The new college was on the Oxford and Cambridge model. However, his successor, Thirlwall, abandoned the English language policy. He not only encouraged Welsh preaching and Welsh literature, but set out to learn the language himself. D'Ambrose Jones, *A History of the Church in Wales*, Carmarthen, Spurrell, 1926, pp.254-6.

16. WDA. Vaughan Diary.

17. Snead-Cox, 1, p.39; McCormack, p.23; WDA. Vaughan Diary: On such occasions he heard the news and gossip of Rome. Once it was a story about Nicholas Wiseman, his future Bishop. "Nicholas Cardinal Wiseman when he was Rector of the English College was a very strong thinker and a bold speaker of his opinions . . . had it not been for Cardinal Weld, in whose house he delivered lectures on Creation he would have been removed from the Rectorship of the English College. When the Cardinals agreed that he had better leave, Cardinal Weld said, 'By all means, but I must first cease to be protector of the English College.' Lord Clifford never has mentioned this to Cardinal Wiseman. Dr Wiseman was much too bold in his opinions for the people of Rome—they used to fear for him." Vaughan's story refers to a course of twelve lectures Wiseman delivered in the drawing-room of Cardinal Weld's palace during the Lent of 1835. They were mainly concerned with geology: "On the Connection between Science and Revealed Religion." The lectures were later published in two volumes. See: *Dictionary of National Biography*, vol LXII, New York, Macmillan, 1900, p.244.

18. McCormack, p.23; Snead-Cox, 1, p.39.

19. MHA. HCV. Box 25.

20. Vaughan, *The Young Priest*, pp.74-5.

21. VFA. "Sales" Convent, 19 January 1853.

22. ibid.

23. ibid.

24. VFA. "Sales" Convent, 29 April 1841.

25. Mary Vaughan, p.58.

26. *Clare Vaughan*, p.2.

27. *Gwladys Vaughan*, p.54.

28. John later studied at Downside and tried to become a Carthusian monk but left due to ill health. He studied at the English College in Rome and the Bruges seminary. He was ordained by his brother Herbert at Salford in 1876. After teaching at St Bede's Commercial College, his health failed again and he went to Australia where his brother Roger was Archbishop of Sydney, and a cousin, Frederick Weld, was the Governor of Tasmania. He returned to England and was called to London by Henry Manning where he became a Canon. After Herbert Vaughan's death in 1903, he edited and had published Herbert's *The Young Priest*. In 1909 he became an auxiliary bishop in Salford and for a few years rector of St Bede's. Finally he became parish priest of Great Harwood, where he died on 4 December 1925. See: *Remembered in Blessing*, pp.119-122.

29. *Clare Vaughan*, pp.3-6.

30. *ibid.*

31. Snead-Cox, 1, pp.29-30,
32. Courtfield Archives.
33. London Records Office, Colindale.
34. VFA. 30 January 1853, Sr Angela to Roger at Downside: "My Dearest Roger, ... it is a great comfort to me to see you practising so faithfully the lessons of virtue taught you by your mother in this most trying of circumstances."
35. *ibid.*: Sr Angela quotes from a letter she received from her brother, William.
36. VFA. Bruges, 29 January 1853.
37. WDA. Vaughan Diary.
38. Snead-Cox, 1, pp.39-40.
39. *ibid.*, pp.40-41.
40. *ibid.*, p.42.
41. VFA. 3 February 1853.
42. Martindale, *Bernard Vaughan*, p.12.
43. MHA. Fr Edmund Langston Hayburn, correspondence, 24 June, 1973; and with the author in January 1993 and January 1995: His great-uncle was Fr Edmund Madden who became chaplain in March 1853. Father Madden was born on High St, Kilkenny, Ireland, around 1825 to Michael Madden and Bridget Cahill. He studied at the Sorbonne in Paris and went to the mission at Swansea before becoming chaplain for John Vaughan at Courtfield. He died in March 1865 at Monmouth in the home of Father Thomas Abbot. Fr Madden had returned from a sick call wet from the rain, fell asleep in front of the fire, and died of pneumonia. He was buried in Coedangred Cemetery; Fr Hayburn has a few letters written to his brother Michael from Courtfield in 1859. "As the eldest son.... He inherited a great deal of property in Kilkenny. His obituary notice remarked that he was always very kind to the poor."
44. Roger was ordained at the Lateran Basilica in Rome, on 9 April 1859.
45. *Clare Vaughan*, p.26.
46. Joseph Vaughan, OSB, *A Monastic Autobiography of twenty-five years*, Salford, Roberts, 1894, p.3.
47. *Gwladys Vaughan*.
48. *Bernard Vaughan*, p.9.
49. Snead-Cox, 1, p.44.
50. *ibid.*, pp.46-7.
51. *ibid.*, p.51; And vol 2, p.375: While he was studying for the priesthood, Vaughan occasionally stayed with his aunt and uncle at Ince-Blundell. On one occasion the governess gave an opinion of some point during a discussion on geography and was challenged "with some heat" by Herbert Vaughan. "That afternoon the school-room door was opened and the tall form of this youth of twenty appeared. He had come to apologise to the governess in the presence of all the children for his rudeness in contradicting her."
52. McCormack, p.28.
53. WDA. Vaughan Diary; David Newsome, *The Convert Cardinals*, London, John Murray, 1993, pp.208-9: Of all the converts, Manning shared Wiseman's concern for London's poor. Wiseman had asked for the help of the Jesuits, the Oratory and the Redemptorists, but received none. He expressed his frustration to Faber. What he wanted was "a new congregation," which would act as "an oratory with external action." At Rome, Manning began to draw up a rule using as a model the sixteenth-century congregation of Oblates founded by St Charles Borromeo in Milan.
54. WDA. Diary.
55. VFA. Crimea Diary; Webb, *Modern England*, pp.304-5: In late October 1854 Russian forces unsuccessfully attacked the British base at Balaclava in the Crimea. Early in November another Russian attack at Inkerman was beaten back. A terrible winter followed. Colonel John Vaughan,

Herbert's father, was among the troops. Poor leadership in the prosecution of the war, lack of food, medicine, fuel, shelter and equipment, great numbers lost to disease, and the heroic efforts of Florence Nightingale and her nurses at Scutari were read about in Britain the day after they happened. War correspondents sent their dispatches by telegraph and so the public received news quickly.

56. Hewitson, *Stonyhurst*, pp.279-80. The regiment still exists as "The Royal Monmouthshire Royal Engineers."

57. Snead-Cox, 1, p.55.

58. *ibid.*, p.57. On Lucca, see: Janet Ross and Nelly Erichson, *The Story of Lucca*, London, J. M. Dent & Sons, 1912. A legend tells that the ashes of King Richard, son of King Offa of Mercia, are buried in one of its churches. Byron had a house at Bagni di Lucca in 1818, and was followed by "a whole population of Britons [who] took up their abode by the riverside in the first half of the nineteenth century."

59. Vaughan's diary at the WDA has, in Vaughan's handwriting, "November 28th" 1854. According to the records of the archive of the Archdiocese of Lucca: "Waughan(sic) Erberto di Newportensis del distretto di Galles in Inghilterra" was ordained deacon on 23 September by Archbishop Giulio Arrigoni of Lucca. On 28 October the archbishop ordained him a priest with "lettere dismissoriali del Suo Ordinario." The diary is the only place the author has seen "November 28th" referred to as his date of ordination. The man who ordained Herbert Vaughan, Giulio Arrigoni, was born at Bergamo in 1806 and was made archbishop in 1849. He attended the first Vatican Council and kept a diary that became an important historical document; Bishop Cornelio de Wit, former Superior General of the Mill Hill Missionaries, was visiting nuns from the Philippines in Lucca and went to the chapel where Herbert Vaughan was ordained. It is in the Archbishop's House near the Cathedral. Conversation, 19 November 1994.

60. VFA. Crimea Diary.

61. Snead-Cox, 1, p.233.

62. *ibid.*, p.57; McCormack, p.30; WDA, Vaughan Diary: The Plowdens had a bank in Rome. Lady Lothian became a convert in 1851. See: Bence-Jones, p.178.

63. WDA. Vaughan Diary.

64. Snead-Cox, 1, p.58.

PART THREE

FILLED WITH THE ECCLESIASTICAL SPIRIT

CHAPTER V

St Edmund's College and the Oblates of St Charles

First Appointment

Herbert Vaughan's priesthood began quietly with his ordination and, two days later, a first Mass witnessed by a few well-wishers. Afterwards he wandered in the Italian hills with only the company of his thoughts, one of which concerned a request from Nicholas Wiseman. After his ordination, Herbert received a letter from the cardinal in which he was offered the vice-presidency of St Edmund's College, Old Hall, Ware, in Hertfordshire.

St Edmund's was a mixed college: that is a seminary which also accepted lay students. Robert Whitty, Wiseman's vicar-general and provost of the Westminster chapter, knew Herbert Vaughan; they had travelled together to Rome in 1852. Whitty was a cousin of Frederick Lucas of *The Tablet*, and had come from Maynooth in Ireland to St Edmund's College to complete his studies in theology. On meeting Whitty, John Henry Newman said: "Mr Whitty is one of the most striking men I have met."[1] Whitty had discussed the training of priests with Vaughan. In his notes Herbert also kept suggestions made by Faber and Wiseman concerning seminary training and the formation of an association for secular clergy, the Oblates of St Charles. Whitty suggested to Wiseman that Herbert Vaughan be considered for a post at St Edmund's.[2] We do not know what moved Wiseman to appoint such a young and inexperienced man to be the vice-president at Old Hall, but the winning personality of Whitty may have had something to do with Herbert Vaughan's acceptance of the post.[3]

St Edmund's College is near to the village of Old Hall Green, about five miles from Ware, in Hertfordshire. The college was founded in France, at Douai in Flanders, by Cardinal Allen in 1568. It first trained young men and boys for the priesthood but soon became a school for English Catholic lay-students who were not allowed to have schools under the Penal Laws. However, there was in England a school at Silkstead near Winchester prior to 1662, which was moved to Twyford in 1695. It was closed during the Jacobite rising in 1745 and then re-established at Standon Lordship, Hertfordshire, in

1769, by Bishop Challoner. Bishop James Talbot, vicar apostolic of the London District, transferred the school to Old Hall Green where it was known as Old Hall Green Academy. When the English College at Douai was closed and confiscated in 1793 during the Reign of Terror of the French Revolution, refugee students from Douai returned to England and went to Old Hall Green Academy. On 16 November 1793, the school's name was changed to St Edmund's. Lay students and seminarians made up the student body. In the 1850s it was the seminary of the two dioceses which at that time covered the whole of the south of England. It was one of Wiseman's priorities on the restoration of the hierarchy in England to improve the training of the seminarians at St Edmund's College.[4]

Nicholas Wiseman

Nicholas Wiseman, along with Henry Manning, helped to determine the path of Herbert Vaughan's career in the Church. One historian recently referred to Wiseman as a genius and a "childlike polymath of unbounded sympathies and generosity of spirit."[5] Another considered him incompetent, mainly for his "tactless handling of ... England's obsessive anti-Papism."[6]

The most inflammatory line written by Wiseman, on the restoration of the Roman Catholic hierarchy, was in a pastoral which also included the announcement of the Pope's Act of Restoration on 29 September 1850. The pastoral read: "At present and till such time as the Holy See shall see fit otherwise to provide, we shall govern and continue to govern the counties of Middlesex, Hertford, and Essex as the ordinary thereof...." Queen Victoria considered the statement from "Out of the Flaminian Gate of Rome," as "a direct infringement of my prerogatives."[7]

Wiseman was born in Seville, Spain, on 3 August 1802. His grandfather, James Wiseman, was a merchant who had come from Waterford in Ireland at the end of the eighteenth century. His father, also James, was a partner in the firm of Wiseman Brothers who were merchants trading between Waterford and Seville. James Wiseman married twice, the second time to Miss Xavier Strange of Aylwardstown Castle, Co. Kilkenny. She became Nicholas' mother. When Nicholas was still a baby she "laid him upon the altar of the cathedral of Seville and consecrated him to the service of the Church."

When his father died in 1805, Nicholas returned to Waterford with his mother, sister and brother. It was in Waterford that he first learned the English language. He attended a local boarding school and then, on 23 March 1810, he went with his brother, James, to St Cuthbert's College, Ushaw, in England's north-east. There were ninety students at the Durham school. Father Thomas Eyre was president but died two months after the boys arrived and was replaced temporarily by the historian, John Lingard. In 1818 Nicholas Wiseman left St Cuthbert's for the English College at Rome to continue his studies for the priesthood. On 19 March 1825 he was ordained a priest.[8]

After ordination, Wiseman was appointed by Pope Leo XII to assist Abbot Molza in compiling a Syriac grammar, anthology and lexicon. Wiseman's work appeared in 1828 under the title *Horae Syriacae* ... and won him an international reputation as a scholar. On 19 May 1828 he was named rector of the English College where he had been a student and vice-rector.

In appearance the young Wiseman was tall, slight and pale, with black hair. He was devoted to Rome and in sympathy with the Romantic Movement. He was enthusiastic about Lacordaire and liked jesting in Latin. He welcomed impulsively each generous suggestion that might advance the Catholic Church in England. After meeting the convert George Spencer in 1830, he was encouraged to think that the conversion of England to the Roman Church was close at hand. In May 1836 he founded, with Daniel O'Connell and Michael Joseph Quin, the Catholic quarterly magazine, the *Dublin Review*.

Wiseman was recalled to England in 1840 to become president of Oscott College and coadjutor bishop to Bishop Walsh of the Central District. In 1848 he became pro-vicar apostolic of the London District and the following year succeeded Walsh as vicar apostolic.

At Oscott he had taken an enthusiastic interest in the Oxford Movement of Tractarians and other high Anglicans. In the opinion of David Mathew, it was during this period that he sowed the seeds of his later miseries as bishop and archbishop. Wiseman, he wrote, had an "essential greatness; he was magnanimous; he had an European scope; he had the strength to carry through his programme, everything except the capacity to make them acceptable."[9]

In Oliver Rafferty's opinion, Wiseman was not well attuned to the spirit and ethos that had marked English Catholicism in its struggle for survival from the Reformation until Emancipation in 1829. And yet, his wide learning and experience enabled him to appreciate the concerns of the Church and the world beyond the parameters of the Catholic community of nineteenth-century England. Rafferty considers the choice of Wiseman to be the first Archbishop of Westminster and leader of the Catholic Church in England, to be, in some ways, an odd one. Although he was thoroughly English in his sympathies and habits, his main qualification was that "he had been completely 'Romanized'" between 1818 and 1840 by his experience as a student and rector of the English College in Rome.[10]

W. T. Gribbin calls Wiseman the "Brunel of Victorian English Catholicism." Manning detected his Spanish roots in the "grandeur of conception in all that related to the works, the creations and the worships of the Church." Wiseman also looked for an influx of new blood into the Catholic Church from the Oxford Movement and "sensed the heady possibilities of a mass conversion of England."[11]

Wiseman in later life was a large man. He told the story of visiting a dying woman while at the parish of St Leonard's. The lady opened her eyes to look at Wiseman "with profound admiration" and addressed him as "Your immense." The convert and future Jesuit, Edward Purbrick, described visiting Nicholas Wiseman for the first time at his Golden Square residence: "On entering he was standing between Mgr Searle and Fr Lythgoe, and they formed a trio somewhat formidable for a timid stranger to encounter. I thought: Is this then the effect of prayer and fasting? There, such mountains of flesh I had never before seen.'" Purbrick thought Wiseman "at first sight forbidding, his shaggy eyebrows ... and wide thick lipped mouth, being neither handsome nor attractive. But the reception he gave was warm and hearty." Wiseman could often be seen with his pets and companions, a big dog he called Hekla and a little dog he named Tiny.[12]

When the hierarchy was restored, Nicholas Wiseman, who was the eleventh and last vicar apostolic for the London District, was appointed archbishop of Westminster in October 1850. Wiseman was weathering the storm of outrage over his "Flaminian Gate" letter and the opposition of many of the Old Catholics to the restoration. Catholics were only about 4 per cent of the population, many of them Irish immigrants, and were still regarded "as outcasts of society in bondage to Rome." Many of the Old Catholics thought the restoration and closer ties to Rome were "totally incompatible with allegiance to our Sovereign and with our Constitution." The same people often regarded the immigrant Irish as debasing the moral and social tone of English Catholicism. Also, over long years of persecution they had learned to be undemonstrative and were therefore "suspicious of the earnest Oxford converts" like William George Ward, Henry Edward Manning and John Henry Newman. They were "at once bewildered and alarmed by the flamboyant enthusiasm of the converts that seemed to embrace what they regarded as devotional extravagances."[13]

Changes were also complicated following emancipation in 1829 by the arrival of foreign missionaries and a movement to centralize authority under the Bishop of Rome, a tendency labelled Ultramontanism. Ultramontanism was one of the most successful religious movements of the nineteenth century. It answered the need for stability and identity by proposing that the papacy stood for authority in a time of revolution and change. It aimed to unify society under a loyalty to the pope.

Old Catholic priests and bishops, for practical and financial reasons, dressed plainly, lived simply, and carried out their pastoral and liturgical duties with the least possible ceremony. The converts and continental missionaries now accused the Old Catholics of lacking devotion, of disloyalty and "Gallicanism," despite the witness of their devotion to the Church by their ancestors over centuries.[14]

Nicholas Wiseman identified himself with the movement to Romanize the Church in England. Although a man of wide vision and optimism, who did more than anyone else to create the modern English Catholic Church, and avoid the dangers of insularity, he must accept a large part of responsibility, according to Derek Holmes, "for the ultimate success of that Romanizing policy which did not have entirely happy results." Edward Norman regards his esteem for the orders, especially the new Italian ones, which he introduced to Westminster as "vital spearheads of the missionary advance in England," as the hardest feature for his own clergy to accept. The Old Catholics disliked what they considered the "Italianate enthusiasms of the missionary congregations such as the Passionists, Redemptorists and Rosminians."[15]

The new converts, on the other hand, considered Rome to be the centre not only of Catholicism, but also of all their religious ideals. They disliked anything that appeared to be nationalism in religion and considered the Old Catholics to be intellectually deficient, which was "the unkindest cut of all." Deficiencies in their intellectual training were admitted but it was a price they had paid for their loyalty to the Church over three hundred years.[16]

Edward Norman considers Wiseman's "Romanizing" and his lack of respect for the independent authority of the bishops to be underlying the problems experienced by the Catholic Church in England in the 1850s.[17] They also underlay the difficulties Herbert Vaughan was to encounter at St Edmund's between 1855 and 1861.

Wiseman had a running dispute for ten years with the chapter of his own diocese concerning the right of the chapter to interfere in matters that were, as they appeared to Wiseman, clearly within the sole jurisdiction of the bishop.[18] He also made an issue with the English Church and its bishops over whether they, like the Westminster chapter, were to have a decisive, or merely consultative voice in the adoption of policies affecting the development of English Catholicism. One of the issues that arose from the disagreement was the position of Catholic colleges. "Wiseman had always believed that the English clergy needed reforming, and that an infusion of a Roman spirit in the seminaries would go a long way to preparing them for the ideal of the priesthood which he imagined to reside in Italian practice."[19]

Henry Edward Manning

Wiseman used the talents of recent Oxford converts in his efforts to Romanize the Church. One of the converts was Henry Edward Manning. David Newsome considers that the genius of Wiseman was to be able to take full advantage of the talents that the Oxford converts brought to the Catholic Church: "One has to say that had any other of the Vicars Apostolic been elevated to the newly created see of Westminster, the careers of Newman and Faber, possibly, and that of Manning most certainly, would never have taken the course they did."[20]

Manning wrote that he owed to "Cardinal Wiseman and Pius IX all that has befallen me in my Catholic life. I never asked of them or of anyone in my former life, anything whatsoever. All that has come upon me has come without any seeking. I was made a rector without being a curate, archdeacon without being a canon, provost (of Westminster) without being a canon also, and archbishop without being a bishop."[21] Had Manning remained an Anglican, such were his talents and his friendship with Gladstone that he might have been appointed archbishop of Canterbury.[22]

Henry Edward Manning was born on 15 July 1808 at Copped Hall, Totteridge, Hertfordshire, to William Manning and Mary Ryan. His father, was a Tory member of Parliament for Eversham between 1794 and 1830. Soon after Henry's birth, Mr Manning was appointed Deputy Director of the Bank of England, and, during the Napoleonic Wars, became Deputy Governor. Manning had made his fortune as member of a West Indian merchant firm.

Henry, the youngest son, attended school at Sevenoaks, Kent. In 1822 he went to Harrow and from there to Balliol College at Oxford in 1827. He had a reputation as an athlete and sportsman, and was exceptional at cricket. In 1829 he was elected president of the Oxford Union. At Oxford he became friends with the future Prime Minister, William Gladstone. He was ordained an Anglican priest on 9 June 1833 and went to Lavington in Sussex. The rector, John Sargent, died and Manning succeeded him. He married the late rector's daughter, Caroline Sargent, in November of 1833. The ceremony was performed by the bride's brother-in-law, and Manning's distant cousin, Samuel Wilberforce. After four years of marriage, on 24 July 1837, Caroline died of consumption. In 1840 Manning was appointed archdeacon of Chichester.[23]

Henry Manning was not closely associated with any of the leaders of the Oxford Movement and did not contribute any tracts. After Newman and William George Ward were received into the Catholic Church, Manning became for a time one of the most trusted of the High Church party. In 1848 he went to Rome and met with Pope Pius IX. On his return to England he found the Church of England in a turmoil over the appointment of the bishop of Hereford despite the unorthodox opinions the bishop held.

Then in March 1850 there was a judgement by the Privy Council about the theological orthodoxy of the Revd George Cornelius Gorham. When Gorham's bishop refused to appoint him to a new parish, he appealed to the highest tribunal of the Church of England, but lost his case. He finally appealed to the Judicial Committee of the Privy Council and won the right to become rector of the parish. Manning was among many of the High Church party who protested. Supported by his friend Gladstone, he wrote a letter to his bishop, titled "Appellate Jurisdiction of the Crown in Matters Spiritual," in which he argued that no such jurisdiction existed. Manning's last official act as archdeacon was to preside over a "No-Popery" meeting at the Chichester cathedral library on 22 November 1850. It was a topic for which he had   no sympathy. After the meeting he resigned the archdeaconry and went to London.[24]

After Manning gave up his Anglican living he wrote to another convert, Viscount Campden, the Earl of Gainsborough. He confessed that he had long been convinced that he "could not continue to hold on, under oath and subscription; but obedience to others made me wait. When this anti-Roman uproar broke forth, I resolved at once. I could lift no hand in so bad a quarrel...."

> What my human affections have suffered in leaving my only home and flock, where for eighteen years my whole life as a man has been spent, no words can say; but God gave me grace to lay it all at the foot of the Cross, where I am ready, if it be His will, to lay down whatever yet remains to me.[25]

On Passion Sunday, 6th April 1851, Henry Manning was received into the Roman Catholic Church, along with his friend James Robert Hope-Scott, a well-known lawyer. They were received separately by Fr James Brownbill in the domestic chapel of the Jesuit residence on Hill St in London.[26] Lady Georgiana Fullerton, whom Robert Gray calls "almost excessively Catholic," wrote that Brownbill taught by his manner "that they could bring to the Church nothing and were to receive from her everything."[27] Manning's old friend, Sir Sidney Herbert, was disappointed. He was the husband of Elizabeth Herbert of Lea, and knew Manning from school days when Herbert was president of the Oxford Union. He wrote to Manning that it would be better, after Manning's going over to Rome, that they did not meet: "As politics part men, how much more that to which politics are nothing."[28]

Herbert Vaughan first met Manning when they travelled to Rome together in 1852. In the party were Henry Manning, William Lockhart and Robert Whitty. At Rome, the man who, perhaps more than any other single person, helped to change the face of modern English Catholicism began a lifelong friendship with Herbert Vaughan. The twenty-year-old Vaughan became Manning's regular server at his 6 a.m. Mass, and "gradually 'the old parson' came to command in the young priest, half his age, 'his highest and intimate reverence,' Manning, in return, thereafter treating Vaughan almost as if he were his own son."[29]

Between Manning and Vaughan, there was a difference of twenty-four years in age, as well as a difference of background and temperament. Herbert Vaughan was brought up, in Edward Norman's words, in "the isolated world of the Catholic gentry" while Manning's world was that of the establishment with its links to Harrow and Oxford. "Vaughan was retiring by nature whereas Manning became so only after his wife's death."[30] According to David Mathew, Herbert Vaughan had a vigorous mind, "neither complex nor original, but clear." There were similarities, but Mathew considered Manning "already singularly capable" with a "positive cast of mind," and all the connections afforded by his education at Harrow and Balliol.[31] Vaughan was an "activist" while Henry Manning was a "thinker and pietist." What their long, and at times shaky, friendship was to "most obviously have in common was a developed interior life."[32]

A. N. Wilson, in his biography of Hilaire Belloc, considers the conversion of Manning to the Roman Catholic Church in 1851 to be one of the "most important events in the history of the English Church." Henry Manning was the friend of Gladstone, the brother-in-law of the Bishop of Oxford, and was at the "very core of the Anglican establishment." After becoming a Catholic he attracted converts, but also possessed, in Wilson's view, the political acumen, the high personal respect and the excellence of mind, needed to organize what had been little more than a sect into a grand and serious rival to the established Church from which he sprang.[33]

Nicholas Wiseman found Manning indispensable to his plans for restoring the Catholic Church in England. Manning became "the supremely able negotiator with the government and the friend of Florence Nightingale in getting Catholic chaplains and nurses to the Crimea," and the "Apostle to the Genteels" who converted duchesses "by fascination."[34]

His conversion also ended friendships and was done at great sacrifice. He left his handsome rectory at Lavington and his archdeacon's stall in Chichester Cathedral. "It was the greatest mortification to him to be obliged to wear the Roman collar in the streets of London. This item of attire, now universally regarded as normal clerical wear even by most Protestant clergymen, was in the 1850s bizarre, foreign and outlandish. It was not something which would be seen on the neck of a gentleman."[35] After his conversion, he spent the years 1851-1854 in Rome, only returning to England to escape the summer heat. During that time, Manning was instrumental in bringing many others into the Roman Catholic Church.[36]

According to Sheridan Gilley, Manning thought that the nineteenth century was faced by two overwhelming problems: the problem of doubt, calling into question all the values by which Christendom had lived since Constantine, and the problem of poverty, threatening the overthrow of society itself. The answer to doubt he saw in acceptance of an "infallible Church," and the answer to poverty in "radical social reform under the guidance of that Church, rescuing rich and poor from the secular socialists who wanted to destroy religion." Manning's views about Rome were shared by Herbert Vaughan, but his political radicalism was not, and yet Vaughan became Manning's "beloved Ultramontane ally" and his successor.[37] "We became very intimate," wrote Manning nearly thirty years later, "and my affection has lasted and grown to this day." In Snead-Cox's view it was a friendship that proved strong enough to "survive the many divergencies of view which separated the two men before the close of Manning's life."[38]

St Edmund's and the Oblates of St Charles

Cardinal Wiseman believed that the English clergy needed reforming. "The training and education of the English clergy during the nineteenth century... reflected the spread of ultramontanism which was frequently associated with the introduction of Roman practices or Italian devotions." For example, the introduction of a statue of Our Lady into Prior Park Seminary near Bath led to the comment, reported by Bishop Ullathorne: "Let us have no Romanizing here. Take it away!" At the same time, new devotions to Our Lady became popular at St Cuthbert's, Ushaw, in the 1840s. Despite some resistance, the teaching and opinions of English priests became "more or less ultramontane." In 1838 Edward Cox was appointed professor of theology at St Edmund's, in the hope that he would "Romanize that Gallican institution."[39] However, Cox became one of the most prominent "anti-Roman" priests in England, and later president of the college.

On Wiseman's first visit to St Edmund's, he was welcomed by Dr Crookhall, an old friend, standing in for Edward Cox. During the reception, Crookhall was all "charm and geniality." On his second visit, Wiseman was met by Cox himself. Cox might have become bishop of the London District instead of Nicholas Wiseman if the Old Catholics had remained prominent. The visit proved "awkward" and witnesses thought Wiseman's attitude towards St Edmund's was never the same from that day. "The associations of the visit made him regard St Edmund's as the embodiment of the old tradition which he wished to displace, and he seemed to the professors to interpret all the college customs by this leading idea."[40]

After he became Archbishop of Westminster, Wiseman replaced Edward Cox as college president in 1851. He wrote to Cox that "the seminary is in no respect what it ought to be and cannot, as now conducted, furnish to this diocese learned, eloquent, and gifted priests such as times require."[41] Wiseman wrote to George Talbot that St Edmund's was "cleared of its terrible obstruction," the whole system reformed and a "sound high-toned ecclesiastical spirit" introduced. It was Talbot's view that the sooner the Old Catholic clergy "die off the better; all we live to hope for, in the regeneration of the Church in England, is from the young."[42] Wiseman appointed William Weathers to replace Edward Cox. Weathers had come to the college at the age of fourteen in 1828. He was prefect of the college from 1840-3 and in 1843 became vice-president. After replacing Cox in 1851, he remained president till 1868.[43]

William George Ward

One of Nicholas Wiseman's first acts to implementing his reform ideas at St Edmund's was to appoint a convert, William George Ward, as lecturer in moral philosophy. At St Edmund's, Ward and his wife, Frances Wingfield, became lifelong friends and benefactors of Herbert Vaughan.

W. G. Ward was born in London on 21 March 1812, the son of William Ward, a financier. His grandfather, George, owned an estate on the Isle of Wight, was a Tory member of Parliament for the City of London and a director of the Bank of England. His father, also William, was a famous cricketer; the most successful batsman of his day, and proprietor of Lord's cricket ground. His mother was Emily Combe. The family settled at Northwood, on the Isle of Wight. William George Ward was educated at Brook Green, Hammersmith, at Winchester College and at Christ Church, Oxford, where he distinguished himself as a powerful debater and president of the Oxford Union in 1832. He took a scholarship to Lincoln College in 1833 and became a fellow of Balliol, Oxford, in 1834. At Balliol he became one of the Oxford Tractarians though he started as a lecturer in mathematics and logic.

Dean Arthur Stanley met Ward in 1833: "There bounced in on Sunday a huge moon-faced man, Ward, once of Christ Church, now of Lincoln." Stanley and Ward became friends at Oxford. "He is very uncouth in appearance, as you know, and also uncouth in his tastes; at least he has no taste for beauty of scenery, and not much for poetry. On the other hand, he is passionately fond of music." What the dean liked very much about Ward was "his great honesty, and fearless and intense love of truth, and his deep interest in all that concerns the happiness of the human race."[44]

Ward developed his dialectical and argumentative skills at the Oxford Union and he also became a powerful and controversial writer. His chief influence in his youth, according to R. W. Church, was social:

> ... (his) bright and attractive conversation, his bold and startling candour, his frank, not to say reckless, fearlessness of consequences, his unrivalled skill in logical fencing, his unfailing good-humour and love of fun, in which his personal clumsiness set off the vivacity and nimbleness of his joyous moods.[45]

Ward was also a music critic, who knew opera, and was an "admirable buffo singer." Accompanying his obvious talents and often with the greatest good-humour he was "unreservedly defiant and aggressive," somehow combining "jauntiness and seriousness."[46]

In the winter of 1844, William George Ward became engaged to Frances Mary Wingfield, the youngest daughter of the Revd John Wingfield, who was once a canon of York Cathedral. She was the sister of one of Ward's contemporaries at Christ Church, William Wingfield, who became a Roman Catholic with his wife in 1845. Frances Wingfield was also a "zealous Puseyite" and frequently attended Frederick Oakeley's services at the district chapel in Margaret Street in London.[47]

In 1844, Ward had replied to a protest against his writings by William

Palmer with the publication of "The Ideal of a Christian Church considered in comparison with Existing Practice." It was a ponderous work of 600 pages, for which he was given the nickname "Ideal Ward." In it he argued that only the Roman Church satisfied all the conditions of what a church ought to be.[48] When the book was widely read, the university decided to censure Ward and portions of his study as inconsistent with the Thirty-nine articles of the Anglican Church. Ward was formally censured on 13 February 1845. He resigned his fellowship and married on 31 March 1845, settling at Rose Hill, near Oxford.

Frances Mary Wingfield found in her husband, for the first time, "an Anglican who absolutely believed in the Church of Rome as the one true Church."[49] They were both received into the Roman Catholic Church at the Jesuit chapel in Bolton Street in London by Father James Brownbill, on 5 September 1845, and confirmed by Nicholas Wiseman at Oscott on 14 September.

With the help of Father Robert Whitty, Ward made an arrangement with Bishop Griffiths, the vicar apostolic of the London District, and Edward Cox, then president of St Edmund's College, for a plot of land within the park in which the college was located. Ward gave a legacy of a few hundred pounds to the school, and had Edward Pugin design a country house in the Gothic style. The architect was at first delighted with Ward. When he visited him he found "hugh folio volumes of St Thomas Aquinas and St Bonaventure on Ward's table and recognized the true medieval spirit."[50] The house was built, and he and his wife moved in during 1846.

At first he did not teach at the college but spent his time in the study of theology. Ward was poor at the time, for he had not come into possession of the family estate on the Isle of Wight. He was called upon by Wiseman in 1851 to teach the seminarians from Westminster and Southwark at St Edmund's. He first taught philosophy and then dogmatic theology. He held the position despite strong opposition both inside and outside the college to a lay convert and married man teaching theology at a school for the training of priests. George Talbot helped to have his appointment approved at Rome, and in 1854 the Pope awarded him a doctorate. His lectures were carefully prepared for his students and aimed at the construction of a systematic treatise "On Nature and Grace," and were clearly ultramontanist in tone.[51] Vaughan met Ward at St Edmund's in 1855.

Herbert Vaughan prepares for St Edmund's

Nicholas Wiseman had another idea which he communicated to Herbert Vaughan through Father Whitty at Rome in early 1854. Wiseman wanted to form a missionary community of secular clergy, "a band of men ready to his hand, willing to devote themselves to whatever enterprise he should point out to them."[52] Despite the introduction of many religious communities to London, he did not find any who were able to implement his plans for the diocese. They answered his requests for help by saying that the conditions he wanted them to work under were contrary to their rule. Wiseman wrote to Fr Faber that he had described his idea to Henry Manning in 1853 as an "Oratory with external action" of men somehow between the "secular and regular state." He had seen such groups while travelling on the Continent, and it appeared to him that "Providence has now given me an opportunity of gathering together such a band. Mr Manning, I think, understands my wishes and feelings and is ready to assist me; several will, I hope, join him...."[53] Several did join Manning. One of them was Herbert Vaughan.

In 1853, while Manning was still in Rome, Wiseman had Whitty write to him asking that he return to England to help in the formation of a congregation of Oblates of St Charles for the Diocese of Westminster.[54] Manning placed the letter before Pius IX and the Pope asked that he remain in Rome. Finally in 1854 Manning returned to England. David Newsome says that Manning was in full sympathy with Wiseman. In 1856 he returned to Rome again with letters from Wiseman asking for the approval of Pius IX and the prefect of Propaganda for the new congregation. With the help of Mgr Cardoni, Manning drew up a rule, using as a model the sixteenth-century congregation of Oblates founded by Charles Borromeo in Milan.[55] According to Snead-Cox, when Herbert Vaughan was appointed to St Edmund's, "he went as an avowed disciple of Manning," and had already offered to join the Oblates.

To prepare for his appointment to St Edmund's, Herbert Vaughan visited some of the principal Italian, French, German and Austrian seminaries. As he would do throughout his career, he prepared for his work very well. Wiseman suggested that he follow his same route of twenty years earlier, and gave him the itinerary he used on his journey in 1835.[56] Herbert travelled armed with introductions from Wiseman.

His first interview took place in Munich on his birthday, 15 April 1855. He left a notebook recording the places he visited and the questions he asked: "His practice was to note the order of life in each seminary and discuss problems connected with the formation of the secular clergy."[57] He wrote down the views of men such as Dollinger and Denzinger. Even at the age of twenty-three he was asking a question to which he returned throughout his life: "What is the perfection proper to the secular priest?" He continued to accumulate information on subsequent visits to the Continent and Ireland, and asked others to do so on his behalf. Before he was thirty, he was to be one of the best-informed men of his time on the "state of the question regarding the secular clergy."[58]

George Errington

While Herbert Vaughan prepared himself for St Edmund's, and shortly before Wiseman re-approached Manning about his plan for Oblates in Westminster, a step was taken that was to be the undoing of the Cardinal's peace of mind.[59] Due to increasing work and failing health, Wiseman chose as his co-adjutor George Errington, bishop of Plymouth. Newsome considers Wiseman's choice of Errington for his co-adjutor to be "perhaps the greatest blunder of his life."[60] Errington had been a contemporary of Wiseman at Ushaw and at the English College in Rome, where he had been his vice-rector. He was a canon lawyer and held in high regard by Old Catholic clergy. Mathew described Errington as a "fine old lion; weather-beaten, rather grim; well read in theology; exacting, determined; of old Catholic stock from High Warden in Northumberland."[61]

Errington was also his prefect of studies at Oscott where they had become close friends. But George Errington was a different kind of man from Nicholas Wiseman. Wiseman could avoid business matters for days "while he was absorbed in writing an article or preparing a lecture." To his vicar general, it was often: "No business today, Dr.Whitty."[62] Errington, on the other hand, was efficient and disciplined in business, more "English" than "Roman" in outlook, and unmovable on points of principle. He was once described by Mother Margaret Hallahan as "hewn out of a rock." He was a stern individual and something of a "martinet." Bishop Grant of Southwark warned Wiseman to be careful of Errington if he wanted his advice. Through his blue-tinted spectacles he viewed the accumulating evidence of Wiseman's attempt, as he saw it, to take over St Edmund's College as a microcosm of the fate of the entire English Church.[63] According to Newsome, Errington distrusted converts; "There would be no favours to the Mannings of this world, if it was left to him."[64]

Wiseman may have mistakenly presumed that their earlier relationship would help them develop a harmonious partnership at Westminster. The collaboration he sought did not develop. Wiseman was also suffering from diabetes and heart failure. The situation was complicated by Wiseman's friendship with Manning.

Opposition to Wiseman had grown following the first Synod of Westminster at Oscott in 1852. He was not helped by attacks made by impatient converts such as William George Ward and Edward Manning on the Old Catholics. Manning once described "the little remnant" as "one of the greatest evils in England." Opposing views of the English Church began to be played out in a conflict at St Edmund's shortly before Herbert Vaughan arrived.

Within six months of his appointment in 1855, George Errington, who, with others, had considered the appointment of W. G. Ward to the college as foolhardy, made an official visit to St Edmund's. Errington "expressed disapproval," and imposed restrictions on Ward's methods, which he considered too Roman. Ward resigned, but Wiseman promptly reinstated him. Errington then suggested that he would submit his own resignation, reasoning that the public would see the issue as a "trial of strength between my influence and one opposed to it."[65] Instead of resigning, Errington was temporarily appointed as administrator of the diocese of Clifton, where he was to remain for about two years. Years later Errington summed up his attitude and that of many London clergy to Ward's appointment: "If Ward were a second St. Thomas Aquinas as theologian, and a St. Charles Borromeo in matters of ecclesiastical discipline, it is so great an anomaly that a married secular should govern, by the influence of his talent, an ecclesiastical seminary, that I do not believe such an arrangement would have the blessing of God."[66]

In 1855, Herbert Vaughan arrived at St Edmund's full of enthusiasm and the ideas collected in his diary during his European travels. He wrote of his admiration for the College of Propaganda in Rome: "Look at Propaganda—a great model for us—where men of all classes and nations, languages and climates dwell in one seminary."[67] What was he to make of St Edmund's? "Let us transplant," he wrote, "the Sulpician or German plant to England with enough earth to keep it alive, but then, let it be planted in English soil, and according to the genius of the country." He also had a strong opinion about the mixing of lay and church students as was done at St Edmund's. He thought that the presence of lay students reduced rather than enhanced the "ecclesiastical spirit," but at the same time he was not in favour of excessive isolation. To accept the post at Old Hall, he had given up his idea of becoming a missionary to Wales in favour of Wiseman's plan to prepare apostolic priests for the "conversion of England." And yet, he did not abandon his thoughts of a missionary life completely.[68]

Cardinal Wiseman had also appointed an Edmundian, William Weathers, to replace Edward Cox as president of St Edmund's.[69] Weathers was not in favour of Wiseman's "Romanish" reforms, nor had he asked for, or welcomed, the appointment of Herbert Vaughan to the staff. Vaughan, at twenty-three, was younger than some of the students. He was a seen as a protégé of both Wiseman and Manning, and therefore the representative of an aggressive faction. His months of travelling around the Continent with Wiseman's letter of introduction clearly made him a challenge to both the administration and some of the college staff members. He was perceived as part of Wiseman's plan to reform St Edmund's, and, it was suspected, to get the training of the clergy into the hands of the archbishop.[70]

Herbert Vaughan displayed his youthful arrogance on the day after his arrival, when he knocked at the door of William George Ward's room. One of the first goals, Vaughan thought, was to replace Ward on the staff. To Vaughan it was unacceptable that theology was being taught to ecclesiastical students by a layman and a married man "who had never gone through a regular course under a trained professor." How Herbert Vaughan came to this view, and acted in the way he did, knowing that Wiseman had championed Ward, is not explained. Herbert Vaughan himself is the source for a description of his first encounter with Ward. He told the story of his own temerity in approaching a man of Ward's stature, perhaps struck by his own pretensions and the humour of the incident.

Ward invited Vaughan for a walk and opened the conversation with a leading question: "Well, what are your views about the college and my relations to it?" Herbert replied that he thought Ward's position irregular, and that he would like him replaced by a priest as soon as possible. Apparently, Ward took the measure of Vaughan immediately, and calmly replied: "How very interesting!; Yes, I quite see your point; Most interesting." In what was characteristic of Vaughan and a habit he was aware of, he spoke impatiently and in a confrontational tone to Ward. Vaughan recalled forty years later that he "blurted out to him during our first walk that I wished him far away, as an untrustworthy, because an untaught, teacher for such a post."[71] Vaughan was speaking to the Oxford convert who is considered by some to be the most prominent English ultramontane intellectual of the nineteenth century.[72] In response, Ward asked Vaughan to attend some of his lectures before judging him. Vaughan did so and "his mind was changed by the very first lecture he heard; so much so that he begged leave to attend as regularly as his duties would permit, and later on when Dr. Ward's pupils presented him with an address on his retirement, Dr. Vaughan signed his name among them." Vaughan quickly changed his opinion of Ward: "Anything like rivalry, or opposition or distrust became impossible and instead of being an opponent, Herbert became a partisan. Because he was not very occupied himself, he took up the post of censor, sitting in on Ward's lectures." Between the two men there sprang up a close friendship, which Ward, writing twenty years afterwards accounted "as among the highest privileges which he possessed."[73]

William George Ward died in 1882. His son, Wilfrid, remembered Herbert Vaughan's eulogy in which he spoke of his father as "the champion of the unpopular truth" and then thinking that this sentiment had become the ideal of Vaughan's own sense of duty. Friendship with Ward and his family became one of the more important influences of Herbert Vaughan's early career.[74]

The confrontational approach the twenty-three-year-old Vaughan took towards William George Ward at St Edmund's on their first meeting was similar to other incidents in Vaughan's public life. Wilfrid Ward thought that Herbert Vaughan "could not move in a mixed crowd without occasionally jostling it, sometimes too roughly to put it in the best temper for understanding him." As for controversy, such as the one he was to be part of at St Edmund's, he admitted that "he had at times too bad an opinion of his opponents' case even to try to persuade them." He was often intent on convicting his opponents rather than convincing them.[75]

Herbert Vaughan preached in the college chapel on Pentecost Sunday, 1856; the theme was devotion to the Holy Ghost. It is the only sermon of his known to be preserved from that period. He urged his listeners, no matter at what stage of intellectual growth they were, to pray to the Holy Spirit for sanctity and light; that "grace and light from the Holy One which is the quickening of vigour to your life." It was a mild appeal, and it fitted Wiseman's theme of raising the standard of seminary training at St Edmund's.[76]

The status of George Errington following the disagreement over Ward's position at St Edmund's was resolved when Ward resigned in 1856. Wiseman requested that his assistant bishop return to London from Clifton, which he did. Once Errington complied, Ward withdrew his resignation.[77] Ward finally resigned his lectureship at St Edmund's in 1858, and moved to Northwood Park on the Isle of Wight, the estate he had inherited from his father in 1849. His stay at Northwood was brief and he returned to his house at Old Hall in 1860 "with a mind made up to wage war" against liberalism in the Church, a crusade he carried on chiefly in the pages of the *Dublin Review*.[78]

Westminster Chapter opposes Wiseman and the Oblates

Cardinal Wiseman's plan to form an Oblate community became a formal petition to Rome in November 1856 and Herbert Vaughan's name was second on the list of members, behind that of Henry Manning. The word "Oblate", from oblation, the act of a religious offering, had been taken on by some religious groups following the Council of Trent in the sixteenth century. One group was that of Saints Ambrose and Charles, a community of secular priests formed for pastoral work in Milan in 1578 by Charles Borromeo. This was the community Wiseman chose to imitate; with a rule modified to suit English conditions.[79]

A centre for the new community was found in Westmorland Road in Bayswater. There had been a small school and a chapel with one priest between Marble Arch and Harrow-on-the-Hill. Two ladies, sisters, had undertaken the expense of building a church on Westmorland Road, but had underestimated the cost, and the work came to a halt. When only the walls and part of a tower were finished the two benefactors died. Manning asked Wiseman to chose the unfinished Bayswater site as the centre for the Oblates' missionary and education scheme for the diocese.

On the Monday after Pentecost, 1 June 1857, Manning, Vaughan, four other priests and two clerics held their first General Chapter in a small house at 12 Sutherland Place, close by the unfinished church. On 2 July the first service took place in a "splendid new gothic-conceived church of Thomas Meyer," and it was blessed by Cardinal Wiseman and dedicated to St Mary of the Angels.[80] The founding members were all admitted as novices on the day of the first meeting. The original group was made up of Manning, then forty-nine years of age, Herbert Vaughan, twenty-five years, William Roberts, William Burke and Thomas McDonnell. At Rome there were two students; converts Charles Laprimaudaye and Augustus Rawes.[81]

The Oblates faced opposition from Archbishop Errington and the majority of Wiseman's own Westminster chapter. Errington returned to Westminster in 1857 and he came into conflict almost at once with Wiseman over the Oblates and their position at St Edmund's. He opposed the idea of a community of secular priests, believing that they would in effect become a religious order and independent of the Cardinal. David Newsome considers Errington's antipathy to converts to be the source of endless trouble. With the eye of a keen canon lawyer, Errington found a discrepancy in Manning's version of the Borromeo rule and concluded that it suggested that the Oblates were intending to evade control of the bishop. Errington wrote to Rome that "Manning was manoeuvring to remove the Oblates from episcopal control." He then challenged the Oblates' right to take over the Bayswater church. Wiseman refused to take any action. "This was the background to a battle royal against the Oblates, aimed at their apparent take-over of the seminary at St Edmund's."[82]

When Herbert Vaughan and two other members of St Edmund's staff became members of the new community, it appeared to Errington and others that "Wiseman's circle" was preparing to hand the college over to the Oblates. In April 1857, Manning was appointed provost of the Westminster chapter ahead of more senior candidates among the canons. Manning and the Cardinal had expected the post to be filled by John Maguire, vicar general and canon theologian of the diocese. Pius IX personally nominated Manning to replace Robert Whitty, who had resigned to become a Jesuit. The old clergy were stunned and many of the chapter were outraged. According to Newsome, Manning's most formidable opponents were Francis Searle, Wiseman's personal secretary, John Maguire and Errington, "who regarded themselves, as of right, to be the Cardinal's inner council."[83]

Errington, along with Grant of Southwark, considered the presence of the Oblates at the college to be an unlawful intrusion, and the Westminster chapter asked Manning to produce the rules of the Oblates for an examination. The two bishops and the chapters of Westminster and Southwark objected that having a religious community in the middle of a seminary for the training of secular priests was contrary to the decrees of the Council of Trent. But the fundamental issue involved the right of the chapter to interfere in matters which, according to Wiseman, were clearly within the sole jurisdiction of the bishop.[84]

In July 1858 the status of Vaughan and the other Oblates at St Edmund's became intertwined in the controversy between the chapter and Wiseman.

According to the Council of Trent each diocese should set up a seminary under direction of the local bishop. Wiseman's critics and his chapter petitioned Rome that St Edmund's did not fall into this type of seminary but was "a mixed college for the education of lay boys and priests." Therefore Trent did not apply and it was not under Wiseman's control. Principles in the dispute were to surface "upon the sea of suspicions and ideological incompatibilities."[85]

The Oblates considered that their vocation was to remain diocesan priests while living in community and at the disposal of the bishop. They were to undertake tasks which the diocesan clergy could not efficiently perform. One such task was the training of priests at St Edmund's. While the controversy continued, Vaughan and his fellow Oblates remained at the college, and the issue of their presence became an expression of a much larger conflict for the local Church.[86]

At St Edmund's, in addition to being vice-president, Herbert Vaughan was novice-master of the small Oblate community. Each Friday, Frs Archibald MacDonald, Henry O'Callaghan, Robert Butler and Vaughan met. The first of these "spiritual chapters" took place on 25 August 1857. Herbert Vaughan was listed as "vicar of the spiritual director."[87] Henry Manning, as the Oblate superior, wrote to Vaughan "urging a policy almost in defiance of that pursued by the President."[88] The Oblates at the college were seen as representing Manning, "a man rightly suspected of wishing to get St Edmund's under Oblate control."[89] It was a conflict of interests for Vaughan. He was effectively Manning's assistant for the Oblates and vice-president of St Edmund's. Therefore to whom was he to give his loyalty, Weathers or Manning? It was never an issue for Vaughan for he recognized Manning as his superior and Wiseman as his bishop.[90] Hostility to his presence and that of his fellow Oblates increased among some of the students, clergy and canons of the chapter.

Herbert Vaughan continued to suffer the effects of heart problems while at Old Hall. A little more than a year after arriving, he wrote in his diary: "The night before last I suffered violent throbbings of the heart. I have been thinking that before long I shall die." It was the heart attack he recalled forty years later, when he suffered another.

In spite of his intermittent ill health and suspected "espionage" on behalf of Manning and the Oblates, Vaughan was seen by the younger students as young, handsome, generous, and open-hearted, with "contagious enthusiasms" that many admired. This was the assessment of Bishop Fenton, who had been a student at St Edmund's in 1855. Fenton told Snead-Cox that Vaughan was a great hero with all the students below Philosophy: "He was a tall, fine, handsome man and a beautiful rider, and the boys were proud of him as vice-president when they saw him galloping over the park on a fine charger that his father the Colonel had given him. He was very popular with the boys and rightly so because he was very kind to them." When they were sick he was infirmarian. When they were poor he gave them money, always quietly, in such a way that no one should know what he was doing. For their part, according to Fenton, the Church students found his monthly conferences encouraging.[91] However, Michael Clifton, in his biography of Bishop Grant, found material to show otherwise, that is, "how unpopular Vaughan was with many of the students at St Edmund's."[92] Vaughan's critics would become more vocal during the summer of 1859.

Herbert Vaughan's activities were not confined to the college. On Sunday mornings he offered Mass at Hertford, Waltham Cross or St Albans, and later at Enfield. There is also a tradition that Vaughan worked occasionally at St Mary and St Michael on Commercial Road in London's East End during 1856-7.[93] He made especially his own the mission at Hertford. The mission was named in honour of the Immaculate Conception and St Joseph and founded by Vaughan in 1858. He collected money from family and friends to build a permanent church and presbytery on St John's Street. Cardinal Wiseman blessed the new buildings.[94]

One Sunday evening, when he was returning to St Edmund's in the college "dog-cart," he was stopped between Hertford and Ware by a man who pointed a pistol at him and demanded money. Vaughan got out of the cart on the opposite side, and going around, "attacked the man from behind with his whip; whereupon the latter got into the cart and drove off in the direction of Hertford." Vaughan was left standing on the road with his whip. The thief did not drive very far. When Vaughan reached Hertford on foot, he found his horse and cart in the station yard; the bandit had probably made his exit on the train.[95]

The dispute over the status of St Edmund's and the presence of the Oblates continued. On 1 July 1858, the chapter began its investigation of the college. At the meeting John Maguire questioned William Weathers, the president. He wanted to know whether there was a plan to hand over government of the college to some congregation and whether some professors were subject to Manning's authority. Weathers admitted that some were directly under another superior but that he had no direct knowledge that the college was to be handed over to a congregation. Weathers and Manning agreed that the president had considered becoming an Oblate.

In August Maguire wrote to Manning asking for a copy of the Oblate Rule. Manning asked for Wiseman's advice. On 1 September Manning advised the chapter that they had no right to initiate an investigation without the bishop's permission. On 15 September the chapter met again. Manning, the provost of the chapter, was asked to leave the hall, but he refused to do so. After an adjournment, the meeting chose Maguire, O'Neal, Searle and Oakeley to see the Cardinal about the administration of St Edmund's. They wanted assurance that problems would be avoided "arising, and likely to arise in a greater degree, from the professorial staff of St Edmund's being formed partly of ordinary secular priests of the two dioceses, and partly from members of a Congregation in a very different relation to the diocese; still more necessary is every guarantee, if it be true (as rumour had added), that there has been some probability of the seminary being entrusted to the new Congregation."[96]

For Wiseman, the proceedings were a revolt against the provost and himself, and so, in December 1858, he annulled the decisions of the chapter and both sides appealed to Rome. Some opponents complained that Wiseman was "acting tyrannically and arbitrarily." One member of the chapter, Canon Maguire, was upset by the estrangement from Wiseman whom he had served "faithfully and assiduously."[97] Maguire, the vicar general, was later dismissed by Wiseman for his opposition.[98] Rome answered the petitions on 7 January 1859, and referred to a previous decision regarding the difficulties of implementing the Council of Trent's norms for seminaries. Wiseman was asked to call a provincial council of bishops to discuss the matter.

The particular issues concerning the Oblates at St Edmund's, Manning and the Westminster Chapter, broadened into a dispute between Wiseman and the other bishops of the hierarchy over control of theological colleges. At the Oscott synod of bishops in the summer of 1859, Archbishop Errington and Bishop Grant were Wiseman's most forceful opponents. David Newsome writes that "the complete breakdown of relations between the Archbishop of Westminster and his coadjutor" was another issue that had to be settled at Rome.[99]

While Manning was scrupulous in trying to avoid involvement, Vaughan was "not slow in expressing his own views," according to Newsome.[100] Vaughan's opinion is clear in correspondence of the summer of 1859, during the heat of the controversy between Wiseman and his chapter. At the same time, although he was at the centre of the conflict, there are no complaints in his diary. Rather it contains concerns about his own failings and lack of progress in the spiritual life.[101]

A Charge of Espionage

At St Edmund's, Vaughan may have been popular with the younger boys, but he was not well received by the senior students, whose immediate superior he was. Many students were nearly his age, or older, and ready for ordination. Bishop Fenton remembered that "he had some trouble with them," perhaps over preservation of discipline in the college. Manning wrote to Mgr Talbot that the Oblates were hated as sneaks at St Edmund's because they tried to enforce the rules. For example, he continued, "Herbert Vaughan was barred from a room where boys were smoking and drinking."[102]

On 13 June 1859 students of Southwark diocese sent a letter to Grant, their bishop, complaining about Vaughan. They charged that an attempt had been made to use the "divines" to support a proposal that the "present Vice-President (Vaughan) is so confided in and beloved by the students generally, that they would hail with the greatest satisfaction his accession to the post of President in the place of Dr Weathers.... However much we respect the present vice Rector, we know that he is a member of a religious order whose partial association in the government of the college has already given rise to suspicion and heart burning ... the oblates have completely failed in gaining the confidence and affection of the students."[103]

William Weathers told Vaughan that there were sufficient grounds for "an odious charge popularly circulated in and out of College to Fr Vaughan's serious prejudice that he had introduced and kept up a system of espionage among the boys." Vaughan called for an investigation by Wiseman and Grant. Wiseman told Weathers that such a meeting could take place only after the July synod.[104]

And so, on 27 August, Cardinal Wiseman and Bishop Grant conducted a visitation of St Edmunds to investigate the charges of "espionage" that had been made against Herbert Vaughan and the Oblates. Vaughan reported what took place in a four-page letter to his Oblate superior, Henry Manning. The meeting was held and the student complaints were brought out into the open. Herbert Vaughan was accused of operating an "odious system of espionage." Vaughan in turn charged that Weathers was an accessory by his silence and consent to the "calumny." He explained at the meeting that he was trying to introduce "a system of confidence and mutual relations between student and superior." He suspected that Weathers was so anxious to find something against him and the Oblates that he asked three students and three priests to gather evidence of "espionage." When Weathers complained that Vaughan disagreed with his decisions as president, Vaughan countered that he had done so in a number of cases which were "justified in the eyes of the Bishops."

Grant and Wiseman called Vaughan and Weathers aside and asked them to reconcile their differences and work in harmony. Vaughan continued in his report to Manning that he promised to do his best, "though expressing my doubts candidly as to the results." The senior seminary students were to be told that the charge of "espionage against Vaughan had been investigated and they (the bishops) had found that the report was without foundation ... a calumny." Weathers told the students of the findings, and that they must all concur in it, "but different impressions seem to have been made on different minds by his words."

Vaughan concluded his report with a boast that "the result of the whole is a complete moral victory." He thought that Wiseman had "carried the whole thing splendidly and I am sure we must all feel very grateful to him for having given us this opportunity of another victory." The victory was that Weathers' authority was not destroyed, and Vaughan had been "exculpated from the charge brought against me and to raise my moral position indefinitely by the formal expression of the 'increased confidence' in me which this investigation resulted in."[105]

Vaughan was to fall from the heights of the "moral position" he was confident of in 1859. Writing to Manning again in 1860 or 1861, he reminded him of the price he paid for his personal loyalty to his superior while at St Edmund's. He wrote that he had always spoken to him "with the most natural simplicity. I have never thought of expressing my ideas to you through hints or of politically furnishing data and leaving the conclusions to be drawn. I have kept back nothing from you—save much fighting I have had for you and much ill-will that I have gained ... through my defence of you personally as well as of principles which are mutually ours."[106]

On 13 June 1859 Herbert Vaughan completed the second year of his Oblate novitiate and on 2 July, along with Manning, William Roberts, Thomas Dillon, Henry Rawes, Thomas McDonnell and Henry O'Callaghan, he made his commitment before Cardinal Wiseman. At their 8 August meeting at St Mary of the Angels, it was formally announced that they had made their "oblation."[107]

In the spring of 1860 Herbert was sick again. It was suspected that he had smallpox. He wrote to his father: "I write because no man knows the day or the hour—mine may be at hand. I never looked at the possibility of death with more calmness, thanks to Our Lord."[108]

Family Matters

While on the staff of St Edmund's, Vaughan was also concerned with the welfare of his brothers, sisters and widowed father. In the spring of 1856 the family had returned to England from almost three years' stay at Boulogne in France. The manor at Courtfield remained closed because Colonel Vaughan found it impossible to make up his mind to return to the scenes of past happiness. Instead, he rented a house in London, at 31 Brompton Crescent, and later in Montague Square. In London the family would be near to both Herbert and Roger, who was a Benedictine monk, ordained in 1859.[109]

Colonel Vaughan brought along most of the library from Courtfield. Their London home was near to the Brompton Oratory, where they attended Mass, and where Clare Vaughan spent her free time "absorbed in adoration before the Blessed Sacrament." The eldest sister, Gwladys, left in 1856 to join the Visitation nuns at Marquera near Boulogne. Clare Mary joined a community of Poor Clares at Amiens—where she was to die on 20 January 1862. Another sister, Teresa, pleaded with her father in 1857 to be allowed to become a Sister of Charity. One sister, Margaret, born in 1851, was handicapped.

Bernard Vaughan left a note describing family life at London and the influence of his brother Herbert: "About this time," he wrote, "Herbert used to ride up to London from Old Hall and exhort and encourage us to undertake works of piety and charity such as our mother practised." Herbert made arrangements with Fr Zanetti, a Jesuit and his former "master" at Stonyhurst, to let the Vaughan children visit a Jesuit poor school at Westminster. Three of the sisters—Teresa, Clare and Mary—would load up once or twice a week with food and gifts for the sick, and those in need, and go out quietly at about 11 p.m. to make their deliveries.[110] Obligations to the Oblate community also required him to go regularly to London. Within two years of its foundation, in addition to the development of the community house and mission at Bayswater, the Oblates were instrumental in establishing three new missions and churches in poor areas, along with seven elementary schools. They also engaged in parish preaching, conducted missions and gave retreats. At the first elections, Manning was confirmed as superior by Cardinal Wiseman. "Dr Manning of Bayswater," as he became known, was simply "Father" in the community. The "oblation" they made was an offering of each person to the work undertaken by the congregation and a promise of obedience to its constitutions. A member was bound to the task given: in this case, the work of the Westminster Diocese.[111]

Vaughan returned in the autumn of 1860 for what was to be his final school year at St Edmund's. His situation, and that of the other Oblates at the college, remained stormy. In Richard Schiefen's opinion, Herbert Vaughan did little to calm Cardinal Wiseman, or the tensions generated by the case pending in Rome over the involvement of the Oblates at St Edmund's. Wiseman felt the need for close friends in whom he could confide during his conflicts with the chapter and Archbishop Errington. The Cardinal turned more and more to those who were younger. "These young men, [such as Herbert Vaughan] while lending him the desired support, did little to calm his spirit." The harshness of their judgements could only have contributed to his sense of despair. Herbert Vaughan, for example, concluded that there was a "movement ... evidently designed to drive the Cardinal out of England," and added that Searle, the Cardinal's secretary, "always did him harm." Of Archbishop Errington, he wrote: he "seems really to care nothing for souls."[112] This is a side of Herbert Vaughan that would surface throughout much of his life, and one that he often acknowledged; that he could be impetuous, contrary, harsh, abrupt and self-righteous.[113]

Vaughan and others, Schiefen continues, "should have moderated their rhetoric in the interest of peace. Instead, they made matters worse by inflammatory judgements and accusations." Those who were at odds over St Edmund's and the Oblates had previously been "thoroughly devoted" to each other. Archbishop Errington, for example, had known Wiseman before Herbert Vaughan was born.[114]

William George Ward and Family

There was another influence at St Edmund's in 1860. William George Ward had returned from running his estate near Cowes on the Isle of Wight. His health broke down, caused, he said, "by a mode of life and duties so uncongenial." His son Wilfrid was born at the Ward house at Old Hall, on 2 January 1856, and came to know many of those who visited his father during his childhood there and at Northwood. "Father Herbert Vaughan was an intimate friend and guide to the family. His frequent visits were the great excitement of our early youth," wrote Wilfrid.[115]

By 1860, William George Ward was enormously fat. He was described as a "combination of Socrates and Falstaff." Aware of his own intellectual power, he once said, "I have the mind of an archangel in the body of a rhinoceros." Inside the Catholic Church Ward fell by temperament into what has been called the extreme right wing of English Catholicism. "There are two views," he once said, "of which I, as usual, take the more bigoted." Ward developed extreme views of Catholic orthodoxy; Bishop Ullathorne called him "*vir super omnia dogmaticus.*" Ward chose Father Frederick Faber as his spiritual director, the London Oratory as his ideal church, and Manning as the leader of his party.[116] As he grew older he became "very narrow and very strong."[117]

Wilfrid Ward recorded his reminiscences in 1913. When he was born in 1856, Cardinal Wiseman wrote to the Wards: "I pray God to bless mother and child." Once, on a visit to Old Hall, he put his biretta on Wilfrid's head saying, "You will be a Cardinal." The nine Ward children came to think of the "world that really mattered somewhat as of a great battlefield with two camps, which we always called 'the right side' and the 'wrong side;' the former consisting of all who took my father's general views on matters ecclesiastical, the latter of those who opposed them." The opposition was a mixed group including Newman, Sir John Acton and the President of St Edmunds, all representing levels of "ecclesiastical liberalism." Wilfrid Ward eventually learned that the "so-called liberalism" at St Edmund's had only "consisted in opposition to the policy of my father and Herbert Vaughan." Vaughan, appointed by Wiseman, guided by Manning, and supported by Ward, "made a party among the divinity students of zealous young men who became Oblates of St Charles. They adopted many habits from foreign seminaries and were regarded by their neighbours as indiscreet and priggish and hostile to the President."[118]

One can detect similarities in temperament and view of the right "ecclesiastical spirit" between Vaughan and Ward, however overpowering Ward's intellect was when compared to Vaughan's. Herbert Vaughan's blunt and intemperate reports to Wiseman, referred to by Schiefen, were those of an inexperienced vice-president of St Edmund's who sounds very much like Ward. At Ward's funeral in 1882, Wilfrid remembered Vaughan as saying: "No one had known Dr Ward's mind more intimately than he ... no one agreed more thoroughly with his expositions and views, no one had better opportunity of marking his character."[119]

The ill-fated enterprise at St Edmund's that aroused the opposition of the Westminster chapter, and the uncompromising hostility of Archbishop Errington, continued to 1861. In March 1860 Manning drew up a memorandum, a defence of the Oblate community against Errington's accusations, and took it to Rome for Pius IX. Among other points, it explained the involvement of the Oblates, at Wiseman's direction, in the teaching and administration of the diocesan seminary. Manning also defended the work of the Oblates and Herbert Vaughan to Monsignor George Talbot, who was in Rome.[120]

The secular clergy, according to Manning's supporters, were losing the spiritual direction of the educated laity, at least in London, to the religious orders. It was felt that the needs of the laity were not being met by the seculars. Therefore, what seemed to be needed urgently was a "Council of Trent" seminary, directed by secular priests "who have learned to live by a common rule, and can act with unity of mind and purpose." Later Manning told Wiseman that he saw the issue as being greater than St Edmund's, the Oblates and the training of secular priests: "It has become a question of episcopal jurisdiction and capitular submission."[121]

The Oblates left St Edmund's in the summer of 1861. On 4 November, Cardinal Wiseman addressed a meeting of the Oblates at Bayswater, and said that "the resignation of four of the Fathers of their professorial chairs at St Edmund's College, he believed to be the best for all parties concerned."[122] In the winter of 1861 Rome ruled that Herbert Vaughan's position, along with the other Oblates, at St Edmund's, was a contravention of the decrees of the Council of Trent. Vaughan's position was an important element in "the most notorious English Catholic dispute of the century."[123]

Henry Manning hoped that a step backward from St Edmund's in 1861 would be followed by one forward in 1862. Meanwhile, Vaughan looked back on his work at St Edmund's with a sense of frustration and disappointment. He had felt lonely and powerless. He had concluded, soon after his arrival, that it was desirable to remove the lay students and make the seminary purely ecclesiastical, but chose to be "very silent about this." No doubt so quiet that Manning accused him of being "led away by Oakeley or the Fathers."[124] Vaughan may have remained "very silent" about the presence of lay students, but not about other issues.

It was one of Wiseman's priorities to raise the standard of the secular priesthood. It was a goal of Manning's and Vaughan's as well. Towards the end of his life, Manning argued that the priesthood is the first and chief of the religious orders, the only such order founded by Christ. In 1883, his book *The Eternal Priesthood* sought to give theological and devotional ground for his ideas. In like manner, so did Herbert Vaughan's *The Young Priest*, written in his final days and published after his death. Owen Chadwick wrote of Manning: "powerful offspring of the Oxford Movement, tried to do for the clergy of the Church of Rome what the entire Movement sought to do for the clergy of the Church of England."[125] Vaughan, more than forty years later, would write: "The distinctive work of the Episcopate is to produce and multiply a holy Priesthood. The Priesthood of Jesus is stored up in the Bishop, and he is bound not only to give it birth, but to feed, train, and perfect it on the model of Christ and His Apostles."[126]

The lamentable controversy probably broke Wiseman; he became melancholic and suffered a heart attack during the proceedings at Rome. It also broke the spirit of the Old Catholics and has been "compared with the defeat of the Celtic Church in England by Rome at the Synod of Whitby in AD 664."[127] The Oblates were removed from St Edmund's, but Errington lost his right of succession and the chapter was defeated.

Herbert Vaughan experienced hard lessons at St Edmund's. At the same time he won a loyal friend in William George Ward who became associated, along with his family, with many of the major events of Vaughan's life. Ward wrote to Vaughan in 1880: "I account your friendship as amongst the highest privileges I possess."[128]

William George Ward's son Bernard wrote on Vaughan's death in 1903 that Herbert Vaughan carried out "several reforms and improvements" during his years at St Edmund's. "But his term of office cannot be considered wholly a success. When Dr. Crookall retired to open the vice presidency for Vaughan, Weathers, the president, had not asked for him. This made his appointment a delicate one." In addition his restless energy "could not find sufficient scope within the walls of the College, and he frequently undertook work outside which interfered with the continuous residence so essential for College life." His Sundays at Hertford, commitments to the Oblates at Bayswater and family responsibilities in London "could not but interfere with the duties he had taken in hand at the College," according to Ward.[129]

Disappointed and frustrated by the circumstances surrounding his tenure at St Edmund's, and finally by Rome's order to withdraw the Oblates, Herbert Vaughan began to dream again of great adventure: "In proportion as I saw I could do nothing at St Edmund's in the direction I wished, the idea of foreign missions grew upon me."[130]

Notes

1. Snead-Cox, 1, pp.454–5: In 1852 Whitty travelled to Rome with Herbert Vaughan; Robert Whitty was born at Pouldarrig near Oldgate on 7 January 1817. When he was fourteen years old he entered Maynooth Seminary in Ireland. He offered himself to Bishop Griffiths, vicar apostolic of the London District. He came to Ware when he was a sub-deacon in 1839 and was ordained at St Edmund's College, on 19 September 1840. When Wiseman became archbishop of Westminster, he appointed Whitty provost of the cathedral chapter and his vicar general. In 1857 he resigned to become a Jesuit. He died on 1 September 1895 at the age of seventy-eight.

See: A. Askew, "St. Edmund's College Conference of the Society of St Vincent De Paul, 1845-1860," *Edmundian*, vol vi, no 35, December, 1904, pp.134-5; *The Catholic Encyclopedia*, XV, London, Encyclopedia Press; Ward, *Sequel*; Whitty had a sister with the Sisters of Mercy in Baggot St. See also: W. T. Gribbin, *St Edmund's College Bicentenary Book, 1793-1993*, Old Hall Press, 1993, p.53: A letter from Newman to Dalgairns, 16 December 1845: "I was but a few hours at St Edmund's. Mr Whitty I like extremely, though an Irishman. He is a very simple, natural, warm-hearted, reflecting person—apparently not thirty—very expectant of great accession of information, instruction etc. from converts....There is apparently little learning or cultivation there—they are behindhand—and have not the worldly set out (I am not using the words in a bad sense) of Prior Park...."

2. W. S. Lilly, "Cardinal Vaughan," *Nineteenth Century*, August 1910, p.241; Edmund Purcell, *Life of Cardinal Manning*, vol 2, London, Macmillan, 1896, p.121: Manning wrote to Whitty on 10 December 1858. Whitty had joined the Jesuits in 1857. "Cardinal Barnabò should know all the personnel of the affair (St Edmund's) ... Father Vaughan was your own selection and you can speak of the whole matter as no other person can...." According to Schiefen: "In spite of widely criticised inaccuracies, one should still consult E.S. Purcell's *Life of Cardinal Manning*. Errors of emphasis, detail and judgement abound, but the author has reproduced a vast amount of contemporary correspondence, some of which has been lost or is not readily available." p.126, fn.5.

3. Hanrahan, "Vaughan," p.717.
4. MHA. "Prospectus, St Edmund's College." HV, Box 45.
5. Sheridan Gilley, *The Tablet*, 11 January, 1992, p.35; See also: David Newsome, "Cardinal Manning and His Influence on Church and Nation," *Recusant History*, vol 21, no 2, October 1992, p.138. And his more recent: *The Convert Cardinals*, London, John Murray, 1993.
6. Seaman, *Victorian England*, pp.124-5.
7. Oliver Rafferty, "Nicholas Wiseman, Ecclesiastical Politics and Anglo-Irish Relations in the mid-nineteenth Century," *Recusant History*, vol 21, no. 3, May 1993, n. 6.
8. Wilfrid Ward, *The Life and Times of Cardinal Wiseman*, London, Longmans,1897. vol 1, p.1; See also: Brian Fathergill, *Nicholas Wiseman*, London, Faber, 1963.
9. David Mathew, *Catholicism in England*, London, Eyre and Spottiswoode, 1936, pp.193-5.
10. Rafferty, "Nicholas Wiseman".
11. Gribbin, *St Edmund's*, p.55.
12. Ward, *Wiseman*, vol 2, pp.163 and 174.
13. Newsome, "Cardinal Manning", pp.138-9; See also: Seaman, pp.124-5.
14. Derek Holmes, *More Roman than Rome*, London, Burns & Oates, 1978, p.48ff; For a helpful summary of ultramontanism, see: Patricia Byrne, C.S.J., "American Ultramontanism," *Theological Studies* 56, June 1995, pp.301-26.
15. Newsome, "Cardinal Manning", p.138.
16. Snead-Cox, 1, pp.67-8.
17. Edward Norman, *The English Catholic Church in the Nineteenth Century*, Oxford, Clarendon Press, 1984, p.130ff.
18. *ibid.*, p.131, fn.88.
19. *ibid.*, p.131.
20. Newsome, "Cardinal Manning", p.138.
21. *ibid.*, p.139.
22. *ibid.*
23. E. E. Reynolds, *Three Cardinals,* London, Burns & Oates, 1958, p.31; See: David Newsome, *The Parting of Friends, The Wilberforces and Henry Manning*, Leominster, Gracewing, 1993, pp.251-4.
24. Anthony Stark, "Cardinal Henry Edward Manning," *Westminster Diocesan Yearbook, 1993*, pp.174-7.

25. "More unpublished letters, Cardinal Manning's conversion," *The Tablet*, Saturday 9 April 1898, p.578.

26. Correspondence with Fr Holt, SJ, Archivist, Farm St: The baptism register for those years is missing.

27. Robert Gray, *Cardinal Manning*, London, Weidenfeld, 1985, p.140; James Pereiro, "Truth Before Peace: Manning and Infallibility," *Recusant History*, October 1992, pp. 236-7: He wrote to Gladstone on 6 December 1850 that he did not believe that the "Church of England is more than a provisional institution." This was not some rash judgement but "the deep conviction of long years of patient and silent thought." Recent events only "precipitated conclusions which for long years have hung suspended." About Manning's reception see also: Webb, *Modern England*, pp.232-3.

28. Newsome, *The Parting of Friends*, p.69.

29. Newsome, *Convert Cardinals*, p.200.

30. Norman, *Catholic Church*, p.354.

31. Mathew, *Catholicism*, pp.208, 222.

32. Norman, *Catholic Church*, p.354.

33. A. N. Wilson, *Hilaire Belloc*, London, Hamish Hamilton, 1984, pp.1-3.

34. Sheridan Gilley, "Mosaic Radical," *The Tablet*, 11 January 1992, p.35.

35. Wilson, *Belloc*, pp.1-3; David Mathew, *Catholicism in England*, 1955, quotes letters of Dr John Lingard to illustrate how much the Old Catholics disliked the new dress and devotions, p.200: "... if I am not allowed to wear my white cravat, I will as a Donation start the Douai collar. Alas, alas, the days of fun are over and therefore to be serious, accept Dr Wiseman's invitation. You may learn something new, at least how to wear purple stockings and silver buckles.": *Life and Letters of John Lingard*, p.309; See: "Memoir of Father Hutton," p.8, quoted in Claude Leetham, *Rosmini*, New York, Longmans, 1957, p.190. Hutton writes of the dress at Downside: "The only habit worn by the Benedictines was blue stockings, knee-breeches, and a long dark blue coat." The Roman collar and cassock worn by Fr Gentili and his brethren were the first to be seen in England.

36. Wilson, *Belloc*: One of the many to attribute to Manning a conversion to the Roman Catholic Church was Bessie Parkes, a woman who had been an active figure in the Liberal Party. Parkes became the mother of Hilaire Belloc. In the early 1860s she called on Manning when he had become "Dr Manning of Bayswater." She found him "severe." After their conversation he wrote down the titles of a number of books concerned with the history of the Reformation. "His look seemed to say, 'you are an unpleasant young woman, one of the stiff old Presbyterian stock, but I will tell you faithfully what I think, and let it take its chance.' I do not think he had any suspicion that I was so impressed and overpowered by his intellect, that when I left the room and the house I ran nearly all the way home with the sense that I was fleeing from an overmastering brain."

37. Gilley, "Mosaic Radical," p.35.

38. Snead-Cox, 1, p.38.

39. Holmes, *More Roman*, pp.170-1; See also: Leetham, *Rosmini*, p.152: Bishop Baines bought Ralph Allen's "palatial building of Prior Park," near Bath for £20,000 with the intention of opening a school and seminary to train clergy. Leetham on p.190 refers to the comment of Ullathorne when he was bishop of the Western District that "Mr. Vaughan told me ... appointed president of St Pauls... put up a statue of the Blessed Virgin; and one of the superiors came up and said, 'Let us have no romanizing here. Take it away.'"

40. Ward, *Wiseman*, p.162.

41. R. J. Schiefen, CSB, "Some Aspects of the Controversy between Cardinal Wiseman and the Westminster Chapter," *Journal of Ecclesiastical History (JEH)*, vol XXI, no 2, April 1970, p.125.

42. Holmes, *More Roman*, p.171.

43. Schiefen, "Controversy," p.126, n.2; Askew, "St Vincent De Paul, *Edmundian*," December, 1904, p.135: He became the first and last rector of Henry Manning's Hammersmith Seminary, and was ordained Bishop of Amycla and auxiliary to Manning in 1872. He is buried in the college chapel at St Edmund's.

44. Notes, "The Life of Dean Stanley," *The Tablet*, 23 December 1893, p.1013.

45. R. W. Church, *The Oxford Movement*, London, Macmillan, 1891, p.295: A former Anglican dean of St Paul's, Church wrote that Ward and his Tractarian colleagues knew about the Latin Church mainly from France where "it was more in earnest and exhibited more moral life and intellectual activity than, as far as Englishmen knew, in Italy and Spain." When English travellers came upon "poorly paid but often intelligent and hardworking French clergy; on the great works of mercy in the towns; on the originality and eloquence of De Maistre, La Mennais, Lacordaire, Montalembert," they were encouraged to break out of "insular ignorance and unfairness." Such ideas "took possession of a remarkable mind, the index and organ of a remarkable character," Mr W. G. Ward. He learned from his association with Dr Arnold and then his friend Arthur Stanley and later by the "intervention of a still more potent affinity, the personality of Mr Newman."

46. Norman, *Catholic Church*, p.131; In argument he was often "unpersuasive, he irritated and repelled in spite of having so much to teach, in spite of such vigour of statement and argument, because on the face of all his writings he was so extravagantly one-sided, so incapable of an equitable view, so much a slave to the unreality of extremes." See: David Milburn, *A History of Ushaw College*, Durham, Ushaw Press, 1964: p.255: "William George Ward ... who ranks with the best theologians the continent can produce."

47. Oakeley later became a Catholic. He held a fellowship at Balliol and cared for the district chapel in Margaret St in "which the services and sermons were conspicuous for a deep spirit of devotion and soon became notorious for their very 'Roman tendencies.'" Gladstone attended his services. After he became a Catholic he spent most of his priesthood in Islington, London. *The Tablet*, 7 February 1880.

48. R. W. Church, *The Oxford Movement*, Chicago, Univ. of Chicago Press, 1970 ed., pp.250-2. See also: Wilfrid Ward, *William George Ward and the Oxford Movement*, London, Macmillan, 1889, pp.248ff.

49. Norman, *Catholic Church*, p.132; Ward, *W. G. Ward*, pp.348-9; Dean Stanley described Ward's "degradation": "The more I reflect upon it, the more simply shocking is the impression left. A mob of 1,200 persons assuming judicial functions, after the most solemn warnings of their incompetency, on a question which it is quite impossible they can have studied, and then proceeding to inflict a sentence such as, in its present form, has never been inflicted on any one in the whole history of the University...." Notes, *The Tablet*, 1893.

50. Michael Trappes-Lomax, *Pugin*, London, Sheed and Ward, 1932, pp.138 and 221. Later Pugin wrote that if he had known "Mr. Ward would have turned out so badly, I would never have designed a respectable house for him." Pugin held strong views about the use of rood screens.

51. Snead-Cox, 1, p.78; *The Tablet*, 15 July 1882, "Funeral of Mr.W. G. Ward," p.113: "His theological lectures were marked by great solidity—the scholastics, Suarez, De Lugo, Ripalda, and Billuart, were his authors." Quoting from the homily given by Bishop Herbert Vaughan.

52. Snead-Cox, 1, p.71

53. *ibid.*, pp.73-4: Wiseman to Faber.

54. Vincent Allan McClelland, "O Felix Roma," *Recusant History*, October 1992, p.180 .

55. *ibid.*, p.181; Newsome, *Convert Cardinals*, p.208.

56. MHA. HV. "Black Book."

57. Hanrahan,"Vaughan," p.717; McCormack, p.36.

58. *ibid*; Bernard Ward, "Cardinal Vaughan," *Edmundian*, NS, vol V, no. 31, July 1903, p.161: "And here at once his English character asserted itself in the questions he used to ask. "What do

you do to train the boys to use their liberty?" would be his first interrogation, and one which led to the utter astonishment of those whom he was addressing. He used to relate that only in two places did he receive answers which showed any perception of what he was aiming at." One was the Dominican house at Auteil near Paris.

59. Lilly, "Vaughan," p.272; Snead-Cox, 1, p.70.

60. Newsome, *Convert Cardinals*, p.209.

61. Mathew, *Catholicism*, pp.200-1.

62. Ward, *Wiseman*, p.162

63. Norman, *Catholic Church*, pp.131-2.

64. Newsome, *Convert Cardinals*, p.209; McCormack, p.43.

65. Norman, *Catholic Church*, p.132,fn:to Talbot.

66. Schiefen, "Controversy," p.127, fn.3.

67. WDA. Vaughan Diaries, VI, p.239; McCormack, p.39.

68. WDA. Vaughan Diaries, VI, p.113: "Left Rome on Dec 18th by the 'Dilly' a packet. 27th at Genoa ..."; p.153: "Feb 9th 1855: Visited the Rector of the Oblates at Nice and talked of the spirit of the secular clergy.... At Nice there is a third ecclesiastical college under the direction of the Oblates where those who have finished their four years course in the grand seminary spend one year... to fill young priests with the spirit of their state...; March 5th: Took a packet to Milan. At Genoa on March 6th.... The Duke of Brignoli established last month a seminary for foreign missions under the care of the Lazarists—opened by the General last month ... might not we get something out of it for England...; March 8th: Milan and the Seminary of St. Charles ...; Innsbruck, Sunday March 18th; Munich March 21st: It strikes me that some day Park College might be made the general seminary for little boys and Old Hall devoted to Philosophy and Theology for two or three dioceses."

69. Arthur Stapylton Barnes, *The Catholic Schools of England*, London, Williams and Norgate, 1926, p.123.

70. Snead-Cox, 1, p.77; Schiefen, "Controversy," p.127; Bishop Ullathorne argued in his book on the restoration of the hierarchy, that colleges which trained clergy and laity under one roof, did so out of necessity, but no longer: "It compels the working of two systems under one roof, and in the hands of one set of superiors. Thus their attention is divided, whereas each of the systems of training demands the whole man ... the establishment of purely ecclesiastical seminaries ... would renovate the Church...." Bishop Ullathorne, *History of the Restoration of the Catholic Hierarchy in England*, London, Burns & Oates, 1871, pp.110-2.

71. Snead-Cox, 1, pp.77-79; *W. G. Ward and the Catholic Revival*, pp.47-52: "I had not at this time any personal acquaintance with Ward, and arrived at the College with strong a priori views. The anomaly of a convert of quite recent date teaching dogmatic theology, of one who had never gone through a regular course under a trained professor, of a married man too, being placed in a position of such trust and importance, struck me as a thing to be got rid of as soon as possible. The day after my arrival I went over to make acquaintance with this singular phenomenon. I found him hard at work in his study. He at once asked me to take a walk in the shrubberies with him.... I had little realized, when I blurted out to him during our first walk that I wished him far away, as an untrustworthy, because an untaught, teacher for such a post, how diligent he had been in educating himself upon the great theologians of the Church, and how sensitive he was to the danger which I had apprehended" [Vaughan became an admirer of Ward].... "The combination of moral and dogmatic teaching which he introduced, and his own intense devotedness to the truths he taught, raised men's minds above themselves, and introduced them into the regions of almost a new estimate of life and the possibilities which were opening before them;" See also: Maisie Ward, *The Wilfrid Wards and the Transition*, London, Sheed and Ward, 1934, pp.12-13.

72. K. Theodore Hoppen, "W. G. Ward and Liberal Catholicism," *JEH*, vol xxii, no 4, October 1972, pp.323-344; Years later Wilfrid wrote about the incident for *The English Illustrated*,

noting how different Cardinal Vaughan's views were in 1893 from those at St Edmund's: "The welcome he has accorded to the cooperation of laymen is instanced not only by the introduction of laymen into committees connected with diocesan matters but by inviting them to take their part in delivering lectures in the Ecclesiastical College." Notes, *The Tablet*, 7 January 1893.

73. Ward, "Vaughan," , pp.161-2; Lilly, "Vaughan," p.272.

74. McCormack, p.46; *The Tablet*, 15 July 1884.

75. Wilfrid Ward, "Cardinal Vaughan," *Dublin Review*, July 1910, p.222.

76. Herbert Vaughan, "Devotion to the Holy Ghost," in Edwin Burton, *Sermons Preached in St Edmund's College Chapel*, London, Burns & Oates, 1904, pp.33-49.

77. Norman, *Catholic Church*, p.132.

78. *Dictionary of National Biography*, p 803; Newsome, *Convert Cardinals*, p.210; See also: Maisie Ward, "W.G. Ward and Wilfrid Ward," *Dublin Review*, April-June 1936, pp.235-52: p.239: "Ward spared no pains and certainly no expense to make his editorship all that was wished by Wiseman and later by Manning; but, be it noted, what they wished was an effective antidote to Liberal Catholicism"; Hoppen, Ward, p.344: "Only an infallible authority could presume to guide the Church in its work for the salvation of souls, and secular science, the study of fallible men, could never attain so impregnable a commanding power."

79. *New Catholic Encyclopaedia*, 10, p.613; John P. Guissano, *The Life of St. Charles Borromeo*, 2 vols, London, Burns & Oates, 1884, trans. from the Italian, first published in 1610, Preface by Cardinal Manning, p. xxviii: Manning wrote that Borromeo's chief work was the formation of pastors. Borromeo "broke through the tradition of worldly ambition, avarice, inertness which crushed and stifled the spiritual life of men and revived ... the image and reality of the Good Shepherd, surrounded by his apostles."

80. Francis J. Kirk, "Reminiscences of an Oblate of St. Charles," in Winifride de l'Hopital, *Westminster Cathedral and its Architect*, 2, London, Hutchinson, 1919, pp.366-7.

81. McClelland, "O Felix Roma," pp.180ff; WDA.

82. Newsome, *Convert Cardinals*, pp.209-10.

83. *ibid.*, pp.208-9.

84. Schiefen, "Controversy," p.125; WDA. *Catholic Directory*: Westminster Chapter: Manning, provost; John Maguire, vicar general and canon theologian; Thomas Long, canon penitentiary; James O'Neal, 2nd diocesan vicar general; William Weathers, president, St Edmund's; Francis Searle, cardinal's secretary; George Rolfe; George Last, chapter secretary; William Hunt; Robert Shepherd; Frederick Oakeley.

85. Norman, *Catholic Church*, pp.132-3.

86. McClelland, "O Felix Roma," p.181.

87. Snead-Cox, 1, p.87.

88. McCormack, p.47.

89. Snead-Cox, 1, pp.86-9: Manning to Vaughan, 7 October 1858: "You, Fr Macdonnell, Fr O'Callaghan, should draw up a statement to review the past state of the College and its deficiencies...." This was practically in defiance of the President, or at any rate an attempt to manage the Seminary without reference to him.

90. "Poem by Cardinal Wiseman," taken from *Baeda*, St Bede's College, Manchester, in *The Tablet*, Saturday 30 April 1898: "Several years ago Cardinal Vaughan, at that time Bishop of Salford, presented to our library the original MS of Cardinal Wiseman's well-known hymn, 'O beate mi Edmunde!' written for St.Edmund's College, Ware, by Wiseman at the request of Dr Herbert Vaughan, then Vice-President of that College." St Bede's gave the MS to St Edmund's and received in return two poems also written by Wiseman. *The Tablet* printed one of them, written two years before Wiseman's death.

91. Snead-Cox, 1, p.90-91; A daughter of the W. G. Ward's became the Abbess of Oulton. She was born and raised at Old Hall in the Ward home, a house now known as St Hugh's. She wrote of her memories of Old Hall from 1852 to 1866 for the *Edmundian* and recalled a story about

Herbert Vaughan that must have impressed the younger boys. "My sisters and I, as children, looked upon St Edmund's as the centre of the Catholic World.... The College clock, though seldom correct, gave the time to the whole neighbourhood, and was far more important to us than the railway time, or, for the matter of that, than the time indicated at Greenwich Observatory.... I remember the Old Chapel and Dr. Crookall seated at the organ, which a boy was blowing with his foot." The Abbess admitted that her father "lived very secluded from his family at this time, and one of the strictest rules of our lives was that we might never enter his study." The children usually saw him kneeling in church. "I once received a severe rebuke from him for passing the window and peeping in at Mr. Michael O'Sullivan," one of the seminarians. Mr Ward kept up friendly relations with William Weathers, the president, according to his daughter, and was disappointed when Herbert Vaughan left, to be replaced by Frederick Rymer. When Vaughan was vice-president and "Mr. Tunstall, Procurator, there was a story told about a bull in the farm which broke loose and became so dangerous that none of the men could manage it. Dr. Vaughan and Mr. Tunstall set off in pursuit and succeeded in getting a rope round its neck, to which they held on at each end till Hakes came with his axe and killed the beast." Abbess of Oulton, "Reminiscences of Old Hall from 1852 to 1866," *Edmundian*, vii, 38, December, 1905, pp.7-10.

92. Michael Clifton, *The Quiet Negotiator*, Formby, Print Originata, nd, pp.59ff.

93. Bernard Vaughan, pp.146-7: His name appears in the baptismal register as baptising infants in July 1856 in the Virginia St Chapel (the new church opened on 8 December 1856). There is a tradition that he had a confessional in the new church.

94. Snead-Cox, 1, pp.92-6; McCormack, pp.50-1; *The Tablet*, 9 April 1881, p.579: Father Edward Watson wrote to the editor from the "Hertford Mission." He had been sent there in July 1880 and "found house, sacristy and church, all well on towards the last stage of substantial and decorative debilitation;" A tablet near the entrance of the present church building commemorates the founding of the mission by "Cardinal Vaughan." The *Catholic Directory* notes that the church was consecrated in October 1866. Visit by the author on 17 November 1994.

95. Bernard Ward, *History of St Edmund's College, Old Hall*, London, Kegan Paul, 1893, p.298.

96. Richard Schiefen, *Nicholas Wiseman and the Transformation of English Catholicism*, Shepherdstown, Patmos, 1984, pp.274 ff.

97. Norman, *Catholic Church*, p.133; Newsome, *Convert Cardinals*, p.212; Clifton, *Negotiator*, p.59: Errington was close to a breakdown and so took a leave. Wiseman, through Mgr George Talbot at Rome, tried to get Errington out of Westminster. A diocese in Trinidad was offered but Errington replied: "I will ask Barnabo for a hearing before being condemned.... Now I would not accept Trinidad ... I do not think I could agree to anything that would contain a tacit condemnation of myself...."

98. Clifton, *Negotiator*, p.60.

99. Newsome, *Convert Cardinals*, p.211.

100. *ibid.*

101. McCormack, p.52.

102. Snead-Cox, 1, p.94.

103. Clifton, *Negotiator*, pp.59-61: From the Southwark Archdiocesan Archives, St Edmund's College papers.

104. *ibid.*, pp.60-1.

105. WDA. Vaughan, St Edmund's, to Manning, Monday 29 August.

106. WDA. Vaughan to Manning. 1860.?

107. WDA. Vaughan papers. Notes concerning Oblates.

108. Snead-Cox, 1, p.93.

109. *Clare Vaughan*, pp.27-8. Col. John Vaughan married a cousin, Mary Weld, on 15 Feb. 1860 in the chapel at Lulworth. He was fifty-one and she thirty-nine. They had two children who died in infancy: Charles and Eliza.

110. *Bernard Vaughan*, pp.12-14.

111. McClelland, "O Felix Roma," p.181.

112. Schiefen, *Wiseman*, p.274.

113. Snead-Cox, 1, p.49.

114. Schiefen, *Wiseman*, p.274.

115. Ward, *Transition*, p.19.

116. *ibid.*, pp.8-9: "The main reason for a party-spirit lay perhaps in the development of an opposite tendency among another group of Catholic writers represented in England by Sir John Acton and Mr Richard Simpson, whose organ was the Rambler.... It is a little difficult today to recall the atmosphere of enthusiastic belief in man, in civilisation and progress which pervaded the mid-nineteenth century. A furious optimism possessed the world, and men believed they had conquered an evil past and were on the high road to a millennium. Catholics strongly possessed by this outlook did tend to the inconsistency of which W. G. Ward complained...."

117. *ibid.*, p.7.

118. *ibid.*, pp.20-1.

119. *The Tablet*, 15 July 1882.

120. Snead-Cox, 1, p.81.

121. *ibid.* p.82; Schiefen, *Wiseman*, pp.258ff.

122. *ibid.* p.94; WDA.

123. Norman, *Catholic Church*, p.357; Gribbin, *St Edmund's*, p.59.

124. Snead-Cox, 1, p.95; WDA. Vaughan papers.

125. Chadwick, *Victorian Church*, p.254; Ward, *Dublin Review*: great work ... raising the ideals of the clergy.

126. Vaughan, *The Young Priest*, Introduction, p.1.

127. Gribbin, *St Edmund's*, p.59.

128. In 1880 Ward dedicated his "Essays on the Church's Doctrinal Authority" to Vaughan: "From the time when our friendship commenced with our united work at St Edmund's in 1855 and 1858, you have been associated, I may say, with every event of my life, public and private." Snead-Cox, 1, p.98.

129. Ward, Vaughan, *Edmundian*, p.162.

130. Snead-Cox, 1, p.95.

CHAPTER VI

Herbert Vaughan and Missionary Beginnings

Attraction to the Missionary Life

Herbert Vaughan was never completely free from the "haunting wish to get away from civilization altogether, and in some far land devote himself, body and soul, to the work of converting the heathen." According to John Snead-Cox, the wish to become a missionary remained at the back of his mind during his days at Rome and later at St Edmund's. It was something he had to resolve.[1]

One of Vaughan's biographers wondered why the overseas missionary idea should have arisen, a question to which, he thought, Vaughan "himself has left no explicit answer."[2] But Vaughan was explicit in specific notes which explained how his ideas had developed, and also in early diary entries.[3]

Vaughan's enthusiasm for the foreign missions remained throughout his life. He came to be respected internationally as a promoter of the missionary work of the Church. In his final days, he explained his understanding of the Church's mission, and the standards expected of the missionary, in a collection of conferences on the apostolic life entitled *The Young Priest*.

There were two categories of missionaries according to Vaughan, those working for the conversion of England, especially priests ordained "ad titulum missionis," and those who were sent into "the midst of the heathen populations of the world." With the latter he had a close relationship through the society he was to found at Mill Hill. Whether working for the conversion of England or overseas for the non-Christian populations of the world, they were missionaries. A missionary, he wrote, especially an ordained priest like himself, was called to a very high standard, an "apostolic standard." It was a standard that filled the mind with "the Apostles and the Saints, and above all with the great doctrines that present to us the Three Divine Persons of the Trinity and Our Lord Jesus Christ and His example...."[4]

Herbert Vaughan tried to enlist the help of others in his commitment to the foreign missions; not everyone shared his, at times, impulsive enthusiasms. Vaughan was the spiritual director of the sisters of St Mary's Abbey, Mill

Hill, in the late 1860s, and remained associated with the community for many years afterwards. The St Mary's nuns remember that, "In season and out of season" he urged the "beauty of foreign missionary work."[5] As late as 1902, a year before his death, he told the abbess that she must provide six sisters for the Uganda Mission. Appalled, she said she did not know where to find them. "Oh, you can make them," said he.[6]

More than one commentator agreed that for Herbert Vaughan evangelization was the hallmark of true Christianity.[7] Even at Salford in Lancashire, where he was leader of the diocese for twenty years, he was regarded by one writer as "essentially a missionary bishop" who treated his diocese as a "small mission field."[8]

Among his many accomplishments, the most romantic and one of the greatest achievements of Herbert Vaughan's life, was the founding of a missionary college in the north-west London suburb of Mill Hill. For Edward Norman, Vaughan's St Joseph's Society for the Foreign Missions "gave an example of Catholic activism to a Church which despite the Roman direction imparted by Wiseman and Manning was still very inward looking." Vaughan's foundation, the first of its kind in the Catholic Church in England, was to help inspire "generations of Catholic young men with noble vocations to a wider service."[9]

During his childhood at Courtfield, whenever Herbert thought of priesthood he thought of the missions as well. At first he dreamed of serving Australia, following the example of Bishop Ullathorne. But the longer he reflected on the idea the "more he became convinced that he should be a missioner to Wales."[10] In this thought, he had the example of chaplains at Courtfield, who were part of the Welsh Mission, his teacher at Monmouth, Father Abbot, Bishop Brown, and the Havards at Brecon.

From the sixteenth century, Rome considered England and Wales to be mission countries. After the Acts of Supremacy and Uniformity in April 1559, Roman Catholics had the choice of conformity or exile on the Continent. The exile movement of Catholics who refused to conform continued without interruption until the French Revolution two centuries later. From 1581 the penalty was death for celebrating Mass, administering the sacraments, and sheltering priests. Under Penal Law, Roman Catholic priests had to lead an underground or at least inconspicuous existence. Most of the Catholic priests were trained on the Continent. William Allen established a college at Douai in 1568. The first missionary left the Douai seminary for England in 1574. The English College at Rome became a missionary seminary followed by Valladolid, Seville and Madrid in Spain, and Lisbon in Portugal. Father Persons founded the seminary at Valladolid, and those at Eu and Saint-Omer.[11]

England, Wales and Scotland were administered by missionary vicars apostolic and divided into districts. Until 1840 there were four for England

and Wales: London, Midland, Northern and Western. The Western District was administered by the Benedictine Thomas Joseph Brown, who was vicar apostolic from 1840. The Benedictines also supplied people to the Australian mission, where Herbert's Benedictine brother, Roger, became Archbishop of Sydney. English priests volunteered to work in Australia and wrote of their experiences for people at home in England. One was William Bernard Ullathorne, later Bishop of Birmingham.[12] Courtfield was also home to a succession of missionary chaplains during Herbert's boyhood. Between 1830 and 1853 there were six.[13]

John Hobson Matthews visited Courtfield a few years after Herbert Vaughan's death and suggested that his youthful ambition to devote himself to the reconversion of Wales was born of the historical association of his home and ancestry.[14] One of the first entries in Vaughan's diary at Rome retold the conversation he had with the antiquarian and historian Daniel Rock about his plan to become, not only a missionary to Wales, but the founder of a seminary for the training of missionaries for Wales.[15]

Expansion of His Missionary Idea

Herbert Vaughan's idea of a missionary life had not dimmed, and his travels in Europe and studies at Rome had broadened his interests. While the Roman Church in England struggled to exist under Penal Law and then became the object of the missionary activity of foreign-trained missionaries—the Roman Catholic Church was referred to derisively as the "Italian mission to England"—the known world was witnessing a spectacular expansion of missionary evangelization. Men and women were inspired by the ideal of a "free, independent and non-political planting of the faith." But in practice, methods—especially of the powers of patronage granted to Spain and Portugal—contributed to abuses in the name of the Catholic missions.[16]

In order to preserve missionary independence, the Sacred Congregation of Propaganda Fide was set up at Rome in 1622. At least ten cardinals under a prefect administered the Catholic Church's missions. They were divided into territories, or "vicariates" and "prefectures," depending on the area's importance. Each territory was placed under a prefect or a vicar. For example, Brown was the vicar apostolic of the Western District of England and Wales.

At first, priests of the older orders served as missionaries. Among them were Franciscans, Jesuits, Dominicans and Carmelites. Later, special missionary institutes were started. The first such institute was the Paris Foreign Missionary Society in 1663. It became the arm of Propaganda Fide—the Congregation of the Propagation of the Faith—especially for India and the Far East.[17]

During the eighteenth century the work of the missions suffered due to the influence of the "encyclopaedists and deists among the French philosophers."[18] Even Spain and Portugal became hostile; the Jesuits were expelled from Portuguese territories and Spain suppressed the order in 1767. The intensity of anti-religious activity had disastrous results for evangelization.

In France the Revolution closed the Paris Missionary Society and smaller communities disappeared or were reduced in size. The uninterrupted wars following the French Revolution made communication between the Rome office of Propaganda and non-European areas almost impossible. When General Berthier occupied Rome and the office of Propaganda in 1798, work was disrupted. Soon afterwards Pope Pius VII was taken prisoner, and the Congregation was almost totally destroyed. Napoleon planned to transfer the Pope and the Congregation's office to Paris. In 1805 Napoleon returned the seminaries of the Paris Missionary Society and the Fathers of the Holy Spirit, allowing missionary activity slowly to begin again. At the same time, the focus for the support of the spreading of the faith began to shift from Spain and Portugal to France. New missionary orders and congregations also began to appear after 1805.

In 1814 Pius VII restored the Society of Jesus; "an act of greatest consequence for the mission." In 1824 the most "important source of money for the missions in modern times," the Association for the Spreading of the Faith, began regular publication of its journal, *Annales de la Propagation de la Foi*. Pauline Jaricot, a young girl from Lyons, was the inspiration for the association started in 1822.[19] By 1841 the *Annales* was publishing 70,000 copies in French and 15,000 copies in English. Each edition brought the work of the missions into Catholic homes,[20] and helped to begin a new wave of interest in the foreign missions.

The missionary zeal of Pope Pius VI in supporting early nineteenth-century ventures prepared the way for the full restoration of missionary work, especially under Gregory XVI, between 1831 and 1846. Pope Gregory's papacy led the way by means of the Congregation for the Propagation of the Faith. For example, he established forty-four new mission bishoprics; the new vicariates in England and Wales were among them.[21] New and revitalized missionary organizations also took up a commitment to overseas evangelization once again.[22]

Between 1835 and 1845 the renewed interest in the foreign missions was felt in England and Ireland; although the British Isles were still considered missionary lands. The emigration of large numbers of English-speaking Catholics to Australia and North America created demands on the home countries for funds and personnel. In addition, the Catholic Emancipation Act in 1829 had awakened many to the challenge presented by the millions of non-Christians in the British Empire. Once new territories and a more structured administration under Propaganda Fide were in place, calls came for more administrators and priests.[23]

Protestant Missions

Along with news from the Catholic missions in the Vaughan household, Herbert Vaughan had the example of ambitious Protestant missionary movements.[24] The growing interest of Protestant England in overseas missions in the nineteenth century developed from a Church revival that began in the eighteenth century. The Society for the Propagation of Christian Knowledge (SPCK) and the Society for the Propagation of the Gospel (SPG) were founded in the eighteenth century. In 1792, William Carey and Andrew Fuller started the English Baptist Society, and in 1795 the London Missionary Society began. They were followed by the Church Missionary Society (CMS) and the British and Foreign Bible Society (BFBS).[25]

The CMS was begun by a group of evangelicals at the Castle and Falcon Inn in Aldersgate St, London, on 12 April 1799. The founding group became known as the "Clapham Sect." The chairman was the Revd John Venn and one of the members was William Wilberforce. During the early and mid-nineteenth century, missionaries such as William Carey, Henry Martyn and David Wilson brought back stories from their labours in exotic places under the British Empire. They sparked the imagination of English Christians. In 1856 Livingstone returned from the rain forests of Central Africa. He toured England, Wales and Scotland in 1857 preaching "commerce and Christianity," describing the evils of the slave trade and Africa's commercial potential. After he visited Oxford and Cambridge, the Cambridge and Universities Mission to Central Africa was organized.[26]

Development of an Idea

Herbert Vaughan was aware of the Protestant achievements in missionary work. It proved an incentive, and part of his argument, for an organized Catholic foreign missionary effort, not only in England, but in the United States. He also read about and witnessed the work of Catholic missionaries and missionary support groups on the Continent and in Ireland. On his arrival in Rome in 1851, he "met with a missionary priest and became fired with a desire to go out to the Foreign Missions with him."[27] His travel and studies expanded his horizons, yet an interest in Wales remained strong.

At ordination he left behind the idea of being a solitary priest on some lonely Welsh coast in order to accept an appointment at St Edmund's. At first it seemed possible that St Edmund's might be transformed into a Tridentine Seminary that could train young men for the foreign missions as well as for England, but the thought of serving the "abandoned" of his own diocese was at first uppermost in his mind.

At Ware he hoped to serve the Church but his dreams were soon eclipsed by events surrounding the appointment, and his "old ambitions stirred."[28] He wrote years later that "on being called to St Edmund's the thought of the want of good and zealous priests and therefore of the absolute need of a seminary led me to give myself entirely to this one idea of seminary life and a stronger ecclesiastical spirit for England." Yet the thought of the overseas missions of the Church persisted. Finally he "secretly determined, in case St Edmund's should be put under my direction, to remove the lay boys and to replace them in part by candidates for the Foreign Missions which would also raise the spirit of the College."[29] As the prospect of St Edmund's being part of his dream appeared less likely, Herbert Vaughan began to meditate on the thought of millions "in Africa, Asia and the Isles of the Pacific" who were "passing to the grave without having ever heard of Jesus Christ."

He thought of "England's influence in the world, of her traffic and her power and he knew what the great Protestant missionary societies were doing." The news of Protestant successes was a reproach to him and, he thought, to the Catholics of England, for doing, in his opinion, nothing at all.[30] The Catholic Church in England was struggling with many internal problems. One was the obvious disunity seen in the conflict between Wiseman and his own cathedral chapter. Despite the problems at home, Vaughan was aware of the remarkable renewal of missionary work by the Continental Church, especially in France. Hesitatingly, before leaving St Edmund's, he began to consider not only the idea of becoming a missionary, but the training of others who would devote their lives to the foreign missions.[31]

The opposition he experienced at the college, and the frustration of the Oblates' plans were also the occasion for reflection on the importance of an "interior life." He tried to impress upon his students the importance of living an inner life of the spirit. As he did, he became more convinced of his own view that when "totally absorbed in external work … we have not a sense of the interior life."[32] While his views and ambitions were tested: "Before even I finally left St Edmund's the thought of the state of the Infidels and Pagans in the world, and the small number of Christians, began more and more to occupy my mind."[33]

Herbert turned to his Oblate superior, Henry Edward Manning, for advice: "I spoke to Father Superior in the Summer of 1859/60 about it in the fear of some delusion, so strong had been my desire to do something. He, however, encouraged my idea by saying something might come of it, and that I need fear no delusion." Snead-Cox adds that it was in the summer of 1859, and that Manning "listened patiently" and "counselled prudence," saying that "something might come of it someday."

With Manning's slender encouragement, Vaughan continued to think even more seriously about the foreign missions, while he remained at St Edmund's for another two years. In the meantime, despite his misgivings, he continued to collect information about seminary training and mission-sending organizations. The notes he kept on journeys during the spring and summer of 1860 show that he pursued his dream in spite of a "torment of doubts" that were to last for the next two years.[34]

Ireland

On 17 May 1860, Vaughan visited Ireland and All Hallows College in Dublin. All Hallows Seminary was not the first college in Ireland to prepare men for the foreign missions but it was a model. It trained men for the secular priesthood in "designated jurisdictions to which they were formally attached at ordination." They were missionaries who were motivated "above all else" by a desire to sustain the faith of fellow Irishmen "at risk through lack of pastoral care" in Australia, America, New Zealand and other places where Irish emigrants had gone.[35]

The path taken by John Hand, a native of Oldcastle in Meath, who founded All Hallows, was similar to the one to be followed by Vaughan.[36] Father John Hand was an "organizer" for the Association for the Propagation of the Faith in Ireland, and from this connection, and his reading of the English edition of the Annals, he was inspired to do something more for the missions.[37] Hand was impressed by how much France was doing for the foreign missions and wondered: "Why not Ireland?" On 15 August 1840, Dr Cullen wrote from Rome that "If there were a College for the Foreign Missions in Ireland it would be well supplied with students."[38] Hand outlined proposals in a "Circular to the Irish Bishops" in 1840. In February 1841 he was given a hearing but the bishops rejected his scheme. However, Archbishop Murray of Dublin and Dr Cullen in Rome urged him to carry on.

In 1841, Hand spent three months in Paris looking for a practical model for Ireland. At Amiens he met the founder of the Association of the Missionaries of the Holy Heart of Mary, Father Franz Maria Libermann. Libermann encouraged Hand to do for the British colonies what he himself was doing for France.[39] In 1842 Hand went to Rome and petitioned the Prefect of Propaganda. In his petition he mentioned only the distress of "our Catholic brethren" and not of primary evangelization. Propaganda approved of his proposal and allowed Hand to open his college in 1842. The college prospectus of February 1842 "envisaged a seminary whose alumni would serve overseas wherever priests were needed." Hand's supporters wanted him to help in places where there were Irish emigrants such as Australia and America, and in mission areas with Irish ecclesiastics such as India, the Cape of Good Hope, the West Indies and Mauritius.[40] Hand's premature death, the increased emigration of the late 1840s, and the overwhelming demands of the Irish diaspora, led All Hallows College away from the training of missionaries for the evangelization of non-Christians.

When David Moriarty, a future Bishop of Kerry, and one of Vaughan's early supporters, became president of All Hallows, he found serious financial problems. The college looked wherever it could for assistance. Moriarty even went to London to petition the British government for a grant to help a "college instituted for the supply of priests to the British colonies." He thought it was in British interests to support the project. Mr Hawes at the Colonial Office told him that there was no help available. Soon afterwards, in April 1854, Moriarty was consecrated co-adjutor Bishop of Kerry.[41] Bishop Moriarty knew Herbert Vaughan and later encouraged his efforts to begin a missionary college in England. They probably met for the first time at the Old Hall home of William George Ward, where Moriarty and Vaughan were frequent guests.[42]

Search for a Model

As Hand had done twenty years earlier, Vaughan searched for information and ideas. He visited All Hallows briefly in 1860 and came away unimpressed by the system that was in place. He thought that the president had no more authority than the most recently appointed professor. "It does not encourage ready submission to authority of the individual which must follow in the mission." he wrote in his diary.[43]

In June 1860, Vaughan went to France and visited more seminaries: the major seminary of Rouen managed by the Picpus Fathers, the college of the French Missions at Lyons, the major seminary of Lyons run by the Sulpicians, and the major seminary of Grenoble. By July he was at Rome and visited, among others, the Jesuit-run German College, the College of Propaganda and the North American College. Travelling to Milan, he met with the Oblate rector of the major seminary, and also visited the Instituto delle Missioni Estere in Milan.[44]

Throughout this period Vaughan used his skills as a keen observer and drew on the experience of many others to formulate a plan of his own. Like those associated with the founding of All Hallows before him, he saw an opportunity for evangelization laid open by an expanding British Empire. They were not the first Catholics to do so. Eugen De Mazenod, founder of the Oblates of Mary Immaculate, sent a newly ordained Irishman named Daly to Liverpool in May 1841 "for the conversion of English heretics and if necessary and if the number of new vocations is sufficient, to branch out into England's colonies or her new acquisitions in America or in any other part of the world."[45]

All Hallows had developed into a missionary-sending college for the Irish diaspora, and Mazenod's hopes had not materialized. Vaughan, at the heart of the empire, continued to plan and dream of an opportunity to begin, and he prayed for direction. On his travels in 1860 he prayed about the project that was slowly coming together in his mind at "one shrine after another." In each place he sought the advice of experienced spiritual guides but returned to England dissatisfied. He experienced an inner conflict between the energy and ambition he had for his dream, and an uncertainty about possible hidden motives; perhaps, he thought, vanity and pride were driving him on. His diaries show a troubled mind, but they also reveal a single-mindedness in his continued effort to gather information in a search for a model for a missionary-sending seminary for England.[46]

Conversation with Cardinal Wiseman

Herbert Vaughan was dreaming of great missionary endeavours, and at the same time was troubled by scruples. Snead-Cox wondered where the "forceful, confident character" he and his friends knew was to be found in Vaughan's diary—"records of hesitations, and doubts, and scruples, and self-distrust!"[47] It was also the time of the impending collapse of the Oblate presence at St Edmund's. In the summer of 1861, four Oblates, including Herbert Vaughan, withdrew from St Edmund's after six years. After he left Ware, he decided to speak to Nicholas Wiseman about his thoughts on the foreign missions: "I for some time wished to speak to the Cardinal ... (to ask) whether he did not feel a necessity to do something for the Foreign Missions, but I felt deterred from doing so." He found an opportunity when the two men were together on the Isle of Wight, probably visiting the Wards' estate, during the summer of 1861.

They were driving along in a carriage and Wiseman was half-asleep. Vaughan asked the cardinal whether he had any interest in the foreign missions. "Yes, why do you ask?" "Because I have something on my mind and I fear to tell you. You will snub me. I believe England ought to do something for the Foreign Missions." Wiseman then told Vaughan of an experience that, he said, he had never told anyone before. Just before he had been made a bishop at Rome he went to speak with Vincent Pallotti. Pallotti had founded a missionary society in 1835.[48] Wiseman took a seat across the table from Pallotti with only a cross between them. "After I had opened my mind," Wiseman said, "and laid bare all its trials to him, he slipped down from his chair to his knees, and after a moment's prayer, said: 'Monsignor, you will never know the perfect rest you seek until you establish a College in England for the Foreign Missions.' These words fell on me like a thunderbolt; I was in no way prepared for them." The topic of missions had not come up between the two men and Wiseman had "no interest at the time in Foreign Missions." No other advice was given by Pallotti. Wiseman left and made a resolution to try to form a group of priests who would form a training college for the foreign missions. When he returned to England, he spoke to Bishop Walsh, the vicar apostolic for the London District. Walsh disagreed and told Wiseman that the Oscott seminary was to be his missionary college. Wiseman decided to wait until someone came along who could take up the task. After saying all this to Vaughan, Wiseman became "bright and cheerful," and the two men spoke about it several times that day, and the following day, but they "determined to do nothing for some time."[49]

According to Snead-Cox, Wiseman's approval did not put an end to Vaughan's concern about possible hidden motives in his own plans. He did note after speaking with Wiseman that he "remained much consoled and the hope of realising the idea became prominent to my mind." Shortly afterwards he went to Courtfield.[50]

At Courtfield he prayed at the tomb of his mother "to beg her assistance to teach me how to begin, if it were God's will that I should begin at all. And after several days of prayer, an answer seemed to come to me in the chapel saying distinctly: 'begin very humbly and very quietly.'" Vaughan remembered the experience as something forceful, like a sudden revelation.[51] His prayers to understand what God wanted of him "increased and became more constant."

Living at the Oblate residence in Bayswater during the winter of 1861, Vaughan became severely ill. At first, it appeared that he was going to die but slowly he regained his strength. His health had broken down, as one friend suggested, because he "over-taxed his strength, as usual," at St Edmund's.[52] Vaughan wrote in his diary that he "entertained a great confidence that something would be done" about his idea to help the foreign missions. While he was getting better, he read the Life of St Francis Xavier "with the greatest interest and on his feast I felt almost beside myself with a desire to carry our crucified Lord to the Heathen as he had done."[53]

Deaths of his Sisters Clare and Helen

In 1861 his sister, Helen Teresa, became the first Sister of Charity to die in England. Herbert had given her the Last Sacraments. In January 1862 Vaughan travelled to Rome and remained away until June. January brought a new sadness to the Vaughan family. On his journey to Italy in early January, he stopped to see his sister, Clare Mary, a nun with a community of Poor Clares at Amiens. Clare was dying, her health weakened by a cold and fever. "The doctor ... had no hesitation in pronouncing it to be a pulmonary attack, from which there was little or no chance of her recovery." Herbert gave her Holy Communion and was "struck with this instance of her profound detachment"—she did not even look at her brother. Clare died on 20 January 1862.[54]

Rome

Arriving in Rome on 5 January, Vaughan wrote in his diary that he was praying for knowledge of God's will about his missionary project and that he wanted to rid it of any personal ambition. He offered to sacrifice his life for the establishment "in England [of] a seminary for Foreign Missions." He worked out a plan of prayer and devotions, visited churches and asked for the advice of understanding people, in a search for peace of mind.[55]

Vaughan did not spend all of his time at Rome in prayer and agonizing self-doubt, as one would conclude from his diary entries. A letter to Wiseman, found in the Westminster archives, dated 10 January, gives us a glimpse of the public Vaughan, who, although unwell, carried his loyal advocacy for Wiseman to Cardinal Alessandro Barnabo of Propaganda. When he met with Barnabo, the first question Vaughan was asked concerned George Errington. Vaughan told the prefect that he had heard that Archbishop Errington had gone to Dublin and intended to stay there until Westminster became vacant, and then, with the help of the chapter, to return to London. Cardinal Barnabo did not think it was possible, "but said that a man who could take down the Pope's words in a private conversation in his presence, was capable of doing many strange things." Vaughan answered that "all were thankful to have got rid of him," and then raised the question of Wiseman's problems with the chapter. He wrote to Wiseman:

> I was sorry to hear that the case had taken something of a personal turn . . . I was obliged to say that several of the bishops have continually spoken against you in the houses of laymen, and upon his [Barnabo's] asking with astonishment, what reason they could have had for so doing, I said I thought it was partly jealousy and partly a desire to stand well with those chief families of the diocese who were anti-Roman in their tradition and spirit . . . also dwelt on Dr Grant in general terms . . . he ended by saying: Who appointed him? He then volunteered a tirade against Searle and the chapter for their opposition.

Before leaving London, Vaughan had written to Manning that he had heard "something of the calumnious chatter which some of the priests, who sometimes see your Eminence, allow themselves to indulge in" at Manning's expense. "This I must say," the letter continues, "that I never met anybody so disinterested and unselfish and whose conduct is simply so all that I could wish it to be and as regards your Eminence, there is no one more really true to you" (*sic*). The letter closes with Vaughan adding: "I have been rather unwell, suffering from palpitations," and notes that Manning was in Rome and was to preach every Sunday in Mgr George Talbot's church.[56]

At Easter he went on a retreat at the "Franciscan Convent of Castel Gandolfo," about twenty miles from the city. His diary entries became more intense. He read the life of St Francis of Assisi and saw that Francis had gone to Rome to pray at the tombs of the apostles, asking whether he should give himself up to the foreign missions. After the retreat, Vaughan drew up a proposal he called "reasons for such a seminary," and sent it to Henry Manning. The paper included a plan for "St Peter's Seminary."[57] He asked Manning to delay giving his decision in order that he "might become quite indifferent to all but God's will." Manning sent his reply some weeks later through Father Dillon, who was in Rome, informing Vaughan that he had decided to begin a seminary for the foreign missions as soon as possible. It was to be called St Peter's Seminary for the Foreign Missions.

On the day of the canonization of the Martyrs of Japan, 8 July 1862, Vaughan made an offering of "myself and of the whole work to God."[58] He began to think that his future might be as a missionary to Japan.[59] On 25 June Vaughan had met the founder of the La Salette Missionaries, who advised him "to find God's will about the missionary college through confidence and prayer to our Lady."[60]

His inner turmoil and depression, viewed through the diaries of this period, are relentless and grim. Perhaps it was a consequence of a forceful, energetic character with a consuming idea, forced to have "one foot on the brake, the other on the throttle." He had no power to implement the proposal himself and so had to submit, wait and have it possibly rejected. Such apprehensions absorbed his energy. Noel Hanrahan calls the years of Vaughan's indecision over the beginning of a college for training missionaries the "radical crucifixion of Vaughan's human powers." Once freed from this, with his project approved, and able to be his own self, Vaughan's remarkable gift for organization was unleashed.[61]

Proposal to the Oblates

Herbert Vaughan left Rome in July 1862 and arrived back at London in time for an Oblate chapter meeting at Bayswater on 28 July. At the meeting, Henry Manning introduced the idea of training priests for the foreign missions as a work for the Oblates. He suggested that the foundation of a "new house of studies," a proposal made in their May 1861 meeting, would be open to students for the overseas missions as well as for other dioceses. Manning thought such a work was "quite within the scope of the Congregation" and it "would bring with it a special blessing as the first institution of its kind in England."[62] A decision was postponed with the majority of those present receiving Manning's proposal with "great coldness." It was soon clear that no practical steps were to be taken.[63] Vaughan wrote years later that "the Congregation adopted the idea in principle. Health and other circumstances rendered the beginning impossible. It then seemed quite out of the question beginning in London, though I had humbler ideas than before. Still a country house seemed indispensable. So greatly is one mistaken when one is often most sincere. Poor man!"[64]

The idea that Herbert Vaughan presented to Manning was part of a major proposal being considered by the Oblates: a plan to move the Oblate novitiate and seminary to a house in the English countryside. Not all members wanted another venture so soon after the failed enterprise at St Edmund's. The added dimension—training candidates for the foreign missions—became part of Manning's proposal, and met with similar opposition. Whatever the reasons, the rejection of the proposal was a disappointment for Vaughan; he sensed a lack of sympathy among his colleagues.

Spain

In the beginning of 1863, Vaughan was ill once again and Cardinal Wiseman sent him to Spain for a complete rest. He planned to spend part of his time at Seville with the Zuluetas, who were friends of Cardinal Wiseman.[65] He was still thinking of Japan when he left England. The stories of sixteenth- and seventeenth-century martyrs and the challenge of recently reopened missions were fresh in his mind. Despite his poor health he was convinced that "something would come of my journey to Spain."[66]

Vaughan first went to Barcelona where he spoke with a priest called Farn about his idea. Farn's advice was to put the project out of his mind, and then rest to restore his health. He added that Vaughan should pray "generally without reference to any particular plan. That God's will would make itself known to me." He tried to follow Farn's advice and "endeavoured to put all thought of the missions out of my head." He was successful in doing so until 20 February 1863, the day he arrived at Seville.[67] From Seville he wrote to his brother, Kenelm, that he had taken a room and was learning Spanish: "An old aunt is my padrona, who cooks and messes for me, and her nephew, who is in minor orders, lives with her. He attends lectures in theology but comes and chatters away incessantly when at home ... so that I think a few months will see me over the first difficulties of Spanish." Snead-Cox added that Vaughan spoke Spanish "almost like a native."[68]

Joaquín Medina, S J

On his arrival in Seville, Vaughan's mind was disturbed once again, still with the thought that he must do something to train missionaries in England for the foreign missions: "The idea soon began to force itself on me again. I tried to keep it away but could not succeed." He went to see the superior of the Jesuit residence at Seville, the Valencia-born Fr Joaquín Medina. The residence was connected with a novitiate and with the church of St Louis of France.[69] The Jesuits, and other restored religious orders, were involved in the work of popular evangelization in Seville. Adapting the modern missions begun by Antony Claret in Catalonia in the 1840s, they followed the traditional formula for parish missions but paid more attention to catechetical instruction and the formation of lay leaders.[70] Vaughan met Fr Medina and explained the advice he had received from Farn in Barcelona. "At first he was somewhat silent," Vaughan wrote, "but after some time he began to say the idea was good...." All during March, Vaughan prayed to St Joseph to help make known God's will for him. He continued to consult with Fr Medina, presenting the difficulties he saw in carrying out such a plan, adding that "the uncertainty was a trial."

Medina did not take Vaughan's health problem seriously, saying "that God could use us for his purposes without such health, as He does continually to many." He told him not to be so apprehensive nor shut out the inspiration of the previous two years. Medina suggested that Vaughan "ought to examine and see how it could be brought into a practical shape and prudently begun." Encouraged, Vaughan waited for a sign that the work should begin. However, at the end of the conversation, he concluded that the Jesuit "appeared to take it all very coldly and I could not determine whether he were fully considering the subject or not."[71]

Vaughan thought that a start might be made in a rented house near the Wards.[72] What made him hesitate was the thought that he would not have the strength to care for the education of seminarians during an English winter. While in Spain he did not "for one whole day" feel "equal to such a work."[73] He was sure that his Oblate community would help but they "would not look upon the work as theirs but as mine if I lived away from them from the beginning." He was also certain that Manning would think it was unwise for him to start on his own: "And so I walked up and down the Plaza del Principe Don Alfonso"—but he was unable to think how to take the first steps to begin.

He asked congregations of nuns to pray for his intention, while he took up works of charity, visiting the local hospital, preaching to the English in Seville, and giving "more alms than usual."

On 20 April something unusual took place while he was offering a Mass of the Blessed Trinity. During the consecration the thought flashed across his mind: "Begin quietly at Bayswater, taking rooms for the candidates for the Missions and letting them go to class with our own Postulants. And in the winter you can go to South America to beg and recruit health." The inspiration left him at peace. "I felt as I went home from the Church and during the day like someone who has found a rich treasure and who longs to communicate his joy to someone else."[74]

Two or three days later he told Fr Medina what had happened. He wrote in his diary that Medina had been reflecting on their earlier conversation, and said that "the thought of England doing something for the Foreign Missions had grown much on him and he thought it very important. This was the first real encouragement I had received from him." When Vaughan brought up the same objections again, Medina scolded him, saying he expected too much and did not trust enough in the Lord and God's Providence. Then Medina suggested that Vaughan make a retreat and apply St Ignatius' test of election to his idea. From that day onwards, Vaughan said a prayer, "*pro gratiarum actione*," during his Mass. In his diary, his depression continued as he wrote of the suspicion that he had been deceiving himself, "year after year," in one way or another, even when "in good Faith and unintentionally."

Puerto de Santa María and Victorio Medrano, S J

Vaughan left at the end of April for Puerto de Santa María, the port city near Cadiz, south-west of Seville. His retreat began on 1 May 1863, under the direction of a native of Navarre—the home of Francis Xavier—Fr Victorio Medrano.[75] Medrano was fifty-one years of age and superior of the Jesuit house at Puerta de Santa María. He had the reputation of being an encouraging and knowledgeable spiritual director.[76] At Puerto de Santa María there was a residence for young Jesuit seminarians from the College "La Victoria" and teachers from the College of St Louis. The year after Vaughan met him, Medrano was appointed superior of the Jesuit residence in Madrid.

Vaughan told Medrano "at once the chief matter which I wished to deliberate on in the retreat and gave him as simply as I could, the antecedents which in any way bore upon it."[77] Medrano helped Vaughan to finally resolve on a course of action. For one, he saw only good resulting from the plan and no reason "for believing that the devil had anything to do with it." He suggested that Vaughan begin very humbly. Vaughan added that perhaps he could at first take only two or three students and have them live outside of the Oblate house, and separate from the community, while attending classes, until they had sufficiently proved themselves. Medrano advised him to have perfect trust in God just as St Ignatius did when founding the Jesuits. "God keeps a part of His Design hidden from us usually in order to exercise His servants in Faith and Confidence in Him." He added that even if the effort were short-lived, "we must often begin good works and bear to see them come to an end after a short time: during their time of existence they have produced good fruit; if their existence is short, we must bear with this as God Our Lord bears with it. Let us do good while we can." Vaughan began his retreat and was directed to use the meditations to put his ideas to the test "especially the test of St Ignatius' Exercise on the Election."[78]

Before the end of the retreat, Medrano advised Vaughan to propose his plan to Manning again and to rest "satisfied if I obtained permission that I was carrying out God's will." One day in the chapel, Vaughan wondered how missionaries might join together with his Oblate congregation. He thought that "they might be called 'Oblates of St Charles' etc. ... but that they might also be called 'Missionaries of the Sacred Heart.' "[79]

Thanks to Joaquín Medina and the practical Victorio Medrano, Herbert Vaughan's mind was settled, and he resolved to do all that was humanly possible to found a college for the training of missionaries in England "for the conversion of the heathen." Snead-Cox concluded: "In such tribulation of soul was born the Missionary Society of Mill Hill."[80]

Herbert Vaughan's old prayer that he might do something heroic for God seemed about to come true. He decided to begin a journey to the Americas in search of funds needed to support the training of priests for the foreign missions. He was inspired by Seville, its cathedral and historic connections with the exploration and evangelization of the Western Hemisphere.[81] But first, he needed the approval of his Oblate superior, Henry Manning. And so he returned to England to see Manning.[82]

Return to England and Preparations for a Begging Tour

By June of 1863, after years of "painful examination of the missionary idea," Herbert Vaughan found that Manning had changed his mind. In a letter to George Talbot, Vaughan wrote that he proposed to Manning and his assistants that the Oblates take "three or four candidates, attaching them to our own house of studies here for the Foreign Missions. My proposition was received with coldness by him and his consultors."[83] Vaughan was told that his work as an Oblate lay elsewhere and he must "give himself to the internal workings of the congregation."[84] Vaughan wrote to Talbot that he set about "cheerfully" to comply with Manning's instruction but Manning again changed his mind. This time he told Vaughan that the Oblates were not at that time prepared to admit students preparing for the foreign missions and to find the means to support such a venture on his own. Despite a lack of support, Vaughan wrote: "At present I am to consider myself charged with the commencement of such a work."[85]

Vaughan went to the Jesuits in Farm Street in London for advice, asking them what he should do next. They suggested that he see Cardinal Wiseman. And so, in June 1863, he approached Wiseman again with the "old and often meditated idea" that had been "impressed on him by a higher and holier mind" than Vaughan's or his own—Vincent Pallotti.[86] He asked Wiseman to have his plan approved by all the English bishops. He wanted to do this in order to make the project known in England, and, afterwards, to go to "South America, Brazil, Chile, etc, where I have some friends...."[87] Wiseman hesitated, thinking that the bishops would not give official approval to the "lonely effort on the part of a single priest." Finally the Cardinal invited Vaughan to join him at a meeting to be held at Oscott in July 1863, where he could make his own presentation.[88]

All of the bishops approved of his proposal, except Bishop Alexander Goss of Liverpool. Vaughan then began to appeal directly to individual bishops. One response hints at the ambiguous support offered by the English bishops: it warned him not to expect "material and personal attention to foreign missions" but they did rejoice that "others find themselves able to stretch out a helping hand." William Ullathorne was one of the early supporters of Vaughan's proposal.[89] Herbert Vaughan may have considered it an achievement to have a hearing and come away with little more than their best wishes.

In August, Wiseman invited Vaughan to join him at the Congress of Malines, a meeting of Catholic organizations on the Continent. Cardinal Wiseman was one of the principal speakers. Vaughan was also allowed to speak of his project and prepared a pamphlet to distribute in order to explain the scope of his proposal. The Congress received him well and passed a resolution that gave moral support to his efforts. Of Wiseman's address, Vaughan wrote that he spoke at "great length … fluently in French" with a "somewhat English" accent and was "enthusiastically applauded." The reaction of Professor Lamy of Louvain was the opposite of Vaughan's: "Wiseman's speech was a complete fiasco." When Wiseman was reading an account of the progress of the Church in England, "people couldn't hear him, were impatient to hear Montalembert, and so tried to choke him off with applause," but failed.[90]

In addition to expressions of moral support, Herbert Vaughan asked for letters of introduction to people in the countries he planned to visit on his begging tour. His preparations were thorough and energetic. He prayed, sought advice and approval, and then laid the foundations for the undertaking. Once he had completed his preparations, he went ahead, with no evidence of his former hesitation and self-doubt. Throughout his life he worked hard and prepared well. He was a dreamer, an adventurer and a romantic, but in addition to these traits, he had a practical approach to challenges and an ability to persevere.

The archives at Mill Hill have copies of the many letters of introduction he solicited in the summer and autumn of 1863. For example, the rector of St Beunos' in Wales, George Lambert, wrote to John Jackson in Buenos Aires on 1 August 1863: "An old and esteemed friend of mine Rev Dr Vaughan who was at Stonyhurst a little before your time … is anxious to obtain help toward the founding in England of a College for the Foreign Missions. Should you be able to assist him in any way by introduction to wealthy Catholics in South America…."

On 25 August he received letters from Archbishop Colina of Pueblos in Spain, the archbishop of Seville and four other Spanish bishops. Letters followed from England and the Continent addressed to, among other places, Trinidad, New Grenada, Venezuela, Ecuador, Salvador, Haiti, Guatemala, Chile, Mexico and Brazil.[91]

Additional moral support arrived during September 1863 in a letter from the Bishop of Kerry, David Moriarty. Moriarty explained that while he was president of All Hallows College, "I wished to see a foreign missionary house like our own established in England." He was convinced that "a missionary college in England will possess several peculiar advantages and it will be a powerful auxiliary in a great cause." He knew of Vaughan's "zeal" and his "wise plans" and the "enlightenment of your views" on clerical education. "I believe that God has called you to begin an institution which will contribute much to His glory." [92]

On 25 September 1863, the Oblate chapter blessed Vaughan's plan to collect funds in order to begin a training college for the foreign missions. He was given a letter in the name of the congregation in which they prayed for "a successful outcome." Vaughan replied that "in going away he still felt united to the work of the Congregation."[93]

On 23 October Cardinal Wiseman authorized Vaughan to travel in search of financial help for the training of candidates for the foreign missions. Included were hand-written letters by Wiseman's secretary, Canon Morris, in Spanish, along with special introductions to the presidents of Bolivia, Guatemala and Venezuela.[94]

Snead-Cox mentions that a newly ordained friend of Vaughan volunteered to accompany him but withdrew from the journey at the last moment.[95]

Rome again

In October, before leaving for the Americas, Vaughan travelled to Rome to ask for the Pope's approval. Pius IX gave his blessing on 9 November 1863: "After the blessing of the Pope, I never felt another temptation to desert it" (that is, the plan for the foreign missions).[96]

During his short stay in Rome he drew up a formal petition for Propaganda Fide. The prefect, Cardinal Barnabo, gave him a letter which recommended Herbert Vaughan and his missionary project. Vaughan was presented as an Oblate of St Charles, commissioned by his community and Cardinal Wiseman to begin a college for training priests in England for the evangelization of non-Christians in areas ruled by Britain. Barnabo requested that Vaughan be assisted, in all the areas he was to visit, by church leaders, to obtain funds for the founding of such a college.[97] Vaughan returned to London by way of Lyons, where he asked the help of the Council of the Propagation of the Faith, the organization that gave financial support to the Church's missionary efforts.

Wilfrid Ward remembered this period in Vaughan's life because Vaughan made frequent visits to his home either at Old Hall, in London or on the Isle of Wight."[98] In his *Dublin Review* article on the publication of Snead-Cox's book in 1910, Ward added that the "sense of romance which his American campaign aroused in Herbert Vaughan's friends was inevitably associated with his extraordinary beauty—far greater in his thirties than at a later period....The portliness of later life and the slight heaviness of feature were not yet in sight. Slim of figure, his fearless blue eyes, aquiline nose and firm set mouth, the expression of sweetness and courage combined, made him in appearance an ideal Sir Galahad, setting forth in his quest of the Holy Grail.... His absolute faith that the work was God's work made his perseverance indomitable."[99]

Vaughan returned to England in December, and made final arrangements to sail from Southampton on 17 December 1863. By that time Cardinal Wiseman was an invalid. The Congress of Malines in August had been his final public appearance. The day before Vaughan left for the Americas, Wiseman wrote him an affectionate and encouraging letter.

> My Dear Herbert: It is only now when you are on the eve of starting for your noble mission, that I seem to realise the greatness of your devotedness and self-sacrifice in separating yourself from home and friends, and from all that is naturally dear to you.... Health even, of which I hope you will be most careful, seems risked in such an undertaking. Indeed did I not feel ... the ... sublimity of our cause, I would hardly allow you to embark in the double ocean of this work and of the Atlantic. But I feel an inexpressible confidence ... God ... will prosper this work, such as I have never... felt in any other. Especially, while I am myself in so much darkness and depression about myself, this feeling shines brighter.... I therefore give you a parting, though, I hope, not a final blessing.... Yours very affectionately in Christ, N. Cardinal Wiseman. [100]

Of Wiseman's letter, Vaughan said that for thirty years he could never read it without tears. It was received at the moment his dreams were beginning to take a visible shape. An idea that had been for many years in his thoughts was going to be a reality. In his imagination this was to make of his life an "heroic enterprise in the one great cause."[101] It really was Wiseman's final blessing, as he was to die before Herbert Vaughan returned.

Henry Manning wrote to Nicholas Wiseman from Rome the day after Herbert's ship had departed. He had learned that Vaughan planned to extend his trip to California and to go on horseback across the Andes. He was alarmed:

> If Herbert is not gone, I could wish that you could keep him from undertaking what I fear he has neither the health nor the strength to go thro'! When he first talked of S. America, I never thought of California and 1000 leagues on horseback. I don't think he knows what this is. He had much better go with you to Spain and S. America after he is stronger.[102]

Manning's letter arrived too late to alter Herbert's plans. For him, all signs of depression and self-doubt seem to have disappeared as he went aboard the steamer.

Notes

1. Snead-Cox, 1, p.104: "for years together it presented itself as a desire which hardly dared to be a hope." Heathen—or pagan—can be defined as one who is not an adherent of any of the world's chief religions; especially one who is neither Christian, Jew or Muslim. See: *The Concise Oxford Dictionary*, London, OUP, 1985.
2. Arthur McCormack, *Cardinal Vaughan*, London, Burns & Oates, 1966, p.55.
3. WDA. Herbert Vaughan: "Notes on the Development of the Idea of the Foreign Missions;" Herbert Vaughan: Diaries, VI.
4. Vaughan, *Young Priest*, pp.2ff, 96, 112.

5. C. C. Martindale, SJ, *An Untold Tale*, London, Falcon, p.15.

6. *ibid.*, p.26.

7. MHA, HV, Box 45, book 2: His message to the founders of the Catholic Missionary Society in 1902: "Convert England and Wales."

8. Charles Bolton, *Salford Diocese and its Catholic Past*, Manchester, 1950, p.131.

9. Edward Norman, *The English Catholic Church in the 19th Century*, Oxford, Clarendon, 1984, p.358; Derek Holmes, *More Roman than Rome*, London, Burns & Oates, 1978, p. 217: Holmes thought that the original spirit of his missionary foundation showed Vaughan's determination to establish "papal and Roman Catholicism not only in England but throughout the world."

10. McCormack, p.19.

11. Hubert Jedin ed., *History of the Church*, Tunbridge Wells, Burns & Oates and New York, Crossroad, 1981, V, p.517. Peter Guilday, *The English Catholic Refugees on the Continent, 1558-1795*, London, Longmans, 1914, pp.2-3.

12. One of the inspiring Benedictine missionaries and an early supporter of Vaughan's missionary college was William Ullathorne. See: Cuthbert Butler, *The Life and Times of Bishop Ullathorne, 1806-1889*, 2 vols, London, Burns, Oates & Washbourne, 1926; *NCE*: William Bernard Ullathorne was born at Pocklington, Yorkshire on 7 May 1806. He traced his ancestry to St Thomas More. He went to sea as a cabin boy but left and entered Downside to become a Benedictine in 1823. After ordination he first taught, and then in 1832 went to Australia as vicar general to Bishop Morris, OSB, where he worked with colonists and convicts for ten years. His pamphlet "Horrors of Transportation" was regarded as a classic indictment of the complacency of the British government concerning prisoners brought out to Australia. Ullathorne's health broke down and he returned to England and a mission at Coventry. He was proposed to be bishop of Hobart-town, Adelaide and Perth, but never returned to Australia. In 1846 he was named vicar apostolic of the Western District where he remained for two years, after which he was transferred to the Central District. He became the leading proponent for the restoration of the hierarchy in England and Wales. In 1850 he became the first bishop of Birmingham and remained there until retiring in 1888. During his career he took a leading role in most of the social and religious movements of the time. See also: Mathew, *Catholicism*, p.196.

13. Courtfield Archives. (CA)

14. John Hobson Matthews, *The Vaughans of Courtfield*, London, Sands, 1912, p.48.

15. WDA. Vaughan Diaries. See chapter IV.

16. Jedin, 7, p.189ff; See also: Edmund M. Hogan, *The Irish Missionary Movement*, Dublin, Gill and Macmillan, 1990. Introduction and Appendix A.

17. *ibid.*, Jedin.

18. Kevin Condon, *The Missionary College of All Hallows*, Dublin, All Hallows, 1986, pp.23ff.

19. *ibid.*, pp.25ff; Lawrence Nemer, *Anglican and Roman Catholic Attitudes on Missions*, St Augustin, Steyler, 1981, p.25; Jedin, p.193, nn.23-4.

20. Jedin, 7, p.204: Bishops or their representatives composed the reports. During its first 100 years it contributed 500 million francs to the missions.

21. *ibid.*

22. Condon, pp.25-7: Jesuits went to India and Africa; the Lazarists (Vincentians) to the Middle East and China; the Paris Mission sent missionaries to China, South-East Asia and North America; the Order of Mary Immaculate, founded in 1816, went to Canada and South Africa; the Marists, 1832, to New Zealand and Oceania; the Picpus Fathers, 1817, to Hawaii and the Polynesian Islands. In 1848 the older Congregation of the Holy Spirit, 1703, joined with the Society of Mary Immaculate under the leadership of Père Franz Maria Libermann and began working in the French colonies, especially in Africa.

23. *ibid.*

24. Seaman, *Victorian England*, pp.6, 15: "If however one looks for the most enduring and distinctive characteristic of the Victorian age (1837-1901) one finds it in its high sense of moral

responsibility.... Victorians were almost always acting with reference to their all-pervading belief in the moral imperatives of personal responsibility, of duty and of living for something other than the satisfaction of immediate needs.... A moral code of duty, high seriousness and dedication to work ... together with the other more tangible factors deriving from the unique economic circumstances of the time which gave the Victorians ... quite astonishing energy."

25. Nemer, p.193.

26. *ibid.*

27. WDV. Vaughan, Notes.

28. Noel Hanrahan, "The Apostolic Spirit of Herbert Cardinal Vaughan," Rome, PhD thesis, no. 2876, 1957.

29. WDA. Notes.

30. Snead-Cox, 1, pp.104–5.

31. Hanrahan, "Vaughan," p.722.

32. WDA. Vaughan notes.

33. WDA. Notes.

34. Snead-Cox, 1, p.108.

35. Hogan, *Missionary Movement*, p.2; Condon, Appendix: Missionaries before the famine were mostly educated in major diocesan seminaries: St Kieran's, Kilkenny, founded in 1782, was the oldest, supplying priests to Newfoundland and the Maritime provinces of Canada. In 1838, Bishop Ullathorne recruited a group for Australia; St Patrick's, Carlow, had a fund set aside for the education of priests preparing for the missions. In 1838, St Patrick's, Maynooth, began sending men overseas, especially to India and Australia. St John's, Wexford, became the major source of priests for Newfoundland in the 1830s and 40s. St Peter's, Wexford, became the chief mission outlet for the Eastern Cape in South Africa. In 1842, St Patrick's, Thurles, was authorized by Propaganda to prepare young men for foreign missions. St Mary's College, Youghal, in Waterford, was started by Fr John Foley for the foreign missions in 1839.

36. Hogan, p.21: The seminary he founded—All Hallows—lacked a clarity of purpose at first. Was it for the evangelization of the non-Christians written about in the Annals or for the care of the Irish diaspora? Edmund Hogan thinks that "Hand envisaged a seminary which would provide priests mainly for the British and French colonies whose apostolate would embrace both primary evangelization of indigenes and the pastoral care of emigrants." Inspiration for the former were the models of missionary organization on the continent that dedicated themselves exclusively to the work of non-Christian missions, whose members, though assigned to missionary jurisdictions, continued to belong to the institute. Ireland already had a model for the latter, well established before the great famine, for training students for priesthood in jurisdictions to which they became attached. The missionary college was no longer responsible for their welfare.

37. Condon, p.14: Irish priests who had been trained in France and Rome knew of the Congregation of Missions founded by Vincent de Paul in the seventeenth century. In France they were known as the "Lazarists" after the Priory of St Lazare in Paris where St Vincent had his headquarters.

38. *ibid.*, p.33: Cullen had written on 15 August that "If there were a College for the Foreign Missions in Ireland it would be well supplied with students."

39. *ibid.*, p.39; On Libermann, see: Jedin, 7, p.197ff.

40. Hogan, p.24.

41. Condon, p.82: Moriarty was from North Kerry. He had been educated at St Patrick's Maynooth, and in France. He was the vice-president of the Irish College in Paris, and was known for his "high idealism and charisma laced with common sense." He became ill with consumption, and returned to stay with his mother at Banna Strand. When he succeeded to the presidency of All Hallows there was no financial support from the Irish bishops, and no promise of help from the Society for the Propagation of the Faith.

42. Maisie Ward, *The Wilfrid Wards and the Transition*, London, Sheed and Ward, 1934, p.19.

43. MHA. Notes on Herbert Vaughan's diary.

44. *ibid.*

45. Jean Leflon, *Eugene De Mazenod*, New York, Fordham, 1970, 4 vols, 3, p.278.

46. Snead-Cox, 1, p.108.

47. *ibid.*, pp.107-8; WDA. Vaughan, Notes.

48. MHA. HV. Box 44: Pallotti's "Society for the Catholic Apostolate" sent its first missionary priests to London in 1844 to care for the Sardinian Oratory and later to Clerkenwell, the German Church, Greenford and the Italian Church.

49. Snead-Cox, 1, p.107. All comments from Vaughan diaries seen by John Snead-Cox; About Pallotti, see: Lady Mary Herbert, *Venerable Vincent Pallotti*, Milwaukee, Pallottine, 1940. One reviewer for *Ave Maria* wrote: "In the middle decades of the nineteenth century the asceticism of a St Francis was blended with the zeal of a Don Bosco in the life of Venerable Vincent Pallotti. A dynamic force in Catholic Action in promoting retreats and missions to prisoners, soldiers and the very poor throughout Italy." About Wiseman's missionary ideas: In the *Dublin Review* for 1837, he appealed for support for the foreign missions, using the same argument Vaughan was to employ when beginning his missionary society: "We know that the first appeal will be met by an outcry about our wants at home. God knows that they are great; and we would coin our heart's blood to remedy them." Wiseman reminded his readers that the "first principle of gospel prudence in matters of gain, is . . . 'Give and it shall be given unto you.' Our conviction is, that besides the divine blessing, which will be drawn upon ourselves by this work of catholic charity, the new impulse which that divine virtue will receive from it, will act with advantage upon our own languishing contributions." See: "Glance at the Institution for the Propagation of the Faith," London. 1837, *Dublin Review*, April 1838, pp.368-93.

50. WDA. Vaughan, Notes; Snead-Cox, 1, p.108.

51. WDA. Vaughan, Notes.; Not the 1861 of McCormack, p.57; Snead-Cox, p.108.

52. Lady Herbert, "Some Further Notes on Cardinal Vaughan's Work when beginning the Foreign Missionary College," London, Wyman, n.d.; Snead-Cox, 1, p.108.

53. WDA. Notes.

54. Lady Lovat, *Clare Vaughan*, London, Burns & Oates, 1887, pp.153,164: Her father, John Vaughan, wrote to her: "How happy you are my child! You are taking leave of earth in order to go to heaven." Also: Sisters of Charity Archives, Notes on Sister Chatelain. "Teresa Vaughan. . . . In her early years she had thrown herself into the pleasures of the world with a zest and enjoyment which alarmed her more serious sister and others. Great therefore was their surprise when Teresa suddenly declared her determination to become a Sister of Charity . . . when she presented herself in Park Street (London), Sister Chatelain told her that it would be impossible for her to endure the life and labours of a Sister of Charity when her health was so delicate. . . . Touched by her earnestness Sister Chatelain could not refuse to put forward her request to the superiors, and to Teresa's great joy she was accepted and began her postulation in Park Street in 1861 . . . the day was fixed for her entrance to the seminary. But this happiness was not to be hers, for she was taken suddenly ill, and when her brother, then Father Herbert Vaughan, went to see her, he found it necessary to give her the Last Sacraments immediately. 'It would have been nice to go to Paris, but it is far nicer to go to Heaven,' she said. . . . A very short time after pronouncing her vows, she died."

55. Snead-Cox, 1, p.109; MHA. Bernard Roes, "Our Founder and Patrons": He also continued to pray to the saints who were to play an important part in the development and realization of his missionary vocation and that of his Foreign Mission College. The saints became models worthy of imitation and friends here on earth and awaiting us in the next life. In St Joseph he had a childlike and unshakable confidence. He even promised to dedicate a future seminary to St Joseph and St Peter.

56. WDA. Vaughan correspondence. 10 January 1862, Hotel della Minerva, Vaughan to

Wiseman: "I arrived here on the eve of the Epiphany, after having suffered like a horse."

57. WDA, Vaughan, Notes; MHA. HV, Bx.2. April 1862: "St Peter's Seminary" was to be open to persons interested in the Oblates, the secular priesthood, and "boys or youths for the foreign missions." There was to be a "little" and a "great seminary." The missionary students were to wear cassocks with red braiding and a red sash, while the others wore Oblate dress. The missionary candidates might be boys and young men, and even priests, "not only English but foreigners ... provided their intention is to serve the foreign missions." Suitable candidates were to be recruited in England, Ireland and "to a certain limited extent in the seminaries of France.... Bishops in the colonies could be invited to "send us subjects to educate and if possible funds for their education." No one under fourteen nor anyone not knowing the "rudiments of Latin" was to be admitted. The "characteristic spirit—in the first place and chiefly—is to be thoroughly Roman in spirit and affection."

58. Francis Corley and Robert Williams, *The Jesuit Saints and Blessed*, Milwaukee, Bruce, 1941, pp.66-70. The Jesuit scholastic, Paul Miki, two other Jesuits, six Franciscans, fifteen tertiaries and two laymen were crucified at Nagasaki during the persecution of Toyotomi Hideyoshi on 5 February 1597. They were canonized on 8 July 1862 and are remembered in the liturgical calendar on 6 February. See also: John Delaney, *Dictionary of Saints*, New York, Doubleday, 1980, p.409; Jedin, VIII, p.192.

59. Snead-Cox, 1, p.113.

60. MHA. Notes.

61. Hanrahan, "Vaughan," pp.9-10, n. 185.

62. McClelland, "O Felix Roma," p.214, n.8.

63. Snead-Cox, 1, p.113.

64. WDA. Vaughan, Notes, no. 11.

65. MHA. Lady Herbert, Further Notes.

66. Snead-Cox, 1, p.113.

67. WDA, Vaughan, Notes; Ward, *Wiseman*, p.171: Clara de Zulueta was the wife of Merry del Val, the Spanish ambassador to the Vatican. Wiseman was born in Seville. The street in which he was born was renamed on his death, by order of the town council, "Calle del Cardenal Wiseman;" See: *Dictionary of National Biography* 62, London, 1900, p.246.

68. Snead-Cox, 1, p.119, fn.1.

69. Joaquín Medina was born in Valencia on 9 April 1811. He entered the Jesuits on 30 July 1826 and made his profession on 2 February 1845. He died at Valencia on 8 July 1885. "Fué muy espiritual y muy emprendedor de muchas obras." Information concerning the Jesuits at Seville and Puerta de Santa María from correspondence with Amancio Arniz, SJ, at Valladolid, the archivist at Grenada, and especially Valeriano Ordóñez, SJ, at the Collegio San Ignacio, Pamplona. Medina was superior of the Seville residence and "prefectus valetudina, operarius."

70. William Callahan, *Church, Politics and Society in Spain, 1750-1874*, London, Harvard Univ. Press, 1984, p.237: "The resurgence of the missions, particularly after 1851, arose from the determination of the Isabelline bishops to deal with 'immorality and indifference' through direct combat. The Jesuits active in Seville took pains to move on foot from parish to parish, even rejecting offers to ride in carriages, and they tailored their activities to the social situations of their congregations;" See: Wilfredo Rincán García, *Monasterios de Espana*, 3, Madrid, Espasa Calpe, 1992, pp.315-27; And: Band y Vargas, *La Iglesia Sevillana de San Luis de los Franceses, Seville*, 1977.

71. WDA, Vaughan, Notes: "I urged the example of St Francis Xavier, who kept hidden in his breast his desire of the missions and was told by St Ignatius that he was to go to Asia, without his having ever manifested his wish.... Father Medina replied that this was a case which was not for imitation: that the duty of St Francis was to manifest his conscience entirely with all his desires to his Superior. And so we should do."

72. The Wards had homes in London, first at Gloucester Square, and later at St John's Wood.

Ward, *Transition*, p.36.

73. We know that Herbert Vaughan had a heart problem from his school-days, and he often "overtaxed his strength" as Elizabeth Herbert observed. Like his sister, Clare Mary, he also had weak lungs. It was perhaps due to an infection caused by winter cold. Of Clare, Lady Lovat wrote that the austerities of the Amiens convent did not kill her but "the terrible hereditary disease which she bore in her veins and which she already knew the slightest cold was ... likely to rouse to an active mischief." *Clare Vaughan*, p.157.

74. Snead-Cox, 1, p.115; WDA. Vaughan, Notes.

75. Jesuit Archives, Valladolid; Jesuit Archives, Pamplona: Medrano was born at Puente la Reina, in Navarre, on 23 December 1811. He entered the Society of Jesus on 8 October 1843. He died at Madrid aged sixty-nine on 16 October 1880; The archives of Andalusia: According to the directory of the Spanish Provinces for 1863, Medrano's name appears in the "Hospitium Missionum el Domus probationis ad Portum Stae. Maria. Es Rector desde el 8-5-1859, y Prefecto de Estudios." The retreat house and the novitiate were in the same place, a house called "Victoria."

76. *ibid*. He became the director of a future saint, Vicenta María Lopez Vicuña, foundress of a religious institute for domestic servants. He was also involved in parish missions, Ignatian retreats, was Director of the Catholic Women's Association and promoter of schools for poor children.

77. WDA. Vaughan, Notes; Vaughan also found time to visit Jerez and find out about the old English hospice of St George at Sanlucar de Barrameda. His source of information was the son of the English consul who had been at St Cuthbert's. The hospice had the same rector for forty years until he was replaced by Fr Beck of the Seville Oratory in 1865. In 1875 Vaughan returned as Bishop of Salford representing the English hierarchy. On that occasion he was welcomed at St George's by the local clergy and a Union Jack. See: Michael Williams, "The English Hospice of St George at Sanlucar de Barrameda," *RH*, 18, no 3, May 1987, pp.263-76.

78. *ibid*; Snead-Cox, 1, p.117.

79. Snead-Cox, 1, pp.118-9; WDA. Vaughan, Notes.

80. Snead-Cox, 1, p.118.

81. One of the altars in the cathedral is dedicated to the "Virgin of the sailors." The cathedral holds many reminders of Catholic Spain's links with Spanish America.

82. McClelland, "O Felix Roma," p.214, n.8: that the training of missionary priests be within the work of the Oblates at a newly proposed seminary.

83. See: Hanrahan, "Vaughan," p.9, n.182: Talbot papers, 703.

84. McClelland, p.183: Perhaps Manning's change of mind was linked with a new proposal he made the following year to locate the Oblate Seminary at Rome, rather than the English countryside.

85. Hanrahan, "Vaughan," n. 182; MHA. HV. Quoted in a letter to Talbot, 20 June 1863: Manning to Vaughan: "I am most willing and glad that you should use all the efforts in your power to collect means for beginning such a work and that when begun you should devote yourself to it."

86. MHA. HCV. Wiseman to Vaughan, 18 July 1863.

87. MHA. HCV. Bayswater, 20 June 1863, Vaughan to Talbot: 3rd proposal: A blessing and sanction of the Holy See would "confirm" ... induce many others to imitate apostolic zeal of the Holy See for countries of the Heathen to whom England owes so great and so neglected a duty."

88. Snead-Cox, 1, p.121; McCormack, pp.62-3.

89. MHA. HV. James Kyle, Preshome, 22 September 1863 to Herbert Vaughan.

90. Schiefen, *Wiseman*, pp.325-6.

91. MHA. HV: Letters are on file. There is no evidence that Vaughan planned at first a visit to the United States. It was 1863, during the Civil War in the United States. A visit to the east coast was impossible.

92. ibid., Moriarty to Herbert Vaughan, St Mary's , Bayswater.
93. McClelland, p.214, n.8.
94. MHA. HV.
95. Snead-Cox, 1, p.120: He was an only son and his parents begged him to give up the idea.
96. *ibid.*, p.121.
97. MHA. HV. Prefect of Propaganda.
98. Ward, *Transition*, p.19: "His frequent visits were the great excitement of our early youth."
Frances, their mother, was "especially devoted to him" and it was through her letters from
Vaughan that we know of many of the experiences he had on his American journey. The
children "regarded him as a saint, and watched his every action looking out for signs for our
guidance.... It was he mainly who put it into our heads that we were all to be priests and nuns.
Every time he visited us, he told us of some exciting scheme of his own for the glory of the
Church, and we were profoundly interested in his plan of going to America in order to collect
money for founding a college for foreign missions. He was to start at the end of 1863, but before
he went he brought to fulfilment the consecration of my eldest sister to the religious life. She
entered the Dominican convent of St. Dominic at Stone as a girl of sixteen in July, 1863."
99. Ward, *Dublin Review*, July 1910, p.15.
100. Snead-Cox, 1, pp.121-2; Ward, *Dublin Review*, p.13: "Vaughan's America campaign for
funds.... Wiseman, to whose large-hearted and enterprising nature the adventurous scheme
especially appealed...."
101. Snead-Cox, 1, pp.121-2; To Frances Wingfield Ward he wrote from on board the ship:
"... But how good is God! He provides for us all, and He leads one in one way and another in
another, by various routes, till at last we shall meet in Him and in the embraces of the Sacred
Heart." See: Ward, *Transition*, p.20.
102. WDA. Manning to Wiseman, 18 Dec. 1863.

CHAPTER VII

Journey to the Americas

Departure from Southampton

Herbert Vaughan went on board a paddle-wheel steamer, the SS *Atrato*, at Southampton, on 17 December 1863. Before sailing, he wrote to Mrs Ward. Frances Wingfield Ward was one of Vaughan's earliest supporters and a faithful correspondent during his absence in the Americas.[1] He had his own cabin and room enough to put up an altar for Mass. On board were "seven or eight Spanish and Italian Jesuits" and two young men from Ushaw College who were emigrating to Vancouver Island in the Pacific Northwest. After some words of encouragement, Vaughan wished that "we shall all be apostles together—you by prayer and I by work," and closed with a greeting for "Ward and the children."[2] He wrote in his diary that two of the Jesuits were students who were going to Guatemala, and that there were also on board: "New Granadian cutthroats, gentle Peruvians, voluble Frenchmen, a German who professed to be an atheist, a Trinidadian planter, whose religion is sugar and polished boots, doctors and surgeons for ships and travellers to Vancouver etc...."[3]

With his assortment of letters from the Pope, Propaganda, Cardinal Wiseman, and from bishops, diplomats and friends, Vaughan began his journey. After a quiet crossing of fourteen days, the *Atrato* arrived at 2 p.m. on 31 December 1863 in St Thomas, the Virgin Islands. St Thomas was governed by Denmark and used English as the official language. His attempts at begging had been unsuccessful on the *Atrato*. He wrote that he had no courage for begging on the ship.[4] During the stopover at St Thomas he recorded his observations in brief notes; a habit he continued during his travels. He met the governor of one of the English islands who flattered him by saying that he appreciated the Catholic priests because "whenever there is a public calamity, the Catholic priests are foremost to the relief."[5]

By 4 January 1864, he was at sea again aboard the *Tamar*. The next stop was the Mosquito Coast, a part of Nicaragua on the Caribbean Sea. At Bluefields he learned about President George Frederick of the Mosquito Republic. Frederick had ruled the Mosquito Indians as a king under a British Protectorate until 1860. "The said George Frederick has no religion, is tolerably well educated ... (a) little man ... (and) Bluefields is beautifully situated and contains some good houses. It is very healthy and free from mosquitos." The tribes had no Catholic missionary but "for fifteen years or more the Moravian Brethren have been settled among them and have some three establish-ments."[6]

Vaughan's companions on the packet to Panama were a group of Brothers of the Christian Schools en route to Tahiti. "They were eleven months at sea last time and arrived at Tahiti ill for life."[7] After a stop at Cayenne they reached Colón on the Isthmus of Panama on 7 January 1864. During the passage, the packet's paddle wheel was smashed twice during storms, and "once the men working on it were carried round with the wheel—no loss of life."[8]

Panama

The autonomous state of Panama was part of the Republic of New Grenada. Colón, the port on the Caribbean side, was linked by rail with the capital, Panama City, on the Pacific. Vaughan wrote of Colón that "nothing could be sadder and more melancholy than the state of religion here." During his visit, he baptised six black children. The city's two thousand inhabitants had not seen a priest in months, and, according to the French consul, the Catholics "live and die like beasts."

On the recently completed cross-isthmus railway, he travelled to the capital through scenery which he described to be "like Milton's picture in Paradise Lost." The town of Panama did not have a port where ships could dock. They anchored in a harbour between the mainland and a chain of islands. The town itself is set on a coral peninsula running into the Gulf of Panama.[9] In Panama, he was scandalized by the "great gamblers" among the priests. He was told of priests taking their chickens right into the sacristy, hurrying through Mass, and "going straight off from the altar to the cockpit."[10]

While waiting to continue his journey, Vaughan found an opportunity to minister: "I said Mass in private houses on the 11th, 12th and 13th of January and the people came in numbers. I attended people dying of small-pox"—part of an epidemic that had killed 1200 already—"heard confessions, and baptised; in private of course."[11]

Governor Santacolumba ordered Vaughan not to "officiate ... in obedience to the Constitution." But he had already promised a Mass and to bring Communion to a dying woman the following day. He kept the commitments, was charged with a criminal offence, and freed on $50 bail. The British vice-consul, Mr Bidwell, tried to intervene on Vaughan's behalf, but the governor gave orders that he was not to leave Panama. The same day, 14 January, Vaughan found a small and slow-moving American steamer, the *Saint Louis*, and left for California. The *Saint Louis* was owned by the Pacific Mail

Steamship Company and captained by William H. Hudson. It sailed between Panama and the Folsom Street Wharf in San Francisco, California.[12]

California

Instead of the normal eleven or twelve days, the *Saint Louis* took seventeen to reach California. There were three hundred and twenty passengers on board, with about seventy of that number in first class. Many were Irish going to California for gold, or men avoiding conscription into the Union armies during the American Civil War. It was "a rough and unrefined set," wrote Vaughan. The "most agreeable man on board" was a Mr Chipman, "a New Englander by birth, but a naturalized Mexican." Vaughan quotes Chipman at dinner: "I hate those Yankees. I had the misfortune to be born in New England.... It's the only mean thing about me, some of the puritanical blood that country has given me. I'd rather be an Englishman than anything else, but they didn't want no more British subjects, or I would have joined them." Captain Hudson objected to his remarks, saying that he had put a man in irons for less. Chipman defended his right to speak freely, and after the captain left said to Vaughan: "I'd shoot him ... if he attempted to touch me, the bullying tyrant. I'd treat him as I would a Mexican reptile."[13]

Herbert Vaughan began his journey with two small notebooks: one had the title: "Names and addresses for introductions to South American trip— Paris;" and the other: "Education fund" containing an account of monies collected. The first entry for the education fund was for January 1864 in Panama: "Feliz Clausel, 20 New Grenadian dollars."[14]

On Sunday morning, 17 January, he offered Mass for the Irish and steerage passengers, and performed a funeral service for a girl he had confirmed the night before. She was committed "to the deep." In the evening he said prayers and "preached on the Holy Name to the Protestants." He was told by the purser that "he had never known a Catholic priest to perform services publicly on board before."

On 22 January the ship reached Acapulco, Mexico. He visited the local parish, a primary school, and the proprietors of the El Dorado Hotel; "a wonderful old couple" who had "travelled together all thro' California and part of Mexico." Of the Americans he met, he thought that they were "a wonderful race of men." He met a dozen businessmen between thirty and fifty years of age: "after dining noisily but moderately and quickly—for they all bolt their food—will sit down over the coffee and sing comic songs and choruses for half-an-hour, like college boys meeting at an inn, or students going on vacation. They all say that the Americans have no time to consider religion much—their life is too fast and they are too busy money making to be religious." Chipman told Vaughan that Americans never exercised without an object: "For health's sake they never consider it, but after the almighty dollar a fat fellow like me will run faster than a greyhound."[15] Vaughan made an entry in his education fund at Acapulco: "Wilson and Doherty" gave a donation of two Mexican dollars.

On 1 February 1864, the *Saint Louis* docked in San Francisco. Vaughan went immediately to see Archbishop Joseph Sadoc Alemany, where he was received "with frigid politeness and given to understand that he was a sort of spiritual poacher." He was told that there was to be no opportunity for him to beg for support in San Francisco. Alemany was born in Spain and had come to California circuitously. After gold was discovered on 24 January 1848 fifty miles east of San Francisco on the south fork of the American River, fortune-hunters set out for California in great numbers.[16] On 20 November 1849, Father Charles Montgomery, a Dominican from the Eastern Province of the United States, was appointed bishop by Rome, but he did not accept the office. In April 1850, Sadoc Alemany, also a Dominican and a delegate from the United States at the order's chapter meeting in Rome, was called for by Pope Pius IX. The pope asked Alemany to become bishop of California. Alemany accepted, returned to New York, and crossed the country to California, entering his diocese on 6 December 1850.

Vaughan expected Alemany to encourage his begging campaign, especially when he saw his letters from Rome. Instead, the archbishop called his council together and they decided against Vaughan's plan. The archbishop gave Vaughan six reasons why the council of the archdiocese had rules against foreign collections. He did make a concession: Vaughan was allowed one collection in a country area. Alemany had faced many problems on his arrival in California. He had written to Moriarty at All Hallows in 1851 asking for help for California, which was then in the grip of "gold fever." His diocese was larger than France, and of his thirty priests, twenty-seven were from All Hallows in Dublin.[17]

Marysville

Vaughan set off for Marysville to meet with Bishop Eugene O'Connell. O'Connell was "a nervous, wiry, ascetical" man and had been dean of All Hallows when he was appointed by Pius IX to become the first bishop of Northern California and Nevada. He asked the pope to change his decision and when the pope would not, O'Connell responded: "*Damnatus sum ad metallia*"—condemned to the mines—referring to a passage in the Roman Martyrology and a form of punishment for Christians under the emperor Diocletian.[18] On 27 September 1860 the Vicariate Apostolic of Marysville was established and O'Connell installed as the first vicar apostolic. Vaughan was welcomed by O'Connell, and allowed to preach for financial help as much as he wished, despite the poverty of the vicariate. The difficulties that Vaughan experienced were more than matched by many blessings, and he was "full of confidence that the work will succeed."[19]

Herbert Vaughan had arrived in Marysville by river steamer from San Francisco. Paddle steamers went up the Sacramento River, first to Sacramento, and then on to Marysville. It is possible that he travelled with Father Dominic Monteverde, a native of Genoa, who had been ordained at St Mary's in San Francisco on 14 February and assigned by Alemany to help O'Connell at Marysville.

It is certain that Vaughan arrived in mid-February 1864. At the time Vaughan visited, O'Connell was trying to pay off a debt on his cathedral, St Joseph's. He wrote in December 1864: "I am in a nice fix, as I have been all along, between the old fabric called St. Joseph's Church—barn would have been a more appropriate title and the heap of debt on it." But he did manage to pay the debt and began to build a tower and finish the interior during 1865.[20]

Soon after Vaughan arrived at Marysville he was invited to give a public lecture at the Marysville Theatre. The *Daily California Express* announced on Wednesday, 24 February, that an "interesting lecture" was to be given by O'Connell's visitor: "Dr Vaughan is engaged in drawing attention to the importance of educating persons as missionaries, who will take up the vast fields that are so loudly calling for immediate attention." The lecture took place on 1 March and the morning paper announced that "Rev Dr Vaughan, a gentleman of fine talent, and an orator seldom equalled, will deliver a lecture this evening." The subject was: "The recent trials and triumphs of Christianity in Tonkin and Cochin China."

His lecture described scenes not in "remote history but to the sufferings and deaths which have taken place within our own day, even so lately as two years," reported the *Express*. The lecture "brought before our eyes so that we have learnt that almighty God even in this day grants to those who suffer persecution for his name's sake the same fortitude which he gave to the early Christians and Apostles." Vaughan spoke of the life of Abbé Venard and read to the audience the letters he wrote to his father and sister before he was executed in South-East Asia.[21]

To support his efforts with their prayers and sacrifices, Vaughan enlisted the help of Presentation nuns at San Francisco and the Sisters of Notre Dame in Marysville. The Presentation community in San Francisco lived on Powell Street. Their foundress in California was Mother Teresa, Bridget Comerford, who was born in 1821 at Coolgraney, Gowran, County Kilkenny. Vaughan said Mass at the Powell Street convent and became friends with Mother Teresa. They corresponded for many years afterwards, and, when he was bishop of Salford, he assisted her in several projects.[22]

The Sisters of Notre Dame conducted a school in Marysville. The Academy of Notre Dame had one continuous session from September to July. There was a staff of eleven sisters and 176 students when Vaughan visited.[23]

All during March the nuns prayed for him, and he to St Joseph. On the final day of March 1864 a letter arrived from Archbishop Alemany which permitted him to preach a sermon in each church of the diocese on behalf of the foreign missions. His first homily produced 200 pounds.[24]

A letter from Frances Ward reminded Vaughan of Manning's efforts to secure a new location for an Oblate seminary. Mrs Ward wrote to say that Manning was away, but when he returned, her husband was going to "settle with him about a country house" for the new seminary. The Wards supported Vaughan's plan to train priests for the foreign missions in the Oblate seminary. Vaughan advised them not to place conditions on their gift, especially not to insist that it be used for training missionary candidates: "The freer he (Manning) is left, and the less he is spoken to about Foreign Missions, till I come home with funds collected, the more easily and certainly will all things work together for good." The letter to Mrs Ward was dated March 1864.[25] Back in England, the Ward household regularly heard about Herbert Vaughan from their mother. The "letters he wrote to her describing his romantic adventures in America, his frequent rebuffs and ultimate success, were listened to by the family eagerly."[26]

Vaughan was unaware that Manning was about to change his mind about the location of a new seminary. Rather than a house in the English countryside, he prepared to recommend that a house of studies be set up in Rome. On 19 January he wrote from Rome to Oblates Thomas Dillon and Henry Rawes asking them to consider the Rome proposal before an Oblate meeting took place in May. On 2 February he wrote that both the Pope and the Prefect of Propaganda Fide had approved of the Rome idea. One of the points stated: "The money the Wards offer would enable us fully to do it."[27] In the meantime, Vaughan, in California, continued to hope that the proposal for his foreign missionary candidates to be part of an Oblate seminary in England was still part of Manning's plan.

Vaughan continued to collect money for his education fund. Among the California entries are: Presentation Convent School, $250; Thomas O'Neill, $20; Students of Santa Clara College, $61.50; Cathedral, Marysville, $170.; Father Congeato, SJ, church collection, $1265. He was collecting "burses," that is, funds to be set aside for the education of individual students. Initially, he hoped to have three or four candidates who would train with the Oblates. He also hoped that the Wards would help him to acquire a property, and that his collections and the interest from their investment would maintain the staff and students for a missionary college.[28] He hoped to collect in San Francisco "four or five burses, possibly six or seven." Each burse was to be worth one thousand pounds. He wanted to be sure that, once training began, the students for the foreign missions would be adequately maintained.

Edward Norman comments that throughout Vaughan's career, begging was "hateful work," and it is a "tribute to the nobility of his character that he gave his life to it—that the Church he served might be institutionally sound in its assault upon the faithlessness of the world."[29]

In early March he tried to invest some money. He joined with nine others in forming the "Harrison Gold and Silver Mining Company." They staked a claim to some promising rock in the hills above Swain's Ranch, about eighteen miles from Marysville, that he and Mr Harrison had discovered. There is no evidence that the claim ever produced a profit for the investors.[30]

Herbert Vaughan's health improved while he was in California.[31] His five months there remained a happy memory until the end of his life. The only passage in all his writings, according to Snead-Cox, in which he ever speaks of natural scenery with anything like enthusiasm, is a description of the Sacramento River as it rolls into the Bay of San Francisco. It was written on 8 March 1864 aboard a river steamer that had just emerged from the river into the bay. One of Vaughan's recorded deathbed remarks, thirty-nine years later at Mill Hill, was about his memory of San Francisco Bay: "For sheer beauty there is nothing in Italy or anywhere in the Old World to touch it." It was on this, the first of Vaughan's three journeys to the United States, that Snead-Cox noted that he felt an affinity with the people of the United States, especially in their "restless energy," "spirit of high adventure," and a willingness to sacrifice "for the success of an undertaking."[32]

On 18 June he recorded some thoughts based on a conversation with a Fr Lootens, a Belgium priest who had worked for several years in Oregon and Vancouver. "The result of his experience," Vaughan wrote, "is that a missionary priest to the Indians ought to be a religious as a member of a congregation, with a centre. He had never heard of others doing much good—the life itself full of trial, temptation and suffering and requiring the support of Rule and centre."[33] It was an idea that would develop into St Joseph's Society for Foreign Missions from beginnings at the seminary he founded in Mill Hill.

Jesuits in California were, in Vaughan's opinion, "the most intelligent and active men ... among the clergy. "They are much respected. Two large Colleges are both deeply in debt but the Society of Jesus has the 'go-ahead' of the people and if they can see their way they don't fear a debt any more than the men of business."[34]

South America

Herbert Vaughan stayed nearly five months in California. On 23 June 1864 he left San Francisco for South America aboard the ship *Uncle Sam*. It was a small packet "ill provided and slow" and leaking! On the way out of the harbour they hit a schooner and then ran up on a rock, and waited until high tide lifted the ship off and then continued out of the port.[35] When he returned to England Vaughan submitted an article to the *Dublin Review* titled: "California and the Church. A Report by Herbert Vaughan, January 1866."[36]

According to Francis Weber, archivist of the archdiocese of Los Angeles: "In my opinion Father Vaughan's observations on the Catholic Church in those early days is without parallel."[37]

Vaughan wrote of Archbishop Alemany, who had not welcomed him or his plan to beg in California, that "no man is more poorly lodged in the whole city [next to Old St Mary's Cathedral in a 'dingy little house'] and no one preaches the spirit of Evangelical poverty, a detachment in the midst of this money-worshipping city, like this Dominican Spanish Archbishop of San Francisco." Dressed in his white habit and with his green cord and pectoral cross he opened his door every day to "all who come to consult him."[38]

Vaughan's friends in San Francisco tried to persuade him against the long journey he planned next. It included an over-the-Andes trip from Chile to Brazil, and possibly on to Australia. They were more apprehensive when they heard a rumour that the Confederate ship *Alabama*, was operating in Pacific waters and had recently captured the San Francisco ship *Golden Age*. But Vaughan light-heartedly wrote: "whether we shall not share the same fate I should not be sorry if we did, for Captain Semmes would favour the mission on which I am travelling and might probably become a Founder of the College for Foreign Missions."[39]

At the beginning of July the *Uncle Sam* stopped at the beautiful anchorage off Acapulco, Mexico; for Vaughan, it was his second visit. In the harbour were French frigates, with one thousand men waiting to go ashore. They had been "frying in the intense heat of the harbour for months." This was during the French adventure in Mexico. Their opponent was the Mexican leader, "Alvarez with some one thousand men," in the mountains around Acapulco, who was trying to cut off the town and starve its inhabitants. Vaughan joined Admiral Bonet and the chaplain, Abbe Soudan, for a meal on board the flagship, *Pallas*. Bonet gave him a donation of sixteen dollars and recommended that he visit a Mr Lesseps at Lima, "the French chaplain in Rio, the Sister Superior of the Sisters of Charity at Rio, the Superior of the Picpus Fathers at Valparaiso and the French teaching nuns in Lima and Callao."[40] At 11 p.m. on 2 July, the *Uncle Sam* sailed out of Acapulco.

On 8 July there was a fire on board, but it was brought under control within an hour. The same day Vaughan wrote from the Pacific coast, off Costa Rica, to Mrs Ward. He was more convinced than ever that the success he was having collecting money was the result of the prayers of others. His experience in California showed him that "the key of all hearts is in heaven—and that prayer is more powerful than eloquence." He had found that money was not easy to get and yet he found individuals were very generous toward the cause of the foreign missions.[41]

In his diary he copied statistics from a report on the work of Protestant missionary societies published in May 1864. They were short accounts of the Church Missionary Society in India and Sierra Leone, and the Wesleyan

Mission Society, Baptist Missionary Society and British and Foreign Bible Society. Such information was often used by Vaughan in his appeal to Catholics on behalf of the foreign missions.[42]

The *Uncle Sam* arrived in Panama but he made no record of going ashore—perhaps he was still regarded as a fugitive by the governor. His diary entry suggests that he immediately transferred from the *Uncle Sam* to another ship going to Lima: "The first thing I saw on coming aboard at Panama was a tall middle-aged man in blue cloth trousers, white socks and low shoes—seated on a chair and his feet over the bulwarks—a Yankee, said I at once."[43]

En route to Lima, Vaughan stopped at Guayaquil, Ecuador. Early on the morning of 14 July the ship entered the "great broad river of Guayaquil, so broad we could scarcely distinguish the opposite bank." It was the chief port of Ecuador. "This republic is so poor and the road to Quito almost impassable now, that I determined not to lose time by stopping to collect in it." Among his letters of introduction was one from Stonyhurst to "Joseph Jackson at Quito." On the stop-over he visited the cathedral and the bishop—who donated one hundred Peruvian dollars—and had a meal with him. "He lives with his old sisters and Chaplain Canon Marriott ... a great dinner in my honour." Vaughan found the bishop to be an "amiable and intelligent man" who had founded a seminary, where there were only twenty students, next to the cathedral. He also met Jesuits who were active in education, operating two colleges, one at Quito, and another in another part of the state. At the Guayaquil school they had 105 students.[44]

Peru

On 18 July, he arrived at Lima, Peru, on board a steamer bound for Chile.[45] He was invited to stay at a friary by a Father Wilson. His room was high up under the roof, and opened into the Chapel of Saint Francis of Solano. For the Feast of Saint Francis of Solano there were "eighteen days of preparation—candles etc. ... as in Spain and Italy. Singing pretty good."[46] Among his contacts at Lima was a French diplomat to whom he was recommended by the Ministry of Foreign Affairs in Paris.

When Vaughan arrived in Peru, the Church and the bishops were paralyzed by an anti-religious government. Because he was begging from door to door successfully, he came under the scrutiny of government security and a "proclamation" was sent around "forbidding me to collect from the inhabitants of Peru." The proclamation had no effect, for when Vaughan went to see the President, "his wife, in the presence of her husband gave me 250$. The President apologised for the decree ... passed against me, saying I could collect privately." Vaughan received donations from expatriates and Peruvians alike: "Mr and Mrs Ramos, W. R. Grace $100; M. P. Grace $10; U.S.

Steamship *Lancaster*, $200; Archbishop of Lima, $300."[47]

He travelled beyond the limits of Lima and, for example, on 29 July he went to the port of Callao to offer a Mass. One of the places in Lima that interested him was the seminary under the rectorship of Dr Juan Ambrosio Huerta. Huerta was a professor and rector of Santo Toribio Seminary, and later became the first bishop of Puno. It was a mixed school—lay and clerical—for philosophy, but "then it becomes purely Ecclesiastical.... There is much piety going on within. It is the hope of the diocese."[48]

He remained for nearly two months in Lima and on Sunday, 14 September, he left from Callao on a coastal steamer, the *Cloda*. "The decks a collection of men, women and children, dogs, fruits...." Five days later, after a stop at Pisco, and other towns along the coast, he landed at a port he calls "Islay." His destination was overland, the town of Arequipa. At Islay he had breakfast at the home of Patrick Gibbons, and at noon he started for Arequipa. He stopped at the ranch of "James Ayres of Exeter ... English beer, beds etc. etc.... in the middle of (a) desert." He began the next day at 2:30 a.m. and rode thirty-three miles before breakfast. In one place, there were the bones of "thousands of dead horses and mules ... in one open ravine filled with boulders the old dried bones in every shape had been fantastically stuck up in a variety of positions, so that looking up the valley from a distance the place seemed alive with horses, mules and asses."[49]

From a distance Arequipa looked like a "patch of beautiful green in the desert. It is a larger oasis, nothing more." He was welcomed by English expatriates; James Ryder and Alexander Sandison of "Fletcher's House (Jack's)" gave him hospitality and two hundred dollars for his fund. Besides Fletchers of Liverpool there were two other English firms in the town; Gibbs Company, managed by James Barry, and Stafford and Ward. A Mr Harmsen promised him "some shares in the Railway between Islay and Arequipa for the Foreign Missions."

Unfortunately, the local bishop, "the best Bishop in Peru," had been buried shortly before Vaughan reached Arequipa. He was Bartolomé Herrera, the best known conservative thinker of the first decades of the republican period in Peruvian history.[50] The English and others that he met were very generous to Vaughan. There is even one entry for two hundred dollars given by "a Spanish sinner."

On 29 September he was back at Islay and boarded another steamer, the *San Carlos*, under Captain Ellis. Ellis gave him a small donation. He left the *San Carlos* at Arica on 1 October and on the next day went by railway to Tacna, a town right on the border between Peru and Chile. It was another oasis like Arequipa, dependent on one mountain stream for its water. Mr Bohl, the head of Gibbs and Company, welcomed him: "Tacna is a thoroughly foreign town, made up of English merchants, but chiefly French, Germans and Italians. Population 12,000—the Cura, Dom Sebastian Sarse, a

Spaniard, said that perhaps 200 go to their Easter duties."[51]

He returned to Arica again and spent the day with Mr Nugent, the vice-consul. Although it was a seaport, he wrote, "the people of Arica are very good and devout while the people of Tacna are the reverse." The reason was a good priest who was clever, zealous and an effective preacher. One source of local wealth was the guano on the hills and rocks nearby that "scents the whole town pungently."

Chile

After a short stay at Arica, he arranged passage on the steamer *El Peru*, under Captain Bloomfield. The captain took up a collection on board and personally gave Vaughan a fifteen-dollar donation. The ship called at Cobija and Coquimbo, and finally reached Valparaiso; from there he travelled overland to Santiago on about 19 October.[52] He had been advised that there was little chance of collecting any money in Chile for "such a quixotic enterprise."[53] Soon after he arrived, he went on a ten-day clergy retreat being given by the rector of the seminary, Dr Joaquín Larraín. He was very impressed by St Joseph's Retreat House, founded by Archbishop Vicuña in 1826. "The retreats are the means of sanctity of the city. Contrast it with the London social welfare meetings.... The poor bring their bedding, sleep four or six in a room—sometimes number 600, or even 750 for ten days—they keep a perfect silence." He estimated that about six thousand people made a retreat each year at St Joseph's and the other houses in the city, out of a population of 160,000 people.[54]

Someone offered to organize a concert to raise money for his fund, but he turned it down, saying later: "such means tend to degrade the purity of charity." Snead-Cox wrote that Vaughan never had "any sympathy" with fund-raising by means of concerts or bazaars. Among the donations at Santiago were one from the archbishop for 250 dollars and one of ten dollars from a "friend of the infidels."[55]

He began to travel from town to town, and, on some days "begging from house to house." Everywhere he was received kindly. Some of the places mentioned in his diary were: Valparaiso, 27 December, 1864; Guayacan, 9 January 1865; Concepcion, 5 February; Talca, 16 February; Curico, 21 February. In some lonely ranches he found fellow Englishmen trying to make a life and generally "he did not depart empty-handed."[56]

His activities were not carried out without opposition. For example, at Valparaiso, where he stayed with the Picpus Fathers, the local newspapers made fun of his begging using "superlatives" such as "fanatismo, estupido, etc." to describe his project for the foreign missions, but Vaughan records that he remained silent.

He also found the "English abroad so much more liberal than at home."

The English merchant houses were afraid to give in the name of the firm, so gave rather in the name of individual partners. It was also at Valparaiso that two ship captains were very kind to him, offering him passage on their steamers. One of the Royal Navy officers, Captain Turner, had been in China and on the African coast. They met at one of the dinners given by several merchants.[57]

At the end of February 1865, hearing that it was very dangerous to cross the Andes on horseback, he decided to travel to Rio de Janeiro on Captain Edward W. Turner's ship, a man-of-war, the HMS *Charybdis*. First he settled his business at Santiago and then went again to Valparaiso. In his diary he entered a notation concerning donations he had received. The first entry was for Doña Trinidad Ugarti de Guzman who promised him twenty thousand Chilean dollars. She had already paid eighteen hundred dollars through her brother, but did not want her name to appear on the marble tablet Vaughan planned for the future missionary college in England. He honoured the lady's request and wrote under burses: "Una Señora Chilena."[58]

To Brazil

At Valparaiso, Vaughan met Captain Turner again and prepared to sail from Chile. While awaiting departure he was invited on board the ship of Rear Admiral Joseph Denman. He had dinner several times with the admiral and his wife—a "very high church" Anglican.[59] On 2 March 1865 Vaughan left for Rio on the *Charybdis*. At the same time, the *Alert* and Admiral Denman's ship left as well. Captain Turner was very kind to Vaughan. He gave him half of his cabin with a cot in the dining area. He ate breakfast with Turner and other meals in the ward room. A "good old Catholic" was on board; William Roche, the medical doctor.[60] The weather turned rough off Chile and so Turner decided to go around Cape Horn under full sail, rather than through the Straits of Magellan. Near the Falkland Islands, a marine lieutenant, Carry Smith, "had the calves brains, goose and joint, porter and beer, into his lap at dinner. I was lashed to the table." [61]

They reached Rio de Janeiro on 4 April 1865. For five days he lived with the Capuchins, "but their height upon the hill and lock-up at 8pm and their food determined me to go to the Lazarists." The Lazarists, or Vincentians, were chaplains to Misericordia Hospital and there was a Dutch priest in the community who spoke English.[62] Brazil in 1865 was an empire and the largest and most populated state in South America. It was 3.3 million square miles with a population of approximately ten million. The Emperor Pedro II ruled from 1831 to 1888. According to Jedin, the time of Empire was "a time of stagnation behind a facade of peace and quiet. In fact more to the truth, it was a period of decay for Catholicism."[63]

Death of Nicholas Wiseman

At Rio he received news that Nicholas Wiseman had died on 15 February 1865.[64] Vaughan wrote: "It left me stunned, though it did not surprise me. I was broken down with sorrow at the thought." In a letter to Mrs Ward, he wrote that he was continually thinking of Wiseman "as I sit, or walk alone, in the midst of this great city." He wondered who was to succeed him: "Who is to put on his armour? ... and, above all, it will need a very clear head ... to meet the disloyal Catholic intellect, which seems to be growing with the luxuriance and the strength of a weed. The only man I see is my Father Superior," Henry Manning.

Back in England, W. G. Ward was so anxious about who would replace Wiseman that "he could not sleep at night." He busied himself writing to the Vatican on the matter while "nearly all the influence of the Bishops and Canons in England was against the appointment of Manning." Manning is supposed to have said that it was a race between Ullathorne of Birmingham and Grant of Southwark.[65]

Vaughan was far away from the activity surrounding the choice of Wiseman's successor; he continued to beg for help to train men for the foreign missions. He considered the prospects for collecting funds in Brazil to be very slim, since the country was at war, there had been a business and financial crash, and because of their involvement, the English were not popular. He was received by the Emperor and spoke with him about Nicholas Wiseman. Pedro II and the Empress became patrons of Vaughan's project and the Empress Teresa Christina gave him one thousand Brazilian dollars for his fund.[66]

For almost one year he had been without any mail. At Rio, a small parcel of letters arrived from the Pacific coast where they had been sent by Mrs Ward. From them he learned that the Oblates were planning to set up a house of studies in Rome. "Would it not be well," he wrote, "to let the Roman arrangements connected with our Congregation be made without me?" That is what took place. The Oblate chapter of 16 May 1864 considered a move to Rome but raised questions about such a decision. By 1 March 1865, private money was given to the Oblates, including a gift from the William George Wards to rent some accommodation at Rome. Father Henry O'Callaghan was sent on behalf of the chapter to make a start.[67]

In Brazil, Herbert Vaughan wondered what his future would be, and decided to make no plans, because "Manning's approval is indispensable and uncertain." It seemed certain that the plan to send a few candidates to a new Oblate house of studies in England had fallen through. He wondered if the Oblate community would miss him if he set out to start a separate foreign missionary college. As more money was donated, he began to feel he had enough to justify the beginning of "a college on his own, separate from an Oblate seminary." He wrote to Mrs Ward in May that: "amid many anxieties and doubts as to the cooperation of others, and uncertainties as to the future decisions of those upon whom it is my duty to depend," he was grateful for the support of the Wards.[68] By that time he had collected a total of about ten thousand pounds, and had promises of more to be given later.

He was clear on a course of action if Manning approved. This was to "make a start at once, hiring a house in or near London. ... If we have not Oblate Fathers for the work, then horse the coach from other stables ... until we can keep our own." He asked the Wards not to mention his plans at Bayswater because they must first be cleared with Manning.[69]

Archbishop Henry Edward Manning

On the 6th of June 1865, Vaughan wrote to Manning. He had just received a note from Mrs Ward that his superior had been named Wiseman's successor. He congratulated Manning, and concluded that his presence "would be of no real value in London and I had better finish my work here as quickly as I can and then go home."[70] That same day, 6 June, at the Oblate chapter in Bayswater, Manning attended his last meeting as superior of the community. He gave an emotional address and added that he would still keep his old room at Bayswater while archbishop of Westminster. The chapter then selected three names to be considered for election as the new Oblate superior. V. A. McClelland writes: "The names in order of preference were Herbert Vaughan, Thomas Dillon and Francis Kirk. Vaughan of course was too busy with his work for the foreign missions to be the right choice."[71] Archbishop-elect Manning chose the second name on the list, Thomas Dillon.

Return to England

Vaughan looked forward to a fruitful visit to Recife, on the north-east coast of Brazil, before returning to England in August, but was abruptly told by Manning to come back to England at once. The same day a letter arrived from Herbert's father, Colonel John Vaughan. Colonel Vaughan repeated a rumour that his son had collected fifty thousand pounds. Herbert wrote to his father on 16 June, soon after his ship left from Salvador, Brazil, that he was "sorry to say, what I have in hand is about eleven thousand pounds." He also expressed his anxiety about what to expect under Archbishop Manning.

On 7 July he wrote "on board the *Guienne* at St Vincent," a ship which stopped at various ports before crossing the Atlantic to her final destination at Bordeaux. Twenty-five passengers came aboard at St Vincent. The ship was already filled with men, women and children, many sleeping on tables. A French officer serving in the Senegambia, who had slept outside Vaughan's cabin in the "wider part of the corridor," asked him if his son, a pale child of about eleven, could use his bathroom. "The scene was broad farce to all but the child. The thought that it was father and son made it at once sadness itself. Poor children!"

In his diary pages he wrote preparatory notes for a life of St Peter that he spoke of for many years afterwards, but never wrote, and "Sheep Farming in Buenos Ayres."[72] While at sea he also wrote to Mrs Ward that he was thankful she had put aside some "personal antipathy" she used to feel towards Henry Edward Manning. He added that he was glad that the Wards had done something for the "Roman squad," probably a reference to their promise to help the Oblates set up a house of studies in Rome and not in England as they had originally agreed to do.[73]

On 16 July the ship was in the Bay of Biscay. Vaughan wrote to his father that he hoped he was "taking good care of yourself ... life is a frail light and easily put out." On 18 July he wrote that the passage across the Atlantic was quick, and the ship "so full, people had to sleep on tables the whole way over." "The immense solitude of the ocean is as God left it and to me is always a peaceful contrast with the petty thoughts of men upon its shores."[74] In the final pages of his diary his thoughts ran ahead to the work on behalf of the foreign missions. One entry gives reasons for a choice of "Asia and Africa for our fields"[75] In another he gives a name to the seminary: "College for Foreign Missions under Patronage of Sacred Heart of Jesus," and adds some notes: all are to be for the "Foreign Missions with an obligation to leave Europe"; sent two-by-two under certain conditions for "their protection and spiritual welfare"; all to be secular priests, but at the same time "bound together for mutual support and advantage by a common rule and spirit"; the rule of the Oblates seemed to be the most suitable; the Holy See to be asked to assign a mission in "say, a part of Japan" for which the "Congregation" will be in a large part responsible, but not for other more established missions; and men to be sent out simply "under the Bishop of the District or Vicariate."[76]

Alone with such thoughts while crossing the Atlantic, he refined his ideas about a missionary college and a congregation of missionaries. It was not, therefore, to follow the model of Ireland's All Hallows, but to be similar to those of the Continent, especially that of the Paris Foreign Missionary Society of Rue de Bac.

When the mail boat reached Bordeaux, Vaughan travelled first to Paris, where he prayed at Notre Dame des Victoires, and then went on to England. It was the last week of July 1865.

Notes

1. See: *The Wilfrid Wards and the Transition* by Maisie Ward, London, Sheed and Ward, 1934, p.5: Frances Wingfield Ward was the daughter of the Revd John Wingfield, "one of the pluralists of bygone days who held at the same time a canonry of York, a prebendal stall at Worcester, the living of Bromsgrove and other preferments.... Soon after their marriage she was copying an article in which her husband recognized the Church of Rome as the true Catholic Church. To Mrs Ward, an ardent Anglican, this came as a thunderbolt—or rather as a

flash of lightning. She had copied half the article, she could go no further. "I cannot stand it," she said; "I shall go and be received into the Catholic Church." They were received into the Church together in September 1845.... She brought nine children into the world and had most of the care of their upbringing. She had to conduct the whole of the practical side of life while W. G. toiled indeed, but always at work congenial to him. Yet the unanimous view of a large family must have something in it, and I imagine that her daily life and its difficulties developed a certain irritability and severity in Mrs Ward, who was even in my childish memories a strongly marked and slightly eccentric personality; See also: Mrs Ward's obituary, *The Tablet*, August 13, 1898.

2. Snead-Cox, 1, pp.122-3.

3. WDA. Vaughan Diary, 2 January 1864, Caribbean Sea, Ship *Tamar*.

4. Snead-Cox, 1, p.124.

5. WDA. Vaughan Diary.

6. *ibid.*, p.10.

7. WDA. Vaughan Diary.

8. *ibid.*

9. Panama was at first part of the old Republic of Colombia, which became independent of Spain in 1819. A year after the liberator Bolívar's death in 1831, three new republics were formed. One was New Grenada and included the Isthmus of Panama. In 1855 the Congress of New Grenada declared The Autonomous State of Panama. Panama City, the Government capital on the Pacific side, was linked by a railway to the new port of Colón on the Caribbean in 1855 after renewed prosperity during the California Gold Rush.

10. Snead-Cox, 1, p.125.

11. According to Snead Cox, 1200 had already died. *ibid*. p.126.

12. *ibid.*: The fare to San Francisco was $10 according to an advertisement for the *Saint Louis* in the 29 March, 1864, issue of the *Daily California Express*.

13. WDA. Vaughan Diary.

14. *ibid*; MHA. HV. Panama, January 1864.

15. *ibid.*, pp.23-4.

16. Henry Walsh, *Hallowed were the Gold Dust Trails*, Santa Clara, 1946, p.13.

17. Condon, *All Hallows*, pp.244ff; John B. McGloin, *California's First Archbishop: The Life of Joseph Sadoc Alemany, OP, 1814-1888*, New York, Herder & Herder, 1966, pp.230-232: "In the early months of 1864 Fr Herbert Vaughan, future Archbishop of Westminster, was on a begging tour for a missionary society which he founded in England. His penetrating eye took in much and the literature of this earlier American period of California Catholicism was substantially enriched by an article which he published in the *Dublin Review*."

18. John T Dwyer, *Condemned to the Mines, The Life of Eugene O'Connell, 1815-1891*, New York, Vantage, 1976, p.76: O'Connell reported to Paris and the SPF on 10 March 1864 that he had nine priests and a vicariate that stretched 480 miles north to south and 420 miles east to west.

19. Snead-Cox, 1, pp.130-1; Condon, *All Hallows*, p.347: "To this day the Catholic heritage of North-east California and Nevada, the handsome frame churches and schools built by priests and nuns to say nothing of the congregations who are their successors today—bear mute witness to the diligence and high commitment of these early pioneers in the diocese of Sacramento."

20. Dwyer, *Condemned*, pp.75-85.

21. *The Express* was the oldest democratic newspaper in the state. It was founded in November 1851. Yuba County Library, *Daily California Express*, 1 and 2 March 1864, Local Matters; The Vaughan report was followed on Friday 17 March, by a note concerning the celebration of St Patrick's Day: 10 a.m. Mass, Rgt Revd Bp O'Connell, assisted by Frs Callan, Nugent and Montevardo, with the Marysville Hiberian Benevolent Society.

22. Ann Curry, PBVM, *Mother Teresa Comerford, Foundress of the Sisters of the Presentation, San*

Francisco California, San Francisco, March, 1980, pp.14-5; pp.21-4: In June 1880 Vaughan tried to help Mother Teresa with her petition to Rome seeking the amalgamation of four convents. Vaughan also promised his support and patronage for a missionary novitiate proposed for Kilcock in Kildare. Archives of the Sisters of the Presentation, Sr Ann Curry. See also: Sr M. Rose Forest, "Hearts of Oak," 1964, MS at Presentation Mother House; See: "California and the Church, a Report by Herbert Vaughan," January 1866, *Dublin Review*, VI, pp.14-35: The Presentation Sisters were from Ireland where they were founded by Nano Nagle in 1775. In San Francisco "from their peaceful enclosure" they went out to teach "one thousand children from infancy up to womanhood." In addition they ran the "only school in the State of California for Indians and Negroes."

23. "Brown's Marysville Directory for the year commencing March 1861," Yuba County Library: There was also a "select school for young men" in St Joseph's church basement, with an enrolment of thirty-seven boys; Mr H. Murphy, MA, was the teacher.

24. Snead-Cox, 1, p.129.

25. *ibid.*, p.131-2.

26. Ward, *Transition*, p.20.

27. Vincent Allan McClelland, "O Felix Roma! Henry Manning, Cutts Robinson and Sacerdotal Formation, 1862-1872," *Recusant History*, 21, October 1992, pp.183-4.

28. Snead-Cox, 1, p.134: "I am collecting funds to form burses for students. You will perhaps build the college itself, or at least in part or its first part or wing."

29. Norman, *English Catholic Church*, p.346.

30. Snead-Cox, 1, pp.132-3: Swain's Ranch, 5 March, 1864.

31. *ibid.*, p.134; WDA. San Francisco, 11 April, 1864: He wrote to Mrs Ward that her "report of the universal expectation of my death among my holy confrères is immensely amusing. I think (though one must never presume) that I shall falsify their predictions. Certainly I do not fail to take good care of myself and I shall neither expose myself to over fatigue or to dangerous climates. I believe I have a work yet to do and plainly more of heavy crosses yet before I shall say 'I have finished.' But we are in the hands of Our Lord and He is not further removed from the shores of the Pacific than from Bayswater Road or Westbourne Grove. So that one is ever equally in his hands." He was staying at St Ignatius College and helping an "excellent Irish community of nuns here . . . who have much to suffer." The nuns were probably the Presentation Sisters on Powell St. It is also possible the community was that of Mother Mary Russell. Russell and six other Sisters of Mercy arrived from Ireland with Teresa Comerford and her Presentation Sisters in November 1854. Both groups were recruited by Fr Hugh Gallagher. Mother Mary Russell was born in Newry in County Down of an old family. Her brother Charles became Lord Chief Justice of England. See: "The Late Mother Mary Russell," *The Tablet*, 10 September, 1898, p.424.

32. *ibid.*, p.135; WDA. Vaughan Diary: "Scene on Bay of San Francisco—coming down the Sacramento, March 8th 1864: I never saw a more beautiful scene even in Italy than that which we have just left behind. The sun was just gone down in a pure unclouded sky—and we just came out of the Sacramento River into the lovely bay of San Francisco. We were in strange contrast with the scenery—an American river steamer built up like a house, several stories high, with the great see-saw engine crowning its heights, and every modern comfort and luxury in the saloons and dining rooms—but one does not see oneself or observe one's own want of harmony, with what surrounds one—and often this is as on the present occasion, an advantage. The mountains to the left, not rugged and tossed about in pointed forms like Sabine or Alban ranges, but, gently undulating and dying away round the bay towards the West, are covered with a blue and purple as deep as that of the purple grape with its untouched bloom upon it—and as the hills stretch backwards and towards the North they become as blue as the blackened thornbush— The tints on the mountains at sunset are certainly finer and deeper than in Italy. Stretched in front in the bay like a sheet of gold which runs away into a beauteous silver colour—and there is

not a ripple to be seen far or near; a schooner with its sails loosely hanging about its masts is waiting for a breeze to carry her on for she stands out in the bay, a little shred of golden water is visible beyond between it and the mountains, and apparently only just out of the silent stream of the Sacramento. Far away a tongue of low land projects right into the bay from the East. At its root sits Beneen, a city of commerce and a tributary satellite to San Francisco. The land gives nought but the bulrush and long grass, oftentimes it is covered over with the great waters which are brought down the Sacramento. Here and there a widgeon or a wild duck rises from the water and skims its surface fast across the bay—And now an owl, the sun going down to bed, appears and with heavy wing pursues [his] various courses until he is lost in the dark shades of the hills. As I stood gazing quietly on this scene, alone and thoughtful, a man came up and said 'You never saw the like of this....' I said 'never' ... 'God has given you a beautiful land.' We only want population, he replied. It reminds me, he said, of certain beautiful lakes in Scotland and of the bay of Naples. I could only say 'Humph', for I had seen neither—and add it was the most beautiful scene I ever remember—and if given in a steel engraving would be thought ideal. One thing alone is wanting—churches and convents, bells summoning to prayer and ringing out Our Lord's Ave." Today one can view the Sacramento entering the bay near Vallejo on the route to Rodeo. The Vallejo–San Francisco Ferry follows the passage into the bay regularly each day. Author, 16 March 1994.

33. WDA. Vaughan Diary: 18 June 1864.
34. *ibid.*
35. *ibid.*
36. Vaughan, *Dublin Review,* January 1866: He wrote this article while returning to England via the Island of St Vincent in July 1865. See: Snead-Cox, 1, p.153.It was reprinted in the U.S. in the *Catholic World*, March, 1866.
37. MHA. Correspondence, April 10, 1865. The article was reprinted in *Documents of California Church History (1784-1963)*, Los Angeles, 1965, pp.102-25.
38. *ibid.*, p.120.
39. WDA. Vaughan Diary; The *Alabama* had been built at John Laird Sons and Company near Liverpool in 1862. She was rigged as a three-masted sailing barque but powered by coal-burning boilers and twin horizontal steam engines. The *Alabama* was one of a dozen or so cruisers used by the Confederacy to counter a Union blockade. Her captain was Raphael Semmes. The report Vaughan heard about the *Alabama* operating in Pacific waters was not true. She was sunk off Cherbourg in June 1864. The rumours Vaughan heard probably concerned the activity of another Confederate cruiser. See: Max Guerout, "The Wreck of the C.S.S. *Alabama,*" *National Geographic*, 186, 6, December 1994, pp.67-83.
40. WDA. Vaughan Diary.
41. MHA. HV.
42. WDA. Vaughan Diary.
43. *ibid.*: "I found however that he was a man from the South. What a life these Americans lead! What energy! He had been a farmer—took to railway making and superintended the Panama railroad when constructing—lived in the swamps, only had one little touch of fever. Went to California round the diggings—then came back to Panama—heard of some old Indian tombs in Cheroqui—300 miles from Panama, went off with a party to open and explore them.... He was led a wild goose chase by a Frenchman who had an island in which gold in abundance. A failure after much labour etc. Now he is going to Peru to set up a cotton plantation. His name is Johnston."
44. *ibid.*
45. *ibid.*
46. *ibid.*
47. Correspondence, J. Peter Grace, 31 May 1992: "W. R. Grace is my great-grandfather and M. P. Grace is my great-uncle. The $110 they sent is worth $1500 in today's dollars, and in

1864, in Lima, Peru, they were just starting with Guano bird-droppings.... My grandfather was a two-term Mayor of New York and founder of W. R. Grace and Ingersoll-Rand."
48. WDA. Vaughan Diary; See: Jeffrey Klaiber, *The Catholic Church in Peru, 1821-1985*, Washington, Catholic Univ. Press, 1988, translation, 1992, pp.62-9: Huerta was a delegate to the First Vatican Council and finally became bishop of Arequipa. True anti-clericalism appeared in the middle of the nineteenth century in most of Latin America, but the most anti-religious attacks came in the person of Manuel González Prada for whom religion was a form of superstition used to justify clerical exploitation of the Indians. For him and other liberals the Church represented an obstacle to social change. At the time of Vaughan's visit, the Church had counter-attacked and it was a period of Church militancy. José Sebastián Goyeneche was the Archbishop of Lima.
49. *ibid.*; Snead-Cox, 1, p.138; Vaughan was still at Lima on 8 September 1864. A letter of the British Legation of that date was addressed to a Mr Lettsama, the Consul General at Montevideo in Uruguay: "I take the liberty of introducing you to Rev. Mr.Vaughan, son of Colonel Vaughan a proprietor in Herefordshire. This gentleman whom you will find a very amiable and distinguished person has been travelling in South America for the purpose of raising funds towards the erection of a Catholic College in London, at the head of which will be Dr Manning, for the conversion of Infidels all over the world."
50. Klaiber, *Peru*, pp.65-6: Herrera was of humble origins. In 1842 he became rector of San Carlos seminary, reformed it, and gave it a definite conservative and ultramontane orientation. At one time he was minister of justice and government and later minister of foreign relations. In 1860 he presided over the constitutional congress. "Although the conservative ideas of Herrera held little attraction for the later generations more enamoured of democratic doctrines... he did not speak for any economic group... (and he had) an intimate knowledge of Peru's Indians, and adopted his conservative position precisely with that knowledge in mind."
51. *ibid.*, pp.70-2; MHA. W.M. Gibbs and Company, $150.; British Consul, G.H. Nugent, $20; J. Lansing, United States Consul, $17.
52. *ibid.*, pp. 73-4.
53. Snead-Cox, 1, p.138.
54. WDA. Vaughan Diary.
55. MHA.
56. *ibid.*: An English rancher wrote to his sister in Portugal about Vaughan's visit. Herbert carried the letter: 12 January 1865: "My dear Mary Ann, The dull routine of our mountainous life has lately been cheered by the presence of Rev Herbert Vaughan, D.D., who will be bearer of these lines ... a chance for a long chat about your faraway brother.... But also because I'm sure that you will derive much pleasure from the acquaintance of one whose short stay amongst us here will be long remembered.... Dr Vaughan has been travelling over our Western Hemisphere on a pious mission for the propagation of our faith."
57. WDA. Vaughan Diary.
58. *ibid.*
59. *ibid.*: Some of the names entered by Vaughan: Captain Nicholas Tourner of the *Clio*; Captain Magindie of the *Alert*; Francis William Davis, MD, of the *Alert*; on the *Charybdis*: Edward W. Turner, Captain, Edward Bateman, 1st Asst; Lovedale C. Singleton; William Childers; Edward C. Hall; George Gily, Master; William S. Roche, Surgeon; Henry Rickard, Asst. Surgeon; H. Glison, Chaplain; Carry B. Smith, Lieutenant of Marines. Vaughan also records a meeting with Dr Davis of the *Alert*. Vaughan was given some skulls by Dr Roche that had been brought back by a scientific expedition up a Peruvian river. Davis had information about them and Vaughan was to meet him in London at "Hallet and Comeny, 14 Great George St., Westminster."
60. *ibid.*
61. *ibid.*: "*Charybdis* March 25, 1865: Every night Captain has a party of all who will to play

cards and smoke, etc.—I chat for awhile and then retire into the other half of the room which is caged off and ... write, say my office, etc. ... join in conversation when I like ... at 10 1/2 cards would end and I join the chat and yarns—brandy and water till 11 all retire and I swing in my cot shortly after."

62. *ibid.*

63. Jedin, 8, pp.153-4.

64. During his final days, Wiseman's thoughts returned to his youth, his mother and friends, and to Aylewardstown. He prayed in Spanish "O Dios, Dios mío." His agony began on Monday and he died on Wednesday at 8.30 a.m.; "no struggle, no change, simply ceased to breathe." See: *Leaves from the Annals of the Sisters of Mercy*, 2, New York, 1885, p.234; Schiefen, *Wiseman*, p.340: "Cardinal Wiseman's last recorded words as he lay dying were: 'I never heard of anyone being tired of the stars.'"

65. Snead-Cox, 1, p.142; Ward, *Transition*, pp.22-3: "What sad news on reaching Rio! I cannot get out of my mind the death of our dear friend, the Cardinal....Of priests he was, as you know, my great friend and supporter.... And now another thought presses—who is to sit in his vacant place? Who is to put on his armour? Who is to continue the work of which he laid the foundations?... It will require very delicate and prudent fingers to draw the threads which must bring into closer relationship the Church and the State; and, above all, it will need a very clear head and a very unfaltering hand, and the seven gifts of the Holy Ghost, to meet the disloyal Catholic intellect, which seems to be growing with the luxuriance and strength of a weed. The only man I see is my Father Superior (Dr Manning). But what are his chances with all the Bishops and the Chapter and Barnabo against his appointment? The Holy Ghost has hard times of it with us English Catholics. I suspect Rome will choose 'Dignus' or 'Dignior' ! Expediency and the Devil hate 'Dignissimus.'"

66. Brazil became independent in 1822. Under the Constitution of 1824, the emperor was the first ecclesiastical authority in the choosing of the hierarchy and in the "supreme judgement of all the laws and decrees of the Popes and Councils." During the long reign of Pedro II the Church was nothing more than a bureau of government.

67. McClelland, "O Felix Roma," p.185.

68. Snead-Cox, 1, p.146.

69. *ibid.*, p.147.

70. WDA. Letter AA 122: "My dearest Fr. Superior, I suppose I should say, Archbishop. Mrs. Ward in a little note sent off by this sailing mail let me hear the good news. Thank God. What a relief and what a realization of all my hopes and prayers.... You have been splendidly trained however to suffering and contravention and public abuse and misrepresentation and I suppose all this side of the grave station.... England wants to see an Archbishop whose house and way of life is such as we read in St. Charles.... You must do for the episcopate what you have done at Bayswater for the clergy.... I look upon this as the final seal upon the congregation. It now may do its work." A slightly different version is found in Edmund Purcell, *Life of Cardinal Manning*, 2, p.245: Hospital Da Misericordia, Rio de Janeiro, 6th June 1865; McCormack, pp.75-6; Ward, *Transition*, pp.123-6: W. G. Ward was very pleased with the choice of Manning: "Te Deum laudamus, good sleep by night, a good Archbishop by day and a good opera in the evening are adequate for human felicity.... When Father Vaughan had gone on his long journey to America, Manning became my mother's spiritual director and over her and his other penitents he had a very great ascendancy. He had made a close study of such French models of direction as Francis de Sales and Fénelon."

71. McClelland, "O Felix Roma," p.215, fn.16.

72. WDA. Vaughan Diary, p.115.

73. Snead-Cox, 1, p.152; Ward, *Transition*, p.124: The personal antipathy of Mrs Ward to Manning might be explained by the "curious mixture" of her husband's feelings towards the new Archbishop. "Manning was by no means entirely congenial to him.... My father was

devoted to French plays, and eventually prided himself on possessing every French play that had ever been written. Manning disapproved of his taste for the theatre, and of the French plays inclusively ... my father lived with four windows open in his study while Manning hated fresh air.... Though he jumped for joy at the news of Manning's appointment as Archbishop, the Archbishop's bodily presence was not so eagerly received. Once when he told Manning that he had been suffering from great depression, Manning, with utmost kindness, said: 'When you feel like that again, come and spend an evening with me at Archbishop's House.' The inextinguishable laughter with which my father repeated that remark told its own story."

74. VFA.

75. WDA. Vaughan Diary: "Asia and Africa our fields for missionary labour because: 1) America is in the hands of the Catholics of N and S America and of many French Priests and Capuchins. No doubt they suffice not. Asia which has the largest population and Africa which is the least known and civilised claim our labours. 2) Then England's influence in Asia and Africa are greatest. 3) The Sects and or Protestants—another phase of the old idolatries of Greece and Rome—are dying of contempt, neglect and indifference. Still to a certain point they witness to Jesus Christ."

76. *ibid.* pp.120-1: "College for the Foreign Missions under the Patronage of the Sacred Heart of Jesus: 1) All educated in it shall be for the Foreign Missions, i.e. with obligation to leave Europe. And the principal aid shall be to send out Priests to the Pagan Missions though at the same time those who may not be considered fit for the more difficult missions may be sent to the Colonies and other countries out of Europe; 2) The Holy See shall be asked to assign to the Congregation: a Mission, say a part of Japan. We shall then make it our principal endeavour to supply Japan. Others who from whatever cause may not be sent to Japan will be sent out *bini et bini* to whatever foreign vicar apostolic may desire to receive them under certain stipulated conditions for their protection and spiritual welfare; 3) All the students educated for Foreign Missions in the College of the Sacred Heart shall be Secular Priests, but at the same time shall be bound together for their mutual support and advantage by a common rule and spirit. An almost universal experience shows the importance of such a condition, and we see it enforced in the Congregation des Mission Etrangers at Paris, in the Italian Congregations for Foreign Missions, not to speak of the Marists and Oblates of Mary etc.... the rule of the Congregation of Oblates founded by St Charles Borromeo appears under the circumstances to be in every way the most suitable, notably on this account that while it is a protection to the spiritual life of the subjects, it puts him at once in the normal relation toward the Bishop or Vicar Apostolic of the district which secular priests hold towards the Bishop for whom they are ordained.... The mission of Japan having been confided to the Congregation will of course be in great measure dependent upon the Congregation and the Congregation will be held responsible for it. Other countries which may be supplied with Priests from the College of the Sacred Heart will have no claim upon the Congregation, and the Congregation on the other hand will exercise no jurisdiction over the Priests whom she will have sent out to them: They will be simply under the Bishop of the District or Vicariate." Although these notes were written at the end of Vaughan's America diary for 1863-5, they are not dated and therefore there is a remote possibility that they were written later, when he returned to England. However, they do represent the development of his missionary ideas up to his return to England in July 1865.

CHAPTER VIII

Foreign Missionary College

Return to England

Edward Norman, author of *The English Catholic Church in the Nineteenth Century*, considers the foundation by Herbert Vaughan of a college to train missionaries for work overseas to be one of the greatest achievements of his life.[1] With funds and experience from his travels to North and South America, Vaughan was about to make his years of planning and hard work a reality.

On arrival in England in July 1865, he immediately reported to Manning, who was no longer leader of the Oblates but Archbishop of Westminster. Errington had been co-adjutor archbishop and was expected to succeed Cardinal Wiseman. However, his position was weakened by his long-standing disagreement with Wiseman. Pius IX also felt that the actions of the Westminster chapter were a personal insult, and he decided to take the matter of the appointment of Wiseman's successor into his own hands.[2] Manning on the other hand, as provost of the Westminster chapter, took Wiseman's side against the allegedly Anglo-Gallican Errington and the canons of the chapter. It was also Manning who, according to Sheridan Gilley, defended the Pope's temporal power "in an England passionately sympathetic to the Garibaldians who would destroy it." The Pope went against the advice of Propaganda, the British government, most of the English bishops, and the chapter, when he selected Manning on the 30 April 1865.[3] Henry Manning received Vaughan with kindness and encouraged him to devote all his energies to beginning a missionary college.[4]

Return to the Oblates

After visiting Manning at Kensington, Vaughan returned to his Oblate community at Bayswater. Oblate Cuthbert Robinson was in Rome when news reached the community, on 6 August 1865, of Vaughan's "phenomenal success in collecting money in America for the Oblates' foreign missionary college venture." He wrote that Vaughan had "11,000 pounds for his seminary and himself. I mean a part left to his own disposition. Providence has blessed his expedition."[5] According to Wilfrid Ward, Pope Pius IX had advised Herbert Vaughan in 1863 about his proposed trip to America: "Don't go, you will get nothing." When his trip turned out to be a success, Vaughan wrote to a friend of the Pope: "Tell his holiness that his blessing was worth more than his prophecy."[6]

On 25 August he recorded a gift of two thousand pounds he had received from Mr and Mrs William George Ward.[7] The Wards also undertook to help him find a suitable place to begin training future missionaries. At first he thought to rent a building near Bayswater, but when the Oblate house of studies was transferred to Rome, he abandoned the idea.[8]

While he searched for a property, Vaughan also began to look for suitable candidates. On 21 September 1865 he visited the Redemptorists and Marists at Limerick in Ireland. In 1866 the Redemptorists directed to Vaughan the first priest to be ordained from his future college. He was a young man named Cornelius Dowling, a native of Fermoy.[9]

Vaughan also continued to refine his thoughts about the nature of the training to be given to missionaries, and other questions concerning the running of a seminary. In the back of one book he scribbled the names of interested young men he had met,[10] along with other points he wanted to think about. For example, he wrote that some "Divines" can be educated as Oblates and others "affiliated" with a bishop. He wondered if there was a decided advantage in having religious missionaries rather than secular. Was it important to separate missionary students from seminarians not preparing for the missions, in this case from the Oblates? And finally, what district or mission territory was he to apply for in Rome?

During his absence the Oblates had nominated Father Richards and himself as official visitors, and on returning to London, he attended a chapter meeting on 4 November 1865 at St Mary of the Angels, Bayswater. At the meeting, Archbishop Manning stated that, "the College for Foreign Missions, under the direction of Father Vaughan, had all his sympathy."[11]

Holcombe House

Mrs Frances Ward continued to search for a suitable place where the college could begin. She found one with several acres at Holcombe House in Mill Hill.[12] Mill Hill Village was made up of two hamlets on Bittacy and Milespit Hills, connected by a string of large houses along The Ridgeway in a rural area about eleven miles from the centre of London. Later settlements were at Mill Hill East and Mill Hill Broadway. In the nineteenth century Mill Hill was still one of the important hay-producing areas of Middlesex County and during harvest time attracted an influx of migrant workers from Ireland and Bedfordshire.[13] Holcombe House was a Georgian home built by Sir John William Anderson on several acres of land he acquired at one end of The Ridgeway, on a place called Holcombe Hill. Today the old house stands between the red brick buildings of St Mary's Abbey and the Missionary Institute, London. The small hamlet on Holcombe Hill was a later addition to the village of Mill Hill, and the road along The Ridgeway was one of the main routes out of London to the Great North Road.

In 1861, Holcombe House was leased to Charles Thomas Druce, a Baker Street businessman. His widow was the holder of the lease in 1865 and 1866 when the Wards and Herbert Vaughan took an interest in the place. In the autumn of 1865, Vaughan visited Holcombe House for the first time and liked what he saw. It is possible that he was also attracted by the resemblance of the facade to that of his home at Courtfield, with its semi-circular porch and recessed arches.[14]

The Druce family was unwilling to transfer its lease. The occupant, probably Herbert Druce, acting in his mother's name, bluntly told Vaughan during a second visit "to go about his business." While he investigated the Mill Hill property, another smaller house became available. Friends told him to take the smaller place but he felt it could not equal Holcombe House. He was uncertain what course of action to take and so he sought the advice of his cousin William Clifford, Bishop of Clifton.

Bishop Clifford had written to Herbert in January 1863 about a nun in his diocese who possessed what he at the time considered to be extraordinary powers.[15] He asked Clifford to consult her about his dilemma. The answer came: "Buy the large piece of ground, for your work will take an extension of which at present, you have no idea."[16]

Vaughan had an interest in mystical phenomena. For example, he consulted a "holy woman" soon after his ordination in Italy about his appointment to St Edmund's. On this occasion, in 1866, the woman was known as Sister Walburga of Taunton in Somerset. The Sisters of St Joseph of Annecy, in a history of their Taunton community, tell the interesting story of a girl named Anne who entered the community novitiate as a lay sister in 1855, and later became Sister Walburga. Beginning with what seemed to be a change of character, she experienced dreams, ecstasies and visions of Christ's passion. "Soon she went into ecstasy every evening, seeming to behold the sins of the world." Years later Walburga left the community and the Sisters returned to the traditional emphasis of their community; "the hidden practice of simple virtues."[17] At the time of Clifford's consultation with Sister Walburga, she seems to have been respected, and certainly her advice to Vaughan was sound.

He decided to try once again at Holcombe House but he had the door "slammed in his face," and "servants were given strict orders never to let him into the house if he called."[18] Vaughan then put the challenge into the hand's of his trusted friend, St Joseph.[19] More than once during his life, Vaughan showed a simple and unshakeable confidence in his patron.[20] The story of St Joseph's help to acquire Holcombe House was not characteristic of nineteenth-century England's pious anecdotes, but Vaughan repeated it to his friends with great simplicity throughout his life. St Joseph became the patron of his Missionary College of the Sacred Heart.[21] Vaughan set about to enlist Joseph's help in what Snead-Cox calls "a sort of spiritual prank."[22] He found a small statue of Joseph and planned to place him in symbolic possession of Holcombe House. He wrapped up the statue and went to see Mr Druce again. Druce was irritated when he saw Vaughan but before he could speak, Vaughan turned to leave, and before going out, asked if he could leave a package in an open cupboard while he visited someone else nearby. Vaughan left the St Joseph statue in the cupboard before receiving an answer. A few days later, on the last day of a novena to St Joseph, the agent for the Druces wrote to Vaughan that they were willing to transfer the leasehold.[23]

Another problem arose when the owners discovered that the house was wanted for a Catholic seminary. The Ward's agent, acting on Vaughan's behalf, discovered a clause that prohibited its use as a seminary soon after the new lease was signed. The owner of the lease, Joseph Shuter, did not object to a seminary being built on the property, but thought that the ringing of bells would lessen the value of the unsold portion of the property. Vaughan decided to try to buy the freehold rather than the lease. At the last moment Shuter's lawyers refused to let the sale go through. Rather than wait any longer, Vaughan decided to begin under the lease he held. He did so even though he knew that Shuter could bring legal action against him for opening a seminary.[24]

College for the Foreign Missions

Before moving into Holcombe House, Vaughan published a letter addressed to the Catholics in England on the Feast of the Martyrs of Japan, 5 February 1866. It was titled: "A statement on behalf of the College for Foreign Missions." He wanted popular support for his new college.

While Catholics in England were struggling with many domestic problems, there was a remarkable missionary movement on the Continent, especially in France. The "Société des Missions Étrangères," founded in 1863, and its missionary college in the Rue du Bac in Paris, became his inspiration.[25] In addition, the revitalized missionary efforts in France had influenced Vaughan. And now, when he was to begin a missionary college in England, he turned to France for financial support and seminary staff. And yet he never underestimated the needs of the English Church. He urged more sacrifice and held to the belief that the sending out of missionaries was the sign of a mature Christianity and would be rewarded at home—the gospel paradox that the one who gives will receive.[26]

In the statement to English Catholics, he quoted Bishop Ullathorne of Birmingham, a former missionary to Australia: "The mission to the heathen is a school of generous heroes whose works of faith and sanctity will bless the country which sends them out."[27] Vaughan wrote that: "The exclusive object of the College is to educate secular priests for foreign missions beyond the seas." From its beginnings he was concerned only with the preparation of clerics for work in mission areas. According to Lawrence Nemer, author of *Anglican and Roman Catholic Attitudes to Missions*, the idea of founding a society, where clerics were governed by clerics, only developed gradually. But it is clear that Vaughan did have an idea that the training of foreign missionaries demanded more than a college. His diary notes made on his journey to the Americas show that he was thinking of a Congregation that provided support to missionaries trained by the school. In April 1862, he wrote that the seminary was to be like an "affectionate mother, striving to provide her children with whatever they may need when on their distant mission ... and in case of their being obliged to return on account of ill health.... The seminary will see to their being properly provided for till death."[28]

The statement to the English Church appealed for men "of solid virtue" with "great generosity of heart and a disposition to embrace the apostolic life," but kept in mind the maxim: "Few men, but good ones." "Youths of every nation" would be admitted but it should be kept in mind that the college was "only provisional and introductory" and the end was to provide everywhere "a good native clergy." "A foreign missionary college," he wrote, "is to work towards its own extinction." He ended the statement with an appeal for candidates and the cooperation of all Catholics. Letters from Wiseman, Manning, Ullathorne, Clifford, Cornthwaite, and Moriarty of Kerry, as well from some Catholic laymen, recommending the project, were added to the letter.

First Steps

Before any more obstacles arose to prevent his entry into Holcombe House, he began the move on 28 February 1866. From Bayswater, Vaughan sent a cart ahead to Mill Hill "with a few blankets, chairs and bedsteads for the night."[29] He and another Oblate, Father Henry Bayley, left Bayswater and arrived that night in a snowstorm. Accompanying them was the first student, Henry Osmond. Osmond left about two years later because of ill health.[30] "We began in real poverty—six mugs, or rather college pudding basins, for our tea and beer, and borrowed a few chairs and plates. We started that night with reading at supper the Life of St Joseph."[31] The next morning, Thursday, 1 March 1865, the first Mass was celebrated at Holcombe House.[32]

Two days later, a letter arrived to say that the owner, Joseph Shuter, was prepared to sell the house and property to Vaughan. The sale was completed on 17 March 1866; Vaughan paid the sum of £5,397 12s. 4d. for the freehold. On Monday, 19 March, the feast of St Joseph, Mass was celebrated "in the best way we could." Manning was present, gave a short talk in the chapel and "declared the College begun." It was to be called St Joseph's College of the Sacred Heart, and became the foundation of an international missionary society.[33]

On 12 July Vaughan wrote to Monsignor George Talbot at the Venerable English College in Rome. In the letter he told Talbot that his own ambition was to work for the foreign missions, if possible in Japan, but his duty seemed to be for the present calling him to the "house for Foreign Missions." He wondered who of the Oblates was going to help him. Maybe, he thought, Henry O'Callaghan or Robert Aloysius Butler—but they were already committed. Vaughan continued: "We are getting on well here. I have four students and more coming."[34]

Life at Holcombe House reflected Vaughan's ideal of the austere life he considered necessary for the training of missionaries. His knowledge of the lives of the saints, the awareness of the missionary training employed in other countries, the experience at St Edmund's College, and his own hardships when begging through the Americas, helped form a model. Throughout his career he was a keen observer who took great pains to prepare his projects, as he did the missionary college at Mill Hill. Although his views changed as the foundation grew, in the beginning he was quite uncompromising in his frugality.[35] An Oblate colleague, Father Cyril Ryder, visited Vaughan after the college had been opened for about twelve months. He found a dozen students, and since cooking was considered an "unnecessary expense," they were eating dinners of tinned meat. The austerity seemed extreme to Ryder.

Vaughan drove about London in a small "roughly built country cart" pulled by a pony. To avoid paying for a carriage license there he had a board on the back on which in big letters was painted "Herbert Vaughan, Mill Hill."[36] Once Ryder was in the cart with Vaughan and they decided to take a short cut across Hyde Park. A policeman stopped them because only licensed carriages were allowed in the park. He was about to let them pass after Vaughan explained that it was "a poor gentleman's" carriage, when he saw the board and Vaughan's name, making it a commercial cart. The two priests along with their cart were told to leave the park.[37]

Mary Elizabeth Herbert, Lady Herbert of Lea

Sometime in 1866 a woman who was to become the foremost benefactor of Vaughan's seminary, and known as the "Mother of the Mill" for her kindnesses to the foundation, visited Holcombe House. Mary Elizabeth Herbert, widow of Sidney Herbert, Lord Herbert of Lea, had been directed to Holcombe House by Henry Manning.

She was one of the notable women of the Victorian era, socially as well as religiously; notable, especially, both as an Anglican and as a Catholic, for her works of charity, and as a prolific writer of Catholic books and pamphlets.

Shane Leslie wrote that Elizabeth Herbert became as deeply knit to Vaughan's life and purposes as "St Paula to St Jerome."[38] Vaughan himself was to compare her to his own mother; she even resembled the late Mrs Vaughan. He considered the relationship that was to develop between them similar to that of "Madame de Swetchine and the Dominican preacher Lacordaire."[39]

The Herbert and Vaughan families were related. Mary Elizabeth Herbert wrote many years later that the "Vaughans are cousins of ours, the Pembrokes and the Vaughans having intermarried." The first was a Gwladys Vaughan, the daughter of Sir David Gain, who had been knighted by Henry V at Agincourt. She first married "Sir Roger Vaughan and then William, Earl of Pembroke. Their arms are in the cloister at Wilton, as ours are at Courtfield."[40]

A press clipping about the settlement of her estate in 1911 contained the following:

> Lady Herbert of Lea, aged 89, of Herbert House, Belgrave Square, S.W., and of Wilton House, Salisbury, formerly an intimate friend of Mr. W. E. Gladstone and of Miss Florence Nightingale, one of the founders of the Foreign Missionary College at Mill Hill, Hendon, and the Orphanage for Girls at Salisbury, writer of numerous books and pamphlets, widow of the Rt. Hon. Sidney first Baron Herbert of Lea, and mother of the thirteenth and fourteenth Earls of Pembroke.[41]

Mary Elizabeth Herbert was born on 21 July 1822. She was the only daughter of General Ashe a Court, a soldier and member of Parliament. He was the brother of the first Lord Heytesbury, a diplomat who served during his career as governor-general of India, and ambassador to Russia. Her mother, Elizabeth Gibbs—an invalid—was the daughter of a West Indian planter. Mary Elizabeth—Lizzie to her family—grew up at Heytesbury House, the Wiltshire home of her uncle. Her father used the home while his diplomat brother was overseas. Another uncle, a naval captain, also lived at Heytesbury. When she was a child, her governess was a Miss Hildyard, who later trained the daughters of Queen Victoria. When her family moved to Staffordshire, their neighbour at Drayton Manor was Sir Robert Peel, the future Prime Minister. Occasionally Mary Elizabeth helped Peel with his correspondence. When she married, Peel told her husband: "You gain a wife while I lose a secretary."[42]

On 12 August 1846, at twenty-four years of age, she married Sidney Herbert, the second son of George Augustus, eleventh Earl of Pembroke, by his second wife, Catherine, the daughter of Count Woronzoff, a former Russian ambassador to Great Britain. The Herbert home was not far from Heytesbury.

Sidney Herbert was educated at Oxford and became a friend of Gladstone at the Union debating society. He was a member of Parliament from Wiltshire, and, briefly under Peel, secretary to the board of control. He returned to office with Peel in 1841 as Secretary to the Admiralty. In 1845 he became a cabinet member as Secretary of State for War. In 1852 he served as Secretary, under Aberdeen during the Crimean War. In 1855, under Palmerston, he became Colonial Secretary. He was a personal friend of Florence Nightingale and instrumental in helping her to improve the condition of hospitals at Scutari. Under Palmerston in June 1859 he again became Secretary of State for War. Unfortunately, he developed Bright's disease and was told that only rest could save his life. Instead he kept at his work, accepted a peerage in 1860, but in July had to resign his office due to deteriorating health. He returned to Wilton House in Wiltshire, "unable to enjoy its beauty—he had gone blind," and died three days later on 2 August 1861.[43]

In private life he and his wife were known for their charitable interests. At Wilton they had a model lodging house for agricultural labourers and were active in helping to promote emigration. They had estates in Wiltshire and at Donnybrook in Dublin. They spent large amounts of money on improvements and helped to build many churches, especially one at Wilton and another at Sandymount near Dublin.[44]

Mary Elizabeth Herbert was often involved in works of charity. One who knew her was Mother Mary Basil, foundress of St Mary's Abbey at Mill Hill, who had been working in Soho with a community of Church of England nuns in 1858. In her memoirs she noted that in 1858, Lord Halifax, at that time Mr C. Wood, Mr and Mrs Gladstone and Lady Herbert of Lea, when still a Protestant, came to help the community and its work for London's poor.[45] Due in part to her friendship with the Herberts, and the efforts of Sidney when he was Secretary of State for War, and Manning after his conversion to Catholicism, Florence Nightingale was sent out to Scutari to nurse the wounded during the Crimean War.[46] It was Lady Herbert who helped organize the sending out of the nurses—among them English and Irish Sisters of Mercy.[47]

When Sidney Herbert died in 1861, she was left with seven children, four sons and three daughters: George and Sidney who became Earls of Pembroke; Reginald who joined the Royal Navy; Michael who became a diplomat and ambassador; and daughters Mary, Maude and Gwladys. Her husband was a great loss to her.[48]

Mary Elizabeth Herbert was born a Protestant, but even in her youth she found "Protestant worship formal, empty and cold."[49] "My Sundays," she wrote later, "were a perfect terror to me."[50] Largely due to the influence of Henry Manning, she was received into the Catholic Church. She had been married about four months when she first met Manning, who was then an Anglican. "My husband one day brought to introduce to me one whom he called his oldest school and college friend.[51]

After what Purcell calls "a prolonged delay, owing to family difficulties," Lady Herbert was received into the Catholic Church on 5 January 1865, by a "holy old canon" in the archbishop's private chapel in the cathedral at Palermo, Sicily.[52] Manning wrote to her from Rome warning her of the storms awaiting her because she had become a Catholic. "But keep as close to God as you can, and humble yourself lower and lower."[53] A few weeks later, she was confirmed in Archbishop Manning's private chapel. Her sponsor was a Sister of Charity and the only others present were the old canon and a "holy missionary priest whose prayers I had especially begged."[54]

Mary Elizabeth Herbert lived on the family estate at Wilton. After becoming a Catholic she was accused by the rector of the Wilton Anglican church of "dissimulation" and a "want of openness." Her grand-daughter, Gwendolen Plunket Greene, wrote that she had "entered a world of wilful misunderstanding and prejudice, utterly alone"; and she was obliged to sacrifice all her interests, her charities, and even her friends in the Wilton home she loved. The children's guardians exercised their office "with almost incredible harshness. They interfered with and humiliated her, at every step.... Her children loved her but seemed to regard her as something quite different from themselves."

In later years, when her grand-daughter was old enough to know her better, she wrote: "She may have been tactless in earlier years ... but she never spoke of these differences of faith nor did she show any of the sadness she felt." So the children all accepted her unfailing kindnesses and countless generosities whilst remaining apart from her. They smiled at "Mama's" many Catholic activities, her Catholic friends, holding themselves aloof from all she loved most. "I have never known a home so full of light, so radiating peace and good cheer as Herbert House."

Lady Mary Elizabeth Herbert had many talents, but the only gift she seemed to use and care for was her writing. "She wrote with much grace and simplicity, though her facility was perhaps something of a snare, and gave the impression of superficiality."[55] Mrs Greene remembered her as "tremendously strong and of great energy, an intensely active spirit." She described seeing her grandmother when she was about seventy years old "sitting at her large and scrupulously tidy writing table by the fire where she wrote letters all the morning in the most lovely handwriting, and always wearing lavender suede gloves." In the afternoon and evening she always took care of her outside interests and responsibilities. Despite her many activities, "she always remained a gentle, peaceful and recollected woman—hating untidiness and disorder." Her home seemed as orderly as herself to the grand-daughter.

She remembered her at Herbert House in London: "On the coldest, darkest mornings before day is up, I seem both to see and to feel the busy presence of my grandmother: be it ever so early she will be there before you, tidying, arranging, embellishing—silent and purposeful, rendering her loving service in devoted attention. My grandmother lived nearly ninety years, and I believe that during all that time it is hardly an exaggeration to say that she never failed any obligation, nor turned a deaf ear to any call. She fulfilled quite simply the words of her Master, 'If you love me, keep my commandments.'"[56]

Herbert House in London had a weekly lunch at which there was "invariably a crowd of people" who were "relatives, children, priests, students, missionaries and even Cardinals." At these lunches the children's old Protestant governess, "Pre" Raekstraw, was always there in her "black shovel-bonnet," along with Uncle Henry, "my grandmother's gentler brother." "Presiding over this festive scene, beneficent, courteous and charming, my grandmother sat at the head of the table, with her constant companion Garry, the fat pug dog, beside her." After many disappointments and sorrows in her life, Lady Herbert "had learnt dependence on God, and a strength which never forsook her."[57]

Lady Mary Elizabeth Herbert became a partner with Herbert Vaughan in his project at Mill Hill, thanks to Archbishop Manning. Each week she travelled from Wilton to go to confession to Henry Manning, who then lived at York Place, in London. One day as she was leaving, Manning said to her: "I want you to go down and see Herbert Vaughan's new little house at Mill Hill where he is beginning his Foreign Missionary work. I confess I do not know how he will succeed but it was a favourite idea of Cardinal Wiseman, and he himself is full of faith and energy about the undertaking."[58]

The local vicar at Mill Hill remembered her visits. She travelled to Mill Hill in a little horse-drawn closed carriage driven by a coachman called Johnson driving a pair of "immaculate, beautiful horses."[59] On her first visit she decided to adopt the Holcombe House community. According to Arthur McCormack, it was just in time, for "the only room with furniture was the chapel" and Vaughan and his one student were sleeping on the floor in the empty rooms.[60] She began to give all that she could of her own resources and tried to interest her friends in Vaughan's project. No other single person did as much for his missionary college.

Her friends and family affectionately used to call Mary Elizabeth Herbert "Lady Lightning" for her quickness. She was now joined in charity to a man later nicknamed the "Scarlet Runner" for a similar trait, but with less affection than sarcasm.[61]

The Ward family also made regular visits to Holcombe House. Manning often joined them for the drive to Mill Hill. Wilfrid Ward wrote of those 1866 visits: "In this enterprise we saw Herbert Vaughan in the mood most characteristic of him, full of keen happiness and varied schemes for the future. The Archbishop took a great interest in the project."[62]

To Rome

In the winter of 1866-7, Vaughan left Holcombe House and travelled to Rome. Between 29 and 31 of January, he became ill at Genoa due to "neglecting an inflamed wound and by the use of arnica," which brought on a streptococcal infection. The infection became life-threatening, and his sister,

Gwladys, wrote a message to their father, Colonel Vaughan, that he "should push on to Genoa" for "his son Herbert is there dangerously ill."[63] Colonel Vaughan wrote to Archbishop Manning from the Hotel Royal in Genoa on 2 February that he found that none of the "fearful accounts" he had received had been exaggerated. "Raving unconscious, his tongue black, and apparently dying. The parish priest came to anoint him." The doctor "used a knife," but they feared another operation on his leg might be needed. Colonel Vaughan continued in his letter to Manning: "From your knowledge of Herbert's character, you can readily believe that he is calm and patient in suffering.... The surgeon says the serenity is in his favour. He has great bodily suffering and mental agony" and is in "a state of delirium." Yet his father was able to see "so much gain and profit in these severe trials and lessons that come from God, that they have a bright and happy side for me."[64] However, although out of danger, even when Herbert Vaughan returned to England, the wound refused to heal.[65]

Throughout Vaughan's career, his energy, when not betrayed by poor health, involved him in more and more work. When he went to Rome in April 1867, he was received by Pope Pius IX. The topic discussed with the Pope was Catholic higher education in England. It touched on the return of John Henry Newman to Oxford with an Oratory mission and the prohibition against Catholics attending Oxford and Cambridge Universities. But the issue was once again far wider and more fundamental. It was an aspect of the struggle between the ultramontanes and their opponents.[66] Vaughan told the pope that there was an immediate danger of "our losing control of our higher studies" and the formation of a "liberal and anti-Roman school at Oxford."

In a letter to Manning on 10 April, Vaughan reported on his audience with the Pope. He had separated Manning, and a few friends, he said, who looked to the Holy See, from the other English bishops, who were weak and timid, though good and devoted to their work. The Pope in turn defended Newman, but Vaughan brought up an old *Rambler* article as evidence that Newman was unreliable.[67]

According to Newsome, the possibility of an Oratory mission at Oxford, and Newman's presence there, would have been an incentive for Catholic families to send their sons to a Protestant university. The complications that arose from this issue can partly be explained by the fact that none of the major figures was free from a touch of disingenuousness. Vaughan had gone to Rome, prompted—allegedly—by W. G. Ward, to resist the Oxford project, and he "had done his utmost to convince all parties, including the Pope himself, that Newman's presence in Oxford would inevitably attract Catholic youths."[68]

St Joseph's Missionary College

The Catholic Directory for 1867 lists Vaughan's missionary college at "Mill Hill, Hendon." The Oblate Fr Henry Bayley had been replaced by Fr P. Reynen.[69] Herbert Vaughan did not receive the help he had hoped for from his Oblate community. One reason was that the new house of studies at Rome taxed their resources. And so Vaughan began to look for others who might take over the running of the college. It had become too difficult for him to do everything himself. While travelling, he made contact with the major missionary institutions on the Continent and in Ireland. Over the next two years he was to make three formal requests to hand over the missionary college "to persons more competent than myself to form and direct."[70] It is not surprising that Vaughan turned to France, for French influence at the time was dominant in Catholic overseas missions.[71] The first missionary society he proposed to hand over his college to was the Paris Foreign Missionary Society of the Rue du Bac.

There is an oral tradition that Vaughan, before 1870, did not have the intention of forming a "society."[72] This has been shown to be inaccurate, for he had already expressed the idea in his diary when travelling to the Americas.[73] The aim of the seminary was to educate secular priests for foreign missions with a distinct preference for "pagan" areas.[74] At the same time he had acknowledged in his notes that the seminary would have an obligation toward the missionaries who were sent out.

It was not modelled on All Hallows, since it sent priests to jurisdictions where a local bishop would be responsible for them as seculars in his diocese. The areas Vaughan looked to in Asia and sub-Saharan Africa would involve primary evangelization and not the care of a diaspora community, and so the missionaries would need special care. Therefore he turned to the missionaries he most admired in the Rue du Bac, the Paris Foreign Mission.

Another pioneer, Charles Martial Allemand-Lavigerie, archbishop of Algiers and Carthage, opened a novitiate for missionary priests in Algeria on 19 October 1868. His organization was called "Missionaries of Our Lady of Africa." Like Herbert Vaughan, he had searched for a model and he too admired the flexible framework of the Paris Missionary Society. Its members made a simple promise to preach the Gospel in the Far East, remained connected with their diocese of origin but were seconded to vicars apostolic, and were more of an association than a religious society.[75] However, Vaughan wanted more than a model from Paris, he needed their help in Mill Hill to form an organization like their own.

His request for assistance from the "Congrégation des Missions Etrangers" in Rue de Bac was unsuccessful. It was probably made in late 1866 or early 1867. He then visited the Lazarists, or Vincentians, in Paris in August 1867, and met with the superior general, Fr Etienne. Vaughan proposed to entrust the "intellectual and spiritual training to the Lazarists" while he remained "procurator." A misunderstanding arose about Vaughan's status. Did "procurator" mean he was to remain "rector" over the students and the Lazarists? Vaughan wrote to the Lazarists in an attempt to clarify his intentions. It would be neither "equitable nor fair to any congregation to invite their members to become the subject of a superior, himself not bound or trained according to their method." He went on to say that he had "many faults" but a lack of "straight-forwardness and frankness [was] not among them."[76] If they were available and willing, Vaughan was prepared to hand over the missionary college to them. Father Etienne visited Mill Hill sometime in mid-November 1867, and left with a good impression. Vaughan was "satisfied that the Lazarists will carry out my views as to the spirit and training of the men in this House, or rather my views are but theirs."[77]

By mid-February 1868 it was clear that negotiations had not gone well.[78] Disagreements surfaced over the way the college was to be run: Vaughan wanted men trained exclusively for "foreign missions" and not for "chaplains etc. in France." Vaughan also wanted no distinctions in the allotment of rooms and food between students and staff, but found that the "Lazarists always make this distinction." The result was that the Lazarists did not agree to come to help Vaughan at Mill Hill.

In an undated letter, probably written in February 1869, Vaughan was despondent over such a "poor beginning for a Foreign Missionary College which looks out on a field of 800 millions." As he walked up to his room at Holcombe House he thought: "weak and incapable that I am, from the beginning of this enterprise till now I have been alone in it." There was no other priest to "bear the burden with me. I cannot do novice master's work which is so vitally important as well as other things." He had also failed to obtain what he had expected from the Lazarists. "Moreover our numbers are very small," he wrote.[79]

In July 1869, Vaughan tried once again to find help. He asked the Congregation of the Holy Spirit, also known as the Holy Ghost Fathers, and, more recently, as Spiritans. He went to France and visited Largonnet in Brittany, where they had two thousand acres of land and an old Cistercian Abbey in a deserted rural area, where the congregation had established a training centre. From Brittany he travelled to Paris to see the superior general at 30 Rue L'Homond. During lunch Vaughan "proposed to make over to him the Mill."[80] Again he failed.

It became clear that since he had "tried all I can to give up the work to others, it is God's Will that we should break our own colts and horse our own team." He decided that he "must be more at the Mill and less engaged in outward works."[81]

Notes

1. Norman, *Catholic Church*, p.358.

2. David Newsome, "Cardinal Manning and his influence on the Church and Nation," *Recusant History*, 21, no 2, October 1992, p.139: "By a strange irony, it was Errington's implacable … opposition even when appealed to by Pio Nono himself, that paved Manning's way … by the personal nomination of the Pope;" Newsome, *Convert Cardinals*, p.212: Pius IX begged Errington to reconsider his refusal to resign and become archbishop of Trinidad. "In fact he went further. By producing a pocket-book to take down precisely what the Pope was saying to him, he so angered Pio Nono as to forfeit all sympathy."

3. Sheridan Gilley, "A Mosaic Radical," *The Tablet*, 11 January 1992, p.35; Newsome, *Convert Cardinals*, pp.248-9.

4. Snead-Cox, 1, p.154.

5. McClelland, "O Felix Roma," p.194.

6. Wilfrid Ward, "New Cardinals," *The Tablet*, De c.1892,

7. Snead-Cox, 1, p.155.

8. McCormack, p.80.

9. MHA. HV. Black Book; Dowling's brother, D. M. J. Dowling, was an assistant at Holy Name Cathedral after his ordination in 1875, and was chancellor of the Archdiocese of Chicago from 1880. In April 1889 he was named vicar general of the archdiocese, a post he held till his death on 27 June 1900 at the age of sixty-six. Harry Koenig, *A History of the Parishes of the Archdiocese of Chicago*, Chicago, 1980, p.79.

10. MHA. HV. Some of the legible names are: Cutler and Walsh, Kilkenny; Michael MacNamara, Limerick; Patrick Williams, Waterford; Ed Gall, Ossery; Pat Healy , Limerick; Pat Kelly, Carrick.

11. WDA. Notes by Francis Wyndam, 16 June 1904.

12. MHA. See: *The Tablet* , 13 August and 20 September 1898: At her funeral Vaughan gave the eulogy: "I well remember in the 50s the charity shown by her in establishing the mission church at Hertford when several hundred pounds were given to that church. And out of her private fortune a large sum (2000 pounds) was given to the founding of the College of the Foreign Missions to the heathen."

13. Graham Roberts, "Mill Hill Village, 1898," Old Survey Maps, Alan Godfrey, Gateshead.

14. Most of the details about Holcombe House are from an unpublished manuscript by Fr Aylward Shorter, "Holcombe House, Home of the Missionary Institute, London," Mill Hill, March 1993. The suggestion that Holcombe House resembled Courtfield was made by the late Bishop Gerald Mahon on 22 June 1989. See also: Snead-Cox, 1, pp.156ff; Very near to Holcombe Hill and Hammer's Lane was the site of a windmill, from which Mill Hill takes its name, which worked as long ago as 1321 but disappeared before the middle of the eighteenth century. In 1775 Sir John Anderson, a wealthy glove merchant, acquired land on the hill which included part of the Great Mill Field and what came to be known as "Hill Field" where St Joseph's College for the Foreign Missions stands today. Anderson completed the house in 1778.

15. WDA. HV, Notes on the Development of the Idea of the Foreign Missions. p.4, no 12: "In January 1863 Dr. Clifford wrote me an account of the vision of a nun. I felt a conviction in spite of health etc. that something would be done: and that something would come of my intended journey to Spain;" Bishop William Joseph Hugh Clifford had returned to Rome on 16 September 1851 with Herbert Vaughan on his first journey. In April 1852 he became Errington's secretary at Plymouth. After studying Canon Law he became the third Bishop of Clifton in 1857. *The Tablet*, 19 August 1893, p.302.

16. *Remembered in Blessing*, p.59; McCormack, p.80, n.1.

17. MHA. Correspondence with the Sisters of St Joseph of Annecy, Staplegrove, Taunton, Somerset. From a community history, "Taunton 1808-93," pp.71-3: "Walburga … The

distressing phenomena connected with that name are sufficient to occasion the utmost caution with regard to ecstasies, visions etc." A change "as complete as it was terrible, suddenly took place. Ecstasies and revelations gave place to what have been manifestations of hysteria, but what the terrified nuns firmly believed was diabolical possession." One summer when he was visiting, Bishop Clifford witnessed Sister Walburga beating some sisters in the school dormitory. She was "removed from the monastery and never returned. On her departure an extraordinary feeling of peace and unity filled the Community." From that time the Sisters showed a great reserve with regard to mystical phenomena. "Any unusual favours are recorded almost apologetically, and the emphasis is always on the hidden practice of simple virtues."

18. McCormack, p.80.
19. Norman, *Catholic Church*, p.347.
20. MHA. St Joseph and other saints were his inspiring models and proven helpers. During his life he looked on them as personal intimate friends. See: MHA. HV Box 25, "Our Founding Patrons," by Bernard Roes.
21. Ward, *Dublin Review*, 1910, p.18.
22. Snead-Cox, 1, pp.156-7.
23. Shorter, "Holcombe House," p.24, n.1.
24. *ibid*.
25. "Souvenirs of a Missionary College," *Dublin Review*, no 28, October 1885, pp.301-24. The article is unsigned, but may have been by Vaughan. He was owner of the *DR* at the time and had written on mission topics. It was occasioned by the publication of "Martyres et Poètes. Souvenirs du Seminaire des Missions Etrangères," Paris, Victor Palme, 1884: "Our copy of its system started most auspiciously, because it set out with the same confidence and a still smaller beginning.... The whole idea of the college, including the beautiful ceremonies at the departure of its missioners, is taken from the French Séminaire des Missions Étrangères."
26. Lawrence Nemer, *Anglican and Roman Catholic Attitudes on Missions*, St Augustin, Steyler, 1981, pp.25-31; See also: Wiseman, *Dublin Review*, 1838: In his article on the Association for the Propagation of the Faith, Nicholas Wiseman stressed that England's needs at home would be met if her Catholics were generous, giving from their poverty, to those in great need. "... has not Divine Providence opened to us a way of supplying our remaining wants, by giving, out of our little, something to those who have so much less?"
27. McCormack, p.84.
28. Nemer, p.35; MHA. HV.
29. Snead-Cox, 1, p.158.
30. *The Tablet*, June 18, 1898, p.879: Henry M. Bayley was a convert who had graduated from Trinity College, Cambridge, and become a Church of England priest. He was a curate at Harlow for a time. After becoming a Catholic he taught at St Edmund's and then joined the Oblates. He was ordained at Bayswater in 1862. As a Catholic priest he was to spend most of his life at Kensal New Town where he cared for the Little Sisters of the Poor, St Joseph's Home, on Portobello Road; MHA. The first student, Osmond, took the "red sash" with the oath of Propaganda Fide, and received minor orders in December 1868.
31. Snead-Cox, 1, p.158.
32. VFA. Herbert Vaughan to Lady Herbert, St Joseph's College, 1 March 1871: "Yesterday then was the anniversary five years ago of my coming down in a snowstorm at night to Mill Hill with one student and today of the First Mass in Holcombe House;" *The Times* for 1 March reported on a petition to the House of Commons that "Roman Catholic inmates of work houses may have free expression of their religion and that Roman Catholic pauper children may be educated out of poor rates."
33. MHA.; Shorter, "Holcombe House," p.24; *The Times* of 19 March reported the suppression of a Jamaican insurrection: "There is no longer any reasonable doubt that cruelties of which it is impossible to think without shuddering were perpetuated in the suppression of the

Jamaican insurrection."

34. MHA. Correspondence, Herbert Vaughan to Mgr Talbot, Venerable English College, Rome, 12 July 1866.

35. Ward, *Dublin Review*, 1910, p.20; WDA. Vaughan Diary, 1866: "St Joseph's College in Honour of the Sacred Heart." Among the notes is the following: "As Religious orders raise the secular clergy and the people, so a Seminary for Foreign Missions must exercise a beneficial result—Every place has an atmosphere and influence independent of any effort, or desire—a virtue going out from it. A Seminary for Foreign Missions would be singular indeed if it did not shew forth 1) A perfection of the Apostolic life—missionary; 2) A witness of self-denial, in renouncing country etc.; 3) Charity and love of God. No unworthy motive could be suspected in those who give themselves up for it.... This will tend to raise and perfect our spirit."

36. MHA. Scrapbook: On Vaughan's sixty-ninth birthday a journalist wrote that the "old-fashioned country cart still occasionally does porterage work between the College and the (railway) station." By 1901 the inscription on a weather-beaten metal plate on the shaft could still be read: "Herbert Vaughan, Mill Hill."

37. Snead-Cox, 1, p.159.

38. Shane Leslie, Editor, *The Letters of Herbert Cardinal Vaughan to Lady Herbert of Lea, 1867-1903,* London, Burns & Oates, 1942, p.vii; In addition see: Shane Leslie, "Missing Letters of Cardinal Vaughan to Lady Herbert of Lea," *Dublin Review*, Autumn, 1947, 220, pp.97-115. Her letters to Vaughan have not been preserved.

39. Norman, p.348: "His close relationship to Lady Herbert of Lea ... followed naturally enough from the devotion he felt for his mother.... Lady Herbert actually resembled her physically."

40. VFA. Scrapbook.

41. Daughters of Charity Archives, British Province, Mill Hill Ridgeway. "Salisbury, original press cutting ... paper unknown." LH, pp.82ff: She left a gross estate of £33,809. "In her will she bequeathed 5000 pounds to the Roman Catholic Bishop of the Diocese of Clifton and the Roman Catholic parish priest of Salisbury for the perpetual maintenance of the Society of the Sisters of Charity of St.Vincent de Paul in their Industrial School at Salisbury, and bequests to servants.... To her son, Sidney Earl of Pembroke ... an ancient ring of the abbess of the Old Wilton Monastery 'which I always wear.' ... To the Most Rev. Herbert Vaughan (who predeceased her), for his own use, the whole of the furniture in her domestic chapel at Herbert House, including marble altar, painted glass windows, plate, vestments, linen, relics, and other ornaments, and such holy pictures as her children shall not desire, or in the event of his predecease then these articles shall be given to the Foreign Missionary College at Mill Hill, near Hendon, for the use of missioners;" The old abbey of Wilton became a religious house for seculars in AD 773. Alburga, sister of King Egbert converted it into a Benedictine priory. She became the first prioress. The king made Wulfthryth abbess from 968 to 1000. She became St Edith. Besides being head of a religious house, the abbess administered law and justice. It was her ring that Lady Herbert wore. See: William Herbert Pembroke, *Survey of the lands of William, First Earl of Pembroke*, Oxford, Roxburghe, 1909, 1, Introduction by Charles Straton, p.xliv. Lady Herbert wrote that "it seemed as if St. Edith were to follow and form part of my life." Sebastian Meynell, "Lady Herbert of Lea," *Catholic World*, vol xciv, January 1912, pp.505ff.

42. Meynell, "Lady Herbert," pp.505-514.

43. Leslie Stephen and Sidney Lee, Editors, *The Dictionary of National Biography*, Oxford, Oxford University Press, 1917, pp.663-5 .Disraeli used him in Endymion as "Sidney Wilton" and Elizabeth his widow is "Lady St. Jerome" in *Lothair*.

44. *ibid*.

45. "An Untold Tale," p.6; Another example of Elizabeth Herbert's charitable interests is found in: Daughters of Charity Archives, Notes left by Sr Langdale, "Salisbury, St Elizabeth's

School.": The beautiful Anglican Church at Wilton was built by her before she became a Catholic. In the year 1868, wishing to help the Catholics of Salisbury, many of whom were very poor, she decided to open an Orphanage there, and confide it to the care of the Sisters of Charity.

46. Webb, *England*, pp.304-5; See also: "The Order of Mercy and its Foundation," *Dublin Review*, March 1847, pp.1-25, for an early look at the Mercy Sisters.

47. Meynell, "Lady Herbert," p.509.

48. Gwendolen Plunket Greene, "Recollections of Lady Herbert of Lea," *Pax*, Spring 1943, xxxi, no 226, The Quarterly Review of the Benedictines of Prinknash, pp.5-13: Gwendolen Greene was the daughter of Lady Herbert's daughter Elizabeth Maude and Sir Charles Parry of Highnam Court. She became a Catholic after the death of her husband.

49. *ibid.*; Lady Herbert, *How I Came Home*, London, Catholic Truth Society, 1893, 1929ed.

50. McCormack, p.92.

51. Greene, "Recollections," p.6, n.1: "It is often said she was "converted" by Cardinal Manning and while it is true that he made a great impression on her... yet in her own account in the CTS pamphlet... 'How I came home,' she shows clearly how very early in her life she felt most unhappy ... in the Established Church;" Leslie, *Letters*, p.vii: She was "carried away by the Oxford movement and the Catholic revival in the Church of England"; Meynell, "Lady Herbert," p.510: In 1864, on New Year's Eve, she was in Rome, and attended a "Solemn Exposition" in the Jesuit church. During the exposition of the Blessed Sacrament she had a religious experience. She had gone with Protestant friends to see the church out of curiosity but she slipped away from them and stood among the congregation. "What happened, I do not know. It seemed to me as if all the people and the lights had disappeared and that I was alone before the Lord in the monstrance and that He spoke to me directly ... asking me 'Why I waited?' 'Why I did not come to him at once...?' At last I looked up and saw that everyone was gone and the lights were put out... the sacristan was standing by me saying he was going to shut up the Church ... somehow I had made a promise to our Lord which I must not break." On 5 January she was received into the Roman Catholic Church in Palermo; Shane Leslie, *Henry Edward Manning*, London, Burns Oates & Washbourne, 1921, 1, p.82: "When Archdeacon Manning visited Rome in the winter of 1847-8, his party included Sidney and Mrs Herbert and Florence Nightingale; Martha Vicinus and Bea Nergaard, Editors, *Ever Yours, Florence Nightingale*, London, Virago, 1989, pp.39-40: "Florence met the wealthy Anglo-Catholic couple Sidney and Elizabeth Herbert, who were to become key figures in her future work. Congenial friends in their circle were the Reverend Henry Manning and Mary Stanley, both of whom later converted to Roman Catholicism."

52. Greene, "Recollections," p 7; Lady Herbert, *How I Came Home*, C.T.S., 1893, p.31.

53. Edmund Purcell, *The Life of Cardinal Manning*, London, Macmillan, 1896, i, p.239: "Be very silent, trust greatly in the Sacred Heart, and not much in anything below it; least of all in friends. When the sun goes in they change colour;" And, p.232: Bayswater, 21 April 1865: "I fear you must look for no other sympathy in your family, for English people on this subject have lost their nature. Even the tribunals of justice are unjust and kindred are the unkindest of all;" Greene, "Recollections": Although she had been left sole guardian of her seven children in her husband's will, one of the storms she faced was over their religion. She hoped they would follow her into the Catholic Church but it did not happen. They were carefully brought up in the Church of England as wards of Chancery." Only one daughter became a Catholic before her marriage to Baron von Hügel: See Michael de la Bédoyère, *The Life of Baron von Hügel*, London, Dent, 1951, p.7: Mary, or Molly, "who married Friedrich von Hügel, wrote angrily of her mother's faith on a trip to Sicily. Watching Lady Herbert pray before a statue of Our Lady: "If this isn't image worship I should like to know what is? That vicious HEM! [Manning]"; Meynell, Lady Herbert, p.511: Two sons became earls of Pembroke; the third, at sixteen, lost his life when the *Captain* sank in 1870; the fourth was Sir Michael Herbert, who served as

British ambassador to the United States; one daughter who became a Catholic and married Baron von Hügel; another became Lady Elizabeth Parry, wife of Sir Hubert Parry; the third became Lady Ripon.

54. Lady Herbert, *Home*, p.32.

55. McCormack, p.92; Meynell, "Lady Herbert," p.513; Elizabeth Herbert did become an active promoter of all Catholic charities and interests until she died in 1911. She used her talents, especially a gift for writing, on behalf of the Catholic Church and became "one of the most prolific Catholic writers of her day." The heroine of one book she edited, Madame de Beauharnais de Miramion, could have been a model for her own long life. It was the story of a woman who "sanctified her widowhood" working for the foreign missions. Elizabeth Herbert continued in the preface: "But where shall we find in London society a woman like Madame de Miramion who trampling under foot the convention alike of birth and fashion, would be willing to sacrifice her whole life in stemming the torrent of evil and saving those for whom Christ died.... What then was the difference between her life and ours? It consisted in her singleness of purpose. She had one objective in view—the Glory of God and this hidden motive activated her in all she said or did, or left unsaid and undone": M Alfred Bonneau, *The Life of Madame de Beauharnais de Miramion, 1629-1696*, Edited by L. Herbert, London, Bentley, 1870, Preface; Greene, Pax, p.8: She played the piano, painted in watercolour and wrote with great ease; The *Catholic Encyclopedia* lists her as "authoress and philanthropist." "The pen more especially was consecrated to the cause, and for many years she produced a large number of books in rapid succession, partly original and partly translations, which found for the most part a ready sale. Among the best known of these may be mentioned: *Impressions of Spain* (1866); *Cradle Lands* [i.e. Egypt and Palestine] (1867); *Wives and Mothers of Olden Time* (1871); *Wayside Tales* (1880)."

56. Greene, Pax, p.7.

57. *ibid.*, p.11.

58. McCormack, p.93.

59. MHA. *Westminster Gazette*, 20 June 1903: "The vicar of Mill Hill Church, one of historic interest ... built by William Wilberforce opposite from the non-conformist school ... (remembered) 'When Dr.Vaughan established his great missionary college ... Sunday afternoon ... I would often encounter Lady Herbert of Lea's dashing pair of horses as she drove to see Dr.Vaughan.'"

60. McCormack, p.93.

61. Greene, Pax, p.12: "Her friends used to call her Lady Lightning, for her quickness, and I notice how often the Cardinal (HV) refers to light in connection with her. To me she stands always as brightness, light seems to be her special quality and element;" Leslie, *Vaughan Letters*, p.243: The nickname seems to have been given her by Fr Garside; Her son-in-law, von Hügel, wrote after her death—on 30 Oct. 1991: "I have known her intimately for 39 years. Never once in all that time did her courtesy and kindness falter. Never a week, often a day, passed but she did me and my three, not to speak of their mother, a genuine kindness. And it has been wonderful to observe how splendid has been the fruit of her long cheerful fidelity to the best lights that God gave her": Bedoyère, *Hügel*, p.252.

62. Ward, *Transition*, p.26.

63. MHA. Gwladys Vaughan; Leslie, *Vaughan Letters*, pp. 166-7: In a September 1869 letter to Elizabeth Herbert he recalls his illness at Genoa.

64. VFA. There is a problem. The date is placed in 1867 but the letter from John Vaughan is dated February 2, 1857, to Wiseman ... from Genoa! But, MHA. Box 5, file a, book 3: 29 Jan 1867 to Gwladys Vaughan, Convent of the Visitation, Boulogne: "Tell Father to push on to Genoa."

65. McCormack, p.87.

66. Norman, p.227.

67. *ibid.*, p.244.

68. Newsome, *Convert Cardinals*, p.261.

69. WDA. *Catholic Directory*, 1867, p.67: "On Sunday and Holy Days, High Mass sermon at 8½; evening service, sermon and Benediction at 6 in summer and 5 in winter. Act of Reparation to the Sacred Heart on Fridays at 5 p.m. Mass on weekdays at 6."

70. Leslie, *Vaughan Letters*, p.157.

71. Adrian Dansette, *Religious History of Modern France*, New York, Herder & Herder, 1961, 2, p.431;

72. MHA. Herbert Vaughan to Benoît; WDA. Diary notes: South American trip.

73. Nemer, p.35.

74. MHA. CB 22, p.18.

75. Francois Renault, *Cardinal Lavigerie*, London, Athlone, 1994, pp.99-112.

76. MHA. HCV. Correspondence, 20 November, 1867.

77. Leslie, *Vaughan Letters*, p.43.

78. *ibid.*, p.63.

79. VFA. Correspondence. undated.

80. MHA. Correspondence, 4 June 1992; Leslie, *Vaughan Letters*, p.157.

81. Leslie, *Vaughan Letters*, p.156

CHAPTER IX

The Tablet, Papal Infallibility, First Missionaries

From 1866, Herbert Vaughan was rector of the foreign missionary college at Mill Hill. He also became increasingly involved with the campaigns of Archbishop Manning and, beginning in 1868, occupied as proprietor of the Catholic weekly, *The Tablet*.

Friendship with Henry Edward Manning and Lady Mary Elizabeth Herbert

Henry Manning confided in Vaughan on matters concerning the English Catholic Church, and Vaughan, in turn, acted on the archbishop's behalf. Examples of the intimacy between the two men can be read in correspondence with Monsignor George Talbot.[1] On one occasion, Talbot had practically "made up his mind to abandon the attempt to rebuild the English Church at Rome." Vaughan wrote him from Mill Hill: "The Archbishop told me two days ago that you were thinking of giving up the work.... This must not be so.... It would never do to abandon it, now that you have done so much and overcome so many obstacles."[2]

On another occasion Vaughan acted on his own. In 1867 Vaughan had spoken with the Pope about John Henry Newman and the proposal that he and his Oratorians open a mission at Oxford. A bitter dispute arose between Newman and Manning over Vaughan's report to Pius IX. In one letter to a friend, Newman referred to Manning, Ward and Vaughan as "the three Tailors of Tooley St." In July, Frederick Oakeley tried to mediate. Manning responded with a statement of the issues, as he saw them, that had divided the two men over the years. Newsome writes that Manning expressed bewilderment over the accusations against his entourage at Archbishop's House, York Place. Manning explained that he had spoken to Herbert Vaughan about the details of his report to the pope, and Vaughan assured him that "all he had said or done had been not only without my direction but without my knowledge. It may be said that I did not restrain them. I could not restrain what I did not know."[3]

It was during this time that the friendship with Lady Elizabeth Herbert grew from benefactress and client, to one of affection and collaboration. There was a regular flow of letters between her and Herbert Vaughan. Almost all of Elizabeth Herbert's letters to Vaughan have been lost but Vaughan's correspondence with her can be found at the Vaughan family archive in Glen Wye, Courtfield, and in the book prepared by Shane Leslie in 1943.[4] Mary Elizabeth Herbert's interest extended to the Vaughan family as well. On one occasion, for example, 16 July 1867, she sponsored Herbert Vaughan's sister, Mary Elizabeth Barbara, at her religious profession in Torquay. Mary became Sister Clare Magdalene and later prioress of St Augustine's Priory at Newton Abbot.[5]

A year after the opening of the missionary college, Archbishop Manning came to Holcombe House at Mill Hill to bless a new chapel—the old one had been in a converted dining room. It was 19 March 1868, the feast of St Joseph. Elizabeth Herbert and one of the Weld-Blundells gave the two hundred pounds needed for construction of what was known as the "Iron Chapel." It was a wooden building only 14 ft by 20 ft and roofed with sheet iron. There were no seats or benches and so all knelt on the floor. Later, a high altar and four side altars, dedicated to the Blessed Virgin, St Joseph, St Francis Xavier and another saint were installed.[6] Before Manning gave his talk, he told Vaughan that on the way to Mill Hill that morning he had an idea to have "a public meeting in support of the College." "If you wish it," he continued, "I will announce in my sermon today that a public meeting shall be held in London for this purpose."[7] Therefore plans were made for a great assembly to take place at St James' Hall in London.

St Mary's Abbey, Mill Hill

One of the tasks Manning gave to Vaughan was to be pro-vicar general for the religious convents of the archdiocese. Vaughan tried to avoid the appointment but could not: "It will," he thought, "help the Mill by the additional power it will give me." Vaughan had been helping a group of nuns made up of women who had left an Anglican religious community and wished to become Catholics. They were the founders of St Mary's Abbey, Mill Hill, who bought Holcombe House when Vaughan built a new college. Over the years they became neighbours, friends and missionary collaborators with Vaughan's community.

In the 1860s the sisters were referred to as the "Hackney Nuns," after the section of London where they worked. Their leader, Mother Mary Basil, and some sisters of an Anglican community had been thinking about becoming Catholics. They wrote to Lady Herbert and asked "if she had ever repented doing so?—that is, becoming a Roman Catholic." When she received the letter Elizabeth Herbert "flew to the Sisters" and at the same time recommended to Manning that Herbert Vaughan become their guide. Manning prepared the Sisters and they were received into the Roman Catholic Church on 10 February 1868. Just before they were to leave their former convent, news reached Vaughan at Moorfields that their superior at the Church of England community refused to allow them to leave in their East Grinstead religious habit. In addition, she asked for three hundred pounds from the departing members. It was money they had already used during a cholera epidemic. To resolve the difficulty, Manning walked to East Grinstead and promised that he would be responsible for the three hundred pounds.

Lady Herbert and Lady Londonderry helped the new community in its infancy. In May 1868 the nuns returned to Ash Grove, Hackney, to resume their work. The community log book begins on Saturday 2 May 1868: "Returned to Priory from Kensington (with) seven sisters who left in February with novices Edith, Ann and Mary Ann Bond." Over the following days Herbert Vaughan's name appears at least twice a week; for benediction, confessions, and "advice." Lady Herbert's name appears as well when she brought the new Franciscan habits on 26 June and when she renewed her Third Order of St Francis promises in the chapel to Father Vaughan on 29 September. Another time she stayed the entire day along with Caroline Hanmer.[8]

Miss Caroline Hanmer is a name quietly associated with Herbert Vaughan, especially at his missionary college, where she would live and serve for more than forty years. In the college's Calvary cemetery, Herbert Vaughan's grave and monument occupies a central place, but other graves are visible to the left and rear, one behind the other and each marked by a simple stone cross: barely legible, they read: on one, Lady Herbert of Lea, "Mother of the Mill," and on the other, Caroline Hanmer.

Caroline Hanmer

Caroline Mary Hanmer was born on 10 May 1818, one of three daughters of Thomas Hanmer of Bettisfield Park, Flintshire, in Wales, and was raised in an evangelical tradition of the Church of England. Her brother was the first and only Lord John Hanmer.[9] She had been a good friend of Henry Manning when he was an Anglican, and, like him, became a Roman Catholic in 1851. When Vaughan expanded his missionary college, Caroline Hanmer, who had already helped the seminary, "to the utmost of her power," came to live at a cottage on the grounds called "Rosary," where she spent the rest of her life. The cottage was built near to the entrance on Lawrence Street and Elizabeth Herbert stayed at the Rosary Cottage whenever she visited Mill Hill. Caroline Hanmer founded a group which supplied church goods to the missions and she cared for the health of the students. According to someone who knew her, she made the success of Vaughan's work "the main object of her life."[10]

Meeting at St James Hall

The great meeting proposed by Manning when he blessed the new chapel at Holcombe House took place at St James Hall, Piccadilly, on 24 April 1868. "As far as rank and numbers went, Catholics in England had never seen anything like it before: ten bishops on the platform, dozens of distinguished laymen, the body of the hall packed."[11]

Manning spoke first, reminding the audience that as members of the British Empire and English speakers, they had the means to spread the faith which others did not have. Vaughan spoke next and he called attention to the generosity of Americans at the beginning of the college, but reminded those who were present that the English now must pay for its success and give their financial support. The most urgent appeal was for a permanent missionary college that would cost six thousand pounds to build. The meeting unanimously passed resolutions expressing sympathy with the work of the missions and recognizing the particular obligations of English Catholics.

The name chosen for the new building was St Joseph's College of the Sacred Heart for Foreign Missions. As a result of the St James Hall meeting, a pamphlet was published. It was prepared by Herbert Vaughan and titled "Our Duty to the Heathen." The pamphlet was distributed in the British Isles and translated into other languages. Lady Elizabeth Herbert prepared one edition in French and it was reprinted several times.[12]

An important outcome of the meeting is mentioned in Vaughan's preface. It was the forming of an organization to allow "thousands of devout persons throughout the country ... to cooperate actively" in missionary work. The support organization was called "St. Joseph's Society of the Sacred Heart for Foreign Missions." The secretary was Mr E. G. Shapscote of York Place in London.[13]

There was such a good response to the appeal that Vaughan prepared to lay the foundation stone of St Joseph's College in June 1869.

The Tablet

The Catholic press in the nineteenth century was combative and partisan. The Catholic weekly newspaper *The Tablet* was no exception. Herbert Vaughan purchased *The Tablet* in the summer of 1868. Unlike so many other newspapers in the nineteenth century, it survived.[14]

On 17 May 1990, Cardinal Basil Hume celebrated a Mass in Westminster Cathedral to mark the 150th anniversary of *The Tablet*, now published in a smaller format. The Jesuit publication *America* reported the milestone with the following commentary: "Many of these readers, including myself, think *The Tablet* is the best Catholic magazine in the English-speaking world as well as one of the best of magazines by any standard."[15]

The first issue of *The Tablet* was published on 16 May 1840. Its editor and founder was Frederick Lucas, a convert from Quakerism who looked for readers among the educated laity. For his motto he chose the words of Edmund Burke: "My errors, if any, are my own. I have no man's proxy."[16]

Lucas was controversial and courageous. In 1842 his opponents, according to Snead-Cox, managed to bring out *The Tablet* under the editorship of Michael Quin, the first editor of the *Dublin Review*. Lucas, "robbed of the paper he had made," found it was "only a fresh incentive to fight." He brought out a rival, the "True Tablet." Between the two factions, wrote Snead-Cox, it was a "war to the death." Within a year Lucas won back his paper.

In 1849 Lucas visited Ireland and what he saw of the famine "made him a changed man." More and more absorbed in Irish politics, he decided to take *The Tablet* to Ireland. "In characteristic fashion he warned his rivals that in leaving England he meant still to hold the field." To those who interpreted his departure as an "opening for some cowardly, truckling, time-serving Government hack, whose congenial business it will be to incite falsehoods and betray the Church, are respectfully informed that no such individual will have the slightest chance of success." If he was a success publishing from Dublin, he promised to "keep the field as clear of these peddlars and their packs as ever I have been able to do in London."[17]

In Ireland, Lucas became a member of Parliament for a local constituency, but when he raised a protest over Archbishop Cullen's order that no priest should attend public meetings or take part in politics, he was defeated for re-election. In championing a cause against the archbishop of Dublin, whom Lucas thought to be deliberately "stifling ... the only articulate voice ever likely to be raised in defence of the unhappy and the oppressed," he hastened his return to England, where he died in 1855.

The Tablet was brought back to London and John Wallis, who had recently been called to the Bar, became editor. "He was a man of brilliant abilities, and to many of his friends it seemed that he was sacrificing a fine future at the Bar for a forlorn hope as a Catholic editor."

Wallis' thirteen years as editor were unsuccessful, according to Snead-Cox, because "He failed to do more than lay down the foundation of the success the paper afterwards obtained." Wallis was a Tory at a time "when nearly all the Catholic families, still cherishing the tradition of the emancipation struggle, were Liberals."

The Tablet remained the forum for semi-official Church communications by means of the publication of papal documents, episcopal letters, directives and so on. It became indispensable to those concerned with Church affairs.[18] Wallis had been on excellent terms with Cardinal Wiseman, but he became a "thorn in the flesh" to Archbishop Henry Manning.

Another conservative Catholic publication was the monthly, the *Dublin Review*, started in 1836. It was not the first Catholic monthly, for one had appeared in 1831. The *Dublin Review* was founded by Nicholas Wiseman with the help of two Irish laymen, Daniel O'Connell, the "Liberator," and Michael Quin. It began as an attempt to counter the influence of the strongly anti-Catholic *Edinburgh Review*. In the 1860s it was edited by Herbert Vaughan's friend, William George Ward, who used its pages to support the views of Wiseman and Manning on issues such as the Roman Question and academic freedom. Roger Aubert, in Jedin's *History of the Church*, considers Ward's *Dublin Review* to be the English emulator of Louis Veuillot's newspaper *L'Univers*, like *L'Avenir* twenty years earlier. Veuillot had campaigned in France to win over the lower clergy to a theocratic idea of society in which "politics would be in the service of religion" and for a Church which would be in "closer contact with the Papacy." The Church would be then better able to withstand the forces of revolution. "Ultimately Veuillot succeeded in creating among French Catholics a 'cult of the papacy' as could be found in no other country."[19] Manning thought that one way to fight a revival of paganism in England was with a Church that spoke through the infallible voice of the Pope.[20]

Opposed to the views of Manning, Wiseman, the *Dublin Review*, and *The Tablet* under Vaughan's ownership, were spokesmen for liberal Catholicism, Richard Simpson and Lord John Acton. Simpson was a former Church of England clergyman, a convert, and editor of a weekly called the *Rambler* and another periodical the two men published called *Home and Foreign Review*. John Henry Newman was an unofficial advisor, and once, briefly, the editor of the *Rambler*.[21]

The Tablet's closest rival was the *Weekly Register*, owned and edited by another convert, Henry Wilberforce, a grandson of the Great Emancipator, William Wilberforce. His uncle, Henry, was a brother-in-law of Manning, who had resigned his Church of England appointment at East Fairleigh in Kent to become a Catholic in 1850. Uncle Henry had founded the paper.

Catholic publications were in financial difficulties by the 1860s.[22] To save *The Tablet*, Wallis became a partner with a Mr Keating in 1862. The arrangement lasted for almost six years, ending early in 1868 when Keating complained that with circulation declining, it was bad for business to make "a spread of opponents" such as the English Catholic Liberals, Irish members of Parliament and the Archbishop of Westminster.[23]

Herbert Vaughan buys *The Tablet*.

In the summer of 1868 Herbert Vaughan had an opportunity to acquire a newspaper when Wallis decided to sell *The Tablet*. Vaughan bought it for nine hundred pounds.[24] According to Snead-Cox, it was the "luckiest investment of his life."[25] However, Vaughan's inexperience and temperament, especially his bluntness, did not endear him to readers. Snead-Cox remarked: "But what an equipment was unworldliness of this sort for a journalist!"[26] In addition to his inexperience, Vaughan did not have the literary gifts of a Ward or Manning. Wilfrid Ward thought that while Vaughan's ideals were identical with his father's, "his practical programme was quite on other lines." W. G. Ward had no business aptitude, "while to Vaughan it was the most congenial subject next to religion. Few people I ever met had a stronger sense of the value of money than Cardinal Vaughan—though he devoted it to the highest objects. On the other hand, the training of the intellect which was so much in my father's eyes hardly counted for Vaughan as anything at all, apart from its market value—which for a Catholic was nil."[27]

This did not mean Vaughan was an ineffective communicator with *The Tablet*. Father Sydney Smith, in his 1910 appreciation of Vaughan, stressed that "if the excellence of a good style are unpretentiousness, simplicity, directness, lucidity, and force, his had these qualities." He was not as good as many of his contemporaries "in intellectual power and erudition, yet, though his active life left him little time for reading, he quickly seized with an intelligent grasp the points of a subject, intellectual and practical, when it was brought to his notice." Smith was a Jesuit and editor of *The Month*.[28]

There is little evidence that Vaughan bought *The Tablet* to keep it out of Liberal Catholic hands[29] or as an exclusive vehicle for his ultramontane views of ecclesial authority, which were "as uncomplicated as his spirituality." However, *The Tablet* did become a proponent for an "exclusivist attitude to that issue which almost at once became the central loyalty test for Ultramontanes—Papal Infallibility."[30] According to Snead-Cox and Walsh, Vaughan's real reason for buying the paper was his appreciation of the importance of the Catholic press.

During his trip to America in 1865 he had been impressed by the influence of newspapers.[31] The best known Catholic publications at the time in the United States were Brownson's *Quarterly Review* and McMaster's *Freeman's Journal*. Isaac Hecker, founder of the Paulists, was convinced of the apostolate of the press and founded the *Catholic World*, which published its first issue in April 1865. Hecker had worked in London when he was still a Redemptorist and stopped to visit Manning in the summer of 1867 on his way to a congress at Malines in Belgium.[32] Vaughan's friendship with Ward and the *Dublin Review* influenced him as well. His father, Colonel Vaughan, had seen the efforts of the Catholic press in France when he stayed at the home of Père Bailly while studying in Paris. Was the idea of a Catholic press planted at Courtfield? *The Tablet* thought so in 1932 when it remembered the centenary of Vaughan's birth:

> The whole life of Vaughan contradicts the notion that he bought *The Tablet* as a sufferer from *cacoethes scribendi* or as a pushful churchman bent on self-aggrandizement. From boyhood till old age and death this man lived *ad majorem Dei gloriam*, and his journalistic work was done in the same spirit as his apostolic work for the heathen, for the poor-law children, and for religious education.[33]

Vaughan's Views on the Catholic Press

In one of Wallis' last issues, Herbert Vaughan proclaimed a new liberalism. He reversed some of Wallis' Tory policies, but the vituperative style remained the same. In his first issue of November 1868 he explicitly refused to tolerate any criticism of episcopal decisions in matters of doctrine, discipline or ecclesiastical government, and, during the time of the First Vatican Council, he refused to publish any letters that did not reflect his Ultramontane position. His opening manifesto declared the paper would maintain without reserve "the great truths which have been so clearly declared to us by Pius IX." Among the "truths," he included the Syllabus of Errors of 1864.[34]

During his first week at *The Tablet* offices in 21 Newcastle Street, Vaughan wrote to Lady Elizabeth Herbert. It was 4 a.m. on a Friday morning and he was to sign some legal papers at Somerset House the next day before returning to Mill Hill. The following week he hoped to hire a sub-editor to help him.[35]

Montalembert wrote of Vaughan and Ward and their publications: "How unfathomable are the designs of God in allowing such oracles as Dr Ward, Mr. Vaughan, and others to be the representatives of Catholic intelligence in the eyes of that immense Anglo-Saxon race which is so evidently intended to cover the whole modern world."[36]

After his first issue of *The Tablet*, there were rumours that Vaughan was being subsidized by Manning and that *The Tablet* was practically under the archbishop's control. Boldly—and badly, according to Snead-Cox—he wrote: "In pure politics, literature, fine arts and every other subject proper to a newspaper I accept no dependence on any person."[37]

Infallibility and the First Vatican Council

Throughout Vaughan's life, there were those who felt he treated them unjustly. More than once, Vaughan's enthusiasm led him into rash criticism of others, especially in the pages of *The Tablet*.

To Wilfrid Ward, his editorship of *The Tablet* during this period, especially during the First Vatican Council, gives us a "psychological picture" of Vaughan.[38] Vaughan's simple test of loyalty "was always and under all circumstances to stand on the side of Rome."[39] On the issue of papal infallibility "Herbert Vaughan deliberately set himself to strangle and suppress any and every utterance in favour of the Inopportunist party." The Inopportunists were those who thought it not the moment to make declarations about papal infallibility. In *The Tablet* there was not a single letter expressing that view, of which Vaughan's cousin, Bishop Clifford of Clifton, and John Henry Newman were the exponents.[40]

Vaughan held that it was his duty as a Catholic editor to oppose these "wrong-headed persons" in the most effective manner possible. On the issue of infallibility the critics of the definition were many and included Bishops

Hefele, Moriarty, and Dupanloup along with Newman, Acton and Friedrich von Hügel.[41] Wilfrid Ward thought that Vaughan was "amazed at their perversity" and seemed to have contemplated solely "the struggles of the simple mind between faith and doubt which did not represent the issues before the universal Church where a greater variety of human emotion and of thought was at work."[42]

Often Herbert Vaughan was criticized not for the views he held, but rather for using *The Tablet* to defend those views in an "odious and unchristian manner." His use of extreme language shocked the old clergy.[43] For example, in the "abstract reasoning of the *Tablet*" he demanded the "execution" of Montalembert. Personal knowledge of Montalembert, wrote Wilfrid Ward, "made such attacks in the case of so loyal and devout a Catholic absurdly too apparent."[44] On another occasion he "enthusiastically" criticized the distinguished bishop of Orleans, Felix Dupanloup. Vaughan's Rome correspondent reported that Napoleon III had offered the bishop the diocese of Lyons "as leader of the Gallican party," which supported the more or less complete independence of the Church in France from Rome. *The Tablet* was accused of libel and Vaughan apologized. However *The Tablet* again accused the bishop of being a Gallican.[45]

On 14 March 1870, *The Spectator* published a confidential letter sent by John Henry Newman to William Ullathorne. In the letter Newman described the promoters of infallibility as an "insolent and aggressive faction." Bishop Brown of Newport, who knew the Vaughan family well, wrote to Newman thanking him for the letter's publication and went on to say that "in regard to the Tablet I have not hesitated to express loudly my disapproval, also my apprehension of the serious evil likely to ensue from the course pursued by Herbert Vaughan and his party in England."

Bishop Alexander Goss of Liverpool wrote that Ward's *Dublin Review* and *The Tablet* under Vaughan and Archbishop Manning, "have taken upon themselves not merely to advocate the infallibility but to denounce everybody else as little less than heretics and infidels and as committing the unpardonable sin against the Holy Ghost whose decision and ruling they forestalled." Cuthbert Butler adds in his life of Ullathorne that the reaction seen in the letters of Goss and Brown shows how "many good people ... were suffering under the intemperate language of (the) foremost advocates of the infallibility."[46] Vaughan answered "with gusto" the complaint that he refused to air other views in *The Tablet*, especially over the different ways of approaching the issue of papal infallibility.[47]

In addition to Vaughan's confrontational style, the ultramontane views defended in *The Tablet* appeared to some to set the authority of the Church above truth. For Owen Chadwick, ultramontanes thought that if the doctrine of the Church and the results of human enquiry disagreed, then human enquiry must give way.[48] In 1864 Pope Pius IX published the Syllabus of

Errors—a catalogue of eighty unacceptable propositions appended to the encyclical *Quanta Cura*—and Catholics argued over infallibility and Galileo. Taken out of context, the propositions were often bewildering; Abbot Butler thought that it "was a most inopportune document." "In the atmosphere of doubt and incipient agnosticism created by the studies of historians and scientists, the Church of Rome stood unyielding, and though this unbudgeable picture of authority attracted hesitant souls, it repelled more." The definition of infallibility which came out of the Vatican Council was thought to be "inopportune" by Newman and untrue by Acton. It also "discouraged all the more liberal minds"[49]

According to David Newsome, although the Church was challenged intellectually and politically in the nineteenth century, it was growing "steadily more powerful, both within and outside Europe, and the prestige of the Papacy had reached a height unparalleled in modern times" under the long rule of an astute pope. And it was the power of "Ultramontanism" within the Church, in a political and intellectual conflict with liberal Catholics, that led Pius IX to call the First Vatican Council.[50]

Roger Aubert adds that Catholic opposition to liberalism was not always confined to negative criticism. While opponents of liberal Catholics might have had a closed mind when maintaining the "right of a Christian society," some did have a "two-fold positive ideal" which was a result of their reaction to what they saw as a timid view that religion was a private matter and without impact on social life. They demanded a "right to the actual state compared to the legal state dominated by a small oligarchy." Manning and Vaughan, for example, undertook more social initiatives than the "liberal" Catholics. They directed their efforts to helping the poor and working class immediately rather than working towards a solution of its [society's] real problems through structural reforms."[51]

Von Arx, in an article titled "Manning's Ultramontanism," gives a positive assessment of the views of Manning, Vaughan and others. In its political aspect he discovered what was "most original and stimulating" about Manning's views. Manning, according to von Arx, had a "vision of the significance of infallibility for the mission of the Church to the new political world in which it found itself." A definition of papal infallibility "would be a powerful attraction for those outside the Church." Therefore it was necessary for the "Church to speak definitively and unequivocally through the infallible voice of the Roman Pontiff."[52]

The opportunity to pursue this vision presented itself with the call by Pope Pius IX for bishops, and those "with a right to participate," to begin a Council at Rome on 8 December 1869. About seven hundred bishops participated. The Council was called "from the pastoral perspective of the reaction to naturalism and rationalism which he had pursued ... since the beginning of his pontificate." Before the Council took place, several bishops, including

Manning, "demanded immediately" that the meeting be utilized to define the truth of infallibility.[53]

The First Vatican Council met in an atmosphere "charged with controversy and emotion." It met at the time of the Italian revolution and ended when Rome was occupied: "Thoughts about the Pope and his doctrine of infallibility were entangled with his treatment by the revolutionaries.[54]

During this period Vaughan made many enemies, and his views cost him many *Tablet* subscribers. Snead-Cox refers to his "peculiar policy," with its dogmatism, its intolerance of all opposition, its impatience with those who feared the consequences of a definition of infallibility, and above all its willingness to discredit opposition with suggestions of disloyalty or accusations of "Gallicanism," which alienated many sympathetic and more moderate people. "They were indignant at what they saw as Vaughan's amazing conceit."[55]

While the Council was meeting, Herbert Vaughan published a supplement to *The Tablet* called "Vatican." Michael Walsh writes that it was so unremittingly ultramontane that it was criticized even in Rome. Even Vaughan's friends protested at the tone of *The Tablet*, and "one less friendly" person denounced *The Tablet* as "bold, abusive and disingenuous."[56] Vaughan's courage and his loyalty to friends hardly compensated for his abrasive style in *The Tablet* over the years 1868-71. Those outside the Catholic Church accused him of "fanatical bigotry" and those within of "narrow-mindedness and intellectual tyranny." Yet he seemed to be remarkably resilient in the middle of the opposition raging around him.[57]

The 19 March 1870 *Spectator* magazine commented on *The Tablet*: "*The Tablet*, like the great Ultra-Montane quarterly, the *Dublin Review*, is, no doubt, exceedingly harsh and as we should think, uncharitable in its condemnations of heresy, or what it thinks so, but both Editors seem to us to set a rare example of candour to Protestants in the perfect freedom with which they habitually confess their own blunders—the rarest and most unwelcome of editorial tasks, and the one which always excites in our minds the most respect."[58]

At times the problems were not of Vaughan's making. In April 1870 he wrote to Elizabeth Herbert complaining about "an awful mess" he found himself in through the negligence of his acting editor at *The Tablet*: "I have been made to pronounce a terrible and false condemnation of the Apologia! What a row this will make.... I wrote at once to Newman to apologise and explain, and shall have to do so in the papers next week! What a mess on me!"[59]

The Tablet did not consume all of Vaughan's energy in its publication and controversy. He brought in an assistant—Eliot Rankin, a convert and lawyer and an old friend—who later took charge of the paper. In 1871 Rankin had returned to England from Rome, where he had been a privy chamberlain to Pope Pius IX. Rankin, according to Walsh, was "perhaps the most unassuming—and, as a Franciscan tertiary—possibly the most devout" editor of the weekly.[60]

Once released from the stress of weekly deadlines, the abrasiveness that characterized Vaughan's writing does not appear in his other activities. Cuthbert Butler, in his life of Bishop Ullathorne, wrote about Vaughan's clashes but found it difficult "to recognize the serene Cardinal whom we knew and revered so greatly in the truculent editor of the Tablet.... It may be thought that, seeing his character and natural temperament and his enthusiasms, Manning and Ward were not the best friends for him in his young days." In Butler's opinion, it was not until Vaughan had gone to Salford as bishop in 1872 that he had a chance to mature into "the noble character he was in the last and greatest phase of his life."[61]

Years later, it was a calmer Vaughan who wrote to William Samuel Lilly— a Cambridge convert, author and writer for reviews—to apologize for criticisms of a speech Lilly gave in Birmingham in 1892. Vaughan wrote from Salford that he regretted a paragraph printed in *The Tablet*. "I will take good care that this matter shall drop. I write this hurried line to express to you my good will and my earnest hope that we may work together for many a year to come." Lilly added: "The hope so graciously expressed in this letter was abundantly realised."[62]

It can also be argued that Herbert Vaughan's principles concerning ecclesiastical journalism did not mellow as much as his temperament in later years. In 1900, George Tyrrell read a Vaughan pastoral on the principles of Catholic journalism and wrote to Wilfrid Ward that he thought they "led to a clericalism of the strictest and narrowest type":

> Vaughan wrote that Catholic journalism needed "to follow the lead of the Church in matters that concern the Church; to strengthen her action upon the world; to defend the faith and Catholic interests with skill and courage; *sentire cum ecclesia* in all things; to inform and convince... readers that they may intelligently and joyfully cooperate with the Episcopate, and thus present to outsiders the spectacle of a Church knit together not only in one faith, but in the discipline of the common spirit."[63]

The Catholic Truth Society

Remarkably, Vaughan had time for other ventures while he published *The Tablet*, cared for his fledgling missionary college at Mill Hill, and travelled to the Continent and the United States. For example, in 1868 he founded the Catholic Truth Society.

Shortly after he became vice-rector of St Edmund's in 1855, he "started an enterprise aimed at distributing inexpensive literature among Catholics and Protestants." After he left Ware, the work was abandoned until he became owner of *The Tablet* and began a more ambitious project.

The idea to produce inexpensive pamphlets about the Catholic faith was not new; the first pamphlets originated at least as far back as 1829, the year of Catholic emancipation. In 1832 there was a Catholic society for the distribution of prayer books and other material, and in 1834 the "Catholic Tract Society," followed by the "Catholic Institute" in 1838. In 1868 Herbert Vaughan revived the idea and through *The Tablet* "presented his prospectus for a Catholic Truth Society, modelled on what he had discovered in America." The aims were twofold: "to instruct Catholics in their faith and to dissipate 'popular prejudice and error' among non-Catholics." He was helped by Lady Elizabeth Herbert and by Fr George Bampfield, a convert.

The Catholic Truth Society offices were at 27 Wellington Street, Strand, in London. In 1869 a branch was started in Manchester, but the Society faltered in 1870 and became moribund. It was revived only in 1884, re-established thanks to the efforts of James Britten. Vaughan later admitted that he had set up the original foundation "before its time." Britten's new society of 1884 had, within the next four years, branches in America, Canada, Australia and New Zealand, India, Africa, the West Indies and British Guinea. A later development was the Catholic Evidence Guild.[64] In 1993 the Catholic Truth Society announced its 125th anniversary in an advertisement that quoted Herbert Vaughan, writing in 1868: "We are in the age of the Press. It can penetrate where no Catholic can enter.... It is an instrument in our hands."[65]

St Joseph's College, Mill Hill

Vaughan's missionary college was housed at Holcombe House for about three years, but it was soon too small for the growing community. In less than eighteen months after the public meeting at St James Hall, Vaughan, with the help of Elizabeth Herbert and other benefactors, was able to collect enough money to begin construction of a new college on property adjacent to Holcombe House called Hill Field, beyond the house garden.[66] The new building was planned to accommodate seventy-two students. And so, on 29 June 1869, the Feast of SS Peter and Paul, Archbishop Manning blessed the foundation stone of St Joseph's College.

From Holcombe House, a procession, led by a cross-bearer, made its way across the fields to the new site; included in the procession were twelve students, each carrying a statue of one of the twelve apostles. Members of the Catholic nobility and gentry carried pictures of Our Lady and St Joseph, and finally clergy and bishops brought up the rear, with Archbishop Manning carrying a relic. After the blessing, the procession returned to the Iron Chapel where Manning gave Benediction.[67] Vaughan employed the architect George Goldie to design a building in "Lombardo Venetian style" and a team of twenty-seven Dutch bricklayers, carpenters and painters, under the building contractor, sixty-two-year-old James Bueyssen.[68]

By 1868 Herbert Vaughan had four nationalities represented at the missionary college. In January 1869 Vaughan visited Dublin and saw Cardinal Cullen while he was on *Tablet* business arranging for a Dublin correspondent. At such times he was always a sharp-eyed recruiter of candidates for his college as well.[69]

In the summer of 1869 Vaughan toured the Continent, appealing for missionary candidates at seminaries in Belgium, France, Alsace, Switzerland, Tyrol and the Netherlands; he also looked for professors to teach at Mill Hill. He had already negotiated for the "swarm of Dutch builders" to come over that August and carry on with the building. He went to Paris, Lucerne and finally Strasbourg. At Mulhouse the bishop and rector of the major seminary recommended a man "with a heart of gold" who had been anxious for many years to become a foreign missionary. "He is an artist, and an architect ... and a gentleman," he wrote to Elizabeth Herbert. This un-named priest was probably meant to replace Fr Reyen, who had fallen ill.[70]

On 27 December 1869, the first priest was ordained from Vaughan's missionary college. Cornelius Dowling was born at Fermoy in Cork on 27 January 1841, the son of Jeremiah Dowling and Mary Sullivan. He attended St Colman's College, Fermoy, and had applied to join the Redemptorists twice but each time failed a Latin exam. Early in 1866 the convert and redemptorist Fr Bridgett suggested that Dowling apply to Vaughan's new college. He became the second recruit. Dowling persevered and was ordained by Bishop William Morris at St Thomas Seminary in Hammersmith.[71]

Only partially finished, St Joseph's College was opened free from debt on 1 March 1871, with a community of thirty-four students. Among the students were some refugees from the College for African Missions at Lyons. Vaughan had moved into the house the day before and after supper each room was blessed during a procession that included a Fr Planque, superior of the Congregation of African Missions, who carried a small statue of St Joseph. Vaughan slept that night for the first time at the new college and in the morning offered Mass in a temporary chapel set up in the common room at an altar dedicated to St Francis Xavier, a gift from Elizabeth Herbert.[72] In the meantime, the vacated Holcombe House was occupied by the twenty-seven Dutch workers.[73]

Among the gifts Elizabeth Herbert gave to St Joseph's College in 1869 were two paintings, one of St Joseph and the other of the Sacred Heart. Both were central to Vaughan's devotional life. At the Vatican Council, where he assisted Manning, he worked to promote a declaration that made St Joseph patron of the whole Church. Vaughan led a campaign that gathered 150,000 petitions, which were sent to the Pope to "do something for old Joseph." On behalf of the Sacred Heart, he encouraged the devotion wherever he went—at a time when the cult was achieving enormous popularity throughout the Catholic world.[74]

So generous was the response to appeals on behalf of St Joseph's Mission-ary College that the cornerstone for a memorial chapel in honour of St Joseph was laid on 19 March 1871.[75] It was a chapel built by English Catholics in gratitude to St Joseph for prayers answered. On top of a tower he planned to place a statue of "the first foreign missionary," St Joseph, with the "Divine Infant in his arms exhibiting His Sacred Heart to the World."[76]

In the summer of 1871 Vaughan was again on the Continent searching for recruits. He visited three bishops and was allowed to appeal for students interested in the foreign missions at their diocesan seminaries. On 6 August, for example, he spoke to the theology students at Utrecht for an hour and a half. He simply announced the existence of the missionary college at Mill Hill "to obtain the confidence and good will of the Bishops and superiors ... for the Dutch are slow to decide and the invitation given now may be accepted in a year hence."[77]

Request for a Mission Assignment

Vaughan pursued his dreams for his missionary seminary, but he did so with many uncertainties. Among them were questions about the legal status of St Joseph's College in the Church, and the placement of his ordained missionar-ies. He needed a missionary assignment and he began to petition Propaganda Fide for one during 1870. Cornelius Dowling was already ordained, but as yet had no overseas mission to go to. Others were to follow him—and where would they work?

At the end of April 1870, Vaughan prepared to travel to Rome, paying for his journey with money given to him by his father. On 1 May he reached Paris and visited the Church of Notre Dame des Victoires, praying that the work at Mill Hill be "the means of saving thousands and millions of others."[78] In May he was in Rome, and on 3 May he met the superior general of the Society of Milan for the Foreign Missions. He wrote that they had the same rule, aim and history—"for they like us sprang out of the Oblates of St. Charles."[79]

During the month of May, Vaughan went nearly every day to the offices of Propaganda to see the prefect, Cardinal Barnabo. The "huge placid" Barnabo asked that he consider undertaking Labuan and Borneo for a mission area. Vaughan thought Borneo would be a good mission but he still wanted a "promise of Japan." On 25 May he wrote that he finally had faculties to ordain students "ad titulum missionis infidelium," but still waited for approval of the "Fundamental Rules and Oath," that would bind the products of the college together, and to have a mission assignment. He wrote to Elizabeth Herbert on 25 May that "Propaganda is a kind of furnace in which our works are placed to be tested and tried to the very top of one's patience. I have now at last got faculties to present our students for ordination."[80]

On the last Saturday in May he met Pope Pius IX but nothing was settled, for the "French refuse to give up an inch of Japan." He returned to England empty-handed. Unknown to Vaughan, events three thousand miles away in the United States were to determine the assignment of Vaughan's first missionaries.

First Mission: Baltimore, United States of America

Before becoming archbishop of Baltimore in 1864, Martin John Spalding was the bishop of Louisville, Kentucky. At Louisville he wrote to Rome calling for the Church to take special care of those being released from slavery. He was very anxious to help those who were baptised Catholics. After he became Archbishop of Baltimore he wrote again and suggested a meeting of all the bishops of the United States. "It is," he wrote to another bishop, "a golden opportunity for reaping a harvest of souls, which neglected may not return."[81] Spalding introduced the topic of what the Church might do for the African-American population at the Second Plenary Council of Baltimore in 1866: "Four million of these unfortunates are thrown on our charity."[82] But the bishops at the meeting "substituted rhetoric for concrete action."[83]

Spalding was disappointed but not discouraged. While he was in Rome during July 1867 he petitioned in the name of the American bishops that the Pope order a European congregation to help. He used the Jesuit Michael O'Connor as his unofficial agent. O'Connor was a former bishop of Pittsburgh who had resigned his office to become a Jesuit. He had worked for the African-American community in Baltimore. At a provincial meeting of bishops at Baltimore in 1869, Spalding achieved some of his goals. The meeting declared in favour of churches, missions and fund-raising on behalf of the African-American population. An appeal was also made for religious to give themselves to the specific work of African-American evangelization. In Europe Michael O'Connor met Herbert Vaughan and asked him, on behalf of Spalding, for missionaries.

Vaughan had written to an Oblate colleague in Rome, Father O'Callaghan, asking him to look into the possibility of a mission in Mexico or South America. About the same time, Vaughan was contacted by O'Connor—who was visiting Ireland on his way back to the United States from the Vatican Council. He and Vaughan spoke about the needs of the newly liberated African-Americans. O'Connor then wrote to Archbishop Spalding, who in turn wrote directly to Vaughan. Vaughan contacted O'Callaghan again asking him to go in person to the Pope and remind him that a mission had not been assigned to his missionaries. Vaughan added a note, repeating Spalding's appeal for help.[84]

At Mill Hill, Vaughan was completing construction of the permanent college. The new missionary college became a symbol, and eventually the *alma mater*, of a slowly developing organization that was to become St Joseph's

Foreign Missionary Society.[85] There were ordinations in 1870, which brought the number to four priests waiting for their first mission assignment.

Vaughan read a biography of the founder of another missionary congregation, Father Francis Libermann. Libermann wrote that no one will ever think of saving the souls of Africans unless "priests filled with the Spirit of the Lord" come to be with them. Vaughan felt a profound peace on reading Libermann's words.[86] Soon afterwards, in the autumn of 1871, the Pope assigned Vaughan's small band of new missionaries to the United States. Vaughan wrote to Spalding to inform him and received a reply that urged his men to come at once from Mill Hill: "In three counties of Maryland, there are sixteen thousand negroes... you have here a field of action already prepared." Spalding appointed Vaughan's missionaries to St Francis Xavier Church in Baltimore. The missionaries went later, for a brief time, to the Upper Marlboro Missions in the three counties.[87] On 29 October the Pope granted "Herbert Vaughan, Superior of St Joseph's Society of the Sacred Heart, Mill Hill, Diocese of Westminster (England) and four Priests ... of the society who are leaving for the United States to evangelize Negroes" the title of "apostolic missionaries." The four pioneers were Cornelius Dowling, James Noonan, Joseph Gore and Charles Vigneront.[88]

The departure ceremony for the pioneer missionaries was arranged for 17 November 1871. Vaughan proposed that they make a special public promise that recalled St Peter Claver, who had worked for the African slaves brought to South America: "To render my work more amply fruitful, I promise and vow that I will show myself a father and servant to the African-American people. I will undertake no other work whatsoever, which could lead me in any way to neglect or give up this special service."[89]

On the day of departure, Archbishop Manning was present and delivered a farewell homily. Seminarians and staff from St Thomas' Diocesan Seminary at Hammersmith were also present. A procession began at the Calvary cemetery and moved to the temporary chapel. Manning gave his farewell message: "I trust that the work ... will not only be to labour among the negroes of the South but to found in America a missionary college like this, in which the African population may there be trained to carry the faith into their own land."[90]

While those present sang hymns, each of the priests, and even the workmen of the Dutch contractor who was building the new chapel, "kissed the feet and faces of the four priests." At 6.30 p.m., after supper, they all left in a procession for the Mill Hill railway station "singing hymns while the college bell was tolling". The small group travelled into London where they stayed the night with the Oblate community at Bayswater. The next day Vaughan and his four missionaries went aboard the ship SS *Berlin* at Southampton, and were joined by the Jesuit Michael O'Connor.[91]

The arrival in the United States of Herbert Vaughan and his companions was an answer to Archbishop Spalding's prayers. He welcomed the party on 5 December 1871: "Here came four missionary priests for the negroes, together with their Superior the Very Rev. Herbert Vaughan, from the Missionary College of St. Joseph at Mill Hill near London." According to the Josephite historian and archivist, Peter Hogan, their arrival marked "a pivotal point in the history of the Catholic Church and the Afro-American."[92] Martin Spalding died two months later. The day before he died, he was heard to say that the arrival of Vaughan and the missionaries for the African- Americans "was one of things which he had asked God to let him see established in his diocese before he died."[93] On the Sunday following their arrival, 10 December, they were officially received by Spalding in St Francis Xavier Church. They made their headquarters at 51 Courtland Street in Baltimore.

Vaughan wrote to James Alphonsus McMaster of New York on 15 December. McMaster, a convert, owned the *New York Freeman's Journal and Catholic Register*. At one time it was the most widely circulated Catholic newspaper in the United States. It had a circulation of more than ten thousand and as many as one in three priests in the United States were subscribers. Not a diocesan newspaper, it was Catholic in its principles and interests, but independent of Church authority.[94] McMaster had published Manning's sermon to the departing missionaries and Vaughan thanked him. He was also grateful for the kind words McMaster had for Vaughan's missionaries on a previous occasion.

Vaughan continued: "No one can appreciate more highly than I do the great mission of the Catholic press in these days of steam and universal education, and I am gratified to find how favourably the American journals on the whole have noticed the mission which I humbly represent." Vaughan was a little amused, and probably embarrassed, that some were referring to the undertaking as the "conversion by London of the negroes of America—as though London as such had a pretension to so holy a mission." Vaughan then explained briefly the background and aims of St Joseph's Society for the Foreign Missions, a title which had first been used for the founding and support organization for the missionary college. "If there be any local idea in the work, it is the broad one of enlisting the English-speaking races of the world into the purely Apostolic work of the Church. This can be done by some of us giving ourselves, and by others giving their substance, so that the vocations which are going to waste may be saved and utilised." Vaughan promised to send McMaster a copy of the pamphlet "Our Duty to the Heathen."[95]

In January 1872, Vaughan "consecrated the mission to the Sacred Heart of Jesus"[96] and the first missionaries began to be called the "Josephites," after their patron St Joseph. Vaughan was still not satisfied for he had not found the mission field he had hoped for in the Far East or Africa. Africa pursued him "like a shadow," for he still had a vision not only of working among the African-Americans of the United States "but to found in America a missionary college ... in which the African population may there be trained to carry the faith into their own land."[97] Vaughan added that he hoped to be acting "not so much upon America as upon Africa," for he recognized the need for African-American leadership for the evangelization of Africans, whether in Africa or the Americas. It was an experience well known to anyone familiar, as Vaughan was, with the missionary work of Protestant groups in Africa, and the "Back to Africa" movement in the United States.[98]

Travels in the United States

After settling his small band of missionaries at St Francis Xavier, Vaughan set out to see what he could of the post-Civil-War United States, especially in areas where his men might be called upon to work. During his travels he not only collected information but also promoted the work of his missionaries, appealed for funds, and whenever possible, recruited prospective missionary candidates. He put forward his aims in a letter to Archbishop Purcell of Cincinnati on 8 January 1872. He was anxious, he wrote, "to consult your wide experience and to take your advice upon matters connected with my mission to the coloured people." He asked for an opportunity, when he visited Cincinnati, to make the work known "by preaching a sermon or your delivering a lecture upon it."[99]

In his notebooks Vaughan recorded visits to Savannah, Vicksburg, St Louis, Natchez, Memphis, Charleston, New Orleans, and Mobile, among other places.[100] What he saw of the treatment by white Catholics of African-Americans shocked him. He wrote to Elizabeth Herbert that "the dislike of Americans" for "the negroes ... far exceeds in intensity anything I had expected."[101] But the pages of his diary are filled with encouragement for mission by those who esteemed and loved the African-Americans, and the promising evidence seen in the work of Protestants and Catholics, whites and African-Americans alike. His notes are a product of his enquiring mind applied to the spiritual and material condition of the African-American population in each of the places he visited.

The clergy gave Vaughan's mission a mixed reception, but overall he considered it to be positive. The bishop of Mobile, Alabama, encouraged him to choose New Orleans as a centre for his work in the South, and would welcome him in Alabama. He felt that Vaughan was coming at just the right moment in history: "Now is the time to begin our Mission. Till now they were in delirium of freedom—their Churches were pandemonium—they would not have listened to Catholic teaching. All quieter now—and the Catholic Church is coming at the right time in coming now."[102]

However, another bishop, the archbishop of St Louis, told him on 25 January that all his "plans would fail; could suggest nothing for the negroes, and refused permission to collect and declined to give him a letter of approval."[103] A priest at St Louis, the Jesuit Fr O'Callaghan, "who has for seven years worked for the negroes, disagrees with the Archbishop," and spoke rather of the "virtue and simplicity of the negro" and offered to give seven thousand dollars he had collected, along with some land, for a church, to Vaughan if the Jesuit provincial would allow it.[104]

Vaughan visited a plantation near Savannah belonging to a Mr McAlpin, a small church at Charleston under Father Folchi for the "2000 nominally Catholic negroes," and the Louisiana State Legislature; he offered Mass "on Mon Louis Island (*sic*) on the coast of Alabama for an exclusively coloured congregation. Father Blake, Pastor: they have morning and night prayers in common—there are about 90 Spanish Creoles;" and even visited Jefferson Davis, the former president of the Confederate States of America.

Wherever he could, he asked about the experience of Protestant-sponsored missions. For example, in Savannah on 19 February, he visited the "Beech Institute for coloured children supported by the Congregationalists of New York." Vaughan wrote that the plan of the Congregationalists was "to educate them in small numbers, give them a coloured clergy and then leave them to take their chance."[105]

He was disturbed by the inequalities he witnessed within the Church and before the Blessed Sacrament. In his diary he complained that the Church also offered little in the way of popular devotions for the African-Americans. "Why," he wondered, "cannot we have catechists or brothers like the Methodist preachers?"[106]

In Georgia he met Sisters of St Joseph "brought over by Mgr. Verot from Pusy in France." They had come on behalf of "coloured children" but their work was "so unpopular with the whites" that they could not live without undertaking some other occupation. "They now have an orphanage of some twenty boys up to the age of fourteen. This is well supported but is of questionable precedence." Vaughan's conversations with men and women working with African-Americans reinforced his conviction that his missionaries needed to restrict their ministry exclusively to African-Americans. He saw the need of separate parishes where they would be free from the humiliations heaped upon them in the white churches.[107]

On 20 February he wrote from a steamer going from Savannah to Charleston. The ship stopped at Beaufort on 23 February and Bishop Lynch told him that Beaufort was the place for his missionaries. It was "a paradise for blacks because for miles of swamp and rice fields none but blacks can live in Summer." At Charleston the bishop and a Fr Folchi, the "priest of the coloured people," were both anxious for Vaughan's help. Vaughan noted that Folchi was told by the bishop that he had missed his chance of success with the African-Americans by admitting whites to his small church. On 25 February he arrived at Richmond, Virginia, where the bishop was ready to give him a three-acre plot with an old hospital building for a "coloured institution." "Richmond is one of the nicest towns in the South—60,000 inhabitants and seven hills like Rome it is said."[108]

When Vaughan returned to Baltimore from his tour of the southern states, he then travelled to New York to appeal for help for the new college chapel at Mill Hill and for the mission to the African-American population.[109] In New York he stayed at St Paul's Church on Ninth Avenue and West 59th Street in Manhattan. His host was Father Isaac Hecker, the founder of the Paulists.

In 1858, Hecker, a convert, and four other Redemptorist priests sent by their congregation to work among the German immigrants in New York City were released from their order and founded a new group, the Society of St Paul. Archbishop John Hughes of New York entrusted them with an area west of Sixth Avenue between 59th and 110th Streets. On 60th Street they built a parish church-rectory and Father Hecker became the first parish priest and superior general of the Society of St Paul, known as the Paulists. Hecker believed that "the parish should be a perpetual mission," and incorporated the key elements of mission into the daily life of St Paul's. He also invited some of the best Catholic preachers of the day to speak in the church. A historian of the American Church, Jay Dolan, considers Hecker's parish to have been the model modern parish upon which every other has been patterned.[110]

When Hecker and his colleagues arrived at 59th Street, the parish embraced an area of New York City called "shanty-town," a rocky swampland dotted with ramshackle wooden shacks where "Irish settlers eked out a meagre existence from their small truck gardens." By the time Vaughan visited in 1872, a transformation was taking place which changed the area into an "urban scene of tenements, railroad yards, streetcar lines, the Elevated Railway, gas storage tanks and docks."[111]

Hecker's biographer Joseph McSorley referred to Vaughan as Hecker's "warm friend."[112] Vaughan does not say where they first met, but David O'Brien writes that Hecker was ordained by Nicholas Wiseman in London on 23 October 1849. His first assignment was the Redemptorist community at Clapham, London, where Vaughan's uncle, Edmund, was assigned for a time. Edmund was also a provincial for the Redemptorists. While Hecker was at Clapham he helped to conduct parish missions throughout the city and received a few people into the Catholic Church. In 1851 he returned to the United States.

In 1867 Hecker stopped to see Manning, Newman and other Church leaders on his way to the Congress of Malines, where he gave an address titled "La situation religieuse des Etats Unis." He was one of the vice-presidents of the Congress.[113] Hecker was also at the First Vatican Council as a "procurator" in the place of Bishop Rosecrans of Columbus and later as a theologian to Archbishop Spalding. But in Rome he associated with liberal Catholics and came away disappointed with the attitudes that lay behind passionate calls for authoritative condemnations. He did return to the United States with—and in this he shared Vaughan's views—a determination "to pursue his life goal of evangelization."[114]

Vaughan was impressed by the Paulist community during the weeks he stayed at St Paul's in 1872. Hecker himself was not well when Vaughan arrived. It was an illness which lasted until his death sixteen years later on 22 December 1888. He wrote to a friend in January 1872 that his body had been weak for several months. Physically he suffered from "habitual exhaustion, headaches, loss of appetite, digestive troubles and severe nervousness."[115] In 1875 Vaughan wrote to Rome that there was a great need in the United States for "priests and communities which would operate in the spirit of the Paulists."[116]

On 18 March 1872, he wrote to Elizabeth Herbert from St Paul's that he was "preaching and collecting" in the principal churches of New York. Although he had the opportunity to preach on behalf of the mission to African-Americans, he thought that "on the whole the people don't care about the salvation of black people and many object to their salvation." Despite the odds against the mission, "we are going to succeed, that is certain." Among the churches he spoke in were St Stephen's, St Paul's and St Peter's. The parish priest of St Stephen's was Fr Edward McGlynn, one of the earliest and most vocal advocates of the social gospel.[117] Vaughan saw in the great violence and tragedy of slavery an outcome that worked for good. In an article published in *The Tablet*, based on a homily he gave at the end of February in St Paul's, he described some of those torn away from Africa returning again "willingly and borne upon the wings of faith and charity."[118]

By 1 May he had collected twelve thousand dollars for the mission to African-Americans and promises of three burses to be paid within two years. It was all for the American mission, for he thought that it was useless to beg in the United States for St Joseph's Chapel at Mill Hill.[119]

John R. Slattery

While Vaughan stayed at St Paul's, he was asked to lecture more than once. At the end of April Father Burke organized a "big lecture" concerning his project to be held in the parish. It was on this occasion, or one similar to it, that a young American named John Slattery heard him speak on behalf of the African-American mission. Slattery later became one of Vaughan's missionaries, and, in 1893, the first leader of the independent American Josephites. Stephen Ochs writes: "During the last two decades of the nineteenth century, the cause of black priests in the Catholic church had no greater champion than the Reverend John R. Slattery."[120]

John Richard Slattery was born in New York on 16 July 1851, the only surviving child of James and Marguerite Slattery, who were immigrants from Ireland living in St Paul's parish. James Slattery began as a labourer and went on to make a fortune in construction and real-estate. John's mother looked after her son's religious education and helped him to develop a "strong sense of devotion," especially to the rosary. He was an altar server at St Paul's and it was Father Hecker "who heard his first confession."[121]

Slattery attended New York public schools and entered the Free Academy of New York, a red brick building on 23rd Street and America's first urban college. It was renamed City College in 1866. He attended the secondary school section. Slattery was one of two Catholics in his class and was often involved in fights over his Irish origins and Catholicism. In 1865, during his third year of high school, he went to St Charles Preparatory Seminary, a school staffed by Sulpician priests at Ellicot City, Maryland. He soon withdrew because of an eye problem, and when he finally recovered, he entered Columbia Law School in New York. It was while studying at Columbia that he heard Vaughan speak at St Paul's.

The reaction was not immediate. Nine months later, in the autumn of 1872, as he was returning from classes at Columbia College School of Law, his path was blocked at the corner of Astor Place and Broadway by a parade of African-Americans, members of the Odd Fellows Society.[122] Slattery recalled the moment years later: "The spectacle of these poor people and the thought that the Society to which they belonged was condemned by the Church moved me profoundly. The idea came to me to consecrate my whole life to the evangelization of this unfortunate race."[123]

Agitated by what he had experienced, after supper that evening he went to his confessor, Father William J. Dwyer, at the Paulist Church for advice. Dwyer knew Vaughan and arranged for Slattery to be admitted to St Joseph's College in Mill Hill to see if he had a vocation. Dwyer also helped Slattery to mislead his parents into thinking that he was training to become a missionary priest for Africa or Asia and not for African-Americans in the United States. His mother was pleased with his decision but his father was disappointed, for he had hoped his only son would become a lawyer and inherit the family fortune. Only two years later did the Slatterys discover the truth of his future ministry and ordered him to return home from England. He refused, and was ordained on 17 March 1877 at Mill Hill.[124]

Slattery was not the only recruit of Vaughan's 1872 visit to the United States and Canada. Years later Slattery wrote that there were seven Americans and seven Dutchmen who were new students at the missionary college in London. Among them were John H. Greene, whom Vaughan had met on a train journey.[125]

Travels to Boston and Canada

In April, Vaughan travelled first to Boston and then on to Canada with Fr Vigneront. At Boston he collected $1100 in one church. On 15 May he addressed the students of the major seminary of Quebec: "The Archbishop has given me leave to take two of his subjects—if any two are willing to volunteer. I have sown the seed. May the Holy Spirit give the increase." The following Sunday he was to preach to a "congregation of 4000 Irishmen in Montreal." One who did respond to Vaughan's Canadian appeal was Theophyle Mayer.

Mayer was born on 15 August 1850 of an old Canadian family and orphaned at ten years of age. He went first to a seminary at Oneida, New York, and later to St Hyacinthe College in Canada. He transferred to St Joseph's at Mill Hill and was ordained on 3 December 1876. He went to India where he became the auxiliary bishop of Madras. He died at Singapore on 9 September 1900.[126]

St Francis Xavier Mission

While Vaughan was travelling, the mission at Baltimore, under the leadership of Cornelius Dowling, was being established.[127] The basement of St Francis Xavier Church was converted into an evening school taught mainly by James Noonan, another Irish-born priest. The others were a Frenchman, Charles Vigneront, and an Englishman, James Gore.[128] Vigneront helped to organize the mission's work: There was a chapel and a school, a home for the aged poor, the beginnings of an industrial school, a projected high school for boys, as well as an inter-racial brotherhood. Vigneront also cared for a short-lived Chapel of the Sacred Heart on Leadenhall Street in South Baltimore.

However, uncertainty and disappointment accompanied the missionaries from the beginning of their work at St Francis Xavier. Archbishop Martin Spalding died on 7 February 1872 and was replaced on 30 July by James Roosevelt Bayley. Bayley had little confidence in a mission to African-Americans. He also had little hope that such a mission "could accomplish substantial good" among them.[129] Spalding's death was followed by that of Michael O'Connor on 3 October. It was O'Connor who had guided Vaughan to the mission in the United States.

The most serious setback for the small group took place on 9 August when Cornelius Dowling died of typhoid fever. Vaughan wrote to Elizabeth Herbert the following day: "I have the saddest of news from Baltimore. Poor dear Father Dowling died last night. The telegram is from the coloured brother and says no more.[130] This is a great blow to our work and a heavy sadness to us all, but to me especially. I knew him so well and trusted him entirely.... I never met a more devoted, zealous and unselfish priest...."[131]

Return to England

Herbert Vaughan returned to England in June 1872. He brought with him three postulants for the Sisters of St Mary's Abbey, Mill Hill. Among them were a Miss McCormack and a Miss Perkins.[132] In a letter to Elizabeth Herbert he referred to them as the "Missionary Franciscan Sisters," for Vaughan always wanted the nuns who settled at Holcombe House to be the nucleus of missionary Sisters.[133]

Before sailing for Liverpool from New York he had left his missionaries under the leadership of the unfortunate Cornelius Dowling, with few guidelines and little formal administrative structure. According to Ochs, this was to lead to trouble almost immediately. Over the next six years, administrative and philosophical difficulties, combined with lack of manpower and money, nearly destroyed Vaughan's venture in the United States. Dowling's death in August, difficulties with the mission's inter-racial brotherhood, and the exclusivity of their apostolate to African-Americans added to the mission's problems. Vaughan gave instructions that Mass was not to be offered for whites. But what of those white Catholics who chose to attend their churches? Vaughan, in his enthusiasm, had also failed to foresee that questions about property and placement would prove more and more difficult.[134]

However, the event that had the most important consequences for the new mission was to take place in the months immediately after his return to England. He arrived home full of hope for the college's first missionary venture and a great affection for his new friends in the United States. His letters made no secret of his feelings: "New York is the most wonderful Catholic city in the world. In no city in Europe is there so loyal and truly Catholic a population and in none are they so destitute of churches and clergy. I can hardly trust myself to speak about all I have seen and heard."[135]

After an absence of seven months, Vaughan was ready to take up his routine again, sharing time between The Tablet, the missionary college at Mill Hill and the various tasks Manning assigned to him in the archdiocese. But he was soon affected by events in another part of England, in Lancashire.

Bishop of Salford

On the morning of Saturday, 13 July 1872, Manchester was experiencing a violent storm and its most disastrous floods on record. As the storm grew in intensity, Bishop William Turner of Salford died peacefully after a short illness;[136] Salford adjoins the city of Manchester in north-west England. While attending Turner's funeral, Henry Manning promoted the name of Herbert Vaughan as Turner's successor. It was not the first time that Vaughan's name had been raised as a possible bishop. Archbishop John Bede Polding of New South Wales in Australia had approached Cardinal Barnabo at Propaganda in August 1866 with a formal petition that he be given a coadjutor bishop. He submitted three names: the first was Roger Vaughan, Herbert's Benedictine brother in Hereford; the second was Herbert Vaughan. The proposal was postponed and not taken up again until the end of 1872, when Roger was appointed.[137]

At the Salford chapter meeting of 7 August, Manning presided. Three names were proposed as candidates to succeed Turner: in alphabetical order they were Robert Croskell, John Rimmer and Herbert Vaughan. A week later the names were submitted to all of the bishops and they forwarded them to Rome. On 25 August Vaughan wrote to his father that he had heard talk of his name being suggested for Salford, "but my mind is bent upon carrying this providential work (the missionary college) out to its completion, and I believe nothing will be allowed to interfere with this."[138]

The first person Manning spoke to at the funeral was Canon Peter Benoit. Benoit was Turner's secretary and "practically" vicar general of the diocese. He was generally considered to be the foremost candidate to become the next bishop despite the fact he was from Belgium. Some of the clergy were not in favour of Benoit because he had a name for being strict and demanding.[139]

By tradition, the bishops of the north of England were drawn from men trained at St Cuthbert's College, Ushaw, near Durham. The leading candidate with an Ushaw background was Robert Croskell, the vicar general and provost of the chapter. He was from the north, had studied at Ushaw and been the parish priest of St Augustine's. Once he had been a candidate for vice- president of St Cuthbert's. His brother, Thomas, was the bursar of Ushaw from 1850 to 1886.[140]

Manning faced formidable obstacles in promoting Herbert Vaughan. In addition to the strong candidacies of Croskell and Benoit, Vaughan was a stranger to Manchester. Manning's first success was to persuade Peter Benoit to withdraw his name and give his support to Vaughan. When three names were submitted in August, Vaughan's name was included, and Benoit's replaced by Canon John Rimmer. Rimmer had been a chaplain to Leagram in Preston, and later, from 1871, for Burnley schools.[141]

Vaughan wrote to Elizabeth Herbert in September that he would try to get out of the appointment if he was chosen, but if "I cannot, I shall hope to be allowed to retain the direction of St. Joseph's and be here often." There were about ninety students and staff at St Joseph's College in September 1872.[142]

On 29 September 1872 Vaughan learned from Manning that Rome had chosen him to be bishop of Salford and that all "resistance could be useless."[143] On 2 October Vaughan heard from the Salford chapter that he had been appointed bishop. He immediately wrote to Rome arguing: "Why I should not be moved from my present work and asking they choose someone else for Salford." On 9 October Vaughan received a telegram saying that the appointment was final but he was to continue as superior general for life of his still unconstituted missionary organization, and that he should choose a vicar who could look after the missionary college as rector. On the 16th he received the official document from Rome naming him bishop of Salford. "This is the will of God, blessed for ever."[144]

After a retreat Vaughan went to Manchester. He arrived at Salford Cathedral the day before his episcopal ordination.[145]

Vaughan's enthusiasms and personal style, seen in the founding of the missionary college at Mill Hill and the introduction of the first missionaries to the United States, were special. The weakness of his effort was that he was soon drawn away, and, as Ochs remarks, his men were left to carry on with few guidelines. His practical genius lay in his personal involvement and hands-on approach to his projects, but his energy and active mind constantly urged him away, so that it was humanly impossible to apply his strengths effectively. The Salford appointment had the same effect; he was drawn away from his missionary college while remaining its head and administrator from his new diocese in Lancashire.

Father Thoonen, the first archivist at St Joseph's College, Mill Hill, left the following comment in his notes: "One cannot but regret that his impending episcopal appointment and work would hinder him completely to undertake similar sorts of tours and investigations (as he did in the United States) in the other countries and races among whom his missionaries were going to work, like India, Borneo, East Africa. Vaughan would have become a direct missionary leader and inspirator not as it had in fact to be—merely an administrative Superior General."[146]

Notes

1. Leslie, *Vaughan Letters*, p.83, n: "a very guileless and indiscreet favourite of Pope Pius IX. His intellect was not strong and he was confined to an asylum near Passy" in 1868. Vaughan wrote that he had "written oddly" to him; See: Fergal McGrath, *Newman's University, Idea and Reality*, London, Longmans, p.110, n.4: Talbot had been vicar of Evercreech, near Bath. When he went to Rome he "played a large and not overwise part in English Ecclesiastical affairs at Rome." He was a thorn in Newman's side, and Manning, to whom he was devoted, described him as "the most imprudent man that ever lived." Ullathorne thought him a very good and kind-hearted man who was notorious for his poor judgement.

2. Cardinal Gasquet, *A History of Venerable English College, Rome*, London, Longmans, 1920, pp.258ff.

3. Newsome, *Convert Cardinals*, p.266. Wilfrid Ward, *The Life of John Henry Cardinal Newman*, London, Longmans, 1, p.154: Newman wrote to a friend on 28 April 1867: "As to clamour and slander, whoever opposes the three Tailors of Tooley St ... must suffer but it is worth the suffering if we effectively oppose them."

4. MHA. HCV. Box 48: Impressions of the Mill Hill archivist Fr Thoonen on reading Leslie's book of Herbert Vaughan's letters to Lady Herbert of Lea: "I arrived at Victoria in 1945 after an absence of six years and went straight to Burns Oates for a copy ... began to sample it on the underground ... puzzled, even taken aback at the intimacy of the correspondence and at the terms of endearment with which some of the letters opened;" VFA. Letter from Alfred Adrian

Weld-Blundell, The Abbey, Fort Augustus, 29 March 1943, to "Alice"(Alice was probably Alice Vaughan Berkeley, the niece of Herbert Vaughan, and daughter of Francis Baynham Vaughan. Her husband, Wolstan Berkeley, died in 1943. Dom Alfred was over eighty when he wrote from the Benedictine Monastery of Fort Augustus. He had spent ten years in the United States, where he helped found two monasteries; in Portsmouth, Rhode Island, and Washington, D C): "Have you read Cardinal Vaughan's letters to Lady Herbert? ... I found them most interesting. I lived off and on for some years with Lady Herbert before and after Herbert Vaughan's death. I can understand why she would not let Snead-Cox have the letters when he was writing his life. I did not know what had become of them and I am so pleased and congratulate Charles on letting them be printed now."

5. Herbert, *Mary Vaughan.*
6. St Mary's Abbey Archive; MHA. Notes of St Joseph's College.
7. Leslie, *Vaughan Letters*, p.78.
8. Abbey Archives, Log Book.
9. Mr Paul Mason, Archivist, Clwyd County Council, 27 January 1994: "The other daughters being Charlotte Emma and Margaret Maria...." In *Burke's Peerage* (1970) and *Pedigrees of Anglesey and Caernarfonshire families* (1914) by E. Griffith ;" In St Joseph's College library is a book titled: *A Memorial of the Parish and Family of Hanmer in Flintshire*, by John Lord Hanmer, London, Chiswick, 1877. The book, according to a note inside the cover, was given to Fr Henry by "Caroline Hanmer, April 1908," a few months before her death. Her father, Lt Col Thomas Hanmer, was killed accidentally in a shooting accident in 1818, leaving four sons and three daughters. The children first lived with their mother at an old house called Whitehall in Shrewsbury.
10. MHA. HCV. Box 25, Fr v d Biesen; St Joseph's Advocate; *Mill Hillian*, 1932; WDA. Scrapbook; There is a story that she was associated with Florence Nightingale's nurses in the Crimea but there is no evidence of this to be found.
11. McCormack, p.88.
12. MHA. HV: *Our Duty to the Heathen. A Sermon by the Archbishop of Westminster with Speeches and Letters by Clergy and Laity*, London, Burns & Oates, no date.
13. There were three conditions for admission to St Joseph's Society of the Sacred Heart for Foreign Missions: "1. Pray for conversion ... and that labourers be sent. 2. Names inscribed in the books of the Society. 3. Contribute an annual subscription. Some persons might undertake to collect among friends." WDA. Directory.
14. Owen Edwards and Patricia Storey, "The Irish Press in Victorian Britain," in *The Irish in the Victorian City*, ed., Roger Swift and Sheridan Gilley, London, Croom Helm, 1985, pp.158ff: "The history of the newspaper press in the nineteenth century is littered with the bodies of newspapers started with high hopes and varying aims which failed for an equally varied number of reasons, like insufficient capital, local indifference to the cause supported and the strength of rival newspapers." Herbert Vaughan's *Tablet* survived and was sympathetic to others who sometimes did not. An example was the *Catholic Times*, acquired by James Nugent, a Liverpool priest, in 1869. Another was the *Catholic Opinion* which was founded in London in 1867 and edited by Fr William Lockhart. When Vaughan was at Salford, in 1873, he acquired and began to use the *Opinion* as a supplement to *The Tablet*. He gave the *Opinion* to Nugent in 1876. Nugent's newspaper was edited and managed by John Denvir, an Irish nationalist. Vaughan was very helpful to Nugent and the *Catholic Times*: "Vaughan's attitude must have made a pleasant change for Nugent and Denvir after the difficulties created by Canon Fisher, the 'anti-Irish' vicar general of the Diocese of Liverpool, when they sought access to Bishop Goss of Liverpool, whose sermons they wished to use in the *Catholic Times*."
15. John W. Donohue, "A Report. The Tablet's 150th Anniversary," *America*, 12 May 1990, pp.467-8.
16. See: Michael Walsh, *The Tablet, 1840-1990*, London, 1990; See also: Edward Lucas, *The*

Life of Frederick Lucas, M.P., London, Catholic Truth Society, 1887, 2 vols; Lucas declared the principles of *The Tablet* in the first issue: "The advocacy of all Catholic rights; the pursuit of justice and truth independently of any political party; and the maintenance of lawful authority and social order. The specific features are a copious chronicle of the events of the week; leading articles on multifarious subjects of interest; notes on topics of the day; a minute Foreign and Irish correspondence; a weekly review of new works; and an extensive supplement devoted to ecclesiastical and educational news...." It was published each Friday by James Donovan of 19 Henrietta Street.

17. See: Snead-Cox, 1, pp.181-191; Frederick Lucas, 2, p.411: Lucas was outspoken in his criticism of Archbishop Cullen.

18. Walsh, *Tablet*, pp.14ff.

19. Roger Aubert, in Jedin,8, pp.293, 311.

20. Henry Manning, *The Temporal Power of the Vicar of Jesus Christ*, London, Burns and Lambert, 1862, p.74: Manning developed his idea of combating a "pagan revival" and a "the old heathenism, which had been subdued in Italy and Rome, and held under by the Christian order of Europe, striving once more for ascendancy, with its impiety, its infidelity, its blasphemy against God," with a Church in Britain that spoke definitively and unequivocally through the infallible voice of the Pope; Jeffrey P. von Arx, SJ, "Manning's Ultramontanism," *Recusant History*, 19, May 1988, p.347, n.11.

21. Ward, *Transition*, p.31; See also: Dermot Quinn, *Patronage and Piety*, Stanford, Stanford University Press, 1993.

22. David Newsome, *The Parting of Friends*, London, John Murray, 1966, pp.4-5.

23. Walsh, *Tablet*, p.15.; Snead-Cox, 1, p.187.

24. Snead-Cox, 1, p.190. Walsh, *Tablet*, p.16.

25. Snead-Cox, 1, p.195.

26. *ibid.*

27. Ward, *Transition*, pp.50-1.

28. Rev Sydney Smith, "The Life of Cardinal Vaughan," *The Month*, July 1910, 116. p.7: For unpretentiousness, simplicity, directness, lucidity, and force, "his had these qualities."

29. Walsh, *Tablet*, p.16.

30. Norman, *Catholic Church*, pp.349-53.

31. Walsh, *Tablet*, p.16; Snead-Cox, 1, p.181.

32. David O'Brien, *Isaac Hecker, An American Catholic*, New York, Paulist Press, 1992, pp.215, 240, n.16: On the early history of Catholic publications in the United States see: Paul J. Foik, *Pioneer Catholic Journalism*, New York, 1930; and Thomas F. Meehan, "The First Catholic Magazines," *United States Catholic Historical Society*, Historical Records and Studies 31 (1940), pp.141-2; O'Brien, *Hecker*, p.218: Vaughan knew of Hecker's publishing apostolate in the United States called the *Catholic World* and the Catholic Publication Society. But "placed against the political and literary press of the country, almost all of which was in Protestant hands, Catholic publishing counted for little." The Methodists produced two thousand volumes and one thousand tracts per year and millions of Sunday school papers. Other denominations had their own programs. *Harpers Review* had 100,000. Only John Boyle O'Reilly had over 10,000 subscribers—but with few agents to spread material.

33. *The Tablet*, 9 April 1932, p.465.

34. Walsh, *Tablet*, p.117; *The Tablet*, 9 April 1932: From the 7 November 1868 issue: "We have taken as our legend the words Pro Ecclesia Dei, pro Rege et Patria, because they express the principles of the paper, and the order in which we shall always place them.... In respect to matters purely political, we shall always uphold the principle of respect and obedience to all legitimate authority.... Even the captivity in error of the last 300 years has not destroyed the Catholic aspiration after truth and justice, which is part of the national character." The editor of the 1932 issue continued: "Vaughan's torch was not of that 'light without heat' kind which some

thin-blooded Catholics would have us carry. The light by which we illumine the dark places of anti-Christian intrigue would be too feeble to search the Underworld if it did not glow forth from an ardent passion for the truth, and for the Church, truth's guardian. Such was the fervid master-passion of both Frederick Lucas and Herbert Vaughan, in their several ways."

35. Leslie, *Vaughan Letters*, p.132; VFA. "November 1868, Friday, Newcastle Street, Tablet Office." Vaughan to Elizabeth Herbert.
36. Homes, *More Roman*, p.134: He quotes from an article on Montalembert in the *Downside Review*, 89, 1971, pp.158-64.
37. Snead-Cox, 1, pp.198-9: It was Manning. "I owe to His Grace more than to any other person my education and formation.... For sixteen years I have lived in close relation with him. It would be strange, then, if my views were not identical with his on many subjects. They are so by choice and by conviction."
38. Ward, *Dublin Review*, 1910, p.224; Walsh, *The Tablet*, p.18.
39. Snead-Cox, 1, p.200.
40. *ibid.*, p.201.
41. Ward, *Dublin Review*, 1910.
42. *ibid.*
43. *ibid.*
44. *ibid.*
45. Walsh, *Tablet*, p.18.
46. Cuthbert Butler, *The Life and Times of Bishop Ullathorne, 1806-1889*, 2, London, Burns Oates & Washbourne, 1926, p.63; Snead-Cox, 1, pp.215ff.
47. Walsh, *Tablet*, p.20.
48. Chadwick, *Victorian Church*, p.416.; von Arx, "Manning's Ultramontanism," pp.332-347; Aubert, in Jedin, 7, p.296.
49. Chadwick, *Victorian Church*, p.417.
50. Newsome, *Convert Cardinals*, p.268.
51. Aubert, in Jedin, 8, pp.298-9; See also n 23: "Considérations sur le liberalisme," by A. Simon, RIS, 4 (1961) pp.3-25. From Aubert: "Pius IX "who almost daily condemned liberalism as the 'error of the century,' was no longer able to see the radical difference between Catholic liberalism and liberalism as such...." But the Pope's approval was reserved for those "who without consideration of intellectual developments or of local requirements, maintained what was supposed to be the 'right of a Christian Society.' His encouragement convinced them that the pope had entrusted them with a mission." An example was the Pope's praise for *The Tablet*.
52. Von Arx, "Ultramontanism": "Just how powerful he thought the appeal of the Church's witness to authority and unity must be to the world at large, Manning made clear at the Council itself. In his great speech in the Council Hall of May 23,1870 in support of the definition of papal infallibility," Manning argued that the definition would more than anything else promote conversions, and the return of the country to the Faith. "The progress of Catholicism in England," Manning argued, "is to be measured not so much by the number of actual conversions, as by the progressive penetration, constant and visible, of the whole English people, by Catholic ideas and Catholic truth, and the change of mental attitude that is being wrought thereby." See also: Cuthbert Butler, *The Vatican Council*, London, Longmans, Green and Co, 1930, 2, p.50.
53. Aubert, Jedin, 8, p.317. See pp.318-330 for a description of the workings of the First Vatican Council.
54. Chadwick, *Victorian Church*, p.417: "The Vatican Council of 1870 defined papal infallibility in a manner bound to cause unsettlement of mind in all the western Catholic groups. For it met in the shadow of the Italian revolution, and was dispersed by the Italian occupation of Rome." Also, Aubert, Jedin, 8, pp.319-20: They wished to emphasize the principle of authority as strongly as possible in a world undermined by democratic efforts, which in their eyes were

nothing more than a milder form of anarchy, inspired in the main by Protestantism, and help the development towards an increasingly centralized organization.

55. Snead-Cox, 1, p.231, n.1: Years later when *The Tablet* was engaged in another controversy, and Snead-Cox was the editor, Vaughan wrote to him the following note: "Go on the same lines; you will never lose as many subscribers as I did in 1869."

56. Walsh, *Tablet*, p.18.

57. Comtesse De Courson, "Herbert Cardinal Vaughan," *The Rosary Magazine*, 40, April, 1912, no 4, Dominican Fathers, Somerset, Ohio, p.389.

58. Snead-Cox, 1, p.238.

59. Leslie, *Vaughan Letters*, p.175.

60. Walsh, *Tablet*, p.20.

61. Butler, *Ullathorne*, p.308.

62. Lilly, "Vaughan," p.283.

63. WDA. ACTA. Herbert Vaughan, "Principles of Catholic journalism," Pastoral, 22 February 1900; The letter from Tyrrell to Ward quoted in: Mary Jo Weaver, *Letters from a "Modernist,"* London, Sheed and Ward, 1981, pp.29-31.

64. Christopher Ralls, *The Catholic Truth Society, A New History*, London, CTS, 1993, pp.1-2; Holmes, *More Roman*, p.240.

65. Catholic Truth Society, 125th Anniversary; *The Tablet*, 9 April 1932, pp.467-8: One of Vaughan's first contributions was the "People's Manual" on St Joseph. Among his published writings probably none has been more widely distributed. When the Catholic Truth Society was revived, Vaughan renewed his interest, became president and published a number of addresses he gave at annual conferences.

66. MHA. HV. Donations came from England and overseas. For example, from Paris Mr Daniel Murphy sent 1000 francs.

67. Shorter, "Holcombe," p.26.

68. *ibid*.; George Goldie was born at York on 9 June 1828. His father was a physician. He went to St Cuthbert's, Ushaw and became a student of A. Welby Pugin who was working at the college. He worked for Weightman and Hadfield of Sheffield to learn his trade. In 1867 he formed a partnership with his assistant Charles Edwin Child. He died at Saint-Servan in Brittany on 1 March 1887. The college, the chapel, St Mary's Abbey convent and chapel, were designed by Goldie and his partners. MHA. From the RIBA library, 11 November 1994.

69. Leslie, *Vaughan Letters*, p.140; VFA. Correspondence, January 27 1869.

70. Leslie, *Vaughan Letters*, p.166; Reyen tried to work as chaplain for St Mary's nuns but his health broke down.

71. MHA. Logbook.

72. Leslie, *Vaughan Letters*, p.213.

73. Shorter, "Holcombe," p.26.

74. Norman, *Catholic Church*, p.347.

75. Leslie, *Vaughan Letters*, pp.214-6: "Well, the College is all coloured, the rooms all in order, the hot water apparatus working perfectly—though the weather is more like summer than March—the community room and library have been turned into a Chapel and all your banners, vestments, paintings, etc., set out there quite charmingly. At 3 1/4 an express train came down from Town bringing seventy or eighty persons: the Archbishop drove down, so did the Gainsboroughs, the Marchese Patrizzi, the Vavasours, Lady Beaumont, etc.. The Lord Chancellor of Ireland and Monsell and a few others made up our swells. The day was mild as May and the ceremony began about 4 of laying the Foundation Stone of St. Joseph's Church. The Archbishop preached from the terrace to a great crowd gathered below, and then we had a beautifully illuminated Benediction with all your candlesticks and vases etc.."

76. *ibid*; MHA.

77. Leslie, *Vaughan Letters*, pp.226-7: From the seminary at Killenburg, Holland.

78. *ibid.*, p.178; Dowling's health was not good and Vaughan considered sending him to Ceylon (Sri Lanka).

79. When did he decide to have a missionary society in addition to a missionary college? Vaughan understood the necessity of a support organization from the very beginning. The ideas took form gradually under the leadership of Vaughan.

80. Leslie, *Vaughan Letters*, p.183: Hotel D'Angleterre, Rome; And p.186, 30 May 1870, Rome; VFA.

81. Peter Hogan, "Josephite History," *Josephite Harvest*, 95, 3, Spring 1992; See also: R. H. Steins, "The Mission of the *Josephites* to the Negro in America, 1871-1893," MA thesis, Columbia University, New York, May 1966; On Spalding: Thomas W. Spalding, *Martin John Spalding, American Churchman*, Washington, Catholic University Press, 1973.

82. Stephen J. Ochs, *Desegregating the Altar*, Baton-Rouge, LSU Press, 1990, p.39.

83. *ibid*, p.42.

84. McCormack, p.96.

85. MHA. HV.

86. McCormack, p.96; The book that Vaughan read was probably: Jean-Baptiste Pitra, *Vie de Francois-Maria Paul Libermann*, Paris, Poussielgue; See also: Adrian van Kaam, *A Light to the Gentiles: The Life Story of Venerable Francis Libermann*, Maryland, University Press, 1985.

87. Snead-Cox, 1, p.167; The Propaganda Archives refer to the assignment of the mission to Vaughan and his four priests but the letter of appointment, or "copy thereof is not in the Archives." G. J. J. Heuthorst, MHM, Rome; The title of "apostolic missionaries" along with "appropriate faculties" were granted on 29 October 1871. Udienze di NS, 1871, p.2, 169, fol. 1142, Audience schedule, n 44, 29 Oct., 1871, Rome, in Anton Debever, "United States Documents in the Archives of Propaganda Fide, a Calendar," vol 9, *Academy of American Franciscan History*, Washington, DC, 1982; An official letter of assignment has not been found in the Mill Hill Archives; JA, Peter Hogan.

88. Propaganda Archives, 29 October 1871, item 23, p.310, n. 2421; MHA. Dowling had been ordained in 1869 and was at first a chaplain to a wealthy family and then procurator for the college. James Noonan was ordained in 1871, as was Charles Vigeront. James Gore, from Lancashire, was ordained in 1870 and remained at Mill Hill until assigned to the first mission at Baltimore.

89. John Rooney, *Struggling to be Prophets*, St Louis, Mill Hill Press, 1991, p.45: In Rooney's opinion Vaughan "had not realized that they might become a missionary institute." He chose a "vow" to "hold them to their task."

90. Hogan, "Josephites," p.5.

91. Leslie, *Vaughan Letters*, p.238.

92. Hogan, "Josephites," p.1.

93. J. L. Spalding, *The Life of the Most Rev. M. J. Spalding*, New York, Catholic Publishing Society, 1873: Spalding wrote Vaughan a letter of welcome: "The archdiocese of Baltimore receives you with open arms and I have no doubt that you will be welcomed with similar cordiality by my venerable colleagues throughout the country."

94. Robert Trisco, *Bishops and Their Priests in the United States*, New York, Garland, 1988, pp.150ff: McMaster was an ultramontane champion of Catholicism. Some journalists likened him to Louis Veuillot, editor of *L'Univers*. Orestes Brownson's son described McMaster as having "the same zeal and earnestness, the same rashness and imprudence, the same deference to papal, and want of respect for episcopal authority."

95. Notre Dame University Archives. Herbert Vaughan, 15 December 1871, Archbishop's House, Baltimore, to James Alphonsus McMaster, New York; O'Brien, *Hecker*, p.110.

96. Rooney, *Prophets*, p.47.

97. Ochs, *Desegregating, pp*.43-4.

98. *ibid.* p.44; See: For example, Richard West, *Back to Africa*, New York, Holt, 1971.

99. Notre Dame University Archives, Herbert Vaughan, 106 Charles Street, Baltimore, 8 January 1872.

100. WDA. Diary;

101. Ochs, *Desegregating*, p.44.

102. WDA. Diary; Vaughan visited Mother Austin Carroll of the Sisters of Mercy in New Orleans. He told her that he hoped to send "sisters over to teach the blacks,"and Mother Austin promised to help them with accommodation if they did come. Vaughan was thinking of the St Mary's Abbey community. He sent her *The Tablet* as a gift for a number of years. Sr Mary Hermenia Muldrey, *Abounding in Mercy*, New Orleans, Habersham, 1988, p.183.

103. WDA. Diary.

104. Snead-Cox, 1, p.170; WDA. Diary.

105. *ibid*.

106. Snead-Cox, 1, p.174.

107. Ochs, *Desegregating*, p.44, fn. 68.

108. WDA. Diary.

109. Had he made two trips to New York? He wrote to Elizabeth Herbert: "my plan is nearly made up to go to New York at the end of January." Leslie, *Vaughan Letters*, p.241.

110. Joseph Scott, CP, "A Century and More of Reaching Out," New York, 1983, p.15.

111. *ibid*., p.34; O'Brien, *Hecker*, pp.174–5; William Barry, "Isaac Hecker," *Dublin Review*, July 1892, pp.63ff.

112. Joseph McSorley, *Father Hecker and His Friends*, London, Herder, 1952, p.188, no 2: "Some light is thrown on Hecker's views by the discussions he held in 1875 with Cardinal Deschamps, who had then come to look on Hecker with new respect, and with Bishop (later Cardinal) Herbert Vaughan of Salford, Hecker's warm friend. Both of them encouraged the idea of a Paulist foundation in Europe."

113. William Portier, "Inculturation as Transformation: The Case of Americanism Revisited," *US Catholic*, vol ii, no 3, Summer 1993, p.119.

114. O'Brien, *Hecker*, pp.225–41.

115. *ibid*., pp.259–60.

116. When Vaughan was Bishop of Salford he was asked by Rome to submit his observations about the Paulists. The Paulists were seeking approval in Rome for their laws and constitutions. Vaughan wrote that the "great need at present in America is for priests and communities which would operate in the spirit of the Paulists." Paulist Archives, APF, SRC, vol 1005, Baltimore, 8 February 1875.

117. VFA. Vaughan to Herbert, 59th Street and Ninth Avenue, 18 March 1872. On McGlynn, see: Manuel Shanaberger, "Edward McGlynn: A Missionary Priest and His Social Gospel," *US Catholic Historian*, 13, Summer 1995, pp.23–47.

118. Hogan, "Josephite," p.5. It was published in *The Tablet* of 20 July 1872: "The branch torn away from the parent stem in Africa by our ancestors, was carried to America, carried away by Divine permission in order that it might be engrafted upon the tree of the Cross. It will return, in part, to its own soil not by violence or deportation but willingly and borne upon the wings of faith and charity." Vaughan wrote to Propaganda Fide on 3 March 1875 suggesting that African–American Catholics under the care of their pastors colonize the Cape Colony in South Africa and be protected by the English government. See: Propaganda Fide Documents, Calendar, vol 10, p.69, no 548.

119. MHA. In his collection book Vaughan recorded: In Washington, among others, "Mrs. General Sherman," $250.; Visitation Sisters, Georgetown, $25; James and Joseph Donohue, $1000; at New York were St Stephen's Church through Fr E. McGlynn, $2000; St Paul's, Fr I.Hecker, $800; St Peter's, Fr William Quinn, $550; In the summer of 1872, General Sherman and his son visited London. Archbishop Manning visited them at their hotel. Joseph Durkin, *General Sherman's Son*, New York, Farrar, Straus & Cutharty, 1959, p.27.

120. Ochs, *Desegregating*, p.49.

121. *ibid.*, pp.49-51; Also see: William Portier, "John Slattery's Vision for the Evangelization of American Blacks," *US Catholic Historian*, 5, no 1, 1986, pp. 19-44.

122. Portier, "Slattery's Vision," p.24; The Free Academy of New York was formally opened on 21 January 1849. It became "one of the great democratizing institutions of an emerging urban culture." It was an "odd combination of high school, college, and trade school" with an average entrance age of fourteen. See: James Traub, "*City on a Hill, Testing the American Dream at City College*," New York, Addison-Wesley, 1994, pp.9, 21-6.

123. Peter Hogan, correspondence, 6 December 1994; Josephite Archives (JA): "Biographie de J.R. Slattery:" William Portier secured a microfilm of Slattery's "Biographie" from the National Library in Paris. The Josephites' have a copy of Portier's, which was made by Fr Cyprian Davis. It is used by Ochs and Poitier: "The inspiration came to him as it had to many evangelical Protestant missionary-teachers who flocked to the South during Reconstruction, to consecrate his life to the evangelization of African-Americans."

124. Ochs, *Desegregating*, p.51: He presented a handsome appearance and excelled in the classroom. After ordination he first taught Logic at the missionary college and was then assigned to Baltimore.

125. One of the Dutch students was John DeReyter of Zeitphen, Zuyder Zee. Vaughan recruited him when he preached at the Jesuit College in Kaylenberg where DeReyter attended. He died in America in 1896. See: J. R. Slattery, *The Catholic Review*. Wilmington, Delaware, 2 September 1896; Another recruit was John H. Greene: Josephite Archives, Peter Hogan, March 1967: At his death in Baltimore on 29 January 1917, *The Sun* ran Green's obituary the next morning: "... former soldier, poet, journalist, lawyer and historian, and the oldest Catholic priest in the Archdiocese of Baltimore." Vaughan met Greene on a train between Baltimore and Washington. Greene was fifty-one years of age and a lawyer employed as a clerk at the Treasury Department in Washington. Vaughan may have been surprised at Greene's connection with Mill Hill—he had taught at the non-conformist Mill Hill School—and shared interests—he had worked with the *Tipperary Free Press* and *Dublin Nation* after leaving Trinity College; later he founded a newspaper in Sligo called the *Independent*. In America he became editor of the *Cincinnati Enquirer* and was a correspondent and private in the 10th Ohio Regiment during the Civil War. Wounded, he returned to Cincinnati, became editor of the *Catholic Telegraph*, and then completed a law course at Cincinnati Law School. It was Greene who was to begin publication in 1883 of the American edition of *St Joseph's Foreign Missionary Society Advocate*. When the American Josephite province separated from Mill Hill, he remained a member of the Mill Hill community. At one time he was chaplain to the "Mill Hill Sisters" at Patricroft, between 1898 and 1900. At the age of eighty-one, he was released from Mill Hill and, in 1902, returned to Baltimore where he died in 1917.

126. MHA. Scrapbook: *The Tablet*, December 1900. His death "evoked wide-spread expressions of grief all over the South of India from Catholics and Protestants alike;" VFA. At Quebec on 15 May: "The Archbishop has given me leave to take two of his subjects—if any two are willing to volunteer. I have sown the seed. May the Holy Spirit give the increase;" Snead-Cox, 1, p.179: He mentions a certain Arthur Bouchard who was recruited and "served on the Foreign Missions until his death." Snead-Cox is mistaken. Josephite Archives: Arthur Bouchard was born at Rivieri, Quebec City, Kamouraska, Canada, to Mathew and Felice Bouchard. He studied at a local college and then the seminary in Montreal. He went to St Francis Xavier where he stayed with the community for eight months. In August 1873 he went to Mill Hill. On 19 March 1876 he received the cleric's tonsure. On 10 March 1877 he left to become a Carthusian; he soon returned to Mill Hill and was readmitted on trial in August but left for good in September.

127. Hogan, "Josephite," p.5.

128. MHA. The English-born were in the minority at the college. James Gore was born at

Woolton, Lancashire on 23 July 1846, the son of Richard Gore and Lucy Cockson. He was ordained at the Kensington Pro-Cathedral on 9 October 1870 by Henry Manning. Gore died at Charleston, South Carolina, on 18 November 1876, aged thirty.

129. Ochs, *Desegregating*, p.45; Steins, pp.24 and 26; MHA, Benoît, March 2, 1875.; Rooney, *Prophets*, p.52.

130. Ochs, *Desegregating*, p.45: Vaughan had established an inter-racial brotherhood under the care of his priests. They were to devote themselves to the service of the religious community where they lived; it usually involved manual work. "The quarrelling, bickering, racial animosity, and lack of leadership that characterized the Josephite brotherhood resulted in its abolition and an early end to the experiment in interracial community."

131. VFA. Vaughan to Herbert, 10 August 1871, Mill Hill.

132. St Mary's Abbey Archives, Logbook; "An Untold Tale;" The Abbey Logbook mentions a letter of 16 April 1872 from America stating that he was bringing some postulants with him. A 12 June entry states that "none of the concessions which Dr Vaughan wanted for them should be granted."

133. VFA. Vaughan to Herbert, 1 May, 1872; "An Untold Tale," p.15: At Vaughan's and Manning's urging most of the professed Sisters had moved from Ashgrove, Hackney to the vacated Holcombe House at Mill Hill. The change was completed on 4 September 1871. They began building to accommodate up to one hundred girls—they already had thirty—for an industrial school for delinquents. In addition, the foundation stone for the new Abbey was laid on 24 July 1872, and the building blessed on November 24th, 1873.

134. Ochs, *Desegregating*, p.44.

135. VFA. Vaughan to Herbert, 2 April 1872.

136. Brian Seale, *The Moston Story*, Manchester, 1983, p.65.

137. VFA. Scrapbook, A. M. O'Sullivan, OSB, letter to the editor, *Evening News*, Sydney, 21 December 1883.

138. VFA. Herbert Vaughan to John Vaughan, 25 August 1872: In the same letter Vaughan reveals a gentler side of his character. His remarks were prompted by a question he had asked his father about some inheritance money: "My dearest Father ... you have been a little pained by my letter. Father I really grieve, for there is no one on earth I love as I do you. My only object was to clear up what appeared to me a misunderstanding." He adds some news that a design has arrived for the statue of St Joseph planned for the College tower and that there were thirty students at Mill Hill with some German Jesuit students on the way.

139. J. De Muelenaere, *"Canon Pieter Benoit,"* Overdruk uit Handellingen van het Genootschap 'Societe d'Emulation' te Brugge, deel CVII (1970), p.9, n.10.

140. *ibid.*: De Muelenaere says he was Provost of the Chapter; Snead-Cox, 1, p.240; *The Tablet*, 20 December 1902, p.980: Robert Croskell died at Levenshulme, near Manchester, in his ninety-fourth year, in December 1902. He was born in Liverpool on 20 January 1808. "His departure," said the *Manchester Guardian*, "removes a remarkable link with the distant past, and his memory will live long with those who knew him, and who for many years had spoken of him as the 'Venerable Provost.'"

141. Charles Bolton, *Salford and its Catholic Past*, London, Hollis & Carter, 1950.

142. VFA. Vaughan to Herbert. 21 September 1872.

143. *ibid.*, 29 September 1872.

144. Snead-Cox, 1, p.241.

145. *ibid.*, p.245.

146. MHA. HV.

PART FOUR

BISHOP IN LANCASHIRE

Bishop of Salford; Dispute with the Jesuits at Manchester, and between the English Bishops and Religious Orders; St Bede's Commercial College

Salford

In the fall of 1872 Archbishop Manning wrote to the Chapter of Salford Diocese about Rome's selection of Herbert Vaughan to be their new bishop: "You will soon learn what I have lost and what you have gained by the appointment of Dr Vaughan.... The surprising success which has attended the Bishop-elect in his previous labours, and especially in establishment of St. Joseph's College, gives us a well-founded hope that he will accomplish great good in the diocese of Salford."[1]

Rome's choice of Herbert Vaughan was controversial. One reason was that he was virtually unknown to the Catholic Church of the north of England, with its line of St Cuthbert's Seminary and Stonyhurst College ecclesiastics. But Manning succeeded, and Vaughan was to spend the next twenty years in Lancashire.

Salford was geographically small but otherwise one of the most important dioceses in England, comprising Manchester, which dominated the area, and the industrial centres of the north-west. J. A. Hilton—using the 1851 religious census—says Salford diocese, in the mid-nineteenth century, had 33,092 Catholics. According to Stephen Fielding, by 1890 Manchester alone had nearly 98,000 Catholics. When Vaughan arrived in 1872, there were about 100,000 Catholics in the whole diocese. The vast majority of them were working class and urban. There was only one aristocratic family, the de Traffords, who owned estates in rural Lancashire. The numbers of Catholics were also swelled by the immigration of Irish Catholics.[2]

The industrial revolution had brought about not only an economic but a social transformation of the Manchester area. Thanks to the cotton trade, Manchester had become one of the great cities of the world, famous for both its industry and its politics. It was called the "chimney of the world" and was also the home of the Manchester school of free traders. There was massive urban growth, which brought with it, according to Alan Kidd, "enormous problems of organization, provision of amenities and maintenance of public order." When Vaughan arrived it had long been one of the "most over-crowded and unhealthy places in the whole of England." It was also developing into the warehousing and financial centre for the cotton industry. The great poverty in Vaughan's time was caused in large part by the operation of an employment market of day or piece workers whose insecurity of income could be worse than low wages. They were especially the car men, porters, messengers, warehousemen and those in the building trades.[3]

Gerard Connolly investigated nineteenth-century historical traditions concerning the "providential re-establishment" of the Catholic Church in England by studying Manchester, "possibly the nineteenth-century 'city' par excellence, together with its Siamese twin, Salford," as the setting for his study.[4] It was an area ideally suited for just the gifts Vaughan could bring: "administrative skill, financial enterprise and energetic construction."[5]

In 1840 there were only four Catholic churches in Manchester and none in Salford and Pendleton. Prior to the 1850s, Bishop James Sharples cared for the area while he was co-adjutor to Bishop George Hilary Brown of the Western District. Bishop Brown came to Salford on 9 August 1848 to open a new church, St John's, which later became the cathedral. Nicholas Wiseman preached at the opening for an hour and a half before sixteen hundred people. When Bishop Sharples died in August 1850, his vicar general was William Turner.

A month later, on 20 September, Salford Diocese was created as part of the restoration of the Catholic hierarchy. There were only thirty missions in the whole diocese. It was perhaps the most overcrowded and financially ill-provided of all the newly erected dioceses. According to Hilton, the division that gave Liverpool roughly twice as many churches, priests, and people as Salford created a serious imbalance between what were originally meant to be two roughly equal dioceses.

The following year, on 25 July 1851, William Turner was ordained bishop in St John's Cathedral. Until the debt was cleared on the building thirty years later, St John's remained unconsecrated. During his tenure, among other accomplishments, Turner laid down a network of schools that proved to be the foundation of Catholic education within the diocese even to this day.[6]

Edward Norman uses a comment by Bolton in his history of Salford to support a view of Vaughan "that has continued to find supporters": that Vaughan was, in his own words, "a poor mediocrity." Even Vaughan's biographer, Snead-Cox, called attention to a general impression that Vaughan was "an estimable but rather narrow-minded prelate whose career had been redeemed from mediocrity chiefly by the unusual energy which had directed it."[7] According to Norman, Bolton's book shares a similar view of Vaughan: "The centenary history of the Diocese of Salford," he writes, "which Vaughan served for twenty years, allocates only one page out of 255 to his achievements—the author regarding him as essentially a missionary bishop who treated the diocese as a small mission field."[8]

However, Norman's assessment of Bolton's view of Vaughan is incomplete, for Bolton writes in the same text of William Turner's successor: "The great Bishop Herbert Vaughan" who was to work hard and wait eighteen years to consecrate the Cathedral Church.[9] Nor was being "essentially a missionary Bishop" a problem, for Bolton concludes the paragraph with: "The diocese was a small mission field for him, but he cultivated it with zeal."[10]

Bolton records Vaughan's tenure: recruiting clergy on the Continent, especially in Holland, establishing a Pastoral Seminary, St Bede's College, The Catholic Rescue Society, The Catholic Truth Society, and more than forty new parishes, among other works. He concludes that in 1892: "It would have been hard for any man to assume the mantle of Bishop Vaughan." National Directories show that at the end of 1873, therefore one year after Vaughan arrived, there were 109 secular priests and forty regulars in the diocese. There were also eighty public churches and chapels. When he left in 1892 there were 178 seculars and fifty-nine regulars, and 118 public churches and chapels.[11]

According to Connolly, it was Herbert Vaughan's incumbency that was the summit of the movement from the "abandonment of consensus in matters of religion" towards a "confessionalism which presented the Roman Catholic Church as the sole institution of religion and as a clerical enterprise under the firm control of bishops." He calls it "the victory of the episcopate over the priest." On the other hand, John Bossy considers Vaughan's work at Salford, and later at Westminster, to amount to perfecting the introverted character of Catholic institutions.[12] At the same time, it can be argued that it was Wiseman, Manning and Vaughan who guided the re-established Church away from the insularity of "Old Catholics" and made it part of the international Catholic institutional community.

When Herbert Vaughan received his appointment to Salford he prepared for his ordination with a ten-day retreat with the Clapham Redemptorists.[13] From Clapham he went straight to Manchester and arrived the day before his ordination at Salford: "With a carpet-bag in his hand, he was met by one of the resident clergy, who asked who he was and what he wanted. 'Oh,' was the reply, 'I am Herbert Vaughan and I have come to be consecrated.'"[14]

Herbert Vaughan was ordained bishop by Archbishop Manning at St John's Cathedral on Sunday 28 October 1872, the feast of SS Simon and Jude, and the anniversary of his ordination to the priesthood eighteen years earlier. Along with Herbert Vaughan, William Weathers, the former president of St Edmund's, Ware, was ordained Bishop of Amycla and auxiliary to Manning at Westminster. The *Manchester Guardian* of the next day reported that the entire Roman Catholic hierarchy, except for the Bishop of Shrewsbury, were present. Two temporary thrones were erected in the chancel for the newly ordained bishops. Music was provided by the organist, Mr McDonald, with a "choir and band." The Mass was Haydn's in B flat, number one. Shortly after 9 a.m. the procession entered St John's. Vaughan and Weathers were in white vestments, and Archbishop Manning in a purple robe with a jewelled mitre and the pallium of his office.

The homily was given by Bishop Ullathorne of Birmingham. He chose a text from Acts 20:28: "Take heed to yourselves, and to the whole flock wherein the Holy Ghost has placed you bishops, to rule the Church of God, which He purchased with His own Blood."

> But where, in this nineteenth century, shall we find the apostolic authority except in the Chair of Peter, and in the line of the Roman Pontiffs? Twelve hundred years ago that divinely-constituted authority sent Augustine to found the See of Canterbury, and Paulinus to found the See of York. But those Sees, with their suffragans, have long departed from the Catholic faith, and with the loss of communion with the Apostolic See they have lost their Catholic jurisdiction, and even their Catholic orders; whilst the same apostolic authority that founded those sees of old, has founded sees anew; and amongst others it sent your late venerable bishop to establish the See of Salford, and has appointed his successor, who is now presented to you. The votes of the Cathedral Chapter commended him to the attention of the Pontiff, the suffrages of the bishops sustained their commendation; the 259th successor of St. Peter has called him to the episcopal office; and notwithstanding his reluctance, has given him his institution, his jurisdiction, and his flock.[15]

Afterwards, at the lunch in the Salford Town Hall, among those present were Sir H. De Trafford, Mayors W. Booth of Manchester and T. Barlow of Salford, and Michael Henry, MP. In his speech, the vicar general, Robert Croskell, responded to a rumour circulating that Vaughan had been forced upon the diocese against the wishes of the chapter. "That was false," he said. The nomination had originated in the chapter and they wanted him. "What was true was that they feared the great work he had in hand would prevent his coming among them."[16]

The "great work he had in hand" was his missionary college at Mill Hill. The chapter had raised objections to Vaughan's appointment when it was learned that the Pope wanted him to retain authority over the college; they thought he would be prevented from residing at Salford. The Pope, however, had not asked him to stay at Mill Hill, but asked that he choose a vicar to be rector in his place.

When Herbert Vaughan rose to thank the gathering he singled out Henry Manning. The *Manchester Guardian* reported: "More than 20 years ago the Archbishop conducted him to Rome and in Rome it was his good fortune to be selected as one of four—His grace the Archbishop being one of the four—to receive an appointment to a place in the Accademia Ecclesiastica or Pontifical College." Vaughan continued: "From that day to the present, the Archbishop and he had been in close fellowship and in most affectionate intercession."[17]

In 1904, Bishop Casartelli wrote to Mary Elizabeth Herbert, asking her for information about Herbert Vaughan when he first came to Salford. She remembered going to visit him "a month or so" after his consecration. Vaughan was living in a "Crescent, of which I forget the name. I arrived on a pouring, wet, snowy evening." He was staying at an industrial school where the master "had been sent away." "Nothing was ready for him: neither fire nor food. A rough maid-of-all-work opened the door and said he had not come back." Vaughan arrived soon afterwards "dripping wet just as I was just going into the kitchen to light the fire."[18]

The *Catholic World* in 1933 called Vaughan's "humility and solicitude for the interior life," the keynote of all his life's work. The article went on to repeat an anecdote about Vaughan that took place soon after he arrived at Salford. A rich friend from the United States gave him "a beautiful sapphire ring worth three hundred pounds," but he would not wear it. Instead he bought a simple cameo with an image of Our Lady on it, and he wore that instead.[19]

Temperance

Temperance movements arose in the nineteenth century to combat the abuse of alcohol. Some, like the Crusade of Rescue, which Vaughan later tried to establish in every parish, and the Church of England Temperance Society, had divisions for moderate drinkers and for total abstainers. Vaughan was a moderate drinker while Manning was a total abstainer.[20]

Two days after his ordination, Bishop Herbert Vaughan made his first public appearance, at a temperance meeting of about four thousand people in the Free Trade Hall.[21] Vaughan sat on a platform between two "teetotalers," Archbishop Manning and the Apostle of Temperance, Father Nugent. As soon as the people saw their new bishop they began shouting. It was more of a welcome than Vaughan had ever dreamed of.[22] He was expected to support the total abstinence plea of his guests but he did not do so and instead he confessed that he was not a teetotaler and encouraged those of his audience who voluntarily pledged never to touch intoxicating drink to do so without reproaching those who did not.

Years later he explained his view to John Snead-Cox, stressing that it would never do, he thought, to divide society into those who took a drink and those who did not. "We must leave some room in the world for people who are temperate." There was, according to Snead-Cox, "consternation" on the platform at the Free Trade Hall but "great delight in the body of the hall. The crowd recognized a man who knew his own mind and was not afraid to speak it." It was to be a note that "echoed through all his life."[23] However, his contention on the occasion that drink was actually food from which the poor could obtain some nourishment was a great scandal to Manning and the other temperance advocates.[24]

Vaughan was aware of the dangers of alcohol, but less concerned about temperance than Manning. According to Snead-Cox, he once told a congregation that he "had never been in any city in Europe or America where the sight of drunken men and women was so common as it then was in Manchester."[25] Over the years, his experience at Salford made him more familiar with the effects of alcohol, especially on the local economy and the working classes. In time he proposed more controlled licensing, rather than prohibition, and eventually organized a crusade against the abuses of alcohol.[26]

Administration

Under Bishop Turner, Salford Diocese had been able to increase the number of missions from thirty to seventy, despite the economic problems caused by shortages of cotton for the local mills during the Civil War in the United States. During the "cotton famine" great hardship was experienced by the Catholic population, concentrated, as most of it was, in industrial areas. Few Catholics lived in the countryside and this was seen as a "great handicap to the diocese." Turner also began the Salford Grammar School in his own house in the Crescent, and, in a modest way, began a school for boys run by Xaverian Brothers from Belgium. He started a girls' school, which later became Loreto College, and established a system of elementary education.[27]

However, the administration of Salford Diocese, except in regard to elementary schools, remained inadequate, especially during Turner's declining years, and its social and pastoral problems were serious. After he surveyed the diocese and decided that Salford was "the grandest place in England for popular energy and devotion," Herbert Vaughan decided on a number of projects. One of them was to make the administration of the diocese more businesslike. He immediately ordered that synods be held annually rather than every seven years. Each dean was told to visit all the parishes of his deanery every three years and was made responsible for the management of all the missions in his area. Vaughan also standardized and centralized the diocesan finances. An administration board was appointed annually to advise him on financial matters, and was, with the bishop, solely responsible for contracting diocesan parish debts. Vaughan insisted that serious efforts be made to reduce the debts of the missions and the diocese. The board was a result of Vaughan's preoccupation with the difficulties of raising money from a predominantly working-class population.[28]

In his diary, describing a plan of personal austerity modelled on the life of Charles Borromeo, who "made his palace like a monastery," he wrote the following: "Dr.Newsham used to say 'the Bishops are Bankers'—Please, God, I will not be a Banker—but will make my Pastorals, instructions, and chief care and thought to be 'pray and preaching.'" Just in case, he noted, "have everything in writing, as much as possible, ... take time to consult before deciding, ... be slow to reform, but very firm, ... and mix freely with the clergy—without allowing extra expense."[29]

Bishop Vaughan refused to go into debt and simply pay off the interest. He always tried to pay off the principal. It soon became a practice to use 15 or 20 per cent of the collections for building improvements to reduce parish debts. In doing this, Vaughan was not universally popular with his priests, "who had to find the money which his policies demanded." He even set a minimum salary for an assistant priest; the average salary for an assistant was forty pounds, and fifty for a parish priest. But a priest's full salary could not be paid "before all current liabilities of the parish" had been discharged."[30]

Herbert Vaughan's Health

Vaughan's health during this period is not mentioned in sources, but it is known that he continued to experience periodic weakness. The only reference to illness during his first days at Salford was made in 1896 by his brother Joseph, the Benedictine: "At Dunedin, New Zealand, I was seized with heart-failure and for some days was swaying between life and death—all my symptoms were precisely similar to those your Lordship laboured under when first made Bishop."[31]

Pastoral Seminary

One of the first major projects Vaughan undertook at Salford concerned the education of the diocesan clergy. Salford clergy came from all parts of Europe. Bishop Turner had established links with Bruges in Belgium and Vaughan recruited priests from the Netherlands, Ireland and Germany for his missionary college at Mill Hill and also for Salford.[32] Vaughan established burses for the education of poor students and restricted the establishment of schools run by religious orders, in order to control recruitment of potential candidates for the diocesan priesthood.

Between 1852 and 1873 the bishops held four provincial synods and had laid down guidelines for those who were training men for the priesthood at Ushaw, Ware and Oscott. The synods generally advocated "a training which

isolated the seminarians from contemporary developments in secular education and which was marked by a deep suspicion of the world." By the time of
the 1873 synod at Ushaw, the attitude of the Catholic Church in England,
according to Peter Doyle, was "hostile, or, at best, defensive."[33] The bishops
thought that they could meet the demand for a better-educated clergy, who
could match the needs of the age and influence it, by increasing the course of
theology from three to four years; a policy of "more of the same." In the 1850s
Bishop Goss of Liverpool tried to raise the educational standard of his priests.
He wrote in 1858 that "it is one of the most discouraging features of the day
that, as a rule, there is no study among the clergy." In another place he wrote
that, "The clergy of Lancashire have long been pre-eminent for their zeal, and
I am anxious that they be pre-eminent for their learning." Vaughan was not a
scholar, as Goss was, but he had his own pragmatic view of education for
secular priests in the diocese.[34]

In 1859, at the third provincial synod, the English bishops had committed
themselves to the creation of Tridentine diocesan seminaries. Each bishop,
according to the decrees of Trent, was to have his own training establishment
for the preparation of secular clergy exclusively.[35] There was a proviso
allowing poor dioceses to combine their resources. England had never had a
seminary on the Trent model; this was illustrated in the controversy over the
status of St Edmund's College, Ware. Each of the colleges that trained
students for the priesthood also admitted laymen who mixed freely with their
clerical counterparts. At no time did Vaughan, after his experience at Ware
and the founding of St Joseph's, Mill Hill, have any sympathy with a policy of
having separate seminaries for each diocese. Salford Diocese had students for
the priesthood scattered about in "five or six different colleges, some in
England and some abroad." When studies were finished at Ushaw, Rome,
Paris, Valladolid or Lisbon, they returned to Salford "almost as strangers,
and to a Bishop who knew practically nothing of their qualities or capaci-
ties."[36] Bishop Vaughan did not decide to start a seminary for students from
twelve years of age onwards, but to establish a seminary of pastoral theology
attached to the cathedral.

In his plan, candidates, after their third year of theology, would spend a
period of one year continuing their theological studies, learning the practical
tasks of a parish priest and becoming known to the bishop and clergy. "In
this way Vaughan hoped to provide an immediate solution for temporary
emergencies in parishes, while enabling his young priests to make an easier
transition from the seminaries to the industrial parishes of the diocese."[37]

After a visit to Rome[38] in March 1873, Vaughan presented his plan to a
diocesan clergy meeting in May. The cost of the project was estimated at
£15,000. One priest who was present described "a contagion of enthusiasm
with which the Bishop's words fired the whole meeting."[39] The clergy present
subscribed £2400. A final £5,000 was raised in time for the feast of St Joseph,

1874. Canon DeSplenter and Canon Beesley were Vaughan's chief helpers in this undertaking.[40]

The Pastoral Seminary was completed, and classes began in 1874. Over the next five years, sixty-five priests passed through its doors. Unfortunately for Vaughan's innovative project, the costs involved and the continued shortage of priests—students were often appointed away before completing the course—eventually forced the Pastoral Seminary to close.[41]

Pilgrimage

Shortly after arriving at Salford, Vaughan joined a pilgrimage of a thousand English Catholics to Paray-le-Monial, France, the centre for the devotion to the Sacred Heart. According to Snead-Cox, it was for Vaughan "another step towards the renewal of the Catholic life of the country in all its fulness ... a part of the Catholic revival." The pilgrimage was a pioneering effort to set an example for the re-establishment of organized pilgrimages to places once venerated in Catholic life and devotion. In September 1874 there was another pilgrimage made up of former students of St Edmund's, Ware, to the shrine of St Edmund's in Burgundy. Not only were pilgrimages a revival of devotion but, as Manning's words at St Edmund's shrine testify, of a claim to legitimacy.[42]

Dispute with the Jesuits

Another priority of Vaughan's at Salford was quality secondary and commercial education, and in this, according to Norman's assessment, he was determined to break the monopoly of the religious orders.[43] In Lancashire the "religious" were the Jesuits who had a secondary boarding school at Stonyhurst and St Francis Xavier in Liverpool. They attempted to open another school in Manchester. And so, in the summer of 1874, Vaughan became involved in a dispute with the Society of Jesus which affected the Catholic world beyond Manchester. There was a fundamental question: What was the authority of a bishop in his diocese?

In addition, Vaughan had in mind the needs of the secular clergy and influence over the growing Catholic middle class. Within a month of becoming bishop he planned not only the pastoral seminary but also a commercial college that would complement the already existing grammar schools.[44] Oliver Rafferty, a Jesuit, argues that "the débâcle in Manchester was, then, but one more instance of the need felt by secular and regular clergy alike to have an influence with the Catholics on their way up the social ladder." It was a struggle for influence over the growing middle-class Catholic community in the nineteenth century. The school the Jesuits opened in Manchester was repeatedly stated to be one for the middle classes. The Jesuit superior wrote to

Vaughan that in opening a new school they were opening a school which was "entirely in conformity with their Institute, the education of the middle classes."[45]

Vaughan had the support of Manning in the dispute. Manning, and Wiseman before him, emphasized that the status of the secular clergy must be raised and that the Church should work towards a system of education for the poor and middle classes.[46] Manning distrusted the Jesuits' alignment with the aristocratic establishment and Newman's converts. In addition, he thought the Jesuit model as a system of education "to be increasingly decadent" and "ill equipped" to deal with the growing secularism of the mid-nineteenth century. Education was not, in the opinion of Manning, Vaughan and others, to be left solely to the religious orders in the revived Catholic Church in England. It was seen as part of the process that would raise the secular clergy in the estimation of the people. Their ability would be demonstrated in a whole range of pastoral work, including education.[47]

The controversy with the Jesuits began at Salford but ended in Rome with a pronouncement by Pope Leo XIII on 8 May 1881 called *Romanos Pontifices*. It was a dispute, according to Vaughan, "on matters of discipline affecting the working of the Church in Great Britain." His eventual victory was a personal triumph, according to Rafferty, because he had "assiduously campaigned at Rome to have the freedom of religious orders restricted, and their operations subject to the supervision of the local bishop." Pope Leo XIII's decision in 1881 "sought to remove any ambiguity in canon law, clearly regulating the power and obligations of the orders and bishops."

Rafferty considers the most important single catalyst in the chain that led to *Romanos Pontifices* to be Vaughan's dispute, beginning in Manchester in 1875, with the English province of the Society of Jesus headed by Father Peter Gallwey.[48] Underlying the dispute was his goal to raise the number and quality of his diocesan clergy. The secular priests of Salford were in a minority, and with secondary education largely in the hands of religious orders, likely candidates often followed the vocation of the regular priests, that is, priests in religious orders, who taught them.

The school in question had its origins in the early 1850s. The Xaverian Brothers opened a school at All Saints, Grosvenor Square, in January 1853. It closed at the end of the year. In the same year, Bishop Turner and the Jesuits agreed on the opening of a small secondary school in Manchester. It began with one priest, one scholastic and a lay brother. By 1854 the school was having financial problems and the Jesuits withdrew. Turner thanked them for their efforts and decided to continue with his own diocesan clergy. In 1862 Turner invited Xaverian Brothers to take over. It was called the Catholic Collegiate Institute. In the same year Turner established the Salford Catholic Grammar School in his own house.

In 1866 the Jesuits again became interested in Manchester. Turner wanted them as preachers and confessors and so they moved into the Oxford Road area in 1867. Bishop Turner attached conditions to their return, stipulating that they "were under no circumstances to have a school other than a primary school for the education of poor children of their parish." Turner made it clear that he did not want them to compete with the educational work being done by the Xaverian Brothers.

In the summer of 1873 Bishop Vaughan participated in the Fourth Synod of Westminster held at St Edmund's, Old Hall, Ware.[49] The meeting opened on Wednesday 23 July, and continued to Monday 11 August. Bishop Ullathorne opened the first session with a talk in which he called attention to the sanctification of the diocesan clergy "as opposed to the regular."[50] Manning was chairman and twelve bishops of the restored hierarchy were present, including Herbert Vaughan and his uncle, William Vaughan, Bishop of Plymouth. Two bishops from the colonies attended; one was Archbishop Roger Bede Vaughan, co-adjutor of Sydney, who gave the closing homily. There were also representatives of at least nine religious orders. Vaughan's friend Mr W. G. Ward was also present.[51]

The bishops resolved to encourage the growth of Catholic secondary education in England. Soon afterwards, Peter Gallwey, the Jesuit provincial, approached Herbert Vaughan at Salford about the possibility of opening a college in Manchester. Vaughan had his own plans for secondary education in the diocese and did not want another Jesuit school. He thought that the Jesuits already had enough schools in north-west England. When the provincial wrote again to Vaughan in 1874, he was met with a "polite but firm refusal."

Gallwey turned to his Roman superiors, Fr Beckx and Fr Weld. Alfred Weld, a relative of Vaughan, met Cardinal Franchi the Prefect of Propaganda Fide. Franchi wrote to the Jesuit General, Beckx, encouraging the Jesuits to do what they could for secondary education in England, particularly in Manchester. On 11 December 1874 Gallwey wrote to Vaughan claiming that it "was perfectly within the powers of the Jesuits to open a school in Manchester attached to their church without the Bishop's authority."[52]

The Jesuits held a meeting at Oxford on 17 December 1874. From the notes that remain from the meeting, one of the reasons for opening the school was to put two scholastics to work as teachers. Rafferty concludes: "One is tempted to speculate that the history of the Catholic Church in England would have been different if the two young men in question could have been found gainful employment elsewhere."[53]

Vaughan contacted Rome and asked if Propaganda wanted the Jesuits to open a college in Manchester. A telegram arrived stating: "Neither order given nor wish expressed. This is official." Vaughan informed Gallwey that he was to be away in the United States until the end of February 1875. He planned to visit his missionaries and to take part in the first chapter meeting in Baltimore of the St Joseph's Missionary Society of the Sacred Heart. He requested that the Jesuits take no action until he returned. Instead, Gallwey opened the school. In response, Vaughan threatened to suspend all the Jesuits in Manchester "*a divinis*" if the school was not closed. Gallwey, among other claims, said that he was acting on "privileges of the order."[54] The school reopened after the Easter holidays in 1875 and Vaughan consulted with his fellow bishops at a meeting being held about the same time. As a result of the consultation, he decided to go to Rome and demand that the college be closed. If he lost the case, he had decided to resign from the diocese of Salford.

Vaughan arrived in Rome on 25 April 1875. In his diary he wrote that Beckx came to see him early the next morning and asked if they could have a long talk about the "Manchester affair." "I replied it is too late," Vaughan wrote, "the matter is before Propaganda. I suppose you could obey but you have not done so in closing the school." On 30 April Vaughan had an audience with Pope Pius IX. He told the Pope that he "was being sacrificed by the SJs," and explained his case: He had published his intention to start a college; the Jesuits had had a college before in Manchester but left; he had an agreement with the Jesuits and had prohibited the opening of their college; the Jesuits claimed they had a right to act; the Bishop of Liverpool wrote to him that boys in the Jesuit college there were "crying victory over the Bishop of Salford;" and that Jesuits and "friends abroad are boasting that they are always triumphant in Rome." Vaughan "urged that if the SJs have their college in Manchester it would be like confining the Bishop to Trastevere and giving Rome to them. (The Pope said that he had not known the relative position of the two towns but had thought them separated)." Vaughan concluded that he would do no good in the diocese if "I'd not form clergy, that my college should be in Manchester and that the Jesuits had Stonyhurst and other colleges in England." The Pope told Vaughan that he would call for the Jesuit General. On 21 May, Vaughan met with Fr Alfred Weld, who argued that there was room in Manchester for five or six colleges and that there was going to be no peace until the Jesuits had a college there.[55]

Finally Cardinal Franchi arranged for Vaughan and Beckx to meet. The prefect wanted a compromise whereby the Jesuits closed the school and Vaughan did not dispute their privileges. The Jesuits were ordered by Beckx to close the college. Beckx promised Vaughan, in a letter dated 25 May 1875, that he would write to the Jesuits at Manchester to close the school at the "end of the current month." Beckx wrote to Gallwey on 27 May that the school should be closed. On 1 June Vaughan sent a telegram to Salford asking if the Jesuits had closed the school as they had agreed. The answer was that the school was still open and so Vaughan went to Beckx and told the general that he was not leaving Rome until he heard that the school was definitely closed. This time Beckx telegraphed Manchester and the Jesuit school finally closed its doors.[56]

On 3 June Herbert Vaughan saw the Pope and was reminded that he should "go more than half-way towards peace and reconciliation" with the Jesuits.[57] As soon as he arrived back in Salford, Vaughan went to Stonyhurst and made his annual retreat and at the same time requested that the Jesuits conduct the annual retreat for his clergy.

Although Vaughan had won his battle with the Jesuits over the Manchester school, both parties knew that the real issue was yet to be faced. The dispute would continue over the privileges of the religious orders and the definition of the permanent relations between the bishops and the orders working within their dioceses. One immediate result was that the English bishops benefited from Vaughan's experience, for the Manchester incident demonstrated that they could engage in a contest with the religions orders and win.

Manning had already proposed to Propaganda in March 1875 that the whole question of the relationship should be made a matter of inquiry for the universal Church. In an 1887 note, Manning traced the beginning of the conflict with religious orders to the synod meeting at St Edmund's in 1873. "In that council," he wrote, "the first seeds of the contests of the Bishops and the Regulars were sown in Gallwey's unseemly speech and Fr G. Porter's theory that the 'Sincere Christian' and the 'Catechismus ad Parochus' are the books for the secular clergy. He did not say, but this means, that all that is higher is for them."[58] The conflict that followed Vaughan's success in Rome concerning the Manchester school, was, according to Edward Norman, due to Manning who went forward with the case against the religious orders, but it was Vaughan who was to carry on the battle in Rome. He collaborated with Bishop Clifford at first, and then remained to fight on alone on behalf of the English bishops between 1879 and 1881 for the decision that became known as *Romanos Pontifices.* Vaughan was to be away in Rome for a year and a half.[59]

Investigation of the English Seminaries on the Continent

In 1875 Vaughan had another task entrusted to him by the English hierarchy. The financial conditions of the English colleges abroad came under scrutiny, and Vaughan was asked to make an enquiry into the condition of each of the schools and their property. Vaughan's travelling companion was his secretary, Mgr Charles Joseph Gadd; Gadd kept a diary during the journey. There is an oral tradition at Salford that Vaughan and his secretary were known as "My Lord and my Gadd."[60]

Vaughan and Gadd travelled through France—where they visited Lourdes and Biarritz—and then continued through the Basque country to St Alban's College at Valladolid in Spain. Vaughan was the first bishop of the English hierarchy to have visited the school. The two men arrived on 16 March and were greeted by John Guest, the rector. Gadd wrote in his diary about Guest: "Nice old man. One of the old school, courteous and a little dogmatic but evidently very good. Scrupulous and nervous, has not said Mass for two years." The two men stayed until 20 March and were able to visit the college property, pay their respects to the Scots College and the archbishop, and assist at the entrance of King Alfonso XII into Valladolid and his reception at the cathedral. They then travelled to Madrid, Córdoba, Seville, Sanlúcar de Barrameda, and Lisbon in Portugal, among other places.

Vaughan's findings were published in the "Report on the English Colleges in Italy, Spain and Portugal" to the bishops, in Low Week, 1876. In his report he praised the service that had been given to the English Church by the colleges in Lisbon and Valladolid. He thought that they should be maintained, as they might be as useful to the Church again, as they had been in the past, and the climate might benefit students in poor health. It was considered a "well written report, containing a history of all the English Colleges, their work for the missions in the days before emancipation and their financial status." Vaughan's observations on the Spanish colleges were so well done that they were taken to be their official history.[61]

St Bede's Commercial College

According to Mary Vaughan, a joke went around that whenever Herbert Vaughan had five spare minutes, he would call his secretary and ask what new project he could start.[62] One of the major projects he undertook at Salford was to found a commercial college.

"High-flying heirs to the vision of Bishop Vaughan" is the headline of a special *Universe* newspaper feature in the 10 October 1993 issue. Vaughan's heirs were the "nine hundred and fifty boys and girls of the independent HMC grammar school, St Bede's College, Manchester."[63] One hundred and thirty years earlier, Salford was at the heart of the Lancashire commercial world, and Vaughan was aware of the growing need for young Catholics to train for business and scientific careers. He decided that part of the answer was to begin a modern school, which would help not only the Catholics of his diocese, but even those who might come to study from overseas. On his journeys he had seen a new type of school that departed from the classical model. In Germany it was the *Realschule*, and in the United States, business colleges such as "Packard's University in New York." In France there were institutes of commerce and *Ecoles Spéciales des Arts et Manufactures*. And so he began a commercial school in Manchester, first at Grosvenor Square, and in 1877 moved it to Alexandra Park. In the 1880s he extended the experiment to St Bede's on the Rhine in Germany.

When Herbert Vaughan began St Bede's, England was unfamiliar with the idea of a business school, *école de commerce* or *Realschule*.[64] The schools conducted on traditional classical lines had no special relation to industrial Lancashire. According to Snead-Cox, despite school-leavers being able to write tolerable Latin verse, they had "failed to acquire those habits of sustained industry, of precision of thought, and exactness of language which were needed to fit them for a commercial career. No better centre for such a commercial or technical school as the Bishop designed could have been found than at his doors in Manchester."[65]

The "Catholic Commercial College" began in 1875 in a former Baptist chapel in Grosvenor Square, Manchester. Only later was it renamed St Bede's Manchester College. It was not far from Owen's College. The school opened its doors to the first students—fourteen boys—in January 1876.[66] The aim of the college was the "education of Catholic boys of the middle classes who were destined for a business or professional career." The first headmaster was Fr Charles Wood, a convert from Anglicanism, who had studied for the priesthood at Rome. He was assisted by James Hayes.[67]

Vaughan's plans did not stop at Grosvenor Square. According to Bolton, following the Platonic idea that the young should be able to see and think about beauty, Vaughan decided to build a college in "as noble and as beautiful a style as his funds would permit."[68]

Vaughan staffed the school with priests of the Diocese of Salford and "gifted laymen, whether English or foreign." He did not invite the help of any religious group because he wanted to retain direct control of the new institution, and because he wished it to be "a means of helping to form a clergy *colto e civile*."

In 1877 Charles Wood was succeeded by Thomas Wrennall, formerly a classics master at St Cuthbert's, Ushaw. Vaughan appointed a "brilliant scholar" as prefect of studies, Louis Charles Casartelli. Casartelli was to become bishop of Salford. One of the other early members of staff was Vaughan's youngest brother, John. After he was ordained in 1876 he taught mathematics at St Bede's. Another teacher was Canon Moyes, who edited the *Dublin Review* for a time and followed Vaughan to Westminster.[69]

The first prospectus, issued in 1876, illustrates how determined Vaughan was to be a pioneer. He wanted the school to be a "more direct and practical preparation for the Civil Service, and such professions as must be entered at an early age, by concentrating the attention of its scholars upon modern languages and the more useful branches of science." In a commercial career the young Catholic would be a good provider for his family, rise up the social ladder, and gather resources "whereby he may be enabled to perform great works of mercy and charity, to the honour of God and the salvation of souls."

Some months after beginning at Grosvenor Square, Oxford Road, Mr Constantine Kelly bought two houses in south-west Manchester facing Alexandra Park for a "bachelor friend," who was Herbert Vaughan. Next to the houses was the Manchester Aquarium. The building was for sale and thought to be suitable only as a music hall. Bolton describes the Aquarium with its "magnificent timbered roof," and the school built by Vaughan against it as "a Florentine palazzo in red terra-cotta, planned in an ample and spacious way, and paved with mosaic." Vaughan, in order to protect the site of his college, decided to buy the Aquarium, but the building had cost £22,000 to build and Vaughan "had not six pence." Kelly was asked to offer £7000 for the building but when the news leaked out that Kelly's friend was Bishop Vaughan, "zealous opponents of Popery urged each other to step into the breach ... in the name of science and Protestantism to avert the catastrophe."[70]

Negotiations with Kelly were broken off, and the property went for public auction. Vaughan was the highest bidder with £6800, and so he took over the Aquarium, fish, refreshment stands, chairs and a stock of sheet glass. An hour after the purchase was settled, Vaughan met with clergy and laity to explain that he felt "strongly that in a few years he might have grave reasons for self-reproach" if he had let the opportunity slip by.[71] Snead-Cox describes the "wonderful time" that followed when Vaughan tried to manage the Aquarium.[72] When the venture failed, Vaughan took on the building as part of his commercial college, and in October 1877 the foundation stone was laid for a new wing. In May he announced to the diocese that the cost of the aquarium and the new addition was £19,000. The new section was opened in 1880 and a central block in 1884. The chief feature of the main floor was a corridor sixteen feet wide and two hundred and eighty five feet long.[73]

In June 1877 Vaughan wrote to Louis Casartelli from a health spa in Flanders that he thought they "must aim rather at a commercial and practical course than a purely technical one in Manchester." The Catholics of Manchester, he thought, ought to make provisions to meet the general need for a Catholic commercial college in the community, and for Catholics who come to study in England "from America, Australia and Europe."[74]

The 1879 diocesan almanac states that two courses were offered at St Bede's: an elementary course which boys could enter at seven years to get a "sound English education and modern languages, Latin and Greek being optional," lasting between four and seven years, and a preparatory class leading to a "first class certificate from the Education Department of the Privy Council."[75]

Among the educational experiments initiated by Vaughan was the establishment of a subsidiary college in Germany. He started St Bede's on the Rhine during the autumn of 1886, in the palace of the Metternich family at Bonn. "English boys were to be given the opportunity of pursuing German and other studies in an atmosphere that would not be entirely foreign, and at the same time a few German students were to be accepted lest the house should remain too exclusively English."[76]

While Vaughan was at Salford, the commercial college was very much the "Bishop's College." Casartelli, years later, recalled the powerful influence Vaughan had over St Bede's when he—Casartelli—was on the staff: "The characteristic note of his relation to the College was his intense personal, minute interest in all that concerned the new school, even down to the smallest details." Much of the system and routine of college life were due to Vaughan's influence. For example, he insisted that staff and students dine together. "When at home, His Lordship always took meals together with us; and what is more, he insisted on presiding and carving, saying he was the Admiral and the Rector was the Captain of the flagship." Casartelli remembered Vaughan giving a hand at manual work in the school: "I can still see him up on a ladder in the first room set apart for a chapel ... hammer in hand, nailing up tapestry behind the space where the altar was to be; or armed with a crowbar, opening large boxes at the front-door containing handsome gifts he had bought or procured for the adornment of his College."[77] Vaughan was not only the "founder but also chief benefactor of St. Bede's."[78]

A reporter for the *Daily Telegraph* visited Herbert Vaughan just before he was transferred to Westminster in 1892.[79] The bishop, he wrote, was staying in a "small villa" attached to the college, and met him in a "little study." He described Vaughan as a "grey-haired handsome gentleman with clear-cut features and keen blue eyes, dressed in a black gown and violet-edged soutane." When the reporter entered, Vaughan was busy writing at a table "covered with papers and surrounded by shelves crammed with books and pamphlets." On the walls were illustrations of the "Life of the Saviour and of the Madonna."

After a brief conversation about Vaughan's views and social schemes the bishop led his guest up a staircase and at the top he pulled aside a heavy curtain before an entrance to a wing of the college, There they met the vice-rector, Francis Hart. A question was asked about the use of corporal punishment: Hart explained that it was given to younger boys, and Vaughan added: "I know that I've received it but suppose I'm too old for it now."[80]

At one point Vaughan showed the reporter his "school of Christian art." It was in a studio "filled with finished and unfinished pictures, sketches and designs." The finished works the reporter described as of "full breath, rich colour, delicate execution." Vaughan had brought an artist named Stopoloni from Italy in 1890 or 1891. The artist's assistant was a young man from Bolton.

As they walked through the college, the reporter noticed that whenever they met a student "the Bishop had a kindly word or a pat on the head for him" and that none of them tried to avoid meeting Vaughan. Casartelli recalled that Vaughan spent fourteen of his twenty years at Salford living simply and sharing the life of staff and students at St Bede's. An 1889 advertisement for the college noted: "The students dine and live with superiors as far as possible in the frank and easy terms of family life."[81]

One of the original benefactors, and a co-founder of Vaughan's Manchester College, was Abbot Hunter-Blair.[82] He pointed out that Vaughan's "commercial education" did not in practice exclude the humanities. This view was clear when Vaughan decided, in March 1891, to amalgamate the Salford Catholic

Grammar School, founded by Bishop Turner in 1862, and St Bede's College. Vaughan recalled that the aim of Turner's school was to foster vocations to the priesthood and to give a sound education to boys of a "respectable class." Some thought that Vaughan's decision to join his minor seminarians and the lay students of the college was one of expediency. But Vaughan justified the union as part of the effort of the Church to enter into "contact with the people of England."[83] The college still has the preparatory school which served as a junior seminary until the 1970s. By then some five hundred priests had received their early training at St Bede's.[84]

When Snead-Cox was preparing his biography of Herbert Vaughan, St Bede's College could claim that more than two thousand boys had been educated there, and that, for the year 1910, there were 180 students. "No one could wish for Cardinal Vaughan a worthier or more lasting monument."[85]

Accademia of the Catholic Religion

Henry Manning visited Lancashire in January 1876 and called attention to the success Vaughan was having in Salford Diocese. It was 10 January and Manning was giving the inaugural address of the "Accademia of the Catholic Religion" in Manchester. During Wiseman's final illness he had asked Manning to take the lead in founding an academy in London. Eleven years later Manning was present to "congratulate the Bishop of Salford that in the city of Manchester in which with a vigorous authority he has already welded together the spiritual organization of the Church, he has successfully founded this intellectual agency." Vaughan's aim was that his people "shall be abreast, at least, with the highest culture of this great city."[86]

Dispute between Local Ordinaries and Religious Orders

The closure of the Jesuit school at Manchester did not resolve a fundamental issue raised by the conflict between the Bishop and the Jesuits; did the bishops have jurisdiction over regulars working in their dioceses? Some thought that a clear definition of the relationship between bishops and religious orders was needed.[87]

At the annual post-Easter meeting of bishops on 12 April 1877, Henry Manning proposed that Ullathorne and Clifford should prepare a petition asking Rome for a new constitution determining relations between the hierarchy and the orders. Manning's resolution was passed and, on 13 April, questions needing resolution were drawn up and approved. At the end they were reduced from twenty-five to twelve.[88] The meeting agreed that each diocese should send the facts concerning their grievances to Ullathorne. Bishop Ullathorne prepared a draft and Bishop Clifford approved it. In May 1877 a party of clergy and laity was in Rome for the jubilee of the episcopal ordination of Pius IX. They carried along a gift from English Catholics of £24,000. Vaughan had arrived earlier and was present at the presentation. Clifford was asked to report to Propaganda on behalf of the English bishops: they were preparing a document to present to the congregation in November 1877. Clifford saw Monsignor Rinaldini, the secretary to the prefect, Cardinal Franchi, and presented the message of the English bishops.[89]

The representatives of the religious orders, or regulars, were already at work presenting their own case. They claimed their colleges were immune from episcopal jurisdiction, and that Jesuit missions should not be divided, that is, new missions staffed with secular priests should not be set up in any place where a Jesuit mission existed.[90] On 10 May Manning wrote to Clifford that "nothing will suffice but a final norm in the form of a constitution."

During the summer Clifford and Ullathorne worked on a final document and it was approved at a meeting of bishops at Birmingham on 30 July. The document, called the *Relatio* in Vaughan's notes, was amended and printed on 19 September. On 5 November Manning went to Rome with Clifford. The Cardinal presented the *Relatio*, and, on 5 December, Cardinal Agnozzi asked for a large number of additional copies. For their part, the Jesuits presented a "statement against the Bishops to Propaganda." The bishops retained a consultor, an ecclesiastical lawyer, Ludovico Martini, while the religious orders used the canonist Fr Ballerini. A decision was to be given at Easter 1878. However, in February 1878, Pope Pius IX died and the events surrounding his death delayed the business of the court.

Before leaving Rome on 26 March, Clifford drew up four papers for the lawyer, Martini, concerning the position of the Church in England. He also left with an agreement that the "case should be treated in autumn." On 18 July the bishops of Scotland formally joined in the controversy on the side of their English counterparts. September passed, and finally, on 13 November, Martini wrote concerning the delays. On 2 December he wrote again to say that he could not be ready until the end of January 1879. Clifford wrote to Agnozzi that he was coming to Rome himself but was told that he could come, but that the "regulars want more time." In February he went to Rome, but was informed that the "regulars had done nothing." The case dragged on and Clifford began to feel that the impartiality of the court was under suspicion since most of the cardinals meeting at Propaganda were religious. Strained relations continued into 1880.[91]

Vaughan was in Rome at the beginning of 1880. Manning wrote to him asking that he remain there until Clifford arrived. "I believe that the whole world of intrigue is up, and the other world of timidity and compromise is ready to give way." On 17 January Manning wrote of the bishop and the secular priesthood: "... instituted both without vows ... to be the example and law of perfection, the light of the world and the salt of the earth in the law of Charity which is the spiritual perfection of God and man. To restore this truth to vigour is to raise the Secular Clergy and to raise the Secular Clergy is to raise the Church throughout the world.”[92] A few days later Manning wrote to Vaughan again: “God has laid on you and the Bishop of Clifton this duty, and in Rome you must stay.” Clifford and Vaughan resolved to stay till the end of the case, believing that they were faced with an organized policy of delay.

Propaganda was under the impression that there would be a swift and amicable solution because the chief characters were cousins: the Jesuit provincial, Alfred Weld, and his relatives, Vaughan and Clifford.[93] The Roman officials described the protagonists for the bishops: Manning was *il diplomatico*, Clifford *l'avvocato*, and Vaughan, due to his persistence during the case concerning the Jesuit college at Manchester, *il diavolo*.[94]

Manning arrived in Rome early in April 1880, but the value of his assistance was somewhat doubtful. It was suggested that he revealed too much and was therefore persuaded to return home.[95] On 17 May 1880 the regulars replied to the commission set up to hear the arguments. The case was delayed again until the courts were to reassemble in November, and so Vaughan remained in Rome through the summer as a “symbol of the unity between the English Bishops.”

On 3 September Vaughan wrote to Cardinal McCloskey of New York asking his opinion concerning what “effect of the admission of such claims” by the religious orders would have in the United States. Vaughan wanted to mention McCloskey's opinion privately to members of the commission: “It would help them form their opinion and realize that the great Church of the United States is as much concerned as we are in the decision.” Vaughan proceeded to lay out the arguments clearly, stressing that if the orders made good their “claim to privileges and exemptions against us in the first place,” they would move to apply them to the United States and Australia. On 5 November 1880, McCloskey wrote to Vaughan stressing the importance of the issue for the United States and Vaughan passed on copies of his letter to the commission.[96]

While the English bishops were united and enjoyed the support of the bishops of Scotland and the United States, the religious orders were often divided and ready to compromise. In addition, the delaying tactics of their lawyers often alienated supporters.[97]

In the beginning of January 1881 the commission decided in favour of the bishops and sent its findings to the Pope, Leo XIII. Between January and May it was still not clear what form the Pope's decision would take, nor when it would be issued. Finally, on 14 May the decision, *Romanos Pontifices*, was published. The document was considered a victory for the English bishops. Manning wrote to Vaughan on 18 May that he could only “thank God for it, and God grant that it may be the last internal conflict in the Church in England. It is the third, and I trust it may be the last. It has been a hand-to-hand fight.” Vaughan and Clifford went to see the Pope on 23 and 27 May.

On 2 June Vaughan left Rome and went to a health spa at Kissingen in Bavaria. He wrote to Caroline Hanmer at Mill Hill: "I have been following the doctor's orders in coming here and drinking these waters for four weeks. I believe it was well that I came, for I felt that in a little while I should fall to pieces, but now I believe I shall be made up again and go on better than before, but quietly." He remained in Bavaria until 5 July when he returned to England. He had been absent for a year and a half.[98] There was a rumour in Rome that he was about to be made co-adjutor to Cardinal Manning at Westminster. Instead he remained at Salford for more than ten years.[99]

The Bull *Romanos Pontifices* of 1881 made only minor concessions to the religious orders. Bishop Ullathorne "read and re-read it with increased delight." He saw the bishop's office strengthened all through the document and even considered it an answer to objections raised about the infallibility issue at the Vatican Council, that is, that it would weaken the bishops' position.[100]

Bishop Herbert Vaughan had left Salford Diocese on 2 December 1879 and returned on 13 July 1881. He was solemnly received by the chapter and clergy at the doors of St John's Cathedral. In his address to those welcoming him, he spoke of Salford: "... the tenderness of the shepherd's care for his sheep, and of a father's love for his children, which God, in His goodness, permits me to feel for the members of my flock, draws me more close to Salford than to any other place in the world, and causes me a joy and thankfulness in returning here which I could know in no other spot on earth."[101]

Notes

1. Snead-Cox, 1, p.240.
2. Norman, *English Catholic Church*, p.361; J. A. Hilton, *Catholic Lancashire, from Reformation to Renewal, 1559-1991*, Phillimore, 1994, pp.92ff. Stephen Fielding, *Class and Ethnicity, Irish Catholics in England, 1880-1939*, Buckingham, Open University Press, 1993, pp.38ff; See: Charles Bolton, *Salford and its Catholic Past, Centenary*, Salford, 1950, p.17: Most of Salford Diocese belonged to the ancient Diocese of Lichfield, founded by St Chad. There were few parishes. Whalley Abbey built by the Cistercians with the help of Norman Lords of de Lacy was the most important institution. Of ancient Catholic life little was left but ruins; pp.27-8: The first weight of systematic persecution of the old faith was felt after 1571 when Parliament imposed severe penalties on "all who used the Pope's authority to reconcile or absolve Catholics who had accepted the Established Church and on all who dared to bring to England the Agnus Dei wax or pictures, blessed by the Pope." Among other laws all priests were ordered in 1585 to leave the country. Those who remained could be condemned to death along with those who gave them shelter.
3. Alan Kidd, *Manchester*, Keele University Press. Keele, 1993, pp.35-6.
4. Gerard Connolly, "The Transubstantiation of Myth: towards a new popular history of nineteenth century Catholicism in England," *JEH*, Jan 1984, 35, 1, p.78ff.
5. Norman, *Catholic Church*, p.361.
6. Hilton, *Catholic Lancashire*, p.100; David Lannon, "Bishop Turner and Educational Provi-

sion within the Salford Diocesan area, 1840-1870," M Phil thesis, Univ. of Hull, September 1994, p.2; SDA. 1878: William Turner was born at Whittingham Hall, Preston, on 25 September 1799. He was educated at Ushaw and Rome between 1813 and 1825 and was ordained at St John Lateran in Rome on 25 December 1825. His first appointment by the vicar apostolic, Bishop Penswick of the Northern District, was to St Augustine's, Granby Road, in March 1832.

7. Norman, *Catholic Church*, p.345; Snead-Cox, 1, p.v.

8. Norman, p.345; Bolton, *Salford*, p.131.

9. Bolton, *Salford*, p.118.

10. *ibid.*, p.131.

11. *ibid*; SDA. *Catholic Directory*, 1873, 1874.

12. Connolly, "Myth," pp.98-9.

13. Snead-Cox, 1, p.241.

14. *ibid.*, p.245;

15. *Manchester Guardian*, 29 October 1872, no 8, 175; Bishop Ullathorne, *Ecclesiastical Discourses*, London, Burns & Oates, 1876, pp.95&97-8.

16. Snead-Cox, 1, p.245; JA. John R. Slattery in his unpublished handwritten manuscript, "Biographie de J. R. Slattery," says that Turner had "completely abandoned in the last years of his life the government of the diocese to his vicar general, Canon Benoit. This resulted in an embarrassment for Vaughan as the new bishop and for those who knew Benoit." Slattery, who arrived at Mill Hill early in 1873, wrote that it was Manning who arranged for Benoit to administer the missionary college at Mill Hill. The original manuscript is deposited in the papers of "Houtin, Oeuvres, t.LIV, Bibliothèque Nationale, NAF 15741-15742."

17. *Manchester Guardian*, 29 October 1872.

18. Salford Diocesan Archives (SDA). Mary Elizabeth Herbert, 14 Via Veneto, Rome, February 12, 1904, to Bishop Casartelli.

19. *ibid.*: "I never heard of Pius IX having given him that ring but I never forgot his speech about it. It was a very poor cameo and Monsignor Dunn has got it;" Francis Bowen, "Cardinal Vaughan," *Catholic World*, 1933, vol 136, p.540: Vaughan remarked:" When people kiss my hand they will kiss her picture and not any part of myself."

20. Gerald Wayne Olsen, "Anglican Temperance Movements, *JEH*, 40, 2, April 1989, p.249.

21. Snead-Cox, 1, p.251.

22. *ibid.*, p.248.

23. *ibid.*

24. Norman, *Catholic Church*, p.353.

25. Snead-Cox, 1, p.249.

26. *ibid.*

27. Bolton, *Salford*, p.130.

28. Holmes, *More Roman*, pp.201-3; SDA. Mission Fund book, Board of Finance. A Board of Finance had been established by Turner on 11 January 1858. According to David Lannon, despite what Snead-Cox writes about the state of financial administration under Turner, it was not so poor. It was more a reflection of Vaughan's organizational mind.

29. WDA. Vaughan, Salford notes, 1872.

30. Holmes, *More Roman*, p.202; SDA. ACTA; Hilton, *Catholic Lancashire*, p.100: "He was an efficient administrator who placed the finances of the diocese on a firm foundation by his insistence on paying off the capital as well as the interest of any debts incurred to build churches."

31. WDA. San Francisco, 15 June 1896, Jerome to Herbert Vaughan.

32. Snead-Cox, 1, p.252; Holmes, *More Roman*, p.172; McCormack, p.137.

33. Peter Doyle, "The Education and Training of Roman Catholic Priests in 19th-Century England," *JEH*, 35, 2, April 1984, p.208: "It reflected a very narrow view of theology and was

partly responsible for the failure to develop a commitment to continued study after ordination in many of the clergy."

34. *ibid.*

35. McCormack, p.137.

36. Snead-Cox, 1, p.252.

37. Holmes, *More Roman*, p.173; It is not clear if those in the seminary were ordained priests or deacons after three years of theology. Probably deacons from the diocese and ordained priests from the Continent and elsewhere were joined together.

38. WDA. Herbert Vaughan, Salford notes. On 21 March 1873, he had an audience with Pope Pius IX: "I asked his direction saying that I had noticed he turned in his discourses to the people and not to Kings and Governments. The Holy Father said 'Yes, the Church is the Church of the people, I turn to them. I could give you many instances of the contempt of Government for religion.'"

39. Snead-Cox, 1, p.254.

40. Bolton, *Salford*, p.131.

41. *ibid*; Snead-Cox, 1, p.258.

42. Snead-Cox, 1, pp.260-7: Snead-Cox quotes from a letter written by Miss Alice Thompson, a convert, who was on the pilgrimage: "It was a pioneer effort, but it set an example which has been followed again and again, so that organised pilgrimages from our shores have long ago resumed their old place among the commonest manifestations of Catholic life and devotion;" The following year another pilgrimage was arranged to France. See: Ward, *History of St Edmund's*, pp.288ff.

43. Norman, *Catholic Church*, pp.361-2.

44. McCormack, p.148; Holmes, *More Roman*, p.203: "In an effort to increase the number of possible candidates for ordination Vaughan restricted the number of schools run by religious orders."

45. Oliver P. Rafferty, SJ, "The Jesuit College, Manchester, 1875," *Recusant History*, 20, 2, October 1990, pp.298-9.

46. *ibid.*, p.303, nn. 39 and 41. See: *Dublin Review*, 1863, pp.139ff.

47. See: Robert Gray, *Cardinal Manning*, London, Weidenfeld and Nicolson, 1985, pp.215ff:

48. Rafferty, "Jesuit College," pp.291ff: The ruling by the Pope that was to follow the line of events from Vaughan and the Jesuits at Manchester "represented a milestone in the development of the Roman Catholic Church in England in the 19th century." The hierarchy was restored but the Church continued to function much as it had under vicars apostolic. Although Wiseman and Manning had as priorities the elevation and professionalization of the secular clergy, for the most part it was undistinguished as a group and diocesan organization tended to be undeveloped. On the other hand the religious orders, especially the Jesuits, were well organized in England and had strong institutional representation at Rome. The English Church lacked finance, personnel and connections at Rome. Bishops depended on religious orders but the orders were for the most part not subject to the authority of the hierarchy. In addition, prior to 1850, as a mission country, many freedoms were extended to the orders. "The restoration of the hierarchy did nothing to effect detrimental change in the privileged status of the religious orders." Tension between the bishops and the orders was inevitable.

49. In 1803 a similar meeting was held at Old Hall, the first attempted by the vicars apostolic. Present were the senior bishop, Gibson, and seven others along with the president of St Edmund's and one representative of a religious order, the superior of the Trappists at Lulworth.

50. Ullathorne, *Discourses*, pp.115ff; Ullathorne, in Burton, *Sermons Preached at St.Edmund's College*, p.80; On page 77 Burton gives a list of bishops and provincials who attended. Included were the "President of the Anglo-Benedictines," and provincials of Dominicans, Jesuits, Passionists, Institute of Charity, and Redemptorists.

51. William George Ward was present for practically the last time. His house at Old Hall was

converted into a preparatory school for younger boys entering the college and known as "Wards" but officially called St Hugh's.

52. Rafferty, "Jesuit College," p.295ff.

53. *ibid.*, p.303, fn.22.

54. *ibid.*, p.299: The exchange between Gallwey and Vaughan was often uncivil. Another author is quoted by Rafferty, p.300: "As Pollen asserts" (*The Month*, "Cardinal Manning and the Jesuits," 137, 1921, p.482) "there is no doubt that the Jesuits must bear the blame (for the Manchester College crisis) of having judged these circumstances as amiss."

55. WDA. Vaughan Diaries. Rome dispute with the Society of Jesus.

56. *ibid.*; Snead-Cox, 1, p.303

57. *ibid.*: Pius IX nicknamed Vaughan his "Bishop of Trastevere" because of the proximity of Salford to Manchester, and pronounced his name "Vou-gan;" McCormack, p.153.

58. Rafferty, "Jesuit College," p.300-301; Snead-Cox, 1, p. 320.

59. Norman, *Catholic Church*, p.354.

60. SDA. Box 179. HV in Spain: copy of a diary of his companion. For the identity of his companion, see: 16 March, Valladolid: "Neither Fr. Gadd nor I ...;" And: Leslie, *Vaughan Letters*, p.277, Rome, March 3, 1876. An example of one of Gadd's entries: At Biarritz "met Fr. Strickland and Fr. O'Connor ... attended Vatican Council with his bishop... after the Council he started for Fiji and Sandwich Islands on which tour he has been about five years.... His tales of the Faith in those parts are very distressing."

61. SDA. ACTA, Low Week, 1876; See: Michael Williams, *St Albans College, Valladolid*, London, Hurot, 1986, pp.166-7; Praise of Vaughan's report is from: Peter Guilday, *The English Catholic Refugees on the Continent, 1558-1795*, London, Longmans, 1914, p.136, fn 1; The apostolic letter *Universalis Ecclesiae* had ended the purely missionary status to which England had reverted after the Reformation ... though England was still under the Congregation, Propaganda Fide, McCormack, p.147; The study was also part of an effort to establish a University College at Kensington in London. Rafferty, "Jesuit College," n.17; In November 1878 Vaughan went on another visitation, this time to Bruges and the English College, founded by the late Sir John Sutton. His companion was Mgr Boone. SDA. "Report on Visitation of Bruges College, 1878."

62. Mary Vaughan, p.103.

63. *Universe*, Sunday 10 October 1993, Special Feature, "St. Bede's College:" The Headmaster, John Byrne, had a mixed staff of seventy-six. The school motto is "Nunquam otio torpebat," i.e. He never drowses in idleness.

64. Snead-Cox, 1, p.305; Bolton, *Salford*, p.131.

65. Snead-Cox, 1, p.306.

66. *ibid.*; See: C. A. Bolton,"Cardinal Vaughan as Educator," *Clergy Review*, October 1947, Vol xxviii, no 4, pp.237-245.

67. Snead-Cox, 1, p.315; See: "Louis Casartelli," *Baeda*, St Bede's, Manchester, 1, 8, January 1913.

68. Bolton, "Educator," p.239.

69. Snead-Cox, 1, p.319: John Vaughan travelled to his brother Roger in Australia. When he returned to England he went to Cardinal Manning at Westminster. Again his health failed and he went to a Carthusian monastery near Lucca in Italy. In 1909 he was ordained auxiliary bishop of Salford and became rector of St Bede's.

70. *ibid.*, p.307; Bolton, "Educator," p.238: In another paragraph classical studies are set aside as being no longer suited to present needs: "The new order of circumstances in modern life requires a new provision in education. Experience daily proves that a considerable number of Catholic youth, whose social position rightly entitles them to a polite, refined, and liberal education, are no longer able to devote those years to study of Greek and Latin literature which are essential to obtain a real mastery of this branch of learning."

71. Snead-Cox, 1, p.308: In the local newspaper it was reported that Vaughan "only got possession of the property on Friday last at 4pm and at 5:30 the Bishop was in the act of giving to an assembly ... the lucid and masterly exposition of his motives."

72. *ibid*, p.311.

73. SDA. Among those who contributed were a Manchester merchant, Lawrence O'Neil, £6000, and Daniel Murphy of San Francisco, £1000.

74. SDA. Hotel de Flandre Spa, 25 June, Vaughan to Casartelli. Vaughan addressed Casartelli as "Lewis" in his correspondence. Casartelli studied at Louvain before coming to St Bede's: "There are I know many practical difficulties in way of the realization of such a project, arising not only from the poverty but from the character many from whom (*sic*) we wish to provide. But every great undertaking is fraught with difficulties. As to salaries for Professors: your best plan will be to ascertain what is expected by them, what they could be satisfied with. My resources will be taxed to the utmost until the school begins and therefore each case must be treated separately and according to its value. At present the salaries of lay teachers range from 60 to 130 or 150 (£);" Vaughan borrowed money for St Bede's from funds invested by St Joseph's, Mill Hill: SDA. "Loans from Mill Hill, total: 7795 pounds, at 5% per ann., repayable 16 months notice, November 1, 1879."

75. SDA. Advertisement, 1879, ACTA.

76. Bolton, "Educator," p.241; McCormack, p.167.

77. Bolton, "Educator," p.240; Casartelli, *Baeda*, 1, p.5, 1910.

78. MHA. HV.

79. MHA. *Daily Telegraph*, 31 March 1892.

80. Bolton, *Salford*, p.153: Hart helped to build St Bede's Chapel and was later parish priest at Padiham till he died in 1915.

81. SDA. 1889, ACTA.

82. Bolton, "Educator," p.244; Abbot Hunter-Blair wrote of Vaughan in 1937. See: *Baeda*, 12, 1, p.6: "My recollections of Herbert Vaughan during his years as Archbishop and Cardinal are those of a grand and noble figure, one that imparted unsurpassable dignity to the Church in England, the figure of a great Prince, who was also a most humble and devoted priest, as we learned (if we did not already know it) from his admirable biography." About the Snead-Cox biography Bolton wrote: "In some countries a similar work would have passed through twenty or thirty editions, and there would have been a much more enthusiastic cultus of his memory and name." See also the tribute by Casartelli in *Baeda*, 1, 1910.

83. Bolton, "Educator," p.243: Salford Catholic Grammar School with its classical studies was also the junior seminary of the diocese. Vaughan justified the move in November 1897 when he wrote: he was "always pleased when I hear that there is a large proportion of the lay as well as of the clerical element in our great diocesan colleges such as Ushaw, Old Hall, and St. Bede's. The advantages of such a union are well divided, and each would be the poorer and the weaker without them." Bolton was quoting Hunter-Blair, pp.3-4.

84. *Universe*, "St Bede's," 10 October 1993.

85. Snead-Cox, 1, p.319; *Universe*, "St Bede's": The Headmaster, John Byrne: "Our founder, Cardinal Vaughan was inspired by a vision whereby the pursuit of educational excellence in the last quarter of the 19th century was open to the Catholic children of Manchester."

86. SDA. Inaugural address, 10 January 1876, Accademia of the Catholic Religion, Manchester.

87. Snead-Cox, 1, p.321.

88. *ibid.*, p.322.

89. WDA. Vaughan Diaries: "Course of events and dates in Bishop's appeal on bishops versus regulars question."

90. Snead-Cox, 1, pp.323-4: Clifford to Manning, 6 May 1877.

91. WDA. Vaughan Diaries.

92. Snead-Cox, 1, p.332.

93. Purcell, *Manning*, p.508.
94. Snead-Cox, 1, p.333.
95. Holmes, *More Roman*, p.204.
96. New York Archdiocesan Archives, MF Roll 7, A 30–A 40. Rome, 3 Sept. 1880, Vaughan to Cardinal McCloskey: "The public question concerns the contention between the English and Scottish hierarchies and the Regulars or more strictly speaking the tenet. The Fathers hope to make good their claim to privilege and exemptions against us in the first place and then to apply them to the US and Australia. The matter therefore concerns the American Church almost as much as it does ours. The claims put forward are briefly and principally thus: 1. The right of the priests to open colleges wherever they please, the ordinary having no discretion to prevent their doing so. 2. The missions served by Regulars are to be treated as parishes; if they are divided, upon the observance of all canonical details required in the division of parishes properly so called, the Regular body has a right to possess and serve the dismembered portion. 3. The poor schools of the mission are incorporated in the order, so that they are entirely withdrawn from the authorities and visitation, and examination, even in catechism, of the ordinary. 4. The monies and coin intuita missionis are free in case of the regular missions from inspection and visitation of the Bishop."
97. Holmes, *More Roman*, p.203.
98. Snead-Cox, 1, pp.354–5.
99. Frederick Zwierlein, *Letters of Archbishop Corrigan to Bishop McQuaid and Allied Documents*, Rochester, Art Print, 1946, p.31: Corrigan to McQuaid: "I learn that Mgr. Vaughan is named Coadjutor to Westminster, cum jure. Manning will not risk the Roman journey this winter on account of poor health." And again on 12 February 1881: "I understand that the decision in Rome is favorable to the Bishops; item that Dr.Vaughan is made Coadjutor, or about to be made, to Westminster."
100. Butler, *Ullathorne*, pp.188–9; Holmes, *More Roman*, p.204.
101. SDA. Acta, 1882; Snead-Cox, 1, pp.355–7.

CHAPTER XI

Growing Foreign Mission Commitments

Peter Ludovico Benoit, Rector of Mill Hill

When Vaughan became Bishop of Salford, the Pope allowed him to become superior general of his missionaries, but he was instructed to hand over rectorship of the college to an assistant. The man he offered the post to was Canon Peter Benoit, the secretary of Bishop Turner at Salford. Vaughan was later to refer to Benoit as the "second founder" of St Joseph's Society of the Sacred Heart for Foreign Missions.[1] At Salford, Canon Benoit was affectionately called "Canon Benite."

Canon Peter Ludovico Benoit was born at Kuurne in the Diocese of Bruges, Belgium, on 1 November 1820. He was the seventh of twelve children of farmer Xaverius Josephus Benoit and Barbara Theresia Tanghe. From 1833 he was raised by his uncle, Philippus Benoit, the pastor of Merkem. He attended a Latin school at Roulers—Rousselaere, West-Flanders—from 1834 to 1840.[2] He became interested in becoming a missionary about the time Father Lefevre, who was working in Missouri in the United States, and later became Bishop of Detroit, came to visit his old school at Roulers in 1840. Lefevre had become a Vincentian in 1826 and then gone as a missionary to the United States, left the Vincentians, and worked for many years in Missouri.

Benoit considered presenting himself as a candidate for Lefevre's mission, but did not. Instead he went to study at the major seminary at Bruges on 1 October 1840. While preparing for the priesthood, he became a teacher, between October 1842 and August 1846, at Duinen College, a school connected with the major seminary, where he taught the fifth-year class. On 20 December 1845 Benoit was ordained deacon, and, after the summer holidays, in October 1846, when the college was moved elsewhere, he remained at the major seminary in order to prepare for ordination.[3]

While Benoit was teaching, he became friendly with the John Weld family of Preston who spent the winter months at their home in Bruges. He had been thinking about becoming a missionary to South Africa,[4] but Mr Weld told him of the great need for priests in England, and so he began to consider a future on the English mission. Probably in the summer of 1846 Benoit travelled to England and was the guest of the Welds for two months in order to learn English, still with the intention of going to South Africa. After his return to Bruges he expressed his interest in the English mission to his advisor, Mgr Faict, and wrote to Bishop George Brown, vicar apostolic of the Lancashire District. Brown wrote back "requesting that he consider working in Lancashire." Brown had been informed that Benoit wished to devote himself "to the great and holy work of saving souls in the town of Manchester."[5]

After Benoit's ordination at Bruges on 29 May 1847 by Bishop Francis Boussen, he asked Mgr Faict to write again to Brown asking about possible work in Lancashire. Brown wrote to Faict on 10 August—he had not given a definite answer earlier because of an epidemic of typhus—accepting Benoit. With his own bishop's permission, on 17 August 1847, Benoit became the first Flemish missionary priest for England.[6]

Benoit's first appointment was to St Augustine's, Granby Row, in Manchester, where the parish priest was William Turner, the vicar general and later first bishop of Salford. When Turner became bishop, Benoit was his personal secretary and a canon of the chapter. In 1852 he became vicar general and "confidential advisor" to Turner. The large extension of schools during Turner's time was due in a great measure to Peter Benoit's zeal and ability.[7]

Benoit was a hard worker, but often ill. For many years he felt a call to become a monk and to a "life where contemplation and caring for his soul would be submitted to a strict rule." Mgr Faict, his former teacher and advisor, had a difficult time persuading Benoit not to go to a monastery. After a retreat at Stonyhurst in 1869 Benoit wrote: "There is only a little time left of life for me, let me go ahead quickly and save my soul."[8]

In 1863 Benoit travelled to Rome in connection with the issue of Catholic education and the Roman Question, and while there he met the pope. In 1869 he attended the Vatican Council as a theologian to assist Bishop Turner.[9] He also assisted at the provincial councils at Oscott, and, at the third council, he was secretary to a section concerned with moral theology.

Vaughan probably knew Benoit for many years. He had stayed at Preston with the Welds, who were his relatives. Vaughan's uncle, William, the Bishop of Plymouth, had asked Benoit to help recruit priests in Bruges for England. De Muelenaere suggests that he met him at Malines where Vaughan presented his proposal for a missionary college in August 1863. Certainly Benoit learned of Vaughan's ideas when Wiseman brought Vaughan to Oscott to address all the English bishops, arguing for their approval of his missionary idea.[10] Benoit became one of the first supporters of the college at Mill Hill. His name and address appear on an 1868 list of volunteers, called "zelators," who collected donations for the college; zelators were able to speak with others about the work, and helped to recruit possible candidates. At the Vatican

Council Vaughan met him once again.[11]

As soon as Vaughan received the telegram from Rome confirming his appointment to Salford, on 9 October 1872, he wrote to Benoit, informing him of Rome's decision and asking him to visit him at Mill Hill. Vaughan asked that he come to London before 16 October, the day he was to begin a retreat at Clapham. At Mill Hill, probably on 15 October, Vaughan appealed to Benoit to take over the administration of the college as rector and to become his vicar. He wrote: "October 16,1872. Today I received the Brief nominating me to be Bishop of Salford. This is the Will of God: blessed for ever.... I have promised to propagate the devotion to the Blessed Sacrament—to Our Lady and St Joseph—and under them I place myself and my whole work and future!!"[12] Benoit returned to Salford to organize preparations for the ordination of Weathers and Vaughan on 28 October.

After the ordination, on 2 November, Benoit travelled to Mill Hill to look more closely at the work he was being asked to undertake. He told Vaughan that he wanted to make a thirty-day retreat in order to discern if the task was God's will for him. Vaughan thought that the young foundation could not remain so long without a rector. He also knew that Benoit was the best man for the task. Thirteen years earlier Benoit had been a candidate for the presidency of the English College at Bruges. In Vaughan's opinion, he had all the skills necessary to run the college and expand it. Benoit reduced his retreat to a week, beginning on 11 November at Manresa Retreat House. Benoit wrote in his journal: "May the Life of Jesus be my example."[13]

As soon as Benoit completed his retreat he took up his new position at St Joseph's College, Mill Hill. He wrote that he "thanked Providence for bringing him back to a seminary where among very pious youths he would be able to serve God according to a rule."[14] At once he applied his energies to the college construction programme. There was already a debt of £1800 on the new memorial church, and Vaughan refused to have the building blessed until all debts were paid in full. To help the college, Benoit made plans to spend his yearly holiday in Belgium seeking donations for the project and recruiting Flemish candidates.

When Benoit died in 1892, Vaughan recalled "the almost noisy discontent" which made itself felt when the time came for Canon Benoit's removal from Salford. Many families depended upon him entirely for guidance and many poor people depended on him for the means of subsistence. His alms were always given in secret. "Those who were helped by him best knew his kindness and benignity ... he was not one who was content to see others did their duty while he shirked his own."[15] Benoit was to serve Vaughan's missionary college and the society that developed from it for almost twenty years.

Expansion of Missionary Efforts

While he was Bishop of Salford, and later as Archbishop of Westminster, Vaughan remained superior of the missionary college and the society of missionaries formed at a meeting in Baltimore in 1875. During the 1870s he also helped to establish a complementary group of women, the Franciscan Missionary Sisters of St Joseph, and in 1875 he admitted the first four lay brothers into his new society.[16]

When he handed the college over to Peter Benoit at Mill Hill, there were ten ordained priest-members of the developing organization. Vaughan tried to keep contact with each individual. Over the years each missionary was obliged to write to Vaughan at least once a year. To one he replied: "I thank you for your communications. They are a natural and most necessary means, whereby to ensure union with the head and peace and blessings upon the members."[17] One member said that Vaughan wanted to know all of his future missionaries at Mill Hill: "As Bishop of Salford it was his custom to spend over a week at Mill Hill for the yearly visitation between Easter and Pentecost." The visitation was not exclusively concerned with the members but also with the "youngest aspirants who were not yet bound to the society by the missionary oath." Each one appeared before Vaughan during his week-long visit. The interview was informal and lasted for about thirty minutes. Vaughan tried to "raise the interview to a confidential conversation that varied according to the nature and character of each student. Yet every conversation, however different from the rest, ended in the same manner with an urgent exhortation to continually beseech God for the true spirit of prayer."[18] Despite his affection for the missionary society and his continued efforts on its behalf up to his death in 1903, he was in charge only from the outside. He was not able to devote all his energy to the work and influence it from within.[19]

Peter Benoit's task as rector of St Joseph's was as a rule confined to the direction of the school, but he soon became Vaughan's collaborator and very often acting superior of the new society. Vaughan had great confidence in his vicar and a good working relationship grew up between the two men. Noel Hanrahan describes them as men of a "kindred spirit" and says that Vaughan trusted Benoit to communicate that spirit to the society.[20]

From Salford, Vaughan corresponded with Benoit at Mill Hill. The early letters touched on subjects such as ideas about the seminary buildings and college staffing. For example, Vaughan met a German-American priest in Rome, and on the recommendation of Propaganda, he took him on as a professor in February 1873.[21] But when Benoit wrote to say he wanted to take on another teacher from Belgium, Vaughan replied on 14 March 1873 that, "with regard a Professor from Belgium ... my only fear is bankruptcy court. You will have to set to work begging." On 6 April, Palm Sunday, he wrote again that Benoit had the "working of the college and my confidence and therefore should have my support as to the choice of persons" but wondered where the money was to come from to support them.[22]

John R. Slattery, the American recruit from Isaac Hecker's parish on the west side of Manhattan in New York, and the man who was, according to Peter Hogan, to become "the moving spirit in black Catholic work" in the United States until 1904, arrived at Mill Hill on 19 January 1873.[23] He described his experience many years later. The seminary course was divided into two sections, theology and philosophy. Slattery spent two or three months doing a refresher course in Latin and then began to study philosophy.

Benoit was rector but also taught church history. The vice-rector was David Charles Nicols, MA, a Cambridge graduate and a convert. He had been born at Mill Hill, where his father was the Church of England priest. He taught philosophy, was master of discipline and choir-master. He was also, according to Vaughan's correspondence, in charge of college finances. He left the college after Easter 1873. For many years he was in charge of the mission at Ongar in Essex.[24] Bernard Chevillion taught moral theology and sacred scripture.[25] The German-American priest from Rome, Fr George A.M. Braun, arrived two weeks after Slattery and began teaching philosophy. He had taught a course at New York University, and earlier at the seminary of Archbishop Hughes on the campus of Fordham University.[26] On the whole, the young Slattery found that "studies at Mill Hill were not strong." Training in the "spiritual life" was left to the individual with time for reading and a half-hour lecture by the rector each Sunday.

In the early days, discipline was sometimes lax. Slattery recalled that when he attended the City College of New York he had a break at noon to go outside for lunch, but he "never saw or heard of a boy abusing the privilege to enter a saloon, whereas at Mill Hill I have known seminarians to return as full as a tick."[27]

Despite its shortcomings, and the absence of Herbert Vaughan, the missionary college prospered and became the headquarters for St Joseph's Foreign Missionary Society of the Sacred Heart for Foreign Missions.[28]

During his summer holiday in June 1873, Peter Benoit went on a begging tour of Belgium. His first stop was to see Adolph Duclose, who prepared a large etching of the new college which was published in the Flemish "Rond den Heerd" along with a bit of history about the missionary venture at Mill Hill and an appeal for help written by Benoit.[29] Under his direction, and with regular reference to Vaughan, the construction at Mill Hill continued. The memorial church was opened on the feast of St Joseph in 1873, and was consecrated on 31 March 1874. On 13 April 1875 a special statue of St Joseph and an altar was dedicated and "crowned" as the national shrine by Manning. Seven other English bishops were present, along with many guests.

During the six years he took part in the formation of missionaries, Herbert Vaughan initiated a spirit through his example, his writings and weekly conferences. It was left to Benoit to try to "consolidate that missionary spirit with his own example and ideals into the hearts of future members of the Society." Vaughan credited Benoit as being not only the second founder of the society but as the "true founder of this house."[30]

Mission in the United States

The initial major problems for the new society soon appeared in the United States. Vaughan had accepted the invitation of the Archbishop of Baltimore to dedicate his first band of missionaries to the evangelization of the African-American population in the United States. But Vaughan saw the American mission as only a preparation for a more ambitious enterprise, that the Mill Hill missionaries in the United States would prepare African-Americans for the evangelization of Africa. He still hoped for work in the colonies of the British Empire and an independent mission territory entrusted to his missionaries. According to Slattery, the evangelization of the African-Americans was hardly mentioned at Mill Hill. In contrast, he recalled the great excitement that broke out when Rome assigned a mission in Madras, India.[31]

In addition, when Vaughan became a bishop and remained superior general, some of the bishops who had been involved in the 1866 provincial council in the United States anticipated jurisdictional problems. They wondered: What would be the status of the Josephites, as the missionaries were called, in a local diocese when their superior was a bishop, and living outside the United States?[32]

In the United States, the three missionaries remaining after the death of Cornelius Dowling were reinforced by two more. The mission had also expanded from Baltimore into Louisville, Kentucky, in 1874 and to Charleston, South Carolina, in 1875.[33] As willing and dedicated as Benoit was at Mill Hill, he was compelled to clear matters with Vaughan at Salford. It proved to be an administrative weakness that "nearly destroyed" the undertaking in the United States. And so, despite the working relationship between Vaughan and Benoit in England, the "long-distance management of the United States' missions through an assistant proved unsuccessful."[34]

First Chapter in Baltimore

The year 1875 was a significant one in the development of Vaughan's missionary society. It was a time when he and Benoit had an opportunity to remedy administrative and leadership problems, and to ease the personnel crisis in the American mission. The American provincial superior, James Noonan, had written to Vaughan in September 1874 urging him to take steps to form his missionaries into a congregation "as at present we are neither regulars nor purely secular priests.... Why should not the members have the advantages of the religious life while they have, if I may use the expression, its disadvantages."[35] Vaughan wrote back in October asking Noonan to discuss his ideas with his colleagues. He urged them to lay down "the official rules of the Society" so that they could be presented to a meeting planned at Baltimore during a visit Vaughan proposed for January 1875.[36]

On Thursday, 7 January 1875, Vaughan, Benoit, four new priests, a deacon, and Vaughan's secretary at Salford, Charles Joseph Gadd, sailed for the United States aboard the *Oceanic*.[37] They arrived at Sandy Hook on Thursday, 21 January 1875. On 22 January they landed in New York after paying a bribe of two pounds to a customs officer. "So much for Republican honesty," Benoit wrote in his diary. The group hired two horse-drawn coaches to carry them to Pennsylvania Station and took a train for Baltimore. Vaughan and his party arrived in Philadelphia at 3.30 p.m. and went to the cathedral. They met the bishop's chancellor and secretary, who still carried in his breviary a picture of St Joseph which Bishop Vaughan had given him during his first visit to the United States. At 6 p.m. they took the train for Baltimore and reached St Francis Xavier later in the evening.

At St Francis Xavier, Vaughan called together the first general chapter of his missionaries. The meeting began on Tuesday, 26 January 1875, and the missionaries soon began to discuss the preparation of a body of laws and procedures for a society whose goal was "to propagate the Gospel among the unevangelized races beyond Europe."[38] Vaughan wrote to Mary Elizabeth Herbert on 2 February that the twelve attending the meeting had been discussing the "constitutions of St Joseph's Society, which were drawn up four years ago and which I had not brought forward." When they finished preparing the document, Vaughan was pleased beyond his expectations at the way everyone accepted it. He quoted from the "Rule," which began with the words: "As the Society is an Apostolic Institution endeavouring to follow as closely as possible in the footsteps of Our lord and His apostles, it attaches the greatest importance to the practice and spirit of Evangelical Poverty, which is properly called the foundation of the Apostolic Life."[39]

The meeting at Baltimore produced the first official body of rules for St Joseph's Society and also a specific hierarchical chain of command. Vaughan was elected superior general for life, and Benoit, who had given up his position as a canon of Salford Diocese, became a member of the new community. On Saturday, 6 March, Benoit wrote in his notes: "We have now resigned our Canonicate.... May I yet be the instrument of the salvation of many souls and thereby be better prepared when my turn comes."[40] In the office of superior general, Vaughan was at the top of the pyramid of administration. Under him were a vicar, who was Benoit, and provincials, who were responsible for areas or provinces of the society. Dowling, and after him, Noonan, had already been referred to as provincials of the mission to the United States.[41]

It was hoped that the missionary society thus constituted had a structure and rules that would solve some of its difficulties, but they did not do so, for some "fundamental problems remained unsolved." Vaughan was superior general, but Salford, and other commitments to the English Church, demanded most of his time and energy. According to Stephen Ochs, even letters from the United States were lost in the paper shuffle between Benoit at Mill Hill and Vaughan at Salford. And so communications between England and America broke down.[42]

Vaughan hurried back to England, where he was in the middle of the controversy with the Jesuits in Manchester, but Benoit stayed on, making an extended tour of the United States. Benoit kept detailed notes of his trip down the east coast, along the coast of the Gulf of Mexico to New Orleans, up the Mississippi to Natchez and Vicksburg, then circled by rail from Memphis to Little Rock, and ended up going through St Louis, Louisville, Cincinnati, Detroit, Niagara, Albany and finally to New York City. In each place he contacted local church leaders and investigated potential mission areas.[43]

The missionaries from Mill Hill in the United States were committed to work exclusively among African-Americans, and for this they suffered "poverty, isolation and exhaustion, which eventually sapped the vitality of many." Death claimed three of the first four missionaries within four years of their arrival, and frustration and despair were to drive the fourth, James Noonan, to leave the society.[44] Schools constituted one of the most taxing responsibilities for the missionaries and so they scrambled "to secure faculty, money, and facilities for them." According to Ochs and Steins, by December 1878 the nine missionaries in the United States had "fallen victim to fatigue, frustration and dissatisfaction." Benoit's notes, made during his tour, had to wait for a much later use, except where they concerned the new stations opened in Louisville and Charleston.[45]

The opening of the Madras mission in 1875 began a process of "subordination of the American province." The provincial in the United States, James Noonan, was proving himself unequal to the task of his office. In his own words, he had developed, "a distaste for the work of being a priest for the coloured people." Never a strong personality, he became increasingly despondent and isolated from his colleagues. Decision-making continued to be delayed and complicated between men on the missions, through the provincial, Noonan, to Benoit at Mill Hill, and finally Vaughan at Salford—and then back again by slow sea post. Morale plunged, threatening the continued existence of the St Joseph's Society in the United States.[46]

India: Madras

While the mission in the United States struggled for existence, Vaughan was called to other overseas commitments. He returned to England on 15 February 1875 and found a request from the vicar apostolic of Madras in India asking him to send missionaries. Benoit was travelling in the United States and did not arrive at Liverpool aboard the *Britannic* till 8 June. Vaughan wrote to him on 16 June: "Welcome home again!" and urged that "we must have some other than the negro American mission. It is only half a mission."[47] According to Peter Hogan, Benoit's hopes and plans must have evaporated on his return to England when he discovered Vaughan had made other commitments, or was about to do so.[48]

In July 1875 Bishop Stephen Fennelly visited Mill Hill and spoke to Vaughan about obtaining some priests for the Telegu Mission in the Madras vicariate. On 15 August Vaughan wrote to Propaganda for approval of a plan to help Fennelly. Cardinal Franchi, the prefect, approved on 31 August and asked that the missionaries devote themselves to the conversion of the "heathen" and "apply themselves to the study of the indigenous languages."[49]

In 1832 the Vatican had attempted to break the hold of the Portuguese *padronado*—patronage—in India by establishing a number of new vicariates. When the vicariate apostolic of Madras was founded in 1834 it was entrusted to priests from Ireland. The mission to South India has also been called the Maynooth Mission to India.[50]

On 2 November 1875 Cardinal Manning presided over the departure ceremony for the first band of four missionaries bound for India. They were led by David Forbes, a Cork doctor, who had given up his medical practice to become a priest. He was given the title of provincial.[51] The other three were: John Sabbe from Belgium, who died in India less than three years later; Joseph Grand, a Frenchman, who never returned home again and worked on the Madras mission for forty-seven years; and Theodore Dieckmann, a German, who was a missionary in India up to his death in 1913. Dieckmann succeeded Forbes as superior when the doctor left after three years because of poor health.[52]

The men travelled overland to Marseilles where they sailed east aboard the SS Meikong. They landed in India on 7 December 1875 and stayed with Bishop Fennelly at Madras. They were to care for the Telegu mission in Guntur District which had an area of 5006 square miles and a total population of six thousand Catholics. There were 1037 families in 162 villages. The priests arrived at their headquarters at Phiringipuram on 28 December.[53]

Cholera, smallpox and a great famine from 1876 to 1878 were to tax the resources of the new missionaries. In addition they had also been asked to care for the Nellore district. In 1878 they reported that they had a total Catholic population of 9912 and that the "number of baptisms from heathenism only amounted to 2,247."[54]

At the end of 1876 four new missionaries were assigned to the Telegu mission in Madras: Mayer from Canada; Krott from the Netherlands; Rettori from Italy; and Hermans from Belgium. A reporter from *Revue Catholique* of Louvain was present at the departure ceremony on 26 December. After the homily the men made their missionary promise to the rector, and those present came forward for the kiss of peace, in which some kissed the feet of the departing missionaries. The congregation sang *L'Hymne des missionaires de Gounod* which had been translated into English. Canon Bamber gave the benediction and a procession carrying cross and banners moved out of the college grounds towards the train station while the rosary was recited and the *Magnificat* sung.[55] By the middle of 1878 there were twelve missionaries in India.

The Canadian missionary, Theophyle Mayer, became vicar general of the vicariate of Madras in 1882 and, on 4 November 1893, auxiliary bishop.[56] Fennelly had died in 1881 and was replaced by Mgr J. Colgan. It was he who named Mayer vicar general. Mayer was also administrator of the cathedral. One other missionary from Mill Hill worked at the cathedral and taught at Notre Dame Seminary while four others worked in the Madras area. Eleven missionaries with four local priests looked after almost the whole of the Telegu mission.

The Madras Archdiocese had a population of 7,085,784 non-Christians and 44,153 Catholics. The Catholics were made up of three groups: the Europeans and Eurasians who lived mainly in Madras and its surroundings of Chingleput and Arcot; the Tamils; and the Telegus who lived in the districts of "Guntoor, Nellore, Cuddapur, Kurnoll and Bellary."[57]

Vaughan hoped that his missionaries might have the Telegu mission entrusted to them as their own, and Franchi's letter in 1875 indicated that a distinct mission might be assigned to Mill Hill. However, it was only in 1928 that St Joseph's Society was assigned its own mission with the establishment of the diocese of Nellore. The long delay and confusion over the role of a Mill Hill provincial in the archdiocese "was a constant source of frustration and annoyance to members working in Madras."[58]

Herbert Vaughan supported one of the achievements of the Telegu mission, the founding of St Joseph's Seminary at Nellore for the training of local clergy. In 1882 John Kleinschneider began the seminary in two thatched huts, one which had formerly housed a cotton press, and an adjoining bungalow. A part of the building was set aside for a church. Vaughan wrote to Kleinschneider in 1890 that: "It is the most important work which can be undertaken. The formation of native clergy roots religion in the country in a way that strangers never can establish it. It was through neglect of this that Japan lost the Faith and that religion in many countries has decayed. The growth of a native clergy must always be slow and needs much patience. But it is in the end the most splendid service that can be rendered to men."[59]

In the same year, 1882, Theodore Dieckmann became the founder of the Congregation of Native Sisters of St Francis. They soon opened schools and convents throughout the Telegu mission. Vaughan considered the founding of the sisterhood "only second in importance to the establishment of a native priesthood."[60]

By the end of 1900, thirty-seven priests from Mill Hill had worked among the Telegu and twenty-three were still active. After more than twenty-five years, Vaughan's missionaries still had no separate mission and the missionaries felt that as long as the Telegu mission remained a part of Tamil country around Madras, their mission would not be fairly treated. In January 1902 John Aelen became an assistant bishop to Colgan with the right of succession. In February Vaughan wrote to Colgan that he was anxious about the work of St Joseph's Society in the Archdiocese of Madras and he asked that an "agreement come to a few years ago to make Bellary a separate diocese should not be abandoned but put forward again before Propaganda." Vaughan wanted to give preference to the Bellary districts in the next appointment of missionaries from Mill Hill, provided they were given their own diocese.[61]

In 1975, Noel Hanrahan, one of Vaughan's successors as superior general, wrote of his impressions of the St Joseph's Society contribution to the Indian Church: "What I found was not a struggling Mission but a well-established and flourishing Local Church. The one mission of the early days had given rise to no fewer than four dioceses, each under the direction of an Indian Bishop and each having as many local priests as ever there were missionaries in the whole area.... This is a success story of which the Society, and our Telegu missionaries in particular, can justly be proud.... Perhaps the key to success was the early emphasis on the formation of native clergy."[62]

Afghanistan, Chaplains, and the British Expeditionary Force

Vaughan, assisted by Peter Benoit, tried to keep pace with requests from Propaganda to provide missionaries for areas under British rule. On 18 January 1879 a request came from the Pope that St Joseph's Society supply chaplains to the British army in the Punjab. The letter came through Mgr H. O'Callaghan, the representative of the English hierarchy at the Vatican. The British army was engaged in a campaign known as the Second Afghan War. The hope was that once the war was over the missionaries would be able to establish military chaplaincies at garrisons in Afghanistan, and from those bases initiate missions among the people of Kafiristan, the part of Afghanistan that had not yet accepted Islam. But the British army had no intention of occupying the whole of Afghanistan. In the treaty of Jacobabad the British had negotiated to place permanent garrisons at Kabul or Kandahar, or both, or place all their forces at Quetta. At first it looked as though garrisons would be kept at all three places. It was into this uncertain situation that Vaughan's men were drawn, and upon subsequent military decisions that the Mill Hill Afghanistan venture depended.

Many of the troops were Irish and so the army needed English-speaking priests, but the government preferred not to have Irishmen, suspecting their political sympathies.[63] The letter from Propaganda asked whether St Joseph's

Society would "take Afghanistan and send out three or four priests without delay." In a letter of 23 January Vaughan told Elizabeth Herbert that the Pope wished to make it into an Apostolic Prefecture. He wrote to Benoit wondering about the area: "I have heard that Peshawar is very unhealthy with temperature of 110 degrees in the shade." Vaughan telegraphed Rome, gladly accepting the request. "So now I suppose we shall have a field of our own and not a very easy one."

On 28 January he wrote Elizabeth Herbert that "Propaganda wants us to get Chaplaincies to the Army in Afghanistan; if the Government won't pay, Propaganda itself will. We shall be glad of any authentic news on Afghanistan."[64] Vaughan hesitated but when he was assured that his society would be given a territory in North India he agreed to assign four priests and did so on 9 March 1879. The leader was George A. M. Browne.[65] The others members were: John Aelen, Richard Burke and John van Eynthoven. The group left for Afghanistan on Tuesday, 15 April 1879. "People have foreseen their martyrdom," Vaughan wrote.[66] Burke was an American from near Rochester, New York; Aelen and van Eynthoven were Dutch; and Browne was American of German origin.[67]

The official reason for not giving a precise territory was that it was not the right time to do so. It may have been planned to carve out a prefecture from possible territory conquered in Afghanistan. According to John Rooney, this was implicit in the correspondence but was not explicitly stated.[68] In addition, the Italian Capuchins would have to be consulted if an area were to be given on the North West frontier. Mgr Jacopi in Agra was at first under the impression that the Mill Hill priests had come to assist him by taking over from his own missionaries a cholera-infested area on the frontier. Rome appointed Browne to be "Prefect of the Afghanistan Mission," but the vicariate was to stand or fall with English rule in Afghanistan.

On 17 May 1879 the little party arrived in Madras and shortly afterwards its members were posted to their stations. A letter to Vaughan from Browne is reproduced in a 1979 booklet by James van der Klugt and Michael Conroy:[69] Jhelum on the Eve of Pentecost 1879, they were at "the northernmost part of the railway. We travelled 2453 miles from Madras." Conroy and van der Klugt point to the problems that were to come up again and again: "The great distances to be covered, the huge areas incorporated in the existing vicariates, the deadly threat posed by disease, especially cholera.... The oblique reference to the difficulty of finding converts to Christianity among the Afghan tribes was ... almost prophetic. A hundred years later the difficulty is just as great as ever. Time does not solve all problems."[70]

Browne assigned Aelen to Kandahar, Burke to Quetta and van Eynthoven to Landi Kotal. By June they were all at work. Van Eynthoven had written to Browne that he was living in a tent and trying to make contact with the Catholic soldiers, and complained of the intense heat. Six days later Captain

1. Eliza Vaughan, 1810-53,
Herbert Vaughan's mother

2. John Francis Vaughan, 1808-80,
Herbert Vaughan's father

3. John Snead-Cox, 1855-1939,
Vaughan's cousin and biographer,
editor of *The Tablet*

4. Cardinal Nicholas Wiseman, 1802-65,
first archbishop of Westminster after the
restoration of the hierarchy in 1850

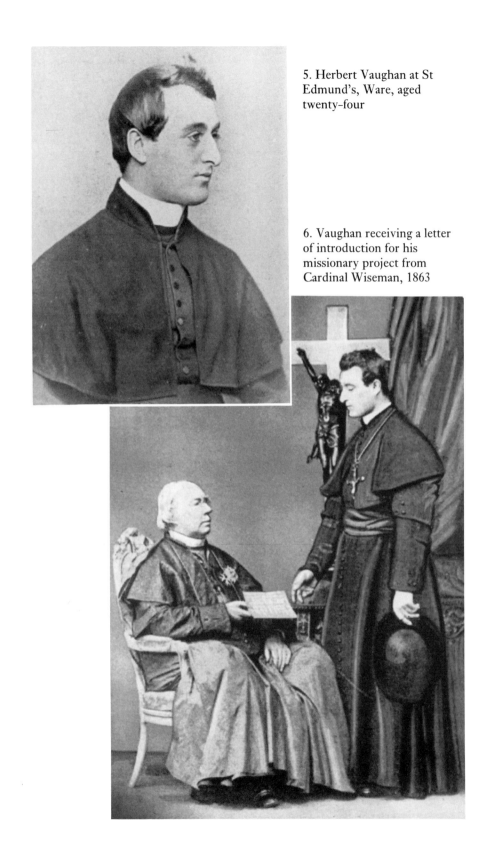

5. Herbert Vaughan at St Edmund's, Ware, aged twenty-four

6. Vaughan receiving a letter of introduction for his missionary project from Cardinal Wiseman, 1863

7. Archbishop, later Cardinal, Henry Edward Manning, 1808–92, in 1868

8. William George Ward, 1812–82, editor and proprietor of the *Dublin Review*

9. Austin Oates, 1859–1912, honorary secretary of Rescue and later Archbishop Vaughan's secretary

10. Canon Peter Benoit, 1820–92, rector of St Joseph's College, Mill Hill

11. Herbert Vaughan as rector of St Joseph's Missionary College, 1868

12. Canon James Moyes, 1851–1927, promoter of Home Rule for Ireland

13. Wilfrid Ward, 1856–1915, writer, promoter of Catholic entry to Oxford and Cambridge

14. Rt Revd Louis Casartelli, 1852–1925, fourth bishop of Salford

15. Revd John R. Slattery, 1851–1926, first leader of the independent American Josephites

16. Alice Ingham, Mother Mary Francis, 1830-90, foundress of the Mill Hill Sisters

17. Madeleine-Marie Justine Dupont, Mother Mary of Jesus, 1851-1942, prioress of the Carmelite Convent in Notting Hill

18. The Mill Hill chapter of 1884

19. John Francis Bentley, 1839-1902, architect of Westminster Cathedral. *From a photograph by his son, Osmond*

20. Bishop John Cuthbert Hedley, 1837–1915, editor of the *Dublin Review* to 1884

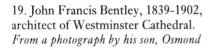

(inset) Lady Herbert *from a portrait at Mill Hill, made shortly after her marriage to Sidney Herbert in 1846*

21. Lady Mary Elizabeth Herbert of Lea, 1822-1911, in a group of the house party at Wilton House on the occasion of the coming of age of Lord Herbert. *Originally published in* The Tatler, *1902. By permission of The British Picture Library*

22. Cardinal Vaughan and the bishops of England and Wales, 1897

Butler wrote to say Eynthoven was very ill. The next day, 18 July, the young missionary died of cholera.[71] On 10 November three more priests arrived from Mill Hill: Thomas Jackson, John Temme and Gerard Raatger. Browne moved from one army camp to the next, spending the larger part of 1880 in Rawalpindi.

At Kabul Browne met Armenian Christians. They were the remnant of mercenary gunners who had been at Lahore, and, in 1735, had been taken by Mohammed Sher Abdali to Kabul. They still had a church and Mass vestments but no priest and numbered only thirteen in 1880.

With the defeat of the British army of the Kandahar garrison at Maiwind by Ayub Khan in July 1880, plans for occupying Kabul and Kandahar were dropped. The British threw their support behind Abdur Rahman's plan to build a united Afghanistan. This decision put an end to any hopes of establishing a Catholic mission. Kabul was left in the hands of Abdur Rakman Khan and the British withdrew to Peshawar and Quetta. Because the few Christians had been favoured by General Roberts, they were forced to follow the British to Peshawar.

Herbert Vaughan asked Thomas Jackson, who had been a hero on the battlefield at Marwind and Kandahar, to submit a report concerning the possible evangelization of Afghanistan. Jackson replied that any British subject who continued to reside in Afghanistan was in danger of death. If the British army kept Kandahar, Jackson felt that the way to Afghan hearts would be through education. With the withdrawl of the army, the presence of the missionaries from Mill Hill began to break up. Van Eynthoven had died. Burke's mind was affected temporarily due to sunstroke and he wandered off from Peshawar and was missing for six months. Finally, Thomas Jackson was chosen to lead a new mission to Sarawak in Borneo. Browne's position became more difficult. He was officially a superior without a territory.

According to Conroy and van der Klugt, Browne was to go through "his own little Gethsemanes before he completed his mission to Afghanistan." Misunderstandings, because Browne did not pursue with the army an award of a Victoria Cross to Jackson for his "undoubted heroism on the battlefields," clouded relations between the two men. Problems with the Capuchins over the status of Mill Hill and with the sisters of a convent in the hills above Rawalpindi added to the difficulties. "These contretemps dimmed somewhat but could not diminish the achievements of this leader of the Mill Hill Mission to Afghanistan."[72]

In February 1881, Bishop Meurin of Bombay wrote to Browne that "Your vicariate stands or falls with English rule in Afghanistan." With British withdrawal, Browne was asked to go to Madras. When that did not work out, he was asked to return to Mill Hill as a professor of philosophy. Conroy and van der Klugt add: "There we leave one who endured much and accomplished much to push forward the frontiers of the Church."[73]

Vaughan travelled to Rome and asked that the Afghanistan mission be closed in order to strengthen the Mill Hill mission in Madras.[74] On 1 May 1881 a letter from Madras informed Browne that for their service as chaplains, the Governor General of India and the officers on the frontier praised the bravery and devotion shown by the missionaries from Mill Hill, especially the bravery of Thomas Jackson.[75]

The involvement of Vaughan and St Joseph's Missionary Society in the Punjab and northern areas of India had come to an end. "Afghanistan still awaits its apostle," wrote Conroy and van der Klught in 1979. After an absence of five years, Mill Hill missionaries would return again to the Punjab and Northern Frontier, and to "the lovely vale of Kashmir."[76]

St Mary's Abbey, Mill Hill

Another of Herbert Vaughan's projects was the search for a foundation of Sisters who would complement the missionary college and St Joseph's Society. His idea was to have a group of religious Sisters who would not only be co-workers in his missionary venture but more immediately take over the domestic care of the missionary college at Mill Hill.

The college population had increased after the school was relocated and expanded. Vaughan first hired lay people to do the domestic work, but it was an unsatisfactory arrangement in the minds of Vaughan and Benoit. For example, Benoit complained that the "two women and serving boy" who were in charge of the kitchen, were a "cause of repeated trouble," and "not infrequently the dinner was held up pending the settlement of a dispute in the pantry."[77]

He hoped that the Hackney Sisters who had settled at nearby Holcombe House were the ones to take up the task. They had been looking for a larger house for their growing community at Ash Grove and finally agreed with Archbishop Manning to move to Holcombe House, which Herbert Vaughan had put up for sale. Mother Mary Frances decided that the professed Sisters should go to Mill Hill, while the novices under Mother Margaret, along with a few of the professed, remained at Ash Grove. Vaughan was pleased that the Sisters were coming to Mill Hill and planned to sell to them, in addition to the house, part of the land he had purchased for St Joseph's College.

He hoped that a working relationship between the Sisters and the missionary college would develop. As their confessor "in season and out of season," he urged them to consider the beauty of foreign missionary work, devoting most of the conferences he gave them at Ash Grove and at Mill Hill to the subject. He visited Mother Frances so often that the occasions were referred to as Vaughan's "twenty minutes to spare?" visits and were made famous in the convent annals in verse and sketch. "It had always been his wish to have the community for the Foreign Missions." It did happen, but not as soon as, nor in the manner that, Vaughan had hoped.[78]

The sisters moved off from Ash Grove in a cab for Holcombe House on 4 September 1871. The cab arrived with Mother Mary Frances and was met by Herbert Vaughan, Father Seddon, Miss Caroline Hanmer and the Sisters who had come earlier. An accompanying van had problems along the way. The owner, Mr Fletcher, had arranged for a team of animals "not at all suited, one being very large and the other very small. It took the ill-matched beasts many hours to reach Bittacy Hill ... but once there, no further persuasion could induce the creatures to mount that truly redoubtable incline."

According to the Abbey diary, in January 1873 Herbert Vaughan offered to sell adjacent land to the new foundation, without the cottages on them, for £7,500. He also offered to reduce the price by £1,000 if the "community would undertake the college washing gratis—it was decided that this could not be done." Negotiations about the property continued. Of special concern were cottages and an orchard on the plot. At one point Vaughan sent an "angry letter about the orchard and thought the community was becoming grasping."

Vaughan tried another tack to involve the Sisters in the running of St Joseph's. The college supplied a chaplain to the Abbey and so Benoit made an offer: he would accept in compensation for the chaplain's services the taking on of the college laundry. Benoit was told that such an arrangement was impossible.[79]

On 4 September 1875, Benoit asked on behalf of Vaughan if any Sisters "could go out to the foreign mission," as the society would be sending a band to India the following month. "Mother Abbess" decided that no one would be ready for at least two years. It was not until February 1881 that the community agreed to send Sisters to Baltimore to care for abandoned African-American children. On 21 March 1881, Mother Frances wrote that the missionaries and others at Baltimore had been looking forward to the time when the Sisters from the Mill Hill Abbey would come out to them, and that this would be putting into practice the original idea of Herbert Vaughan. Four Sisters finally left from Liverpool for Baltimore aboard the *Caspian* on 6 December 1881.[80]

The Sisters of St Mary's Abbey did not become those of Vaughan's missionary plans. According to Arthur McCormack, "For the first twelve years of its existence Mill Hill never succeeded in finding a satisfactory answer to its domestic needs. Like Vaughan before him, Peter Benoit often thought wistfully of seminaries abroad where the house ran smoothly because the work was done by nuns." There were also the demands from missions for Sister co-workers. But Vaughan's plans for the Abbey Sisters were successfully resisted by a determined Mother Mary Frances, and the community remained under the jurisdiction of the local bishop, independent of St Joseph's College and Society.

Mill Hill Sisters: Franciscan Missionaries of St Joseph

On 5 December 1872, a Franciscan priest, Father Gomair, wrote to Alice Ingham at Rochdale in Lancashire asking her to make an appointment to see the new bishop of Salford, Herbert Vaughan. A friend, Mother Mary Paul Taylor, wrote to Vaughan on behalf of Alice early in 1873: "In the town of Rochdale, four women, zealous members of the Third Order of St. Francis, have been living together in strict observance of that rule for the last two years, and these form the nucleus of the undertaking I have so much at heart."[81]

Five years later, on 5 March 1878, Alice Ingham and three of her companions were on their way to Mill Hill where they joined the college household. Vaughan's hope to have an "order of nuns which will be to the priests of my foreign missionary society what the holy women in the Gospels were to Jesus and his apostles" was realized.[82]

Alice Ingham

The same year that the Catholic Emancipation Act was passed, a new church, St John the Baptist, was opened at Rochdale. The parish priest was the future Bishop of Salford, William Turner. On 8 March the following year, 1830, a daughter was born to a cotton mill worker, George Ingham, and his wife Margaret Astley.[83] She was baptised Alice on 21 March by William Turner.

Alice and her older sister Sarah found a silent example in their mother's patient, uncomplaining hard work. The strong attraction to prayer which set Alice apart in her adult life can be traced to her mother: "From her too she inherited an unfailing cheerfulness and a deep trust in the goodness of God. "Blessed be God! How good He is!" was the expression that always came to her lips."

Alice and Sarah attended St John's primary school for four years. The school was a room in the cellar of the church presbytery and was in session for not more than two hours a day. William Turner arranged for religious instruction to be given in the parish each Sunday afternoon with the help of two volunteers.

When Alice was twelve years old, her mother died giving birth to a baby boy. She lived only long enough to "clasp him in her arms and then closed her eyes forever," Alice wrote. On a winter's afternoon, soon after her mother's death, Alice had an experience that made a lasting impression. She was watching Thomas, the newborn child, when she looked up to see her mother bending over her. Alice was never certain whether she dreamed what happened or not. Her mother put her arms around both of her children and whispered, "Do not be sad over me, child. I am perfectly happy and very soon this little baby will be with me forever." The baby, Thomas, died less than a week later.

Alice's father then married a childless widow named Elizabeth Cheetham.

Elizabeth was a dressmaker and milliner at 155 Yorkshire Street in Rochdale. By the time Alice was twenty-one she too was a milliner, making and selling women's hats. About the same time, in 1851, her father became a Catholic.

When Mr Ingham died in 1865, Alice was thirty-five years of age. She had not married and was a companion to her stepmother and a partner in her business. She was also active in the parish and a friend of Mother Mary Paul who belonged to a new community of nuns called the Cross and Passion Sisters. Alice met a Franciscan priest, Fr Gomair Peeters, a Belgian who was appointed to Gorton Monastery in 1865. He had been a missionary in Suez. He became one of Alice's spiritual directors.[84]

Alice tried to join the Cross and Passion Sisters, but returned home after a short time and renewed the rounds of acts of charity she had become known for in her neighbourhood. Mother Mary Paul and Fr Peeters thought Alice had a special call and so helped her to begin a small community, using the shop on Yorkshire Street, on 2 May 1871. She and her stepmother were joined by two other women, Mary and Bridget. Alice became a member of the Third Order of St Francis and in October 1874 she made a private vow of chastity. In the shop the hat-making business continued, along with the sale of confectionery. At the same time the women had a place for prayer and recreation and a room to seat twenty to thirty children who came for an hour each evening for religious instructions.

Rochdale had its share of poverty in the 1870s. "The poverty and over-crowding of the poor, their plight and the need for relief" must have meant that even the smallest help that Alice and her companions brought to the sick and dying was welcomed.[85]

Their friend Father Peeters helped the community, but he knew that they needed the bishop's approval to develop further. He told them first to see Bishop Turner. Turner acknowledged the small group and set a probation period for them, but he died soon afterwards. The women continued in their quiet way to work in the town. Father Peeters referred to them as the "little saints of Rochdale" and there is a story that Alice was called the "Threepenny Bit Lady" because she had a practice of giving "church money" to people who were ashamed to attend Mass on Sundays because they had no money to put in the collection.

In 1873 Bishop Vaughan wrote to Alice acknowledging the community, but took no action on their behalf. In October 1874 he told Mother Mary Paul that the community had been in his thoughts but he still thought it too soon to give them a special rule.[86] Meanwhile Father Peeters was transferred to Glasgow, Alice's stepmother died and the two early members left. But young women who shared Alice's ideals joined her, and a new shop was opened.[87] Vaughan finally paid them a surprise visit in 1876. While he was visiting Rochdale, the bishop "in characteristic fashion walked up to the shop in Yorkshire Street, accompanied by a schoolboy whom he had recognized in the street as an altar server,

Freddie Holt." Vaughan walked "so fast that he was panting for breath by the time they reached" the shop. In his own words: "I decided to call on them. Nothing could have exceeded their quiet joy. They placed themselves entirely at my disposal." Two more years passed before they heard from him again.

By January 1878 it seemed that there was to be no future for the little group. At a community meeting, one Sister said of Bishop Vaughan: "I'm sure he has forgotten all about us." Alice suggested that they all make a novena to the Sacred Heart, and at the end of it, each person could choose what she wanted to do in the future. Six days later Vaughan sent a letter to Alice asking her to come to his house on Chapel Street in Salford. When she arrived, "two minutes later the Bishop appeared, greeted her warmly and then plunged straight into business."

In the official history of the Franciscan Missionary Sisters of St Joseph there is the following tribute to Herbert Vaughan, claiming him as "their co-founder, for although he did not call together the women whom God chose to be the nucleus of the new congregation, it was he, as Bishop of Salford, who gave the community begun in his Diocese of Salford, the blessing and approval of Ecclesiastical authority. As Superior General of the St. Joseph's Society to which the Sisters were 'auxiliatrix' until 1930, he was superior, guide and kindly father."[88]

During their conversation in Salford in 1878, Vaughan asked Alice to go to Mill Hill and "undertake the domestic economy of the Missionary College." Later he advised her to go to Mill Hill first and talk it over with Peter Benoit. Benoit had already visited Alice and her community at Rochdale and so knew them and their work. On 2 February Alice Ingham arrived at Mill Hill. While she was there her sister Sarah died. Alice, like the Abbey Sisters, had misgivings about the laundry. It was not unusual for religious congregations to have the washing done by Sisters but laundry work was to become the *bête noire* of Mill Hill College and other places. Among other humiliations, the community was warned by Canon Purcell that "if his advice was not taken the Sisters would be nothing but pious laundresses."[89]

The first group—Alice, Helen, Margaret and Agnes—set off for Mill Hill on Ash Wednesday, March, 1878. Alice was still not certain she had done the correct thing in leaving Rochdale and going to Mill Hill to work in the kitchen, bakery, sewing room and laundry. Father Peeters advised her that it was her opportunity to form the group into a religious community. According to their community history, Alice and her companions persevered with fortitude and resolution and gained much: "The blessing and thanks of the newly ordained missionaries, the regular and beautiful liturgy, the opportunity, eventually, to go to distant lands themselves for the sake of the Gospel and, of course, the fulfilment of their hope to become recognized by the Church."[90]

On the Feast of the Immaculate Conception, 8 December 1878, their friend and spiritual director the Franciscan Fr Gomair Peeters died in Glasgow.

Peter Benoit then became their director and he in turn asked the help of Father Francis Larive, a Salesian from Malmesbury.

Before going to St Joseph's, Mill Hill, the Sisters had no distinctive dress. As early as 1873 Alice decided that they should not have a special habit, so as to have easy access to persons of all classes. But that changed at Mill Hill. A tradition among the Sisters has it that the clothing day, that is, the day they did take on a distinctive religious habit, was 19 March 1880. Bishop Vaughan was interested in what form the religious habit would take. There is an anecdote that a Sister went to see him at Salford, bringing along the proposed dress: Vaughan chose his secretary, Charles Gadd, as the model, and put the headdress on his head, "rearranging it himself and fitting it himself on his Secretary's head so that Sister could see how it looked."[91]

Alice and her companions had made a great sacrifice in moving from Rochdale, where they were known and respected, to become servants at Mill Hill. They exchanged their freedom to be generous to the poor for the dependence and silence of a subordinate place at the college. And yet, Vaughan is referred to as "our Cardinal" in their official history, "the humblest and kindest of men." He is also remembered as "a product of his age and class and this comes through in his directives regarding the Sisters. Paternalism was a virtue and those priests who had care of the infant Congregation appeared to operate without much reference to the people concerned, the Sisters." But somehow their views were made known and they influenced the formation of their community. Alice Ingham constantly repeated that it was all God's work: "Blessed be God, how wonderful are his ways."[92]

Crisis for St Joseph's Missionary Society

Sister Germaine suggests that there was more than one reason why Vaughan turned to Alice Ingham for help at Mill Hill in January 1878. At Rochdale the women were restless about the undetermined state of their small community and Vaughan's call came at just the right moment. But there were other problems at Mill Hill itself. The very existence of the college was threatened in 1877 when the Society for the Propagation of the Faith withdrew its annual grant of £400. The new rule of the Paris Council was "not to divert any portion of their money to the maintenance of colleges in Christian nations." Benoit would not be able to continue running the college household.[93]

The boarding allowance per student had already been reduced to 7s 6d per week. Vaughan wrote to Benoit that he would not allow the college to run up bills: "Rather than prolong its existence for a few years on credit, it were better to close it at once in honourable poverty and solvency." Vaughan turned to Mary Elizabeth Herbert and asked her to write to Paris appealing for a change in the Society's decision. An appeal was sent to every priest in England with Vaughan's letter attached, asking for help. Henry Manning called a meeting at

Willis' Rooms in London on 13 April 1877. A correspondent of *Revue Catholique* was present. He had often been to the college and found the circumstances of the meeting very sad. In addition to Vaughan, Manning and Weathers, the bishops of Beverley, Plymouth, Liverpool, Nottingham and "*la noblesse Catholique*" also attended.[94]

Manning told the gathering: "If the faith is to be extended at home, it must be by our aiding to carry it abroad." Not only did donations increase but an organization was formed to publicize the work of the new society and collect funds. A new council was formed: Mary Elizabeth Herbert was named treasurer and Peter Benoit chosen as secretary. The aim of the council was to increase the number of supporters and collect 5s from each one per year.[95] The Marquis of Ripon and Elizabeth Herbert led the fund-raising through 1877 and into 1878. Finally, on 22 January 1878, a large public meeting of approximately four thousand people took place at the Free Trade Hall, Manchester, in support of the foreign missions. Benoit was present and he repeated the difficulties experienced in operating the college. After the meeting, Vaughan sent for Alice Ingham and asked her to "undertake the domestic economy" of the Mill Hill community.[96]

Another outcome of the financial crisis was the publication of an illustrated monthly. Each year since 1868, friends of the college, and later of the society, received an annual report. In 1878 the new council decided to publish a monthly. And so *The Illustrated Catholic Missions* was published but it was a failure. Austin Oates, Vaughan's Rescue secretary at Salford, recalled that it was an English edition of *Les Missions Catholiques*. He helped Vaughan edit the first edition. "The night previous to going to press we worked very late . . . references to Gazeteers and Atlases were frequent."[97] The successor to the *Illustrated*, St. *Joseph's Advocate*, was not a failure. The *Advocate* published its first edition of forty thousand copies in 1883. Additional financial help also came from profits from *The Tablet* which Vaughan directed to Mill Hill.[98]

Gwladys Vaughan

Herbert's eldest sister, Gwladys, a Visitation nun, died on 3 February 1880. She had been a member of a community at Boulogne for twenty years as Sister Clementine Elizabeth, and suffered for much of her adult life from poor health. In a letter to Herbert's brother Reginald, their father wrote that "It is a pang to lose a sister, but is a deeper pain to lose a beloved daughter, so devoted to me as dear little Gwladys was. . . . And now, dear child, the worries and pains are past! I have one tie less to earth; one motive more to think of heaven."[99]

Death of Herbert Vaughan's Father

During Bishop Vaughan's absence in Rome, his father, Colonel John Vaughan, and his stepmother, Mary Charlotte Weld, died at Biarritz. Mrs Vaughan died on 7 December and his father on 16 December 1880.

On his return to Salford, Vaughan's first public remarks alluded to the loss of his father. Snead-Cox quotes him as saying that "death has made more than one place void during my absence." Not only were members of the clergy and laity gone, but also "the most loved ones of my own innermost circle of domestic affection have closed their earthly career. Now henceforth they call me to meet them in another world. God grant that by fidelity to duty and perseverance unto the end I may become at last worthy to join them in the home of eternal peace and rest."[100]

Colonel John Vaughan had written to Herbert from Courtfield on 6 September 1880: "Thanks most deeply my dearest Herbert for your consoling letter and doubly grateful am I for your masses and prayers." Shortly after he and Mary Weld Vaughan, his second wife, went to Biarritz, they both became seriously ill. After encouraging Herbert in the "gigantic task" of "ecclesiastical education," he concluded: "You, in all events, are not one of those who expect great triumphs without long struggles and hard blows. I will write again before long. I am quite tired now."

By the end of November it was clear that death was near for both John and Mary. Herbert travelled from Rome to Biarritz to see them for the last time. He wrote to his youngest brother, Father John Vaughan, on 26 November, that he had to return to Rome within a week. He saw that there was no chance of recovery for their father: "He gets no sleep and suffers alternately from the heart and fainting. The longing for sleep which will not come is the most distressing feature of his illness." He asked John to come out to replace him at the deathbed. Bernard Vaughan was also with his father and stepmother.[101]

On his way back to Rome, Herbert wrote from Marseilles. Snead-Cox says he was lost for what to say and so added a meditation on suffering: "The more we endure for Christ the greater the merit. Suffering is as a crucible, it intensifies ... the adhesion of our will with that of Christ.... May God bless and console you my dearest old Father. Your most loving son, Herbert." Less than a week later Mrs Vaughan died after a stroke, and nine days later John Vaughan followed her. Herbert had written to his father from Rome on 8 December: "Courage then, dearest old Father, courage—you may yet have to endure. God and the Blessed Mother are with you to strengthen and console you. 'The sufferings of this time are not worthy to be compared to the glory which is to come.' Pray for me your most devoted son."[102]

Father John Vaughan was at the bedside with his brothers, Francis and Bernard, along with two nuns, the doctor and the footman, when Colonel Vaughan died in his rooms at the Hotel de Paris in Biarritz. John wrote to his sister, Mary Clare, two days later, describing the scene. At one point his father recounted what he had seen once in his imagination during prayer: "I was at my prayers one time and I saw an old grey-headed fellow die and go to purgatory, but bless me! When he came out again he was quite a smart young fellow." When Bernard and John heard the story from their father, repeated so seriously, they "did not know what to think. I know I simply burst out laughing." On the morning of Wednesday, 16 December, Colonel Vaughan predicted he would die between six and seven that evening, and he did. A Mass for the dead was offered in the parish church at 10 a.m. the next morning, and soon after both bodies were brought back to England.[103]

The bodies arrived at Bristol on Friday 7 January 1881, and were accompanied by Captain Francis Vaughan to Courtfield where the coffins were placed in the manor chapel, side by side just outside the sanctuary, covered with one pall. The funeral Mass was offered on Tuesday, 11 January, at 10 a.m. About two hundred people crowded inside the chapel while others remained outside. The Solemn Dirge was sung by sixteen monks from St Michael's Priory in Hereford. Herbert Vaughan was not present and so his uncle, the brother of Colonel Vaughan, Bishop William of Plymouth, was the main celebrant. He was assisted by three of Herbert's brothers: Joseph, who was prior of Fort Augustus in Scotland, Bernard as the deacon and John as sub-deacon; Canon Fleming was master of ceremonies.[104]

At the end of the Mass, Bishop Hedley gave the eulogy, which was later published as "Loyal in Life and Death." He chose the words: "Be thou faithful to death and I will give you a crown of glory." In the eulogy Hedley remarked that a note written in Colonel Vaughan's prayer book by Pope Pius IX "summed up his whole life." It read: "Initium sapentiae timor Domini."[105] After the blessing—first by Hedley and lastly by the Bishop of Plymouth—a procession, made up of the sons and brothers of Colonel Vaughan, escorted the remains to a vault beneath the sanctuary for burial.

On the death of his father, Herbert Vaughan succeeded to a life interest in the estate at Courtfield. However, of Colonel Vaughan's eight sons, six were priests at the time of his death, and among the six were the four eldest. Herbert, Roger, Kenelm and Joseph gave up their right of inheritance and Courtfield passed to another brother, Francis Baynham Vaughan. Herbert agreed to renounce his inheritance and receive instead £1,000 per year. According to Snead-Cox, Herbert Vaughan allocated the annuity to some of his Catholic projects, so that long before his death he "ceased to regard it as in any way at his own disposal."[106]

Notes

1. Although the missionary college was founded in 1866, Vaughan considered 2 February 1875 to be the "real birthday of St. Joseph's Society of the Sacred Heart." It was the day that the first chapter meeting closed in Baltimore and the rules were finally accepted. See: Leslie, *Vaughan Letters*, pp.265-6.

2. SDA. *Canon Peter Benoit*, translated from the Flemish and French; MHA. *The Tablet*, 10 September 1892; See also: J. De Muelenaere, *Canon Pieter Benoit—overdruk uit Handelingen van het Genootschap*, Société d'Emulation, Brugge, deel CVII, 1970.

3. De Muelenaere, p.41; JA. and MHA. Peter Benoit, Diary of a trip to America, January 6, 1875 to June 1875.

4. On South Africa see: William E. Brown, *The Catholic Church in South Africa*, edited by Michael Derrick, New York, Kenedy; Also: J. B. Brain, ed., *The Cape Diary of Bishop Griffith*, Cape Town, 1988, p.9ff.

5. MHA. Bishop George Brown to Benoit, 30 November 1846.

6. De Muelenaere, p.5.

7. Conversation with the archivist, Salford diocese, Fr David Lannon, August 1990. Benoit became very influential in the Salford diocese, although he was from Bruges. He was the first of many priest-missionaries from West Flanders to work in Salford.

8. De Muelenaere, p.12.

9. MHA. During a debate in the columns of the *Manchester Courier* on papal infallibility, Benoit wrote: "Salford, August 15, 1870. If they were to apply to the nearest Catholic clergyman they would soon learn that there is a very wide difference between infallibility and impeccability."

10. Snead-Cox, 1, p.120.

11. De Muelenaere, p.11, n. 17.

12. WDA. Herbert Vaughan, Notes on Salford Diocese, 1872.

13. De Muelenaere, p.12, n. 18.

14. *ibid.*

15. MHA. *St Joseph's Advocate*, October 1892.

16. MHA.

17. MHA. Benoit, 38, 1872-92.

18. MHA. Adrian v d Deijssel, Hoogland, 28 April 1944, translation.

19. Interview with Father Noel Hanrahan, Mill Hill, 19 November 1991.

20. *ibid.*

21. MHA. Herbert Vaughan to Elizabeth Herbert, 1 March 1871. Vaughan had as architects the firm of Goldie and Child. The contractors, Buissens and his partner Zegers, were Dutch; He signed a contract for the church, tower and remaining cloister, the whole amounting to £3900. "St Joseph will have to pull us through this as he did through the first undertaking."

22. MHA.

23. Josephite Archives (JA). Notes of Peter Hogan. See also: William L. Portier, "John R. Slattery's Vision for the Evangelization of American Blacks," *US Catholic Historian*, 1986, p.20; Ochs, *Desegregating the Altar*, pp.50-1.

24. Slattery, Biographie; WDA. *Catholic Directory* for 1873; On Nicols: Obituary, *The Tablet*, 3 July 1898, p.184.

25. (JA) Rev John R. Slattery, Copy book 2, 1889-Reports, Communications and Society History to 1928, p.6: "Dr Vaughan, as soon as he had men ready, started for Rome to put himself and his men at his Holiness' feet. There he found no opening for Mission work but was told that 'Le Missions Etrangers de Paris' might give him a mission. Although failing this, Dr V. secured Fr. Chevillion. They met at dinner at the Seminary in Paris.... Fr. C. had just returned hors-de-combat from Birmah after 10 years of service. A native of Bayonne and son of a Physician, young Chevillion had received an excellent education. At 20 he was teaching

Hebrew in a seminary conducted by the Jesuits." He joined the Paris Missionaries and went to Burma in 1860. After ten years he returned to Europe, met Vaughan and joined the staff at Mill Hill. "The personnel of the students at Mill Hill January 1873 were: Rev. Tardy, Priest; Sub Deacon: Wm. Hoonan, P. Riodan, R. Gore, A. van Vaal; Ministers: David J. Forbes, John Crowley, John Greene; Tonsured: D.Hurley, Edward Murphy; Philosophers: Hennan, Knoot, Mayer, Edward Murphy; Theologians: McCarthy, Walsh, Kelly, Murphy, and one other. Beside them, Capt. Mann, (and) a youth named McShane from Belfast were studying Latin. Of them Greene, Hurley, Walsh and Mayer are from America."

26. Henry Gabriels, *Historical Sketch of St Joseph's Provincial Seminary*, Troy, New York, U S Catholic Historical Society, 1905, pp.34-5: The priest Vaughan recruited at Rome was Browne, or Braun, whose real name was Rimsal or Ruhmsal. He had been a priest of the Archdiocese of New York and then a professor at a seminary at Fordham started by Archbishop Hughes. He left the priesthood, studied law, and then enlisted as a private soldier during the American Civil War. He had a change of heart and his Jesuit confessor, Father Joseph Shea, advised him to go to Rome for his penance. At Rome he stayed at a Passionist monastery under the name P. Georges. "In view of his notoriety, he was advised not to return to the United States." After teaching at St Joseph's College, Mill Hill, he led the first missionaries to Afghanistan. When the missionaries were withdrawn, it is uncertain where he went. It is said that he became a faith healer in Scotland; another report had him becoming an Episcopal clergyman.

27. JA. Slattery, Biographie.

28. MHA. Notes, Herbert Vaughan: Founder of St Joseph's Foreign Missionary Society.

29. De Muelenaere, p.25.

30. MHA. Notes, HV.

31. JA. Slattery, Biographie.

32. JA. Josephite Newsletter, November-December 1966- January 1967, p.10.

33. JA. *Josephite Harvest*, Autumn, 1892, p.6: Louisville was not an easy assignment with a bishop who could not get along with most of his priests and religious.

34. Ochs, *Desegregating*, pp.44-5.

35. JA. HV Collection, p.7, book 1, folder 17.

36. *ibid.* p.4, book 1, folder 11.

37. Ochs, *Desegregating*, p.47; De Muelenaere, pp.26-7; Bolton, *Salford*, p.251: Charles Joseph Gadd was born at Salford in 1838. He studied at Lisbon and Ushaw and was ordained in 1861. He was appointed to the Cathedral parish. Bishop Vaughan chose Gadd as his secretary and confidential messenger, sending him on long journeys connected with mission work in Canada, the USA, Spain and Portugal. For six years he was also vice rector at St Bede's. He died at Barton in 1907; A passenger on the same ship was Fr Joseph Rettori. (Another example of Vaughan's success at recruiting and the effect of what some have called "contagious enthusiasm.") He was from Brescia, Italy and wanted to become a missionary but his bishop would not release him. Finally he did and he was on his way to work in America. He met the young priests from Mill Hill and became interested in what they told him of the new society. "He begged Bishop Vaughan to allow him to become a member." He was sent to Mill Hill and later to Madras. He returned from the mission to teach at St Joseph's College. On Sundays he made appeals for the missions and for many years did the painting and decorating in St Joseph's Chapel. During the last year of his life he became ill but continued painting, trying to finish the chapel. He returned to Brescia, Italy, three weeks before he died on Sunday 8 May 1898. See: "Father Rettori of Mill Hill," *The Tablet*, 14 May 1898, p.780.

38. Present were John Greene, William Hooman, Richard Gore, Frederick Schmitz, Deacon Murphy, Peter Benoit, Herbert Vaughan, and Vaughan's secretary at Salford, Monsignor Gadd. JA. MHA; Benoit's Journal. MHA. "Hasty notes of a journey to America."

39. McCormack, p.193; Leslie, *Vaughan Letters*, pp.265-6.

40. De Muelenaere, p.27; MHA. Benoit, notes.

41. Ochs, *Desegregating*, p.47. A recognized province required ten priests or three mission stations. Rectors were priests in charge of churches or institutions, such as seminaries, and were at the third level of authority. The Baltimore Chapter also established the office of "vicar," or vicar-consultor and elector, of the society, to assist the superior general and exercise authority in his name. Peter Benoit officially became the first vicar, and James Noonan was appointed by Vaughan to be the first provincial of the American Province.

42. *ibid.*; MHA. For example: In a letter to Vaughan dated 2 January 1875, McCloskey of Louisville urged the removal of both Richard Gore and Tardy as prerequisites for a successful mission. Vaughan did not act on the Bishop's request and the issue languished for several months with each side growing more and more hostile.

43. MHA. Benoit. For example: On 25 May 1875 Benoit visited the nephew of Archbishop Spalding who was at St Michael's in New York City. According to Spalding: "While they (Mill Hill) have done nothing as yet in the way of erecting churches and schools, their coming has thrown the work backwards. For many priests who were ready to devote themselves to the work have kept back as the Society of the Sacred Heart professed to undertake it. He (Spalding) considers it a mistake that the work should have originated in England. The work would be looked upon more favourably if it had started either in Ireland or Belgium. Bishop Vaughan had displeased many running counter to the commonly received notions of social propriety by mixing familiarly with the negroes and he had disappointed all by doing nothing at his last visit, while his visit had been heralded thro' the length and breath of the country." Benoit thought his remarks were too severe and Spalding agreed that "the next three years would be a better test of the Society's usefulness than the past three;" In New York Benoit stayed with the Slatterys at 57th St. and Seventh Ave. There he heard an anecdote about Bishop Vaughan: When he stayed with then he would walk back and forth on the carpet in order to generate enough electricity "in his system to light the gas lamps to the great amusement of all."

44. Ochs, *Desegregating*, p.46; Steins, pp.33-37.

45. *ibid.*, p.47.

46. *ibid.*, p.48; Peter Hogan, *Josephite Harvest*, p.6-8: By the end of 1877 Noonan had reached the end of his endurance. Two of his band were dead and two were preparing to leave. Of the missions, only Charleston was encouraging. Noonan was released from St Joseph's Society, joined the Jesuits and spent much of his later life on their Jamaica mission.

47. De Muelenaere, p.38

48. Hogan, *Harvest*, p.6.

49. "The Telegu Mission, 1875-1975," in *Millhilliana*, no.4, 1975, pp.201-2; India was not the only area offered to Vaughan's missionaries. Propaganda Fide wrote to Vaughan on 10 December 1874 asking him to take charge of the vicariate of Montana in the United States. Vaughan replied on 3 March 1875 giving "a geographical ethnographical description of Montana, reports on ecclesiastical conditions, and makes various suggestions." But Vaughan regretted that St Joseph's Society could not take charge of the Montana vicariate, suggesting that it be entrusted to the Jesuits. See: Propaganda Fide Documents, calendar, vol 10, p.69, no 548.

50. Telegu Mission, p.200.

51. *ibid.*, p.201.

52. *ibid.*, p.202.

53. *ibid.*

54. *ibid.*, p.204.

55. A. Lacordaire, "Chronique religieuse de l'Angleterre, Londres, 1 Fév. 1877," in *Revue Catholique*, xliii, pp.180-2.

56. Snead-Cox, 1, p.445; McCormack, p.202; Herbert, *Short History*, p.17.

57. "Telegu Mission," p.207.

58. *ibid.*, p.201.

59. *ibid.*, p.206.

60. *ibid.*

61. *ibid.*, pp.209-10.

62. *Millhilliana*, "A Message from the Superior General," p.187.

63. John Rooney, unpublished MS notes: The needs of the army had dictated the choice of Vaughan's missionaries. The majority of the Catholic troops were Irish but for a good many years "the army was quite happy to provide chaplains who were Goan, French or Italian, in fact any priest who was not Irish." The troops complained that their priests could not speak English well. Rome decided to assign the northern part of the diocese of Lahore to Herbert Vaughan's missionaries.

64. Leslie, *Vaughan Letters*, p.304.

65. See 24 above.

66. Leslie, *Vaughan Letters*, p.305.

67. MHA. Burke was born in 1854 at Canadaigua near Rochester, New York. He studied at St Hyacinth near Montreal and went to Mill Hill in 1874. Van Eynthoven was born at Vianen and arrived at Mill Hill in 1872. Aelen was born at Tilburg and studied for six years at St Michaelgestel before going to Mill Hill in 1875.

68. See: John Rooney, *On the Heels of Battle*, Rawalpindi, Christian Study Centre, 1986, pp.96-101.

69. See: James v d Klught and Michael Conroy, *The Opening Door, Mill Hill Mission to Afghanistan: 1879-82*, Rawalpindi, 1979.

70. *ibid.*, p.12.

71. *ibid.*, p.15.

72. *ibid.*, p.24.

73. *ibid.*, p.56.

74. Rooney, *Battle*, p.97.

75. McCormack, p.203.

76. *Opening Door*, p.57.

77. St Mary's Abbey Archives, p.64 Log Book.

78. *ibid.*

79. *ibid.*

80. *ibid.*

81. McCormack, p.198; The history of the "Mill Hill Sisters," can be found in two publications: By a Sister, *Light after Darkness*, Glasgow, Burns and Sons, 1962; Sister Germaine, *The Franciscan Missionaries of St Joseph*, Glasgow, Burns and Sons, March 1983; See also: *Franciscan Sisters of St Joseph, Letters of the Foundress, Mother Mary Francis (Alice Ingham)*, 1983; *The Preparation Period, 1870-1880*, Mill Hill, 1983.

82. McCormack, p.199.

83. George Ingham, Alice's father, was an Anglican, born and baptised in the Whalley District. He was a widower at twenty-one with a son, George, when he married Margaret Astley, who was a Catholic.

84. Germaine, *Franciscan Sisters*, p.8: Father Gomair Peeters, OSF, was a Belgian Friar appointed to Gorton Monastery in 1865, after ill health prevented his return to the Suez mission where he had worked for twenty years.

85. *ibid.*

86. *ibid.*, p.9: "For several years I did nothing but try and prove them, and during all that time nothing could have been more edifying than the cheerful patience with which Alice accepted the delays, mortifications and humiliations with which I thought it right to test the thoroughness of her vocation."

87. *ibid.*: Some of them were Catherine Prescott, Helen Downs, Agnes Taylor-Egglebody. Margaret Manning and Mary Dougherty went on to form another community.

88. *ibid.*, p.87.

89. Germaine, *Franciscan Sisters*, p.11: "It seems that Alice had queried the laundry work, for, man-like he went on: 'About the washing, I do not see much difficulty, there are many religious Congregations where the washing is done entirely and for larger numbers by Sisters of the community.' ... The laundry was, however, at Mill Hill and elsewhere where it became necessary to take it on, the *bête noir* of the early Sisters. Miss Hanmer at the lodge in Mill Hill, who was to have Sister Xavier for twelve years as companion-maid-nurse, complained to the Bishop of the 'washing hanging out' and it had to stop." Letters tell of the Sisters having to stay up all night before holy days to finish the laundry.

90. *ibid.*

91. *ibid.*: "Father Rector gives 20th February 1879 as first Clothing Day but tradition has it as the feast of St. Joseph, 19 March 1880."

92. *ibid.*

93. Elizabeth Herbert, *A Short History of the Origin of St. Joseph's Society of the Sacred Heart for Foreign Missions and of the Foreign Missionary College at Mill Hill*, London, St Joseph's, 1901; Also: McCormack, p.196.

94. Lacordaire, "Chronique," *Revue Catholique*, Louvain, xliv, 1877, p.76.

95. Herbert, *Short History*: "Collection boxes became a feature in many Catholic homes and on Christmas Day, the time for opening the box, many a Catholic child would clap its hands with delight as it counted the coppers and thought of the poor far-away pagans who would now be told about the child Jesus.... The proceeds became the main-stay of Mill Hill;" *The Tablet*, 12 November 1881, p.784: At a meeting in 1881 Lady Herbert encouraged the council and supporters to collect small sums wherever they could "by having alms boxes in their homes." She cited the example of the large sums collected from France by halfpenny subscribers and what the Methodists had done at Wilton: £120 for the missions from mission boxes. Caroline Hanmer had purchased a number of them the previous year for distribution.

96. Germaine, *Franciscan*, p.13: From 1879 until the death of Mother Francis in 1890 Fr Rector (Benoit) took the place of Fr Gomair as staunch supporter and mentor in close collaboration with the Bishop (Vaughan) who throughout his life took a deep and personal interest in each Sister. In January 1880 the Sisters started a foundation at Malmesbury, Wiltshire, where a friend of Benoit, Fr Larvie, had a mission. Another place was opened at Grove House in Hampstead. Canon Arthur Purcell had the parish and soon asked them to take charge of his orphanage for boys at Holly Place as well. In 1881 St Joseph's Society opened a minor seminary at Kelvedon, Essex, and a community went to staff it.

97. WDA. Austin Oates, Anecdotes.

98. An American edition was also published. See: *Irish Ecclesiastical Record*, vol 7, 1886, p.765: "This little organ of the Society is well printed, copiously illustrated and sold at a very low price. It does not confine itself to forwarding mission work among the negroes but also watches jealously everything that may affect their temporal interests ... we find ... articles on the Soudan War (*sic*) and on the presidential elections viewed from a negro standpoint as well as interesting accounts of the spread of the Faith among the heathen."

99. Mary Vaughan, pp.114-5.

100. Snead-Cox, 1, p.372; Snead-Cox, *The Tablet*, and a letter from John Vaughan give the date of Colonel Vaughan's death as 16 December. Mary Vaughan has 17 December and the burial vault in Courtfield has 20 December 1880.

101. *ibid.*, pp. 368-370.

102. *ibid.*, p.370.

103. VFA. John S. Vaughan to Mary Clare Vaughan, 18 December 1880.

104. *The Tablet*, 15 January 1881, p.115: "Funeral of Colonel and Mrs Vaughan."

105. VFA. Hedley, *Loyal in Life and Death*, London, Burns & Oates, 1881.

106. Snead-Cox, 1, pp.372-3.

CHAPTER XII

Salford Diocese, 1881 to 1892: Rescue; The Irish Question; Education

Courtfield

At the end of 1881 the Vaughans gathered once more at Courtfield. The occasion was a Mass formally opening the new chapel on Wednesday, 28 December. John Cuthbert Hedley was among the guests and wrote about the occasion; he was a regular visitor to Courtfield, first as auxiliary bishop and then as ordinary. Following the funeral of Colonel John Vaughan the previous January, Hedley had been appointed to succeed Bishop Thomas Brown of the Diocese of Newport and Menevia in Wales.[1] The evening of 27 December, he arrived at the Ross Railway Station at the same time as Herbert Vaughan, two of his brothers and some others. There were seventeen at the evening meal in the manor.

The next morning the first one to rise was Herbert Vaughan's Redemptorist uncle, Edmund, who in turn woke another uncle, Richard Vaughan the Jesuit. Two altars were prepared and the visiting priests set about offering their private Masses. At about 9.15 a.m., Benedictine monks arrived from Downside Abbey. Hedley wrote of the Mass: "Herbert of Salford preaches, alludes to Bethlehem and compares the newly painted chapel to the stable where our Lord was born (to the advantage of the chapel)." After the Kyrie the organ broke down and remained silent until the Gospel when it began to work again. "All the uncles seem uncommonly well," Hedley's notes concluded.[2]

Two of Herbert Vaughan's brothers had married. Francis lived at Courtfield and Reginald about seven miles away. Francis Baynham Vaughan succeeded to Courtfield after his elder brothers, Herbert, Roger, Kenelm and Joseph, decided on a vocation with the Church. He and his American-born wife, Caroline Pope, lived at the manor with their three sons and three daughters. Francis became a colonel of Monmouthshire Militia just as his father had been before him; he was a captain in 1881. According to one who knew Courtfield and served under Colonel Francis Vaughan, a large number of the enlisted men in the militia, as well as several officers, were Roman Catholics. Some of them were from mining valleys in Monmouthshire, but most were from collieries in the Forest of Dean across the Wye valley. On Sunday mornings nearly half of the battalion would march to the "little Roman Catholic Church in the town which was filled to overflowing with red-coats. For this reason some facetious people bestowed the nickname 'The Pope's Own' on the Royal Monmouthshire." When the author of *Squires of South Wales* joined the militia in the 1890s, he found Francis Vaughan "a delightful, kindly man," although he was "sometimes a little vague." But, he went on: "Colonel Francis Vaughan was a fine man and I pay my deepest respects to his memory."[3]

The author of *Squires* once visited Francis Vaughan at Courtfield. He found many interesting old portraits, "but nobody seemed to know whom they represented." He thought that the whole house, "though not large or imposing, breathed past romance." Once he went to a ball given at the manor which was attended by about two hundred people: "I have wondered since where all their carriages and horses could have been stowed away on that narrow peninsula overlooking the Wye."[4] Of Francis' and Caroline's children, Francis and Herbert became priests, and Mary, a nun. Francis became bishop of Menevia in Wales and Herbert was the leader of the Catholic Missionary Society.

Another brother of Herbert Vaughan, Reginald, went to Australia after he left the seminary, and stayed for a time with his brother, Archbishop Roger Vaughan, in Sydney. He is said to have worked as a hand on a sheep ranch. He married Julia Shanahan while in Australia and when he returned home to England with his family, they settled nearby at Glen Trothy, Abergavenny. One of his daughters, Julia, became a Poor Clare nun. She recalled how her father began each day with Mass and meditation in the family oratory "which was served by a resident chaplain." Like their grandmother, Eliza, and uncle, Herbert, "his ten children—three became religious—were brought up in a spirit of profound reverence for the Blessed Sacrament. Each day they took turns gathering fresh flowers for the altar and trimming the sanctuary lamp. On their frequent visits by pony trap to their cousins at Courtfield, seven miles away, they would recite the rosary en route."[5]

Death of William George Ward

In July 1882 Herbert Vaughan lost his friend of twenty-seven years, William George Ward. The funeral Mass was offered at Weston Manor on the Isle of Wight by Bishop Weathers and the homily was given by Vaughan.

Herbert Vaughan chose the text: "I have had a zeal for good and shall not be confounded. My soul has wrestled for her and in doing it I have been confirmed." He thought that all the published remarks about Ward had missed one thing: "the position which he occupied in the Catholic Church in

England and in the extraordinary services which he rendered to her." Vaughan told the congregation that he had agreed "thoroughly" with Ward's "expositions and views."

According to Vaughan, the keynote of Ward's life was expressed in the words "loyalty to the God of truth as He had revealed Himself and his purposes to mankind." Ward, he said, had singlehandedly for seven years, as editor of the *Dublin Review* from 1863, "waged a continual war against Liberal Catholicism," and in his final years he devoted himself to understanding and refuting the "atheism and rationalism of the day." His work in Catholic philosophy became the "object of his prayers and all his thoughts." Ward had two characteristic virtues, a humility that "in its childlike simplicity was most extraordinary in a man of his gigantic intellectual powers—and his piety," which expressed his personal love for God, for Jesus Christ, and for the Blessed Virgin.

Vaughan continued: "He used to inculcate nothing more upon his pupils than this, that all intellectual power and mental cultivation were dangerous and worthless before God unless they were accompanied by real personal piety and love of God." He thought that there were only two living men whose influence on the Catholic Church in England was greater: Manning and Newman.

The reviewer of *William George Ward and the Catholic Revival* in 1893 wrote that Ward was a person "who desired above all things the glory of God and the good of souls. This true Christian quality so permeated all his character, that it seems to have made it easy for him to brave human respect and suffer gladly real poverty and hardship in his early Catholic life without thinking he was doing anything more than his mere duty. It was this characteristic that caused Cardinal Wiseman and Father Faber, no mean judges of the spiritual life, to open their whole hearts to him at times." Ward was never "betrayed into personalities, and manifestly wrote in the spirit of the utmost candour and sense of duty."

William George Ward was buried in a new vault prepared at Weston Manor.[6]

Death of Archbishop Roger Vaughan

In 1883 there was another personal loss for Herbert Vaughan. On 18 August, his brother Roger, Archbishop of Sydney, died shortly after returning to England for a rest. He had written to his Aunt Teresa, Mrs Weld-Blundell, when his ship arrived at Liverpool, that he would be at Ince Blundell Hall, near Great Crosby, the following day: "I am coming to Ince for a long, long rest! I got little sleep on board, for the berth was as short and narrow as the coffin for which I shall soon be measured." Members of the Vaughan family were on hand to welcome Roger when he arrived at Ince Blundell Hall on the

Friday for lunch. Herbert arrived just before dinner and thought that Roger "looked yellow and weak and said he was very weary and had only left Sydney in time to save his life by a good rest, which he was looking forward to."

Roger had complained of some "abnormal action of the heart" and went to bed at 10.45 p.m. after Herbert walked him to his room. The next morning, the family and village Catholics waited for the archbishop to offer a 9 a.m. Mass in the hall's chapel. When he failed to appear, they decided to have breakfast and allow him to sleep longer. After breakfast, at 10 a.m., Herbert knocked at the door of Roger's room but heard no sound. Alarmed, Charles Weld-Blundell used a ladder to climb through a window and found the archbishop "cold, stiff and dead."[7]

On 23 August there was a Solemn Mass at the Ince chapel. Five bishops were present and the preacher was a Jesuit, Father Morris. Herbert wrote on 1 September: "I cannot get the thought of poor dear Roger out of my mind. Had I lost all my other brothers together I should not have felt it half as much."[8] On 10 September he wrote to Archbishop Corrigan to tell him of "the death of my favourite brother."[9]

The events that followed the death and temporary interment of the body of Archbishop Roger in the vault of Ince-Blundell Hall were to cause additional sorrow for Herbert and his family. The administrator of Roger's diocese at Sydney wrote asking that burial take place in Australia, but Herbert did not answer quickly enough. Roger Vaughan's successor was chosen, and, according to Snead-Cox: "In the light of subsequent events it must be regarded as unfortunate that the reply to the Administrator's request, that the burial should take place in Australia, was not sent by cable but in the ordinary way, by post. Those weeks of silence, perhaps, made all the difference."[10]

Roger Vaughan's successor, Cardinal Patrick Moran, wrote to Herbert from Venice on 12 August 1885 that the administrator of the archdiocese, who had been vicar general to Roger Vaughan, assured him "that no one in Sydney would wish the matter spoken of (the return of Vaughan's body to Australia) and not one penny would be contributed towards that purpose." Correspondence between Herbert Vaughan and Moran was published, first in Sydney newspapers, and afterwards in London. Roger Vaughan had left a large sum of his own money to the archdiocese of Sydney and Moran argued that it had all been used and the whole matter of the translation of the remains was the responsibility of the Vaughan family and the Benedictines of Downside. The final letter from Moran stated plainly that the family could place his corpse anywhere they wished "but it certainly will not be done at my expense."[11]

The Benedictine Henry Norbert Birt wrote that the incident inflicted deep pain and "great indignation in England especially amongst his religious brethren who felt that an unworthy return had been made for much good works done in Australia." The acting administrator of Sydney wrote to the *Evening News* in Sydney denying that he had ever used the language that

Cardinal Moran attributed to him about the transfer of Vaughan's body back to Sydney.[12]

Like his predecessor, Archbishop Polding, Roger Vaughan was opposed by his fellow bishops and some members of the clergy in Australia. Like Polding, according to C. J. Duffy, Vaughan—English and Benedictine—dreamed of a "diocese which would bear witness to the best of the traditions of the Church of Rome and be unimpeded by the legacy of mistakes, ignorance, and bitterness of the religious situation that had torn England and Ireland apart."

Despite his poor health, Roger won over many of those who had opposed his selection by his hard work on behalf of Catholic schools and "two full rounds of visitation and devising a method of keeping up-to-date returns that is a treasure house for researchers." St Mary's Cathedral owes its "inspiration and erection to Vaughan. In his own handwriting he sent out some two thousand personal appeals, often embellished with pen sketches."

However, Roger Vaughan aroused opposition by the kindness he extended to Mary MacKillop, the foundress of the Josephites—the Sisters of St Joseph of the Sacred Heart—who was beatified by Pope John Paul II in Sydney on 19 January 1995, and his recommendation to Rome arising from charges made against "the moral character" of one of the bishops.[13]

In February 1887 Roger Vaughan's body was taken to Belmont Abbey from the vault at Ince-Blundell, and placed at the east end of St Michael's Church. Bishop Hedley led the funeral service. It was not until 1946 that Archbishop Vaughan's remains were transported to Sydney and reburied in St Mary's Cathedral.

In Snead-Cox's opinion, Vaughan's experience with Moran taught him once again that it was worthless to seek popularity. "There is little doubt that the whole painful incident helped to strengthen that singular independence of temper and indifference to public opinion which so marked the later years of his life."[14]

Death of May Vaughan

In 1884 Herbert Vaughan lost his sister Mary, or May, who was Mother Clare Magdalen of the Augustinian Canonesses of the Lateran at Newton Abbot.[15] When May was a girl she had suffered from scarlet fever, and she remained in poor health for most of her life. At St Augustine's Priory, "in her zealous pursuit of religious perfection she never really learnt to exercise proper regard for health." Bernard Vaughan visited her once in 1866 and thought she looked well: She was "happiness itself, as gentle and pretty as ever—she seems the life and soul of the Community and the Nuns are devoted to her. She has no headaches or pains in the back, which formerly used so to worry her." But she was actually "on the verge of a serious lung collapse. The treatment of that time prescribed, amongst other things, hermetically-sealed windows, so her recovery, when at last she did get better, might almost be ascribed to a miraculous intervention."

Despite a history of illness and her own protests, she was elected prioress in 1883. During an influenza epidemic in 1884 she did not become sick but wore herself out caring for other nuns. At Easter she was very weak and by summer she was little better. When Herbert, her "much-loved eldest brother" spent a week with her in December 1884, she had been in the infirmary for a long time. After Christmas, on the Feast of the Holy Innocents, she felt better but died the very same day. She had been prioress for a little more than twelve months.[16] *The Tablet* reported: "After edifying her spiritual daughters by her patience and resignation and leaving behind her many lessons of childlike confidence in God and deepest love, she left the land of her exile, and went home on December 28th 1884." [17]

Herbert Vaughan's Health

Herbert Vaughan continued to experience periodic bouts of illness during the 1880s, one symptom of which was insomnia. Monsignor Gadd wrote to Archbishop Corrigan in 1885 that Vaughan was not well: "I notice that he gets languid and tired sooner than he used to do. A sleeplessness is coming on again."[18] Snead-Cox mentions that his doctor insisted that he walk six miles a day to recover his health.[19] One person who joined him on some of his walks was Thomas Jackson, the prefect apostolic of Northern Borneo.

In 1884 Jackson returned to England to attend a general chapter of the St Joseph's Missionary Society at Mill Hill. While in England he used the opportunity to visit local churches asking for help for the Borneo mission. Jackson went to Manchester and stayed with Bishop Vaughan at Salford for several months. Jackson wrote many years later that Vaughan walked for several hours each day to cure his insomnia, "which threatened to ruin his health. He generally managed to walk the allotted distance in visiting hospitals and other institutions."[20] There were twenty-six churches in Salford and Manchester and the bishop visited two or three of them every time he went out. Before he returned home he might also call on a businessman and "cross-examine him as to the state of trade, or the condition of this or that market, or as to the prospects of industrial prosperity or depression."[21]

Vaughan continued his wanderings about Manchester and Salford and the exercise did give him some relief from insomnia. Gadd wrote Corrigan once again: "Our good Bishop is very well. I really think that the more he does, the better his health is."[22] Probably as a result of what he saw and heard on his walks, and the example of Manning's concern for the poor children of Westminster, he gradually became aware of a serious problem in his diocese. He discovered that the less fortunate Catholic children of the diocese were being neglected by the Church.

Catholic Children's Rescue Society

Away from family and mission concerns, Vaughan became engaged in a project that was a reminder of personal failure and at the same a public achievement. He regretted that he had unknowingly failed to care adequately for the poor Catholic children of his diocese during his first years at Salford. At the same time the success of the organization he founded for their relief has been one of his lasting achievements.

It was towards the end of 1884 that Vaughan became aware of a serious problem affecting the Catholic children of the working-classes in his diocese. "A horrible suspicion forced itself upon his mind" writes Snead-Cox, that Catholic children were being "lost to the faith every year by the thousands." As he realized the seriousness of the problem, he blamed himself for spending his time on things that were much less vital.

His information indicated that there were many Church members being lost. The term popularized at the time was "leakage." The problem of leakage of baptised Catholics from the Church gradually emerged, according to Sheridan Gilley and Roger Swift, to become, for some commentators and bishops, the central problem for the Church in the nineteenth century. Especially alarming to Vaughan was that poor children were being lost to the Catholic Church due to the charitable works of other Christian bodies who were helping orphans and the homeless.[23]

It is surprising that Vaughan waited so long. According to Kidd, from the 1860s to the 1890s there were many charities for the poor, including orphans, street children, juvenile criminals and others. The Boys and Girls Welfare Society, founded in 1870, had pioneered techniques later used by Dr Barnardo to rescue "street arabs." Even the term "rescue" had been used by Fr Quick in the 1860s. Not only did he rescue Catholic children, but he also had a devotion to St Joseph as Vaughan did. The problem was addressed in a *Tablet* letter of 20 August 1881 from "an anxious priest": "The fault lies with ourselves if we allow our children to remain in workhouses. Our first duty is to build and enlarge and multiply our Poor Law Schools and secondly to use every effort to get our poor Catholic children out of them."[24]

Vaughan's regret a few years later that he had been so busy with non-vital issues that he failed to recognize the seriousness of the problem, was not self-indulgent. It was a fair judgement, especially when one knows that his mentor Manning had been struggling, from the time of his consecration in 1865, on behalf of Catholic children.

When Henry Manning succeeded to Westminster, he informed Bishop Grant of Southwark that he wanted "no disputes about money" between them and took steps to see that the Diocese of Southwark received all the funds legally theirs which had been withheld by Westminster when London was divided. He then proposed to Grant that they unite in a campaign to rescue the Catholic children in London workhouses.

In June 1866 Manning wrote a pastoral in which he called attention to children "baptised but robbed of their inheritance by the sins of fathers and mothers, by the cruelty of oppressors or by the apathy of Christians." According to Manning, more than one thousand Catholic children were being "detained in workhouses and workhouse schools of London." Even *The Times* published a letter in the 12 June 1866 edition, which stated that Roman Catholics in London were not "looked as well after as they are in Ireland. Great numbers of them live and die in actual if not formal separation from the Church—parents are at the root of the evil under question."[25]

Manning held a meeting at St James Hall on 14 June 1866 and established the Westminster Diocesan Education Fund. The plan was to open thirty-five new schools, two reformatories and two more industrial schools for Catholic children. Manning even asked that churches be used as schools to care for the large numbers. Catholic children were to be rescued from workhouses and elsewhere in the diocese. The success of the plan was due, according to V. A. McClelland, to Manning's choice of Fr Thomas Seddon as the Fund's secretary. Seddon worked with a convert, Lord Archibald Douglas, son of the Marquis of Queensbury.[26]

In 1882-3 Manning was still reminding Catholics of their duty to care for the children: it was sixteen years since he was moved by a sense of justice about Catholic children placed by state guardians into Protestant schools. His chief appeals had always been "for means to support the orphans and destitute children who are continually thrown, by the death or misery of their parents upon our hands."[27] The action Vaughan finally did take was to form the Catholic Children's Rescue Society.

Snead-Cox wrote in 1910 that after Vaughan left Salford, the Rescue Society continued to carry on its "beneficent mission in Salford and Manchester as though the inspiring presence of its founder were yet in their midst." Snead-Cox does not mention that Vaughan's departure to Westminster in 1892, and the loss of the organization's chairman, treasurer and secretary, were to create an organizational and financial crisis that the society barely survived. But Vaughan himself was the greatest loss, for he was the force behind it from the day it was founded until the day he left Salford.[28]

In 1986, the centenary year of the Rescue Society, Patrick Kelly, Bishop of Salford, gave a tribute to the work begun a hundred years before and the "selflessness of those who have sought to serve" its aims. During a conversation in 1992 Bishop Kelly attributed the longevity of the society in part to the foresight of Herbert Vaughan.[29]

For Herbert Vaughan, the loss to the Church of Catholic children of the diocese was, for some of them, due to their parents, and for others, because of the efforts of non-Catholic organizations. The non-Catholic organizations were mainly Dr Barnardo's Homes and the Wesleyan Methodist Institution and Boys' Refuge. Not only was Vaughan convinced that he had failed to lead his diocese in efforts to care materially for Catholic children, but also in the duty to care for their spiritual welfare—a duty undertaken in the baptismal promises of parents and godparents—which had been neglected.

He immediately applied his energy and diocesan resources to the problem. In September 1885 he asked each parish to take a census and to note the condition of any Catholic under the age of twenty-one. The results more than confirmed his worst fears, "filling him with sadness and dismay and causing him to reproach himself for not having been aware of the situation earlier."[30]

During the 1880s there was remarkable growth in public concern over the question of child welfare. Two acts of Parliament were passed providing children for the first time with effective safeguards against neglect, cruelty and exploitation. This was followed by the establishment of the National Society for the Prevention of Cruelty to Children. Much has been written about these developments but not, according to D. E. Selby, about the part played by Manning in helping to form public opinion on the matter of children's rights and securing the passage of protective legislation for them. Manning did not address the condition of children with his full energies till 1885,[31] that is, about the same time Vaughan was realizing the seriousness of the problem.

During the final years of his life Manning devoted more and more of his time to the cause of poor children and other social concerns, so much so that one writer suggests that those years "were in many aspects the most fruitful of his life, especially in his attempts to apply Christianity to social problems."[32] Vaughan and Manning disagreed over the approach to social issues, but in the case of poor and neglected children—although belatedly for Vaughan—they were stirred to action by the sorry conditions of the times.

Manning was also capable of broader sympathies and understanding of social problems than Vaughan. Herbert Vaughan lacked Manning's life experience and his awareness of the underlying causes of society's ills. This became apparent near the end of Manning's life, when Vaughan became disturbed by his old friend's radicalism. But the straightforward Vaughan was touched by what he saw in his diocese; his sense of duty and fidelity to the old faith and his conscientiousness were to mark his concern for the Catholic children.[33]

N. Middleton, in an article in the *British Journal of Educational Studies*, maintains that "the mandate of complete responsibility obviously accorded to parents was discarded as it dawned on thinking people that the home should be invaded in the cases of neglect, cruelty and exploitation" of children. By the end of the century, he adds, "the position of the child had radically altered from being the least considered member of society towards a position of privilege which allowed a safer passage through immaturity and gave facilities to prepare for life."[34] Henry Manning played an important part in bringing about the change. Manning, who, with Vaughan, worked so hard on behalf of parental rights in education was among the first to admit "that the state might come in when parents failed to fulfil their protective and educational role."[35] While efforts were under way to address the deeper attitudes of society towards the rights of children, Vaughan threw all his energy into what he knew best how to do, rallying his diocese and organizing the means to help Catholic children in need of immediate attention. His answer was the Rescue Society.

From its beginnings, Vaughan was the "head and the hand, and the heart" of the Rescue Society. During the first years he used to set one night apart every week in order to ask to dinner people who might help him with advice or information. "Priests and inspectors of police and guardians of the poor were all made welcome." With the help of the police he made a series of visits at night to the worst and most disreputable quarters of the city. He saw things during his midnight walks that he never forgot.[36]

The situation was put clearly before the people of Salford Diocese in a pastoral letter in 1886 entitled: "The Loss of Our Children." The letter was later published as a pamphlet. He announced that a board of inquiry he had set up reported that ten thousand Catholic children were "in peril of their souls" through either "the vice or neglect of their parents" or the "effects of the workhouse system," and in some cases due to the efforts of the "Protestant proselytising societies." Thirty-seven institutions caring for children, he said, were "hotbeds of proselytism." Snead-Cox remarks that the report did not conceal the stressful conditions under which it was prepared. Finally Vaughan put himself forward as the public champion of the distracted parents who did not look after their children because of poverty, and he promised to fight their battles for them.[37]

In another letter, entitled "Why Rescue?," he explained the background of the system of workhouses and workhouse schools: in England and Wales in 1886 there were about 647 unions, or workhouses, made up of 14,827 Poor Law parishes, each with its Board of Guardians under provisions of the Poor Law Amendment Act of 1834. In the Poor Houses, Catholic children "were brought up aliens to their faith, and were almost inevitably lost to their religion." By the 1880s, the Catholic poor in workhouses were permitted some religious liberty. For example, Catholic priests were allowed to enter some unions. Vaughan thought that Manchester and Salford might be considered examples of toleration in the matter of religious freedom, but he was concerned about poor Catholic children who came to institutions "for food, maintenance and education."

What Vaughan wanted was help for Catholic children by Catholics, a concern that expressed his spiritual values and devotion to the old faith: "All Catholic children have a natural right to be brought up in the faith of their parents and their Baptism. It would be impossible to estimate the number of Catholic children who in the past 100 years have been robbed of this sacred right, and despoiled of this their lawful inheritance." In conclusion, he asked for help to employ Catholic children, for it was "a work of charity and religion and means the salvation of souls."[38]

When the work of Rescue officially began, Vaughan called on all priests and people of his diocese to accept the effort as "not of temporal but of eternal, not of worldly but of divine interest," and, "In the name of God take it up and make it your own."[39]

Bishop Vaughan collected large sums of money, year in and year out, by means of "Rescue Saturday" and other appeals. For example, on 18 February 1887 he addressed a St Patrick's night gathering at the Manchester Free Trade Hall. Each year since 1874, whenever he was at home, he had presided at the meeting and the money raised had been used for the education of poor and abandoned children. But by 1887 the new work of "Protection and Rescue" was "assuming vast and—looking at our resources—I must say alarming proportions." He asked them to respond to the urgency because the cost "will become a very serious matter, but the work is an inevitable duty."[40]

Herbert Vaughan's brother John thought that more than money was needed. He wrote an article for the *Irish Ecclesiastical Record* in 1887 entitled "The 'leakage' in the Church in Great Britain," in which he argued that the fault was mainly with the clergy. In his opinion the "chief cause of our failure" was a lack of a "spirit of prayer and a spirit of mortification."[41]

A most remarkable outcome of Rescue was the personal service Bishop Vaughan enlisted for the cause, since many lay people participated. Before he left Salford in 1892, more than two thousand people were helping in the work of "protecting and rescuing Catholic children, seeing that they went to their religious duties and to a Catholic school." Snead-Cox commented that if he were not writing Vaughan's biography, and rather a history of Salford Diocese, it would be necessary to tell the story of Herbert Vaughan's fellow workers. One he singled out for special mention was Austin Oates, a name that will appear again when Vaughan became Archbishop of Westminster and Oates his personal secretary.[42]

Austin Oates was born in 1859, the son of Wilfrid Oates, one of the original partners of the publishing firm of Burns & Oates. Austin had been educated at Stonyhurst and the Jesuit College at Alost in Belgium. His wife Odilia was from Flanders and they had two sons, Herbert and Austin. Vaughan invited Oates to join him during the time he was collecting information about the problem of poor Catholic children in Salford Diocese. When Vaughan launched the "Salford Catholic Protection and Rescue Society," Oates was appointed honorary secretary. He held the post till 1892, when he left for Westminster. He was known for his hard work and good humour, evident in the notes he left containing anecdotes about Cardinal Vaughan when they were together at Westminster and earlier at Salford.[43]

The aims of the organization, according to Oates, were to rescue Catholic children in institutions where the practice of their faith was denied; to find homes for those who would be forced by circumstances to enter public institutions as Protestants; to watch over the religious interests of our children when entering or leaving the workhouse; to secure when necessary their committal to Catholic industrial and reformatory schools; to find homes and work for destitute street boys; to protect the young and helpless from irreligious and cruel parents.[44]

Oates went around the diocese, parish to parish, enlisting support. He spent time among the poor, and might stay in a "common lodging house." He wrote about his experiences in a monthly called *Harvest*, which ceased publication only in 1970. He also wrote for other publications. One article for the *Dublin Review* in 1887 was entitled: "The lost, strayed and stolen of our Catholic poor children."[45]

Austin Oates had his office at Bishop's House in Salford. Every morning at 9.30 the hall outside was crowded with people looking for help and others who worked for the Rescue programme. Mr Smart was the Society's long-serving investigating officer. One by one, Oates recorded each interview in his secretary's journal.[46]

Before special residences were opened by the Rescue Society there were other Catholic institutions caring for children. One was St Bridget's Orphanage, founded by three laymen in 1841 and first handed over to the Presentation Sisters in 1844, then later to the Daughters of the Cross, and finally to the Cross and Passion Sisters. The Good Shepherd nuns had also established a home for women at Blackley. In 1886, one of Vaughan's relatives, Miss Weld-Blundell, set up "The Catholic Girls Mutual Aid Society." There was also an evening home for working boys opened by the St Vincent de Paul Conference of St Chad's, Cheetham Hill, in Angel Meadow.

Vaughan negotiated with nuns and brothers from Ghent to come to help in Salford. The Brothers of Charity established an independent home at Rochdale, Buckley Hall, and the Sisters of Charity of Jesus and Mary began Holly Mount in Tottington during 1888. The Rescue Society opened two of its own homes for boys, one in Tipping Street, Ardwick, and the other in Tonman Street, Deansgate. In 1886 a home for workhouse girls was opened in Victoria Park by the Sisters of Charity. The Sisters of the Cross and Passion housed nearly fifty girls at Byrom Street, Manchester, and Hulme Street, Salford; at Bolton they supervised a hostel for homeless girls. In 1886 the Catholic Needlework Guild was founded to help the Sisters to clothe the poor.[47]

Rescue Sisters

One group of women has a special place in the story of the Rescue Society. The name of Alice Ingham's community, established at Mill Hill to care for the seminary, and share the work in overseas missions, became synonymous with the rescue work of Salford. On the 8 September 1883, Alice and eleven other women made their vows, and so founded a community known today as the Franciscan Missionaries of St Joseph. It was to Mother Alice Ingham that Vaughan turned for help to care for the children of Salford Diocese. Alice and her first companions had given up their work among the poor of Rochdale as lay members of the Third Order of St Francis. She had done so with serious misgivings in 1878 in order to take on domestic duties at Vaughan's St Joseph's Missionary College.[48] Now her sacrifice seemed to be rewarded. Called to help at Salford, she began an association between the Rescue Society of Salford and the "Mill Hill Sisters." So closely did they identify with the poor children of Salford that they became known as the "Rescue Sisters."

In order to begin, one of Alice Ingham's nuns, Mother Elizabeth, with one novice Sister, took over Ardwick Hall on a cold and gloomy November night in 1886. "The first children were admitted the very next day; a little hunch-backed girl of eight and a baby of eight months." Soon there were 150 children. The boys were transferred to Buckley Hall, where they were cared for by Brothers of Charity from Ghent. In 1888 the Rescue Sisters took over a small house in Paradise Street, Blackburn. A nearby house was added, a place known as "Granny's Castle." Later they rented two fairly large buildings on Princess Street.

In 1889 Monsignor Kershaw of Barton donated a building and plot of land at Patricroft to replace Ardwick Hall. Mother Elizabeth was the first one to look at Patricroft at the request of Bishop Vaughan. Mgr Kershaw was happy to have the Sisters and often told parishioners: "For forty years I have wanted nuns in the parish and now I have them." He remained a friend and benefactor to the Sisters for the rest of his life. Alice Ingham's religious Sisters began to renovate Patricroft with the support of Bishop Vaughan.[49]

Herbert Vaughan continued to regret overlooking the condition of Catholic children in his pastoral care, even after Rescue was well established. The work of Rescue for the unfortunate children, according to Snead-Cox, had changed Vaughan's outlook. It was a "revelation, a challenge, and an inspiration," which "altered and coloured the whole trend of his thoughts and the activities of his episcopate," first at Salford and then at Westminster.[50] Mother Elizabeth recalled one of Vaughan's extraordinary acts of penance connected with Rescue. He visited Patricroft many times as their bishop and superior general since Patricroft also served as the Sisters' mother house and novitiate. More than once he was found on the doorstep replacing his boots: "He had walked barefoot from the train terminus in Eccles, his feet hidden by his cassock and cloak. It was his personal act of reparation for his negligence in failing to establish the Rescue Society sooner." He also publicly apologized.[51]

Vaughan was anxious that perhaps something was being left undone for abandoned children because of a lack of funds. On one occasion he told the Rescue Council to plan for the best ways and means as if money were no object. "When it was a question of saving souls he had no patience with the wisdom which bids us cut our coat according to our cloth—he had a sublime faith that the cloth would be given if he designed the coat boldly enough."[52]

In 1887 Bishop Vaughan cancelled the dinner he usually had with his clergy after the annual diocesan synod. The provost of the Chapter announced that the priests would understand when they realized that the savings could help maintain five or six children for a year.[53]

As early as 1888 Vaughan considered the possibility that some children might be helped to emigrate to Canada. In June arrangements were completed with the Salford Board of Guardians for Catholic orphans to leave the country. In Canada they would be adopted by Catholic families and taught a trade.[54] Fr Rossall, chancellor of the diocese, was chosen to accompany the first group of children. Vaughan wrote to Rossall that the project was to help those "who cannot help themselves, but who may become, if wisely assisted in their early youth, the strength and honour of the Church as well as of the state."[55]

On Thursday, 21 June 1888, the first small group of thirteen—eight boys and five girls, between the age of six and eleven years—left Salford Cathedral. It was to be the first of many such journeys for Rossall over the years. He brought the children to Alexandra dock at Liverpool, where they were met by Fr Thomas Seddon, secretary to Cardinal Manning; Seddon was also secretary of the Westminster Diocesan Education Fund for Destitute Children. Seddon had a group of forty-eight boys gathered from some of the orphanages in and around London; it was his seventh trip. When they went on board the ship, the *Polynesian*, they were met by Henry Manning, who wished them all a goodbye and safe journey. Between 1888 and 1908 over six hundred children from the Salford Diocese emigrated to Canada.[56]

In the early years of the Rescue Society, Vaughan asked Rome for permission to keep as the feast day of the society the one commemorating the finding of the child Jesus in the Temple. He saw in that event from Jesus' life a likeness to the search undertaken for Catholic children throughout Salford diocese. The first year it was kept on 8 January 1886.

In 1892 Manning died and Vaughan was appointed Archbishop of Westminster. Austin Oates left Rescue and joined him in London. "By this time Rescue was well established but a great era in its life and the life of the Diocese of Salford ended," according to Snead-Cox. Unfortunately for Rescue, the loss of Vaughan and with him the income from many upper-middle class donors, along with the departure of Austin Oates, was a blow to the organization.[57]

The Irish

The "Irish Question" dominated English politics in the nineteenth century from the popular campaign for Catholic Emancipation in the 1820s to the calling of William Gladstone to form a government by Queen Victoria in 1868 and beyond.[58] According to G. M. Young, author of *Victorian England:*

Portrait of an Age, problems concerning Ireland "went deeper than the age could reach. The twin cell of English life, the squire administering what everybody recognizes as law and the parson preaching what everybody acknowledges to be religion, had no meaning in a country where the squire was usually an invader and the parson always a heretic."[59] In David Newsome's view, this was exactly what Manning, Gladstone's old friend, tried to drum into the heads of English statesmen. In his "Letter to Earl Grey," published in 1868, Manning wrote that "England treats its colonies, in education as well as in religious equality, better than it treats Ireland."[60]

English confidence had been shattered in 1865 by an uprising led by the Irish Republican Brotherhood, or Fenians, a secret society dedicated to the independence of Ireland. Irishmen felt great bitterness towards England, especially over evictions from their land in the post-famine period. The Fenian violence ended in 1867, but the movement had awakened some Englishmen, including Gladstone, to the problems of Ireland.[61] The first step he took was to propose to disestablish and disendow the Protestant Church of Ireland. As leader of the opposition he announced to the House of Commons on 16 March 1868 that the Church of Ireland must give up its attachment to the State and a week later he introduced the resolutions. According to Newsome, the first significant service that Manning rendered to Ireland was his support of efforts to disestablish the Church of Ireland.[62] The proposal took on wider dimensions and became a constitutional struggle between the elected House of Commons and the hereditary-based House of Lords. Over the year that followed, Gladstone captured the Prime Minister's post from Disraeli and a set up a disestablishment conference to work out the details of the bill, which passed in 1869. Gladstone wrote to Manning that the government appreciated the "firm, constant and discriminating support which you have afforded our Bill." The land laws were to be reformed next. The Land Act of 1870 fell short of expectations, but at least introduced protection against indiscriminate eviction.[63]

Gladstone was defeated on a bill to set up a Catholic university in Ireland in 1873,[64] but stayed in office for another year because Disraeli refused to become Prime Minister without a general election. Parliament was dissolved in 1874 and a February election returned the Conservatives. The Conservatives undertook no constructive measures for Ireland; Disraeli was the head of a party "committed to conserving institutions, sympathy for the landed interest and now the maintenance of Empire."[65]

In Ireland a catastrophic agricultural depression began around 1873. It led to new evictions, which were the cause of renewed violence among poor farmers still on the edge of famine. The misery and bitterness of Ireland found a champion in the Land League founded by the ex-Fenian Michael Davitt in 1879.

The new crisis in Ireland was also brought about by political activity. In

1874 fifty-six Irish members were returned to the Parliament at Westminster. Led by a conservative Protestant, Isaac Butt, they were committed to Home Rule for Ireland, arguing for a separate Irish legislature to deal with Irish affairs. They made little progress and so some turned to "obstructionism" in Parliament. In 1877 Butt was succeeded by Charles Stewart Parnell, a Protestant landowner who had entered Parliament in 1875. In the 1880 election, which returned Gladstone and his Liberals to power, sixty-one Irish members were also elected. However, only twenty-four were supporters of Parnell.

Gladstone's government moved to strengthen law enforcement in Ireland and introduce some reforms. Gladstone was almost alone in opposing coercion and so the Chief Secretary for Ireland was able to introduce a coercion bill in 1881, which provided for the suspension of *habeas corpus*, therefore allowing arbitrary arrest and preventive detention. Gladstone introduced a new Land Bill that seemed too radical for some English but did not satisfy the Irish. Parnell was arrested and imprisoned under the Coercion Act. An agreement was reached by the government with Parnell that coercion would be tacitly abandoned and defects in the Land Act remedied. Parnell re-emphasized his loyalty to parliamentary methods of reform. Unfortunately, soon after his release from prison the new Chief Secretary for Ireland, Frederick Cavendish—a close friend of Gladstone—and his chief civil servant, the Irish under secretary, were stabbed to death while walking in Phoenix Park. Parnell had no connection with the act but the moderate Irish cause was set back, and another measure of coercion was introduced. Gladstone's government was defeated after the death of General Gordon in the Anglo-Egyptian Sudan in 1885, and he resigned.

The Marquess of Salisbury had taken over leadership of the Conservatives in 1881 after the death of Disraeli. Parnell sought their support for Home Rule. Randolph Churchill, a Tory radical, promised Parnell that coercion would be abandoned. In addition, a number of the Conservatives were convinced that land-purchase was an acceptable solution. Lord Carnarvon, the second-in-command of the Tories, was also in favour of Home Rule. Parnell also thought the Conservatives had a better chance of getting Home Rule through Parliament than the Liberals. Salisbury called for a general election in November of 1885. Parnell ordered the Irish to vote Tory.

According to Newsome, Manning had been an advocate of "dominion self-government, but not total separation," after reading Isaac Butts' *Land Tenure in Ireland*. His letters to Gladstone in the early 1870s suggest that he was more sympathetic "than either the Prime Minister or his ecclesiastical colleagues" to the Home Rule movement. Archbishop Cullen of Dublin opposed any suggestion of separation. John Henry Newman was also not in favour. Despite his sympathy for Ireland, it seemed to Manning at the time to be a blow against "the power of England as great as it is retributive."[66]

Privately, Gladstone had become convinced of the necessity of Home Rule in the 1880s.[67] He thought that a Conservative government had a better chance of having it passed by the House of Lords than the Liberals. Nonetheless, he kept his views to himself, even at the risk of losing Parnell's support, because of the hostility such views would arouse in his own party. The Liberals won the November 1885 election with a majority balanced by the Irish party. But in December Gladstone's son, Herbert, innocently told a news correspondent of his father's change of heart in a confidential interview. The "Hawarden Kite" was published and the country was shaken. The Conservatives felt free to go back to favouring union while Parnell shifted his support. Gladstone was left facing a largely hostile Liberal party.

For Henry Manning, Joseph Chamberlain's concession to Ireland—"a measure of self-government ... while retaining Irish representation in the English Parliament"—was closer to his view than Gladstone's idea of a separate Parliament.[68]

In January 1886, Salisbury was defeated on an amendment to the Coercion Bill and resigned. Gladstone returned to power and when he put an Irish Home Rule Bill to the Cabinet, Chamberlain resigned. The bill called for a separate Irish legislature and executive, with power over all Irish affairs except imperial matters. No Irish members were to sit at Westminster, a provision that Gladstone was willing to modify, and there were to be two sections of an Irish Parliament, including an upper house of twenty-eight life peer members.

An important role in the outcome of the Home Rule Bill was played by Chamberlain. He did not like Parnell. His emissary, William O'Shea, husband of Parnell's mistress from 1880, was part of the problem, as was Parnell's alliance with the Tories in 1885. In spite of his interest in a reformed, active, and responsible local government in Ireland, he was opposed to breaking the union.[69]

Cardinal Manning was present in the gallery of the House of Commons to hear Gladstone's three-and-a-half-hour speech on 8 April 1886, and saw the bill defeated.[70] *The Tablet* reported Gladstone's motion in its 10 April edition: "The Government intended to propose the establishment of a legislative body to sit in Dublin to legislate for Ireland and to control Irish administration." At the end of Gladstone's speech the "members poured out of the House in a dense stream, and three or four luckless orators addressed the almost empty benches."[71]

Herbert Vaughan had become owner of the *Dublin Review* and initiated its Third Series in January 1879. Bishop John Cuthbert Hedley was the editor to the end of 1884, when Vaughan became editor as well as proprietor, just as W. G. Ward had been before him. His acting editor was Fr W. E. Driffield. In April 1886, the *Review* published "A Symposium on Home Rule."

Canon James Moyes wrote "The Claim for Home Rule, Upon General Principles," in which he called for the right and freedom to remove the "disaffection" of Ireland; "we may say that they dislike legislative Union; they dislike their rulers; they dislike the system and method in which they are governed," and Home Rule should be given "as a willing work and gift of the conscience and strength of the British people."

Opposing Moyes' view was an "Irish Catholic Barrister," who wrote "The Probable Consequences of Home Rule." To his mind Home Rule was a question "beyond the range of discussion" and what Gladstone was proposing was "the disintegration of the empire," which would lead to disaster for one or both countries. "In one form or another the discontent of Ireland with the 'Saxon yoke' has for half a century been before the English public; and whether the demand was for Repeal or Home Rule, it was always regarded by statesmen on both sides of the House, and by Mr Gladstone himself among the number, as lying beyond the range of discussion."[72]

Gladstone gave the closing speech in the debate on the second reading of the Home Rule Bill on 8 June 1886:

> Ireland stands at your bar, expectant, hopeful, almost suppliant. Her words are the words of truth and soberness. She asks a blessed oblivion of the past, and in that oblivion our interest is deeper than even hers. My right honourable friend (Mr Goschen) asks us to-night to abide by the traditions of which we are the heirs. What traditions? By the Irish traditions? Go into the length and breadth of the world, ransack the literature of all the countries; find, if you can, a single voice, a single book—find I would almost say, as much as a single newspaper article, unless the product of the day, in which the conduct of England towards Ireland is anywhere treated except with profound and bitter condemnation. Are these the traditions to which we are exhorted to stand? No, they are a sad exception to the glory of our country. They are a broad, and black blot upon the pages of its history, and what we want to do is stand by the traditions of which we are heirs, in all matters except our relations to Ireland.... Think, I beseech you—think well, think wisely, think not for a moment but for the years that are to come, before you reject this Bill.[73]

The ninety-three Liberal members whose votes defeated Gladstone's Home Rule Bill on 8 June were led by Chamberlain; Home Rule was defeated by 343 votes to 313. The next day Parliament was dissolved.

The results of the July 1886 election showed how far the voters agreed with the anti-home-rulers by voting in 316 Conservatives and 78 Liberal Unionists against only 191 Liberals and 85 Irish Nationalists. In Ireland, the majority were confirmed in their bitterness against England. In addition, the vote resulted in a collapse of the two-party system and the temporary paralysis of English government for the twenty succeeding years.[74] It is within this context that Vaughan's views on Ireland, and his personal opposition to Irish Home Rule, need to be considered.

Herbert Vaughan and the Irish Question

The label "anti-Irish" has been applied to Herbert Vaughan. For Arthur McCormack, the suggestion that Vaughan was anti-Irish had its origins in his ownership of *The Tablet*: "a paper very pro-Irish under its founder Lucas, but just the opposite under his successor, Wallis."[75] Vaughan's views on the political issues of his time, notably on the question of Home Rule for Ireland, were undoubtably not those of a very large number of his fellow Catholics. His outspokenness on the issue, and the linking of Catholic interests in the Education Question with that of Home Rule probably had more to do with it than editorial positions taken by *The Tablet*.[76]

A story repeated by Snead-Cox captures something of the depth of feeling shared by many about Vaughan, and his detachment, when the care of the Catholic community was at risk. An "eager and devoted" Irish priest, when he learned that Herbert Vaughan was to succeed Manning as archbishop of Westminster in 1892, decided that it was time that he returned to Ireland. When Vaughan heard about the man's intentions and his feelings about Vaughan's opposition to Irish Home Rule, he sent for the priest and tried to persuade him to remain in England. Vaughan's final argument was: "In Ireland they are all Home Rulers—stay here and work for Westminster and you may have the whole of the diocese to convert." Vaughan usually got on well with his Irish priests. Whatever their political opinions, he wanted "good and zealous priests, men willing to devote their lives to work among the London poor, and if he could get that nothing else mattered very much."[77]

Vaughan was not alone among the hierarchy in being distrusted by the Irish. Oliver Rafferty, in an article on the cardinal in *Recusant History*, asks the question about Nicholas Wiseman: "Did his cast of mind and sympathies lead him to certain anti-Irish dispositions in the conduct of the affairs of English Catholicism?" Wiseman's father was Irish, and, at least on the surface, he seemed sympathetic to the Irish.[78] Rafferty argues that, already in the 1840s, the hereditary Catholics and converts in England were alarmed by Catholic political radicalism in Ireland. They feared that in any adverse encounter with the British government, Catholicism in England and in Ireland would suffer. It was Daniel O'Connell who clearly stated that while the Irish took their religion from Rome "we take our politics from home."[79]

Wiseman could not see any advantages for the Catholic Church in the repeal of union between Ireland and England. He believed that all England might return to Rome and this hope determined his strategy for managing the affairs of the Church. In this effort he was more concerned, says Rafferty, to avoid division in the emerging Catholic body than he was with the intrinsic justice of righting Irish grievances. Furthermore, he considered any English political antipathy to Ireland to be the greatest block to their acceptance of the average mid-Victorian Englishman. The political strength of Ireland, especially in the English Parliament, needed to be "harnessed for the advancement of Catholicism" in England, where his sympathies lay.[80]

Paul Cullen, Archbishop of Dublin, distrusted England, but not on the grounds of abstract right and legitimacy of rule. He disliked England, according to Edward Norman, because he considered that the English view of the Irish troubles was a Protestant view.[81] Much of what is written of Wiseman's views on Ireland can also be said of Herbert Vaughan, then his young associate, and later successor, in the work of restoration of the Catholic Church in England.

Like Wiseman, Vaughan's views were not necessarily inspired by any antipathy to Ireland or the Irish. He attempted to distance the English Church from Irish radicalism, which would fuel the anti-Catholicism of the later Victorian era among his countrymen, and to secure the position of Catholics in England.[82.]

The *Dublin Review* in 1870 posed the question, "Is Ireland Irreconcilable?" and argued that the key question of the century was: "Whether it was possible to combine the sentiment of Irish nationality with loyalty to the Crown." To advance the renewal of the Roman Catholic Church in Britain, Vaughan did his utmost to show that it was possible.[83]

One example of Victorian Protestant anti-Catholicism was in the movement instigated by Charles Newdegate, a senior member of Parliament, representing North Warwickshire, to investigate and inspect convents and monasteries. Walter Arnstein in his study of Newdegate presents a Roman Catholic Church at mid-century that was held in "awe or fear of its pretensions," views that were not diminished later in the century by those who felt, like Newdegate, that a "cherished heritage" was being threatened.[84].

According to Snead-Cox, Vaughan had a reputation of being resolutely opposed to Home Rule. Snead-Cox exaggerates when he writes: "It was a question which was outside his life and had only the vaguest interest for him. He never voted against it, or wrote against it, or spoke against it in his life." One can also point to his roots in a landholding family to help explain his opposition. He was of that stock and his father even had holdings in Mayo from immediately after the first years of the famine to the 1870s. Some of his letters from Ireland are quoted in Mary Vaughan's book. Yet the more one knows of Vaughan's life, the clearer it is that whatever his inherited sympathies and experience, he usually rose above them and did not let them interfere with what he saw as his duty as pastor and bishop.[85]

In a letter to Mary Elizabeth Herbert in 1881, Vaughan mentions the difficulty an Englishman had in saying "a word which displeases the Irish." This stemmed from his experience, especially in his ownership of *The Tablet*: "The fact is the Irish are very indignant with the Tablet, that is, a great many of them are—for its having refused to take up the League and for its criticisms of some Irish proposals ... also in three leading articles pointed out the dangers."[86]

Vaughan published a pastoral letter at Salford in 1883 entitled: "Irish Distress and the Action of the Catholic Church in Ireland." In it he appealed for help for the suffering in Ireland while holding up the example of the Pope in Italy, "himself a victim of injustice and persecution without parallel," preaching "patience, obedience to law, respect for authority."[87] He quoted Pope Leo XIII's apostolic letter—published in Ireland by the bishops on 1 January 1883—in which an appeal was made to all Catholics that "the national cause should be distinct from the aims, purposes, and deeds of Secret Societies." According to Vaughan, the sufferings of the Irish poor and the impoverishment of Irish tenant farmers as a result of the disastrous agriculture depression, bad harvests, evictions and an intensified political battle for Home Rule resulted, in 1882, in nearly one hundred attempted assassinations and twenty-six murders. Attacks were also made on Irish who did not follow the directions of the underground resistance organization.

On 3 January 1881, Pope Leo XIII sent a letter to Archbishop MacCabe addressed to all the Irish bishops, endorsing a condemnation of terrorist acts, and blaming them on the "secret societies." After MacCabe became a Cardinal, the Pope wrote the letter referred to by Vaughan, asking the bishops to act together and for the clergy to obey their bishops.[88]

Vaughan's Salford pastoral reported that branches of secret societies "by whatever name they have been called" were planted in England and in his diocese. "But be not deceived. The clothing of these Secret Societies, in outward profession, may be that of the lamb; inwardly they are ravening wolves. It is in Secret Societies that deeds of violence, sedition, treason, and murder are hatched, while no single man seems responsible."

Before Vaughan arrived at Salford, in November 1867, the "Manchester Martyrs" were sentenced to be hanged at the Salford Gaol. This resulted in an attempt by armed men to free two Fenian organizers, in which a policeman was killed. Vaughan's secretary, Charles Gadd, was chaplain to the prison. Fenian activity among the Irish of Salford aroused opposition against them and Catholics, as shown by the anti-Catholic demonstrations led by William Murphy in 1867. And so when Vaughan spoke of or prepared a pastoral about secret societies he was not doing it from a distance.

He thought that little notice had been taken by the secular press of the peaceable work of the Church and her priests in Ireland. "Coercion laws and physical force cannot calm a whole nation, without the influence of religion. That Englishman must be blind to facts and human nature, or steeped in bigotry unworthy of consideration, who does not recognize upon the Irish people the powerful influences of the Catholic religion."[89]

Henry Manning's views on Home Rule and the Irish, prior to his change of mind, were known by Vaughan. To appreciate Vaughan's position it is necessary to understand where Manning stood before 1886. In a letter to Vaughan on 7 March 1881, Manning wrote that he was looking forward to a meeting of all the bishops after Easter. "The human and the diabolical spirits have been making havoc among us. I have seen your Fenian Priests in the *Nation*. The state of the Irishman is preternatural. They cannot hear a word against their own notions and they take the Decalogue as an affront. This is all very sad. We are entangled on every side. And there is a sadness on everybody."

Manning was concerned about unity and solidarity among the Catholic bishops. On 19 May 1883 he wrote that he was to call a meeting of bishops at Birmingham but hesitated until the bishops of Ireland were consulted: "Any apparent division between the English and Irish Episcopates would bring evils of every kind here, in Ireland, in the whole British Empire. The greatest cause has been treated in the narrowest way: and the danger is great. If I can go to Rome I will speak, but I can do nothing from here. I will read your article. You remember that I spoke and spoke alone about Secret Societies in 1868."[90]

Manning, according to Emmet Larkin, in his study of the Catholic Church and the Home Rule movement in Ireland, was "one of the few English Catholics in the nineteenth century who appreciated and worked with the realities of the Irish position in the British political system." The political power of Catholics was related to the number of parliamentary seats they controlled and therefore the Irish, within the Union, with their parliamentary presence, were the "basic factor in the British parliamentary power equation." The *Directory* of 1904 estimated the number of Catholics in Ireland to be 3,310,028 while England had less than half that number, or 1,500,000. In the House of Commons there were only four Catholic members from England and seventy-one from Ireland. Manning understood political power exercised in Parliament and was also able to reach across the cultural divide to the Irish immigrant population in England in a way that others were unable to do.[91]

Sheridan Gilley considers the political role of the immigrant Irish the most serious issue, "which soured relations between the leaders of the Catholic Irish immigrants and the British Catholic establishment." The political objective of most Irish immigrants in the nineteenth century was "a broad nationalist one" which was not accepted as legitimate by the British public.[92]

Vaughan shares this view most forcibly in a letter to Manning of 27 November—no year given, but probably 1885. He first refers to the "Irish Alliance" proposed by Bishop Bagshawe of Nottingham, who, he thinks, is "on a wrong line." Vaughan continues: "he is proposing an alliance with allies whom he is seeking by every means in his power to cast out of the only parliament with which the Catholics of England can ever have do. How far it would also be an alliance with sedition and disloyalty may be a question for dispute. Certainly it would be an alliance with nationalism and particularism and that in opposition [to] the sense of the country we live in." Vaughan thought that the Catholic bishops needed to be cautious about "the danger of merging our office and our Church in the political aspirations of the foreign section of our flock. We are Bishops to represent the Church to the English people and ought to be on our guard against presenting it to them in a colour which will be prejudicial!" He wanted the attitude to be one of "independence of all parties whatsoever—allowing individuals to gravitate as they please to this or to the other, but the Church preserving principles...."

Turning to the activities of the Parnellites, he thought that they would do "anything to strengthen themselves in England and if they could secure the adhesion of the Catholic Church in England, their purpose will be served, though not ours." Finally, he argued: "Where shall we be in the minds of Englishmen, when Parnell and his friends have shaken the dust of Westminster off their feet and have never more a word in the legislation of England?"[93]

Manning counselled Vaughan not to involve himself and *The Tablet* in opposition to the dissolution of the union proposed by Gladstone. "*The Tablet* is a Catholic paper and it commits the Catholics of England in the eyes of the world and the people of Ireland. Eight-tenths of the Catholics of England are Irish. Two-tenths—say two hundred thousand—are English, but a large number are in sympathy with Ireland. *The Tablet* has divided us and will divide us more if it writes politically. The unity of the Church has been committed to us." Gladstone's Home Rule bill was, for Manning, a bad one and "a break in the Empire."[94]

According to Newsome, it was ironic that only a year later Manning came around to Gladstone's way of thinking. Manning wrote to a friend in America: "The time is come when Ireland shall be handed over to itself. Its people have attained their majority."[95]

Vaughan showed Manning's letter to his editor, John Snead-Cox, for comment, and Snead-Cox replied that it would be unacceptable to remain silent "on the most urgent public question." Vaughan thought that nothing that concerned the nation "should be regarded as alien to a Catholic paper." it was the same advice Manning had given when he was in a position to influence the publication of another Catholic paper, the *Weekly Register*. Vaughan insisted that his editor have a free hand to print what he wanted, as long as Vaughan was not asked to study and judge every political issue that arose.[96] Vaughan encouraged the editor to use *The Tablet* as a forum for both sides of the issue of Irish Home Rule, as he had done in the *Dublin Review*. An example is *The Tablet* issue for 20 March 1886. It had two articles, side by side, entitled: "Why I am not a Home Ruler," by Mr C. Langdale, and "Why you ought to be a Home Ruler," by Lady Florence Dixie.[97]

According to Snead-Cox, Vaughan did not try to "coerce the staff of *The Tablet*" to follow his personal position on Home Rule. He was also scrupulous about his activities as bishop, that they should not "in any way compromise his authority or influence" with his people. During the 1886 election he wrote to a Catholic layman expressing his personal opinion: "I occupy a dual position—a private and personal one, and another that is public and official.

Personally I am opposed to Gladstone's measure as it stood before the House.[98] The views expressed by the Tablet pretty fairly represent my opinions." He was aware that, of his people in Salford diocese, "four-fifths are ardent Home Rulers," and that he had "no power whatever over their national aspirations." He put forward two questions: "Is it lawful before God to advocate Home Rule? Is it a question that the Church has decided?" "Yes" was the answer to the first, and "No" to the second. "If that be so, am I not bound to allow the people their freedom, specially when I know that on this subject they would not believe an Angel from Heaven if he contradicted them?"[99]

The alliance Vaughan referred to was between Gladstone's Liberal Party and the Irish Home Rulers in 1886. Parnell threw in his lot with the Tories in November 1885. When it became public that Gladstone secretly supported Home Rule, Parnell changed back again. According to Gearoid O Tuathaigh, in the context of the weakening of political obstacles to the integration of immigrant Irish into British society during the 1880s and 90s, Gladstone's "conversion" to Home Rule can be considered a turning point: "It effectively legitimized their political aspirations and objectives" by "stitching Home Rule into the Liberal Party banner." How far this is true is disputed. In the opinion of Stephen Fielding, Gladstone's embrace of Home Rule did not give legitimacy to the Irish claim, but split his party. It did lead to a Nationalist-Liberal alliance and made Gladstone an object of Irish loyalty and affection, but the Irish were not treated as ordinary Liberals by other party members. It was a tactical relationship because the party offered the prospect of Home Rule. In Manchester Home Rule became a liability in all but the North division.[100]

While Vaughan might attempt to maintain his independence, this was not possible for the Irish, for their nationalism was fused with their religion. It can be argued that the Irish used the Church to achieve assimilation in Britain while preserving a traditional apartness. It was also a feature of the Irish in England that they belonged partly to two kinds of minority, "one which wants integration but whose urge to integrate is restricted by the majority, and another which resists integration in order to maintain its own distinctiveness."[101]

In addition, Steven Fielding argues, Irish Catholics became part of a Church in England that, despite its best efforts, remained detached from the rest of English society. Behind the campaign to establish the Church's patriotic credentials was "the hope that one day Catholicism would assume its position as the country's established religion." Irish Catholics, especially nationalist leaders, did not entirely approve of the Church's English emphasis.[102]

Vaughan's personal view of Irish Home Rule was complicated by his advocacy of denominational education.

Education and the Voluntary Schools Association

In 1861 a Royal Commission reported that the children of the working class, although they were receiving some schooling, "received no systematic training, learned little, and often forgot what they did learn, even elementary skills." It was recommended to set up local school boards with the power to levy rates and examine schools applying for grants.[103]

The State saw the need for reform in education as a result of the Reform Act of 1867 and due to the advances of popular education in Germany, England's competitor, a national system of education had to be devised.[104]

With the passage of the Education Act of 1870, primary education became compulsory. State grants to denominational schools were doubled to enable them to become part of the system. An education rate was paid for the public-controlled Board schools. But when the Act became law, a clause forbade the teaching of any "religious catechism or religious formulary—distinctive of any particular denomination." Manning fought for proportional aid for the Catholic voluntary schools, but Catholics had to face the burden of providing for their own schools out of their own funds. He persuaded the bishops to take the limited aid offered by the Education Act and cooperate with the government. Catholics had a heavy financial burden to carry. By 1884 more than a thousand voluntary schools gave up and were handed over to the School Boards. Some thought denominational schools were about to disappear.

When Vaughan studied the problem he found that not one of the schools that closed was a Catholic voluntary school. Government reports for 1883 showed that Catholic schools had by far the largest percentage of free admissions offered to poor children. Snead-Cox says that Vaughan came "to the conclusion that a new and drastic departure must be made. Cardinal Manning had done immense work for Catholic education in relation to Certified Poor Law, Industrial, and Reformatory Schools, but he had no organization to his hand fitted to make a direct appeal to the constituencies." To redress this deficiency, Vaughan established the Voluntary Schools Association in Salford Diocese, with the intention that it be extended across the country. He wrote in *The Tablet* in April 1884 that the decision to establish the association had been made at the bishops' annual meeting.[105]

In an 1885 pastoral letter entitled "Education Really Free: A question for the General Election," he asked Catholics to "send such men to Parliament as will pledge themselves to take the one only clear and fair course, which is open to the Legislature": that the Catholic, Anglican and Wesleyan religious bodies whose "members demand as an indefeasible right that their religion shall preside over the daily education of their children." Their demand was "a simple one, based on reason and justice" that they have free education.[106]

The campaign on behalf of voluntary schools became involved with the issue of Home Rule for Ireland. The Home Rulers who felt they had been betrayed by the Liberal party in 1885 called on their estimated 150,000 voters in Britain to vote Conservative in the next election. On 21 November, Thomas Power, "T. P." O'Connor, a member of Parliament from Liverpool, drafted a manifesto signed by seven leading Home Rulers, and Parnell told large gatherings of Irish in Liverpool that Irish Catholics should vote Conservative in the election. "This was in spite of the Conservative Party having given no pledge to Home Rule." Catholics in turn feared that the Liberal demands for free education revived in their programme would threaten denominational education.[107]

Vaughan's pastoral letter, and a circular issued on 1 October 1885, made it clear that he considered the question of elementary education was a matter of "life and death." Manning, who privately opposed Home Rule at that time, gave his views in an article published in newspapers and in a pamphlet: "How shall Catholics vote at the coming Parliamentary Election?" He wrote that the preserving of Christian education was vital, and that "all who believed this should ask candidates two questions: would they do their utmost to place Voluntary Schools on equal footing with Board schools," and strive to "obtain a Royal Commission to review the present state of education in England and Wales?"[108] *The Tablet* sent the questions to the parliamentary candidates of the London area. All but three of the Conservatives replied, and only about two-fifths of the Liberals. And so the Education and Home Rule causes coincided in their electoral interests.[109] In the 1885 election the Liberals obtained 335 seats, the Conservatives 249, and the Home Rulers held the balance with eighty-six. In Manchester, Conservatives won five of the six seats.[110]

Vaughan tried to keep his own views private and did not publicly support or oppose Home Rule. He did, however, favour the Tories because of their stand on denominational education. This was despite the alliance of the Tories in the 1885 election with the Home Rulers. His secretary, Charles Gadd, wrote to Archbishop Corrigan on 17 November 1885 that Vaughan was busy with the matter of Education "as it will be affected by the General Election." Vaughan was proving, he continued, to be the "very soul of the Voluntary School Association and it is acknowledged on all hands that the action and work of that association has brought many a reprobate candidate to his knees." Gadd wrote that Vaughan had met a "Protestant gentleman" and asked: "How do you think the election will go in these parts?" The man replied: "Well, My Lord, it will go very much as your Lordship directed it to go." Gadd concluded: "That was an acknowledgement! Wasn't it? But I think the gentleman was right. The conservatives and nationalists have won every seat in Liverpool and yesterday we won every seat but one in Manchester."[111]

After the defeat of Gladstone's bill in 1886, and the fall of his government, Manning was finally converted to Home Rule for Ireland. But Vaughan did not follow Manning's example. Vaughan continued, according to Edward Norman, not "to appreciate the importance of the Irish question, at a time when a large section of the Church over which he was called to preside was in a state of extreme excitement about it," and this was a "substantial contribution to his lack of popularity with Catholics of the parishes."[112] Manning had become convinced that Home Rule in some form was the only means of pacifying Ireland. This was a view unacceptable to Vaughan and many of the Catholic aristocrats who were "trying to cultivate respectability in an environment still distrustful of Catholicism."

An American visited Manning at the end of 1887. In the record of their conversation, Manning's view was that "the legislative body to be created for Ireland should not be one with the pre-rogatives of a Parliament as commonly understood, but a chamber which should have control of legislation affecting local matters only.... The feeling in favour of Home Rule was growing rapidly every day in the country ... it would eventually be strong enough to control both houses of Parliament and force justice to be done to the Irish."[113]

It was over this issue, and others, such as temperance and Manning's "radicalism," that he and Vaughan continued to differ.

Up to 1920 the issue of Home Rule for Ireland remained unsettled. The constitutional relationship with Ireland was still at issue, with all the Irish politicians and most officials believing that the machinery of government under union was defective.[114]

Vaughan carried to his death the unpopularity aroused by his opposition to Home Rule for Ireland. At the same time, unfair criticism aroused tributes to his fairness. On one occasion in 1894 it was charged that he "governed the diocese in the interests of a political party," a statement that aroused Irish priests of the archdiocese to issue a "manifesto": "That we hereby declare that under Cardinal Vaughan we have full political freedom and have frequently and publicly exercised it."[115]

On behalf of voluntary schools, he continued to work for equal treatment during his years at Westminster, and finally shared in the successful passage of the Education Act of 1902.

Re-establishment of the Catholic Truth Society

The original Catholic Truth Society became defunct when Herbert Vaughan became Bishop of Salford in 1872. It was re-established in the 1880s due almost entirely to the work of one person, James Britten. Britten was born in Chelsea in 1846 of a High Church tradition in the Church of England. At the age of twenty-one he became a Roman Catholic. "The absence of authority and of definite teaching—these were the reasons which induced me to leave the Church of England," he later wrote.

In 1884 Britten was employed in the Botanical Department of the British Museum. He was also a Fellow of the Linnean Society, editor of *Nature Notes* and the *Journal of Botany*, and had already written several books and monographs. One day he showed a Fr Cologan "half-a-crown's worth of cheap Anglican publications" he had purchased in Paternoster Row in London. Cologan showed them to a few other priests and finally about a dozen people agreed to contribute a pound each and bring out three small Catholic publications; two prayer cards and "A Little Rosary-book." The sale of the publications made a small profit. Bishop Robert Coffin of Southwark was interested, placed sizable orders, and became their first episcopal patron.

Early in 1884, another friend of the small group, Wilfrid Oates, invited them to meet at the publishers, Burns & Oates. The meeting was not altogether successful and the members left without having come to any practical conclusion, including a name for the group. Britten wrote to Bishop Herbert Vaughan for his support and received an invitation to visit him in Salford. Vaughan promised to help and was willing to serve as president. He also suggested that Britten take up the name and work of his defunct Catholic Truth Society. At the same time he presented him with the entire stock of pamphlets of the original Catholic Truth Society he had started in Lancashire.[116]

Lady Mary Elizabeth Herbert welcomed the group to a meeting at her London home—Herbert House—on 5 November 1884. With Herbert Vaughan presiding, the Catholic Truth Society was formally re-established; Vaughan was president, George Whitlaw was the treasurer, and Fr Cologan and James Britten were secretaries. Britten attributed to Herbert Vaughan the general recognition that the Truth Society received. Vaughan obtained the blessing of the Pope and helped to establish the Annual Conferences of the Catholic Truth Society.[117]

The conferences resulted from a suggestion made to Vaughan in 1886 that a small annual meeting might be held in connection with the Society's activities. Vaughan was always ready, Britten writes, "to encourage any movement which would bring the Church before the people." Support for such a general meeting was not unanimous, but the first one was held, with the approval of Cardinal Manning, in Westminster, in October 1888. The next year it was held in Vaughan's diocese, in Manchester. What impressed Britten about the Manchester Conference was "the hospitality which was freely and generously extended by the clergy and laity of Manchester, not only to their acquaintances from a distance, which would be in no way remarkable, but to those who came to them as strangers, although they left them as friends."[118]

For the remainder of his life Herbert Vaughan was an active supporter of Britten's Catholic Truth Society. During his years at Westminster he often addressed the annual conference on topics close to his heart and the work of the Church in England. Britten concluded his essay on the history of the Society with a quote from Vaughan: "Say not that to scatter books, pamphlets, tracts, and leaflets is waste and loss, if you have a grain of faith in the

Gospel parable of the sower." "God," he continued, "is always sowing His grace over the world of men, and what is the history of His sowing? Is greater fruit to spring up under the hand of the servant than of the Master? But for every effort we make, there is an eternal reward."[119]

Notes

1. Herbert's brother John wrote in the *Ampleforth Journal* in 1916 that Hedley was a friend of the Vaughan family for many years: "The late Bishop Hedley has been known by me ever since I was a small boy, puzzling over my first Latin theme at Downside College, considerably more than forty years ago. I have a distinct recollection of his coming to preach the Annual Retreat, somewhere in the 'sixties, and of the impression it produced on the delighted students.... When, at an early age, the mitre dropped on his own head, he used often to come to Courtfield.... The "Bishop's Room" was always ready for him, and he did not hesitate to make use of it, for he knew he was more than welcome.... The truth is, he was much more like one of the family than a guest; addressed us all by our christian names; and asked for what he wanted without any apology.... He was always playful and kind.... He was always outspoken.... He was devoted to music... and was not adverse to sitting down himself at the piano and delighting us by his really clever performance ... he was always gay and amusing and ready to beguile the tedious day with a joke or an anecdote ... he will long be remembered as a most genial and lovable friend and superior." Judging from two of John Vaughan's anecdotes, Hedley could also use sarcasm on the unwary. See: Bishop John Vaughan, "Reminiscences of the Late Bishop Hedley," *Ampleforth Journal*, 22, 3, May 1916, pp.291-3.
2. J. Anselm Wilson, *The Life of Bishop Hedley*, London, Burns & Oates, 1929, p.91.
3. Herbert M. Vaughan, *The South Wales Squires*, London, Methuen, 1926, p.47: The author tells the following story of Francis Vaughan: A march was planned to Wyaston Leys. The owners of a large park invited him to have lunch. On the "blazing morning in July" the men were in full dress with full packs and rifles while the officers wore fatigues. When they reached Wyaston Leys "our sappers were very weary, perspiring and exhausted." The hosts had prepared refreshments; but for officers only. When Vaughan asked what was to be given to the men, he was told there was nothing prepared for them. And so he "gave orders to march straight out of the park onto the road where the exhausted sappers refreshed themselves with water from cottages." The author wrote that he would "never forget the mortified looks of our would-be host and his house party at Colonel Vaughan's very proper action."
4. *ibid*., p.49: The author included a ghost story told about Courtfield: Francis Vaughan was trying to rent the manor house. An interested person arrived and Vaughan was showing him through the manor when they came to "a remote chamber upstairs." Suddenly there was an "icy current of air" and a sort of "fog or mist appeared to rise from the middle of the floor and ascend to the ceiling." When Colonel Vaughan saw the "opaque pillar of fog" he "sank to his knees and prayed while the guest stood beside him in dumb amazement." Slowly the fog dissolved and the temperature returned to normal. The author adds that "Courtfield never was let."
5. MHA. Scrapbook. *Universe*, 20 October 1961.
6. *The Tablet*, 15 July 1882, p.113, Funeral of Mr W. G. Ward; "William George Ward and the Catholic Revival by Wilfrid Ward," *The Tablet*, 17 June 1893, p.928.
7. Leslie, *Vaughan Letters*, pp.356-8; Snead-Cox, 2, p.280ff; MHA. Correspondence. 21 Oct. 1957. Miss K. Knowlton, 24 East Cliff, Dover, Kent: "My dear mother who will be 90 next week remembers him quite well when he was bishop of Salford. She lived in the village of Ince Blundell and he used to come sometimes to visit his cousins at the Hall. She tells me she has seen him many times walking along the lanes saying his office. She was also present in the chapel on

the morning his brother the Archbishop of Sydney was expected to say Mass and he was found dead in bed. Her father was farm bailiff to Mr. Weld-Blundell."

8. Leslie, *Vaughan Letters*, p.357.

9. NYAA. Correspondence, Salford, 10 September 1883.

10. Snead-Cox, 2, pp.281-2.

11. *ibid*.

12. Henry Norbert Birt,O S B., *Benedictine Pioneers in Australia*, London, Herbert and Daniel, 1911, 2, p.466; Moran was Cardinal Paul Cullen's nephew. He had been the vice-rector of the Irish College in Rome until he returned to Ireland to become his uncle's assistant secretary in 1866. He was made bishop of Ossory in 1871 and finally Archbishop of Sydney on the death of Roger Vaughan. See: John Healy, *Maynooth College, Its Centenary History*, Dublin, 1895. pp.541-2.

13. C. J. Duffy, "An Aristocrat in an Unaristocratic Community," *Footprints*, March 1979, 3, 8, pp.23-24; Roger Vaughan judged that "the case was not proven" against Bishop Timothy O'Mahoney, and recommended that he go to Rome until the situation cooled; Correspondence, Sr Kathleen Burford, Archivist, Mary MacKillop Place, North Sydney NSW, 20 December 1994: Mary MacKillop's Institute decided in its First General Chapter on a form of central government that was rejected by Bishop James Quinn of Queensland.(She had been excommunicated briefly in 1871-2 by Bishop Lawrence Sheil of Adelaide because of her commitment to the central government of her Sisters.) The Sisters had to withdraw from Quinn's diocese and found a welcome with Vaughan in Sydney. In 1880, Mary MacKillop wrote to her mother: "The Archbishop is more than kind, God has raised up a true and powerful friend in him, and just when we most needed such aid as his." Vaughan also accepted their constitutions and treated Mary with, she wrote: a "trusting kindness that goes to my heart after the past in Queensland." The memory of Dr Vaughan's kindness she kept alive for the remainder of her life. From exile she wrote to the Sisters on 17 December 1883: ". . . You should also remember how in the face of all the cruel things said of the Institute and of myself, the late lamented Archbishop (Vaughan) took up our cause, fought for us, at first single-handed, defended us with his priests and asked them to try us, raising by his kindness my spirits and hopes which had nearly been crushed out of me. Well the good Archbishop did all this, and in so doing he supported and maintained the Mother House authority"; Paul Gardiner, SJ, "Love was the soul of Mary MacKillop's virtues," *L'Osservatore Romano*, 4 (1375) 25 January 1995, p.1: Mary Helen MacKillop was born in Melbourne in 1842 to Alexander MacKillop and Flora MacDonald; See also: *The Catholic Weekly*, 21 March 1968. MHA. HCV. Box 46; See also: Carl L. Hemmer, "MacKillop, recently beatified, first Australian," *National Catholic Reporter*, 10 February 1995. Hemmer reviews *Mary MacKillop Unveiled* by Leslie O'Brien, and *Mary MacKillop: An Extraordinary Australian*, by Paul Gardiner, SJ.

14. Snead-Cox, 2, p.286; Mgr Duffy wrote in 1979 about Roger: "Today a balanced verdict is being given to him. The wheel has turned full circle and historians regret that the tolerant kindly rule of this wise man was replaced by the rigid, authoritative regime which only now has come to an end."

15. See: MHA. Elizabeth Herbert, *Mary Vaughan*, London, Wyman; And: E. Scully, "May Vaughan: 1845-1884," *The Month*, 117, April 1936, pp.354-357: The Augustinian Canonesses were started as an independent English foundation at Louvain in 1609. They were forced to leave the Continent during the French Revolution, returned to England and finally settled at Newton Abbot, and St Augustine's. William Vaughan, the Bishop of Plymouth and uncle of Mary, helped settle the new arrivals. Mary joined in 1863. Her playfulness and enthusiasms became part of priory traditions. Later in life her "contagious enthusiasm " and "passionate love of the Blessed Sacrament" helped to establish firmly the perpetual adoration of the Blessed Sacrament at Newton Abbot; See also: Martindale, *Bernard Vaughan*, p.24: Bernard visited his sister in October 1866.

16. *Mary Vaughan*, pp.356-7.

17. *The Tablet*, 3 January 1885, p.26.

18. NYAA. C-5-C9, no.9, Gadd, Bishop's House, Salford, 5 October 1885, to Corrigan, New York.

19. Snead-Cox, 1, p.440.

20. WDA. Anecdotes. Thomas Jackson, St Joseph's Home, Patricroft, Manchester, no date.

21. Snead-Cox. 1, p.440.

22. NYAA. Gadd to Corrigan, 27 November 1885.

23. See: Snead-Cox, 1, pp.403-29, "For the Children's Sake;" Chadwick, *Victorian Church*, pp.410-11: "In the *Dublin Review* of 1884 (ii,65) Mivart wrote a daring article asking why their progress was so slow and why the expectations of 1850 had not been fulfilled, despite the growing number of churches and chapels and convents.... This talk of slow progress or even recession, though at first disreputable, was given justification when Bishop Vaughan of Salford issued an enquiry (1885) into the state of the Roman Catholics in Manchester and found leakage; so that the word leakage became fashionable, and was discussed in *The Tablet* and the *Month*;" Gearoid O'Tuathaigh in Roger Swift and Sheridan Gilley, *The Irish in the Victorian City*, London, Croom Helm, 1985, pp.24-5: Catholic commentators and bishops, such as Bishop Vaughan of Salford were unanimous in their view that "leakage was the major challenge facing the Catholic Church in Britain, and that it was increasing as the century got older. What they meant, of course, was the regular attendance at Mass and the sacraments, and particularly the performance of Easter duties, was not satisfactory when related to the total number of nominal Catholics resident in Britain." In Vaughan's concern about poor Catholic children, he considered them "lost to the Church and perhaps joining Protestant charitable groups;" Henry Charles Kent, Kensington. "The Third Archbishop of Westminster," *Catholic World*, vol 55, June, 1892, pp.385-96; p.395: "In 1885 a new evil forced itself upon his attention—an evil which had already come under the keen eye of Cardinal Manning in London—that, namely, of the 'insidious and active proselytism' whereby thousands of Catholic children were being robbed of their faith. As a result of the investigations of a special board of inquiry it was shown that the district of Manchester and Salford was 'honeycombed by proselytizing agencies.' 'I believe it to be no exaggeration to say,' the bishop declared, 'that Catholic children are lost to the faith by thousands every year in Great Britain, through agencies and societies professedly philanthropic and neutral, but secretly animated by an anti-Catholic proselytizing spirit.'"

24. Kidd, *Manchester*, p.151; Lannon, *Turner*, p.202; *The Tablet*, 20 August 1881, p.291.

25. Edward St John, *Manning's Work for Children*, London, Sheed and Ward, 1929, p.29.

26. *ibid.*, p.66, n; V. A. McClelland, "The Making of Young Imperialists: Rev Thomas Seddon, Lord Archibald Douglas and the Resettling of British Catholic Orphans in Canada," *Recusant History*, 19, 1989, pp.509-29: Thomas Seddon was born in Liverpool and educated at St Edmund's, Ware, when Herbert Vaughan was vice president. After his ordination, in January 1862 at St Patrick's, Soho, he spent five years in Soho and Commercial Road. Manning then invited him to become part of his household and appointed him secretary of the education fund.

27. *ibid.*: The first pastoral letter concerning orphans of the London vicariate was issued on 29 October 1848.

28. Snead-Cox, 1, p.429; Salford, *The Tablet*, 21 January 1892, p.111.

29. Thomas Mulheran, Secretary, Catholic Children's Rescue Society Centenary, 1886-1986, Glasgow, John S. Burns, 1986; Conversation with Bishop Kelly, Wardley Hall, Manchester, 1992.

30. Rescue, Centenary, p.5.

31. D. E. Selby, "Cardinal Manning, Campaigner for Children's Rights." *JEH*, 27, 4, October 1976, pp.403-412.

32. H. Asububel, *In Hard Times: Reformers among the Late Victorians*, London, 1960, p.124.

33. David Mathew, *Catholicism in England*, London, Eyre and Spottiswoode, 1955, pp.222-3.

34. N. Middleton. "The Education Act of 1870 as the Start of the Modern Concept of the Child," *British Journal of Educational Studies*, xviii, 1970, p.177.

35. SDA. 3rd Report 1887, p.404.

36. Snead-Cox. 1, pp.428-9.

37. *ibid.*, pp.407-8.

38. Rescue, Centenary, pp.6-11.

39. *ibid.*, p.2.

40. SDA. Herbert Vaughan, Bishop's House Salford, 18 February 1887.

41. John Vaughan, "The 'leakage' in the Church in Great Britain," *Irish Ecclesiastical Record*, 8, 1887, pp.343-50: "An hour spent at the feet of Christ present on our altars in the Blessed Sacrament would do more to help us reclaim our wandering sheep than many hours of trudging along the narrow streets and dirty alleys of London, Liverpool, Manchester or Birmingham, Glasgow or Edinburgh."

42. Snead-Cox, 1, p.427.

43. Centenary, Rescue, p.12: The Society retained its original title until 1966 when the Rescue Council decided to change the name to "Catholic Children's Rescue Society;" SDA. Harvest, March 1912, pp.63-4: After Austin Oates left Burns & Oates he travelled abroad and in 1882 married Odilia Plettinck of Moulebeke, Flanders. After his return to Manchester he joined Rescue. In Jan 1891 his was awarded a KSG by the Pope for his work for Rescue. He was Vaughan's private secretary. Shortly before Vaughan's death he went to Liverpool and became involved in the work of Fr Berry's homes. He died suddenly of heart failure at his home on Birchdale Rd, Waterloo, Liverpool, on Sunday 21 January 1912; WDA. Oates, Anecdotes: "Vaughan had a "keen interest in the smallest detail of rescue work." For example, he wrote from Oldham to Oates about "Timothy ——, 57 Trinity St, Oldham, and his wife Margaret, have no children and desire to adopt a little girl between three and four years of age. I have told him that you will write and probably let him choose a child for adoption."

44. Centenary, Rescue.

45. *ibid.*, p.15: Oates wrote: "In the one short night we passed in this lodging house and in visiting others we came across at least three hundred boys over sixteen and under twenty.... Left to themselves they are helpless;" Austin Oates, Art.IX, "The Lost, Strayed and Stolen of Our Catholic Poor Children," *Dublin Review*, January 1887, pp.157-176.

46. ibid., p.18: Oates described in his journal "a weak tottering old woman slowly comes forward; two little mites follow her .... The poor mother was a Catholic. Non-Catholic relatives seek the children; "wont ye take them; you'll not give them up? I promised the dying darlint they should be brought up Catholics. Ye'll help me keep my promise?"

47. Sr Frances McHugh and Sr Ambrose O'Connor, *Caritas Contact, Holly Mount, 1888-1988*, Sisters of Charity of Jesus and Mary, Brussels, 77, 3, September 1988, pp.9ff: A presentation to commemorate the centenary of the arrival of the sisters in Salford begins with a scene of Herbert Vaughan arriving at Ghent in Belgium to request help from Mother Gervaise. There is a story that he was so tired that he fell asleep while waiting in the convent parlour. Vaughan had written to a Belgium friend, Fr De Gryse, whom he had probably met during his student days at Brugelette, asking him to help him find a community to assist at Salford. "The poor law boards of Guardians can now lawfully cede us the Catholic children under their care and pay for their maintenance, provided we have here and now a certified school to receive them." He added that the need was greater than in London where another community from Liège had already gone. On 18 March 1888 Vaughan wrote to the superior general of the sisters, Canon Janssens: "We want a house for girls, and one for boys. There is a great field, a full harvest, and I invite you to come in the name of God and gather it in. It is a singular coincidence that tomorrow will be the feast of St Joseph, under whose special care I have placed the whole material part of rescuing and protecting our poor children." The sisters compared the energetic zeal of Bishop Vaughan with that of their founder, Canon Triest. It was from Holly Mount that the Anglo-Irish Province of

the Sisters of Charity of Jesus and Mary developed.

48. See the story of Alice Ingham and her companions in Chapter XI.

49. Rescue, Centenary, p.22: Vaughan wrote to a friend about alterations the sisters had started at Patricroft: "St. Joseph's Missionary Sisters are busy building at Barton in Manchester, for one hundred and fifty children from two months to ten years old, who are all Rescue children, now in the charge of these sisters in Manchester. I am going to make this new place their Mother House and Novitiate. They work famously ... they have looked after a hundred and fifty with eight, and done it well. But it has been overwork."

50. ibid.; There is a lonely-looking Vaughan in one of the group photos of emigrating children.

51. ibid. p.43; Snead-Cox., 1, p.411; and 2, p.9: Before he left Salford for Westminster, Vaughan spoke twice in public and each time reproached himself before his listeners about his late awakening to the problems of Catholic children in his diocese. At a meeting of the Rescue Society in the Free Trade Hall he said that "though their bishop for fourteen years, he had been ignorant of what was going on around him and he ought to have known, and he begged his hearers to atone for his neglect by new efforts."

52. Snead-Cox, 1, p.427.

53. ibid., p.426.

54. Rescue, Centenary, p.24: Letter from Bishop's House, Salford, 20 June 1888.

55. ibid., p.24: "Much as we may regret the need of sending abroad any of our small Catholic population, we have the consolation of feeling that we shall be assisting the development of the Church in such a country as Canada which has such a great future before it."

56. ibid., p.32: Rossall kept an account of the voyage. The Salford group's destination was Toronto and St Nicholas' Home established by Archbishop Lynch for the reception of orphan boys. "But the attainment ... is due in the main to Father Seddon—my cheerful companion, who was with me on all occasions and assisted everywhere, both by his past experiences and personal influence;" McClelland, "The Making," p.522: Seddon was a compassionate man whose advice helped to humanize the system of emigration for children "which in other hands had almost degenerated into a form of white slavery." And: Obituary, The Tablet, 1 October 1898, p.544: Thomas Seddon was secretary to the Fund for Poor Children for thirty-two years. He died on 22 September 1898, while on his annual voyage with emigrant children for Canada, two days before the steamer reached Quebec; St John, Manning's Work, p.135: Emigration had been used as a cheap way of reducing the numbers of children in workhouses. An agent visited workhouses offering to take children for a fee and when reaching Canada charged another fee to any person willing to take one of the emigrants. Manning decided to help emigrate suitable children and older school boys. He was not the first to do so; James Nugent of Liverpool took twelve boys and twelve girls to Canada in 1870. Thomas Seddon, his secretary for the Westminster Diocesan Fund for Destitute Children and Archibald Douglas were to take on the work. In 1874 the Canadian Catholic Emigration Committee was formed. By 1902, out of fifty thousand children helped by all the agencies, five thousand were emigrant Catholic boys and girls.

57. ibid., p.35; The Tablet, Salford, 21 January 1892, p111: Mgr Gadd in a sermon at St John's Cathedral in December of 1892 on behalf of the annual appeal of the Rescue Society presents a less triumphant picture: The loss of Herbert Vaughan's interest and "continual appeals to the wealthier members of the upper middle class, and his personal influence with them, which brought in many large donations—most of which, unfortunately, had since fallen off; his personal sacrifices, which edified and encouraged both clergy and laity, giving to the Society his mensa and private subscriptions, amounting to over 500 pounds a year, were such a sustaining power to the Society that to lose them was a blow which any society, older and more firmly established than the Catholic Protection and Rescue Society, must necessarily feel.... But the greatest loss of all was that of the secretary, Mr. Oates. If an intimate knowledge of every phase of the work which had been created by him and grown up with him, and which embraced a

lawyer's office, an accountant's books, an emigration agency, a criminal investigation department, an editor's desk, and a begging-letter writer all rolled into one; if Mr. Oates's wonderful power of initiative and organization, and his indomitable perseverance as exemplified in some of the lawsuits he had won; if his self-sacrifice, which never asked for, and would never accept, any salary for his services, but was always ready to work—if all these qualities and qualifications were of untold value to the Rescue Society and were always at its command, it was not difficult to conceive the wrench that must have been caused by his abrupt appointment to his present position in London." The reason why Rescue existed, was, Gadd concluded, "not to relieve the poor, but to save the children's faith." He ended with a quote by Vaughan that "We want nothing more, and we shall be satisfied with nothing less," than ensuring for "every Catholic child, a Catholic education;" The crisis passed and the Rescue Society survived.

58. Webb, *Modern England*, pp.335-6; John D. Fair, "The Irish Disestablishment Conference of 1869," *JEH*, v.xxvi, no.4, October 1975, pp.379-94: The Reform Bill of 1867 inaugurated a new era in the political history of Great Britain. It enlarged the electorate and increased the possibilities for party organization.

59. George Malcomb Young, *Victorian England, Portrait of an Age*, Oxford, OUP, 1949, p.44, in Newsome, Manning's Influence, *RH*, October 1992, p.143; Stephen Fielding refers to an ingrained hostility to Catholics and the Irish which was "deeply embedded in English society." The hostility to the Irish "enjoyed a lineage even longer than that of anti-Catholicism. Since at least the time of the Norman Conquest those who lived beyond the realm of the Kings of England—the Scots, Welsh and Irish—were roundly despised by the English. In dramas, poems, novels and histories the English depicted these Celtish peoples as primitive, tribal, violent and backward. By the eighteenth century this practice of satirizing the Celts had systematically poisoned the public mind: they could be seen only in a negative light." To suppress, annex and forcibly anglicize was more difficult to accomplish in Ireland than in Wales and Scotland. The Irish remained a threat to the English State due to their sustained hostility to constitutional incorporation. And by demanding Home Rule the Irish were "open to the accusation that they sought the destruction of the Empire." By the middle of the nineteenth century the "English anti-Celtic prejudice had been reduced and concentrated into enmity for the Irish." By the late nineteenth century the "struggle for Home Rule ... determined attitudes to the Irish. To many English the struggle of Irish Catholics to win independence from the State "appeared to be most perverse...." See: Steven Fielding, *Class and Ethnicity, Irish Catholics in England, 1880-1939*, Buckingham, Open University Press, 1993, pp.5-10.

60. David Newsome, "Cardinal Manning's Influence on the Church and Nation," *RH*, October 1992, vol 21, no 2, p.143: "One of the most significant spheres of Manning's influence was Ireland. He was not only the champion of the ever-increasing army of Irish immigrants, flooding the slums of English cities, in his tireless efforts to secure an effective ministry for them and to improve their social conditions, but he also played a significant role in the affairs of the Irish Church and of the fortunes of the Irish people."

61. See: David Bebbington, *William Ewart Gladstone*, Grand Rapids, Eerdmans, 1993, pp.224-5: Christianity coloured all of Gladstone's public life. Lord Rosebery said that "The faith of Mr.Gladstone, obvious to all who knew him, pervaded every act and every part of his life."

62. Fair, "Irish Disestablishment Conference;" Newsome, *Convert Cardinals*, p.314ff: The "Letter" was an "all-embracing indictment of the injustices inflicted upon Ireland." He called for "religious equality" and immediate reform of the "infamous land laws" and touched upon "the vexed question of Ireland being allowed to have its own parliament in Dublin."

63. Newsome, *Convert Cardinals*, p.315.

64. J. D. Parry, *Democracy and Religion, Gladstone and the Liberal Party, 1867-1875*, Cambridge, CUP, 1986, p.4: Parry considers the 1873 Irish University Bill to have been all but neglected by historians except perhaps by Edward Norman. Disraeli wrote that an attempt to deal with the question of Irish Education had "broken up two governments."

65. Webb, *Modern England*, p.359.

66. Newsome, *Convert Cardinals*, p.316.

67. W. E. Gladstone, "History of an Idea—Why I became a Home Ruler," in Thomas Power O'Connor and Robert McWade, *Gladstone—Parnell and The Great Irish Struggle*, Philadelphia, Hubbard, 1890, p.823ff; p.838: "... preceding the election of 1885. It had now become morally certain that Ireland would through a vast majority of her representatives present a demand in the National sense.... Under the circumstances I conceived that my duty was clear.... To do nothing to hinder the prosecution of the question by the Tory government if it should continue in office,... avoid any language which would place the question in the category of party measures...."

68. Newsome, *Convert Cardinals*, p.316

69. Bebbington, *Gladstone*, p.218: The relationship between Parnell and Catherine O'Shea became public when her husband divorced her in 1890; Fielding, *Class and Ethnicity*, p.81: "The scandal led to nearly ten years of bitter conflict, which in turn led to many Irish in England abandoning the cause of Home Rule in despair."

70. Newsome, *Convert Cardinals*, p.316.

71. *The Tablet*, 10 April 1886, p.583: "There would be securities for the union of the Empire and adequate protection for what was called the Protestant minority."

72. L. C. Casartelli, "Our Diamond Jubilee," *Dublin Review*, April 1896, pp.245-271; "A Symposium on Home Rule," *Dublin Review*, April 1886, pp.374-403.

73. The Earl of Oxford and Asquith, *Fifty Years of British Parliament*, Boston, Little, Brown, 1926, 1, pp.163-4.

74. Gibb, *Modern England*, p.366.

75. McCormack, pp.215-6.

76. *Catholic World*, June 1892, p.395.

77. Snead-Cox, 2, p.386.

78. Oliver Rafferty, "Nicholas Wiseman, Ecclesiastical Politics and Anglo-Irish Relations in the Mid-Nineteenth Century," *RH*, vol 21, no 3, May 1993, p.383.

79. *ibid.*, p.382.

80. *ibid.*, p.398.

81. E. R. Norman, *The Catholic Church and Ireland in the Age of Rebellion, 1859-73*, Ithaca, Cornell, 1965, p.9.

82. Rafferty, "Wiseman," p.382ff.

83. "Is Ireland Irreconcilable?," *Dublin Review*, April 1870, p.481; Quoted in Norman, *Catholic Church and Ireland*, p.2

84. Walter L. Arnstein, *Protestant versus Catholic in Mid-Victorian England*, London, Univ. of Missouri Press, 1982, pp.8-9.

85. Snead-Cox, 1, p.470: "I am afraid the fact that he was the owner of the Tablet in this respect created a prejudice against him."

86. VFA. English College Rome, 19 February 1881, Vaughan to Elizabeth Herbert: "It is an extremely difficult thing for an Englishman to say a word which displeases the Irish, be it ever so true—because he is an Englishman and because they are so ready to misunderstand and take offence. What I have written ought not to offend the right-minded—it will prepare the way for a more direct expression of opinion later if necessary. But it probably will offend."

87. SDA. "Letter on the Irish Distress and on the Action of the Catholic Church in Ireland by the Bishop of Salford," Manchester, Walker, 1883.

88. Jedin, *History*, 9, p.144. The letter of 1 August 1882, addressed to the entire Irish episcopate, endorsed the condemnation of the terrorist acts. However in blaming them on the "secret societies," he showed "little understanding of the necessity for organized resistance in such a situation, even though the Pope generally approved of the desire for justice."

89. Kidd, *Manchester*, pp.173-4; SDA. Vaughan, Letter on the Irish Distress.

90. WDA. Manning papers: Vaughan/Manning letters.

91. WDA. *Directory*, 1904. The figures were based on the 1901 census; Emmet Larkin reviewed the attitudes of Manning and Cullen to Home Rule. See: Emmet Larkin, *The Roman Catholic Church and the Home Rule Movement in Ireland*, 1870-1888, Dublin, Gill & Macmillan, 1990, pp.108-9: When Manning articulated the constitutional legitimacy of Home Rule as a political programme Cullen argued that "the leadership of the movement was at once too Protestant and too Fenian" rather than there being anything intrinsically bad in the principle of Home Rule itself.

92. Swift and Gilley, *Irish in the Victorian City*, p.28.

93. WDA. Herbert Vaughan, Bishop's House, Salford, to Cardinal Manning, 27 November; Snead-Cox identifies the letter in 1, p.473, as "to a Brother Bishop."

94. Snead-Cox, 1, p.470: "It would lengthen my life to say this in Hyde Park, but being as I am, I will not be Pastor and Politician, and I hope you will let the Tablet leave Gladstone's Bill to Chamberlain and Lord Hartington. I am very anxious that the Bishops of Ireland should have no shadow of complaint about you or myself;" Newsome, *Convert Cardinals*, p.316; Ward, *Transition*, pp.108-9: Wilfrid Ward met Gladstone at the house of Mrs Agar, later Lady Clifden, in early 1885. Hartington, Vaughan and a few others were present. After the dinner Gladstone and Hartington argued while the rest remained listeners. Gladstone began to talk theology, which bored Hartington and Vaughan: "Vaughan had no idea of talking theology with a heretic and to Lord Hartington such conversation was unintelligible and boring. He ended by moving over to the other side of the table and sitting next to Vaughan and they kept up an animated conversation on sport and the other interests of country gentlemen, while the rest of us continued our theology. I believe this was the beginning of the acquaintance between Lord Hartington and the Bishop which afterwards developed into a friendship."

95. Newsome, *Convert Cardinals*, p.316-7.

96. Snead Cox, 1, p.471; In *The Tablet* for 11 January 1992, a letter from Archbishop Walsh is quoted as saying: "The Tablet was almost wholly to blame" and that it was a "Tory Anti Home Rule organ."

97. *The Tablet*, 20 March 1886: Langdale argued from what improvements he had seen in Ireland between his first visit in 1853 and again in 1879; Dixie referred to a speech given in Belfast by Randolph Churchill in which he appealed to the "loyal" Roman Catholics of Ireland to unite with the Orangemen in opposition to Home Rule.

98. Snead-Cox, 1, pp.471-2.

99. *ibid.*, p.472.

100. Gearoid O Tuathaigh, in Swift and Gilley, *Victorian City*, p.29; Fielding, *Class and Ethnicity*, pp.88-9. Fielding points out that some Nationalists did find a prominent place within Liberalism; for example see the careers of Boyle and McCabe.

101. *ibid.*, introduction; Sheridan Gilley, "The Roman Catholic Church and the Nineteenth-Century Irish Diaspora," *JEH*, vol 35, April 1984, pp.188ff., p.199.

102. Fielding, *Class and Ethnicity*, pp.40-41.

103. Webb, *Modern England*, pp.337-8: In 1869 Joseph Chamberlain founded the National Education League. A significant number decided that "both voluntary activity and sectarian education were irrelevant to a new democratic age;" Supporters of religious education helped carry the Education Act of W. E. Forster in 1870. The original proposals put voluntary schools on the rates. The revised proposal left them in receipt of Exchequer assistance only. In most state schools religious instruction was given. The Cowper-Temple clause excluded the religious teaching of any denomination in board schools, but permitted the teaching of religion in them by school teachers, and a great majority provided it for their children. In 1876 elementary education was made compulsory. The Act of 1870 had left England with a dual system of schools: the board schools, supported by the State and free after 1891, and the voluntary schools, usually denominational, supported by fees, endowments and state grants of the kind

given since 1833.

104. Newsome, *Convert Cardinals*, p.319.

105. Snead-Cox, 2, pp.87-140; NYAA, Corrigan correspondence indicates that Vaughan was trying to find a place for denominational education within a state school system as early as 1881. Salford, 17 December 1881: "My object will be to bring before the public mind of England the experience of the common school system or government education without religion. What are you doing in the way of providing popular education to the Catholics of New York? I remember when I was there last, such a great mission as St.Stephen's was without a Catholic school." On 2 February he wrote to thank Corrigan for books he had sent to Salford on education. "Here we are going very fast in the direction of the common school system in the United States. We shall have a difficult and dangerous future."

106. "Resolutions of the Bishops. A Letter on Education, Really Free?: A question for the General Election by the Bishop of Salford," Manchester, Walker, 18 November 1885.

107. G. I. T. Machin, *Politics and the Churches in Great Britain, 1869-1921*, Oxford,Clarendon Press, 1987, p.162.

108. *ibid.*, p.163; See; H. E. Manning, "How Shall Catholics Vote at the Coming Parliamentary Election?" London, 1885, pp.13-4.

109. *ibid.*, p.164.

110. *ibid.*, p.165.

111. NYAA. Gadd to Corrigan, Salford, 17 November 1885.

112. Norman, *Catholic Church*, p.355.

113. John Oldcastle, editor, *Memorials of Cardinal Manning*, London, Burns & Oates, 1892.

114. Eunan O'Halpin, T*he Decline of the Union, British Government in Ireland, 1892-1920*, Syracuse, SUP, 1987.

115. *The Tablet*, 10 November 1894, p.60.

116. Christopher Ralls, *The Catholic Truth Society*, London, C T S, 1993, p.3ff; James Britten, "The Catholic Truth Society," *Dublin Review*, no 34, April 1887, pp.408-14; CTS Archive (CTSA), James Britten, "The Catholic Truth Society," A paper read at the Catholic Conference in Manchester, 22 September 1909, pp.13-17; The Catholic Truth Society Archive has indexed publications written by Herbert Vaughan and Lady Herbert. Among those of Herbert Vaughan: "Anglican Archbishops and the Pope," "Who is St Joseph?, "Blessed Peter and the English Church and People," "Leo XIII and the Reunion of Christendom," "Conversion of England and the Power of Prayer," "What is the Mass?," "Our Father and Patron St Joseph," "The Reunion of Christendom," "Devotions to St Peter;" Lady Herbert had sixteen titles in addition to her very popular "Wayside Tales" series 155-184.

117. CTSA, Britten, 1909, p.18.

118. CTSA, Britten, "The Catholic Conference of 1889," pp.31-2.

119. CTSA, Britten, 1909, p.28.

CHAPTER XIII

Missions and Missionaries

Father Maurice McGill, former missionary to the Cameroons in West Africa, rector of the missionary college at Mill Hill, and, from 1988, Vaughan's successor as superior general of St Joseph's Missionary Society, was one of the principal guests at a ceremony at the Catholic National Shrine in Washington, DC, in September 1993. The occasion was the centenary celebration of the Josephites. The shrine was filled to capacity with Catholic African-Americans who had come from all parts of the United States to honour the four hundred and eighty-three members of the Josephites who have served their community.[1] The Josephites trace their origins to a small band of men, led by Herbert Vaughan, which arrived at Baltimore in 1871.

The National Shrine is near to the Catholic University of America. It was to a similar ceremony—the centenary of the establishment of the hierarchy of the American Church—which took place between 10 and 12 November 1889, and the inauguration of the Catholic University in Washington on 13 November, that Herbert Vaughan was invited; he was unable to attend and sent Mgr Charles Gadd in his place. On the Feast of SS Simon and Jude, 28 October 1889, Vaughan wrote a reply to Cardinal Gibbons' letter of invitation. John Tracey Ellis, in an article in the *Catholic Historical Review*, called the letter "a remarkable challenge to the Cardinal of Baltimore and the American hierarchy to realize their obligations to the task of the Universal Church."[2] After Ellis published the letter in 1944, the *Clergy Review* called the document "of great interest to all students of the Catholic revival in England." Ellis had found Vaughan's letter in the archives of the Archdiocese of Baltimore. To Ellis it revealed "all the fervour and courage of Vaughan as a missionary pioneer" and was of interest to the English readers of the *Review* because, in pleading with the American bishops for a missionary enterprise, it revealed "a most impressive continuity of missionary policy, in a deep conviction that, no matter how slender were the resources of the Catholic Church in England, nor how overwhelming the demands upon its clergy, the Church could never hope to fulfil its end if it did not generously contribute to the expansion of missionary labours in pagan countries."[3]

Vaughan had read Cardinal Gibbons' centenary pastoral issued on 8 October 1889. In it, Gibbons gave a view of the history and achievements of the American Church to that date. Based on the information given by Gibbons,

Vaughan launched an appeal from his desk at Salford: "And now my Lord Cardinal, in the presence and commemoration of these facts, what is the thought that emboldens me? It is covered under this question. Has not the time come for the American Church to take its share in the great Foreign Missionary work of the Church? Can you expect that the second century of your existence will be as blessed & magnificent in its religious history as your infancy has been, if you do not send forth your heroic missioners to bear the torch of faith into those dark regions which are now possessed by the enemy of man's salvation, & by over twelve hundred millions of pagans & unbelievers?" Vaughan then traced missionary policy in the nineteenth-century English Church from Ullathorne, through Manning, and to the establishment of a missionary-sending society at Mill Hill. But, he continued: "For who are we? a mere handful compared to you.... Your population numbers 9 millions and is expanding with all the vigour of its youth in wealth and power." In addition, the "whole of the East" was being "overrun with Protestant American Missionaries. For energy, self-sacrifice, skill & intelligence, they are generally represented as outstripping the agents of all the great English Protestant missionary societies." Catholics of the United States shared the same national character and therefore must go even beyond them to become heirs to "the great missionary spirit of St. Patrick." The American Church "ought to produce a race of foreign missioners which should take the lead during the next century in the evangelisation of the heathen world."

Vaughan turned his attention to Africa, and reminded the bishops in Washington that Pope Leo XIII, in 1888, had spoken of the continent.[4] In 1884 the "scramble for Africa" began, and Europe, according to Vaughan, was being enlightened by "a noble desire to raise and enlighten that race—to destroy slavery, to establish liberty, to promote humanity." "Is the Catholic Church of the United States alone to remain a stranger to this movement?," Vaughan asked. "Upon what other nation does this duty towards Africa press with more urgent, more natural, more expectant claims than upon yours?"

The idea of colonization and evangelization by African-Americans was not new. It had been tried in Liberia by the Catholic Church, but was abandoned.[5] Vaughan had proposed the idea in a lecture he gave in New York in 1872 soon after he had arrived with his first four missionaries in Baltimore. On that occasion he said: "We have come to evangelize the coloured people of America, but our mission does not terminate with them. We are travelling, through America, to that great, unexplored, unconverted continent of Africa."

The college for preparing prospective missionaries that the society from Mill Hill had started in Maryland in the 1880s was the seed, "which in time, under God's blessing, will stretch its branches over the coloured race of two continents, if such be the will of the American Church." Manning's appeal at St James' Hall in 1868 was that the surest way to multiply a community's material means at home was "by not limiting the expansion of Charity and by not paralysing the zeal of self-denial;" and an appeal based on the ascendancy at that time of the "English-speaking race" around the world. Vaughan concluded his letter: "Would it not be possible to give expression to some determination on the part of the Catholics of America, to participate to the full in the sufferings & martyrdoms, the triumphs & conquests of the Church's Apostolate throughout the world, during the second centenary of the American Episcopate?"[6]

Vaughan hoped for a mission statement from the gathering of bishops at Washington. The meeting did not make one, but Cardinal Gibbons took Vaughan's challenge very seriously. Until he died thirty-two years later, Gibbons was one of the most influential members of the American hierarchy in helping to transform the American Church into a mission-sending and mission-supporting community.[7]

Herbert Vaughan's influence on James Gibbons is acknowledged by Jean-Paul Wiest in the circumstances which led to the founding of the Maryknoll Fathers and Brothers—the Catholic Foreign Mission Society of America. When Father Thomas Price saw Gibbons in 1911 about opening a national seminary for the foreign missions, the Cardinal approved and rallied support by writing to all the archbishops in the United States. In his appeal he urged his colleagues to follow the advice that Vaughan gave in 1889: "The priests of the United States number more than 17,000, but I am informed there are hardly 16 on the foreign missions. This fact recalls a warning which the late Cardinal Vaughan gave in a kindly, brotherly letter to me 20 years ago, urging us American Catholics not to delay participation in foreign missions, lest our own faith should suffer." At a meeting in Washington, DC, on 27 April, 1911, the archbishops approved of the establishment of an "American seminary for foreign missions." The Catholic Church in the United States had finally answered the challenge underlined by Herbert Vaughan.[8]

Vaughan was impatient with the reluctance of the American Church to act. He wrote a letter to Louis Casartelli, then at St Bede's, Manchester. Vaughan was annoyed with a request of Bishop John Keane, the first president of the Catholic University in Washington. Keane had written to Casartelli inviting him to the United States. "It is quite useless for Bishop Keane to seek my assent to your going to America. I should like to know on what principle the United States should draw continually on Europe when it does nothing whatsoever for the Foreign Missions of the Church. The States are big enough, boastful enough, rich enough and strong enough to provide for themselves. Why should they 'covet their neighbour's ass?' Let them try. Date et dabitus vobis."[9]

A few months before his death in 1903, Vaughan wrote to one of his foreign missionaries, Terence Joseph Cullen; Cullen was in the United States collecting money: "I long to see the time when that great and vigorous Church will found a Foreign Missionary College and send hundreds of Catholic apostolic men to work among the heathen." In Vaughan's opinion, Cullen's efforts would help to "stimulate the desire to begin an American Missionary College, I have no doubt, among the Catholic laity and clergy."[10]

Another person who came under Vaughan's influence was James Anthony Walsh, one of the founders of Maryknoll. In 1903, soon after he was made director of the Society for the Propagation of the Faith in Boston, Walsh went to Europe and visited St Joseph's College, Mill Hill. Vaughan was dying and Walsh was received by Francis Henry. Henry was rector of the college and would succeed Vaughan as superior general of the society. It seems likely that, while he visited Mill Hill, Walsh saw a copy of the 1889 letter of Vaughan to Gibbons.[11] Walsh wrote to the Paulist, Walter Elliot, in August 1904, about Elliot's idea to start a seminary for training missionaries: "Now as for a seminary for Foreign Missions in the United States, you have simply touched the tender spot in my heart. I have thought of it often in the past year, and more than ever since my recent visit to Freshfield and Mill Hill in England where I have learned to revere the character of Cardinal Vaughan."[12] In 1904, at a conference of the Catholic Missionary Union in Washington, Walsh repeated Vaughan's challenge to the American Church made in 1889.

In his address, Walsh said that Vaughan had struck the note that slowly awakened the American Church to the need to face its missionary responsibilities abroad. In a short article in "The Sacred Heart Review" in 1905 he reproduced the conclusion of Vaughan's letter confronting the American bishops.[13] Pope Pius X approved the plan of Thomas Price and James Anthony Walsh to begin a foreign missionary seminary on 30th June 1911.

At Home in Salford

In his position as Bishop of Salford, Vaughan's pastoral concern was not narrowly parochial. For example, in 1877 he published a pastoral letter entitled: "The Indian Famine and Apostasy in Europe." What he considered the moral obligation of English-speaking peoples towards the unconverted compelled him when he founded St Joseph's Missionary College at Mill Hill, when he travelled in the United States in the early 1870s, and even in his appeal to the Bishops of the United States in 1889. People were becoming more and more aware of the colonies; between 1871 and 1900 around 66 million people and 4.5 million square miles were added to the British Colonial Empire. It was realized by some that this "great accession of peoples and territories, though obtained at a time when France, Germany, Italy and Belgium were all for the first time simultaneously involved in the race for colonies, was greatly in excess of the gains made by any of these powers."[14]

Borneo

Vaughan was at Propaganda Fide in May 1870, requesting that Cardinal Barnabo assign a territory to the missionaries trained at St Joseph's College. He wrote to Mary Elizabeth Herbert that Barnabo had offered Labuan and Borneo, but he asked for some time to learn more about the place. Vaughan read over letters to the secretary of the congregation from Mgr Cuarteron. A few days later he wrote of Borneo "with its continuous malignant fevers," and thought that "China and Japan are preferable: perhaps even the 500,000 Indians of Texas and New Mexico, who have no priest at all among them."[15]

The subject of a Borneo mission is not mentioned again in correspondence until 1876. On 15 October 1876, Mrs E. Rodway wrote to an English Benedictine priest, Father McKay, complaining that her son, an officer in the Sarawak service, was not able to fulfil his religious duties. McKay sent the letter to Mill Hill and Vaughan wrote immediately to Propaganda asking that they reconsider the proposal to assign the Borneo mission to St Joseph's Society. On 25 March 1879 Vaughan wrote to Elizabeth Herbert that he had some "curious news from Rome. The whole of the north-west portion of the island has been made over to an English Company by the Sultan. There will be a better opening there than there has hitherto been."[16] In June 1879, Peter Benoit was sent to discuss the matter in Rome and it seems that a decision was made to entrust Borneo to the missionaries from Mill Hill. However, the decision was not to be finalized until Mgr Cuarteron reached Rome. Cuarteron arrived about the end of 1879 and was asked to resign; he did so, and the way was open for the start of a new Borneo Mission.[17] It was to be the first independent mission assigned by Rome to Vaughan's missionary society.[18]

On 15 February 1880, Vaughan wrote to Peter Benoit asking for his advice about who should be the leader of the new mission. Benoit was cautious and suggested that the Afghan mission's affairs be settled before sending people to Borneo. Vaughan disregarded Benoit's advice and requested three names of possible leaders in order that a candidate's name could be sent to Propaganda. On 15 March Vaughan submitted the name of Thomas Jackson to Rome. Jackson was still in India and so he was asked to complete his commitments and proceed to Borneo via Singapore.

Thomas Jackson was named prefect apostolic of Labuan and Northern Borneo on 10 March 1881. On 14 August 1881 he arrived with five priests. The centre for their work was Kuching, Sarawak.[19] Jackson found three other missionaries from Mill Hill already at work: Aloysius Goossens, Edmund Dunn and Daniel Kilty. Goossens was a Dutchman who had taught briefly at St Joseph's. Dunn was from Dublin and Kilty from Liverpool. They had set off from London in March, and, accompanied by Vaughan, travelled to Rome where they met the Pope. Pope Leo XIII dedicated the new mission to St Francis Xavier and St Michael the Archangel. He also made them a gift of a large print of "The Mission to Borneo" by Antonio Ventimiglia. Vaughan travelled with them to Trieste where they set sail for Singapore. Kilty remained at Singapore while a priest of the Paris Missionary Society accompanied the others with a Chinese catechist to Kuching.

They arrived on 10 July 1881 and were met by the private secretary of Rajah Charles Brooke, whose wife, Margaret, was a Catholic. The next morning they met with the Rajah and he gave them ten acres of land in Kuching but suggested that their mission effort be directed to Upper Sarawak and the Rejang. When Jackson arrived, he asked Goossens to work out of Kuching and Dunn to search for a suitable base on the banks of the Rejang. The early movements of the small group can only be regarded as exploratory and there was little attempt to put down firm roots in any one place. Jackson saw his role as supervisory, and spent most of his time travelling, visiting the others and trying to share out the financial help he received from the Society for the Propagation of the Faith in Lyons. Goossens was recalled in 1883 to teach at St Joseph's College and did not return to Borneo for five years. Fr Kilty requested a transfer to the Indian mission in 1884.

In the meantime others began to arrive from London. By 1885 there were seven mission stations: at Kuching, the Singhi, Kanowit, Labuan, Putatan, Bundu Kuala Penyu and Sandakan. Between 1885 and 1895 six more priests and one lay brother were assigned to Borneo. In 1895 there were around one thousand Catholics in the whole territory, along with eight schools and a total of 175 pupils.

Thomas Jackson, the Borneo pioneer who, in retirement, became chaplain to Alice Ingham's Mill Hill Sisters, appealed to Vaughan for Sisters to help with education. Benoit in turn wrote to the Alice Ingham community. They replied on 4 July 1883 that six of the St Joseph's Missionary Sisters of the Sacred Heart—their title at the time—from Grove House, Hampstead, volunteered. When Jackson was in England for a meeting in 1884, he made arrangements for the Sisters to travel to Borneo. Mother Francis saw her first missionaries off on the SS *Breconshire* on 15 May 1885: "Sister Helen, barely twenty-five years of age, to lead the group, then Sisters Aloysius, Mary of the Cross, Josephine, and Teresa, aged twenty-one, niece of Mother Francis." On arrival at Kuching, they were met by Jackson and immediately went to the church, where they gave thanks for their safe arrival. Within a year a convent was built, and to its chapel Margaret Brooke, convert wife of the Rajah, came privately to Mass.

The Sisters began a school for girls, which grew into one of the largest the missionary Sisters from Mill Hill had anywhere. For fifty years they were the only Sisters to work in the prefecture. A few years after their arrival they became the first nuns to work among the Dyaks, and, according to reports, the first white women the Dyaks had ever seen. By 1891 there were 761 baptised Catholics served by twelve priests in nine mission stations. There were also sixteen Mill Hill Sisters at four stations at Kuching, Kanowit, Singhi Mountain, and Sandakan in the north.[20]

In August 1884, when Thomas Jackson was in England for a meeting of the missionary society, he stayed for some time with Vaughan at Salford. He and the Bishop spent most of one Sunday afternoon talking about Borneo. When it was almost 6 p.m., Bishop Vaughan said: "There will be a great crowd of people in the cathedral this evening, so I want you to go into the pulpit and repeat some of the beautiful and interesting things you have told me this afternoon. The people will be greatly moved and edified." Jackson tried to get out of the invitation by saying that he had never preached a formal sermon; he protested that he was sent to the missions three days after his ordination and had been wandering ever since, and besides, he had no time to prepare. Vaughan laughed at Jackson's argument and said he would arrange for him to take the place of the priest who was to preach. As Vaughan left, he told Jackson: "Now I will leave you quiet. You don't require preparation. You have only to tell the people what you have just been telling me. Say a few Hail Marys. God Bless you." Vaughan did not come back but Jackson found out he was in the cathedral as he spoke that evening.

A few days later Vaughan told Jackson: "I think we priests don't do enough to show the people that we care for their bodies and their temporal interests as well as for their souls. I have been thinking that you might do some good by making a speech to the Manchester Chamber of Commerce and telling them—as you have told me—that Borneo may become later on a market for Manchester cotton. You can give them your reasons for saying so. Tell them what is going on in Borneo, what minerals are found there and anything which will cause them to take an interest in that country." Jackson wondered how he could speak to such an audience who he could not imagine were interested in a Catholic mission. Vaughan told him: "You need not be afraid of them. Most of them are very nice people. Don't talk to them about mission work unless they ask you. I know the president. I will get him to send you a formal invitation to address the Chamber. I will also write a letter to the *Manchester Guardian* on the subject, and, if I can, I will go with you and back you up when you speak at the Chamber." Vaughan's letter was published and Jackson received the president's invitation. However, at the last minute Vaughan could not attend and so Jackson "had to face the ordeal alone." [21]

Jackson remained for fourteen years as prefect in Borneo. He was often away to collect funds for the mission. In 1895 he resigned and, soon after returning to England, became chaplain to the Mill Hill Sisters' Rescue Home at Patricroft in Manchester, where he remained until his death in 1916.

New Zealand and the Maoris

The first Catholic missionaries to evangelize New Zealand were French Marist Fathers, led by Bishop Jean Baptiste François Pompallier, who landed at Totara Point in 1838. Pompallier had been vicar apostolic of Western Oceania since 1836, and New Zealand had been part of that vicariate. The Maori people whom they met were not those of Tasman or Cook, but had already been changed by contact with European civilization. The Catholic Church was already present, too, in Catholic seamen, traders, settlers and even a few Maori converts. The approximately fifty Catholics living in northern New Zealand had earlier looked to Bishop Polding in Sydney, Australia, for their needs, and he offered encouragement.[22] Large-scale European settlement began in 1840 when some Maori chiefs signed the Treaty of Waitangi, ceding sovereignty to Queen Victoria. By the 1850s the European population increased to around 79,000 while the declining Maori population, concentrated in North Island, was about 55,000.[23]

Therefore, long before the arrival of missionaries from Mill Hill, the Marists had started Catholic communities throughout the islands, including mission stations among the Maori people. However, over the years before Mill Hill missionaries arrived, the Maori mission work was left in the hands of a few secular clergy.

The first missionaries from Mill Hill came to the Maoris of North Island in 1886, during the time of the fourth bishop of Auckland, John Edmund Luck, a Benedictine. Luck was born in Peckham, London, in 1840, one of seven children of Alfred Luck, a convert. Bishop Luck was concerned about the work among the Maori but he could not spare any priests for the task. In the north there was only James McDonald, "the itinerant missionary of the Maori," and he was growing old.

In 1883 Luck began to search for English-speaking priests to carry on the mission among the estimated forty thousand Maoris on North Island. In July he wrote to Benoit asking that Mill Hill take over the Maori missions in the Auckland Diocese. Benoit and Vaughan were not certain whether to accept the invitation or not. They asked a friend in Australia, Father James Patterson, to visit New Zealand and report back to them about the situation of the Maoris. Meanwhile Luck asked Rome about the formation of a separate Maori vicariate.

During a visit to England in 1884, Luck spoke to several meetings of the council of the Society and supporters of Mill Hill. The meetings encouraged Vaughan to accept the mission, but he was privately against doing so. Vaughan would only agree to send missionaries if the Maori mission became a separate vicariate. At Auckland on 24 August 1885, the Diocesan Council accepted Vaughan's terms and notified Rome. But in August 1886 Rome appointed James McDonald.

The original agreement between Vaughan and the diocese was that Mill Hill missionaries were entrusted with the whole Maori mission and were to set up an industrial school for boys at Takapuna. It was decided that McDonald be left with the north of Auckland and Mill Hill would take the south of the city. Vaughan decided to take on the work but the society could send only two missionaries, Fr James Madan, editor of the mission magazine, *St Joseph's Advocate*, and Fr John Becker. They arrived in Auckland on 23 December 1886. According to E. R. Simmons: "In spite of its uncertain beginnings the Mill Hill mission turned out to be perhaps the most important gift of Bishop Luck to his people. From now on the Maoris would be very well provided for and the Mill Hill Fathers, by their dedicated service and their uncomplaining sacrifice, would give an outstanding example to all and a constant leadership to the Maori people."[24]

Accompanied by Bishop Luck, the two men travelled by sea to Tauranga and then inland by horse and buggy. They reached Matata and were warmly welcomed by the Maoris when the Bishop introduced them as their own priests. After some time they moved into an old disused church that had been transported seven miles and converted into a presbytery. They studied the language and customs of the Maoris and before the end of 1887, "more proficient in the language and with more confidence in themselves," they began to visit other stations.

The daily routine of the pioneer missionaries followed a pattern: "Mass, followed by breakfast, instructions in the Catechism, the teaching of prayers, building, if any was being done, Confessions, etc." They continued to study Maori and began a translation of the Catechism. "By word and example, by their charity, patience and selflessness, the two pioneers formed a truly Catholic community among the Maoris."[25]

On 1 January 1888 a new church was blessed at Maketu and the "two priests preached in Maori, rejoicing with their people on this solemn occasion." Not long afterwards, Becker left for the mission station at Rotorua. He found there was no church or priest's house; the mission had been founded by the Marists years before. "To get some idea of the hardship of travel, we must forget the Rotorua-Taupo districts of today.... We must think of the treacherous area covered in scrub and tea-tree, with narrow, winding tracks instead of tar-sealed roads, where one false step could mean severe scalding or even death. In this way we shall know something of what Fr. Becker could and did endure in his missionary duties."

Becker told the story of visiting a dying man, an old Christian named Toma. Becker would chuckle and say: "Let me finish: let me tell you: Old Toma left a will, written on a piece of note paper, and addressed to me. It read: 'I will leave my soul to God, my body to my tribe, and my love to you, Father. Please pay sixpence I owe for tobacco, lest I go wrong in the next world.' "[26]

In May 1888 two new missionaries arrived; Adrian Holierhoek and John Smiers. Holierhoek went to join John Becker at Rotorua and Smiers went to Matata. Towards the end of 1889 Bishop Luck asked Becker to go to help

Bishop James McDonald on Hokianga, but they never met as McDonald died before Becker was settled in. In June 1889 Bishop Luck appointed Smiers to open the Tokaanu-Taupo area as a parish, which meant that the four missionaries were in four separate mission stations.

Some time during 1892 or 1893 Becker wrote to Herbert Vaughan asking that he be relieved of the office of society superior. Vaughan and his consultants at Mill Hill agreed and appointed in his place Albert Lightheart, who had been chosen for the Maori mission but had not yet left England. With three other priests—John Broomfield, Charles Kreijmborg and Peter Oud—Lightheart arrived in New Zealand in November 1893. By 1900, despite the many growing commitments of their missionary society, eight more priests were assigned to New Zealand. With additional help, Lightheart was able to extend the work of the mission. New churches were opened at Kaihu and Matata in 1895, at Rotorua in 1896, Pawarenga in 1898, Whangape and Te Kopura in 1899 and Te Puna in 1900; presbyteries were also constructed. "These simply designed, set-pattern churches and presbyteries—and later, schools—symbolised the ideals and aspirations of the early Mill Hill Fathers."[27] Fr Charles Kreijmborg is singled out as a priest-builder to whom the "Maori Mission and the Auckland Diocese owe a debt of gratitude." He was an "expert carpenter and builder" and possessed of "boundless energy." It should be remembered that missionaries did not accomplish anything without the help of the often nameless catechists and labourers. For example, one photograph shows Lightheart with twelve unnamed catechists outside a thatched house at Whangaroa in 1895.[28]

On 23 January 1896 Bishop Luck died and was succeeded by George Michael Lenihan, who was ordained bishop on 15 November 1896. In December 1897 two new missionaries arrived: Bressers and van't Westeinde. Bressers had been on his way to Uganda when he became ill on the two-month trek inland from Mombassa. He was carried back to the coast and returned to Europe. When he had recovered, he was appointed to New Zealand. "Africa's loss was New Zealand's gain, for Fr Bressers was an expert carpenter and builder, and a gifted scholar with a retentive memory."[29]

The records of the journeys and appointments of the early years of the New Zealand mission are often bewildering. With few personnel, illness might mean moving one to replace another. "One year, a few years, in a mission station, friendly relations established with the local Maoris, a few converts instructed and received into the Church, and then, a move to a new mission station miles and miles away. But there was no resentment. Every such change was seen as necessary and accepted as such by the Fathers."[30]

Between 1900 and 1907 five more missionaries arrived from Mill Hill, bringing the total number to seventeen. They helped in the expansion of the mission, especially among the northern Maoris. During that time their superior general, Herbert Vaughan, died, and was replaced by Francis Henry.

Kashmir and Kafiristan

After the failed mission to Afghanistan, a suggestion was made that a new prefecture for the Mill Hill Missionaries be carved out of the Punjab in northern India. Vaughan agreed to send new chaplains to the British army, provided that the district assigned had missionary possibilities. Propaganda agreed and the search was on for personnel. In 1887, Mill Hill became responsible for the Prefecture Apostolic of Kashmir and Kafiristan, which had been carved out of the diocese of Lahore. According to John Rooney, the names Kashmir and Kafiristan did not signify precisely defined political or geographical realities, but were merely labels. The four stations assigned at Peshawar, Rawalpindi, Nowshera and Murree, were to be bases for chaplaincy work. Rome's position in 1887 was that missionaries could go out from the stations to the north and west; territory to the south was cared for by Belgium Capuchins. Later on, Vaughan's missionaries were asked by Propaganda to report on the areas of "Kashmir and Kafiristan."[31]

The leader and prefect apostolic of the new mission was from the Madras mission, thirty-seven-year-old Ignatius Brouwer. The others were: Francis Mansfeld, who was newly ordained; Dominic Reijnders, aged forty-two; Frederick Schmitz, forty-two; and Jan de Ruyter, thirty-four. Together with Brouwer they formed the first mission group. Schmitz and de Ruyter had been withdrawn from the United States. The men began their work in early September 1887 soon after arriving at Rawalpindi. Vaughan had signed an agreement in July with the Capuchins that set out the details of a hand-over to missionaries from Mill Hill. Brouwer was annoyed with Vaughan for having signed a document that was "general, vague and capable of both restrictive and expansive interpretation." Despite being overwhelmed with debts, the first group was able to initiate small missions around Rawalpindi.

In 1888 seven new missionaries arrived: Daniel Kilty—who was to die on 23 April 1889—Gerard Wiersma, Peter Ord, John Broomfield, Edward Revely, John Waterreus and Br Robert Coleman. Two more priests and a brother came in 1889: Dominic Wagenaar, Joseph Cunningham and Br Henry Rogers. They were followed by three more priests and two Brothers.

Vaughan and Benoit defined three objectives for the mission within the general aims of evangelization. They were committed to chaplaincy work with the British army, to education at St Thomas College, Murree, which they reopened, and for primary evangelization among the peoples of Kashmir and Kafiristan.[32]

According to John Bray, the missionaries were never able to establish a foothold in Kafiristan, and therefore concentrated on the northern Punjab, Kashmir and—at first—Ladakh.[33]

Mission to the United States: the Josephites

John Slattery was ordained on Saint Patrick's Day 1877 in St Joseph's College chapel by Bishop Weathers, Cardinal Manning's auxiliary. On the same day Weathers blessed a side altar of Our Lady, given by the wife of Colonel Jervis. On 10 June Slattery took the Society oath of obedience and was at once appointed to teach logic at college. He objected to the appointment, saying that he had not come to England to be a professor but a missionary. In May he had written to Benoit arguing that if the society needed teachers they should be found at Louvain or Rome, adding: "My whole soul is with the Negro." During the summer holiday he visited his family in New York and a few mission stations in the United States. He returned to Mill Hill and taught during September and October, but finally, on 28 October, Vaughan and Benoit agreed to appoint Slattery to the United States.

With Evaste Proth, who had been ordained with him, he left for America on 1 November 1877, and on arrival became the rector of St Francis Xavier in Baltimore. His first task was to put the financial accounts in order and attempt to pay off a $23,947 debt. With hard work, and the help of his family and friends, Slattery succeeded in reducing the debt to $1,500 by 1883.

With the departure of James Noonan in 1878 to become a Jesuit and work in Jamaica, the Mill Hill missions floundered, despite the success Slattery had at Baltimore. Slattery's straightforward reports had impressed Vaughan. In an attempt to instil new life into the American mission, Slattery, at the age of twenty-seven, was appointed by Vaughan to be its leader, while he also continued as rector of St Francis. The decision was made during the first provincial chapter of the society in the United States on 13 December 1878.[34]

Three more men arrived in 1878. They were John DeRuyter, Charles Giessen, and Alfred Leeson. Slattery had nine men in his province and parishes at St Francis Xavier in Baltimore, St Augustine's in Louisville, Kentucky, and St Peter's in Charleston, South Carolina. According to Peter Hogan, Slattery's position required that he serve four interests: the members of St Joseph's Society working in the United States; his superiors in England, Vaughan and Benoit, who were a potential source of manpower, as well as of financial and psychological support; the American bishops, whose opposition could hinder the growth and development of the community; the groups of nuns who could support evangelization with a supply of teachers, nurses, catechisers, and parish visitors. In addition, there were the members of the African–American community they had promised under a special oath at Mill Hill to serve exclusively.[35]

Slattery served as provincial from 13 December 1878 until 28 February 1883. According to Stephen Ochs, he provided strong leadership, personally visiting each mission and securing the help of several teaching orders of Sisters for the Mill Hill-Josephite Schools in Baltimore. He acted decisively in connection with a mission at Marlboro, handing it over to the archdiocese in 1879 in order to ensure that the missionaries would work only for African-Americans. Slattery did so well that he won the confidence of James Gibbons, the archbishop of Baltimore. He also found space for African-Americans in a Catholic cemetery that had excluded them because of race.

While in Baltimore he also began to lay the groundwork for what became his most controversial plan: the development of an African-American clergy.[36] Vaughan was willing to accept African-American students into St Joseph's College. When he began at Mill Hill he had defined its long-term goal to be the providing of every mission area served by his missionaries with a good local clergy. His emphasis after 1871 was to train African-Americans on the American mission for the evangelization of Africa, a goal which "certainly suggested black catechists, if not priests." In a letter to Michael O'Connor, the man instrumental in arranging for his missionaries to go to Baltimore, Vaughan evidently asked about the feasibility of black priests. O'Connor responded on 6 October 1871 that he should train catechists as soon as possible but cautioned: "as to priests, it is another question which must be left to circumstances and the development that will take place under the influence of Providence." Vaughan went ahead six months later and accepted into St Joseph's College a young African-American, Medard Nelson, who had been recommended by Archbishop Napoleon Perche of New Orleans. Vaughan stipulated in a note on 25 June 1872 that Medard needed to pay his passage and first year's tuition; it amounted to $200. Probably for financial reasons, Medard Nelson never went to England and Mill Hill.

After he visited the United States in 1875, Benoit was more cautious. On 6th April 1875 he recorded in his diary "a canard" frequently repeated by whites that "All admit that a Negro-Priest w'd find no favour with his race." On the same day a Franciscan priest in Illinois was writing to Noonan, who was still at St Francis in Baltimore, to recommend a twenty-two-year-old African-American named Augustine Tolton. Tolton was "very desirous of becoming a missionary for the people of his race." Benoit made a note on the letter asking if he was ready to remain a catechist, and if not, would he serve in Borneo. Benoit and Vaughan were willing to admit local candidates to the missionary seminary at Mill Hill, based on the recommendation of men working on the missions and provided they guaranteed that such local clergy could work effectively on the missions.[37]

The information Benoit received from the missionaries working in the United States revealed that they did not support the recruitment of seminarians from among African-Americans.[38] It was Slattery who altered his earlier views about the suitability of African-Americans for the priesthood. In 1883 he took steps that eventually resulted in the ordination of Charles Randolph Uncles.[39]

Slattery soon came into conflict with Vaughan, Benoit, and his colleagues on the American mission. He complained to Vaughan about the quality and number of missionaries on the American mission, and of the society's insistence that the American province pay the transportation costs of candidates sent to England for training. He also urged Vaughan to agree that all Americans sent to Mill Hill would be sent back to work in the United States after their training, but Vaughan was not willing to make such a commitment. After 1878, and until 1884, only five new men were added to the American mission, and two were immediately reassigned to England. Slattery began to resent what he considered a diminished interest in the work in the United States and a greater emphasis on the Afghanistan, India and Borneo missions. Vaughan wrote to Slattery on 29 January 1879 that he was pleased with the report Benoit had brought to him about the province. Concerning the problems with certain members, he pointed out that "we are what we are in God's sight and we shall succeed as He, not as men, pleases."[40]

However, by July the tone of their correspondence deteriorated. Slattery's suggestion that the province be dissolved if Vaughan could not commit Americans to the American province and approve of the forming of a house of studies in America to train missionaries for the African-American mission, was answered by Vaughan on 24 July 1879. Vaughan accused Slattery of "a want of loyalty or a want of appreciation of the gravity of the questions upon which you have had to communicate with me."[41]

Slattery's relationship with his fellow missionaries was characterized by a directness that had all the "impatience and arrogance often characteristic of talented young men suddenly thrust into leadership roles, though in many cases he certainly had reason for dissatisfaction." Michael Walsh, who was rector of St Augustine parish in Washington while Slattery supervised the finances—there was an inherited debt of $58,000—wrote to Slattery: "You heap on us rebukes and reproaches.... Permit me to say that I so heartily hate your ways and manners." In an election held during November 1882 the members did not re-elect Slattery but instead chose Alfred Leeson as provincial. Vaughan thought Slattery was the most capable of the group in the United States, but, since the men had not chosen him, after a four-month delay, he appointed Leeson in February 1883. Vaughan wrote to Benoit about Slattery: "He will be a great loss in every way ... except his temper with the men."

Slattery felt humiliated and wrote to Vaughan that his "removal was certainly a disgrace." Early in 1884 Leeson managed to get Slattery out of Baltimore by assigning him to a new mission in Richmond, Virginia. Bishop John J. Keane held services at Richmond Cathedral for African-Americans. He also organized catechism classes. Keane wrote to Benoit for help, and Benoit in turn appointed Slattery at the new provincial's request. Richmond had a congregation of less than forty, no church, no rectory, and a small school with one teacher in the basement of the cathedral rectory. Although he was still angry, Slattery applied his energy and skill to his new assignment and built up the Richmond mission. The first Catholic church for African-Americans was dedicated on 22 November 1885. It included a school and rectory and was free of debt. The school was staffed by four Sisters from St Mary's Abbey at Mill Hill. Slattery started a school at Petersburg in September 1885, and, in 1886, a new station at Keswick, followed by another mission at Union Mills. Eventually Richmond became a central mission for eight churches and five parishes in Virginia.

Slattery began writing a series of articles, beginning in 1881, for the *Catholic World*, the publication of Isaac Hecker's Paulists. He had a friend among Hecker's disciples. At his home parish, St Paul's in New York, he had become acquainted with Walter Elliot, Hecker's disciple and biographer. In one letter that was probably intended to calm Slattery's bitterness towards his Mill Hill community, Elliot wrote of the affection he had for the "Fathers, especially the old ones," among the Paulists: "I would sooner go down on a plank of my own shipwreck than ride the seas on the frigate of others' powers."[42] On another occasion he advised Slattery to promote the province as one with an American identity: "You are a wretch Slattery ... if you don't put your miserable shyness right under foot and make yourself an advertising agent for your own good people. Everywhere you go tell them who you are, where you were born and where your parents live so that people will not think that you or your fathers are British."[43] In June 1883 an article by Slattery, "The Catholic Church and the Colored People," one of several, was published. David O'Brien, Hecker's most recent biographer, called Slattery's series remarkable.[44]

In 1884 Propaganda insisted that the Third Plenary Council of the United States bishops must address the "Negro problem." Vaughan considered making some recommendations through Cardinal Gibbons. At Benoit's request, Slattery was asked to prepare a memorandum on the needs of the African-American apostolate to help Vaughan. On 7 March 1884 he sent a memorandum to Vaughan which contained, in addition, a prospectus for a Mill Hill seminary in the United States. The Plenary Council met between 9 November and 7 December 1884. It did not consider the possibility of African-American priests but did take up the suggestion to have an annual collection for the Negro and Indian missions and formed a Commission for Catholic Missions Among Colored Peoples and Indians.

Cardinal James Gibbons wrote on behalf of the Plenary Council concerning "Home and Foreign Missions." The letter was published in *The Tablet* on 3 January: "The duties of a Christian begin with his own household and his own parish but they do not end there.... In nearly all European countries there are Foreign Missionary Colleges and also associations of the faithful for the support of the missions by their contributions." *The Tablet* reported that the Council urged that a Society for the Propagation of the Faith be started in every parish and every diocese have a collection for the missions each year.[45]

In his writing, Slattery criticized the poverty of American Catholic missionary efforts and documented, much as Vaughan did in his efforts on behalf of overseas missions, the greater investments of Protestant churches in the evangelization of African-Americans. He continued to argue with Vaughan and Benoit for an American seminary to train missionaries. He felt that the seminary at Mill Hill produced missionaries who understood neither the United States nor the Negro missions.[46]

In a discussion with Benoit during his visit to the United States in 1884, Cardinal Gibbons had been enthusiastic about developing such a seminary in the United States for the African-American mission, and suggested that Slattery and Giessen undertake such a project in cooperation with the Sulpicians, who staffed St Mary's Seminary in Baltimore. Slattery took a vacation in Europe, ostensibly to rest due to his nerves, poor eyes and a kidney problem. On his journey he stopped at Mill Hill to promote the idea of an American seminary, and visited Vaughan in Salford. His approach must have been less than diplomatic. Vaughan wrote to Slattery on 29 December 1885 that a letter he had received from him was "as painful to answer as it was to receive." He asked Slattery to "get the last root of bitterness out of your heart and cast it away forever. Do this for the love of God and of His Blessed Mother."[47]

John Slattery worked on the proposal, and finally, Gibbons, returning from Rome in May 1887, stopped at Mill Hill to see Vaughan on his behalf. Vaughan could hardly refuse Gibbons, and, at his insistence, agreed to open a seminary in Baltimore. Slattery was appointed the first rector and returned to Mill Hill to make arrangements to begin. Vaughan wrote to him on 28 August 1887:

> You have devoted yourself with so much zeal and intelligence to the best interests of the Coloured people and God has so visibly blessed your efforts, that I am anxious to see you carry out the work of our society still farther by establishing a College in America for the education of men to be wholly consecrated to what I venture to call the purely missionary work of the Church in America.... The first mission undertaken by our society was at the invitation of Archbishop Spalding and Bishop O'Connor S.J., to the coloured people, and now the Cardinal Archbishop of Baltimore and the Bishop of Richmond, Virginia, to both of whom you are well known, desire to see you employed in founding a missionary house of studies adjoining the Sulpician Seminary at Baltimore, especially for that race. I say then, Go in the name of God, with the permission and blessing of the bishops, collect all that is necessary for your purpose in men and means ... the house of studies under the charge of St. Joseph's Society in America will be naturally American in its character...."[48]

Slattery returned to the United States in September with a list of proposals to be communicated to the American bishops. On 20 October 1887 he wrote to each of the bishops from St Mary's Seminary in Baltimore and announced the opening of St Joseph's Seminary. The Sulpicians agreed to allow students from the American St Joseph's Seminary to attend classes at St Mary's. Two days earlier, Slattery had purchased an old hotel which adjoined the grounds of St Mary's. It was renovated and opened to four students, Charles Uncles among them, who studied free of charge with the Sulpicians. Cardinal Gibbons dedicated the seminary on 9 September 1888. A parish was also established as a training facility for the seminarians; St Peter Claver's Church and School were also dedicated in 1888.

The following year, Epiphany Apostolic College, a minor seminary and feeder school for St Joseph's, opened on 9 September. Before the opening of Epiphany, three African-American students had been sent for their training to Freshfield, the minor seminary Vaughan opened near Liverpool. One of them, James Brown, died of typhoid fever at Epiphany College on 17 September 1890. The first rector was a Baltimore diocesan priest, Dominic Manley, who had joined St Joseph's Society. The money for the original purchase came from Slattery's father and the preparation of the building from the Drexel-Morrel family of Philadelphia.

The example of mission growth seen at Richmond was a pattern repeated in Delaware. John DeRuyter arrived in the United States in 1878, but he became ill and returned to Europe. He then spent some time in Kafiristan, before arriving back in Baltimore in January 1889. The Society was asked to open a mission at Wilmington, Delaware, and he was appointed. He arrived on 9 October 1889 with two dollars and began St Joseph's Mission in the basement of St Mary's Church. In 1890 he built Wilmington's first St Joseph's Church, and in 1891, a rectory, which was later turned over to Sisters for use as a temporary orphanage. In 1892 he built a permanent orphanage.

By 1892 Mill Hill was caring for three churches in Baltimore: St Francis Xavier, St Monica and St Peter Claver, and also St Joseph's Seminary and Epiphany Apostolic College; at Washington, DC, St Augustine Church; at Louisville, Kentucky, there was another St Augustine's; at Charleston, South Carolina, St Peter's; at Richmond, St Joseph's and its mission stations. Josephite-Mill Hill missionaries also staffed St Joseph's in Wilmington. By the middle of 1892 there were sixteen Mill Hill missionaries in the United States, caring for eight mission parishes and two seminaries. Also, under John Greene's editorship, *St Joseph's Advocate* was published with an American supplement; it was later replaced by *The Colored Harvest*. The *Harvest* supported St Joseph's Seminary and work in the United States only.

The first African-American to be ordained in the United States was a Mill Hill-Josephite member. Charles Uncles was ordained by James Gibbons in Baltimore Cathedral on 19 December 1891.[49]

Finally a decision was made to create an independent society out of the Josephite-Mill Hill mission to the United States. In practice, a division had begun long before. For some missionaries, the commitment to the African-American population had eroded. Others were unwilling to leave the United States for other overseas missions undertaken by Vaughan. Still others felt committed to the evangelization of the African-Americans and wanted to bind themselves together more completely to achieve this end.[50]

On Easter Monday, 30 March 1891, Slattery addressed to Vaughan what he titled a "Memorial." In it he outlined his experience with Mill Hill and the African-American mission from the time he was appointed provincial by Benoit in December 1878. He quoted a letter of 12 July 1879 in which Vaughan replied to a letter Slattery had written to Benoit. Slattery wrote that he agreed to pay £40 a year for each student he might send to Mill Hill provided he return to America after ordination. Vaughan himself, according to the letter quoted by Slattery, proposed a better solution:

> I could not help seeing many years ago that it would be a natural and fitting thing that the great American Church should have its own Missionary organization, both for the evangelization of American blacks and for foreign missions and that it should cease at an early date to continue to be dependent upon centres in Europe.... A centre in America for the Mission to the American blacks and for the preparation of American subjects for Foreign Missions would be more serviceable to the Church than the dependence which exists at present upon Mill Hill.... You may not be ready at the present moment to be formed into an independent Mother House, but the time may not be far distant and it might be well that you should be taking measures in preparation.

Slattery recalled Vaughan's 1889 letter to the American hierarchy, and his recurring theme of an American commitment to missionary evangelization. On the opening of Epiphany Apostolic College, Vaughan wrote: "That College is a seed planted in Catholic Maryland, which in time, under God's blessing, will stretch its branches over the coloured races of two continents, if such be the will of the American Church." Gibbons, he wrote, would not initiate or even suggest such a division but promised to give his approval if it was made by Vaughan.[51]

Much had happened to make Vaughan less enthusiastic, not about the theme that he often raised, that America should do more to help the missions both at home and overseas, but concerning Slattery's approach and the many problems that faced the American Province from its beginnings. On 3 November 1891 Vaughan wrote to Gibbons about Slattery's proposal to make the two seminaries independent. He had reservations about allowing the formation of what might seem a rival institution to those who wished to remain part St Joseph's Society from Mill Hill. He thought the execution of the proposal was premature, and wondered if, despite Slattery's good will, high aspirations and splendid energy, he would have the tact and judgement needed to manage men on the missions. "It has always seemed to me that not only is it desirable that such an institution should become naturalized in America but that it should become thoroughly and exclusively American." Vaughan added that "government from England over the American Province must always be either weak or blundering. Were I to interfere much at this distance, blunders would be the consequence." Vaughan concluded his letter to Gibbons: "Sad are the thoughts which are passing through my mind and as such I lay them before you for consideration." In a postscript he offered to transfer to Gibbons his jurisdiction over Slattery, and the other missionaries who joined him, in the United States.

On 28 January 1892, Vaughan wrote from Mill Hill to each member of the American Province. He reminded them that differences had arisen in history which had divided religious orders into many branches. He felt that in "our American Province there have been deplorable defections, and that Satan has seemed determined to sift and winnow us as wheat." Looking back, in Vaughan's opinion, there had been laxity in observance of their rule from the beginning. The spirit of obedience was especially weak: "self-indulgence in small things and neglect of fraternal charity have often split and shivered the union, which should have grown up amongst us, like the life and strength of a tree, which has been fed from one fruitful source of healthy sap." Addressing Slattery's petition, he wrote: "All efforts seem ineffective to heal the breach of confidence and of union that has ceased to grow and widen, it is better that the separation petitioned for be granted. It may indeed be in the design of Providence that an independent society should be called into existence, and that Father Slattery, and those associated with him, should develop a purely American Missionary work among the Negroes of America and Africa."

On 5 February 1892, Vaughan wrote to Gibbons on the death of Manning: "My old friend of over 40 years," who had a great affection for Gibbons, "and often spoke of you and your work." At this point he thought that there was no action or visit by him that could change the course of events. "There are cases of incompatibility of temper between husband and wife even, which an angel must accept and yield to." He added that he hoped that the separation would "turn out beneficial for the coloured people." Gibbons wrote from Baltimore on 14 April that he was ready to accept the missionaries who wished to be released from Mill Hill to form "a society independent of your own community," and would appoint John Slattery as superior. Also involved in the negotiations were ten students at St Joseph's Seminary in Baltimore, and sixty in Epiphany Apostolic College.

By June 1892, Vaughan had transferred to Westminster to be installed as Manning's successor. The final correspondence connected with negotiations over the formation of a separate society was a letter by Vaughan to Gibbons, on 30th May 1893. In the letter Vaughan released Slattery, DeRuyter,

Dominick Manley, Lambert Welbers, and Charles Uncles from the vow of obedience and from all obligations to Mill Hill.

The members in the province had been given a year to make up their minds what they wished to do. Gerard Wiersma, who had been in America, but was then on the India mission, joined the American group. Three chose to return to Mill Hill, but one, John Greene, changed his mind and eventually joined the Baltimore archdiocese. The eight remaining members joined dioceses in the United States.

Peter Hogan wrote that "a door closed on Mill Hill in the African-American missions, but a door opened for St Joseph's Society of the Sacred Heart, or Josephites, to grow in strength in service to the Black Catholic community of the United States."[52]

Apostolic Schools and Minor Seminaries

Epiphany Apostolic School in Baltimore was founded as a feeder school for the new American major seminary. Vaughan had already begun a similar school in England.

When St Joseph's Missionary College was started, candidates who had not completed their minor studies were sent to apostolic schools elsewhere.[53] In 1879 Vaughan and Benoit decided that the time had come for the society to have a preparatory school of its own in England. One was started in August 1880 in a church presbytery at Coedangred, a small mission in Monmouthshire, with two priests and seven students. It was called St Joseph's Apostolic School of the Sacred Heart and was a preparatory school for boys aged sixteen to twenty who had not studied any classics. The students were supposed to have an intention of serving in the foreign missions and were asked to pay £40 a year. After the first year, money was needed to enlarge the presbytery in order to accommodate more students, and so, rather than invest in renovation, it was decided that the Society should find a larger place elsewhere.[54]

In 1881 the school was moved to Kelvedon, Essex. At Kelvedon, a former Protestant school, with seven acres of land, was purchased by a benefactor and handed over to Henry Manning in trust. The Protestant school had once accommodated one hundred boys. One of the classrooms was being used as a mission chapel and attended by thirty Catholics from the neighbouring area. Vaughan arranged for the society to rent the property from the trust for £50 per year. He also suggested a possible use for the new school: "Should the council ever deem it necessary and opportune to conduct the schools of our Fathers—the buildings of Kelvedon are large enough to accommodate a number of such teachers, if money can be found to maintain them during training—probably a three-year course." The apostolic school began on 20 August 1881 with nine students, two priests and a Brother. Francis Henry was appointed rector and Frances Ingham's Mill Hill Sisters sent a small community to keep the household.[55]

In 1884 the Kelvedon school was closed, and then reopened at Freshfield, a station on the railway between Liverpool and Southport. There were fourteen students, two priests and two substitute teachers. St Peter's Minor Seminary was to remain open until 1971. The building had been a Protestant boarding school. It had six acres of land and a further twenty were acquired with the help of the Weld-Blundells of Ince-Blundell Hall, Crosby, Vaughan's relatives. The school was officially opened on 11 August 1884.[56]

Thomas Jackson made a day trip from Manchester to Freshfield with Vaughan in 1884. They were walking in Manchester when Vaughan suggested that they go to "see how Freshfield is getting on. We can just get a train for Southport now." Freshfield, wrote Jackson, is a "place about six miles from Southport on the Liverpool side."

> A while before our visit the Bishop had bought a house there and started a preparatory school for Mill Hill. The land in which the home stood belonged to Mr. Weld-Blundell, who generously made a present of it to St. Joseph's Society; the building had been a private boarding school. As soon as the Bishop got possession of it, he invited some Catholic ladies to look over it, with a hope that they would help him to pay for it. He had ordered two students to be sent from Mill Hill to prepare the house for the visit of the ladies. One of these students, when he was a priest in Borneo, told me that, on the morning of the day when the ladies were expected, the Bishop arrived from Salford, and, finding the house very dirty, he took off his coat and spent a long time in sweeping the walls and floor, so that he became nearly as black as a sweep, and had great difficulty in getting himself clean by the time the ladies arrived in the afternoon.[57]

Vaughan wrote to Elizabeth Herbert that St Peter's College at Freshfield was to open on Monday 11 August 1884: "The place is most suitable and now it is in fair poor order—just as we need it for the present." The school dining room was in the basement, above it a study, above that a dormitory, and on the top floor of the building, a chapel sixty feet long. Elizabeth Herbert visited Freshfield, looked at the kitchen, and arranged for pots and pans to be supplied. Fr Henry was appointed rector.[58]

The Tablet reported the opening of St Peter's: The students arrived on Friday, 8 August. On Monday, Vaughan offered a Mass of the Holy Spirit, and in the afternoon a formal service for the opening took place. After Benediction, Bishop Vaughan addressed the gathering:

> What could have induced them to visit—nothing to gratify the senses.... Certain great facts were always pleading with devout and earnest Catholics and these had drawn them—facts such as the existence of 900,000,000 of heathen who knew not the name of their Redeemer—such as the duty of Catholics of this Empire towards the 200,000,000 of heathen who are our

fellow subjects. There is the strange dispensation of Providence which makes the salvation of men dependent upon the faith and charity of other men.... From the earliest times in the Church, the foreign missionary and apostolic spirit was active. No sooner was Jesus born in Bethlehem than Joseph took the child and his mother into the land of Egypt. He has ever been the type and model of the apostles and of apostolic men till now. The work of foreign missions today is a continuation of that example. The Church is ever seeking out the most benighted lands and preaching to the most abandoned peoples.... It is not that the foolish and weak things are in themselves capable of triumphing over the pride and power of the world; they are generosity, charity, and the spirit of faith—which are divine gifts—that obtain the victory."[59]

Between the new feeder school and St Joseph's at Mill Hill there were forty-nine students in September 1884. On 11 April 1890 Vaughan wrote that another school was planned for the Netherlands: "We are going to build a little College at Roosendaal for about twenty candidates for Mill Hill." He also announced that there was a prospect of making a foundation in the Tyrol.

Vaughan had visited Dutch seminaries in 1871 to recruit students interested in the missions. As a result of a second tour in 1876, and of similar visits by Benoit, "there began a fairly regular flow of vocations from Holland."[60] On 1 January 1890 he wrote that the society had a house "in Holland for the new Seminary, close to Roosendaal—twelve hours from Mill Hill." It was rent-free for the first year. While in the Netherlands he had also met four Dutch bishops at a dinner "which lasted from 1:15pm to 5:30pm!" On the same trip he went to Amsterdam and the Hague. On 20 August 1890 Vaughan again went to the Netherlands to finalize arrangements for the college, a small building close to Roosendaal, in North Brabant.[61] After a short time a building was erected, large enough to house thirty students. The first rector of Roosendaal was Jan Aelen, who had been working in the diocese of Madras, since 1880.[62]

In May 1891 another missionary training centre was started in the Tyrol, at Brixen—now Bressanone—in northern Italy, but at that time part of Austria. Vaughan had first visited the Tyrol in the spring of 1855. At Brixen, a daughter of William George and Frances Ward had married a Schonberg and lived at Castle Pallaus, three miles south of Brixen. He had written about Brixen in October 1889 and again in October 1890; the idea was to have a Freshfield-type college for the Tyrol. Vaughan sent the Tyrolese Fr Aloysius Stotter to Brixen in 1890. Mrs Schonberg approached the Bishop of Brixen about the idea and wrote to Vaughan on 23 July that the local bishop had no objection. In November 1890 Vaughan stopped in Brixen on his way to Rome. On 11 and 12 November he stayed at Castle Pallaus, and, while there, he met the director of the diocesan seminary, Dr Mitterhausen. Vaughan also made a visit to the Elephant Hotel. He wrote to Benoit on the same day to inform him that he had leased a house near the Brixen railway station for £120 a year, beginning in May 1891. The house would accommodate fifteen or twenty students. He wrote to Elizabeth Herbert that it was the only furnished house available.

From Brixen he went to Innsbruck to see the Governor of the Tyrol and settle matters about the college with the authorities. Before seeing Governor von Merveldt, he visited the bishop who told him he would support Vaughan's application. On 15 November the Governor of the Tyrol met with Vaughan; he was "very friendly and favourable" and congratulated him on the foundation at Brixen. Vaughan assigned John Kleinschneider from India to be the first rector, and the school opened with at least six students.

Kleinschneider was from Lette near Coesfeld. He had gone to Mill Hill in 1873, was ordained in 1878, and sent to India. In 1883 he had taken steps to open a major seminary for local priests at Nellore, a work much appreciated by Herbert Vaughan. Kleinschneider did so well, that, in 1893, after visiting Brixen, Vaughan went on to Vienna, confident enough in the school to discuss its future with the Emperor. His aim was to get state approval for the mission school and to have it acknowledged as an Austrian seminary.[63]

St Joseph's Society

The overall government of the missionary society remained with Vaughan till his death. He was superior general but much of the everyday affairs were in the hands of the rector of St Joseph's College at Mill Hill—first Peter Benoit and then, on his death in 1892, Francis Henry. A periodic event that set the future course of the society was the meeting of representatives of the members, called chapters. One took place in August 1884, and Vaughan wrote: "For sixteen days we have sat five hours a day going over all the work in the various missionary provinces, devising rules and regulations for the colleges at home and for the members of the Society everywhere. We have revised our Rules and improved things by experience." The chapter was made up of six nationalities, he concluded, and they came from missions in the United States, India, Borneo and England: "They are all one and united in the early training of Mill Hill and in one aim and one spirit."[64]

Notes

1. *The Josephite Harvest*, 96, 3, Autumn, 1993, p.18: "Thus, on September 11, 1993, in the Basilica National Shrine of the Immaculate Conception in Washington,D.C., when 100 years of Josephite endeavour were celebrated, in the presence of more than 3000 persons, most of them from Josephite parishes throughout the nation, with a Cardinal, Apostolic Pro Nuncio, Bishops, and dozens of clergy and religious in attendance, there was a sense of reward, a sense of faith and trust that have been fulfilled. The mere handful of Catholics among the four million

African Americans a century ago has grown to more than three million, including a dozen Black Catholic bishops and hundreds of African American priests and religious"; p.16:"In the past 100 years, there have been 451 Josephite priests and 32 permanently professed Josephite brothers dedicated to the African American apostolate. A total of 174 parishes and missions have been established by Josephites and in these churches, 337,000 baptisms were performed of which 90,000 were converts to the Catholic Faith. More than 100 elementary and high schools provided education to hundreds of thousands of young people"; "Josephite Centennial Celebration," September 11, 1993: Letter from the Vatican Secretariat of State: "His Holiness sees the apostolate of the Josephite Missionaries as an authentic testimony to faith in Jesus Christ and as a much needed witness to the dignity of the human person"; Letter from the President of the United States: "Your valuable work as spiritual leaders has enlightened millions of people and has helped strengthen the faith of our nation"; Fr Maurice McGill presented the Josephite superior with an ikon of St Joseph on behalf of the Mill Hill Missionaries. The author was also present at the ceremonies.

2. John Tracey Ellis, "A Challenge to the American Church on its One Hundredth Birthday," *Catholic Historical Review*, 30, October 1944, pp.290-8.

3. Denis Gwynn, "England and the Foreign Missions," *Clergy Review*, (NS) 26, 2, February 1946, pp.46-65; Herbert Vaughan may have been influenced by the Centenary Conference of the Protestant Missions of the World held in London, June 9-19, 1888. It was held in Exeter Hall and was the largest of its kind to that date, with 1,579 delegates from 139 different denominations and societies representing ten countries. Thomas A. Askew, "The 1888 London Centenary Missions Conference: Ecumenical Disappointment or American Missions Coming of Age?," *International Bulletin of Missionary Research*, 18, 3, July 1994, pp.113-8.

4. Ellis, "Challenge," p.295 n.6: He was most likely referring to the Pope's letter of 5 May 1888, *In Plurimis*, addressed to the hierarchy of Brazil, in which he congratulated them on the suppression of slavery in Brazil. In his letter, the Pope took occasion to dwell on the evils which the slave trade had brought upon Africa; In August 1888 Cardinal Lavigerie addressed a meeting of the British and Foreign Anti-Slavery Society, in Prince's Hall, London. He was convinced that the slave-trade presented a radical obstacle to development of any kind in Africa. The abolition of slavery in Brazil and the Pope's encyclical letter presented him with a further opportunity to denounce the slavery that still existed in Africa. On the platform, among the civic and religious leaders, was Cardinal Manning. See: Renault, *Lavigerie*, pp.367-385.

5. *ibid.*, n.7; See: Henry Fisher,"The Catholic Church in Liberia," *Records of the American Catholic Historical Society of Philadelphia*, XL (1929), pp.249-310: Between 1821 and 1867 the American Colonization Society transported free African-Americans from the United States to Liberia; 13,136 Americans and 5,732 recaptured Africans. The Society was supported by Protestant missionaries who saw in its work an opportunity to benefit the African-American in the United States and to be the source of evangelization on the African continent. The Catholic Church tried to establish a mission in Liberia. Bishop England saw the need to support the Catholics who were among the African-Americans who went to Liberia, and so Fr Edward Barron of Philadelphia, John Kelly of New York, and a lay catechist, Dionysius Pindar, sailed in December 1841 for Africa. Barron's health broke down and by mid-1844 the mission was abandoned; A letter from Edward Barron was published in the *Annals of the Propagation of the Faith*, vol.IV, in 1843: "Missions of Africa, Mission of Liberia, Extract from a letter of his Lordship the Right Rev. Dr. Barron, Vicar-Apostolic of Guinea, to the Members of the Central Councils of the Association," pp.242-5.

6. Ellis, "Challenge," p.298.

7. Gibbons had addressed the needs of the foreign missions in 1884 at a Plenary Council meeting on 7 December in Baltimore. See: *The Tablet*, 3 January 1885, p.26: "In nearly all European countries there are Foreign Missionary College and also associations of the faithful for the support of the missions by their contributions. Hitherto we have had to strain every

nerve in order to carry on the missions of our own country, and we were unable to take any important part in aiding the missions abroad. But we must beware lest our local burdens should make our zeal narrow and un-Catholic. There are hundreds of millions of souls in heathen lands to whom the light of the Gospel has not yet been carried, and their condition appeals to the charity of every Christian heart;" Gibbons' health was not good but he outlived all who had worried over him. Before he died, at eighty-seven, in 1921, he was asked what was the secret of his long life. He made the reply: "Acquire an incurable ailment in your youth." William Shannon thought him a paradox. Notwithstanding that he seemed to have little talent, "he was an extraordinary man and the greatest figure the Church has produced in America." Gibbons loved the pageantry of the Church and saw that all was done with dignity and splendour, but in Baltimore his rectory was always open. One remarked that "he reigned in Baltimore like a king, but he met every man like a comrade." He was a serious walker and liked eating out "because Christ dined out." He loved horseracing and baseball, and sometimes placed a bet at the track. He liked cards and smoked cigars. Once he visited his native parish in Ireland and stayed with the parish priest who disliked smoking. While there Gibbons smoked discreetly in his room. When a visitor asked if the Cardinal was at home, the parish priest replied, "Yes, don't you smell him?" Once an obnoxious person asked him at a social gathering how far he thought the Pope's infallibility extended. Smiling, Gibbons said, "That is not an easy question. All I can say is that a few months ago in Rome His Holiness called me 'Jibbons.'" When Vaughan wrote to him in 1889, James Gibbons was at the peak of his powers and influence in the United States. See: William V. Shannon, *The American Irish*, London, Collier-Macmillan, 1963, p.114ff.

8. Jean-Paul Wiest, *Maryknoll in China*, New York, Sharpe, 1988, pp.15-18; See also: John Tracey Ellis, *American Catholicism*, Chicago, Univ. of Chicago Press, 1969, pp.130-2. "By the end of the nineteenth century Catholics here had become numerous and relatively well off, they had as yet done relatively little to repay these benefactions by way of help to less favored areas of the world. The American hierarchy were pointedly, if politely, reminded of this fact in 1889 on the occasion of their centennial. In a letter addressed to Cardinal Gibbons, Herbert Vaughan, the Bishop of Salford, England, who had already made a name for himself as a promoter of the missions, conveyed his congratulations" and called on the Bishops to do their part. Personnel were not given but money was.

9. Salford Diocesan Archive (SDA). Vaughan, August 13 (no year), Weston Manor, Freshwater, Isle of Wight, to Father Lewis (*sic*) Casartelli.

10. Maryknoll Archive (MA). Vaughan, Mill Hill, to Cullen, 16 January 1903. In Vaughan's recommendation for Cullen, dated 15 August 1902, he states: "I have, therefore, conceived the idea of inviting Catholics in countries that have not yet founded their own Foreign Missionary College to cooperate with us by giving alms to plant the Church in heathen countries."

11. Wiest, *Maryknoll*. p.16.

12. MA. Walsh, Society of the Propagation of the Faith, Boston, August 21, 1904 to Fr Elliot.

13. Wiest, *Maryknoll*, pp.17-8.

14. SDA. Pastoral letter, Bishop of Salford, "The Indian Famine...," 1877; Seaman, *Victorian England*, p.331ff.

15. Leslie, *Vaughan Letters*, p.181, 184.

16. *ibid.*, p.304.

17. For a history of the Catholic Church in East Malaysia and Brunei see: John Rooney, *Khabar Gembira*, Tunbridge Wells, Burns & Oates, 1981, p.23ff. By the late 1870s, British influence, Rajah Rupert Brooke in Sarawak and the Chartered Company in North Borneo, demanded English-speaking missionaries; only the Anglicans had a Borneo mission, from 1847.

18. *The Tablet*, 18 February 1882, pp.274-5.

19. General Primrose wrote of Thomas Jackson when he was on the North West Frontier of India: "I cannot overvalue the services rendered on the 6th and on many other occasions by Fr. T. Jackson, who was always in the foremost of the fight, attending upon and offering every

assistance to the wounded both European and native." See: *Opening Door*, p.26ff.; Rooney, *Khabar*, pp.26-7: Jackson was born in Preston, Lancashire, in 1846. After leaving his parish school he worked as a general handyman and for some time was a servant at Stonyhurst. He was sacristan at a South London church when he decided to study for the priesthood. Benoit accepted him at St Joseph's College and he was ordained on 28 September 1879. He was assigned to Afghanistan and was mentioned in dispatches for his heroism. He was also popular with the troops and when he was to leave for Borneo they collected £200 for him as a gift.

20. *Franciscan Missionaries of St Joseph*, pp.22-6.

21. WDA. Jackson, Anecdotes.

22. E. R. Simmons, *Pompallier, Prince of Bishops*, Auckland, Catholic Publications Centre, 1984, pp.7-16; *idem, In Cruce Salus, A History of the Diocese of Auckland, 1848-1980*, Auckland, CPC, 1982, p.7.

23. John A. Williams, *Politics of the New Zealand Maori*, Auckland, Auckland Univ. Press, 1969, p.12.

24. McCormack, pp.202-3; Snead-Cox, 1, pp.445-7; MHA, "The Mill Hill Fathers in New Zealand," Centenary, pp.12-23; Simmons, *In Cruce*, pp.179-80; One of the first missionaries, James Russell Madan, was a convert, son of an Anglican vicar. He was born in 1841 at Cam Vicarage, Gloucestershire, and educated at Marlbororough College, Wiltshire, and The Queen's College, Oxford, where he took an MA in 1867. On Madan see: Joan C. Gorham, "The Reverend James Russell Madan, M.A. (1841-1905)," *Millhilliana*, no 1, April 1994.

25. Mill Hill, New Zealand, p.14.

26. *ibid.*, p.15.

27. *ibid.*, p.19.

28. *ibid.*, p.21.

29. *ibid.*, p.22.

30. *ibid.*

31. MHA. Rooney, MS, nn.104-5.

32. *ibid.*, pp.13-14.

33. John Bray, "The Roman Catholic Mission in Ladakh, 1888-1898," *Millhilliana*, no.4, 1993, pp.124-30.

34. JA. Copy book 2. Reports and Society History to 1928, p.12: The chapter meeting lasted three days and reported: "A few years experience among the Colored people has convinced our missionaries that if the millions of negroes now in the U.S. are to be brought into the Church, it can be done efficiently and perseveringly only by societies, that, with regard to our society, it is absolutely necessary to adhere strictly to the vow by which our fathers pledge themselves to be always the fathers and servants of the negro, and to undertake no work whatever which might interfere with the evangelizing of the poor Africans; and finally it is not enough to gather congregations and form day and Sunday schools, but they must also aim at raising eventually orphan asylums and industrial schools for the young and seek admission for the aged into the houses of the Little Sisters of the Poor and other public institutions."

35. Hogan, *Josephite Harvest*, August 1992. pp.8-9.

36. Ochs, *Desegregating*, pp.51ff.

37. *ibid.*, p.54. Benoit wrote to Ignatius Brouwer on the Madras mission on 15 April 1880: "We are guided by you," ... If not in the way of usefulness, all might be for us."

38. *ibid.*, pp.56-8. Benoit sent a questionnaire to the members in the United States, on 15 July 1878, in preparation for the first provincial chapter in December. Headings were: the Negro race in the United States, means of conversion, obstacles to conversion, government of the society, and temporalities. Under the first, he asked about the possibility of African-American priests; six of the eight dismissed the idea. Only John H. Greene expressed optimism about recruiting black priests. Even Slattery displayed a condescending attitude to African-Americans. "Although he never completely shed his racial stereotypes, Slattery's daily contacts with

blacks eroded his prejudices."

39. Uncles was a tall, bespectacled, young mulatto parishioner who expressed a desire to become a priest. Born in 1859, he attended St Francis Xavier School, Baltimore public schools, and the Baltimore Normal School for Colored Teachers, and taught in Baltimore County public schools from 1880 to 1883. Slattery was impressed by what he described as Uncles' "vivid intelligence," and so he tutored him, and another African-American named Joseph Johnson, in rhetoric and logic, two requirements for seminary applicants. Uncles at first was unwilling to become a Society member, perhaps fearing to be sent to the Far East. Slattery tried to find a bishop to sponsor him at the Urban College in Rome or entrance into an American seminary. He failed in this and so and arranged for him to go to St Hyacinth's College in Quebec. Uncles' education was paid for by Slattery with the generous help of Slattery's father.

40. JA. Vaughan, Salford, 29 January 1879, to Slattery.

41. JA. Vaughan, Salford, 24 July 1879 to Slattery; Ochs, *Desegregating*, p.57: Vaughan and Benoit regarded Slattery's stinging letters as intemperate. In one letter Slattery virtually denounced Vaughan, called Benoit a liar, and condemned the charges paid by American students at Mill Hill as monstrous. Vaughan wrote about Slattery's letters to Benoit: "I believe Father Slattery to be very undisciplined and that he speaks as he does from want of knowledge of what is common civility." Slattery seems to have cared more for justice than for civility, according to Ochs.

42. JA. Elliot, New York, 28 August 1883 to Slattery: (Hecker's influence) "would not have been sufficient, I think, to so fill up all the vacant chambers of that haunted house I call my heart.... We know that we have passed from death to life because we love the brethren."

43. JA. Houlton, Maine, Elliot to Slattery, 25 May 1883.

44. O'Brien, *Hecker*, p.328: "Even more remarkable was a series on the 'Negro Problem,' written by the pioneering Josephite missionary John R. Slattery. Presuming general ignorance among Catholics of the condition of freemen, Slattery presented statistics and descriptions of the increasing numbers and importance of the Black population. He defended strenuously the equality of all people before God, the special responsibility of the church toward the unfortunate, and the unique opportunity presented to the church by this large, religiously uncommitted population, many of whom had strong, clear ideas of Christianity but no definite church affiliation."

45. *The Tablet*, 3 January 1885, p.26.

46. R. Scott Appleby, *"Church and Age Unite!" The Modernist Impulse in American Catholicism*, Notre Dame, University of Notre Dame Press, 1992, pp.189ff; JA. Copy Book 2, pp.13-14: "Archbishop Ryan of Philadelphia: can not but feel convinced that the young levites destined for this peculiar mission should be educated in this country" (no date).

47. JA. Vaughan, Salford, 29 December 1885 to Slattery.

48. JA. Copybook 2, pp.15-16.

49. Ochs, *Desegregating*, pp.3, 81-2.

50. Hogan, *Harvest*, Autumn, 1992, pp.15-16.

51. JA. Copybook 2, pp.22ff.

52. Hogan, *Harvest*. Winter, 1992-3, pp.1-11; On Slattery, see: Appleby, *Modernist Impulse*, pp.191: "Encouraged by the recognition and respect that his new post brought him within the American church, and by his friendships with members of the progressive wing of the American hierarchy, Slattery continued his campaign to strengthen Catholic commitment to the black missions"; Ochs, *Desegregating*, p.120ff: After engineering the erection of St Joseph's Seminary and Epiphany Apostolic College and becoming the superior general of the Josephites, Slattery moved in the first ranks of the Baltimore clergy. From 1890 to 1902 he assisted Gibbons as the deacon of honour at all ordinations. He accompanied Gibbons to Rome in 1895 and convinced him that Church authorities were "power hungry politicians who were determined to exert their control over the American Church." In the United States he contended daily with the scandal of

the Church's treatment of blacks. All hope of change was crushed with Pope Leo XIII's condemnation of Americanism in 1899—*Testem Benevolentiae*. When he returned to America from Rome, he began to distance himself from the ecclesiastical world. On June 22, 1902—1902 was the 25th anniversary of his ordination—at the ordination of African-American Henry Dorsey, he gave what he later called his "farewell to the Church." The sermon was published in the *Baltimore Sun*. African-Americans commented favorably, but many white clergy thought it outrageous. In 1903 he decided to resign from the Josephites. Gibbons held discussions about the possible dissolution of the Josephites. A $40,000 mortgage on St Joseph's Seminary, which no one wished to assume, helped keep them afloat. In 1904 Thomas Donavan was elected the new superior general. In September 1905 Slattery announced in the *Independent* that he renounced the Catholic Church and that he had married. "If anything in this world is certain, it is that the stand of the Catholic Church toward the negro is sheer dishonesty." Modernism was condemned in 1907 in the encyclical *Pascendi dominici gregis*. Slattery continued criticizing the Church in books and articles until 1911, when he abandoned religious polemic as well as Christianity. He had inherited his father's estate and been admitted to the California Bar in 1916. He died in 1926 in Monte Carlo. The bulk of his $1.5 million estate went to the New York Public Library. (John Slattery's name can be seen on the left pillar of the entrance hall in the Fifth Avenue Library: author.)

53. MHA.

54. *The Tablet*, 21 August 1880, p.242.

55. *ibid.*, 12 November 1881, p.794.

56. *ibid.*, 16 August 1884, p.246, "Opening of St. Peter's School for Foreign Missions, Freshfield."

57. WDA. Jackson, "Anecdotes." On another occasion Jackson travelled with Vaughan to Ince-Blundell, not far from Freshfield, to see his uncle, Mr Weld-Blundell. At the end of the visit Vaughan's aunt and uncle brought them to the railway station. Just before they reached the station, Vaughan handed Jackson some money for the tickets and asked him to hurry to buy them. His aunt saw the amount and said that it was not enough to get them to Liverpool and then on to Manchester. "Oh yes," said Vaughan, "but that is first class." When she asked by what class he travelled, Vaughan answered: "Father and I are missionaries, we always go 3rd class." When she answered that it was most edifying, but, "Please remember you are a bishop," Vaughan replied, "I am not likely ever to forget that." Some months later Vaughan was in London for a meeting and Jackson went to meet him at St Pancras Station before he set off for Manchester. "It was Saturday afternoon when there were many passengers. He asked me to look out for a place for him in the train, in the 3rd class, while he got his ticket. The only vacant place I could find was in a carriage where all the passengers were railway navvies, with their spades and pick axes. When I showed him the place, he seemed quite pleased and said it was just what he liked."

58. Leslie, *Vaughan Letters*, pp.364-5.

59. *The Tablet*, 16 August 1884, p.246.

60. Leslie, *Vaughan Letters*, pp.396-7.

61. WDA. Oates, Anecdotes: Austin Oates travelled with Vaughan to Roosendaal when he was Cardinal. Oates wrote that Vaughan was never convinced that smoking tobacco had any "soothing or calming influence or effect on anyone." Oates only saw Vaughan smoke once and that was at Roosendaal in 1893. "The cigar—a Dutch one!—he soon allowed to go out. Yet he was most tolerant. In driving or travelling with him, he would even invite me to 'light up.'"

62. F. U. Ros, *Mill Hill, 100 Jaar in Nederland 1890-1990*, Roosendaal, Bijeen, 1990.

63. MHA. HV. Othmar Rink, 1966; And: WDA. Vaughan Diary, 1890.

64. Leslie, *Vaughan Letters*, 31 August 1884, pp.366-7.

CHAPTER XIV

Relationship between Herbert Vaughan and Henry Manning; Death of the Cardinal

John Snead-Cox devotes a section of his biography to the "friendship and differences" between Herbert Vaughan and Henry Edward Manning.[1] In the opinion of Arthur McCormack, Snead-Cox, "unfairly, though not wholly inaccurately," summarized the "differences between the outlook of Vaughan and that of Manning on social questions." Therefore, "by devoting much space to the differences between the two men, writers have exaggerated their importance."[2] In fact it seems that what we know of their differences helps us to know both men better.

In the February 1896 issue of *The Nineteenth Century*, Vaughan described the publication of Purcell's biography of Henry Manning as "almost a crime." However, as he went on to defend Manning's memory, he offered a personal opinion that Manning had been senile in the last years of his life. According to Robert Gray, this "only shifted the grounds of hostile speculation" about Manning, and about Vaughan's relationship with him.[3] Snead-Cox quotes from the same article by Vaughan:

> While my high estimate of him is based upon a friendship of forty years, I always appraise the last few years of his life apart, as not representing the whole man. It is said that there is one faculty which extreme old age seldom spares. It may spare the senses of the body, the intellect, the memory, and the will, but rarely indeed does it spare the delicate balance of that sensitive faculty called the judgement. During the last short period of the Cardinal's long life the process of senile decay had set in.[4]

Snead-Cox thought that Vaughan came to this conclusion as he "watched with misgiving the Cardinal's growing absorption in great public movements" of the time, especially the part Manning played in the London dock strike of 1889. In addition, he looked with "positive disapproval" on the Cardinal's relationship with the Salvation Army.[5]

Vaughan's disagreements with Manning, and the doubts he expressed about Manning's judgment in his final years, have opened to question the

331

closeness of their friendship.[6] Vaughan, it seems, "was genuinely astonished when he found that the phrase 'senile decay' was bitterly resented." When he asked Snead-Cox about it, he was told that "the word 'senile' had such unpleasant associations that one would not willingly use it of a friend." Vaughan then said simply: "Well—I don't understand; I suppose we shall all be senile if we live long enough." Snead-Cox was illustrating how Vaughan's "sense of the values of words would sometimes fail him in the oddest way."[7]

Manning's Social Radicalism

Manning was always remarkable for his sympathy with the poor. Even in his Lavington sermons, when he was still an Anglican, he tried to encourage his listeners to help lessen the sufferings of the poor.[8] As he grew older and studied more closely the causes of the miserable conditions of the working classes, and the potential political power they had to bring about change, he realized that the future of the English Catholic Church depended largely on the attitude it assumed towards them. In 1874 he spoke at the Mechanics' Institute in Leeds on "The Dignity and Rights of Labour." Newsome writes that the speech became his manifesto.[9]

In his 1880 analysis, "The Catholic Church and Modern Society," he identified himself with the cause of the industrial worker. In 1891, his lecture on "The Rights and Dignity of Labour" pointed out the abuses of capitalism, which could only be remedied by state legislation. He advocated the social priority of labour over capital. In a letter of 25 January 1891 he wrote: "The coming age will belong neither to the capitalists nor to the commercial classes, but to the people. The people are yielding to the guidance of reason, even to the guidance of religion. If we can gain their confidence, we can counsel them, if we show them a blind opposition, they will have power to destroy all that is good."[10]

In 1891 Pope Leo XIII issued his social encyclical *Rerum Novarum*. Before Easter of that year Archbishop Walsh of Dublin wrote to Manning saying that the Pope had spoken to him about the encyclical and asked that Manning make the English translation. Manning in turn asked Bishop Hedley to do it with his collaboration. "It was Manning who insisted upon using the word 'strike' and other modern terms, in order to make the document apply all the more directly to the actual conditions in England."[11] Pope Leo XIII had credited Manning for his encyclical condemning slavery in 1880: "It was he who put the idea into my head to do something for the slaves." According to Newsome, Manning inspired parts of *Rerum Novarum*: sections could almost have been taken from Manning's letter to the Catholic Congress at Liège in 1890.[12]

In 1887, Manning supported Cardinal Gibbons of Baltimore in his efforts to secure toleration for the Knights of Labor in the United States and Canada.

Newsome considers that the support he gave to the Knights under T. V. Powderley was "more controversial and ultimately more decisive" than anything he had done on behalf of workers to that date. James Gibbons, supported by Manning, convinced the Pope not to condemn the Knights of Labor and a crisis that threatened to become an ugly confrontation was averted.[13]

Great London Dock Strike

On 14 August 1889, two hundred thousand London dockworkers went on strike after their moderate demands—for better pay, fairness for casual workers and a reasonable settlement of hours—had been turned down by the dock directors. They asked for six pence, rather than four or three per hour, and for casual workers to be hired for a minimum of four hours. The crisis nearly became a catastrophe when the employers threatened to bring in foreign labour, and the dockers threatened to call a general strike for the whole country. Manning—whose father and brother Frederick had been directors of a dock company—convinced the Lord Mayor to call for a committee of reconciliation.

Manning feared the worst but "acted with calmness and coolness." One advantage he had was that he knew the leader of the dockers personally and was in contact with them through a journalist called Margaret Harkness, who wrote for a radical newspaper, the *Star*. One day, Ben Tillett, the dockers' leader, returned to his rooms in Poplar and was told by his landlady that an old priest was waiting to see him in the kitchen. He went in to find the Cardinal, reading the latest adventure of Sherlock Holmes in the *Strand Magazine*. "Let's see what I can do," he told Tillett.

The Lord Mayor of London, Manning, and the Anglican Bishop of London, Frederick Temple, were members of the committee of reconciliation which searched for a settlement. The committee had officially abandoned arbitration when the dockers refused to accept a compromise settlement. Once they were deadlocked, the bishop withdrew, but Manning persevered. When the talks finally collapsed, he single-handedly approached the leaders of the dockers at a meeting of the Strike Committee in Wade Street School. He met with them for four hours, arguing that a compromise was to their advantage, and succeeded in winning them over. He was then chosen by the strikers to be their arbitration representative.

Tillett remembered the part Manning played in the strike: "From the first the Cardinal showed himself to be the dockers' friend, though he had family connections in the shipping interests.... Our demands were too reasonable, too moderate, to be set aside by a spirit so lofty, as that which animated the frail, tall figure with its saintly, emaciated face, and strangely compelling eyes." At the final meeting with Manning before the settlement, Tillett, although opposed to Manning's suggestions, could not resist his argument:

"This gentle old man, bowed with the weight of years, who bent his tall stooping frame over the school desk and talked to us about the sufferings which the strike inflicted on the workers' families, recommending the settlement he had secured, as a business arrangement which gave us all we had demanded or nearly all." The strike over, the Port of London was reopened a few days later after being closed for four weeks.[14] The dockers got their sixpence per hour. The "dockers' tanner" was attributed entirely to Cardinal Manning's work with both their leaders and the employers.

In the first London May Day procession in 1890, banners with portraits of Marx and Manning, painted side-by-side, were carried by marchers. The procession was a great labour demonstration in favour of an eight-hour day.[15] The London Trade Council passed a resolution: "The Cardinal, by his tender sympathy for the poor, and his fearless advocacy of justice, especially for the poor, and by his persistent denunciation of the oppression of workers, has endeared his memory to the heart of every true friend of Labour."[16]

On his death, *The Tablet* wrote that some were a little shocked by what one called his "State-socialism," but that "there was no resisting this spirit in its flights towards what he conceived to be justice and freedom." Manning never separated "his work for the world from his work for the Church, his work for good from his work for man."[17]

Wilfrid Meynell wrote in *The Tablet* of 6 February: "In the love of God and man he performed his indifferent actions, talked politics and read newspapers, went each afternoon to the Athenaeum Club, and lectured before the Royal Society, loitered in the House of Commons, and wandered among the crowds at Marlborough House garden-parties; nor would he have flinched to meet at any moment the messenger which came to him at last so calmly—almost collusively." Meynell then repeated an anecdote: The question, "What he would do were he not a priest?" was put to Manning and two others. "A doctor," said one, still dreaming of the set service of man. "A temperance advocate," said another, with becoming solemnity. "And I," said the Cardinal, "Radical member for Marylebone"—at the time politically the rowdiest of metropolitan areas.[18]

Herbert Vaughan could not accept what he considered Manning's radical point of view. He had written in 1887 to Corrigan in New York about Manning's change of heart over Home Rule for Ireland and his support for the Knights of Labor: "My dearest old friend of Westminster is incurably radical in his sympathies but I hope he will ... write no more on this subject. His letter on Henry George, like his canonization of Parnell, was alike unfortunate."[19]

After the London dock strike, *The Tablet* observed that "even in more sober quarters there seems to be an uneasy feeling that it would have been better if the peacemaker had been another." In Arthur McCormack's opinion the reason Vaughan did not congratulate the victor was because, to his way of thinking, dedicating so much time to worldly matters was falling short of the ideal of the priesthood that Manning upheld.[20] According to Michael Walsh, the *Pall Mall*, and everyone else, knew that the Pope's encyclical "reflected Manning's own attitudes and concerns on social issues, attitudes which Bishop Herbert Vaughan, *The Tablet*'s owner, did not share."[21]

Manning was very fond of Vaughan. In 1875, when he spoke at St Joseph's Missionary College, Mill Hill, he recalled their meeting in Rome in 1852: "From that time to this there has not been the shadow of difference between us—our friendship and confidence have deepened from day to day." Shadows of difference existed, and correspondence supports this fact, but the friendship endured. The first time Vaughan and Manning were seen to disagree seriously was about ten years before Manning's death, over the purchase of the *Weekly Register*.

During Vaughan's 1881 absence in Rome, where he represented Manning and the English hierarchy in their case against religious orders, Manning had a chance to purchase the *Weekly Register*, a Catholic newspaper which, according to Manning, "supplied what our soft-headed and pious middle-class Catholics wish to know about their Bishops, priests and dioceses etc.," from Mr De Lacy Towle. The price was reduced to three hundred pounds, and rather than let it disappear or "run the risk of seeing it pass under control of the Jesuits," Manning bought it and offered to make it over to Vaughan if he wished. In further correspondence he made it clear that he had bought the paper and was running it on behalf of Vaughan.

On 29 May 1881, Manning wrote: "My dearest Herbert, Your telegram yesterday was a great relief.... I hope you will be home soon and time enough for us to decide what is wisest and best to do with it. You shall decide, for I am making you my heir in many things, and am winding up." On 2 June, Manning wrote that he would announce his intentions on 25 June. After this, Snead-Cox says, the record fails. Further negotiations followed, and *The Tablet*'s publisher went to Manning, on Vaughan's behalf, with a cheque as payment, but it was handed back. Manning had made a gift of the paper to Wilfrid Meynell. He gave a written statement that in view of political and other issues, especially those that concerned relations between the Catholics of England and Ireland, Meynell was the one man in England to whom he would entrust it. Vaughan was hurt and perplexed and wrote to William George Ward on 6 January 1882: "As to the W.R., I confess I have been pained and surprised more than I can say. I am unable to reconcile the Cardinal's letters to me with his acts. To start the W.R. with the programme, the size, the form of the *Tablet*, and to sell it for a halfpenny or half the price, is the American way of clearing rivers of well-established companies—running a boat for nothing till ruin brings an end to the competition."[22]

Manning considered his friend at Salford to be his probable successor at Westminster, but, at the same time, he was aware of Vaughan's limitations.

Yet he never ceased to encourage Vaughan to widen his interests in order to become "more human and less ecclesiastical," and told him that he would be a "better Christian when his sympathies are capable of being enlisted in causes which have no direct concern with his work." In an 1881 letter Manning wrote: "When I am gone do not let the Old Testament close over you and bury you in the sacristy." Manning used the term "Old Testament" to refer to the old hereditary Catholics. He continued by saying that he had "held and, I hope, acted upon this law" as an Englishman and a member of "our Commonwealth."[23]

Henry Manning disliked the "meddling of intriguers" among the laity. One example of the "meddling" he referred to concerned the question of diplomatic relations between the Vatican and the British government. He thought a diplomat was unnecessary, for the natural intermediaries between the Government and the Vatican were the English bishops, and not a diplomat in London. For some Catholics, having a papal diplomat was a tactic to limit Manning's authority and freedom of action. Newsome considers this to be the case, in order to curb Manning's influence, especially in his efforts to persuade the Pope not to condemn the Land League and nationalist movement in Ireland. The Duke of Norfolk was "fiercely antagonistic to Manning's sympathy for the nationalists" and thought he saw a way to attack Manning by joining the negotiations. Norfolk believed that having a papal nuncio in England would nullify Manning's influence at the Vatican. Pope Leo XIII sent an old friend of Manning's, Mgr Persico, to Ireland to investigate. Persico emphatically endorsed Manning's view that the "establishment of a papal nunciature was unnecessary and undesirable" and that Irish bishops were neutral in their position on militant nationalism.[24]

Herbert Vaughan disagreed with Manning and wrote an article for the *Nineteenth Century* in which he called for the resumption of diplomatic relations. He used the example of an agreement signed between the Vatican and the Portuguese government concerning episcopal sees in British India and how they might be manipulated "to our disadvantage, because we had, through some puerile fear or insular bigotry, stood aloof from diplomatic relations which no one else was afraid of." Vaughan saw the problem in less subtle terms than Manning.

Snead-Cox quotes extracts from Manning's letters to Vaughan between 1886 and 1888 about the points he made in the article—which Manning had not read yet—in which he told Vaughan that the first effect would be "the meddling of all intriguers in the nomination of Bishops, and a clandestine veto for the Government." As an example, he reminded Vaughan of the layman Errington's mission to Rome on behalf of the British government over the Irish Question. "Mr. Errington misled the Holy Father" about the facts. "I had the whole affair in my hands." But despite their differences, in Snead-Cox's view, the question never seriously affected their relationship. When people asked Manning about Vaughan's opinion, Manning was noncommittal because "I am not willing to say that we differ."[25]

Manning warned Vaughan about the influence of the upper-class Catholic laity in 1886 over the issue of Catholics attending Oxford or Cambridge.

My dear Herbert, I agree with you, for I hold that whenever the laity go wrong, Bishops and Priests go first. But in this case, true as it is, that B.V. Nottingham (Bishop Edward Bagshawe), Newport etc. and Company have acted weakly, nevertheless the laity from your good uncle [Ince] down to Denbigh, Braye and Elwes have gone against explicit and known injunctions. There has been a worldly gang of the upper class whispering and intriguing in Rome. There is one point on which I have always tried to convince some of our friends. The Holy See has gone to the utmost bound in its injunctions. It is often said "If it will prohibit we will obey." I do not believe it. I am confident that they would not. The Holy See can not issue prohibitions where the matter is not intrinsically contrary to the law of God ipso facto. To go to Oxford is not so.... But a large number of the laity— men and women—have all along acted in a seditious and scandalous manner, misleading Rome and undermining the acts of the Bishops. However my time is running out. You will have to look to it—I wish you would read again Bishop Milner's life— ? went wrong— Vicars apostolic dragged, and terrorized by the laity—as old Charles Langdale used to tell me. We need to be calm, kind, just, and considerate towards the laity—but we have a higher duty and if needs be we must suffer for it.

On another occasion Manning wrote of a "string of lies and disinformation" over an administrative decision of the archdiocese. It concerned a congregation which wanted to take over a chapel on King Street "200 or so feet from Spanish Place." Manning asked Vaughan to keep Elizabeth Herbert out of it. It was the second time she "was in the hands of the congregation." "Row there may be, but if I am to hold care of souls I will not brook such deceit." A petition against Manning's action was sent to Rome "signed by dames, laiquer et estemi Clerge." "I hope her name, and Lady G. Porter's may not be there," he wrote. However, Manning concluded that "I am too old for all this and will be quiet." Manning advised Vaughan to read about the problems experienced by Bishop Milner with leading Catholic lay people in the early nineteenth century. If not for Milner, "Catholic Emancipation might have been shackled and hampered with a veto."[26]

Manning advised Vaughan to be less practical and more human in a letter of 24 September 1883. He promised to return Vaughan's *American Canon Law* and advised him to read Sheridan's *Critic* and *School for Scandal*. "You would be holier and happier if you would enter into such things with patience and learn to laugh. You are grim and truculent." At an exhibition they attended together, Vaughan was bored by the pictures, and Manning never saw him "excited until you took me among the Tiles and Stoves and Drain

Pipes. This makes you sharp and inhuman to your fellow-creatures, and if you are so in the Green Tree, what will you be in the Dry."

On another occasion, he told Vaughan to give up his grinding away at work and take intervals of rest. "You rush about, and at, and in, everything. You are just now in a crisis. If you strain your health it may not return.... You are really doing more in being less active, because you are being more thoughtful. We are weak and the Episcopate is weak, because our Bishops are parish priests. They must be broader and have a bird's-eye view of the Church and the English people. You are bound to study this, come what may, for you can by word and writing make yourself heard. It has been a good school to be a Mitred Editor."[27]

In 1890 Manning wrote to Vaughan again: "I remember you asked me to write down the reasons of my Radicalism"—Manning chose the label for himself, "Mosaic Radical"[28]—"I did so briefly at the time and I will do so more fully hereafter. Get and read 'The Last Fifty Years of the House of Lords.' Nobody can understand our present condition without knowing this history. I have seen it and touched it."[29]

Less than a year before his death Manning wrote to Vaughan: "My dearest Herbert, I am sending you *Il Socialismo Cattolico* by Francesco Nitti. It is the best book I have seen on the subject: full of matter, of quotations, very accurate, and in wonderfully clear and easy Italian. It would be well if you would read it out."[30]

Francesco S. Nitti was a professor of political economy at the University of Naples. In the second edition of Nitti's book, published after Manning's death, he notes that Manning "boldly defended the rights of the poor dockers" as a "true socialist" who carried his convictions to "most daring conclusions." Manning thought that society had been "strangled by an exaggerated form of individualism and the coming century will show that human society is grander and nobler than anything merely individual." Not only was the individualism that Vaughan admired challenged, but the rights to private property, for Manning would maintain "as do all Socialists, the right even to theft, as the necessary complement to the right to existence, in all countries in which the state has not established the right to assistance."[31] It was in this spirit that he tried to inspire Vaughan .

There were other differences of opinion. For example, Vaughan had publicly contradicted Manning's views on temperance at Salford when he first became bishop. Vaughan changed his mind over the years but he did not embrace total abstinence. According to John Snead-Cox, Manning was more impatient with Vaughan over his views on temperance than he was with him over Home Rule or Vivisection or the Deceased Wife's Sister Bill.[32]

Vaughan never saw eye-to-eye with Manning on the temperance issue and held that total abstinence was not the answer to the abuses connected with alcohol. He sought the cooperation of the sellers to reduce the alcoholic content of beers and exert more control over the places where it was consumed. Snead-Cox wrote that "Cardinal Manning's indignation knew no bounds." A low point in their friendship was reached when Vaughan supported the introduction of "winter gardens and the consumption of light lager beers and finally, with that object in view, was present at a Licensed Victuallers' dinner in Manchester."

The "Manchester and Salford Licensed Victuallers Association" invited Vaughan once again to speak in 1894, after he became Cardinal. Vaughan told his personal secretary, Austin Oates, to decline the invitation, remarking that he "had been present at one a few years before much to Cardinal Manning's dismay and disgust."[33]

According to Snead-Cox, after a heated discussion about the temperance issue with Manning during one of Vaughan's visits to Westminster, Manning made a decision. After he succeeded Manning at Westminster, Vaughan told Bishop Fenton:

> In the last years of Cardinal Manning's life he seems to have lost his old power of judging men aright. You know he and I were for years and years the closest friends living. We consulted one another and told one another everything. Well, he had appointed me to be one of his executors. On one occasion when I was staying with him in London, we got into a discussion; I could not accept his views, and I suppose, on the contrary, strongly maintained my own. I saw he was a little bit put out—but what do you think he did? He went upstairs, took out his will, and struck his pen through my name as executor. It was a mistake: if I had been his executor, his private papers would never have fallen into the hands of Mr. Purcell.[34]

Death of Henry Edward Manning

During the last two years of his life, Cardinal Manning was infirm and very often ill. At the time of Cardinal Newman's death, on 11 August 1890, he was too weak for the journey to Birmingham and so he presided at a Memorial Requiem at the London Oratory. His strength was failing but he continued to work. In his final winter, 1891-2, he was working on a scheme to provide maintenance for retired teachers. He had often been among the people addressing open-air meetings, joining Booth of the Salvation Army on the platform of a temperance gathering and opening the old Archbishop's House on Carlisle Place to whoever needed help.[35] Shane Leslie described the old barrack-type building on the corner of Carlisle Place and Francis Street as being like a "Dissenting chapel doing duty as a railway waiting-room."[36]

A dockworker wrote that he had gone to see Cardinal Manning at eight o'clock one evening and conversed with him for more than one hour: "I must say there seems to be a kind of magnetic attraction attached to His Eminence for I could have sat with him all night talking."[37] According to the *Euston*

Daily Press, Manning was not always held in such affection by Londoners. When he first became Archbishop, some "found him cold and unsympathetic and christened him 'The Marble Arch.' This was apt, if undeserved, for while the face of the Cardinal was ever immobile as marble, a warmer heart never beat in man."[38] For the *Liverpool Mercury,* Manning had become "a conspicuous illustration of the capacity of a great mind and generous heart to shake off the trammels of tradition which would have otherwise kept him out of immediate touch with the struggling and somewhat neglected masses."[39]

On the silver jubilee of his episcopal ordination, Manning received many gifts, but promised that all of them should go to good works. "Much has passed through my hands in these five-and-twenty years. Nothing has stayed under this roof; all has gone into the work which is entrusted to me. My desire is to die, as a priest ought, without money and without debts."[40] J. E. C. Bodley wrote:

> [Manning] had none of that unctuous air with which some of the clergy, of all denominations and of all races, seem to notify that they are agents of the unseen, and, in doing so, excite the mistrust of their less-favoured fellow-mortals. He was free from all such pious affectation. Yet in close contact with him one felt that he was always living in the presence of an unseen Power, not as its pompous agent, but as its simple and humble messenger. It has been my lot to witness some of the most imposing religious ceremonies of modern Christendom; but nothing so impressive, so faith-inspiring has ever met my eyes as the sight of this noble old Englishman in his threadbare cassock kneeling alone before the altar of his bare chapel.[41]

The figure that inspired Bodley in the chapel seemed a sad one to another visitor when before a fireside. A reporter wrote of his final visit to Manning: "I recalled the dim, misty winter afternoon when in the fading light I had last seen the bent figure of the old Cardinal as he sat gazing into the red embers of the dying fire, a very lonely, a very pathetic figure. The hum and roar of the great, weary city rolled around him though he heeded it not."[42]

On Thursday, 7 January 1892, Henry Manning experienced an acute attack of bronchitis. He stayed at home but did not call his doctor, Sir Andrew Clarke. He was sitting for his portrait even as the end neared. Once he looked at the artist's work and remarked "Have I really grown as old as that," and referring to the old cassock he was wearing, said: "Mind you don't put in these rags."[43] The next day, John Vaughan, Herbert's brother, came to see him. He found Manning seated in his armchair before a roasting fire, and "looking very much as usual, though somewhat weaker." He had been reading Cardinal Wiseman's *Fabiola.* "It still lay open on his knees." Manning remarked that he had not read it since 1852 or 53: "It is very beautiful." About his own writing, he said: "I think I could write a novel. There is material for at least one in every man's mind."[44]

On Saturday he was so ill that he stayed in bed. When he did not improve by Monday, his doctor was called. The Cardinal was suffering from lung congestion and could not eat. Sir Andrew diagnosed broncho-pneumonia. On Wednesday morning there were signs that his heart was failing and he was given the last sacraments. Later in the day he requested that he be dressed in his full cardinalate robes and made his last public profession of faith in the presence of the canons of the Westminster Chapter. He told those present that he was "glad to have been able to do everything in order."

Herbert Vaughan and Canon Gasquet stayed with him through the night. They gave him the last blessing at four o'clock, and at six said the prayers for the dying.

He remained alert until 7.30 on Thursday morning, when he lapsed into unconsciousness. His last coherent words were in Latin: "I have laid down the yoke, my work is done." At twenty minutes past eight, Henry Manning died peacefully. It was 14 January 1892. He was in his eighty-fourth year and it was seventeen months after the death of John Henry Newman.[45]

Whenever Vaughan went to Archbishop's House at Westminster, he stayed in his own small room. It was one that he had used from the time Manning went to Westminster. In early January 1892, Vaughan was staying at Westminster for a few weeks' rest, and so he was with Manning before he died. Vaughan was amazed when Manning, on his deathbed, took from under his pillow a "small worn volume" and handed it to him saying, "I leave it to you. Into this little book my dearest wife wrote her prayers and meditations. Not a day has passed since her death on which I have not prayed and meditated from this book. All the good I may have done, all the good I may have been, I owe to her. Take precious care of it." It is thought that Vaughan placed the book in Cardinal Manning's coffin.[46] Vaughan wrote to Louis Casartelli that between 4 a.m. and 7.30 a.m. those present—Vaughan, Johnson and Gasquet among them—had prayed with the dying Cardinal. He refused to take any more drugs. "At 7.30 I said it was time for Mass, and asked whether he would like me to go and say it for him—he was still clear and conscious." Before Vaughan's Mass was over, Canon Johnson had given the Cardinal final absolution and Henry Manning was dead; Canon Gasquet closed the dead man's eyes.[47] On his deathbed Manning had also made one of the first phonographic recordings to be preserved as a historic document. It was a message to posterity.[48]

Funeral arrangements were to be made by Vaughan. He wrote on 17 January that he had "not even chosen an undertaker" yet and did not propose to go to Kensal Green where Manning was to be buried.[49] After a lying-in-state at Carlisle Place that reportedly attracted more than 100,000 mourners, his body was removed to the London Oratory for the Requiem Mass. According to David Newsome, the scenes at his funeral, and the crowds, mainly of the London poor, that lined the streets along the four miles between the Brompton Oratory and the cemetery at Kensal Green, had no precedent since the death of the first Duke of Wellington. "Forty years earlier, a Cardinal dignitary seen in the streets of London might have been pelted with mud."[50] Manning was buried among his brother Oblates of St Charles in St Mary's Cemetery. His remains were later transferred to the crypt of Westminster Cathedral, built by his successor and friend of forty-one years, Herbert Vaughan.[51]

Notes

1. Snead-Cox, 1, pp.454–9, 483.
2. McCormack, pp.222–4.
3. Robert Gray, *Cardinal Manning,* London, Weidenfeld and Nicholson, London, 1895, pp.6, 249.
4. Snead-Cox, 1, pp. 476–7.
5. *ibid.,* pp.477–8; WDA. Oates, anecdotes: Vaughan disapproved of the Salvation Army, or at least Manning's public profession of admiration for General Booth. Vaughan considered them a religious proselytising agency but did not object to using their techniques as a source for his own ideas. When he was still at Salford, he once asked Austin Oates to call at the "Church Army Labour Colony, St. Mary's Hall, near Edgeware Road, to examine their work. Rev. J. J. Chambers is Secretary. We might learn something useful." St Bede's, Jan 27, 188?(illegible).
6. "Manning and the Tablet," *The Tablet,* 11 January 1992: "*The Tablet* was owned by Herbert Vaughan, his supposedly close friend."
7. Snead-Cox, 2, p.377.
8. Newsome, *Convert Cardinals,* pp.328ff: The problems of the poor bothered Manning so much that during his time as Archbishop ... with a glad heart he chose to become a fool for Christ's sake in order to rouse his generation to a consciousness of the grievous nature of their plight. He became at Westminster the ... lonely pioneer of social Catholicism in England.... In his efforts he learned from the French social reformer, Frederick Le Play.
9. *ibid.*
10. Jedin, *History,* 9, p.138.
11. WDA. Newspaper-clippings, *Public Eye:* "The close resemblance between certain passages of the Encyclical and others written by Manning himself shows how closely Pope Leo had considered the economic situation in England. Through Manning, the Encyclical was brought strongly to the attention of many prominent Labour leaders. Among these, Ben Tillett wrote at once to say that he regarded it as 'a very courageous one indeed.' 'I hardly think,' he added, 'our Protestant prelates would dare utter such wholesome doctrine.'"
12. Newsome, *Convert Cardinals,* p.331.
13. *ibid.,* pp.329–30: The Knights of Labor under the leadership of T. V. Powderley had expanded in industrial areas of the United States and Canada. The Union began to make radical proposals such as the nationalization of the railways and mines. In 1886, Cardinal Taschereau, Archbishop of Quebec, excommunicated members of the Knights of Labor, suspecting them of being a "secret society" tainted with Freemasonry, and sought papal support. Gibbons opposed any official censure and asked Manning's support; *Irish Ecclesiastical Record,* 8, 1887, p.461ff: Manning agreed with Gibbons and wrote to Rome. He pointed out that guilds—associations of labour and crafts—are recognized in antiquity. Unlike under Latin and Imperial law—which rigorously prohibited them, England and Teutonic lands recognized, favoured and charted guilds; p.475: To Manning, Gibbon's argument was "irresistible." "The Church is the Mother and Friend and Protector of the people. As our Lord walked among them, so His Church lives

among them"; James MacCaffrey, *History of the Catholic Church in the Nineteenth Century, 1789-1908*, 2, Dublin, Gill, 1909, pp.68-9; Concerning the Knights of Labor see John Tracey Ellis, "James Gibbons of Baltimore," in *Patterns of Episcopal Leadership*, Gerald Fogarty, ed., New York, Macmillan, 1989, p.133: "Gibbons aligned himself with the workingmen who composed the majority of the Catholic community, and in doing so declared *inter alia*, 'To lose the heart of the people would be a misfortune for which the friendship of the few rich and powerful would be no compensation.' It was a striking stand that endured and set the American church on the right road toward the tradition of social reform. True, in the composition of the letter he had the assistance of John Ireland, John Keane, and Denis O'Connell, but Gibbons alone signed the document."

14. Gray, *Manning*, p.306ff; Newsome, *Convert Cardinals*, pp.332-4; David Newsome, "Cardinal Manning and His Influence on The Church and Nation," *Recusant History*, October 1992, 21, 2, p.147; WDA. Newspaper clipping, no name, date: "Ben Tillett Describes Manning's Part in Dockers Strike"; Also see: Jedin, *History*, 9, p.139, "Catholic Self-Awareness in the British Empire," by Oskar Kohlar.

15. Anthony Stark, "Cardinal Henry Edward Manning," in the *Westminster Diocesan Yearbook*, 1993, pp.174-7; Francesco Nitti, *Catholic Socialism*, trans. Mary Mackintosh, London, Swan, 1895, p.315.

16. Newsome, *Convert Cardinals*, p.333.

17. "Henry Edward Cardinal Manning," *The Tablet*, 16 January 1892, p.84.

18. Wilfrid Meynell, "Some Reminiscences of Cardinal Manning, in 'The Contemporary Review,' *The Tablet*, 6 February 1892, p.6.

19. NYAA. Vaughan, Salford, to Corrigan, 25 June 1887: Vaughan was writing to comment on a pastoral of Archbishop Corrigan; Meynell tells of bringing Manning one Sunday afternoon to visit Henry George and listening while Manning told George that "his love of the Lord led him to love man" and George, who favoured the "nationalization of the land," said that "his love of man led him to love our Lord—the Mount, whence came the Sermon, being the beginning of the spiritual journey of the one and the end of that of the other." *The Tablet*, 6 February 1892.

20. McCormack, p.223.

21. Michael Walsh, "A Poser for 'The Tablet,'" *The Tablet*, 11 May 1991, pp.570-1: "Curious letters, all signed 'A Liberal' and probably by Vaughan, in the issues for 15 August, 5 and 19 September.... The first two display hostility to strikes and to what the encyclical insisted on calling workers's 'associations.'" That of 15 August stated: "According to the Pope's judgement the principles of socialism are evil principles and the organisers of strikes are socialist to a man."

22. Snead-Cox, 1, pp.459-65. He dates the letter to Ward in 1881; WDA.

23. *ibid.*, pp.457-8.

24. Newsome, *Convert Cardinals*, p.317.

25. Snead-Cox, 1, pp.465-8. George Errington was a Catholic and moderate Home Rule M. P. for Co. Longford. In 1881 he was commissioned by the British government as an unofficial envoy at Rome to try and persuade the Pope to discourage clerical support for violent nationalist agitation. His efforts caused a condemnation by the Pope of a testimonial fund for Parnell, but this papal intrusion was resented by many Irish Catholics. G. I. T. Machin, *Politics and the Churches in Great Britain, 1869-1921*, Oxford, Clarendon Press, 1987, p.135;

26. WDA. Westminster, 24 July 1886, Manning to Vaughan; WDA. Westminster, 23 January 1884, Manning to Vaughan; See: *The Tablet*, 17 April 1886, p.608, Review of *The History of Catholic Emancipation* by W. J. Amherst, SJ, London, Kegan-Paul: Milner, on one occasion in 1810, had been invited by Lord Clifford to dine with some friends at a hotel in Dover St—at the end he was asked to sign a resolution drawn up at a meeting of leading Catholic laymen. He refused to sign and for more than a hour "was baited and tormented on every side." At another meeting of the "Board of British Catholics" he was voted out of the meeting. He read his protest that he did not act on behalf of the laymen present but on behalf of the thirty bishops and five

million Catholics "whose religious business I am authorized to transact." He left the group. "I hope you will not turn me out of the Catholic Church, nor shut me out of the Kingdom of Heaven." Only two laymen left with Milner—a Vaughan relative, Weld of Lulworth, and Bodenham of Rotherwas.

27. Snead-Cox, 1, pp.458-9.

28. Newsome, *Convert Cardinals*, p.339: The label Manning chose for himself was "Mosaic Radical," by which he meant a "combination of deference to divine law and divine will, and identification with the best interests of the people; a fusion of religion and humanity, Church and People."

29. WDA. Westminster, 28 June 1890, Manning to Vaughan.

30. WDA. Westminster, 22 February 1891, Manning to Vaughan.

31. Nitti, *Catholic Socialism*, Introduction and pp.315-31: Nitti's book was first published in 1890; *Il Socialismo Cattolico*, Rome, L. Roux. The translator, a Catholic lady living in Rome, noted on page vii: The label Liberalism meant at the time the principle of laissez faire in regard to economic matters and often "free thinking" or "secularism" in regard to religion.

32. Snead-Cox., 1, p.474; Wilfrid Meynell, "The Cardinal and the Drink Traffic," *The Tablet*, 6 February 1892, p.6: "And when men told him calmly (I give the statement from his standpoint only) that they feared spiritual pride dogged the steps of teetotalism, he had no patience left in him. He asked for water, and they gave him the sour wine of pedantries. I think it was not altogether without a qualm that he allowed the sherry he had renounced to be put on the table at that open early dinner at Archbishop's House; but a Bishop must by the gospel rule, be 'given to hospitality;' and how does he know, anyway, that there is not among his guests one to whom St. Paul himself would command a little wine for the stomach's sake? So there the hated decanter stood, and there, if nowhere else, a guest had an approach to experience of what may be called furtive drinking; for he was unwilling to meet the eye of his host while his lips touched the banned liquid."

33. WDA. Oates, Anecdotes, 27 September 1894; WDA. A Manning scrapbook of newspaper cuttings contains many that report on the temperance meetings attended by Manning around the country. Several included Vaughan on the same platform. *The Tablet* of 6 November 1878, p.627, reported on the "Great Meeting of the Total Abstinence League of the Cross at Exeter Hall." Manning was president. Six branches were present. They met to celebrate the birthday of Fr Mathew. They aimed to send to Parliament members who would support their views and "turn men to sobriety."

34. Snead-Cox, 1, p.475.

35. Newsome, "Manning's Influence," p.147; Sheridan Gilley, *Newman and his Age*, Westminster, Christian Classics, 1990, p.421: "He died as he had lived, a Catholic but an Evangelical as well, firm in 'those great and burning truths, which I learned when a boy'." On 9 August 1890, Newman received his niece, Grace. "The following day he fell ill with pneumonia, and died on the evening of Monday 11 August 1890. His last discernible words were to Neville: 'William, William'. He was in his ninetieth year."

36. Newsome, *Convert Cardinals*, p.358.

37. Vincent McClelland, *English Roman Catholics and Higher Education, 1830-1903*, Oxford, Clarendon Press, 1973, p.366.

38. MHA. Scrapbooks. Box 33. HCV.

39. *ibid.*

40. McClelland, *Education*.

41. J. E. C. Bodley, *Cardinal Manning and other Essays*, London, 1912, p.29, in McClelland, *Recusant History*, October 1992, Foreword and p.135; See: Newsome, *Convert Cardinals*, p.358ff; "A Personal Friend" wrote in the *St James Gazette*: "He felt the cold very much as he grew older, and he laughingly compared his favourite room, which was always kept at a high temperature, to the warmer regions of the south. 'This is my Riviera,' he used to repeat,'and I

need not travel five or six hundred miles to get there.' ... That his own simplicity of living amounted almost to asceticism is well known; and the tall venerable figure, bent with age, clad in the long black cassock, the thin keen face with its piercing eyes, surmounted by the pink biretta, formed a picture not easily forgotten." *The Tablet*, 23 January 1892, p.139.

42. MHA. Scrapbooks: "Raymond Blathwayt."

43. *ibid.*, *St James Gazette*.

44. John S. Vaughan, *The Tablet*, 23 January 1892, p.139.

45. "Henry Edward, Cardinal Manning," *The Tablet*, 16 January 1892, p.81ff; Gray, *Manning*, pp.320-1.

46. Leslie, *Vaughan Letters*, p.403; Newsome, "Manning," *RH*, p.136; Friedrich von Hügel wrote to *The Times Literary Supplement* on 24 March 1921 in reference to Leslie's *Cardinal Manning*. Vaughan said to Von Hügel, "Well, this is what happened shortly before his death. I was at his bedside: he looked around to see that we were alone; he fumbled under his pillow for something; he drew out a battered little pocket book full of a woman's fine handwriting. He said 'For years you have been like a son to me, Herbert. I know not to whom else to leave this—I leave it to you.'" Newsome, *Parting of Friends*, p.411, n. 1; Friedrich von Hügel, *Selected Letters 1896-1924*, editor, Bernard Holland, 1927, p.256: "Sir George Sutton heard from his grandmother, Elizabeth Herbert, that Vaughan had placed the book in Manning's coffin. Reginald Wilberforce wrote of the death of Manning's wife on 24th July 1837. Caroline Sargent's early death "deeply affected" Manning's character for, "It set a seal on his character that was never afterwards effaced. After her death he found himself unable to dwell on the past except in direct acts of devotion; *The Tablet*, 20 February 1892, p.301, quoting from *The Nineteenth Century*: "The heavy days, the long evenings, leisure changed into loneliness. The sad nights, and sadder days, when the reality of our bereavement breaks in upon us."

47. Snead-Cox, 2, p.1; George Beck, editor, *The English Catholics, 1850-1950*, London, Burns & Oates, 1950, p.164.

48. WDA. Newspaper clippings, n.d.: "The death of Edison recalls the interesting fact that one of the first phonograph records to be preserved as a historic document was one made by Cardinal Manning—and made on his deathbed. ... The late Lady St. Helier describes in her Memoirs the most impressive occasion when the late Cardinal Vaughan, the late Duke of Norfolk, and many representatives of the great Catholic families of England, assembled at Colonel Gouraud's house to hear Cardinal Manning's 'message to posterity' spoken on his deathbed— the first voice to be heard from the other side of the grave."!!

49. Newsome, "Manning," *RH*, p.155.

50. Newsome, *Convert Cardinals*, p.362.

51. Someone visited the Cardinal's grave on All Souls Day in 1892: The temporary resting place was "neatly planted over with a stone-crop, evergreen, and moss, and is enclosed by a simple solid wooden railing which is painted in dark red, and which is ... having around it kneeling boards where the devout friends of the late Cardinal may kneel.... At the head of his grave stands a large plain solid wooden cross painted light blue, on which is written in Gothic letters R.I.P." To the Editor, *The Tablet*, 5 November 1892, p.74.

PART FIVE

ARCHBISHOP OF WESTMINSTER

CHAPTER XV

Westminster and Westminster Cathedral

Henry Edward Manning's Successor

In Rome in 1881, when Vaughan was representing the English bishops during their dispute with the religious orders, there was a rumour that he was going to be appointed Manning's coadjutor bishop.[1] According to Snead-Cox, there was never any doubt who would succeed Manning.[2] There may not have been any doubt, in Snead-Cox's opinion, but there was opposition.

An article titled "English Romanism," in the 12 September 1882 issue of the *Daily Chronicle*, reported that a "strong effort is now being made to secure the succession of the 'Archdiocese' of Westminster for Bishop Herbert Vaughan of Salford." Leading what the Rome reporter called a "crusade" was Lady Mary Elizabeth Herbert of Lea. The Roman Catholic clergy of England, in the opinion of the *Chronicle* were "sick of priests who have never been seminarists," and "they bitterly resent a conspiracy worked out by a titled lady who has quite enough to do at home, but prefers canvassing amongst the Roman princes and other influential personages to bring about a domination of refugees from a hostile camp and mushroom congregations of priests, whose members are intended to act as instruments for the increase of the already too great authority of the Romish Bishops in England."[3]

In March 1885 the *Evening News* took up the same issue: "Who will be the next Archbishop of Westminster?" The writer admitted that Herbert Vaughan was "the man above all others whom the Cardinal himself would wish to see by his side." But, it continued, "a more unpopular appointment could hardly be made; and we do not hesitate to declare that were the Cardinal to absolutely fix upon this prelate as the successor to the headship of the Roman Catholic Church in England, there would inevitably be something akin to a revolt in the ranks of the London priesthood."

Throughout his career Vaughan was not generally popular with his priests nor is there evidence that he courted popularity. His reputation was established for many among the clergy and hierarchy when he was at St Edmund's, by his immaturity and unrestrained criticism of opponents to the Oblates. Schiefen quotes the following from Vaughan about the opposition: "Is it that with other gifts is vouchsafed to them a special and abundant gift of stupidity, or that there is something inherently wicked in truth and honesty themselves." The impression the clergy took away from Ware was confirmed for many by the often unchristian tone *The Tablet* took during the years he was editor prior to the First Vatican Council.

At Salford there was little evidence of the sharp edge of his temperament in his dealings with others. But his attempts to increase the powers of the Board of Finance by ordering regular detailed reports from each mission and the auditing of mission and school accounts, among other controls, were hard on his clergy. Snead-Cox devotes an entire chapter to his efforts to raise them to his ideal of what a priest's life ought to be. He was strong on discipline and control by the bishop and his administration. At the same time Vaughan's earnestness and generosity generated positive responses to appeals for his various schemes in Lancashire. It was due to the cooperation of his own clergy and many lay people that he was able to do so much throughout his years as bishop. And also his championing the cause of the hierarchy against the privileges of the Jesuits and other regulars won him the respect and gratitude of church leaders and clergy not only in England but internationally. So it is not surprising that the move of Vaughan to Westminster was not happily received by many, nor that his appointment to Westminster was assured.

The *Evening News* article went on to say that Vaughan and the Anglican Bishop of Manchester, Dr Fraser, had between them "the foot and mouth disease." In addition Vaughan had shown himself "excessively imprudent," and his "imprudence," according to the *News*, "horrifies the Roman Curia." "We are not aware that the candidature of the Bishop of Salford has any supporters either in Rome or in England." Manning would not name his protégé "in face of opposition which such an appointment would undoubtedly provoke." The man whom the *Evening News* proposed was Manning's vicar general, Monsignor Gilbert. He "must be next Cardinal Archbishop of Westminster."[4]

However, despite Vaughan's unpopularity, at least as expressed in the secular press, Vaughan was chosen. In Maisie Ward's opinion, there was not a succession problem as there had been at Wiseman's death twenty-seven years before; Herbert Vaughan was an obvious choice. "For one thing, no one else could show a lifetime of such cooperation with the great friend of Rome who had just died." Despite the fact that cooperation between the two men in Manning's final years had not been as close as it had been earlier, Manning knew that Vaughan was to follow him. "In all things that mattered most in the eyes of Rome," Vaughan and Manning were at one.[5]

The Westminster chapter met at the Kensington Pro-Cathedral on 9 February 1892. They sent forward three names in alphabetical order: Gilbert, vicar general of Westminster; Hedley, bishop of Newport; and Vaughan. The next day, a meeting of bishops, with Vaughan's uncle, William, as president, adopted the three names sent to them by the chapter, and forwarded the list to Rome, recommending Vaughan.[6]

Herbert Vaughan was almost sixty years old, not in good health, and it was known that he had neither the taste nor the appetite for the metropolitan office. For years Manning had made it clear that he hoped Vaughan would be his successor, and so it appeared that only a decision against the choice by Vaughan himself would prevent his transfer from Salford.[7] In addition to being Manning's choice, Vaughan had the advantages of a place in national life because of his family connections, an international standing as a promoter of missions, mainly due to the success of St Joseph's Missionary College and Society at Mill Hill, his achievements as Bishop of Salford, and his representations on behalf of the English bishops.[8]

At the same time, Vaughan had seen the faces of the London poor at Manning's funeral and was aware of his own limitations. When he learned the results of the Westminster chapter and the bishops' meeting, he wrote a letter directly to Pope Leo XIII. He requested that Pope Leo choose someone else for Westminster and that he would gladly continue at Salford where he had been for twenty years. In the letter he recognized that the qualities needed by a bishop of Salford were very different from those asked of an archbishop of Westminster:

> The See of Westminster ought to be occupied by a Bishop distinguished for some gift of superior learning or by remarkable sanctity, for he ought to be commended to the Church and to the people of England (for whose conversion he may be able to do more than any one else) by some manifest superiority or excellence. Holy Father, it is no mock modesty or fashion of speech which makes the confession that I have no qualification of learning for such a post. I do not excel as a preacher, an author, a theologian, a philosopher, or even as a classical scholar. Whatever I may be in these matters, in none am I above a poor mediocrity. It will be very easy in such a position as the See of Westminster to compromise the interests of religion in England by errors of judgement—and the very quality of a certain tenacity and determination would make these errors still more serious.[9]

On 23 March he wrote to Mary Elizabeth Herbert telling her about his letter to the Pope, in which he thought he had placed clearly and simply "my disqualifications and my consequent desire to remain here. Who could have done that better than I, who have the most intimate knowledge of them." He was not going to be placed in a position without first stating "the strong reasons which exist for leaving me where I am. Having thus relieved my own conscience, I have been in perfect peace and rest ever since." Whatever the decision of the Holy See, he decided to treat it as an "indication of God's will for me."[10] On 21 March 1892 the cardinals of Propaganda Fide met, and, on the same day, their recommendation was passed on to the pope. On 29 March Herbert Vaughan was appointed archbishop of Westminster.

The *Manchester Guardian* announced on 31 March that the newly named archbishop "is a representative of one of the most ancient of the untitled noble houses of the Kingdom." *Pall Mall* on 30 March compared his family to the Bickersteths of the Anglican community."[11] The *Morning Advertiser* announced on 31 March that Vaughan might not have the "same alluring quality as Manning but he is a man of strong character, high culture and generous aims." The *Daily Telegraph* reporter who interviewed Vaughan at St Bede's wrote on 31 March: "... by the translation of this courteous gentleman, this energetic churchman, this hard working philanthropist and above all this thorough Englishman, the loss of Manchester will be as hard to estimate as the gain of London." The *Leeds Mercury* on 1 April said that Vaughan's appointment would not give universal satisfaction to his co-religionists. At the same time he was, they thought, "a brilliant administrator, a fine scholar with a decided leaning towards modern science and method, a good preacher of the plain and practical style and in private life a benevolent man."

As often as Manning pleaded with Vaughan to maintain an independence of political issues, especially in his ownership of *The Tablet*, he was seen by newspapers, such as the *Mercury*, to be disapproved of by the "Irish portion of the community and a group of Englishmen whose sympathies incline to Liberalism in religion as well as politics." Vaughan, the article continued, "glories in the name Englishman," "supports Tory principles," and "his journal *The Tablet* has opposed Home Rule from the beginning." He was for them "a Unionist from Conviction and Tradition." On 1 April the *Catholic Standard* wrote that "his political sympathies are with the Tories and against Mr. Gladstone on the Home Rule question" and this was the "one blot" on his record. However, the article went on: "Whatever Dr. Vaughan's private opinion may be on the Irish Question, we have never seen or heard of any remark from his pen or tongue adverse to Ireland." The *Western Watchman* in the United States faulted him for his "political creed:" "Many cannot understand how a man so enthusiastic respecting Church affairs can be so conservative in political life." The report ended with a quote from Alexander Pope: "Who'er expects a faultless priest to see, Expects what ne'er was, nor is and ne'er shall be."[12]

Herbert Vaughan continued to honour his commitments at Salford. At the end of March he addressed the Salford Sanitary Association; he was president of the "Working Men's Sanitary Association." He urged them to purchase an old military barrack in Eccles New Road and convert it into a place where the people could amuse themselves during the winter, rather than spending their time in a local "drinkshop." A delegation went to the Mayor of Salford and he approved; the members expected that soon there would be "a grand recreation hall and winter garden in the borough."[13]

In the middle of April Mgr Charles Gadd sent a circular to all the priests of the diocese asking them to meet after the blessing of the oils on Holy

Thursday to discuss, if they wished, the preparation of a testimonial for Archbishop-elect Vaughan.[14]

Bishop Herbert Vaughan was aware of how difficult it would be for anyone to follow Henry Manning. He decided to spend a few weeks at Salford before leaving for Westminster in order to prepare himself. One afternoon when Vaughan was feeling "more despondent than usual" he went into St Bede's College chapel and knelt in a side gallery. Louis Casartelli, the rector, was preaching about the mission of St Patrick. Suddenly Casartelli caught Vaughan's attention with a statement that Patrick was sixty when he first set foot in Ireland. As soon as the sermon was over Vaughan left the chapel to find out on what authority the rector had concluded that Patrick was sixty years old when he began his work in converting the people of Ireland. "He listened to the reply, and then said eagerly, 'Then I may take courage about Westminster.'"[15]

On Easter Sunday, 17 April, Herbert Vaughan delivered farewell addresses in the morning at St John's Cathedral and in the evening at Holy Name Church. "He did not know what he could say to them, for leave-taking was never a time that was easy either for those that left or for those that remained. He had loved that cathedral, and with his whole heart he had loved his people, and he had gladly worked according to his poor ability in their behalf ... and would gladly die for them, but the voice of Christ had been heard, and His fiat must be obeyed." Concerning the recent press reports: "He felt overwhelmed with the kindness and generosity with which they had spoken of him ... in terms far and away beyond anything that he could ever claim to be entitled to." He closed by asking for the prayers of the congregation.[16]

One Londoner, Ellis Schreiber, wrote to Father Daniel E. Hudson in the United States on 29 April: "There has been much sickness in England during the winter, at one time almost a panic with regard to the influenza but thank God, that is quite over now." He inclosed some anecdotes about Cardinal Manning and added: "The appointment of Dr. Vaughan as our new Archbishop seems to give general satisfaction. He is much liked personally, but the ascendancy thus given to the Vaughan family is regarded in some quarters with a slight feeling of suspicion."[17] One wit described Westminster during the Herbert Vaughan years as "Vaughanitas, Vaughanitatum et omnia Vaughanitas."[18]

When Vaughan left Salford the clergy had increased during his tenure from 138 to 237, and public churches and chapels from seventy-nine to 118. According to the Almanac for 1893 Vaughan opened thirty new missions and another ten were reopened on older sites. There were 208,340 Catholics in the diocese in 1892, and 1,770,000 non-Catholics. Also there were 221 primary schools, twenty-one higher and middle schools, with 946 teachers and 44,024 children.[19]

Herbert Vaughan left Salford and Manchester by train on Tuesday, 26

April 1892. He sent a telegram ahead to John Snead-Cox asking him to meet him at St Pancras Railway Station in the early afternoon. Snead-Cox was waiting on the platform when Vaughan's train arrived. The archbishop-elect smiled at Snead-Cox: "'You are not in a hurry, are you?' and then without waiting for a reply he went on, 'They don't expect me at Archbishop's House for some time, so let us have a good talk.' Then, giving his luggage in charge of a porter, he led the way to the broad drive in front of the Midland Station Hotel, and there for the best part of two hours we paced up and down." Vaughan poured out his plans, hopes and fears about the task before him at Westminster, based on what he assumed might be ten years of life left to him. Snead-Cox listened to his scheme for a central seminary, plans for bringing clergy and laity together, a Catholic Social Union, the Society of the Ladies of Charity, and "above all, Westminster Cathedral."[20]

When Vaughan arrived at Westminster, the estimated Catholic population of England was 1,500,000. In Scotland there were 365,000, and, according to the 1891 census, 3,549,956 Catholics in Ireland. In the diocese of Westminster there were 253 secular and 103 religious priests, and nineteen orders or congregations of men and forty-seven of women. Over the whole diocese there were 129 public churches. His pro-cathedral was Our Lady of Victories in Kensington. At Bayswater, the superior of the Oblates was Francis Wyndham, while at the Jesuit Church, Farm Street, near Berkeley Square, Vaughan's old friends William Eyre and Robert Whitty were in residence. He had two auxiliary bishops, James Patterson and William Weathers. Weathers also served as rector of St Thomas Seminary in Hammersmith. Vaughan had three secretaries, Canon Johnson, his assistant Fr Howlett, and Austin Oates, his private secretary. There were four colleges: St Edmund's, Ware; St Charles, Notting Hill; St Mary's Teachers' College at Hammersmith; and St Joseph's Missionary College in Mill Hill.[21]

London had grown from a population of about one million in 1800 to the world's largest city by the end of the nineteenth century, with over four million. Its growth was largely unplanned. The forces of free trade, industry and imperialism which made the City and the West End spectacularly rich also created to the east "an expanse of poverty and wretchedness as appalling as, and in many ways worse than, the horrors of the industrial north." The East End was the site of massive dock buildings, toxic industries and "sweated" trades.

When Vaughan arrived, all the conditions existed for what the wealthy feared most, a revolt by the poor. There was dreadful poverty in which highly skilled artisans were reduced to "sweated" lowly paid labourers. And the City of London, where wealth and political power resided, jealously guarded what it held. Some social commentators saw the conditions of the poor in London, especially the East End, as symbols of urban disintegration and even the end of civilization. Even "improvement" and slum clearance brought great hardship to the poor, for it demolished their housing to make way for new roads and railways. Despite its terrible conditions, especially during the winter months, London continued to draw the destitute and displaced from all over Britain, Ireland, Russia and the world. Until 1888, when the London City Council was formed, the principal means by which the wealthy tried to do something about the poverty on their doorstep was through charity and all the organizations it generated.[22]

Vaughan wrote from his new home at Carlisle Place the next day. Sitting in Cardinal Manning's old house he expected "to meet him on the stairs." It was a good omen, he concluded, "to have arrived on the Feast of Our Lady of Good Counsel."[23] That Wednesday evening he spoke at a meeting in the Westminster Palace Hotel. The Duke of Norfolk was chairman and the purpose was to propose a memorial to Henry Manning. On Friday he met the Catholic Truth Society at his residence. The following Tuesday he was back in Manchester where he presided at a chapter called to choose three names of possible successors to Salford, and, in the evening, he spoke at a meeting of the Rescue Society at the Free Trade Hall.[24]

Enthronement

On Sunday, 8 May, Herbert Vaughan was enthroned at the Pro-Cathedral, Kensington. At the entrance gate two flags were flying and inside, the Archbishop's throne, draped in scarlet and gold, was placed to the north of the altar, which was beautifully decked with flowers. A welcome address from clergy and laity of the Archdiocese was read by Mgr Gilbert while the Duke of Norfolk stood at his side: "We know what have been your zealous labours, as a priest and as a Bishop. Your labours during the seventeen years of your priesthood, especially in your great work for the foreign missions; and the labours of the twenty years of your episcopate, in your constant watchfulness over your diocese, in your preaching and your Pastoral Letters, in the multiplying of churches and schools, in the establishment of colleges, and in your noble work for the protection and rescue of poor Catholic children—all this adds to the joyful confidence with which we welcome you as henceforth our own pastor and Father in God."

In his reply, Vaughan reminded his listeners of the qualities of his predecessors, Wiseman and Manning, who were like "Moses and Josue." One was a "leader out of the darker days, our organizer and our lawgiver" and the other was the "captain who led us over the Jordan, bringing us home again, after three hundred years of exile, into the public life of England." That he was chosen as their successor was "a cause of profound humiliation on account of the disproportion between the feebleness of the instrument and the magnitude of the responsibility" to which he had been raised. At Salford he had some success due to the "hearty cooperation between clergy and all classes of the laity, in everything we undertook." In London, with its millions, people experienced evils that were "more acute and dangerous." With the agreement of the Duke of Norfolk and the welcoming committee, it was decided to have, as a memorial to the late Cardinal Manning, a "platform" or plan of action for the diocese in which the "poor and their welfare" would be "one of the chief planks."[25]

On Tuesday, 10 May, Archbishop–elect Vaughan held his first reception at Archbishop's House. A letter to the *Pall Mall Gazette* reported that he had never seen such "a crush in the great room and ante–chamber." The writer described Cardinal Manning's old butler taking hats and coats and "at the top of the staircase in the doorway of the Conference room, stood the Archbishop, stately and dignified, and with a smile for every one he had ever met before. As each name was called out, he extended his ring for the kiss of the faithful; many bent the knee before him; some bowed and passed on, for there were present numbers of non–Catholics."[26]

Vaughan's entry into Westminster may have been modest, but he was resolved to make as much as he could of the ceremony in which an archbishop is officially installed by Rome. He was to receive the Pallium from Pope Leo XIII, a symbol of his jurisdiction. He could have gone to Rome for the ceremony but asked that it be sent to London to "provide an ecclesiastical pageant which should serve as an object–lesson reminding the English people of certain vital truths in the story of their own past."

The selection of Herbert Vaughan for Westminster was controversial and he was never shy about using the office to fan the fires of speculation. The last one to receive the Pallium was Cardinal Pole on 25 March 1556. Snead-Cox quotes Pole's sermon at Bow Church: "An archbishop cannot exercise this power given to him by the act of consecration until he receives authority to do so by means of this Pallium, taken, as I have said, from the body of St.Peter and transmitted to him by Christ's Vicar."[27] Vaughan thought that the opportunity was "too good a trump card against the Anglican to throw away."[28]

In August, Vaughan went on retreat at St Edmund's College, Old Hall, and then was officially invested as archbishop at the Brompton Oratory Church on 16 August. The ceremony was as solemn and ceremonial as possible, in the presence of the English bishops, the heads of religious orders, four hundred priests, diplomats and members of the Catholic nobility and gentry. Archbishop Edmund Stonor, the resident English Papal delegate to Leo XIII at Rome, brought the Pallium from the Pope. It was the first time the symbol of the archbishop's office had been brought to England since the Reformation. Abbot Francis Aidan Gasquet gave the homily.

After the Mass Vaughan came to the front of the high altar, removed his mitre and knelt at the feet of Stonor, who sat with a book of the Gospels open on his knees. Every one in the church stood as Vaughan "renewed once more on English soil the traditional act of homage of the English Church to the Apostolic See, ending with the words that give to the protestation the form of an oath: 'So help me God and His holy Gospels.'" Stonor then took the woollen Pallium from the altar and put it around Vaughan's neck as the sign of his dignity and authority in the office of archbishop. A few minutes later an old Canterbury Cathedral ceremony of kissing the Pallium by clergy and laity took place. At the end of the ceremony Archbishop Vaughan rose, and with his cross carried before him, blessed the people as he left the church.

The Times reported the ceremony the following day as "significant," for it involved the direct intervention of the Pope, and was of the opinion that the occasion marked an important stage in the development of a more tolerant public attitude towards Roman Catholicism. The Daily Chronicle considered the ceremony to be a triumph for the Catholic Church: "Archbishop Vaughan has made his entry into a Primacy of English Roman Catholics with more of the pomp of ecclesiastical circumstance than is usual on such occasions, even on the continent."[29]

Vaughan's installation was to set the tone of his ten years in London. He engaged in a series of controversies with the non-Catholic world, especially with the Anglicans, while at Westminster. According to Maisie Ward, the "series of rubs" by the end of his term "saw the beginning of that Modernist episode which was to disturb the peace of his own province as of the Church at large. And if the breach was in no way due to him, the earlier frictions most definitely were." [30]

Cardinal Vaughan

In December 1892 Herbert Vaughan was informed that he was to become a cardinal. In January 1893 he began his journey to Rome to receive the red hat from the Pope. On 5 January he wrote to Mary Elizabeth Herbert from Paris with the comment that Christian art might be a medium for the Church to reach the English people "whereby prejudices may be dissipated and minds attracted. How much depends on the power of prestige." From Paris, Vaughan went to Cannes and then on to Rome.[31]

On 11 January, the day after Vaughan arrived in Rome, he had an interview with the Pope. Pope Leo wanted to make him the patron of the Church of San Crisogono; it had been the Pope's titular church when he was made a cardinal. Vaughan, during the visit, which lasted for forty-five minutes, asked rather to be given the Church of St Gregory and St Andrew, a name that "England knows," on the Coelian Hill. The Pope agreed to Vaughan's choice, for St Gregory and St Andrew had been Cardinal Manning's church and was also the place from which St Augustine and his companions had set out on their mission to England. Vaughan thought that the Pope was "wonderful" and that it was said that "he is likely to go on talking for two hours after death."[32]

During a consistory meeting on the morning of 16 January, the pope raised him to the rank of cardinal. The pope made fourteen new cardinals: six Italian, two French, two Prussian, one Irish, one Hungarian, one Spanish, and Vaughan from England. Eight were present in Rome to receive the honour and join with pilgrims celebrating Leo XIII's episcopal jubilee. The message of his appointment was sent to Vaughan, who was staying at the English College.

Soon after midday, the messenger, who was the Master of Ceremonies of the Vatican, was received in the great hall of the college which was "crowded with many English and American Catholics and non-Catholics, besides many ecclesiastics, both foreign and Italian." They were present for the reception in Herbert Vaughan's honour.

A crimson-robed Archbishop Vaughan stood in an arched doorway leading from a gallery decorated with the portraits of former British and Irish Cardinals; paintings of Manning and Howard were the first seen by visitors.

Following the ceremony, Vaughan spoke in Italian: "Two thoughts occupy my mind on this solemn occasion and give to me in my weakness, both courage and joy. The first is the thought of the singular devotion to St Peter and his See which characterized my beloved countrymen for a thousand years, until a miserable schism, born of lust and greed, broke up our peace and religious unity." The other thought, Vaughan added, was that it was a privilege to stand by the Pope "while his barque is tossed in a furious tempest." "In a stormy age of socialism, revolution, and violence, he is a beacon of safety for Christendom, as a lighthouse on a dark night in an angry sea." He stressed that the honour was due not to his own merit but to Wiseman, Manning and the English nation.[33] The final official public announcement was made at a public consistory held on Thursday 19 January 1893.

Vaughan wrote to Caroline Hanmer about his official visit to St Gregory and St Andrew where he was welcomed by a "tremendous crowd." On that Tuesday morning he said Mass at the St Francis Xavier altar and in the afternoon was formally received in his titular church. Among those present were fifteen members of his own family.[34] He was also given a formal reception in the English College at the beginning of March where there were "two thousand guests and all the black Roman nobility. They had seen nothing like it since 1870."[35]

Cardinal Vaughan returned to England on 31 March 1893. The vicar general, Mgr Gilbert, and the Duke of Norfolk welcomed him on behalf of clergy and laity. Vaughan responded with two words—his motto—which seemed to him to sum up "the programme which is before us—*Amare et Servire*. Love must be the root out of which service must spring up. Without love, service demanding care and self-sacrifice will never endure."[36]

Snead-Cox quotes extracts from Vaughan's spiritual diary in order to "lift the veil for a moment" and allow the reader to see another side of the man and not the "haughty prelate," an impression Snead-Cox attributed to his "stateliness of manner and bearing," which he always conveyed by the "striking and imposing figure" dressed in cardinal's robes. The man seen by some who were not close to him as "cold and unapproachable, and generally too magnificent, to sympathize with the troubles and difficulties of ordinary people," also had a "fibre of hardness" in his character. Others also found the Cardinal socially either distracted, preoccupied or dull. Despite these traits, those who knew him well found him to be a person of "infinite tenderness," and a man of the spirit.[37]

The hardness of Vaughan's character was related to the grim seriousness Manning had spoken to him about. One who experienced Cardinal Vaughan's hard side was his brother, Bernard. Herbert Vaughan attended the solemn opening of Holy Name Hall in Manchester on the occasion of the church's silver jubilee in April 1893. Herbert was a guest of Bernard's from Wednesday to Friday. On Thursday there was a luncheon party for guests to meet him and in the evening the hall was opened. "At 8:30 the Cardinal, accompanied by the Bishop of Salford and Mgr Gadd, VG, appeared on the platform.... Down the broad flight of steps which led from the throne to the body of the hall, the Cardinal, robed in black and crimson, passed to mingle with the invited guests." Included in the celebrations was a fund-raising bazaar. Martindale writes in his biography of Bernard that Herbert Vaughan, "with the sense of rigid justice that characterized him ... somewhat dashed his brother's feelings by an announcement made from the Holy Name pulpit just before his sermon" that there was a decree of the Westminster Synod which "forbade any publicity, as by means of advertisement, being given to the music which was to be sung at religious services, a decree which had been violated wholesale on the present occasion."

He said afterwards that he had to speak because Bernard was his brother and he did not want to seem to be engaging in favouritism. "However he preached a magnificent sermon," wrote Martindale, and the bazaar attracted 45,000 visitors.[38] Herbert Vaughan had made a statement in Salford in 1881 on the topic of bazaars. It is an insight into his view of charitable giving. He asked others to keep in mind that the intention was the important aspect for the "Eye of God is upon the heart," and went on to commend almsgiving "simply and solely for love of virtue" and asked his priests to "instill the true principle of charity into the minds of the faithful." Any lesser motives for giving, he thought, "have neither the mentality nor even the character and taste of the higher." Bernard Vaughan had tested his brother when he knew what the reaction might be.[39]

Vaughan sometimes irritated non-Catholics; one example was the public dedication of the English Catholic Church to St Peter. He wrote on 7 June 1893 that "St. George has found champions in the Protestant Press—they like his horse and the snake so much better than St. Peter. Of course, he remains where he was, one of the three principal patrons of England." A service was planned for Brompton Oratory at which one priest would speak about Our Lady and he about St Peter. "The Holy Father's proposal has given great satisfaction," Vaughan concluded.[40]

Not everyone was as satisfied as he thought. The *Manchester Examiner* on 30 May ran the following: "For cool impertinence, the following is difficult to surpass: Rome, May 27—The Pope has granted the private request made by Cardinal Vaughan, Archbishop of Westminster, when in Rome, asking that St. Peter might be made the patron saint of England. A solemn ceremony placing England under the protection of St. Peter will take place at the Oratory, Brompton, in the beginning of July." The writer went on to say: "The impertinence of the proposed transfer passes belief. Only think of it! The Pope and Cardinal Vaughan treating England as if they had proprietary rights! Is it the old story? 'Whom the gods wish to destroy they first make mad.' "[41]

Centenary Celebrations at St Edmund's College, November 1893

Bishop John Douglass arrived at Old Hall with two students, William Beacham and John Law, on 12 November 1793. On 16 November, the Feast of St Edmund, archbishop of Canterbury, studies at the new St Edmund's College began. One hundred years later, thanks to the hard work of a new president, Fr Bernard Ward, the son of William George Ward, the school was revived and the centenary was celebrated. He had published a history of the college at the end of 1892. Herbert Vaughan let it be known that "if the College could not be made to pay its way, it would be closed." Ward was appointed president in January 1893. The celebration he planned to mark the centenary was "a dramatic demonstration of what St Edmund's meant for Catholicism in England." He aimed to "rally all Edmundian forces round the College and heal all the sores and wounds of past conflicts." Rymer, Weathers, Patterson, Akers, Fenton and Lloyd were there. Only John Crook, of the six past presidents, did not attend.

An elaborate reception was planned for Cardinal Vaughan, the unsuccessful vice president of more than thirty years earlier. A carriage and a pair of horses waited for him at the railway station. Acolytes and a cross-bearer were ready to receive him at the college gates, but Herbert Vaughan "defeated all the plans by walking from Ware and getting a lift in a greengrocer's cart in which, to our dismay, he drove up from the Lodge. But that was Vaughan's way." The celebration lasted for three days, and, according to the *Edmundian*, the "bitter memories of the past struggles were all obliterated in the Refectory," at a grand banquet presided over by Cardinal Herbert Vaughan. "And the wonderful thing was that with all these memories of past conflict, the dominant note was one of rejoicing because Ward had resolved them into harmony by his intense love of Alma Mater."[42]

Archbishop's House

In London, Cardinal Vaughan lived first at Archbishop's House, Carlisle Place, the barrack-like building purchased by Henry Manning. Abbot Hunter-Blair described it as Vaughan's "big ugly house." At Westminster, Vaughan was "a grand and noble figure, one that imparted unsurpassable dignity to the Church in England, the figure of a great Prince who was also a most humble and devoted priest." At the Brompton Oratory, the abbot had watched Vaughan on feast days "sweeping majestically (and always rapidly)" up the steps. Hunter-Blair recalled Vaughan's grand evening receptions at which Vaughan's cousin, Alice Lady Lovat, served as hostess,[43] while Herbert Vaughan received everyone with a "word of genuine welcome and a smile on his beautiful face."[44]

Westminster Cathedral

Vaughan's efforts to secure recognition for the Catholic Church in Britain differed from those of Henry Manning, according to Derek Holmes. On his arrival in London he announced that a cathedral was to be built for Westminster. The building of Westminster Cathedral was to be both symbolic of his general attitude as well as an example of his administrative ability.[45]

The laying of the foundation stone for Westminster Cathedral took place on Saturday, 29 June 1895. The day began overcast, chilly and threatening rain. The site of the cathedral was the land of a long-deserted prison. On that Saturday morning in 1895 it was "gay with awnings of scarlet and white and fluttering flags of Empire and Papacy, mingled with those of nations whose generous purses had contributed to the realization of this great day."

At 11 a.m. a procession began from Archbishop's House in Carlisle Place to the music of Mendelssohn's *Athalie*, "The War March of the Priests." The group leading the procession was made up of priests and students from St Joseph's Missionary College at Mill Hill, "Cardinal Vaughan's earliest and most beloved work." They were followed by bishops from France, the United States and India. The cross-bearer was John Vaughan, the Cardinal's youngest brother. Cardinal Logue, Archbishop of Armagh and Primate of Ireland, sang a "low Mass."[46] The largest offertory on record was given at the laying of the cornerstone: seventy-five thousand four hundred and ninety-two pounds.[47] At a luncheon afterwards Herbert Vaughan proposed a toast to Pope Leo XIII and "Her Majesty the Queen," observing that none of Queen Victoria's subjects were more loyal "than the Catholics of this country."[48]

The building of the cathedral during the final eight years of his life was symbolic of his personal attitude and also considered a "symbol of Catholic resurgence, a visible monument to the triumphalism of the ultramontane church." Thanks to the determination and financial acumen of Herbert

Vaughan and the architectural genius of John F. Bentley, the main structure would be completed by 1903.[49]

In Owen Chadwick's opinion, the construction of the cathedral was also a symbol of something else, the Roman Catholic community's ability to "at last build well and expensively."[50] At least one Irish priest working in London connected similar expenditures with the problem of leakage from the Catholic community.[51]

Cardinal Wiseman had considered building a cathedral and spoke of it a few months before his death.[52] When Henry Manning was elected archbishop he held a public meeting, on 25 May 1865, at which he asked that the cathedral project be undertaken as a permanent memorial to the late Nicholas Wiseman. "The See of Westminster needed a Cathedral proportionate to the chief diocese of the Catholic Church ... in the British Empire," Manning said. But before this could take place, he continued, the thousands of poor Catholic children of the diocese, especially those in non-Catholic workhouses, industrial and reformatory schools must be provided for.[53] As a result of the meeting a cathedral account was opened, contributions solicited, and a search for a site begun.

Purcell quotes Manning asking whether he could "leave twenty thousand children without education and drain my funds and my flock to pile up stones on bricks."[54] However, it was Manning who acquired a plot of land at Carlisle Place for £16,500. He then bought an adjoining property for £20,000; paying £14,000 cash and taking a mortgage on the balance for about £1,000 a year. In 1872 Manning used his own money to buy a building called the "Guards' Institute" on the south side of the cathedral plot. After alterations, he moved in during March 1873 and it became Archbishop's House, where he lived till his death. Mr Henry Clutton designed a cathedral with dimensions of four hundred and fifty feet by two hundred and fifty feet, and Manning approved of his plan. Although he had no funds available he was pleased to have at least safeguarded a future building site and an architect's plan.

In 1882 a potential benefactor—at least that is what he appeared to be—Sir Tatton Sykes, whose wife was a convert, offered to build the cathedral at his own expense. The plans proposed for the building were modeled on "a votive church in Vienna." In 1883 Manning paid off the debt on the property. Then a new four-acre parcel of nearby land came up for sale; it was part of the old Middlesex County Prison of Tothill Fields. With the help of legal and financial advisors, Manning paid for the four acres with the land he had acquired earlier, along with a £20,000 mortgage.

Manning wrote to Vaughan on 23 February 1884: "We are now legal owners of the prison land. I went over it yesterday—I can hardly believe that the Middlesex magistrates are out and the Catholic Church is in." Manning's hopes were not realized. Cardinal Manning's cathedral benefactor disappointed him, and, according to Snead-Cox, the disappointment was a bad one. It came as that "worst of all the forms of disappointment, the disappointment which presents itself as final," and for the remainder of his life Manning left his plans for a cathedral in abeyance.[55]

When Herbert Vaughan arrived at Westminster he immediately decided to take up the cathedral project once again and to build one that would be a liturgical, pastoral and intellectual centre for English Catholicism.[56] De l'Hopital says that "he plunged almost immediately with characteristic vehemence into the labour of cathedral building."[57] Vaughan often described his vision of a cathedral that would be very much alive as the "head and the heart of the life of the Church in England and the vivifying centre of its spirit and worship. It was to be the home of a companionship of priests, the example of whose lives should colour all the ideals and activities of the diocese." Above all it should be a "splendid and fitting shrine for the Sacred Liturgy."[58]

When Vaughan and Snead-Cox paced up and down the drive in front of the Midland Station Hotel in May 1892, he told Snead-Cox of his plans to build a "great cathedral." John Snead-Cox, in silence, thought such a project was beyond Vaughan's strength. He knew that the criticism would be that the Church had so many other commitments, so why was money being wasted "upon bricks and mortar." But Vaughan felt certain that the revival of the Catholic Church in England had reached a point in its development when the restoration of the life of a cathedral was a necessity. It was an opportunity to bring to completion the work begun at the restoration of the hierarchy in 1850.[59] First and foremost, according to Snead-Cox, Vaughan committed himself to the idea because "it made possible the most perfect and devotional rendering of the great prayer of the Church." According to Peter Doyle, whatever else might be subject to compromise in Vaughan's vision of a cathedral in central London, one remained untouched: "the full, daily Divine Office would be carried out there with as much dignity and ceremonial as possible."[60]

Vaughan faced criticism about building a cathedral just as Manning had before him. Among the comments: money lavished on such a project robbed the poor, and the time of cathedrals was the Middle Ages. The project had also failed to capture the imagination of the greater part of the Catholic population who would be expected to finance its building.[61] In addition, English Catholics might be embarrassed if it was never completed or was done poorly in such a short space of time. Vaughan envisioned a cathedral "roofed and fit for service within five years." Some wondered how this could be possible "when our devout forefathers sometimes took a century."[62] Opponents to the project also doubted Vaughan's ability to complete it, leaving an "unfinished folly."[63] While critics were sceptical of Vaughan's ability to collect the enormous sums needed, he had no doubts at all. It was his "confidence in God" that formed the "dynamics of Herbert Vaughan's life, and the secret of his success."[64]

John Francis Bentley

Another aspect of the dynamic at work in Vaughan's life was that he acted with the decision of a man who experienced neither doubts nor hesitations. He knew exactly what he wanted a cathedral for. For example, it was for the use of a congregation and therefore he wanted a great open space, capable of accommodating a large number of people with a view of the high altar.[65]

On 29 May 1894 Vaughan sent Mary Elizabeth Herbert proofs of an appeal he planned to circulate, at first privately, among persons likely to contribute to the project. Sir Tatton Sykes, the person who had disappointed Manning, was included in order to bring him "to the point of giving or refusing—giving that is, not the whole cathedral but a substantial donation."[66]

The Duke of Norfolk had already promised £10,000. On 20 July 1894 Vaughan wrote that the cathedral collection was going on privately and there were already promises of over half the amount needed. In the private circular he sent out in July, he proposed a building that would not "drain and exhaust all our resources to erect it, starving and stunting growth in all other directions." This was his response to the policy of the late Henry Manning.[67]

To cut costs, he proposed to use the site acquired by Manning and to build the shell of the cathedral big enough for "all practical purposes," adopting the "ancient Basilica style, taking Constantine's Church of St. Peter in Rome as the model." Vaughan looked for an architect and first thought to select one by means of a competition among Catholics. He abandoned the idea of a competition when he saw how often the name of John Francis Bentley was recommended. In July he wrote to his secretary, Austin Oates, that he had preferred a competition but the "Finance Board and others want me to appoint the architect without competition—in that case I shall choose Bentley, I think."[68] Ten days later, he did.

Bentley immediately travelled to Italy to revisit some of the finer examples of Byzantine architecture, but he would have preferred a Gothic structure, as would many others. Generally the idea of a Byzantine cathedral in London was "at the outset unpopular." But Vaughan also saw the wisdom of avoiding any sort of comparison with Westminster Abbey.

In the meantime, Vaughan threw himself into raising funds, a "work that was intensely distasteful to him," but he persevered, repeating to himself: "I must have the courage of my cause."[69]

Bentley returned from his tour and suggested a synthesis that was a "combination of the idea of a Roman Basilica with the constructive improvements introduced by the Byzantine architects."[70] From the day the foundation stone was laid in 1895, construction of the cathedral went ahead relentlessly until it was opened for a public service eight years later to receive the earthly remains of its founder Herbert Vaughan.[71]

The Benedictines

On the day that the foundation was laid, Vaughan included in his address a dream of Benedictine monks returning to Westminster. They would carry out the liturgy "in all its fulness" as it was "of old in Westminster and Canterbury." It was an imaginative plan, but it led Herbert Vaughan and his cathedral project into another controversy. René Kollar, the author of a recent history of Westminster Cathedral, concludes that Vaughan's problems with the cathedral, and with the Benedictines he hoped might staff it, arose from the Cardinal's personality: "By nature a romantic, he planned the construction of his new cathedral complete with a contingent of Benedictines." For Vaughan and some "pious Catholics" it was to be a new Church arising from the "destruction of the Reformation."[72] Snead-Cox considered the idea of the return of Benedictines to Westminster as one that appealed to Vaughan's historic sense, and that he also believed there was no other body of men in the country capable of rendering the sacred liturgy "with reverence and stately splendour." To him it seemed so natural that he announced that the English Benedictines would come to Westminster without having made a definite arrangement with them. But soon he began to see the problems such an arrangement would cause if the Benedictines were to be given two missions that would be combined to form a cathedral parish.[73]

The Benedictines had been evicted from Westminster by Elizabeth I in 1558. Vaughan's dream did not appreciate the difficulties the restoration of the order would cause among his own clergy. The perception was that the diocesan clergy were not up to the task of performing the Cathedral's liturgy and so the Benedictines were being called in.[74]

In May 1896 Vaughan contacted Hugh Edmund Ford, the superior of St Gregory's Benedictine Abbey at Downside, to arrange for the return of their community to Westminster. He planned to have them take over a mission and purchase property where monks could live and travel to the Cathedral to celebrate the liturgy. The place Vaughan offered was at Ealing in West London on the main railway line to Paddington; it was also on the District Line to Victoria. Ford had his own dream for the Benedictines and it involved more than supplying the ceremonies at the Cathedral.[75]

According to Kollar, Ford was a prudent man who was cautious of "any rash or unplanned action" that might be harmful to his community.[76] He insisted that the Ealing mission must also include pastoral work. Ford's position was clear: he would gladly assign monks for Westminster Cathedral, but only if pastoral duties formed part of the agreement.[77] Vaughan agreed to these and other conditions proposed by Ford, if the monks would provide the singing of the divine office at the cathedral.

Richard O'Halloran

In 1897 Ealing mission was officially handed over to the Downside Benedictines. Unfortunately for the monks and Cardinal Vaughan, Ealing mission was still in the care of Father Richard O'Halloran. O'Halloran had been ordained a priest of St Joseph's Missionary Society in 1880. He promptly left the society, and for much of his life became the "adversary and enemy" of Herbert Vaughan. When Vaughan was appointed to Westminster, he found O'Halloran in the diocese. He assigned him the mission of St Joseph and St Peter at Ealing, which O'Halloran was now asked to vacate and hand over to the Benedictines in 1897. However, the Benedictine Bernard Bulbeck met a defiant O'Halloran on his arrival at Ealing on 12 March 1897. "Death alone removes me from the Rectorship here," said O'Halloran.[78]

It was not long before the London newspapers became aware of the controversy. The *Daily Chronicle* wrote in July 1897 of Vaughan's "arbitrary episcopal action" and the "resistance of secular priests to the encroachments of the religious orders." Readers were told that Vaughan had "lent himself to methods which however familiar they are to the monkish fraternity, seem out of sympathy with his own geniality of disposition."[79] According to Kollar, the Roman Catholic Press refused to waste much ink on the antics of Richard O'Halloran.

O'Halloran, for his part, continued to criticize Vaughan and the Downside Benedictines publicly. "The Cardinal has no more right to send monks into my mission and attack me ... than a highwayman has a right by violence to knock down and plunder a respectable citizen." He tried, but failed, to enlist the support of secular clergy in his campaign against the Cardinal. He portrayed Vaughan as a bigot and himself as a persecuted Irish priest, alleging that Vaughan had told an associate that he wanted to "starve out the beggarly Irishman."[80]

While the problems with the angry O'Halloran continued, the Benedictines worked to establish their new foundation at Ealing. On 5 January 1899 Dom Gilbert Nolan arrived, purchased land, and began to build a new church. Soon afterwards, he urged Downside to build a school. O'Halloran remained at Ealing until 1914, when he was excommunicated by Rome.[81]

Solesmes Benedictines

Other problems arose from the proposal that Downside Benedictines help at the new cathedral. The request by Downside that a monastery be built to house the monks and that they were to have the "use of one of the chapels in the cathedral for their private offices in perpetuity" was part of it. In addition, their request for missionary work at the cathedral posed what seemed an insoluble situation: "a double set of clergy serving under separate superiors" at Westminster.[82]

Looking for a way out of the difficulty with Downside, Vaughan turned his attention to another Benedictine congregation at Solesmes in France. He thought they might be ready to devote themselves exclusively to a "life of prayer and work of singing the Divine Office." In December 1900 he wrote to Abbot Gasquet at Downside that he "could not expect a religious congregation like yours to sacrifice the missionary character of their constitution by confining its members to the choral service of the cathedral." He explained that he understood that the Solesmes community confined their "vocation to the solemn singing of the office." He had visited France but had made no decision about the matter. Vaughan enclosed a letter from Père Paul Delatte, Abbot of Solesmes.

Unfortunately, writes Snead-Cox, if Solesmes was to be of any assistance, they would be dependent on the help of Downside. The answer from Downside was decisive. They had never taken the initiative in the matter of the cathedral and the new scheme was something else again. What Vaughan thought was to be an act of fellowship between Benedictines working for a common cause appeared in a different light to the English Benedictines. The plan was "set aside" by Downside and the English Benedictines "as quite unworkable." According to Snead-Cox, when Vaughan heard that the negotiations had fallen through, he was relieved.[83]

Finally he decided on a simpler solution: The black cowls of Benedictine monks would not return to Westminster, but instead the liturgy was entrusted to the secular clergy. In the spring of 1901 the Westminster chapter "uniformly declared its entire concurrence with the proposal made by his Eminence with respect to the Choir service of the Cathedral."[84] Vaughan announced the decision to call in the secular clergy and to form the Cathedral Choir School in a June 1901 issue of *The Tablet*.[85]

Herbert Vaughan had seriously underestimated the English Benedictine congregation. Like Wiseman fifty years earlier, he too miscalculated the homage, reverence and tradition attached to Westminster. Therefore, it should be served only by English monks, and to invite a French group was unacceptable. In this matter Vaughan misread the sensitivity of the English Benedictines. Abbot Gasquet, on the other hand, accused Vaughan of deception in dealing with Solesmes and claimed that the Solesmes congregation had broken ecclesiastical protocol.[86] Gasquet's long letter excused Vaughan of any "malicious intent," for it was "obvious to everyone of us that you could not have understood the proposals made by the Abbot of Solesmes." Gasquet suggested as a solution that secular priests perform the ceremonies and a choral school be established.[87]

On 7 May 1902, the eve of the Feast of the Ascension, the Divine Office was sung by the new cathedral choir for the first time.[88] And so Herbert Vaughan had achieved his goal of plainchant being sung in the new cathedral, ensured the loyalty and gratitude of the cathedral chapter, and peace between the religious and secular clergy over the liturgy performed, if not the services of the Benedictines.[89] In the summer of 1980, on the fifteen hundredth anniversary of St Benedict's birth, three hundred monks joined for a special Mass at the Cathedral. "Cardinal Vaughan's dream," writes Kollar, "of uniting the Benedictines with Westminster was finally realized."[90]

Kenelm Vaughan

The Cardinal's brother, Kenelm, was also associated with the cathedral project. In 1896 he left for Spain and the Americas to collect money for a "chapel of expiation and adoration" in honour of the Blessed Sacrament. He was away for eleven years.[91] Kenelm spent two years in Spain and collected £4000. King Alfonso XIII and Queen Mother Maria Cristina were among his benefactors. In 1898, during the war between the United States and Spain, he went to South America where he spent nine years and collected a total of £18,634. The Blessed Sacrament Chapel at the cathedral was to be a gift of the people of Spain and the Spanish nations of South America.[92] Kenelm wrote an account of his travels in South America, which was published in Spanish in the United States. An article in the *American Catholic Historical Society* called it "a treasure store of information with regard to the attitude and mind of the people generally towards the Church in nearly all the countries of South America."[93]

One letter to Kenelm expressed the attraction some Spanish-speaking Catholics felt for the project of building a Catholic cathedral in London. It was from ex-president Batista of Bolivia: "It has been a magnificent thought to set this solidarity in the service of religion for the foundation of a chapel which will attest to the piety of Spaniard and Spanish-American in the very heart of the protestant metropolis of England."[94] Kenelm Vaughan continued to travel and was away when his brother died in 1903. Kenelm died on 19 May 1909.

The Relics of St Edmund, King and Martyr

Vaughan was to be disappointed in another dream he had for the cathedral. It was to be not only a symbol of Catholic resurgence in England, but also a shrine for the holy relics of St Edmund, 841-869, king of East Anglia, martyred by the Vikings. Westminster Abbey held the relics of Edward the Confessor; the new cathedral would have those of Edmund, martyr and king. Furthermore, Vaughan's visions for Westminster Cathedral included Benedictine monks; adding a display of the relics of a major English saint would have had the effect of presenting a cathedral that was the heir of the Benedictine cathedrals of medieval England.[95]

In 1893, a Benedictine priest, J. B. MacKinlay, published a book entitled *St Edmund, King and Martyr*. MacKinlay stated that the body of St Edmund had been taken by French soldiers, after their defeat at Lincoln in 1217, from its shrine at Bury St Edmunds to Toulouse and placed in the basilica of Saint Sernin. According to the story, in 1664 the bones were transferred to a silver shrine in the basilica. When Herbert Vaughan heard about the English saint and martyr's remains being in the south of France, he resolved to do whatever he could to bring them to Westminster Cathedral. Henry Manning had already shown interest in the relics and had obtained some bones. Vaughan never thought to question their authenticity.

However, even if the Church authorities at Toulouse could be persuaded to part with the relics, it was doubtful that the French government would allow their transfer to England. In secrecy, Vaughan negotiated for Toulouse to give the remains to Pope Leo XIII, knowing that he would in turn give them to England. In July 1901 the relics were taken to Rome. Mgr Merry del Val was chosen to bring them to Cardinal Vaughan. Only after he had started for England, an English priest at Rome heard about the arrangement, and, knowing something of the relics and of Toulouse, warned that they ought not to be offered for public veneration until their authenticity was verified. But it was too late: they were already on their way to the Duke of Norfolk's Arundel Castle, where they were to remain until a shrine could be prepared at the new cathedral.

The Tablet of 27 July 1901 contained the first of a series of articles by MacKinlay entitled "The Return of St Edmund." "So far all had gone well," wrote Snead-Cox, but soon a "storm of controversy" broke out in the newspapers. The bones, it turned out, were certainly those of someone venerated for ages as a saint but it was suspected they "were not those of the Saxon king."[96]

Cardinal Vaughan read letters to *The Times* about the relics, morning after morning, especially one by Sir Ernest Clarke, with the "saddest sense of frustration. He had worked so hard and succeeded so well—and all in vain."

Vaughan prepared to speak at an annual conference in Newcastle on 9 September 1901, where he would respond to the questions raised about the relics. Before he slept, on the night before his speech, he had Ernest Clarke's letter in front of him. "He was alone with the truth," wrote Snead-Cox. He thought of the friends at Toulouse who had given their treasured relics and the people at Rome who had helped. The next evening not only did he accept that he had made a mistake, but he thanked the man who had destroyed his illusions. "Having built a cathedral, the thought ... occurred to me of enriching it with the relics of St. Edmund the King. To me ... without experience ... the matter seemed to be certain.... Shortly after their arrival in England two learned authorities, Dr. James, of Cambridge, and Dr. Bigg, of Oxford wrote letters to *The Times* calling in question their authenticity.... I determined to submit the whole question to experts.... But last Thursday, Sir Ernest Clarke published the report." Clarke's evidence seemed "overwhelming and conclusive" to Vaughan and he offered him his "hearty and sincere thanks for the services he appears to have rendered."

At Toulouse many thought he acted with "unnecessary haste, and perhaps even with less than due regard for his own dignity." Snead-Cox adds: "I think his own countrymen were wiser."[97]

Cathedral Construction continued

While the problems over the return of the Benedictines continued and the controversy over the authenticity of the relics of St Edmund came and went, the construction of the cathedral continued. The foundations were completed in September 1896, and, in November, a contract was signed with Shillitoe and Son for the superstructure.[98] Bentley was working under immense pressure. At one point he produced a set of designs for the marble pavements. Instead a decision was made to substitute wood-block flooring in the nave and aisles that was based on utilitarian and economic grounds; this was seen by Bentley as a climax of previous disappointments at the hands of Cardinal Vaughan. For example, Vaughan ordered at Rome, without consulting Bentley, an "entirely unsuitable pulpit and throne." Vaughan mentions in a letter of 15 May 1902 that he had as a gift from a Mr Kennedy a "beautiful Byzantine pulpit which Cavaliere a Leonori has designed in Rome." De l'Hôpital philosophizes: "Rare indeed is the architect whose vision finds its perfect fulfilment. To Bentley was given a great opportunity and he used it nobly."

Bentley did not listen to those who called the building a "wedding cake," or "Cardinal Vaughan's Railway Station," or the "Roman Candle." At the same time there were some who called his work "a great artistic triumph."[99] Once Vaughan was showing a friend around the unfinished cathedral when his guest said "candidly that he thought the architectural style a mistake, and the campanile in particular, 'hideous.'" Vaughan only laughed at his friend: "There are plenty of people who agree with you, although I do not myself."[100]

Some thought that Westminster Cathedral, especially its unfinished interior, had a special dignity. More than sixty years later a writer for *The Universe and Catholic Times* thought that the "brickwork and high undecorated domes have created an atmosphere that causes many who visit Westminster to hope that further progress will halt until after they are dead."

There were delays in construction. One was a bricklayers' strike. Another was a war between Greece and Turkey, which held up the transportation of columns from an ancient Thessalonian quarry; the columns were captured and held as spoils of war. In addition, a severe winter made progress on the exterior walls impossible.[101]

Bentley died in 1902, and at his funeral Vaughan said that he was a "poet; he saw and felt the beauty, the fancy, the harmony and meaning of artistic recreations. He had no love of money, he cared little for economy; he had an immense love of art, a passion for truth and simplicity in his work." Vaughan concluded that he had a "critical but kindly humour.... One always felt that there were an elevation and inspiration in his mind and character that were due to his religious instincts and to his unworldly standard of life."[102] Vaughan wrote to Mary Elizabeth Herbert that Bentley's death came when the whole of his architectural work was completed and only the decorating remained to be completed, for which he left some drawings. Near the end Bentley's "nerves were shattered and his memory almost as affected as his speech. He put the whole of his life and soul into the Cathedral and it killed him, not the designing but the carrying it out." Leslie writes in a footnote that "Bentley certainly designed and enclosed the 'space' ordered by the Cardinal. His nerves led him to believe the Cathedral domes would collapse."[103]

The first "public body" to enter the cathedral were the children "Crusaders" of the Crusade of Rescue. In 1901 Vaughan had determined to receive the children and their alms at the cathedral in April. The Crusaders came to his old house in Carlisle Place, where Vaughan gave them buns and oranges. After they handed in the money each group had collected, he led them through the sacristy into the cathedral. They turned half of the building into a playground. "Being gloriously human, in spite of their passionate philanthropic zeal, they had a thoroughly happy time—upsetting loads of mortar, overturning piles of bricks, and mixing sand with putty, to their hearts' content." When the workers reported the damage done by the children, Vaughan was not annoyed: "He was content to feel that for those children their first recollection of his cathedral would be associated forever with a happy memory."[104]

On Ascension Day in May 1902, for the first time the whole of the Divine Office was prayed and Mass offered in the Chapter Hall which was attached to the cathedral. The Chapter Hall was arranged like the Sistine Chapel. The following month the archbishop's throne was moved from the Pro-Cathedral to the Chapter Hall.[105] On Lady Day in 1903, the area that was to become the Cathedral's Lady Chapel was screened off in order to use it temporarily for the local parish mission community.[106] On 11 June a concert was given of works by Wagner and Beethoven. Vaughan was assured afterwards that "the Church is good for sound, both for the singer and the speaker."[107] On 6 June 1903 there was a second musical presentation, Newman's "Dream of Gerontius," set by Sir Edward Elgar. It was the first time a London audience had heard the work. The composer was present, along with one hundred performers and Ludwig Wullner as Gerontius.[108]

Not many days passed before Cardinal Herbert Vaughan's funeral took place in the cathedral's vaulted space. On the centenary of his birth in 1932 *The Tablet* wrote: "The final great material work of Cardinal Vaughan was the building of Westminster Cathedral. Into the vast spaces of that unfinished church his body was taken, in 1903, for the solemn requiem which—unforeseen—was to constitute the Cathedral's opening ceremony. Thence back again to the beloved College at Mill Hill, where a few days previously this same servant of God had prepared to meet the Divine Judge and breathed his last sigh."[109]

Later the remains of Wiseman and Manning were brought from Kensal Green cemetery to the crypt of the cathedral. A small chapel of St Thomas of Canterbury contains an effigy of Vaughan and is known as Cardinal Vaughan's Chantry.[110]

Wales

In an address given at Courtfield in 1986, Daniel J. Mullins, Bishop of Menevia, stated that "all the important developments of the Church in England and Wales in our time owe much to the inspiration and vision of . . . Cardinal Vaughan." When he was a young man Vaughan had looked to Wales as the possible place where he could be a missionary priest. He never forgot his early dreams.[111]

In September 1893, at the opening of a new church in Llandudno, Herbert Vaughan talked about the possible reorganization of the Catholic Church in Wales. Apparently, he was accompanied by the Lord Mayor of London for the occasion. At a dinner that evening he spoke to the guests and told them they would soon have their own bishop. Since the restoration of the hierarchy in 1850, the southern half of Wales, together with Herefordshire, had formed the diocese of Newport and Menevia—north Wales was part of the diocese of Shrewsbury. Vaughan understood that such organization did not make adequate provision for an apostolate to Welsh-speaking Wales, despite the fact that the "post-Restoration Church saw itself in unambiguous missionary terms."[112]

In a letter to the prioress of the Carmelite Monastery, Notting Hill, he wrote that one of his first acts on going to Westminster was to get the bishops "to agree to petition the Holy See to make Wales independent of England by giving it a Welsh Bishop and a chance of conversion."[113]

The Liberal government that came to power in 1892 set up a commission to study the "Land Question" in Wales. It did not result in legislation but aired the problems of rural Wales. At the same time Welsh Liberals concentrated their attention on Church Establishment. It was a time, according to John Davies, when, although religion was still central to large numbers of the Welsh people, "Nevertheless, as commitment to Calvanism was on the wane, the differences between the denominations were slight"; an "Evangelical Concord" included almost all Nonconformists and Low Church members of the Established Church. High Church members and Roman Catholics were outside the "Concord."[114]

Herbert Vaughan, and others in the Catholic Church, saw the 1890s as a time of opportunity and so promoted a renewal of interest in Wales. *The Tablet* published a series of articles on "Catholicism in Wales," beginning in September 1892. The same month the Catholic Truth Society held its annual conference in Liverpool. One of the papers was titled: "Relation to the Catholic Church in Wales." On 20 September a trip was organized to St Winifride's Well and Pantasaph.[115]

In May 1893 Vaughan wrote to Elizabeth Herbert that he was busy working on the "Welsh Church question" and hoped that there might be a good solution.[116] He began to work on proposals concerning the "principality of Wales" during 1892-3. His seventeen pages of handwritten notes preparing a petition for Rome are in the Westminster Diocesan Archives. After tracing the history of the Church in Wales from the fourth century, he argued that it died out in the seventeenth century because of a lack of priests and Catholics "fared in this respect worse than England."

> The Welsh people never liked the Church of England and its cold services. They took warmly in the last century to dissent; and the population is now more largely under the influence of dissent than under that of the Church of England.... Though the Church of England had been altogether ne-glectful of the Welsh during more than two centuries, it has during the last twenty years become very active. The Protestant clergy learn the Welsh language and endeavour to identify themselves with the Welsh feeling and tradition.

On the other hand, the Catholic Church, according to Vaughan, had not undertaken the care of the Welsh people since the sixteenth century "in a serious, systematic and determined manner." Vaughan thought that the character of the Welsh was so different from the English that unless the Church were to make separate provisions for Wales there could be "no way of converting them so long as they are simply as it were tacked on to an English diocese." In his view, the time was opportune because there was a "most bitter contention" going on between the Dissenting Church in Wales and the Church of England.

> While these are equally matched and politically and religiously tearing each other to pieces, it is the time for the Catholic Church to come in and to say: We are the Old Church of Wales. We indeed died out through the persecu-tion of the English, but we have revived and behold the Pope has again looked upon Wales and given to Wales a Welsh leader and has recognized Wales as worthy to be treated separately from England and to stand by itself upon its ancient nationality.... No time should be lost if we are not to be too late.... The hope for Wales is in treating it purely as a missionary district.

Vaughan was preparing the petition on behalf of the English bishops. If Rome appointed a missionary bishop for the evangelization of Wales, the bishops thought it wise to "detach the eleven Welsh counties from England in order to more surely to concentrate attention upon their needs and to satisfy the national feelings of the Welsh people." That is, the six counties of north Wales and the five of south Wales, except Glamorganshire, should be detached from the dioceses of Shrewsbury and Newport to form a new diocese.[117]

The plan that Wales should have a vicar apostolic of its own had been proposed by Vaughan and taken up by the bishops. He considered Wales to be more of a missionary country than England. "It was more sparsely inhabited, Catholicism was more feeble, and the Welsh people had a peculiar national character of their own." Therefore Vaughan urged that Rome give Wales a missionary bishop of its own, a vicar apostolic, "who might have a free hand to deal with it as a missionary country."[118] Within a short time, in March 1895, the Church in Wales was reorganized.

Vaughan wrote to Notting Hill in August 1895 that the following month he was "to consecrate a Welsh Bishop—a young man full of zeal and piety and activity and good sense." The new vicar apostolic was Francis Mostyn. He promised Vaughan that he would print his pastoral letters in Welsh and English and "to identify himself in all things with the Principality. So curiously does God realise the desires He inspires! He does not forget them even after 40 years and more!"[119]

The boundary of the diocese of Newport was established and the rest of Wales was made into a vicariate apostolic; it included the whole principality except for the county of Glamorgan. Vaughan hoped that the Jesuits might take on the role of missionaries to the new Welsh vicariate. Bishop Mullins thought that such a move would have been supported by the historical connections the Jesuits had with Wales and also their presence at St Beuno's, in north Wales. "This is one of the 'ifs' of history," said Mullins. The vicariate existed for only three years and then became the diocese of Menevia on 12 May 1898.[120]

Mother Mary of Jesus

The archive of the Carmelite convent at Notting Hill in London contains approximately one hundred letters written by Herbert Vaughan after he arrived at Westminster in 1892. He became, over the final years of his life, a close friend of the community and of its prioress, Madeleine-Marie Justine Dupont, Mother Mary of Jesus.[121]

As a young girl Madeleine-Marie had prayed for direction at Notre Dame des Victoires in Paris. She found her answer and entered the Carmelite monastery of Rue d'Enfer. It was the first house of St Teresa of Avila's reform to have been founded in France. She became a postulant in 1872 and was professed on 8 September 1873. Meanwhile, in England, Cardinal Wiseman and Father Faber knew of the monastery as "the cradle of reform in France." Faber sent three candidates he had been directing to the Paris community, to apply for membership.

One of them was Sister Mary of St Joseph, a daughter of the Duke of Norfolk. She arrived with her inheritance as a dowry. Part of the money was set aside in a trust by the community for a future foundation in England. Manning, on his way to Pontigny in June 1874, stopped at Rue d'Enfer and gave permission for Sisters to come to England. In the spring of 1877, a building for a new English monastery was started on a plot next to Manning's own St Charles College in Bayswater. On the feast of St Michael in 1877, Cardinal Manning celebrated Mass for the first time in the Sisters' new home; Oratorian priests served as chaplains to the community.

When Manning died in January 1892, the nuns felt a great loss, for he was "truly a father to them during these first difficult years," and they wondered what would happen with a new archbishop. Vaughan's arrival coincided with a period of consolidation for the community and he became their "Father in God." "The most outstanding feature of this period was," according to Mother Mary's biographer, "the friendship of Cardinal Vaughan."[122]

When he was appointed to Westminster, Vaughan was a complete stranger to the community, except to Sister Mary of St Joseph. The first impression he made was not a good one. One day in June 1892 the "turn bell rang violently at 4 o'clock in the afternoon and the Archbishop was announced. Mother Mary of Jesus, taken by surprise and desperately shy, as she always was of strangers, faced the very intimidating person of her new superior through the grille." It was Vaughan "at his most formidable." He sat, to borrow her own inimitable description, "with his feet very far away, firing a series of staccato and disconcerting questions: What sort of place is this? You have a good deal of building outside, do you keep a school? Why not? The Poor Clares in Ireland keep schools, I believe." The prioress answered "humbly and nervously, but at the end of the ten minute ordeal (he was only out on a voyage of discovery) she sought out Mother Mary of the Blessed Trinity (Elizabeth Thomson) and said forlornly: 'Oh Mother it is not the Cardinal?!' "[123]

On his next visit in September, they saw another side of Vaughan. This time he entered the enclosure and saw the community, giving them a short talk "which opened out a new aspect of his personality and rejoiced the Prioress' soul." A few days later, the parents of Mother Mary of Jesus, on their way back to France, stopped to thank Vaughan: "I know that my daughter and all her daughters have a Father," said the old Frenchman, and "I can go away content." Vaughan, in turn, walking along to the door as they were going told them: "Your daughter is a little saint, I know it from everyone who has spoken to me about her."

For the next eleven years Mother Mary of Jesus was to experience "one of the deepest intimacies of her whole life with the Cardinal, marking these years as very happy ones indeed." Vaughan's impact was upon the general life of the community and upon the soul of the prioress. His most obvious contribution to the life of the community was his "painstaking and thorough revision of the

English translation of the Rule and Constitutions and the preface he wrote for it." Vaughan's discourse on the meaning of the Carmelite life "is still an inspiration to those who read it."[124] He sent it to the community as his Christmas gift in 1897.

Not only did Vaughan take an interest in his capacity as archbishop, but in other "homelier ways" too. When the monastery building was being completed, Vaughan went inside to see the work and insisted that the nuns install at least basic central heating. He dismissed pleas by the nuns that heating would not be in keeping with the ideal of the "Primitive Observance" by telling them he felt sure "St. Teresa would have supported him wholeheartedly if she had ever experienced the English climate. London was not France nor Spain, and the exposed situation of the house would render the damp a deadly and invincible enemy." In 1895 Vaughan sent his birthday cake to the monastery with a note: "To be eaten entirely by the daughters of Mt. Carmel, with all Easter joy and recreation."

The community was able to return Vaughan's kindnesses in many small ways. For example, for several years the nuns took care of cutting up, sorting and posting the "maxims" and "virtues" which formed Vaughan's usual Christmas cards to the priests and religious of the diocese. The Carmel community also began to share in the life and work of the archdiocese. Looking through Vaughan's letters it is clear that there was "hardly any event or decision of importance in his eleven years as Metropolitan that was not explicitly and firmly entrusted to Carmel's prayer."

There was another work that definitely fell within Carmel's scope, namely, Vaughan's "care for his young priests and the development of the true sacerdotal spirit within them." He did not hesitate to send Mother Mary of Jesus any of his priests who were in doubt or spiritual suffering. Her ideals were very much like his own. A priest, to her, was essentially one chosen from among men, set apart for God, "a thing sealed," as she once said.

She corresponded, for example, with one young priest who thought he had a call to become a monk: "I wish that God was putting in your soul a light to tell you of the mission in the hands of secular priests just at this moment in England. You are in just this position at this very hour; not only you are there, but your Archbishop, at the same time that he gives you freedom, advised you not to use it. Why not be a saint where you are? Why not a contemplative priest?" In a letter two weeks later she wrote: "I think He wants you to be a contemplative priest, an apostle, not in a cloister but on a mission." The priest remained a secular and years later he told of speaking to Vaughan about the matter and mentioned the advice Mother Mary of Jesus had given him. Vaughan said of Mother Mary: "She is a very superior person, she lives with God."

Herbert Vaughan asked for the prayers of the Carmel community and the offering up of their sufferings to "help me and the Church in England." The

Sisters in turn were grateful for his "many services and unwearied kindness." Because of this relationship and the urgency of his many requests for prayers, on 20 March 1895, the Feast of St Herbert, he was formally affiliated to the monastery. This made him "a participant of all the prayers, communions, vigils, fasts, abstinences, mortifications, solitude, silence and other spiritual exercises which are or shall be made in the monastery."

Mother Mary of Jesus had found the guide and counsellor she needed in Cardinal Vaughan and she submitted all important questions to him.

Perhaps, writes her biographer, the whole spirit of their mutual relationship was expressed in the carving of Vaughan's motto—*Amare et Servire*—on the back of her processional cross. In one letter he wrote that it was only through Mary of Jesus that "God speaks to me and helps me upward."[125]

In the same letter he refers to "Mother Mary of St. Teresa." This was not one of the sisters at Notting Hill but a pseudonym for Mrs Charlotte Weld-Blundell. Her name appears in a number of letters. She was Charlotte Lane-Fox, the eldest daughter of Charles D'Arcy Lane-Fox. She married Charles Weld-Blundell of Ince-Blundell, Vaughan's cousin, on 14 May 1884, at Brompton Oratory. Herbert Vaughan was the officiating priest.[126]

In his letters there are glimpses of Vaughan's own spirituality and the *fornax ardens caritatis* that was his interior life. "How has the legend of the remote, aristocratic, 'a very great prelate indeed,' persisted so long?" wonders Mother Mary's biographer. "There is little great or palatial here; only fatherly care for the soul that trusts him and a boundless desire to further its sanctity."

The Scarlet Runner

Vaughan often discussed his progress in the spiritual life with Mother Mary of Jesus. One letter written just ten days before his death thanks her "for the help and encouragement you gave me some years ago when God was beginning to draw me closer to Himself."[127] The period that Vaughan refers to was a humiliation he experienced towards the end of December 1894 when someone told him that he had scandalized others by the way he rushed through liturgical ceremonies. Snead-Cox quotes him as saying that he "looked into himself and had a revelation." He concluded that during all of his time as a bishop he had been irreverent, and for some time afterwards "he often completely broke down when saying Mass." Those who gave him the nickname of "The Scarlet Runner" did not know the agony of contrition into which the revelation plunged him.[128]

On 26 April 1895 Vaughan wrote to his successor at Salford the following letter:

I beg to avail myself of your kindness in order to bring before the clergy of my old Diocese a matter which is one of sincere grief to me, because, among other reasons, it is a wrong which I have been guilty of in their presence and to their disedification. A few months ago it was clearly brought home to my mind that during the 22 years of my Episcopate I was in the habit of performing certain sacred ceremonies and of administering the Sacrament of Confirmation with such extreme haste and hurry as to deserve the censure of scandalous irreverence. While there is yet time, I desire to make what reparation I can for such habitual misconduct and bad example. A Priest in the Sanctuary does not act in his own personal capacity nor is he there in discharge of any private office of his own. He is the Representative of Our Lord Jesus Christ and he is bound to comport himself as such before God and the people. The Council of Trent leaves no doubt as to what should be our conduct and behaviour.... I therefore beg to express before the clergy to whom as their Bishop I ought to have been an example of reverent and religious deportment in the Sanctuary, my deep and sincere grief and regret for the disedification which I gave to them during so many years by the conduct referred to. I commend myself to their charitable prayers and in return I promise ever to remember them at the altar."[129]

Vaughan had written from Rome to Carmel on 20 January 1895 "Pray for me—my 22 years of wicked and bad example in the sanctuary burns me like a hot iron." He wrote from Mill Hill on 6 May: "When you pray for this poor Father, remember unceasingly that for 22 years he betrayed his Master—the chosen representative of Christ chose deliberately to misrepresent Him by his inhuman and cruel conduct in the Sanctuary ... for me I shall never be sorry enough. I am glad you know my misery because the very sight of misery moves the heart to charity."[130] On 11 May he wrote that he was not unaware of the way he behaved because once at Salford someone had sent him a letter complaining of the way he rushed about during religious services. "It mortified me, and I resolved to keep it and read it from time to time and I did so but somehow or other it brought no amendment."[131] Snead-Cox refers briefly to the story but does not mention that he wrote an apology to Salford and apologized publicly to his priests in a synod at Westminster, nor how it nearly crushed Vaughan's spirit.

In Vaughan, Mother Mary of Jesus met what her biographer calls "the inner soul of traditional English Catholicism." The others she had known were either converts or those who owed much to the spirit of Fr Faber and the London Oratory. Here she met other characteristics: "hidden springs of tenderness and piety that had produced the Jesus Psalter in days of old, with its simple love and homely phrasing, and the silent, unadorned sanctity of men like Bishop Challoner." She needed this insight for the work she was to embark on in founding other Carmelite communities—the first in Lancashire. Before her death, thirty-eight Carmelite monasteries were founded, twenty-eight of which are still in existence.[132]

Joseph Jerome Vaughan, O.S.B.

Herbert Vaughan's brother Joseph, a Benedictine priest, died on 12 September 1896. *The Tablet* wrote that the great work of his life was the foundation of Fort Augustus Abbey and the revival of monasticism in Scotland. Joseph was suffering from dropsy and finally had a fatal stroke.[133] It was a sad end, for he had left Fort Augustus in 1887 a broken man.[134]

After he left Scotland, with Herbert's approval from Salford, he founded St Peter's Priory at Chorlton-cum-Hardy, a suburb of Manchester. On 12 March 1892, Bishop Vaughan said the first Mass in a small temporary home. On 19 March the house was opened. The following November it moved to a permanent residence on Barlow Moor Road. It was to be a new congregation: St Gregory the Great's Society for the Conversion of England. Its members were to devote their lives exclusively to the "Conversion of Our Spiritual Brethren and of the Heathen at Home."[135] Herbert Vaughan hoped the congregation would work to evangelize the non-Catholic population of England, but before long Jerome's health broke down completely.

Jerome's departure from Fort Augustus had not been cordial and to defend himself, in 1894, Joseph, or Dom Jerome as he was called in religious life, had printed a reply to an article he considered unfairly critical of him when he was at Fort Augustus. The article he found offensive was printed in the *Pall Mall Gazette* of 17 and 20 April 1894. Dom Jerome called his reply: "A Monastic Autobiography of Twenty-five years."[136]

The prospect of Dom Jerome's book reaching the public alarmed his Benedictine colleagues. He was writing to defend his actions when he was prior at Fort Augustus. A note in an extract from his book says that "as for the Prior's position—it was unique in the history of English monasticism very much so indeed, as is this booklet as an autobiography."[137]

Dom Oswald Hunter-Blair wrote to Vaughan's successor at Salford, Bishop Bilsborrow, on 18 June 1894, asking him to "prevent the scandal to religion" and a cruel wrong to himself and others by printing and circulating a "document of such a nature." Hunter-Blair thought it "incredible" that any priest was capable of printing and disseminating injurious and calumnious statements gained through Vaughan's "confidential knowledge acquired as superior" of Fort Augustus.[138] On 22 June Adrian Weld-Blundell of the Fort Augustus Abbey School wrote to confirm that Dom Jerome had obeyed his brother Cardinal Vaughan's order not to publish such a "scandalous, disgraceful pamphlet." Dom Jerome was also told by his brother Herbert to send to him the copies of the booklet he had printed. Dom Adrian continued: "I believe Father Jerome usually holds his brother, the Cardinal, to be his immediate superior but the latter seems to support the Bishop of Salford (as the ecclesiastical superior of Prior Jerome)."[139]

To recover his health, Dom Jerome left for Australia. He wrote to his brother, Herbert, from San Francisco three months before his death: "The long sea voyage to Australia did me much good. When I left Chorlton you will remember that I was a wreck unfit for any work at all, and that your kind instructions in your letter of permission to leave Chorlton was that I had better not return until I had quite regained my strength."[140]

In Australia and New Zealand he was well received and lectured and collected funds for what the *Tasmanian Mail* of 15 February 1896 called "a great philanthropic scheme for the uplifting of humanity."[141] While in New Zealand he had a heart attack and for "some days was swaying between life and death." In San Francisco he was struck with "general prostration and dropsy below the knees" caused by a "malfunction of the heart." Jerome asked his brother for news of St Peter's Priory: "It is for your Lordship's Diocese that I have in reality been spending myself and my aim and hope was to have built at Chorlton, St. Peter's Church of Intercession for England's Conversion. If God spares me I may yet accomplish this!"[142]

Jerome died soon after returning home. He was not able to honour the obligations of the Congregation of St Gregory at Chorlton, but his estate did so after his death. Hugh Ford at Downside wrote to Salford immediately after Jerome's death instructing that all copies of his suppressed autobiography were to be burned "except for six which you can bring away."[143]

All that remained at Chorlton were two pictures, of St Benedict and St Scholastica, and a set of priory chairs.

Notes

1. Zwierlein, Corrigan to McQuaid, p.31; cf. chapter X.
2. Snead-Cox, 2, p.2; J. Anselm Wilson, *The Life of Bishop Hedley*, London, Burns & Oates, 1929, p.158: John Cuthbert Hedley was a name that was "in the minds of many as a possible if not a probable choice."
3. WDA. Manning scrapbook: "Here in Rome, the Bishop and her ladyship are spoken of as 'the two Herberts.' The widow of the late Mr Sydney Herbert is noted for her feats of ecclesiastical bloomerism." The article reflects a meanness probably rooted in anti-Catholicism, and, among Catholics, in the old struggles of Wiseman with his chapter. It continues: "She gives herself the allure of a mitred abbess unattached, and created considerable annoyance during the incidents surrounding the giving of the 'hat' to Cardinal Newman by reading an address before the assembled English College. The Roman Catholic clergy are however determined to struggle against this scheme of centralisation of Cardinal Manning;" in having Vaughan as his successor.
4. WDA. Manning scrapbook: *Evening News*, Thursday 26 March 1885: "... Bishop Vaughan is anything but popular, because when he was officiating in the Archdiocese of Westminster, he was always to the front in discussions of questions of discipline." The only support he had, according to the article, was among the "aristocratic set, not including the Duke of Norfolk;" Schiefen, *Wiseman*, p.255; Snead-Cox, 1, pp.374-402.
5. Ward, *Transition*, p.260.
6. Snead-Cox, 2, pp.2-3.
7. McClelland, "English Roman Catholics," p.365.
8. Cf. Chapter XIII; Ward, *Transition*, p.260.
9. Snead-Cox, 2, pp.3-4.; Holmes, *More Roman*, p.200.

10. Leslie, *Vaughan Letters*, p.404.

11. One of the Bickersteth family was Edward, who, in 1815, while a solicitor in Norwich, became formally associated with the Church Missionary Society. He was ordained and sent out to visit Sierra Leone. On returning to England he became assistant secretary of the C M S.... See: Jocelyn Murry, *Proclaim the Good News*, London, Hodder and Stoughton, 1985, p.13.

12. MHA. HCV. Box 33. Scrapbooks; Some years later a Catholic paper in the United States commented on the choice of Vaughan: "He differs, of course, in some things from Cardinals Wiseman and Manning. He lacks the personal magnetism which the first archbishop of Westminster possessed, and he is more of an aristocrat than was Cardinal Manning, who found himself more at home in his study or arbitrating in behalf of striking London dockmen than attending royal receptions. He is the owner of the London *Tablet*, whose antagonism to home rule for Ireland makes that paper anything but acceptable to the Irish people, but whose journalistic ability and excellence cannot be denied even by those who dislike it most." *The Catholic Transcript*, Hartford, Conn., Friday 3 February 1899; Newsome, "Manning's influence," *RH*, p.144; Newsome, *Convert Cardinals*, p.318.

13. *The Tablet*, 2 April 1892, p.552.

14. *The Tablet*, 16 April 1892, p.632.

15. Snead-Cox, 2, pp.8-9.

16. "At St John's Cathedral," *The Tablet*, 23 April 1892, p.662; *The Tablet* also reported the annual "Consular Dinner in Manchester," where Vaughan spoke. The chairman introduced him: "They were honoured by having with them as a guest one whom they all loved and revered—a gentleman who for long had held high rank in his Church, and whose elevation to a still higher rank ... they all felt to be an honour personal to themselves and to their city. His Grace the Archbishop of Westminster had, as Herbert Vaughan, Bishop of Salford, done great work for his Church, its schools, its waifs and strays, and for its charities." Vaughan responded: "... he loved the open-hearted and breezy atmosphere, moral as well as physical, which characterized this part of Lancashire. One always knew when one was in Manchester, or at least if one did not one was very soon told." He admitted that "he did not quite know how it might be amongst the courtesies and refinements and the critical modes of thought which were found in the South of England;" On Sunday 24 April, Vaughan spoke at St Francis Church at Gorton. A brass band welcomed him and he entered after Mass. He had first visited Gorton years before "one winter's night, not as Bishop of a district, but as a poor priest, in order to collect alms for the education of priests to go to the foreign missions." He also reminded the three hundred supporters of the Rescue Society that it was now in their hands. *The Tablet*, 30 April 1892, p.712.

17. Notre Dame University Archives. Ellis Schreiber, London, 29 April 1892, to Father Daniel E. Hudson, CSC.

18. See: *The Month*, April 1936, CLXVII, no.862, pp.354ff, fn.1.

19. SDA. *Almanac*, 1893; *Laity Directories*, 1873.

20. Snead-Cox, 2, pp.10-11.

21. WDA. *National Catholic Directory*, 1893.

22. Gavin Weightman and Steve Humphries, *The Making of Modern London, 1815-1914*, London, Sidgwick and Jackson, 1983.

23. Leslie, *Vaughan Letters*, p.404.

24. At the meeting concerning a Manning memorial: He called for a collection for something that was "thoroughly practical" to be established in memory of Manning in the midst of the poor of London, especially in the East of the city where people from all over the world "in hundreds and thousands mingling with our own poor suffering fellow country-men," lived. *The Tablet*, 30 April 1892, p.689; The meeting at the Manchester Free Trade Hall was attended by about six thousand Catholics with "no fewer than 200 clergy of the diocese." It opened with a concert given by a boys' choir and "artistes." In the middle of the performance, Vaughan

entered the hall "and received an enthusiastic reception, the vast audience cheering again and again." At the end of his talk he repeated an anecdote of St John Fisher: When he was bishop, Rochester was not a wealthy diocese, but when, after ruling there for many years, it was proposed that he be moved to another see, he said: "Ah, I love my poor old wife too well, and have no desire to change her for any widow that may be going, however rich she may be." *The Tablet*, 7 May 1892, pp.739-40.

25. SDA. "Reply by the Archbishop-Elect to an address of the clergy and laity of the Diocese of Westminster," Salford, 1892; Herbert, Vaughan Letters, p.405: 15 May 1892. Vaughan kept up a practice he began at Salford of having his pastoral addresses printed and sold at all church-doors. In this address he found "people very kindly disposed towards it (the reply) and there seems to be a disposition to prepare to work." Over eight thousand copies had already been sold by 15 May.

26. *The Tablet*, 14 May 1892; Over the following weeks, Vaughan preached his first sermon: at the opening of St Stephen's Church, Shepherd's Bush, in which he called upon parishioners to make themselves into a model mission; He attended the wedding of relatives in June: Charles Clifford and Cecile De Trafford: "His Grace said weddings usually had a tinge of sorrow, because they generally meant the loss sustained by two families in order to create a third.... The Archbishop had known the bride since she was a child in arms, and had watched over her innocent education, and he knew what Lady Annette de Trafford would feel in losing her presence from her happy home." *The Tablet*, 4 June 1892, p.902.

27. Snead-Cox, 2, pp.15-21.

28. Leslie, *Vaughan Letters*, pp.405.

29. McCormack, pp.232-3; Holmes, *More Roman*, pp.200-201; *The Tablet*, 27 August 1892, pp.337-8: On Wednesday 24 August, Vaughan consecrated Mgr Bilsborrow Bishop of Salford. At a luncheon in the Salford Town Hall Vaughan spoke: "He said it was just 20 years ago since he stood in that very place and had to thank those present for their kindness in drinking to his health. Twenty years had passed and the old Bishop of Salford had disappeared. (Laughter and cries of 'No.') He had been changed into another character and removed to another sphere, and they were there that day to drink to the health of his successor."

30. Ward, *Transition*, p.261: "Herbert Vaughan was absolutely straightforward, and of great simplicity of mind. He knew exactly what he wanted and made straight for it. When the situation was uncomplicated—or the obstacle easily comprehended, even if not easily over-come—he was at his best. But "when people's aims were mixed or outside his own definite but restricted purview, he might totally misconceive the position of affairs, and consequences followed which he did not foresee or desire." Most of the things that "irritated outsiders were due simply to misconceptions of this sort, with its natural corollary of a total failure to perceive how his words and actions would appear to others. With regard to Anglicans, for instance, he wanted to be sympathetic: he thought he was being sympathetic: while he was wounding them in their deepest convictions."

31. Leslie, *Vaughan Letters*, p.407ff; Snead-Cox, 2, p.22.

32. Snead-Cox, 2, p.22; *The Tablet*, 21 January 1893, p.102; MHA. Scrapbooks.

33. *The Tablet*, 21 January 1893, "From Our Rome Correspondent, January 16, 1893," pp.101-2; MHA. Scrapbooks.

34. Snead-Cox, 2, p.22; The Tablet, 21 January 1893, p.102; MHA. Scrapbooks.

35. Leslie, *Vaughan Letters*, pp.410-11; The late Edmund Gibbons, Bishop of Albany, New York, told Fr Peter Dirven, professor at Mill Hill, in the 1950s: On the day that Vaughan was made a Cardinal in Rome, 19 January 1893, he visited the old North American College near the Gregorian. He was made Cardinal in the morning and visited the college in the afternoon. "He told us off. America with such a large Catholic population did not do a thing for the missions." Gibbons went from Pittsburgh to become Bishop of Buffalo. In 1918 he became Bishop of Albany where he remained until 1954. Gibbons never forgot Vaughan's remarks. When he was

approached in Buffalo by Cushing to help the missions, he began a section of the Propagation of the Faith. In 1951 he welcomed Mill Hill to open a training centre in his diocese, at Slingerlands. Peter Dirven, September 1990, Mill Hill.

36. Snead-Cox, 2, p.23; "Cardinal Vaughan in Manchester," *The Tablet*, 29 April 1893, pp.659-60.

37. *ibid.*, pp.26-33.

38. Martindale, *Bernard Vaughan*, 1924, p.49.

39. "The Bishop of Salford on Bazaars," *The Tablet*, 10 December 1881, p.954; See also: Snead-Cox, 1, pp.441-5. John Snead-Cox wrote to inform Vaughan that *The Tablet* was responsible for one of the stalls at a Press Bazaar in aid of the London Hospital in 1898. He wrote to the Cardinal to say that Mrs Snead-Cox hoped he would visit her stall. He replied that he could not now break a rule which he had held for so many years. At the same time he said he was glad that *The Tablet* was helping the hospital and sent a cheque for fifty pounds to furnish the stall. On another occasion he admitted that "it had been a positive pain to him even to appear to be insensible to the zealous activity and self-sacrificing exertions of the clergy by imposing restrictions on bazaars."

40. Leslie, *Vaughan Letters*, 7 June 1893, pp.412-13.

41. WDA. Newspaper clippings.

42. W. T. Gribbin, *St Edmund's College Bicentenary Book, 1793-1993*, Ware, Old Hall Press, 1993, pp.83-86.

43. *The Catholic Who's Who, 1939*, pp.292-3: Alice was the daughter of Thomas Weld-Blundell of Ince-Blundell. In 1866 she married the fifteenth Lord Lovat, who died in 1887. After her husband's death she continued to write and helped her cousin Herbert at Westminster. In 1917 she became a nun of the Convent of the Visitation, Harrow-on-the Hill. Ten titles are listed under her name and she was also compiler of "In Praise of Divine Love." There is correspondence at Courtfield in the Vaughan archives between Alice Lovat, Glencoe, Fort Augustus, and Dom Oswald Hunter-Blair, St Benedict's Abbey, Fort Augustus. Alice Lovat insisted that Vaughan had asked her to write his biography and that she had known him better than anyone else due to the help she gave at Westminster. The executors chose Snead-Cox. VFA.

44. VFA. Hunter-Blair.

45. Holmes, *More Roman*, p.201.

46. Winifride de l'Hôpital, *Westminster Cathedral and its Architect*, 2 vols, London, Hutchinson, 1919, 2, p.1ff. The Cathedral was to be dedicated to the Most Precious Blood of Jesus Christ, to His Blessed Mother, His Foster-father St Joseph, and St Peter, His Vicar. Secondary Patrons were St Augustine and all the Saints of Britain, and St Patrick and all the Saints of Ireland.

47. Daughters of Charity Archive. Notes on Lady Herbert and the Sisters of Charity of St Vincent de Paul, Carlisle Place, Westminster.

48. De l'Hôpital, *Westminster*, 2, p.1ff.

49. Norman, *Catholic Church*, pp.368-9.

50. Chadwick, *Victorian Church*, 2, p.242: During the last twenty years of the nineteenth century the standard of the Roman Catholic churches built and especially the furniture inside those churches was no longer cheap like the little sheds forced upon them in the age of Irish immigration.

51. Letters, *Irish Ecclesiastical Record*, vol xiii, 1892, pp.705-6: "People may live in London most of their lives and never see a Catholic church for the ... reason that none, except the Brompton Oratory, can be said to be upon a public road.... If half the money spent in England during the past few years in building beautiful and costly churches in places where they are not wanted, had been devoted to freeing the poor missions from debt and securing suitable sites for new missions in the suburbs, we should not hear so much about 'leakage' from the Catholic Church. If the wealthy Catholics of the West End would pay more attention to the appeals from Silvertown, to secure a church for three thousand labouring people, or Poplar to save a really

beautiful specimen of Gothic architecture from the ravages of the London climate, they may rest assured they would be advancing the cause of Catholicity more than by pouring gold into the offertory plates of pet churches...."

52. William Anthony Johnson, "History and Description of the Building," reprinted from an account for the Eucharistic Congress of 1908, in *The Construction of Westminster Cathedral and Attendant Services*, Abbot Bergh, OSB, editor, London, Burns & Oates, June 1910.

53. Snead-Cox, 2, p.314.

54. Purcell, *Manning*, pp. 354-5.

55. Snead-Cox, 2, p.319.

56. René Kollar, *Westminster Cathedral—from Dream to Reality*, Edinburgh, Faith and Life, 1987, p.33.

57. De l'Hôpital, *Westminster*, 2, p.20: "and on taking high office set this legacy of his predecessors into the forefront of his responsibilities."

58. Snead-Cox, 2, pp.319-20.

59. *ibid.*, p.11.

60. Peter Doyle, *Westminster Cathedral, 1895-1995*, London, Chapman, 1995, p.18; See also: Ian Dickie, "Herbert Vaughan and his Cathedral," Westminster Cathedral Centenary brochure, 1995, pp.11-21.

61. Kollar, *Westminster Cathedral*, p.34.

62. Snead-Cox, 2, p.324.

63. Kollar, *Westminster Cathedral*, p.34.

64. Snead-Cox, 2, p.326: "I can remember now as if it were yesterday, how sometimes, in those first years of his stay in London, some chance remark would often leave me in silent amazement at his absolute confidence that all the money he wanted would be given to him. Of all his anxieties and perplexities about the cathedral, certainly that about the money to finish it with was the least."

65. *ibid.*, p.327: From a paper-cutting with the words "just my views" written by Vaughan in the margin: "The primary purpose of every building, which is not a mere monument is that something should be done inside it.... A cathedral or parish church ... is a place of assembly and instruction and a place of common prayer. To these inward needs the outward form should be subordinated."

66. Leslie, *Vaughan Letters*, p.416, n.2: "Nobody ever induced Sir Tatton Sykes to give a yea or nay answer in anything. He was only induced to marry Lady Sykes by the decided action of her mother née Penelope Leslie, who proposed, booked Westminster Abbey and brought the reluctant groom in her own carriage to the ceremony. Even Lady Sykes could not nail him to his Cathedral promises."

67. Snead-Cox, 2, p.328; WDA. Notes of Austin Oates: Oates commented that Vaughan's interest in building was not always appreciated by the architects: "They always dreaded his visits in fear of innovations being sprung upon them—not always practical."

68. De l'Hôpital, *Westminster*, 2, pp.358, 654-5: John Bentley was the son of a wine merchant. He was born at Doncaster on 30 January 1839, the third surviving son among the seventeen children of Charles and Ann Bentley. Bentley was received into the Catholic Church on Wednesday of Holy Week, 16 April 1862. He took the baptismal name Francis. He married Mary Fleuss, the youngest daughter of Henry Fleuss of Düsseldorf. She was an Anglican and was received into the Catholic Church and given confirmation by Cardinal Manning. Bentley died in March 1902. His funeral was at St Mary's, Clapham, and he was buried at Mortlake between the graves of his two little children; See also: WDA. Helen E. Smith, "J. F. Bentley, An Introduction to His Life and Work," a paper given at Westminster Cathedral, 3 May-5 June 1976, Victorian Society and Westminster Cathedral, arranged by Helen Smith and Geoffrey Fisher.

69. Snead-Cox, 2, p.332: "It used to be said that very often his letters and personal solicitations

showed want of tact. It is likely enough that he blundered sometimes. But if you ask a man to give you 1000 pounds it is always possible that he would think it would have been more tactful if you had been silent."

70. Snead-Cox, 2, pp.335-6; See: Robert Ensor, *England, 1870-1914*, Oxford, Oxford University Press, 1993 (first published in 1936), pp.323-5.

71. *ibid* p.338.

72. René Kollar, *The Return of the Benedictines to London. Ealing Abbey: 1896 to Independence*, Tunbridge Wells, Burns & Oates, 1989, p.118: "Vaughan eventually emerged from the problems he created successfully but one can see his ecclesiastical naivety and unreasonable idealism in that he actually believed that the secular clergy would relinquish their claim to officiate in the new Cathedral to the Benedictine monks."

73. Snead-Cox, 2, pp.345-60.

74. Kollar, *Benedictines*, p.118; *The Tablet*, 20 June 1893, p.983: On June 20th (1893) he attended the Annual Dinner of the "Old Boys" of St Gregory's College, Downside. He told the gathering that he was always happy to attend their annual gatherings and hoped that the sons of St Gregory "would be able once more to establish themselves in the diocese of Westminster."

75. Kollar, *Benedictines*, p.38: Hugh Ford was born on 23 March 1851 at Clifton Park. His parents sent him to Downside at the age of ten. In November 1868 he entered the Benedictine novitiate at Belmont Abbey. He took as his religious name, Edmund. In 1873, due to poor health, he went to Australia returning only in 1876. He was ordained deacon in 1877 and priest in 1878. In 1884 he went to Rome with two others to begin a house of studies for the congregation. From 1885-8 he was prior of Downside. In 1889 he went to the Benedictine mission at Beccles. In 1894 he was again chosen prior of Downside.

76. *ibid.*, p.39: "Ford was not mesmerized by the imagination and idealism of Cardinal Vaughan."

77. *ibid.*, p.40.

78. René Kollar, "Bishops and Benedictines: The Case of Father Richard O'Halloran," *JEH*, 38, 3, July 1987, pp.362-85: Richard Joseph O'Halloran was born at Ballyhindon, Co. Cork, on 24 December 1856. He went to school at the French College in Dublin and St Colman's in Fermoy. On 9 September 1875 he entered Vaughan's St Joseph's Missionary College. He was ordained deacon in 1880. Before ordination he became "master of discipline" at a new junior seminary, called an apostolic college, for Mill Hill, in Wales. His "reckless and impulsive behaviour" led to many complaints. In spite of negative reports about him, he was ordained priest by Bishop John Hedley in December 1880. By January 1881 he had left the society. His departure was hastened by his reluctance to take the oath required by all members to work in the overseas missions. After he left, he refused to repay the society for his education. This "ignited a long and fiery conflict between himself and Herbert Vaughan" and marked his "long search for a friendly bishop and clerical employment." He first found work with Bishop Bagshawe of Nottingham. After some time he surfaced at Westminster where Manning offered him a small mission. But "any hope of tranquillity and stability soon disappeared." His "adversary and enemy Herbert Vaughan" succeeded Manning. "Dr. Vaughan had scarcely placed the symbol of jurisdiction around his neck," O'Halloran later recalled, "when he sent me a peremptory order to leave the diocese." Kollar, p.368; Propaganda Fide told Vaughan that he could "do with this priest what you think suitable in the Lord." O'Halloran was allowed to stay in the diocese until he found other employment so that, as Herbert Vaughan said, he "might not be inconvenienced by being suddenly thrown out of work." He gave O'Halloran a mission in the fashionable suburb of Ealing.

79. Kollar, "O'Halloran," p.374.

80. *ibid.*, p.378.

81. *ibid.*, p.385: He remained at his residence for another ten years before dying, unreconciled to the Church, of pneumonia, on 13 October 1925—the rebel church was finally closed; Some who

left Mill Hill were not so disgruntled. Father Joseph Andreas Amrhein, OSB, the founder of the Benedictine Congregation of St Ottilien, came from St Beuron's Monastery in Germany in March 1882 with permission from his abbot to enter St Joseph's Missionary College. He came into personal contact with Herbert Vaughan and it was suggested that Amrhein might take on the foundation of a house at Wimbledon for the training of lay brothers; he felt they should support the priests and be active in education. Amrhein took the temporary oath and received the red sash, but after only six months he returned to Germany. Amrheim founded a congregation in 1884 and today "it is one of the bigger congregations in the Benedictine Confederation, with missions and monasteries in Europe, East and South Africa, Asia and the Americas." Jeremias Schroder, OSB, The Presbytery, Callow End, Worcester, 6 March, 1993; See: Frumentius Renner, *The Five-Branch Candlestick*, Rome, 1984, pp.14-19; Father Schroder is a chaplain at Stanbrook Abbey.

82. Snead-Cox, 2, p.349.

83. *ibid.*, p.356.

84. Kollar, *Westminster Cathedral*, p.116.

85. *ibid.*, p.120.

86. *ibid.*, p.94; WDA. Gasquet to Vaughan, 17 February 1901.

87. Kollar, *Westminster Cathedral*, pp.105-12.

88. Snead-Cox, 2, p.360; De l'Hôpital, *Westminster Cathedral*, 1, p.302: "On October 1st he welcomed his first choir-boys, a little awe-stricken group of thirteen, in their temporary schoolroom, the lower sacristy. The welcome was brief and characteristic. 'You,' cried he, with that large and expressive sweep of the arm he invariably used when in emphatic mood, 'You are the foundations of the cathedral!'"

89. Kollar, *Westminster Cathedral*, p.112; p.120: Hugh Ford wrote that the services were carried out "in a manner comparable to the great abbeys of England before the Reformation." The College of Cathedral Chaplains was formed.

90. *ibid.*, p.124.

91. Chadwick, *Victorian Church*, 2, p.255: "Kenelm Vaughan was a priest such as the Roman Catholic community of an earlier generation could not have produced, and those who have studied the family attribute something to the Welsh evangelicalism of the mother before she was a convert. He founded an order of expiation which was impossible because it aimed to combine active missionary endeavour with a life of severe asceticism and perpetual adoration; lived a hermit life in a back garden in Chelsea or at Hatfield; devoted much time to encouraging the study of the Bible among simple laity, after a controversy in which the Roman Church was accused of hindering the study of the Bible; wandered through South America distributing copies of the New Testament and there were rumours that he exorcised devils; collected fragments from every abbey or shrine suppressed at the dissolution and made an altar from them."

92. De l'Hôpital, *Westminster Cathedral*, 1, p.183.

93. It was published in Spanish by the Christian Press Association of New York.

94. James J. Walsh, "The Catholic Church and Popular Feeling in South America," *Records of the American Catholic Historical Society of Philadelphia*, vol xv, 1904, pp.182-3.

95. Norman, *Catholic Church*, p.368; Correspondence with David Hugh Farmer, August 1995. He has been on a Commission meeting at Arundel Castle to examine the relics and the hagiographical tradition of St Edmund; See also his *Oxford Dictionary of Saints*, Oxford and New York, O.U.P., 3rd ed. 1993, pp.147-8.

96. Snead-Cox, 2, pp.290-1.

97. *ibid.*, pp.293-4. In correspondence between Father Ethelred L. Taunton and Father Daniel E. Hudson, CSC, Editor of *Ave Maria* magazine in the United States. 9 September 1901, 57 Gt Ormond St., London W: Taunton writes: "Cardinal Vaughan has made another mess over St. Edmund's body—I think there were many of us who could have saved him, but he is so ruled by

'Ours' that he won't listen to anyone else—They, as usual, have misled him and the Pope."
However, not everyone shared the opinion that Vaughan had been misled about the authenticity
of the relics. Dudley Baxter, in a letter to Father Hudson on 19 September 1904, Shemming
Grange, Birch, Colchester: "I am now sending you another manuscript about our other St.
Edmund which I greatly hope will appear during the anniversary of his martyrdom—November 20th ... about the probable authenticity of these relics from Toulouse. I have special
permission from our new Archbishop (Mgr Bourne) to publish his own opinion—that is that
this matter is by no means settled—while Cardinal Merry del Val, Archbishop Stonor, and
others have all written to me as stated in this MS. There seems to be a wide feeling now that our
late beloved Cardinal acted too hastily and very injudiciously in practically rejecting the Relics."
Notre Dame University Archive; Correspondence, David Hugh Farmer: the cult of St Edmund
at Toulouse was a comparatively well-approved one from at least the sixteenth century and
there is a written record of the bones at S. Sernin in the fifteenth: "I personally think that at least
some of the relics in the Arundel casket came from the Edmund relics at S. Sernin, Toulouse.
After the great row, a Commission met in Toulouse and concluded that the Toulouse relics were
indeed genuine."

98. Johnson, "History and Description," p.11.

99. Leslie. *Vaughan Letters*, p.445; De l'Hôpital, *Westminster Cathedral*, 2, p.308. One professional opinion: *The American Catholic Historical Society*, 1904, vol xv, p.171: "In certain
modern buildings there seems to be evidence of much and of well applied artistic thought ...
instance in the Roman Catholic Cathedral of London now approaching completion in the
district south of Buckingham Palace.... A few such buildings there are; a few works of art which
show that the power of thoughtfully working out a complex design is not wholly lost to the
world." Quoted from Russell Sturgis, *Dictionary of Architecture and Building, European Architecture*, New York, Baker.

100. Snead-Cox, 2, p.419; Unfavourable comment was also in the Press: "Westminster Mon-
strosity," *The Tatler*, no 24, 11 December 1901, p.475: "There is much indignation in
Westminster and especially in Ashley Gardens at the extraordinary ugliness of the new Roman
Catholic Cathedral. It combines the architectural features of a modern music-hall with the
peculiar graces of an exaggerated factory chimney. Why, with so many beautiful examples of
English gothic to choose from, the promoters should have preferred to go one worse than Keble
Chapel it is hard to understand. It is still harder on Westminster."

101. *The Universe and Catholic Times*, 27 December 1963, p.8, "Death was the Uninvited
Guest," by Edward MacDonald.

102. De l'Hôpital, *Westminster Cathedral*, 2, p.680.

103. Leslie, *Vaughan Letters*, pp.444-5, and n.2. In the same letter Vaughan wrote that he was
not going to make a public appeal for the new Archbishop's House because he was still asking for
money to finish the Cathedral. He planned to rely on private donations to build a house.

104. Olive Katherine Parr, *The Children's Cardinal*, London, Burns & Oates, 1905: When the
contractors, as a joke, sent a bill for the damage caused by the children he responded: "I don't
care what the damage is or what I have to pay, now that the children have been the first public
body to enter the Cathedral." Vaughan, when he addressed the children, "was unusually
bright" and told them a story of how he had been stopped in a Mill Hill Lane by "two little
highwaymen who unaware of his identity demanded from him 'a penny for the Cardinal's poor
children'" Snead-Cox, 2, pp.455-6.

105. Leslie, *Vaughan Letters*, pp.445-6.

106. Johnson, "History and Description," p.12.

107. Leslie, *Vaughan Letters*, p.446.

108. De l'Hôpital, *Westminster Cathedral*, 2, p.313.

109. *The Tablet*, 9 April 1932, p.468.

110. Johnson, p.20.

111. Daniel J. Mullins, "The Welsh Harvest: Where are the Labourers?," *Millhilliana*, no 1, 1987, pp.19-22: "If we are to mount an effective missionary apostolate to the Welsh people at the end of the 20th century, it will pay us to look to the vision of Cardinal Vaughan at the end of the 19th. Either an existing Order or a new one must take on Wales in its whole variety, including Welsh Wales, as its own apostolate. It will have to take the language and the culture of this people seriously.... It would be a fitting fulfilment of his own dream of doing something important for his beloved Wales."

112. *ibid*.; Correspondence, 22 October 1992, Bishop Daniel Mullins to the author: "It was apparently his view that since the Jesuit priests looked after most of the Mass centres across North Wales, that they would take on responsibility for supplying suitable priests for the area. He is reputed to have approached the Jesuit Provincial asking him to accept a commitment to send some of his best men to Wales, and to ensure that they would learn Welsh as an essential preparation for their work under a new Bishop. In fact, in 1895, Rome created the Vicariate of Wales with Francis Mostyn as the Vicar Apostolic. The Jesuits apparently had not taken on the role that the Cardinal wanted. The source of my information is Bishop Hannigan of Wrexham. He had received the information from Canon Pozzi, who had been a curate to the man responsible for the building of the new church (at Llandudno) ... Cardinal Vaughan.... He remains one of the most significant figures in the Catholic Revival in England since the restoration of the hierarchy."

113. Carmel Archives, Notting Hill (CANH). Llandrindod, 15 August 1895.

114. Davies, *History of Wales*, pp.460-4; pp.501-2: "The Roman Catholics were also outside the "Concord." In 1907, 65,000 Roman Catholic worshippers were recorded in Wales, ten times as many as in 1851. They were concentrated in the main towns—Cardiff, Swansea, Newport, Merthyr and Wrexham—and the overwhelming majority of them were descendants of immigrants from Ireland. The Catholic Church, however, was eager to attract the native Welsh back to the Old Faith; in 1889, the Society of Saint Teilo was founded and a translation of the Prayer Book was published; a mission from Brittany was launched in 1900 and the *Cennad Catholig Cymru (The Welsh Catholic Messenger)* was published from 1900 to 1914. In 1895, the Pope recognized the unity of Wales by creating the diocese of Menevia (that is, St David's) side by side with the diocese of Newport. The diocesan structure was reorganized in 1916 when Cardiff became an archbishopric, four years before the Anglicans consecrated an archbishop in Wales."

115. "Catholicism in Wales," *The Tablet*, 17 September 1892, p.450: "Few or none ... influenced in religion by preaching or teaching in a foreign tongue;" *The Tablet*, 8 October 1892, Catholic Truth Society Conference, p.566.

116. Leslie, *Vaughan Letters*, p.412.

117. WDA. Vaughan Notes, for a petition on behalf of a bishop for Wales: "The country was divided into four Bishoprics, which still remain though occupied by Protestants ... but they were united in the 11th and 12th centuries: St. David's and Llandaff in the South and St. Asaph and Bangor in the North. The actual population is 1.360.000;" The Welsh Edition, *Manchester Guardian*, 27 June 1903, Professor Ernest Rhys: "Cardinal Vaughan formed at one time the idea of a new Catholic Crusade to recall the Principality to its ancient faith ... progress was even made I believe, with a volume of essays intended to state the historical basis and conditions of the Roman Church in Wales. The late Mr Lionel Johnson often spoke of his share in this uncompleted undertaking."

118. J. Anselm Wilson, *The Life of Bishop Hedley*, London, Burns & Oates, 1929, p.136.

119. CANH.

120. Mullins, *Millhilliana*; *The Tablet*, 26 February 1898, Catholicism in Wales, Interview with Fr James Carnarvon: Carnarvon arranged with the St Teilo Society—the Welsh Catholic Truth Society—for the "publication of a Roman Catholic Welsh version of the collects, epistles and Gospels for Sundays and feasts," in addition to a prayer book already translated by Jones; "Father Metcalfe's 1837 prayer book is out of print;" Vernacular literature was needed to keep

alive the knowledge and spirituality of Catholics.It was a pressing need that was not satisfied right into the 19th century. Most of the literature supplied to Catholics in Wales from the Continent, even to the Jesuit library at Cwm, was not in the vernacular. See John R. Guy, "Eighteenth Century Gwent Catholics," *Recusant History*, vol 16, no 1, May 1982, pp.85-6; *The Tablet*, 1 November 1902, pp.714-15: In October 1902 Breton Oblates arrived in Merionethshire: "A zealous missionary priest probably stands a better chance of martyrdom in rural Wales than in any other portion of the King's domains." The *Welsh Press* wrote: "The Papists ought to have fair play, although they must be watched."

121. *In the Silence of Mary, The Life of Mother Mary of Jesus, Carmelite Prioress and Foundress, 1851-1942*, London, Notting Hill, 1964, p.208ff; and CANH.

122. *ibid.*, pp.208-21.

123. *ibid.*, p.198.

124. *ibid.*, p.208; From the preface by Cardinal Vaughan to the English translation of *Primitive Constitutions*, Carmel, Notting Hill, p.11: "Thus I conclude this letter by saying that your great apostolic mission is to be accomplished through a more intimate union with Our Lord Jesus Christ than the world can form any idea of."; p.13: "Put a living will into your observance, study the Spirit of God, come to the Rule and Constitutions with God dwelling within you, as 'one spirit,' and your rule will chasten, mortify, vivify, sanctify and beatify you.'Serve ye the Lord with gladness;'" On 8 November 1994 the Prioress, Sr Mary of St Philip, wrote to the author: "Only a couple of days ago, whilst examining the contents of an old bookcase here in the Prioress's office, I found a handsomely bound book, carefully wrapped in a silk case, of the edition of our Carmelite Rule and Constitutions which Cardinal Vaughan had helped to translate and revise, and for which he wrote a long and inspiring Preface, dated Christmas Day 1897. When I opened this little volume, I found that it was not printed, as I had expected, but contained that text, with the Preface, in Vaughan's handwriting, and the rest in M. Mary of Jesus' hand. They must have compiled it between them, in manuscript whilst preparing for printing."

125. *In the Silence of Mary*, p.215; CANH. Rome, 25 February 1895.

126. *ibid.*, CANH: "I am now quite happy about Char (Mrs Weld-Blundell). This morning in the crypt of St. Peter I had a strange distraction during Mass—it was to call her Mother Mary of St. Teresa. I put the thought away—but it quite bothered me. I shall probably send her a letter tomorrow about it—but you may tell her, if you like. I feel quite overcome with the tenderness of Our Lord and his Mother. I feel it must be owing to your prayers and Char's. Certainly I have never merited such treatment;" *The Tablet*, Saturday 17 May 1884: Vaughan married them.

127. CANH.

128. Snead-Cox, 2, pp.380-1: "Mgr. Dunn, writing of a period which was some months later, says: "Very shortly after I had joined his service, in 1895, we were in Rome at the English College, when one morning he suddenly called me into his room. He was evidently much distressed and I wondered what could have occurred. He told me in all simplicity that he had come to realise how much scandal and disedification he had caused by being too hasty and impatient at public functions.... But tears welled up in his eyes, and before he had completed his self-accusation he completely broke down ... but he had gained a knowledge of his fault and it was never repeated.... I was little more than a boy who had been in his service less than a year;" See: MHA., "Cardinal Vaughan's Centenary," by Archbishop Goodier, SJ: "Pictures that show the Cardinal in repose, a splendid figure of calm dignity, give the wrong impression. He could never be still in mind or body.... So swiftly did he perform religious ceremonies— little train bearers had to run to keep pace with him—that many people thought him irreverent and called him the 'scarlet runner.'"

129. CANH. Vaughan to Salford, 26 April 1895.

130. *ibid.*, Mill Hill, Vaughan to Mother Mary, Carmel, 6 May 1895.

131. *ibid.*, 11 May 1895.

132. *In the Silence*, p.221 and appendix; In November 1966 Gerald Mahon, superior general of the missionary society at Mill Hill, sent copies of the preface Vaughan wrote to all the Carmel monasteries: "Our Founder noted particularly that the sanctification of priests—which was specially dear to his own heart—fell very definitely within the scope of St. Teresa's daughters."

133. Mary Vaughan, *Courtfield*, pp.98-100.

134. MHA. HCV. Scrapbooks: From the *Pall Mall Gazette*: "His life was a long series of enthusiasms ... fervidly tinged with a religious emotion. His religion was, like himself, not so much intellectually continuous in its character as a succession of momentary outbursts occurring with great frequency."

135. *ibid.*: "Finally there was nothing for it but to found an order of his own and death has caught him in the height of his enthusiasm for his new venture."; and SDA: "The Conversion of Our Separated Brethren and of the Heathen at Home," by Prior Vaughan, *The Tablet*, 14 May 1892, p.745; *The Tablet*, 30 April 1892, p.712: At St Peter's Priory "Masses are said there every day at seven and eight o'clock." Devotions were also held before the Blessed Sacrament on Wednesdays, dedicated to St Joseph, praying for England once again to become an "Island of Saints."

136. SDA. Joseph Jerome Vaughan, *A Monastic Autobiography of Twenty-five years*, Salford, Robert, 1894.

137. *ibid.*

138. SDA. "Private and confidential," Oswald Hunter-Blair to the Bishop of Salford, 18 June 1894.

139. SDA. Adrian Weld-Blundell, 22 June 1894.

140. SDA. Jerome Vaughan, OSB, Prior CSG, St Mary's Church, Paulist Fathers, 628 California St., San Francisco, 15 June 1896, to Herbert Vaughan.

141. *ibid.*

142. *ibid.*

143. SDA. Hugh Edmund Ford, Downside, 12 Sept 1896.

CHAPTER XVI

Anglican Orders, Higher Education and Catholic Intellectual Life

Roman Catholic Pronouncements on the Validity of Anglican Orders

When Herbert Vaughan was Archbishop of Westminster, he became involved in an issue that, in Edward Norman's opinion, was both "unnecessary and irritating."[1] In order to initiate a discussion between Anglican and Roman Catholic theologians, the French Catholic Abbé Portal, and a leading layman of the Church of England, Lord Halifax, chose a topic which instead became the focus for suspicion and misrepresentation. The "device," as it was later referred to, was the validity of the orders of the Anglican priesthood. They hoped that a discussion of Anglican orders would initiate a gradual rapprochement between the Churches that might one day lead to a corporate reunion. Instead, it resulted in the Papal Bull *Apostolicae Curae* of Leo XIII on 13 September 1896: "We pronounce and declare that Ordinations carried out according to the Anglican rite have been and are absolutely null and utterly void." It was, according to John Jay Hughes, Herbert Vaughan "on whose stubborn and unyielding opposition the soaring hopes of Halifax and Portal were to suffer shipwreck."[2]

The problem of Anglican orders for the Roman Catholic Church did not begin with Portal, Halifax or Vaughan. It was, according to George Tavard, "a creation of the past two centuries." It became a topic among several French theologians in the early eighteenth century when they studied the history and ritual of ordinations in the Church of England. Their debate was reactivated in the nineteenth century. In 1852, at the first synod following the restoration of the hierarchy in England, it was suggested that Anglican ordinations be "solemnly declared null and void." The synod did make such a declaration, for the members believed that Anglican ordinations had already been declared invalid by several popes. The central question concerned the rite of ordination: "Is it capable of doing what is done by the corresponding rite in the Pontifical" of the Roman Church?

"What had been a question turned into a problem when, urged from both sides, Leo XIII examined the thesis of the validity of Anglican orders and found it wanting."[3] He disappointed the expectations of many Anglican clergy who were obliged to be ordained unconditionally if they wished to enter the Catholic communion as priests, and others, both Roman Catholics and Anglicans, who hoped to move towards a corporate reunion. The legacy of the controversy, and the disappointment of many who looked forward to reunion, remains alive.[4]

Herbert Vaughan was a leader of opposition and therefore he did not stand alone. He represented the English bishops, and the commission he set up to study the issue in 1895 was made up of Canon James Moyes, Abbot Aidan Gasquet, and the Franciscan David Fleming. They concluded in their 1896 report that Anglican orders are null, and convert Anglican clergy must always be ordained again absolutely and not conditionally. In Rome the future Cardinal Raphael Merry del Val acted as the agent for the English bishops at the Vatican and lobbied on behalf of a negative answer by the Pope to the proposition.

There were English Catholics who did not share that view. Among the upper classes some were sympathetic to the English Church Union, a society of Anglican clergy and lay people formed for the defence and maintenance of Catholic principles in the Church of England. The Union was founded in 1844 by Anglo-Catholics within the Anglican Church. From 1868 its president was Charles Lindley Wood, the second Viscount Halifax, a man personally inclined toward the Roman Catholic Church.[5] The Pope had censured Roman Catholic members of the Union in 1865. Between 1894 and 1897 the old schemes of the Association for the Promotion of the Unity of Christendom (APUC) were revived, "despite the censure of its attitudes and assumptions by the Holy See in 1865."[6] In the 1890s Anglican sympathizers initiated the idea of reunion, and it was Halifax who was its leading promoter.

While on the island of Madeira with his family in the winter of 1889-90, Halifax met a French Vincentian, thirty-four-year-old Abbé Etienne Fernand Portal, a student of the reforming Bishop Félix Dupanloup of Orleans. Portal was on the island partly for his health and partly in connection with some work he was doing for the Sisters of St Vincent de Paul. Halifax found him extremely kind and also one of "the quickest and most intelligent persons I have ever met." According to Snead-Cox, the men soon discovered they had many common interests, and took long walks together discussing the condition of religion in their own countries. Portal was equally impressed with Halifax. "Here was a representative of the Anglican Church, the President of the English Church Union, and yet what a little seemed to separate him from Catholicism!" Following their meeting, for the "astonished Abbé, all things seemed possible, while the work of doing everything that could be done to put the position of the Anglican Church fairly before Catholic Europe became an imperative duty. To bring about a reunion between England and Rome seemed a project which required only patience and good-will."[7]

Halifax, however, represented only a very narrow section of his co-religionists. Within the Church of England, ritualism and Anglo-Catholicism were attractive to some, but aroused fierce antagonism on the part of many others. One faction called it "Anglo-Romanism," and felt that the movement did not belong within the Protestant establishment. Ritualism, especially in the use of the confessional, was unpopular among the middle classes and evangelical churchmen.In addition, there were divisions and tensions within the Anglo-Catholic movement, which surfaced later in the Cavalier case of 1899. Therefore, Lord Halifax was representative of an ambiguous position within the Anglican Church.[8]

Nonetheless, during 1892, Portal and Halifax corresponded and searched for a way to unify the Roman Catholic Church and the Anglican Church in the near future. They decided that a discussion about the validity of Anglican orders was one way to reach the goal of corporate reunion. According to John Jay Hughes, theirs was a daring idea for the time—"too daring as the sequel was to show."[9] In July 1892, Halifax visited Cardinal Vaughan at Westminster and presented his plan. From the outset, Vaughan made it clear that the recognition of the Pope's primacy was the decisive element and not the validity of Anglican orders. According to Hughes, Vaughan was honestly convinced that Halifax's movement was a threat to the Roman Catholic Church and faith. "He made use of every means at his disposal to thwart what Halifax and Portal were attempting. Given his convictions, it is difficult to see how Vaughan could have acted otherwise." Vaughan wrote in February 1894:

> Halifax and his party are anxious to get some kind of recognition— anything that can be twisted into a hope of recognition will serve their purpose. They wish to keep people from becoming Catholics individually and tell them to wait for a corporate reunion. This will never be till after the Last Judgement—and all the poor souls that will be born and die in heresy before the reunion must suffer in their own souls for this chimera of corporate reunion. They are also most anxious to get some kind of assur- ance about their Orders, at least the statement that they are possibly valid! But this again is to keep souls back from submission to the Church.[10]

What Hughes terms Vaughan's "ruthlessly logical approach" finds support in observations made by Snead-Cox and Wilfrid Ward. Snead-Cox noted that Vaughan's application of some theological proposition to everyday life often had "little regard for the special circumstances and without a thought for such an irrelevancy as the feelings of the person concerned." Wilfrid Ward saw Vaughan as a man with "a curious combination of romantic ideals with intensely unromantic details." He had seen a Vaughan who could override, "almost brutally, the romance of ordinary home life and human love if they stood in his path. Nothing could be more practical than the means he took. He followed the well-known General's advice to his soldiers," for according to Ward, "he kept his powder dry while he said his prayers."[11]

In the meantime Portal had thrown himself into the scheme and published in France, under the pseudonym F. Dalbus, a pamphlet entitled "Les Ordinations Anglicanes." In it he called the consecration of Matthew Parker, who had been appointed Archbishop of Canterbury in 1559 by Elizabeth I, valid in terms of the "historical facts," but expressed doubt concerning the "intentions" of the consecrator. The pamphlet achieved "an astonishing popularity, and attracted the attention of many scholars on both sides of the English Channel" when it was reviewed by Abbé Louis Duchesne, a church historian and author of the *Liber Pontificalis*, in the *Bulletin Critique*. Duchesne used Catholic teaching on the sacraments to argue against Portal's treatment of intention and said that "the conclusion is that Anglican Orders may be regarded as valid."[12] Hughes considers the purpose in bringing up the issue of intention as a tactical move to get the discussion moving.[13]

Just as Ambrose Phillipps de Lisle had convinced Nicholas Wiseman, who had in turn convinced Pope Pius IX, that a substantial part of the Church of England was ready to reunite with Rome,[14] so also did Portal and his supporters in Rome convince Leo XIII that the Anglican Church was ready to submit. "I hear they are on the point of coming over," Pope Leo told Vaughan, who, Edward Norman writes, "had to bear the onus of seeming to be unresponsive and unopen to the daring vision of a wider movement of opinion." Even the historian Abbot Gasquet, "with realism that was like Vaughan's—whose opinions he was representing in Rome on the question—was lectured by Leo on 'how the whole nation was being drawn to Catholicism.'"[15]

In an interview on his first day as archbishop, Vaughan was asked about Protestants and the Church of England. He stated clearly that "I recognize Protestants as fellow Christians but I do not recognize their religion as the true faith." He continued: "There are two currents even in the Church of England itself today—one towards Catholicism and the other towards rationalism. It is only what I would expect in a church of so many inconsistencies."[16]

In September 1894 Portal visited Halifax in England and was introduced to Anglican bishops. The Archbishop of Canterbury, E. W. Benson, was very cool to the idea, and just as sure of his convictions as Herbert Vaughan. At the same time Vaughan was annoyed that Portal did not come to visit him at Westminster. Vaughan, writes Hughes, could understand the Church of England as a "thoroughly Protestant and Erastian institution" but not the position of an Anglican like Halifax, nor Portal's advocacy of "friendly theological discussions" that might lead one day to corporate reunion. The Church of England, as he saw it, was a familiar enemy he could come to grips with, "an age-old foe which had oppressed his forefathers." He would not accept dealing with a Church that claimed to be "the ancient Catholic Church of this land," whose archbishop and others denounced him and other Roman

Catholics with scorn as "the Italian mission," and "claimed to feed its children in the eucharist with the true body and blood of Christ, and to forgive their sins in the sacrament of penance as truly as the pope himself— this was too much for Herbert Vaughan."

Vaughan's answer to calls for a "gradual 'rapprochement' was characteristically simple and straightforward: submission." He was to repeat it time after time "with a sublime disregard of its negative psychological effect. Individual submission to the see of Peter, he said in a speech at Bristol on 9th September 1895, was the only hope there was for reunion, and the greatest obstacle to this submission was pride." Any other path suggested for reunion was to him a snare and a delusion, a "trick of Satan to keep people back from the truth."[17]

Portal went to Rome and saw Cardinal Rampolla, the Vatican Secretary of State, to whom he gave his impressions of the Church of England. The next day he met with Pope Leo XIII for an hour. Portal suggested that the Pope call for a conference between the Anglican and Roman Catholic Churches. He returned on the third day in hope of receiving a letter from the Pope for Archbishop Benson of Canterbury, but instead he received one from Cardinal Rampolla. The Secretary of State's letter praised Portal's efforts and expressed a hope that England "return to the only centre of unity."

Portal then travelled to England to visit the Archbishop of Canterbury again and received an even cooler reception than the first time. Benson considered it imprudent for such a momentous interview with Halifax and Portal to be just sprung upon him and was "deeply annoyed, and made no attempt to dissimulate his feelings." Snead-Cox quotes Benson: "Portal had seen only one side of English Church life with Lord Halifax; and that the Pope could have no complete view of England before him."[18]

Halifax met Pope Leo XIII and proposed a direct offer to the Anglican bishops, bypassing Cardinal Vaughan. Abbot Gasquet brought the news to Vaughan that the Pope had decided to write such a letter to the Archbishops of Canterbury and York. Vaughan asked Gasquet to return to Rome, and the Cardinal came close behind, arriving on the evening of 19 January 1895. The next day he saw the Pope at 12 noon.

Vaughan wrote to Fr Farmer at Mill Hill about his visit to the Pope. He had gone first to Cardinal Rampolla and suggested that if the Pope wrote the letter *Ad Anglos*, he should do it as an appeal to all who were seeking the truth in England, just as Jesus did when he taught his disciples how to pray. "I urged upon him the need of trusting more thoroughly to the supernatural in the central government of the Church."

On 28 January 1895, Vaughan went to see the Pope. He had been warned by Gasquet through Moyes that the Pope had been convinced by Dalbus and the "French influence" in Rome about the possibility of reunion. "One idiot," Gasquet continues, "advised the Pope to write to the Archbishops of Canterbury and York." "We Catholics have all along misjudged most unfairly the position of these good men," the Pope wrote in a letter received privately by Gasquet. In the matter Gasquest thought "it a most fatal policy to give home authority away like it has done. No doubt the Cardinal will hear about it when he goes to Rome."

Vaughan gave Farmer an unflattering description of Pope Leo's appearance during his visit: "When he opened his mouth there appeared here and there some rather unpolished tusks—probably not over four or five—a great mouth ... and dark eyes deeply set—face crumpled and not well shaven." Vaughan was greeted "affectionately" and asked if he had anything interesting from England. "I said I had brought him the results of the bishops' meeting of January 4th." Vaughan first spoke of their request to withdraw the prohibition against Catholics attending Oxford and Cambridge.

He then commented to Farmer about the conversion of England: "If he appears before England as the Doctor of prayer like his Divine Master, no better preparation could be made for any doctrinal encyclical he might issue later on. This is a matter that needs much prayer." The "great work for the conversion of England is thus now in the balance and next week or so may determine whether I am under a delusion or not as to one of the measures that have to be adopted by the Holy Father." Halifax "and his party" were looking for recognition. "They are also most anxious to get some kind of assurance about their orders, at least a statement that they are possibly valid! But this again is in order to keep souls back from submission to the Church. I have my hands quite full with pressing these facts on people here. At the same time it is most important to keep in touch with these people and if possible to lead them to the truth."[19]

In his conversation with the Pope, Vaughan emphasized that there was no chance of corporate reunion and the only prospect was in the increasing number of converts who were coming into the Roman Church. He warned the Pope of Anglican intentions and that they were "all opposed to the supremacy of the Pope, and that his letter could not alter that." Leo XIII finally told Vaughan that he would issue an "Encyclical on the Church and her Head in the middle of this year, if he lived so long."[20]

From the English College Vaughan wrote to Carmel, Notting Hill, concerning the issue, on 25 February 1895: "It has been an unspeakable consolation to me to find that the Vicar of Christ has fully entered into the supernatural way of dealing with England by means of prayer.... Lord Halifax is coming out to see and argue! with the Pope. I am in correspondence with him and he is in great need of prayer. Though so good and earnest, it will be a miracle if he—the head of a sort of sect—is converted. But what cannot prayer do! 'If Stephen had not prayed, Paul would not have been converted' says St. Augustine." On 13 March he wrote again from Rome that "Lord Halifax arrived today and came to me at once to have a good talk. The Holy Father will see him, but I have not much hope of a good result."[21]

Abbot Gasquet had seen the Pope at the end of January in the presence of the new Secretary of State, Rafael Merry del Val. After the Pope finished speaking, Gasquet took the opportunity to support the warning given earlier by Vaughan. Merry del Val, part English himself, supported Gasquet. According to Hughes, without the assistance of Rafael Merry del Val, "none of those who worked so hard for the condemnation of Anglican orders—not Gasquet, nor Moyes, nor even Cardinal Vaughan himself—could have achieved the outstanding success which ultimately crowned their efforts." By 1896, for example, Merry del Val, a confidant of the Pope, was convinced that Portal was "spreading heresy and poisoning people's minds." The Pope called in Rampolla, and Gasquet repeated what he had told Pope Leo. "That interview was decisive, and the Pope knew that the dream of corporate reunion was not to come true in his time."[22]

On 14 April 1895 the Pope issued an apostolic letter, *Amantissimae voluntatis*, addressed to the English people, urging that a discussion of the validity of ordinations might lead to a conference which could start the process towards reunification. According to Derek Holmes, it is clear that this call by the Pope for the English people to pray for the light to know the truth in all its fulness was influenced by Gasquet, Vaughan and Merry del Val. The letter was published in England on 22 April. It was not addressed to the Anglican Archbishops or to the Church of England, but to the whole nation: "To the English people who seek the Kingdom of Christ in the unity of the Faith." It was an invitation for England to pray for the truth. Towards the end of the letter *Ad Anglos*, the Pope urged Roman Catholics to pray the rosary for the conversion of England and granted indulgences for doing so.[23]

In general the letter was well-received in England and even Archbishop Benson spoke of its "honest appeal" but noted that it made no mention of the Anglican Church.[24] Vaughan wrote to Carmel from Paris on 11 May 1895, informing Mother Mary that had he been that day to see the Cardinal Archbishop about an appeal he planned to make throughout the convents of Europe for prayers for England; he had already begun at Orleans. "I have today recommended you and your anxiety to the Mother at Notre Dame des Victoires. I spend my mornings there, not without fruit...."[25]

Vaughan explained to Fr Farmer that he had written directly to the Pope: "My letter to him has been a very bold thing to do—but I have done it deliberately." The letter referred to was probably that of 25 August 1895: "The extreme importance to the Church in England of the way in which the Anglican question is treated by Rome is my apology for writing direct to your holiness." Vaughan warned that it would be a serious mistake if a decision on Anglican orders were made in Rome, "reversing the practice of the Church from the very beginning of the Anglican heresy," without having fully heard from the theologians and historians of the Catholic Church in England. He did not object to "French Ecclesiastics identifying themselves with Lord

Halifax," but asked that the Pope allow the English hierarchy to "see their statements and their arguments." "We fear lest matters closely concerning the Church in England should be discussed and carried on towards a decision without our knowledge and behind our back."

Vaughan was in favour of an examination of the question but "if the representatives of the Catholic Church in England are excluded, while foreigners who are partisans obtain a place and a dominant influence in certain quarters, the discontent and mischief in England will be of the gravest kind." He then reminded the Pope that the previous April he had asked that if a commission on the subject of Anglican orders were formed, he would be informed and the Pope would appoint two or three English experts to the commission.[26]

Shortly after an announcement at the Preston Conference, in September 1895, that Rome was going to reopen formally the question of the validity of Anglican orders, a committee was formed in London to consider the evidence. The year 1896 was also to see the publication in June of the encyclical *De Unitate* addressed to all the bishops of the Church. In March 1896 Pope Leo XIII appointed an international commission to meet in Rome to look into the question. Cardinal Mazzella presided and Merry del Val was secretary; Merry del Val kept Vaughan informed. The members of the commission were Gasquet, de Augustinis, Duchesne, Gasparri, Fleming, and Moyes. The pro-validity members also had the help of Anglicans, Lacey and Puller, who supplied them with information from England. Two more members were added: Fr T. Scannell and José Calasanzio de Llevaneras.[27]

On 30 April 1896 Vaughan wrote to Archbishop James Smith in Scotland asking for his support:

> The English Bishops have unanimously desired me to express to the Holy See their opinion on Anglican orders. They consider that any departure from the tradition of 300 years, during which the Church has treated them as invalid, would be a shock and a scandal to the faithful. They hold that Anglican Orders are not valid and would pray the Holy See to declare them invalid, if such be its judgement. They consider that this modern pretention of Anglicans to possess sacerdotal powers is being pushed, and that recognition of them by Rome is being sought, in order to give colour (*sic*) to the Anglican Communion to be an integral part of the Church Catholic, and hinder conversions. It would be exceedingly valuable if we could add the adhesion of the Irish and Scotch Archbishops to our letter to the Holy Father. I should, therefore, be very grateful if your grace would give me your adhesion to this letter, or a letter which I might use—not of course for publication.[28]

The commission met on twelve occasions between 24 March and 5 May 1896. Vaughan's letter, in the name of the bishops of England and Wales, accompanied by letters of support from Archbishop Smith and the bishops of Ireland

and Scotland, was sent to Mazzella on 10 May 1896. Tavard considers the document disingenuous: "It showed both a ferocious determination to stop any recognition of Anglican orders, and a great ignorance of the theological mood of the Church of England past and present." In his opinion the emotional appeal of the letter needs to be remembered. The devil was "at work in the Anglo-Catholic movement," and a happy result might be expected from a condemnation; a large influx of converts. It was a line of thought that could not be dismissed "by a pastorally-minded pope, who lived before the start of the ecumenical movement."

The final vote took place on 7 May 1896. Voting for recognition of Anglican orders were Louis Duchesne and the Jesuit Emilio De Augustinis. Pietro Gasparri and another member said that the orders were doubtful. "The Vaughan group voted against it." According to Tavard, the commission could not reach a conclusion and handed its documentation to the Dominican Raffaele Pierotti. Leo XIII asked him to sum up the commission's work and present the findings to the Holy Office, which would make a formal recommendation to the Pope.[29]

On Thursday, 16 July, the Holy Office met in the presence of the Pope and voted unanimously that Anglican orders were not valid. Only the Secretary of State, Mariano Rampolla, was absent.[30]

On 10 August Vaughan wrote to Mother Mary of Jesus from Llandrindod, Wales:

I am having a novena to our Lady to help the Holy Father in the matter of Anglican Orders. It is important that nothing should be said of his intentions, because your Abbé Portal, and my Halifax and one of my own colleagues in Rome would exert every effort to hinder the condemnation of Anglican Orders, if they thought a condemnation likely. I hear all over the country they are resting in their sacerdotal offices and care very little for the Encyclical compared to the idea that they are sacrificing priests. This is the last ruse of the devil to keep the people in heresy and schism. Much prayer is therefore needed just now."[31]

The validity of Anglican orders was formally rejected in the papal document *Apostolicae Curae* of 13 September 1896. It was composed by Merry del Val.[32] The expectation that the numbers of conversions would increase if submission to the authority of the pope was clearly demanded was not fulfilled.[33] The Pope, one month after the decision, sent a letter to Vaughan concerning the economic hardship experienced by converted Anglican clergymen. Leo XIII expressed his own ideas on conversions from the Anglican Church and, from his initiative, the Convert's Aid Society was formed.[34]

Herbert Vaughan was the leading public figure of the events surrounding the papal rejection of Anglican orders. At the same time he was representative of the feelings of many Roman Catholics who very often looked on the Church of England with "distrust rather than of hope, of contempt rather than of sympathy."[35] In Hughes' view, Vaughan, like many of his co-religionists, was "quite simply ignorant" of the realities of contemporary Anglicanism. A convert, Fr B. W. Maturin, was asked by Vaughan what he thought was the chief obstacle which kept people from coming over to the Roman Church: "If you want me to be perfectly frank with your Eminence, I should say it was yourself." Vaughan, writes Hughes, was a genuinely humble man, to whom one could say that sort of thing. It was Maturin who wrote on Vaughan's death in 1903: "The Cardinal is a great loss. I shall miss him very much.... He was really a saint. I think one of the humblest and certainly most un-worldly men I ever met, perfectly simple and as straight as a die."[36]

There were other, more severe, judgements of Vaughan and his part in the matter of Anglican orders. Portal thought that "Vaughan and his lieutenants were wrong not to conduct themselves like christians" and, in addition, they did not show any "genuine intelligence." Edmund Gosse, a friend of Halifax, who was at the time librarian of the House of Lords, read the proofs of Halifax's book, *Leo XIII and Anglican Orders*, and concluded that it was all very interesting, human, generous and ardent: "Only wooden old Vaughan comes out as the villain of the piece. And I think he was a villain, a holy villain of course, one of those strange people who employ for sacred ends methods which applied to civic ends would be seen to be infamous." A few weeks after the condemnation, Halifax wrote of Vaughan that he was a "person quite apart. No one can the least understand him who does not know him. He is quite the oddest mixture of things that ever was. He is absolutely impervious to new ideas and combines with a great deal of magnanimity and stupidity a capacity for blundering which is marvellous. I like him and cannot help doing so despite all his enormities."[37] But these, of course, are the views of those who did not share Vaughan's outlook.

In 1901 Herbert Vaughan wrote an introduction to a book titled *Roads to Rome*, in which sixty-five men and women gave testimony to their "return to the Catholic Church." Vaughan wrote: "There are hundreds of thousands all round us, lay and clerical, men and women, who feel the foundations of Protestantism have broken down under them; who are secretly asking them-selves whether there be any solid and divinely inspired religion; who are half and more than half convinced of the claim of the old Church to their submission." Submission in prayer, humility and self-denial were but "ante-cedent conditions" to the supernatural gift of faith.[38]

He wrote to Halifax on 5 October 1896 that submission to the Church, of which the Pope is the legitimate head, was the test. The real question was "where is the Divine Teacher to be found? In a small but respectable section of the Church of England or in the Church of which the Pope is the Head?" He urged Halifax to devote his attention to this question in "earnest and humble prayer."[39]

On 9 December 1896 Vaughan sent a letter to the Pope from the bishops.

At a meeting on 10 November they had agreed on its composition. The Pope asked that each bishop sign it rather than having Vaughan send it on in their name. The letter to the Pope was dated 8 December, the feast of the Immaculate Conception. It was to thank the him for the publication of *Apostolicae Curae.* "When the truth shall shine much more clearly upon our beloved fellow countrymen than it does at present, it will be owing to the frank and unambiguous declarations of Catholic Doctrine and practice which your holiness has given in the face of the whole world."[40]

In a pastoral letter of 1897 on the Confraternity of Our Lady of Compassion, Vaughan recalled the history of the prayer movement aimed at the conversion of England to the Roman Catholic Church. He called attention to his favourite church in Paris, Notre Dame des Victoires, and the work sixty years earlier of the Passionist convert Fr Ignatius Spencer. Of Spencer, *The Tablet* wrote: "In the present world-wide movement of prayer for the Conversion of England, Father Spencer's name is the centre and example. Indeed no more remarkable missionary has appeared in our times; and a reputation for sanctity is on his name."

In 1838 George Ignatius Spencer had devised a plan for a movement of prayer for Christian unity. It was the first significant step in the English-speaking world. In 1844 he took his crusade of prayer for unity to the Continent. It was to be the great work of his life. His was, however, not a crusade for conversion, a recent pamphlet professed, but "rather for the unity of Christians through prayer and mutual co-operation," although the aims of his crusade are more direct than a prayer for cooperation. Jozef Van den Bussche's study of Spencer says of his trip to the Continent in 1844: "Spencer pursued a restless campaign of spending three months telling people about the religious situation in England and asking their prayers for the return of England to the Catholic Church."[41]

Vaughan quoted correspondence between Nicholas Wiseman and Spencer in 1838 that identified two points which England in each generation declared idolatrous and superstitious: according to Wiseman they were "Transubstantiation and the work of the Blessed Virgin." In 1838 the priests of Paris were asked to offer a Mass every Thursday for the conversion of England. In 1897 one was arranged to be said every month at the altar of Notre Dame des Victoires. England would never be won by controversy, Vaughan wrote, but by "calm expositions that satisfy the reason and the heart, and by the power of united prayer for Divine faith which is the gift of God."[42]

Notre Dame des Victoires was a place of pilgrimage for Vaughan and many others who prayed for the conversion of England. A marble plaque is inscribed to the memory of Ignatius Spencer, the "Hon. and Rev. George Spencer," who began prayers at Notre Dame des Victoires in October 1837 for the conversion of England and died on 1 October 1864. He is one of many English converts remembered in the Church. For twenty-seven years Spen-

cer worked for the "return of English heretics and schismatics" and prayed to
Our Lady of Victory to conquer all heresy.: "Par Votre Toute-Puissante
Intercession Hâtez La Conversion Complète De Notre Pays," reads an in-
scription of 8 December 1864.[43]

The idea of prayer for the conversion of England to Roman Catholicism
was not new to Vaughan's writings. A paper Vaughan gave at the Catholic
Truth Society's annual conference at Birmingham was entitled: "England's
Conversion by the Power of Prayer," and aimed at "reviving the spirit and
practice of prayer for the conversion of England," promoted by Father
Ignatius Spencer. Vaughan responded to the question of his understanding of
"England's conversion."

> When I speak of the conversion of England, I do not mean that materialists,
> rationalists, and various phases of heresy will cease to exist; but I mean that
> the Catholic Church will become the most conspicuous, the most re-
> spected, the most trusted by the people of England; that its adherents will
> be composed of great masses of the working, of the educated, and of the
> best classes of the population; that its teaching and influence in restraining
> men's passions and appetites, and as spiritualizing and elevating their lives
> will be fully recognized and applauded by the nation; that Protestantism as
> a State system and a national religion will pass away, while the Old Church
> will continue to expand and to win the hearts of the people, until it becomes
> the great citadel of religious truth, standing alone amid the errors of
> materialism and unbelief.[44]

While he was at Salford he had written to all of his clergy to pray "that God
may grant to our brethren outside the Church a "love for the truth," and a will
to believe it."[45]

Vaughan had at first regarded the controversy over corporate reunion and
Anglican orders with amusement, then with impatience and finally with
dislike. In 1894 he joked that the Archbishop of Canterbury "is going to get
himself declared Patriarch within the next two years!" Holmes considers
Vaughan to be a man who had neither the character nor the history to
sympathize with the efforts of a Halifax or Portal. Vaughan's vision was
simple and straightforward. To him the reunion movement was either a
threat to the Roman Catholic faith or a means of saving the Anglican Church
from collapse. His views and his harsh and, to some, "disreputable methods"
are reminiscent of the apologetic considerations that dominated his thinking,
and by his own admission, were sometimes "brutally" put, during his involvement with the Oblates and Wiseman in their disputes with Errington
and the cathedral chapter. The same apologetic style was seen later in his use
of *The Tablet* to defend ultramontane views, especially at the time of the
Vatican Council.[46]   The only corporate reunion that could take place in
Vaughan's view was the corporate submission of the Anglican Church to
Rome. He considered it wrong to offer an impossible hope that delayed

individual conversions. By 1896 Vaughan was openly hostile and denied the validity of Anglican orders, not only because of historical or liturgical problems, but also because the sacramental powers of the Catholic priesthood were also denied by most Anglicans.

Pope Leo XIII held a similar opinion for on one occasion he referred to Anglican bishops as the employees or creatures of the State, and on another said that he regarded the movement of Portal in France as "a continuation of Gallicanism and a danger to the Church." Once he repeated the complaint contained in a Vaughan letter that "certain Frenchmen have been interfering in this matter. They are *des têtes légères* and act without sufficient knowledge."[47]

Merry del Val, Gasquet, Moyes and Fleming celebrated their victory over the Anglicans with a private dinner party in London. Not all Catholics rejoiced and some were ashamed of the "controversial attitudes and policies, the polemical tone and jubilant crowing sometimes adopted by Vaughan and his supporters."[48]

The papal bull on Anglican orders was sharply condemned by Halifax, the *Church Times* and the *Manchester Guardian*. At a Lambeth Conference in February 1897 the Anglican archbishops of Canterbury and York issued a Latin address to the bishops of the world, "the whole Body of Bishops of the Catholic Church," in response to the "Apostolic Letter of Pope Leo XIII on Anglican Ordinations." The letter confined itself to general declarations about the desirability of reunion.[49] The Roman Catholic Bishops of England and Wales replied with a "vindication of the Bull *Apostolicae Curae*." The Archbishop of York, W. D. Maclagan, responded to Vaughan on 12 March in the York diocesan magazine:

I should be very ungrateful if I did not acknowledge with much thankfulness the excellent spirit which Churchmen, both clergy and laity, have received the letter issued by the Archbishop of Canterbury and myself on the subject of Anglican orders.... The reception which it has met with the Roman Catholic community in England is very remarkable. The English Cardinal, passing by the whole of the arguments contained in the Papal Bull, and the detailed confutation of them one by one in our letter, has taken an altogether new departure. He now puts forward as the root of the whole matter, as the absolute essential for the validity of Holy Orders, the *sine qua non* of all true ordination, the acceptance of the mediaeval doctrine of transubstantiation.... And this is the doctrine the non-acceptance of which is to render null and void the Holy Orders of the Church of England. We need not be much disquieted by such a contention. We are content to make our appeal to the Holy Scriptures, the Apostolic Fathers, to the early Councils, and to the ordinals of the whole Christian Church for more than 1,000 years.[50]

Many in the Church of England were pleased with the rejection by Rome of the hopes of High Church members. The validity of Anglican orders was of little interest to them. Portal and the French churchmen who were connected with the *Revue Anglo-Romaine*, founded at Paris in 1895 to promote reunion, were disappointed by the encyclical. They had hoped, if not for a favourable decision, at least for some more time, and when the condemnation came they gave it a mild interpretation. They even hinted that it might not be final. But on 5 November 1896 the Pope wrote to the Archbishop of Paris about the writers in the *Revue Anglo-Romaine* and declared that Catholics should accept the decree as fixed, definitive, and irrevocable.[51]

In September 1897 a Catholic Conference was held in Ramsgate. The meeting was opened on Monday evening, 13 September, in the Granville Theatre. Vaughan presented the inaugural address. Thirteen hundred years earlier, St Augustine and his missionaries, sent by Pope Gregory to evangelize the Anglo-Saxons, had landed at Thanet. Prior to the Ramsgate conference, there was a Catholic commemoration of the event, which was attended by Cardinal Perraud of France, bishops, priests, monks, Catholic lay people, the secretary of the Catholic Truth Society, James Britten, Elizabeth Herbert, the Duke of Norfolk and others. In his address Vaughan pointed out the parallels he saw between the scene in AD 597 and the one they had participated in that week. Like St Gregory, Pope Leo looked to England:

> As the pagan Anglo-Saxons had formerly all but exterminated the Catholic Church in Britain by a persecution that lasted a century and a half, so later, had the Protestant English attempted to sweep the Catholic Church out of the land by a persecution which lasted three centuries. But finally, toleration, a spirit of inquiry and of good will supervened after the storm.[52]

At one time during his last years at Westminster a rumour circulated that Cardinal Vaughan might be raised to a peerage. In a sermon at City Temple, Rev. Joseph Parker argued for "ennoblement all round," if that was to be the case. According to Parker, the rumour at the House of Lords was that Vaughan was to become a member. "It is the biggest Dissenter," Parker said of Vaughan. "A man who has told the Archbishops they are laymen, the Ecclesiastical Commissioners, thieves, and the whole of the English clergy that they are usurpers and shams. Protestantism is spat upon. The constitution is defied. Liberty to worship God is trodden underfoot. The whole coach is being driven to Rome." The news writer ended the report with the comment by Parker that he was "not saying a word against him as a man for he believed there was not a finer gentleman in Europe."[53]

With a bent for controversy, Vaughan aroused more than his share of excitement, which is why Wilfrid Ward could have a deep personal affection and immense admiration for him, but at the same time lived "in constant fear of what the Cardinal might do next." The feeling was, according to Maisie Ward, "on the whole reciprocated."[54]

In the opinion of Derek Holmes, Vaughan always tended to be narrow and dogmatic when he thought the faith of the Roman Catholic Church was touched upon, but in spite of the fact that he lacked the intellectual gifts of a Manning, he appreciated the pastoral, social and even political implications of the positions he defended. He tried to remain on friendly terms, especially among Catholics, with those with whom he disagreed. In a letter to Lord Acton, Vaughan made what Holmes calls the astonishing admission that he realized that Acton must have gone through "awful trials" and suffered perhaps more than other men "by your great learning and knowledge of the human," in the Church to which Acton had been "faithful and loyal." Vaughan may have recognized that he was, for many among the more thoughtful Catholics of his day, one of the prime movers in the trials he referred to.

For Maisie Ward, when the "bitterness of the moment" faded into history, Vaughan stood out as "one of the great figures of the nineteenth century—not so much in his intellectual equipment as by sheer force of sanctity." She quotes a letter from her father, Wilfrid, to Lord Halifax, written during the controversy over Anglican orders and reunion: "If his words are not always rightly chosen, he is nevertheless a leader of whom for single-minded intention one may well be proud." Ward was reacting to a comment in the *Church Times* that referred to the "swaggering and ostentation" of Vaughan. Ward considered that "swaggering and ostentation are quite foreign to him. I know what is meant but it is a curious misinterpretation. He is a true Englishman and there is more mere bluntness of form than you fancy in sentences which have annoyed you." One example of his bluntness was his public statement on two occasions in 1898 that Anglicanism was a "false religion."[55]

Higher Education: Catholics at Oxford and Cambridge

One of the first major problems to confront Vaughan at Westminster was the university question. Although Oxford and Cambridge Universities were open to Roman Catholics, the Church had forbidden Catholics to enrol.[56] The prohibition included Trinity College, Dublin. Some Catholic laymen of the upper classes chose to send their children, acting against the official policy of their Church authorities. Others applied to their bishops for a special permission to do so. A few Irish Catholic parents held that a prohibition issued through the English hierarchy did not apply to them.

A project close to Wilfrid Ward's heart was to bring about a lifting of this prohibition. If there were certain qualities in Vaughan that created problems, there was one which Ward admired and which made a change possible: Vaughan's tendency to "make straight for the object that seemed right. And he was very strong and tenacious. But if experience caused him to change his mind, he simply changed it. Quite simply, with no worry about saving his face, he reversed his policy." This was what happened, according to Maisie

Ward, in a final settlement of the question of Catholics attending Oxford and Cambridge.[57] Gordon Wheeler saw in Vaughan's approach a change of heart, a realization that "the experience of thirty years had shown that Oxford and Cambridge did not present to well-trained Catholic young men the proximate occasions for a loss of faith and morals which were the grounds of objection laid down by the Holy See." According to V. A. McClelland, Wheeler's view attributes to Vaughan "a perspicacity which history shows he did not possess."[58] Herbert Vaughan's change of heart from one in opposition, who had been Manning's emissary at Rome on the question in the 1860s, was slow and reluctant. It was due more, perhaps, to pragmatism, and to the resistance to the prohibition, and to Vaughan's schemes for a Catholic University, by leading laymen of the Catholic Church.

Vaughan's first reaction in 1893 was to try to set up a Catholic University soon after one was established in Washington in the United States by Leo XIII in 1889; they also existed at Louvain in Belgium and Angers in France. The vision he had for England was to renew the plan for Kensington, which was started in 1874, and by 1882 had ended in debt. It failed due to an ill-chosen rector, Mgr Capel, and lack of financial and moral support.

A Catholic University College had been opened by Manning at Kensington in 1875.[59] It was an outcome of the provincial synod of Westminster held in the summer of 1873. The bishops responded to the request from Propaganda that urgent steps be taken for providing Catholic higher education. A federation of Catholic colleges was proposed that would have as its centre a college of higher studies at Kensington in London. It was to be ruled by an academic senate and aimed at taking academic degrees at the University of London. Newman was invited to become a member but he declined to join. The staff had excellent credentials but had trouble attracting students due to the opposition of the Jesuits, who had their own plans for Richmond. But the final blow to the scheme was the disastrous appointment of Mgr Thomas Capel as rector.

The only relevant correspondence between Elizabeth Herbert and Herbert Vaughan on the subject is a letter that Vaughan had written to her on behalf of Manning in 1874, asking for the support of wealthier Catholics for the university project. She repeated the opposition of the Duke of Norfolk and others to a university at Kensington: "Everyone is agreed as to the importance of having such a College of Higher Studies to counteract the infidel teaching of the day, but then its practical usefulness will depend on the way it is started and the man at the head of it." Manning's plan had aroused strong opposition to the college. In addition, the choice of Capel, according to Lady Herbert, was a mistake:

> The Rector . . . , if he be worth anything he should be the soul of the House, not only its director but its moving spirit. What would have become of your Foreign Missionary College if you had not infused your own spirit into

your men? It is far more important in a college than a monastery, because in the latter, the spirit of the Rule supplies to a certain degree any lack in the superior. Now all the young men I have ever seen detest Mon.C. They think him a charlatan and a tuft-hunter and they don't respect (him), because they don't believe in him. Now I ask you, what sort of effect or influence would such a man have in guiding and moulding youths...?

Lady Howard had told her that she still regretted the failure of Newman's scheme at Oxford: "Rome spoke against it on account of the Archbishop's strong, one-sided representation.... Suppose Dr. Newman for one year in Dr. Manning's place, and Rome would undoubtedly reverse her decision."

Mary Elizabeth Herbert ended her letter with a warning that Vaughan was to hear again in 1893, long after the failure of the Kensington project, and which probably contributed to the reversal of Church policy.

Absolutism of this sort will in my opinion defeat its own end. You can't make the people give either money or their sons when they have no faith in the plan or the system. Whereas, if it were modified to suit the need of the laity, you would, as it were, ride "at the top of the wave" of the Education Movement and by letting them take the lead in the matter, in reality direct and guide it. Then money and men would flow in freely and the end we have all at heart would be attained.[60]

Nineteen years later Vaughan sounded out the hierarchy and influential laity about the possibility of trying again to begin a Catholic university, but neither group was enthusiastic about "another attempt to resuscitate the Kensington College or to establish a new foundation on similar lines."[61] He turned to Bishop Hedley for help. The reason for the urgency was that he recognized that "forces were gathering for yet another assault upon ecclesiastical policy." He even thought to ask Rome for a more stringent decree in favour of the exclusion of Catholics from Oxford and Cambridge.

In the same year, Vaughan saw his fears taking shape in two plans. One was the proposal to organize a summer school for Catholic teachers at Oxford, which had been approved by the Bishop of Birmingham. It was abandoned in 1894 due to the personal intervention of Vaughan. He declared that such a plan would help to foster "mixed education and the frequentation of Non-Catholic universities by Catholic youth." The other plan was the determination of Anatole von Hügel, the curator of the archaeological museum at Cambridge, to present an address and a gift from the Catholics in residence at Cambridge University to Pope Leo XIII in February 1893. Von Hügel intended to make the presentation wearing his Cambridge academic robes. McClelland quotes a story told by von Hügel of his approach to Vaughan, who was a family friend, and his "Ecclesiastical Chief," to inform him of his intentions. It reveals Vaughan's temperament in an astonishing way.

Von Hügel went to Vaughan at about ten o'clock at night, "knowing he knew nothing about the University." Vaughan greeted him very affectionately and then asked:

"What is it about?" I said, "I have two or three questions to ask you." I think I said "Cambridge" or the "University"; before I had finished the word he was up on his legs walking round and round in a fearful state of mind. I said, "I am only asking you two questions." "Stop a moment, stop a moment," he said; and he said "You know what I think of you being at a University. Of course, it is allowable for you; but I am sorry, but I am sorry." "What is it?" I said, "I have a gift for the Holy Father from the undergraduates and an Address." "An Address! What about?" "A book." "I would rather not look at it." I said, "I went into this thing nicely"—and things to this effect. So at last I showed him this Address. He would not read it. He said, "Who did it?" I said: "I had very little time and I had forgotten." ... He said, "Who has looked at it?" I said, "Bishop Hedley. I am no scholar. He had added one or two words. He said I should take it to one or two of my friends in Cambridge. So I took it to Henry Jackson who helped me." And I said, "Your Eminence, of course, I have brought my gown and hood." ... I asked him how I was to set about it. He said, "I will have nothing to do with it. You know how I feel about it." The upshot was: "You just ask Cardinal X. He knows all about it. You take it and ask him." And I said: "May I mention your name?" "Yes." I felt it was not very satisfactory; so I went back and said, "Do put yourself into my position. It is very unpleasant to make a fool of myself." He said: "Don't talk like that to me!" I said, "I am very sorry, but can you dictate to me how I am to talk to him?" So then he laughed. He suddenly got up and he said "Look here. Do whatever Cardinal X says about the book. When your turn comes, kneel in front of the Holy Father, hold it—that sort of way—but not a word." I said, "I beg your pardon. I do not understand." He said, "I will speak." [62]

At von Hügel's audience with the Pope, Vaughan was present. He stood at the Pope's side when von Hügel came forward but spoke hardly a word. The Pope was waiting for something more to be said after he presented his gift but von Hügel said nothing. Vaughan was determined that no public appeal was to be made to the Pope on the university question.

McClelland thinks what happened to von Hügel that February gave birth to a "brilliant strategic plan." Von Hügel would help the Duke of Norfolk draw up a petition to Rome asking for the question be reopened. In June 1894 the duke presided over a meeting of interested laity and it was decided to send the formal petition to Rome while a memorandum containing the chief arguments be addressed to the English hierarchy so that they might assume the initiative if they wished. Four hundred and forty-eight signatures were collected, including those of a number of priests and religious. Heading the list were the names of the most prominent Catholic families.

Vaughan's view on the question when he arrived at Westminster is reflected in a letter to his nephew, Charles, in October of the previous year, and quoted by Snead-Cox: "If there were no future state, and if Catholics in your position had no mission as Catholics to the English people, I would say go to Oxford or Cambridge—whichever you like." But, he went on, "Oxford and Cambridge can only give you what they have. They have a false philosophy so far as they have any; and they are essentially in mind, heart, and influence, alien to the Catholic standards of thought and aspiration." In a postscript he quoted the devil's "recipe to make a loyal, leading, powerful Catholic": "Send him in the most critical period of life to a Protestant University, plunge him into an atmosphere of worldliness, prevent his having a sound course of Catholic Philosophy, and trust to a practical philosophy issuing from familiar contact with the world, the flesh, and the devil."[63]

After the meeting of lay people in June, and the drawing up of their petition, the Duke of Norfolk approached Vaughan. The Duke wrote to Wilfrid Ward: "I had a long talk with the Cardinal two days ago.... I thought it better to tell him in confidence what we were thinking of doing." Vaughan replied that he had heard "I had a meeting, that he thought the present state of affairs most unsatisfactory, that he would welcome anything that would rectify it, that if the Holy See thought well to change its policy he would be quite willing to concur, etc...." The Catholic laity agreed with Vaughan that a Catholic University was desirable where there were enough capable Catholics to support it but since "this was emphatically not the case in England, life in the world must be held to begin on leaving a Catholic public school."[64]

The memorandum and petition he received in September 1893 "left him quite cold" in its arguments. What did impress him was the favourable testimony of the Jesuits at Oxford, and of Mgr Scott and Anatole von Hügel at Cambridge. According to Snead-Cox, Vaughan had to face a situation in which, in spite of every official discouragement, the number of Catholics at the universities had increased and was likely to continue to grow.[65]

Vaughan made a last effort to reach a compromise when he privately asked the opinion of a number of leading Catholics about a renewal of the Kensington experiment. But, Snead-Cox writes, "It was his homage to a dead ideal." He wrote to Hedley on 26 September asking for his thoughts on the state of Oxford and Cambridge and "the ever-increasing number of Catholics going there." In his notes preparing for a meeting of the six northern bishops on 14 October, and for consideration by all the bishops at their meeting on 4 January 1895, he considered the position of about fifty Catholic undergraduates at Oxford and Cambridge as intolerable. In addition, neither the Irish nor the Scottish bishops had taken any action on the prohibition. He knew then that "a negative policy was impossible, and he regarded the continuance of the state of things then existing as impossible."[66]

There was another factor at work in the question of higher education, the growth of a strong middle class. Manning, Vaughan and the English bishops had provided educationally to help the Catholic middle class, a policy that was paying rich dividends in the 1890s. At Salford, Vaughan had followed Manning's policy and committed himself to the ideals of professional education at St Bede's College. After leaving Salford, he encouraged the rector, and later bishop of Salford, Louis Casartelli, to prepare his boys for entry into the local university colleges rather than having them take London external degree examinations. The development of provincial university colleges, after Manchester in 1851, along with London and Durham Universities, attracted Catholic students and from them was emerging the nucleus of a strong Catholic professional class. When Vaughan arrived at Westminster, the demand for higher education became more urgent and was stimulated by the example of Catholics reaching positions of national importance for the first time since emancipation.

For McClelland, the chief question facing Vaughan and the bishops, when the petition was finally delivered to Westminster in December 1894, was "whether or not the Catholic aristocracy were to be given the same opportunities to acquire a higher education as were becoming increasingly available to Catholics of the middle classes." They would not go to the provincial colleges. Some individuals received permission from their bishops more easily than in the past. McClelland quotes a story from Anatole von Hügel's papers about a young man being presented to the Pope by his father for a blessing, while the Pope "hoped that he would be a credit to the University of Cambridge." Therefore the Pope himself was implicated in the growing disregard of Propaganda Fide's prohibition.[67]

At a special meeting of the hierarchy on 4 January 1895, Vaughan proposed that the bishops petition Rome to the effect that attendance at Oxford and Cambridge be tolerated provided there were adequate spiritual safeguards. The voting was close, but the majority favoured Vaughan's proposal. The bishops would petition to remove the prohibition and place themselves at the head of the movement to accomplish this.

In opposition, Bishop Gordon of Leeds had written to Bishop Wilkinson in December 1894: "I do hope that you will stand out against this pandering to the modern and worldly spirit. I would sooner cut off my right hand than help in the least degree to forward the Cardinal's scheme—Fancy our Colleges being turned into preparatory schools for these heretic and infidel-making shops ... we can't be called upon to give money to help aristocrats and snobs on the High Road to Hell. His Eminence is going to Rome and he will play pranks if we are not firm and united."[68]

The opposition to the majority decision resented Vaughan's later assertions that the university question had been reopened at the request of the bishops as if they had been united on the issue. They saw that Vaughan's hand had been forced by the "powerful pressure tactics of an exclusive social set." These were the individuals Manning had warned him against. They were also the people Elizabeth Herbert advised him to "modify" his views to suit during the first Kensington experiment. According to McClelland, Vaughan had been forced to act by the tactics of influential laity; the evidence supports this assessment. When Vaughan saw von Hügel and told him that the lay petition had been endorsed and would be submitted to Rome; "he added bitterly, 'it would be best if I took it and tore it and threw it in the fire.'"[69] Vaughan tried to make the best of the situation and soon wrote to Hedley that the Church was about to embark on a new policy in England, and "though we shall find rocks and shoals, we shall, I doubt not, be entering upon the work that God requires of His Church in this country."[70]

The laity's petition had been sent to Rome in December 1894. Vaughan went with the bishops' letter on the topic in January. He wrote to Fr Farmer describing his visit to the Pope on 28 January: when Leo XIII asked him if he had "anything interesting from England," Vaughan told him that he had brought the results of the bishops' meeting of 4 January. "Tell me quickly. What is it? Is it on education?" "Yes, Holy Father," replied Vaughan. He then outlined what had been decided to ask of Rome: "Bishops' petition ... Holy See to withdraw prohibition as to Catholics frequenting Oxford and Cambridge; propose that Catholic lectures in Philosophy and Religion and History be provided." The Pope then asked: "But how will you secure the attendance of Catholics at the lectures?" "Only by moral force," replied Vaughan. "Were there any Catholic professors in the Universities?" "No," answered Vaughan, "but we can do as they have done at Amsterdam where a Dominican lectures on Thomistic philosophy and many non-Catholics attend."[71]

On Tuesday 26 March 1895, the question was discussed by the General Congregation of Propaganda. They decided in favour of the petition and their decision was then approved by the Pope on 2 April. On 17 April the Jesuit prefect of Propaganda, Cardinal Ledochowski, wrote to Vaughan that the "Congregation had decided that the attendance of Catholic youths at the Universities of Oxford and Cambridge might be tolerated," subject to "the conclusions and precautions recently proposed by the Bishops of England for the removal of the danger of lapsing from the Faith."[72]

A council of fifteen persons was formed on 24 April 1895. It was called the University Catholic Education Board, and its task was to implement the Roman directives.[73] The board was to finance special conferences for the Catholic undergraduates: "in which Philosophy, History and Religion shall be treated with such amplitude and solidity as to furnish effectual protection against false and erroneous teaching."[74] The bishops also announced the appointment of Catholic chaplains.

The first meeting of the council was held at Archbishop's House, Westminster, on 18 June. There were four more meetings before a document announcing the decision to English Catholics was issued on 1 August 1896. It was addressed to the parents, superiors and directors of "Catholic Laymen who desire to study in the Universities of Oxford and Cambridge." It concluded with a warning: "It will be an evil day for the Catholic community when its members make light of the dangers which beset education given in a non–Catholic atmosphere."[75]

Snead-Cox says that Vaughan was able to write to Propaganda five months before his death in 1903, referring to the permission given first to Catholic laymen and later to ecclesiastics to go to Oxford and Cambridge: "I must report most favourably of the effect of these two permissions. Catholics have done themselves great credit in both Universities."[76] In 1896 St Edmund's House was opened at Cambridge and the Jesuits started Campion Hall at Oxford, followed by St Benet's Hall, opened by the Benedictines.

St Thomas Seminary and a Central Seminary at Oscott

Henry Manning had established a seminary for the diocese of Westminster at Hammersmith on land owned by the archdiocese. It had formerly been a Benedictine convent. There was a large house on the property. On the land, Manning built a permanent seminary. When Vaughan arrived at Westminster he could never be "induced to embark upon the enterprise of a separate diocesan seminary."

Before he left Salford he had made up his mind that if he could convince the Westminster chapter that Hammersmith seminary was a mistake and a burden, the school would be closed. On 29 December 1892, the feast of its patron, the seminary was closed. Vaughan looked for "an immediate amalgamation with some existing seminary as a going concern." A few days after he was made cardinal he presented the plan for a central seminary to the Pope. On 1 February 1893 the Pope wrote: "encourage you to begin." Vaughan's plan was to unite the resources of a group of dioceses in the south of England for the support of a central seminary at Oscott. The last lecture at St Thomas Seminary was given on 14 March 1893 and four days later Westminster's students transferred to Oscott in the Birmingham diocese.

Bishop Edward Ilsley was in the position of being both bishop of the diocese and rector of St Mary's seminary, Oscott. Negotiations over the establishment of a central seminary were, therefore, never easy for Vaughan. At one point he considered making St Edmund's, Old Hall, the site for such a school, but in the end accommodated Ilsley and agreed that the existing staff—all Birmingham clergy—should be retained. Mary McInally suggests that Vaughan handed over control of staffing to Ilsley without realizing the possibility of later difficulties.

In April 1895 Vaughan noted that the pope urged him to make the seminary his great work and a university of classical studies. When the seminary was reconstituted with seventy-four students, twenty-nine were from Westminster and twenty-six from Birmingham. However, the Oscott central seminary became a grave disappointment to Vaughan in the years of his failing health. In November 1898 he brought a matter of internal discipline to the attention of the Board of Bishops, of which he was chairman. He was openly opposed by the staff. There was "open and united opposition of the whole staff," according to Snead-Cox.

At the same time he believed that he had done his best to provide for the spiritual and intellectual preparation of priests when he founded the central seminary, whatever the later disappointments.[77]

Problems facing Catholic Intellectual Life

When Manning died, Anatole von Hügel's brother Friedrich, who was married to Mary, the daughter of Sidney and Elizabeth Herbert, complained to Herbert Vaughan that the late Cardinal Manning had left English Catholics without any real guidance in dealing with the intellectual problems of the day. In Derek Holmes' opinion the same might equally have been said about Vaughan, "who was unfamiliar and did not sympathize with intellectual difficulties. Vaughan's attitude was essentially negative, defensive or simply apologetic."[78]

During the closing years of the nineteenth century, Vaughan was involved in a controversy with Catholic intellectuals, especially with the biologist Jackson St George Mivart. Vaughan, along with fifteen of his bishops, responded, as the new century opened, with "A Joint Pastoral Letter on the Church and Liberal Catholicism." According to David Schultenover, the pastoral was approved by the pope, was "unassailable in its force" and was similar in style to the 1907 encyclical, *Pascendi Dominici Gregis*, of Pope Pius X, condemning "modernism."[79]

The intellectual questioning that was perceived to be a challenge to the authority of the institutional Church at the end of the nineteenth and beginning of the twentieth century had been a cause of tension at the heart of English Catholicism since the 1860s. The Louvain historian Roger Aubert, in Jedin's *History of the Church*, thinks the questioning arose from a search for "a synthesis between loyalty to the Catholic Church on the one hand, and the affirmation of modern culture and academic freedom on the other."[80]

The "modernism" condemned by the pope four years after Vaughan's death, and the "Liberal Catholicism" addressed by Vaughan and the bishops in 1900, are abstract terms for models used to define tendencies and movements in conflict with the Catholic faith. Aubert writes of the term "modernism" used in the Encyclical, that it "embraced a series of concepts reflecting, in the opinion of contemporaries, the liberalism of the nineteenth century."[81] However, almost a century after the papal condemnation, there is still no generally accepted definition of modernism. One view is that its roots are in the work of late nineteenth-century Catholic scholars who tried to revitalize theology and exegesis in the light of other disciplines. Liberalism and modernism were terms used to describe many disparate initiatives that the pope would finally present as "an organized subversive movement" whose purpose was to leave "nothing stable, nothing immutable in the Church."[82]

Aubert uses the term "progressive Catholics" to describe those intellectuals with whom Vaughan came into conflict during his time at Westminster: Friedrich von Hügel, George Tyrrell, Mivart and others. Von Hügel had an international standing, and was an important connection with "progressives" of other countries and between them and the Church authorities, at least at the beginning of the crisis.

In November 1893 the encyclical *Providentissimus Deus* was published. It stated that a defence against the rationalistic enemies of Holy Scripture, the "sons and heirs" of the Reformation, was especially urgent, since there were some men among them who wanted to be known as Christian theologians.[83] After its publication, Vaughan, as a result of a memorandum from von Hügel, wrote to Rome advising the Holy Office against issuing any "instruction" on the practical implications of the encyclical. On another occasion he protected the right of open discussion for practical, rather than academic, reasons. Nevertheless, Holmes writes, "Vaughan's faith in ecclesiastical decisions was unquestioning."[84]

Jackson St George Mivart

The man whose writings prompted Vaughan to issue the pastoral against liberalism was Professor Jackson St George Mivart. Mivart was a convert, a scientist, Fellow of the Royal Society and Master in Biology. For Snead-Cox, St George Mivart was to be another "cross" for Vaughan, "in some ways the most perplexing and painful of all." St George Mivart had received his doctorate from the pope and held a chair at the University of Louvain. He had also been on the staff of Manning's university at Kensington, and had completed his formal education at St Cuthbert's, Ushaw. His scientific contributions to the controversy about evolution were acknowledged by Charles Darwin himself.[85]

In 1884 Mivart published a challenging article (already referred to in Chapter XII concerning the Rescue Society) in the *Dublin Review*. He attempted to answer the questions: why was the progress of the Catholic Church so slow and "why the expectations of 1850 had not been fulfilled?" He proposed the following answers: Catholics were being assimilated into the rest of the community, especially through mixed marriages; they were in a world that was moving away from religion; they were alienated by the aggressive behaviour of the ultramontanes on the Continent; the great revival of the Church of England was completed, with a liturgical life richer and more reverent than their own. Mivart and "old Catholics" doubted if the Romanizing movement in the English Church was wise, and advocated a return to the

English traditions of Catholicism.[86] Mivart's argument that progress was slow, if any, and in some areas ground was being lost, was vindicated in 1885 by the results of Vaughan's inquiry into the state of the Church in Salford Diocese.

In 1884 a writer to the *Irish Ecclesiastical Record* denied that an orthodox Catholic could accept the theory of evolution. The following year Mivart replied that a scientist might have a better understanding of scripture than the Church authorities. He was not censured and so took on a new topic, trying to reduce the horrors of hell, and wrote three articles for *The Nineteenth Century* in 1892 and 1893. They were put on the Index of forbidden books by the Holy Office and Mivart submitted to Rome. When *Providentissimus Deus* was published in 1893, some Catholics who had accepted Mivart's theory of a physical, as distinct from psychical, evolution, were forced to retract and Mivart came to the conclusion that "Catholic doctrine and science were fatally at variance."[87] When his articles were included in the 1899 edition of the Index, he asked which propositions were being questioned and was refused an answer. At that point, Mivart withdrew his submission to the Holy Office and denounced the Roman Congregations. He also called for some changes in the force of the doctrine of infallibility, in view of past errors the Church had made in controversies between science and religion.

Mivart demanded an apology from Vaughan for remarks made about him in *The Tablet*. Instead, Vaughan sent him a Profession of Faith, which he refused to sign. In their correspondence, Mivart accused Vaughan of not having read the articles he was condemning. In a letter of 14 January 1900, Mivart wrote to Vaughan directly out of an "old and valued friendship" concerning the "insults of *The Tablet*." "I make no objection to criticism of my writings," he wrote, but objected to "the imputation to me of personal defects as to ordinary courage and honesty. I repeat that my appeal is to your Eminence both as proprietor of *The Tablet* and as a gentleman as regards family and sentiments." Mivart felt that Vaughan had imputed to him "calumnious mendacity and cowardice" through his subordinates on *The Tablet*.

In addition, Mivart was "astonished" to find that Vaughan "can never have read the Articles you condemn." Furthermore, he could not see "how it is possible for the human intellect to set bounds to possibilities as to the absolute *potestas* of the Almighty with respect to matters so utterly inconceivable." What had been written about his articles reminded him of "the attack made by Kingsley on Cardinal Newman. As to much I have been saddled with I can truly exclaim, as Newman did, 'I never said it!'"[88] On 16 January Vaughan replied with a brief letter: "I regret that I must call upon you a third and last time to forward to me, with your signature attached thereto, the form of profession of Faith, which as your Bishop I felt bound to send to you, in consequence of the Articles published by you in the XIX Century and Fortnightly Review." Vaughan told Mivart that he was trying to evade his duty by referring to what was written in *The Tablet*: "If you have a grievance against the Tablet, you must go to the Editor. I am responsible neither for its language nor its arguments."[89]

In a paper, titled the "Case of Dr. Mivart," found in the Westminster Diocesan Archive, the unnamed author writes that Vaughan had "to take action of a decisive kind in the matter." "Besides," it continues, "we have reason to know that the Cardinal was impelled by higher authority to move in the affair on account of the great scandal caused...." After a lengthy correspondence, Vaughan "pronounced as he was bound to do, the sentence of excommunication."[90]

In the opinion of Derek Holmes, Vaughan's correspondence illustrates that, in spite of a genuine sincerity and kindness, which Mivart himself recognized, the Cardinal lacked the ability, or perhaps more significantly, the attitude, that might have been helpful in resolving the problem. Mivart also believed that Vaughan was constrained by the doctrine of infallibility, which would "eat away" the substance of the Church and reduce it to a "mouldering, repulsive skeleton."

The circular letter in which Vaughan declared Mivart suspect of heresy and denied him the sacraments until he proved his orthodoxy brought a strong reaction from Wilfrid Ward. Ward believed that Church authorities would "tend to identify one form of liberalism with the other, and meet the situation by sheer intolerance." Another reaction came from the Jesuit George Tyrrell with whom Vaughan had earlier suggested that Mivart consult: "How horrid all this about Mivart. It will throw everything back a decade and leave the Ark of God in the hands of Philistines."[91]

The Joint Pastoral

According to Maisie Ward, St George Mivart's actions gave Herbert Vaughan a great shock. Not only did Mivart refuse to retract his statements but he was later to die under excommunication.[92] Mivart's excommunication was followed by articles in various papers, including *The Times* and *The Tablet*, ostensibly by Catholics, all written in a tone of defiance of Church authority. There was correspondence in the *Weekly Register* responding to the topic "A Plea for *Habeas Corpus* in the Church" and the Catholic Union of Great Britain protested against the tone of the *Osservatore Romano* when it was dealing with English problems.[93]

The turbulent reaction to the defiant attitude taken by letter-writers in the Press was another indication that a pro-Reform attitude was emerging in some Catholic circles in England. Aubert says that at this point the Church authority hoped to take control of the situation, defend the Roman Congregations and emphasize the difference between the teaching Church and the learning Church. But the predominantly negative character of the document only increased anxiety despite a covering letter by the Pope.[94]

Wilfrid Ward thought that the pastoral condemning liberalism had an almost determining influence in driving George Tyrrell to the far left. But Vaughan had already written to Mother Mary of Jesus in March 1899 that a book written by Tyrrell would certainly be suppressed, because the "Censor in Rome to whom I sent it has given it to the General S.J.—who is not at all pleased with the theologians of the English Province." In the same correspondence he thanked her for her "words on the subject of liberal Catholicism," and continued: "we need many prayers, because the venom is to be found in many places and there is always the probability that the liberal Catholics will make appeal to public opinion and form a dangerous party." But, Vaughan concluded: "I am quite prepared to meet them in a public contest, if need be." The next step was a response to "liberal Catholics" in the form of a pastoral letter.[95]

Vaughan drew up a plan for a response to the views of Mivart, and sent it to Merry del Val. The Roman authorities had also linked George Tyrrell to Mivart. Merry del Val replied that he brought the matter to the Pope but thought that it was Vaughan's "place and duty to speak first in defence of Catholic principle in your own diocese, together with the other Bishops or at all events with the support of the majority of them." Merry del Val then offered to help:

> Would it not be well then, either that you should draft the document and then send it here to be revised by competent persons with the knowledge and approval of the authorities; or that you should allow such person to draft the document and send it to you for your sanction, and final publication? I could get this done for you without anyone appearing in the matter.[96]

According to David Schultenover, what Vaughan finally did is unclear, but a revised version of the proposed pastoral did reach Merry del Val in November 1900. Merry del Val wrote to Vaughan on 7 November that the Pope had spoken of the pastoral "and the evil it is intended to counteract." The Pope had commented on the "causes which have given rise to these liberal tendencies and the evil effects upon Catholics of living in a Protestant and rationalistic atmosphere where almost in spite of themselves they must gradually assimilate so much that is wrong."[97] Schultenover asks the question: "In the end, who bore final responsibility for authorship of the joint pastoral?" From his study of the *Memorias* of the Jesuit General, the Spaniard Luís Martín, he suspects that Martín had other ideas about authorship of the pastoral.

Both Martín and Merry del Val did not regard Herbert Vaughan as firm enough in his views on liberalism to be trusted to write against it. Neither of them "would be inclined to consider Vaughan the effective author." The final proofs of the pastoral arrived from Vaughan and were given to Martín on 20

November. Martín "noted two or three quite defective points and notified Fr Meyer of them. He met Frs Hughes and Brandi on 24 November and discussed the corrections that ought to be made in the pastoral, and these with unanimous accord were sent by Merry del Val to Cardinal Vaughan. He received them gratefully, and, having approved the new redaction, sent the pastoral to Rome." Martin considered Merry del Val the chief executor and *sub rosa* author of the pastoral with the assistance of two others and himself. By 21 December the document was with the pope and after he approved, it was then signed by the English bishops. Dated 29 December 1900, it was published in *The Tablet* on 5 and 12 of January 1901. At the time, Vaughan was in Rome for his official *ad limina* visit.[98]

James Britten, secretary of the Catholic Truth Society, was a friend of Fr Bernard Ward. When the pastoral was published, Ward was president of St Edmund's College, Ware. Britten told the Wards a joke about the joint pastoral: "The story reached us of the gradual declension in the title of the Joint Pastoral. On appearance it was called "the joint," after its reception "the cold joint," after discussion of it "the hash." We told this back to Bernard, who laughed more than he might have done a few years later when he himself was a bishop."[99]

According to Holmes, the pastoral described the nature of ecclesiastical authority in the most extreme and unqualified terms. Tyrrell thought it illustrated the bishops' ignorance of contemporary difficulties. He wrote to von Hügel: "The bishops have mounted on metaphors as witches on broomsticks." Wilfrid Ward thought that it was "an ungrateful task to be continually protecting those in authority from the consequences of their own utterances." He also thought it was a scandal to have bishops signing such documents that at least two did not agree with, but feared giving scandal if they did not. Holmes considers Vaughan's part: "A concern for a narrow uniformity out of a sense of pastoral responsibility or conceived as an apologetic weapon became almost typical of English Catholics as a result of the example of leaders like Vaughan who was rigid and ruthless with himself as well as others and in every sphere of life, intellectual, administrative or devotional."[100]

In the light of Schultenover's conclusions about authorship of the document, Martín and Merry del Val were probably the real masterminds. It is they who are suspected of having manipulated Vaughan and the bishops into issuing the document. Vaughan's own views were too moderate for Martín and Merry del Val, but he was trapped, in Holmes' words, by his pastoral concern for uniformity, and has suffered for it.[101]

Maisie Ward considered the pastoral and the reactions to it to be especially important, and not because it was issued on the eve of the modernist crisis. What impressed her was that it gave an early look at the two latent forces that were to make for insurrection in the Church on the one hand, and the resurrection of Catholic thought and life on the other.[102]

There were other minor examples of Herbert Vaughan's apologetic concerns and his effort to control dissent in the Church.[103] Holmes concludes that it would be unfair to be too strong in criticism of his narrowness. In his view, "A convinced minority finds it difficult to resist the temptation of unduly indulging in self-justification and this becomes almost impossible when there is a real practical need to do so." Vaughan, he continues, struggled "continually with internal difficulties which resulted from the fact that the administrative system remained unsatisfactory." This in turn gave rise to "apologetic considerations because of the danger of scandals and their effect on the Church's public image."[104]

There is a revealing exchange betwen George Tyrrell and Vaughan in Nicholas Sagovsky's *Life of George Tyrrell*. When Tyrrell visited Vaughan he found him cordial and kind. According to Tyrrell, a convert, Vaughan asked him: "Why don't you honour Old Catholics by adopting their time-honoured way of putting things" The time-honoured way of putting things was represented by Canon Moyes, Vaughan's theologian, a man who stood for everything Tyrrell loathed about most theologians. Von Hügel wrote of this conversation: "I know well how, with all his admirable devotedness and also kindness of disposition, it will never be our way of putting things that he will spontaneously understand."[105]

Notes

1. Norman, *Catholic Church*, p.369.
2. John Jay Hughes, *Absolutely Null and Utterly Void*, London, Sheed and Ward, 1968,p.45; And: *idem*, *Stewards of the Lord*, London, Sheed and Ward, 1970; Fielding, *Class and Ethnicity*, pp.40-1. Vaughan represented a hope that one day Roman Catholicism would resume its position as the Country's established religion. The effort to establish the Church's patriotic credentials, down to the building of Westminster Cathedral, were used to implant the impression of a "national church-in-waiting;" Vaughan's opposition, therefore, was both logical and consistent.
3. George Tavard, *A Review of Anglican Orders*, Collegeville, Glazier, 1990, pp.8-9.
4. Correspondence, Kisii, Kenya, 14 May 1992. A member of Vaughan's missionary society wrote to the author in 1992 criticizing Vaughan for being true to form in condemning Anglican orders; A conference on *Apostolicae Curae* was held on 20-22 April 1995 at the General Theological Seminary in New York. See: "Anglican Orders as Bones of Contention," *National Catholic Reporter*, 28 April 1995.
5. Jedin, *History*, 9, p.140ff; Hughes, *Null and Void*, p.28: Lord Halifax was an extraordinary man. He lived till 1934, when he died at the age of ninety-four. "A son of the old Whig aristocracy, born to wealth and privilege, a close friend of the Prince of Wales, later King Edward VII, Halifax was an aristocrat to his fingertips. He was brought up as a Low Church Anglican, but contact with Dr Pusey and with the successors of the Tractarians at Oxford converted him to the Anglo-Catholic view of the Church of England and its heritage. This led him to join the English Church Union.... He was elected president of the Union in 1868 at the age of only twenty-nine. For fifty years he was to hold this post, which provided him with the one all-absorbing interest of his life. Halifax was a masterly and imperious man, conscious that

he was born to lead and command, but also to serve. He was also a deeply religious man, possessed, as his son's biographer has written, of "a deep and pathetic humility." He was a man of prayer and never missed daily Mass if he could help it. He had a personal chaplain who was once offered the bishopric of the Windward Islands when Halifax was in his late eighties. The chaplain was "torn between his loyalty to Lord Halifax and his desire to accept the offer." He sought advice and was told "Halifax is the greatest layman the Church of England has produced for at least a century: you should stay with him to the end." The chaplain remained. Although he was the object of Catholic "convert makers," Lord Halifax never thought for a moment of becoming a Catholic. "In his unshakable belief in the reality of Anglican sacraments he was at one with the overwhelming majority of faithful Anglicans, then and now."

6. Norman, *Catholic Church*, pp.369-70; On the APUC see: E. B. Stuart, "Roman Catholic Involvement in the APUC," *JEH*, 41, January 1990, no 1, pp.40ff: Vaughan addressed a Catholic Truth Society Conference on the topic of reunion in 1894 and said that although Catholics had been invited to join the association when it was founded in 1857 "they had never been able to accept the invitation;" p.63, quoted from *The Lamp*, xlvii, 1894, p.613: Stuart writes that Vaughan's statement, "so convinced and yet so wrong, reveals the extent of the neo-ultramontane victory over English Roman Catholicism. Thirty years after the condemnation, it was believed that no Roman Catholic had ever belonged to the APUC." The association was a joint Anglican-Roman Catholic association of prayer. It had Catholic members. It was condemned by Rome "for encouraging indifferentism by claiming that the Roman, Greek and Anglican Churches had an equal right to the title 'Catholic,' the distinct mark of the true Church." One member was Bishop Moriarty of Kerry. Another was Ambrose de Lisle, who wrote to Nicholas Wiseman asking for his advice. See: WDA. De Lisle, Longcliffe Lodge, Loughborough, December 29, 1864, to Cardinal Wiseman.

7. Snead-Cox, 2, p.146; WDA. Memorandum, Lord Halifax, Summer, 1895; Hughes, *Null and Void*, p.32: Portal was in touch with the younger clergy in the French Church who were working for intellectual and spiritual reform, among whom were Duchesne, Klein and Loisy. He was a man of deep spirituality, with a ready wit, gaiety, charm, and boundless enthusiasm. From Halifax he learned about the Church of England, which he had previously regarded as just another Protestant sect.

8. See: Martin Wellings, "Anglo-Catholicism, the Crisis in the Church, and the Cavalier Case of 1899," *JEH*, 42, 2, April 1991, p.240ff; p.241: Protestant opposition to the policies and practices of Anglo-Catholics in the Church of England, silenced to some extent by the failure of the Church Association's prosecution of Bishop King in 1888-92, took on a new vigour in 1897-8 due to the combination of four factors. One was the promotion of schemes for reunion with Rome by Lord Halifax."

9. Hughes, *Null and Void*, p.33.

10. *ibid.*, pp.38-9.

11. *ibid.*, pp.40-1.

12. Snead-Cox, 2, pp.146-8; Jedin, *History*, 9, pp.140-1.

13. Hughes, *Null and Void*, p.35.

14. See: Margaret Pawley, *Faith and Family: the Life and Circle of Ambrose Phillipps de Lisle*, Norwich, Canterbury Press, 1993.

15. Norman, *Catholic Church*, p.370.

16. MHA. HCV. Scrapbooks. Newspaper clippings. Article by Raymond Blathwayt.

17. Hughes, *Null and Void*, p.43.

18. Snead-Cox, 2, p.156: Taken from a book by "Professor Mason, who was present," titled *Edward White Benson, Archbishop of Canterbury*, 2, p.597; In another letter addressed to Halifax on 14 December 1894, Archbishop Benson wrote: "I am afraid that you have lived for years so exclusively with one set of thinkers, and entered so entirely into the usages of one class of churches, that you have not before you the state of religious feeling and activity in England with

the completeness with which any one attempting to adjust the relations between Churches ought to have the phenomena of his own side clearly and minutely before him." Snead-Cox, 2, p.180.

19. WDA. Ditcham Park, Petersfield, 5 December 1895, Francis Gasquet to Moyes; MHA. HCV. Fr Farmer's letters from Cardinal Vaughan and others.

20. Snead-Cox, 2, p.177.

21. CANH.

22. Snead-Cox, 2, pp.178-80; Hughes, *Null and Void*, pp.223-7: In 1885 Merry del Val came to the attention of Pope Leo XIII. He was made a monsignor while still a sub-deacon, and sent on diplomatic missions to the courts of Vienna and Berlin before his ordination at twenty-three. He was an archbishop at thirty-five and Cardinal Secretary of State at thirty-eight. Under Leo XIII, his gratitude, combined with a loyal and generous nature, would "stifle his critical faculties with regard to the institution of the papacy or the person, policies, and utterances" of the Pope. "And by inevitable corollary Merry del Val was quick to see a dangerous heretic in anyone who suggested plans or ideas which seemed to threaten, however remotely, his own exalted view of the papacy."

23. *ibid.*, p.185; Derek Holmes, *More Roman*, p.218ff.

24. Jedin, *History*, 9, p.142.

25. CANH.

26. WDA. Correspondence, 8 August 1895.

27. Snead-Cox, 2, pp.195-6.

28. Scottish Catholic Archives. Vaughan to Smith, 30 April 1896.

29. Tavard, *Anglican Orders*, pp.92-7.

30. *ibid.*, pp.96-8.

31. CANH.

32. Jedin, *History*, 9, p.142.

33. Hughes, *Null and Void*, p.182ff: Canon Moyes lived in the same house with Vaughan for twenty-seven years and wrote that, despite the fact that Vaughan had spoken of a period of "grace and conversion" following the condemnation, he did not entertain an expectation of increased conversions: "It was said that Cardinal Vaughan seriously expected that hundreds of Anglican clergy would enter the Church if Anglican Orders were condemned. There was certainly a rumour to that effect, but, as far as I know, the Cardinal never attached importance to it, nor treated it as anything more than a rumour 'much too good to be true'"; An essay by Sheridan Gilley is helpful in understanding the context in which nineteenth and twentieth century conversions have taken place: Sheridan Gilley, "Loss and Gain: Conversions to Catholicism in Britain, 1800-1994," in *Friends of Cardinal Newman Newsletter, Christmas 1994*, pp.4-8. See: p.7: "But conversion to Rome was, despite all protestations to the contrary, an act of secession from the national tradition to one involving rites of separation (conditional rebaptism, confession, confirmation), more belief (the extra clauses of the Creed of Pope Pius IV), more prayer (all those rosaries and devotions) and more money (in a church with no large inherited endowments, as many as four collections at a single Mass!). To some devout Anglicans, Roman Catholicism simply seemed a way of being more religious; and even today, when Popery no longer attracts total social ostracism, and a change of religion is widely regarded as merely moving over to a different brand name, Rome still seems exotic or eccentric."

34. Jedin, *History*, 9, p.143.

35. Hughes, *Null and Void*, p.227.

36. *ibid.*, pp.236, 240. Quotation from: Maisie Ward, *Father Maturin, A Memoir*, London, 1917, p.52: "Of the High Church position in particular the view of the two men was diametrically opposed, the Cardinal regarding it (as) a dangerous and specious substitute keeping men back from the Church, Father Maturin looking on it as a teaching of Catholic truth educating them gradually to receive the fullness of truth in the Church."

37. *ibid.*, p.242: Gosse to Halifax, 8 August 1911; Halifax to Athelstan Riley, 6 October 1896.
38. Various, *Roads to Rome*, London, Longmans, 1901, Introduction.
39. Hughes, *Null and Void*, Appendix. pp.305-6.
40. WDA. Memorandum, Archbishop's House, 9 December 1896.
41. Jerome Vereb, "Ignatius Spencer, Apostle of Christian Unity," London, C T S, 1992; "The Conversion of Father Ignatius Spencer," *The Tablet*, 26 March 1898, p.498: Pope Leo XIII, in his Encyclical Letter issued in 1895, *Ad Anglos*, mentions Father Spencer by name as known to him when in Belgium; Jozef Van den Bussche, C P, *Ignatius (George) Spencer, Passionist (1799-1864)*, Louvain, University Press, 1991, pp.91-2; pp.244-5: "He pointed out ... three basic qualities needed for every attempt at reconciliation regardless of time: the need for personal contacts in mutual understanding; the indissoluble bond between unity and truth; the need for prayer."
42. WDA. 8 December 1897, "A Letter on the Confraternity of Our Lady of Compassion" by Herbert Cardinal Vaughan, London, Burns & Oates, 1897.
43. G. Breffy, *Notre Dame des Victoires*, Paris, Librairie Letouzey & Ane, 1925, pp.31-33.
44. SDA. Bishop of Salford, "England's Conversion by the Power of Prayer," *Papers Read at the Catholic Truth Society Conference, Birmingham, June 30, July 1st and 2nd, 1890*, London, pp.99ff: Vaughan reminded his readers that the conversions which had occurred had been the work of prayer: "During the last 50 years, 550 clergymen and ministers, thousands of hard-headed men of business, including 250 lawyers and physicians and about 100 admirals, generals and field officers.... It has been the work of grace, the triumph of prayer."
45. SDA. Bishop of Salford, "A Letter on the Duty of Catholics towards the Anglican Movement," Manchester, n.d.
46. Holmes, *More Roman*, pp.218-9.
47. *ibid.*, p.222.Quoted from correspondence between Canon Moyes and Vaughan.
48. *ibid.*, p.223.
49. Tavard, *Anglican Orders*, pp.115-7.
50. General Theological Seminary Library, New York: A private collection of pamphlets and pastorals with a handwritten table of contents. No.13: "The Archbishop of York on the reply of Cardinal Vaughan to the Archbishops."
51. James MacCaffrey, *History of the Catholic Church in the Nineteenth Century*, 2, Dublin, Gill, 1909. pp.70-74; Some years after Herbert Vaughan's death his brother Bernard became involved in an issue that resulted from a conference at "Kikuyu," a Church of Scotland Mission in East Africa. Bernard Vaughan wrote that in most questions of doctrine and discipline "her members agree to differ." But on one point they were united, their "rejection of the claims of blessed Peter and his successors." He summed up what he thought was wrong with the Church of England: "It does not know what to believe and there is no living person to tell it. A church without authority must lapse sooner or later into what Bishop Weston says it has already lapsed, 'a state of mental chaos.'" Like his late brother Herbert, Bernard continued: To the "members of the Church of England we offer our trust, sympathy, pity and love; but to the Church of Henry, Edward and Elizabeth we cannot pretend to express much respect." See: J. J. Willis, Bishop of Uganda, "The Kikuyu Conference," London, Longmans, 1914; Bernard Vaughan, "Kikuyu or 'A House Divided,'" Manchester, London, Burns & Oates, 1914; In response to criticism of the Kikuyu Conference, Hensley Henson, the Dean of Durham, gave a sermon at St Mary's Anglican Church in Oxford on 1 February 1914. For him, the issue was not over ceremonies but over a point of view. "Which shall it be? Backwards always to a receding past? Or forwards to the increasing future? A creed of sterility or a creed of growth? A Religion of the letter or of the Spirit? Phrase it how you will, that is the issue as clearly presented to the Church of England today as when St. Paul stood like a Rock against St. Peter at Antioch. That was the issue of the Reformation, and the Fathers chose Freedom, with all its shadows and risks." See: Hensley Henson, "The Issue of Kikuyu," Sermon given at Oxford, St Mary's, 1 Feb.1914,

London, Macmillan, 1914.

52. WDA. "Report of the Catholic Conference, 1897, The St. Augustine Celebration," London, CTS, 1897.

53. MHA. Scrapbooks. Box 45. Book 2, newspaper, no name or date.

54. Ward, *Insurrection*, p. 150.

55. Ward, *Transition*, p.290; "The Archbishop of Westminster and the Lord Mayor's Election," The *Tablet*, 8 Oct. 1898: Vaughan wrote a letter to the *Globe* which was published on 30 September. He had been asked if under any circumstances a Catholic might attend an Anglican place of worship in an official capacity: "... I may say, however, that the general principle underlying the answer is, that a Catholic may not take part in the religious services of a false religion." He went on to give examples of where it might be allowed. "Scandalized Protestants" wrote to other newpapers including the *Globe* to express indignation that Anglicanism was referred to as a "false religion." *The Tablet* concluded: "Certainly if there are many Protestants who were under the illusion that Catholics regarded their religion as the true one, or anything but one among many false ones, it was exceedingly well that the error was corrected" by Vaughan; In another letter from Vaughan quoted in *The Tablet*, 10 September 1898, p.419, he denied a report that there were "about 50 clergymen in the Church of England being Jesuits." Vaughan wrote: "Were any dispensation ever granted to any Catholic to act as a clergyman of a false religion for the purpose of furthering the supposed interests of the Church of Rome, these dispensations would be known...."

56. Chadwick, *Victorian Church*, 2, p.453ff.

57. Ward, *Transition*, p.260ff; p.267: Up until 1854 a law had barred Catholics from the Universities. With its repeal it seemed they would be free to attend but then it was not the State that barred Catholics but the choice of many Catholics. The chief promoters of the view that a barrier must be maintained to "keep faith and zeal intact" were Catholic converts who were themselves old university men—Henry Manning and William George Ward. During Manning's lifetime there was no hope for a change of policy. "Even the discovery that the handful of Catholics at Oxford were all practising their religion left him unmoved. 'There is abundant mischief,' he said, 'short of losing faith, such as losing humility, modesty, respect for authority, and in a word, the *sentire cum ecclesia*.'" Quoted from Leslie, *Manning*, p.186.

58. Vincent A. McClelland, *English Roman Catholics and Higher Education, 1830-1903*, Oxford, Clarendon Press, 1973, pp.372-3; See also: Holmes, *More Roman*, pp.224-34: For background to the prohibition: In 1863 an article in the *Dublin Review* pointed out the need to provide for Catholic higher education. In 1864 the majority of English bishops discouraged Catholics from attending the older universities. In Holmes' opinion the ultimate issue was wider and more fundamental than the return of Newman to Oxford, Catholic attendance at the universities or even the danger to their faith. It was another aspect of the contest between the ultramontanes and their opponents. It was Vaughan who had gone to the Pope in 1867 and told him that there was immediate danger of losing control of higher studies and the formation of a liberal and anti-Roman school at Oxford. The English bishops decided to establish a university but it only amounted to an examining board for the existing Catholic colleges. In 1874 Manning made an attempt to begin the Kensington college. Wilfrid Ward called it a "ludicrous failure."

59. Snead-Cox, 2, p.70ff.; Newsome, *Convert Cardinals*, p.323; SDA. One of only two letters found written by Mary Elizabeth Herbert to Herbert Vaughan. Dublin, 15 September 1874, signed: "Your devoted Child and Sister M. E. Herbert." Vaughan had written her about the university that was "meant for my host and his friends as much as for me and in consequence I gave it to them and the subject was discussed almost all day in consequence.... Ever since this question was started, I have felt that the Catholic Clergy, as a Body, wanted one thing and the laity another. That the former in their position as Priests, naturally feel that they speak from Authority and should be obeyed but that they have failed to enlist the sympathy or the reason of the laity in their proposed scheme."

60. SDA. Elizabeth Herbert, 15 September 1874.

61. McClelland, *Education*, pp.372-3; Chadwick, *Victorian Church*, 2, p.454.

62. McClelland, *Education*, pp.373-4.

63. Snead-Cox, 2, pp.70-86; especially pp.79-80.

64. Ward, *Transition*, pp.268-9.

65. Snead-Cox, 2, pp.70-80.

66. *ibid.*

67. McClelland, *Education*. pp.375-79.

68. *ibid.*, p.383.

69. *ibid.*, p.384.

70. Snead-Cox, 2, pp.83-4. A letter to Hedley dated 5 January 1895.

71. MHA. HCV. Fr Farmer's letters from Vaughan.

72. McClelland, *Education*, pp.384-5. Letter from the Farm St Archives.

73. Garrett Sweeney, *St Edmund's House, Cambridge, The First Eighty Years*, Cambridge, St Edmund's, 1980, p.2.

74. Holmes, *More Roman*, p.234.

75. McClelland, *Education*, pp.386-7. Document from the Brompton Oratory Archive.

76. Snead-Cox, 2, p.86; See: Vincent A. McClelland, "Herbert Vaughan, The Cambridge Teachers' Training Syndicate, and the Public Schools, 1894-1899," *Paedagogia Historica*, xvi, 1975, pp.16-38: Vaughan continued to oppose the influence and interests of the English Catholic aristocratic families and their associates on two other issues. "One of these was concerned with an attempt to provide a training institute in Cambridge for those Roman Catholic women who were about to teach in secondary schools—an apparent and urgent need on the eve of the Education Act of 1902—and the other was an attempt on the part of the aristocracy to enable their sons to attend the greater Protestant schools...."

77. Snead-Cox, 2, pp.34-69; Mary P. McInally, "Edward Ilsley; Man of the People," unpublished MS, 1995, pp.132-50: Based on original research, Vaughan's part in the central seminary project is discussed. The matter of discipline was the serving of spirits at professors' weekly meetings "and that they placed them on the table whenever there were visitors."

78. Holmes, *More Roman*, pp.234ff; James J. Kelly, "The Modernist Controversy in England: The Correspondence between Friedrich von Hügel and Percy Gardner," *Downside Review*, January 1981, vol 99, p.56 n.2: Baron Friedrich von Hügel (1852-1925). Born in Florence, he moved with his family to Torquay, England, in 1867. After undergoing a religious crisis following his father's death in June 1870, he began a course of "moral and religious training" and subsequently determined to devote himself "to the study of 'Biblical Criticism and Religious Philosophy.' His friendship with so many important modernists in England, France, Germany and Italy led to him being designated "the lay-bishop of the movement."

79. David G. Schultenover, *George Tyrrell—In Search of Catholicism*, Shepherdstown, Patmos, 1981, pp.144-5; Mary Jo Weaver, "George Tyrrell and the Joint Pastoral Letter," *Downside Review*, January 1981, vol 99, p.19: "The immediate provocative context for the pastoral may well have been the so-called 'Mivart affair.' Jackson St George Mivart (1827-1900), a Roman Catholic convert and biologist, was eager for a reconciliation between modern scientific principles and Roman Catholic doctrine. In 1892, he published an article, 'Happiness in Hell,' in *The Nineteenth Century*, which caused quite a controversy, and resulted in several subsequent articles, all of which were placed on the Index;" p.36: For Tyrrell: "Toward the end of the nineteenth century it became clear to him that there was an 'authority fever' in the air, and that his modest programme of mediating liberalism was not going to work."

80. Roger Aubert, "The Modernist Crisis," in Jedin, *History*, 9, p.442; See: Josef L. Altholz, *The Liberal Catholic Movement in England, The Rambler and its Contributors, 1848-64*, London, Burns & Oates, 1962, p.1: "The liberalism of Liberal Catholicism consisted rather in its view of the relations between theology and politics: it was an intellectual liberalism, characterized by an

emphasis upon the legitimacy and value of intellectual sources independent of the authority of the Church."

81. Aubert, p.420: Nineteenth-century liberalism: "renewed questioning of the traditional conception the Church had of the political and social order; the aggiornamento of the ecclesiastical institutions; the forms of the pastoral and the life style of the Christians living in and committed to this modern world; and the restoration of exegesis, theology, and religious philosophy. In this very general sense, modernism could be defined as 'the meeting and confrontation of a long religious past with a present which found the vital sources of inspiration in anything but this past.'(Poulat);" See also: Roger Aubert, *The Church in a Secularized Society*, New York, 1978, p.187; And: Gabriel Daly, *Transcendence and Immanence: A Study in Catholic Modernism and Integralism*, Oxford, 1980, p.3; "Liberal Catholicism," *The Tablet*, 7 May 1898, p.739: The article quoted from *The Month*, and George Tyrrell, SJ: "There is no more pressing problem just now than the precise relation of Catholic Christianity to the cause of civilization and progress.... The true Liberalism is really for the very few who are capable of thinking widely, deeply, and temperately.... It is when Liberalism becomes 'popular,' when it is affected by the half-educated, and is made the catch-word for party, that it becomes ridiculous, shallow, and irritating...."

82. See: Thomas Shelly, "John Cardinal Farley and Modernism in New York," *Church History*, vol 61, no 3, September 1992, pp.350-361, n 1; Thomas Shelly, *Dunwoodie*, Westminster, Christian Classics, 1993, pp.148-170.

83. Jedin, *History*, 9, p.328.

84. Holmes, *More Roman*, p.234.

85. Snead-Cox, 2, pp.300ff; See also: J. W. Gruber, *A Conscience in Conflict, the Life of St George J. Mivart*, New York, 1960.

86. Chadwick, *Victorian Church*, 2, p.410

87. Holmes, *More Roman*, p 235.

88. WDA. 14 January 1900, 77 Inverness Terrace, Mivart to Herbert Vaughan.

89. WDA. 16 January 1900, Vaughan to Mivart; Another letter addressed to Vaughan by "Gandolfi," Villa Gandolfi, San Remo, January 16, 1902, is an example of one kind of advice Vaughan received over the issue: "I read the outrageous and impudent article of "Dr." St George Mivart in this XIX Century review as soon as it was issued.... Though I am not a Cardinal, Doctor of Theology, or a Wilfrid Ward, I am what I am; and descended as ... (like yourself) from the most aristocratic Catholic houses.... I could not stand a man who is not even a Christian much less a Catholic masquerading as a teacher of Religion so I wrote him a letter most plainly giving Mr Mivart my opinion as to both his views and as to himself. I wound up by reminding him of the fable of the Fox who lost his tail in a trap (the trap of intellectual pride compressed into too small a head) and who advised the other foxes to cut off their tails... which they did not care to do; and I told Mr. St. G. M. that he had ceased to be either a Christian or a Catholic, that I repudiated for one, all he had written ... he removed himself from the Church that the Church would remove him...."

90. WDA. Case of Dr Mivart; Holmes, *More Roman*, pp.236-7.

91. See: Jedin, *History*, 9, p.445-6: George Tyrrell was a respected preacher, spiritual director, author of devotional books and apologetic essayist. According to Aubert, he came under the influence of Friedrich von Hügel and through him became familiar with biblical criticism and Neo-Kantian philosophy. He was of Irish descent, born in 1861, and converted from Anglicanism when he was eighteen. He joined the Jesuits and in 1896 was assigned to the editorial staff of *The Month*. Some of the articles he wrote were published in 1901 in a book entitled *The Faith of Millions*. He experienced difficulties with Church censorship. Aubert continues: "Tyrrell, overly sensitive and irritable by nature, even more irritable because of the first symptoms of Bright's disease, of which he eventually died, was highly incensed by the narrow-minded limitations imposed upon his intellectual pursuits. Consequently he began to doubt the

authority of the ecclesiastical hierarchy."

92. Ward, *Insurrection*, p.134.

93. Holmes, *More Roman*, pp. 237-8; Ward, *Transition*, p.323.

94. Jedin, *History*, 9, p.443.

95. Ward, *Insurrection*, p.134; CANH. Vaughan, 22 March (probably 1899), to Mother Mary of Jesus.

96. Schultenover, *George Tyrrell*, pp.144-5.

97. David Schultenover, *A View From Rome, On the Eve of the Modernist Crisis*, New York, Fordham, 1993, pp.148-9.

98. *ibid.*, pp.150-1: "Of course, had the public known the true story of the genesis of the pastoral, who really wrote it, how 'frankness and unity' had been arranged, and therefore why it all had to be executed with absolute secrecy, the reception even among those who praised it would probably have been not a little different. The pastoral's content and reception by Tyrrell and like-minded readers has been covered at length elsewhere. Suffice it to say that the pastoral harbingered the content and style of *Pascendi Dominici Gregis*. The similarity is not surprising, now that historical evidence has established Rafael Merry del Val as the principal fabricator of both documents, with executive and editorial assistance on the joint pastoral by Luís Martín;" About Luís Martín, See: *The Tablet*, 8 October 1892, p.566.

99. Ward, *Insurrection*, p.142.

100. Holmes, *More Roman*, p.240.

101. Schultenover, *View from Rome*, p.84: Vaughan's testimony in defence of Tyrrell, saying he found nothing offensive in "A Perverted Devotion" and held Tyrrell in "great regard and appreciation," to Martín, counted for little, "as the cardinal had already been discredited for his softness in dealing with the Dreyfus affair." He was not anti-Semitic enough; p.150: Merry del Val and Martin also thought Vaughan had been too lenient dealing with "liberalism."

102. Ward, *Insurrection*, p.134.

103. WDA. Circular for Lent 1898: no.8: "I regret to say that a work has recently been published in this Diocese, entitled 'Steps to Re-Union,' by the Rev James Duggan. I have considered it my duty to delate it to the Holy See. I deem it to be offensive to pious ears, temerarious, and scandalous. The writer in his introduction declares that he submits his work to the judgement of the Church."

104. Holmes, *More Roman*, p.240.

105. Nicholas Sagovsky, *"On God's Side": A Life of George Tyrrell*, Oxford, Clarendon Press, 1990, p.95.

CHAPTER XVII

The Missions, Rescue and Education

Home Missions

1. Mission to London

During Lent of 1894 Cardinal Herbert Vaughan organized a general mission for all the Catholic parishes of London. It began on Quinquagesima Sunday and lasted for four weeks: the first was devoted to children but adults were also encouraged to attend; the second and third weeks were for adults; and the final week was set aside for following up on the adults participating. A house-to-house religious census had already begun when Vaughan addressed his letter: "To all the Fathers engaged for the Simultaneous Mission, London, 1894," on 14 January. What the census returns had already revealed to Vaughan was "an alarming defection." The total number of Catholics from the census of thirty-one London missions should have been "75,745 i.e. 25,084 more than the number registered or known to the clergy. What must be the spiritual condition of these?" Therefore he asked his priests to care for the practising Catholics and then "go out into the highways and byways and by repeated visits and persuasive charity to compel that still larger multitude, which is leading the life of the heathen to come into the feast prepared for them by the Merciful Lord." They were reminded that they were also sent to the non-Catholic population.[1]

Vaughan asked the priests who were giving the mission to remind the people of the "disastrous" consequences which resulted from mixed marriages.[2] They were also asked to point out the vital importance of hearing Mass on Sundays and holy days. The attendance figures he had already received indicated that "a state of spiritual languor or paralysis is creeping over us." Other points to be stressed were the value of a good home life and the relative duties of parents and children. Finally he asked for their cooperation in the formation of a system of help for the young after they left school and reminded them that they needed the cooperation of the educated and devout laity: If not "we shall always remain unable to deal successfully with the enormous difficulties before the Church in this country particularly in respect to the training of the rising generations of the working classes."[3]

427

In a letter to Mary Elizabeth Herbert on 7 April he mentioned that about 60,000 had gone to confession and received communion for Easter during the "General Mission" and that there were 450 converts and catechumens who presented themselves.[4]

The following year, in March 1895, he wrote to Mother Mary in obvious distress. He was in Rome and had been assured by Pope Leo XIII that he would write an encyclical on prayer concerning the question of Reunion. "This is a great grace gained and I perhaps ought to be satisfied with this but I am not." Then he returned to his thoughts about the 1894 Mission: "In London we have 24,000 young Catholics between the age of 13 and 21 who are practically lost to the Church; we have 80,000 Catholics who are practically unknown to the Clergy; we have at least 1,000,000 people who practise no religion and are like heathens. I am sent to all of these, to do the work of Christ for their Salvation."[5]

2. Catholic Social Union

One of the ways he tried to reach the young was through the Catholic Social Union and the Clubs the Union established. McCormack considers the Catholic Social Union Clubs started by Herbert Vaughan as one of his most important, though not so well remembered, enterprises. After his first visit to the East End of London in May 1892, he decided with the help of benefactors to start a youth club, the first of many under the name of The Catholic Social Union, at Mile End Road. By 1894 four others were formed, giving a total enrolment of 1250. Austin Oates acted as organizing secretary and Mgr Dunn was the treasurer. Lady Mary Talbot, sister-in-law to the Duke of Norfolk, later became the honorary secretary to the central committee. From the beginning the idea was taken outside the archdiocese as well.[6]

But the youth clubs did not do enough to satisfy Vaughan completely. He continued in his letter to Mother Mary of Jesus: "But the 80,000 and the 1,000,000—I am sent to all of these and I know not what to do. I tell Our Lord continually that with the best will I do not see my way clearly at all. In two settlements— that of Lady Margaret Howard (Norfolk) and the Duchess (Newcastle) are good; but hardly touch these last two categories—a little the first—but not at all the second. They need to be multiplied by 100." Vaughan asked that Carmel help by praying and offering their sufferings on his behalf. He had prayed himself "but light comes not." He was sure that he would not see his way "till some of us—you and the Prioress perhaps—have gone through much suffering."

> The work is enormous—a mission to the East End millions. How to begin! How to go on! What to say! What to do! The amount of sin and crime to be encountered with their deadening traditions and habits, all this and much more, can never be overcome except by proportional suffering with the prayers of faith.... But are we to shrink? Are we to leave this immense

multitude of abandoned souls without making a supreme effort to save them? Are we not to desire, most earnestly to desire the death of a martyr of Charity, age, and faith in such a cause? Many of my predecessors have taken a much more circumscribed view of their mission to London; may I, can I, follow their example? Am I under some wild delusion—grasping after the impractical and the impossible?"

Vaughan concluded with the request that if Mother Mary, or the Prioress of Carmel, had "any lights in prayer as to all this" they should write to him at Rome.[7]

3. Mission to Polish and Lithuanian Immigrants

There were other groups of Catholic immigrants in his diocese besides the thousands of Irish. The numbers of Lithuanian and Polish Catholics, and especially their children, concerned Herbert Vaughan just as much as the large numbers in East London whom he felt were drifting away from the Church. With parents whose language was not English, the young might be also be lost to the Church if not taught the catechism in their own language. Vaughan found an answer to this problem while he was in Rome during March of 1893 and heard about a new Polish congregation of nuns.

The Sisters of the Holy Family of Nazareth were founded by Frances Siedliska; in religious life she became Mother Mary of the Good Shepherd. The congregation had been established in Rome in 1875 and devoted themselves to catechizing children, instructing converts, and conducting retreats for women. In 1885 they opened a convent in Poland, and in 1891 in the United States. Vaughan told Mother Frances Siedliska about his concerns for the Polish and Lithuanian immigrants in London and invited her to visit England to see their needs for herself. She accepted his invitation and travelled to London in the middle of 1894.

She and her companions were welcomed on arrival by Mary Elizabeth Herbert. Lady Herbert escorted Mother Mary around London and they discussed the possibility of opening a convent. It was Elizabeth Herbert who shared Vaughan's special interest in the immigrant community and helped the Polish Sisters to begin their first English mission in 1895. In a letter to Mary Elizabeth on 7 June, Vaughan said he would be very grateful to have them establish themselves in the archdiocese to work among the Lithuanians and Poles: "There are at least 3,000, probably more, in London. I can give the sisters nothing but the field of work and harvest in a blessing. Money I have none."

Mother Siedliska was in Paris in July and Vaughan asked Elizabeth Herbert to visit her on his behalf and ask that she urgently open a house in London. Mother Mary, along with another Sister and her spiritual director, Fr Lechert, went to London to meet with Vaughan. This time she was able to rent a house and promised to send her Sisters. The first nuns arrived soon afterwards to take up the teaching of catechism to children. Cardinal Vaughan also appointed Father Lechert to be the rector of the Polish Mission.[8]

On the weekend of 12-13 November 1994, the Poles of England and Wales celebrated the founding of the Polish Catholic Mission. Today there are thirty-eight churches served by one hundred and twenty priests, as well as a Catholic publishing house and a weekly newspaper.[9]

4. Catholic Evidence: Town Hall Lectures, Historical Research Society and Diocesan Missionary Society

In April 1932, the centenary of Herbert Vaughan's birth, the editor of The Tablet recalled the Cardinal's work in the cause of Catholic Evidence. "Other pens will do justice to the Cardinal and Bishop and Archbishop, Cathedral builder, missionary worker and—on a more domestic note—proprietor and for a long period editor of this paper." Catholic Evidence was Vaughan's "apostolate for the diffusion of knowledge of the Church, her history and her teaching, by the spoken word."

After he came to Westminster he "challenged the age ... and the doubters ... in the public halls of north-east and west London ... to listen to the Catholic case and put their objections. The Town Hall lectures would attract "anti-Catholic stalwarts" who were not really considered "unwelcome visitors."

A former soldier would often keep order with a "sense of military power and sternness." With troublesome "Dissenters: a minatory finger and 'One word more from you, Sir, and out you go.'" "Great times!," the editor concluded.

The Historical Research Society was another project of Herbert Vaughan's. "He not only sanctioned and encouraged the work, but himself took an active share in it by presiding at the meetings." They began at a tea party given by Vaughan at the old Archbishop's House. The idea came from the "Watch Tower" section of the Guild of Our Lady of Ransom. At first, every month there was a lecture that followed a yearly theme. They were held "in that spacious upper floor of the Cardinal's house which was partly library and partly ... bedrooms. Among them Herbert Vaughan's humble cell."

Vaughan's aim was to encourage "all who would come under his roof." Members were enrolled and the general public invited; a red cord was stretched across the room to separate the two groups. The Historical Research Society was a work which was "conceived, watched over, and witnessed by the great Cardinal whose centenary we are to keep, with prayer and thanksgiving Friday next."[10]

Near the very end of Herbert Vaughan's life he founded the "Westminster Diocesan Missionary Society of Our Lady of Compassion." Its title was later changed to the Catholic Missionary Society. The society celebrated its ninetieth anniversary in 1993. Over those ninety years, wrote Cardinal Basil

Hume, the "Catholic Missionary Society has preached the Gospel in our land seeking always to bring our Blessed Lord's message clearly to our brothers and sisters."[11]

Vaughan wrote on 13 February 1903 that although there were three hundred priests working in the archdiocese, there were millions outside the flock but "within our reach." Their spiritual condition was like that of the "inhabitants of China, Japan, or Central Africa. It is probably worse, for they are descendants of forefathers who were devout Catholics, whereas the latter are not children of apostates from the truth, but of those who have never known the mysteries of faith and the truths of redemption. It is especially to these millions that I send you to preach the Gospel." The man Vaughan entrusted the work to was Charles Rose Chase, a convert, who had been an Anglican minister for many years. Chase studied at the Beda College in Rome and was ordained a Catholic priest. Illness delayed his taking up the post, but he recovered, and was finally appointed the superior of the new society.

Chase made Long Court, Gunnersbury, the society's headquarters. He was also urged by Vaughan to cooperate with members of the Confraternity of Our Lady of Compassion, whose members were a "zealous and intelligent band that has for eight or nine years been delivering Catholic Evidence Lectures to non-Catholics in London." Chase was succeeded as superior by the Cardinal's nephew, his brother Reginald's son and his own namesake, Herbert Vaughan. Herbert had been educated at the Oratory School, Oscott, and in Rome before his uncle ordained him in 1900. Under Fr Herbert Vaughan the organization became the Catholic Missionary Society.[12]

5. The Wholesale Loss of Souls

Cardinal Herbert Vaughan was beset near the end of his life by thoughts similar to those that troubled him as a young priest. This had been especially the case when he was in Spain wondering if he had a missionary vocation, and, if he did, how he might take practical steps to begin a missionary college. The thought that there were men, women and children in London, or far away in Madras, Borneo, New Zealand or in Central Africa, who were not being reached by the Catholic Church, was a weight he could not escape. In this state of mind he wrote of the "heathen" of London as well as the unfortunate of India or Africa, in a letter to Carmel on 13 March 1895:

> How to tackle our heathen population is no new question—come up during the last few weeks or months. I have been at it now for nearly four years. Six months before I left Salford, once a week I held conferences with priests and laymen in the hope that we might devise measures. Nothing came of that but a plan for circulating a certain kind of tract.... In London ... I appealed twice to the clergy in Synod and read to them a letter from Propaganda on Indian missions—but all has been so far in vain. No response. And now I have been three years in Westminster and have done nothing. Meanwhile

I realize more keenly than ever the loss of souls that is going on by wholesale. Speaking to the Bishop of Southwark of 1,000,000 unbaptised heathen in London, he said at once: "You underestimate the number."—he does not admit that 1/2 the population is Christian. I think he is right. And I have done nothing.... For 3 or 4 years I have been discussing, consulting and hoping but heaven is hard as brass.

Recalling his twenty-two years of "irreverence" when he ran through the liturgy, he felt that he was the reason why he had failed to accomplish more at Westminster. He asked that the Sisters pray and make up for his shortcomings. To seek advice about his work in London, Vaughan had gone to speak with the Cardinal Prefect of Propaganda and was urged to "find apostolic men, who care for neither place nor comfort, nor promotion, not anything but souls." The prefect told him to try "a chosen band of Benedictines—as they had the early tradition and converted the Anglo-Saxons—(or) perhaps Franciscans. But more prayer and light are needed—as he admitted." Vaughan was "prepared to devote my annuity of 1000 pounds a year to this work and take it from other things and to make any personal sacrifice that may be useful. But this is of little use unless one has light to see the way in which we are to walk."[13]

The Foreign Missions

1. Africa

Vaughan endeavoured to keep reminding the Church of England of the needs of the unevangelized world outside of Great Britain. On the Feast of St Thomas of Canterbury, 29 December 1898, he wrote to his priests concerning a special collection that was to be made on the feast of the Epiphany 1899 for the "Evangelization of Africa." His letter was commented on in *The Tablet* on 7 January. The money was to be used by Propaganda Fide "to put down the curse of African slavery and to establish in its place the voluntary and sweet service of Our Lord Jesus Christ." Vaughan stressed a special obligation: "To boast that the British Empire has grown to be by far the greatest in extent that the world has ever seen is folly. All boasting is vanity and weakness ... whatever the character of the conqueror or the intentions of their government, a great and wise and loving Redeemer overrules secondary causes and utilizes them for ends of mercy."

What had brought him to make such an urgent appeal was the reconquest by Britain of the Sudan and the country between Khartoum and Uganda. "It ought to inspire every faithful Catholic among us with a renewed fire of enthusiasm for the salvation of souls." Vaughan had a vision of the Catholic Churches in the United States, Canada, and "the old Irish and British Churches" in a new enterprise "to vie with each other in organizing missionary bands for Africa and the Far East—to become more generous in their gifts for the propagation of the Faith abroad; in a word, to create within their own centres armies of apostolic men and women ready to leave home and kindred and die in the propagation of the Faith, ready to obey the voice of the Vicar of Christ, as armies obey the command of their General." Vaughan continued with a description of the tribes of the Upper Nile and ended with the appeal for funds by the Pope who had taken up "the grand work of the regeneration of Africa" fifteen years before.[14]

Herbert Vaughan returned to a similar theme in his Christmas message on 17 December 1899. More than any other, the thought of the English Catholic Church's duty towards Africa had been his mind for the previous six months.

> Some are satisfied by the acquisition of power, some by the development of British common interests, some are carried away by the idea of Imperialism and so forth.... What in the Divine dispensation is the mission of our Great British Empire—say towards Africa and the African races? She is advancing, conquering, settling, laying down her roads by land and water—iron, steam and electrical. She proposes to civilize, does she propose to Christianise? She everywhere establishes liberty and order, will she allow Christianity to use the liberty and order she establishes in order that the Gospel may be preached and constant efforts put forth to make disciples of all men?[15]

Herbert Vaughan's interest in the evangelization of Africa goes back to the early days of St Joseph's Missionary College at Mill Hill. He had hopes that his first band of missionaries at Baltimore would someday prepare African-Americans to become missionaries and return to Africa. According to Arthur McCormack, his interest in Africa as a mission-field for his new missionary society began when he first met the explorer Henry Morton Stanley, who had returned from a journey to Central Africa in 1876. Vaughan was a vice-president and one of the original promoters of the Manchester Geographical Society when he was at Salford, and so had opportunity to meet people like Stanley.

Soon after meeting Stanley, Vaughan and Peter Benoit went to Brussels to speak with Leopold II, King of the Belgiums, about a mission in Central Africa. No commitments resulted from the interview and the King's invitation to join an expedition to Central Africa. The president of the missionary support group, The St Joseph's Society, had its own advocates for Africa. One was the Marquis of Ripon, president of the Royal Geographical Society and an explorer and specialist in African geography. Another was Manning, who, in one of the society meetings at Willis Rooms, had called for an African mission.[16]

Vaughan wrote to Louis Casartelli from a health spa in Flanders about his visit to Leopold II and the prospects of an African mission:

> Fr Benoit will have told you of our interview with the King and of the effect it produced on us. I should be much obliged if you would write to [?] M. Abbadie or speak to Father Schafer and say that if there be an opening for

us in the African expedition and we have timely notice we shall be glad to cooperate as far as we may be able. Our mission to the American blacks was with an ultimate view of using them for Africa. The transportation of Africans to America may have been intended by Providence as a means to convert Africa, after the descendants of the slaves have received the grace of Christianity.

However, there was a strong feeling among the missionaries at Mill Hill that they should support a mission to India. To convince them, Vaughan felt that a "much stronger inducement must be held out than that which the King offered to prove that Africa is the field on which we must fix our eyes at present. The immediate importance of knowing at an early date whether we have to go to Africa is ... so that our men might unite scientific with religious efforts in Central Africa."[17]

Vaughan not only had an interest in Africa but he was also very knowledgeable about the continent. He showed this in an article he wrote for the *Dublin Review* in January 1879 titled: "The Evangelization of Africa." It was the first issue of the *Review* under his ownership and with Bishop Hedley as editor.[18] In twenty-six pages he outlined a history of Africa, and then suggested that commerce and science might aid the work of evangelization. His essay reflects the literature of the time on Africa: a mid-Victorian view of the world that "was suffused with a vivid sense of superiority and self-righteousness, if with every good intention," for the evangelization of Africa. However, Vaughan's aim was not for a Church ruled by Europeans but by African Christians.[19]

Vaughan continued:

Here is a vast, unknown country, with an enormous population of intelligent human beings, having an area more than 240 times the size of England and Wales, dependent for salvation upon the same number of bishops as form the Province of Westminster, and upon less than half our number of priests.... Worse than this: these priests are chiefly upon the mere fringe of the continent; they are scattered along immense coasts, at intervals of space in which there are, even on the coast, millions of souls unknown and uncared for, while the vast interior is teeming with many more millions, who will remain plunged in utter darkness until Catholic charity shall permanently settle down amongst them.... Where, then, is the Catholic who refuses light and help to these millions of his brethren? How long shall we remain deaf, stone-deaf, to their claim upon our souls? The God who made us dependent upon those who preached the Gospel of salvation to our souls has made them dependent upon us.

Vaughan urged that Europe promote the missionary enterprise to Africa by doing as "Palestine did—send out Apostles and missioners until they have founded everywhere native priesthoods." But he was convinced that the only hopeful, promising, and effective way of procedure in respect to Africa is that which may be summed up in the words, "the conversion of Africa by the Africans." He saw "Christian black settlements' all over Africa "after the difficult and costly manner followed by Mgr. Comboni." He concluded the article with a quote from the address he gave in New York in 1872 after accompanying his first mission band to Baltimore. Vaughan hoped to see members of St Joseph's Missionary Society at work in Africa, "aided, multiplied, and extending their labours through the generous and loving co-operation of coloured people from this country. Catechists, sisters, and missioners will arise among them."[20]

In 1894 Herbert Vaughan realized his dream of participating in the evangelization of Africa. It was not done with African-Americans recruited by the independent Josephites in the United States, but by his missionaries from Mill Hill.

2. Death Of Peter Benoit

Vaughan lost his vicar and "co-founder" of St Joseph's Missionary Society, Peter Benoit, after a long illness, on Sunday, 28th August 1892. On September 3rd Vaughan gave the funeral oration at the college chapel. He called Benoit the true founder of "this House.... No more apostolic man could be found than Canon Benoit. He was the perfect model of the priesthood."[21] Benoit was succeeded as rector of St Joseph's College by Francis Henry. Fr Henry had been in charge of the minor seminary, the "apostolic school," at Freshfield.[22]

3. The Vicariate of the Upper Nile; East Africa

In 1894 Vaughan's missionaries were invited to go to East Africa. After the explorations of Livingstone in the 1870s, three missionary societies offered to work in the region. The Lyons Missionaries settled at the mouth of the Nile. Four days after the election of Pope Leo XIII, Cardinal Lavigerie's White Fathers were assigned to regions of Central Africa and finally Daniel Comboni, the vicar apostolic of Central Africa in Khartoum, promised to establish missions in the area of the great lakes.

In 1878 the first caravan of White Fathers started for the interior of Africa. One group established a mission with the help of King Mutesa of the Baganda; they later left temporarily. In October 1885, the Anglican Bishop Hannington was murdered and the following May a large number of Christians—including the martyrs of Uganda— were killed during a persecution.[23]

Vaughan had invited Bishop Livinhac, Cardinal Lavigerie's successor, to visit him when he was in London at the request of the government, in 1892. Livinhac had told Vaughan that it was urgent to have English missionaries in Uganda. He had been to see Lord Rosebery and then visited Vaughan. Livinhac proposed that the White Fathers would give up the north-eastern portion of the Nyanza vicariate to Vaughan's St Joseph's Foreign Missionary Society. Early in 1894 Vaughan was asked to supply missionaries to the new British Protectorate over the Baganda of East Africa.

Herbert Vaughan wrote on 7 April: "we are likely to have a mission in Central Africa, and to send out three men." On the 15th he wrote: "The country is somewhat interested in Uganda and I am doing what can be done with Lord Kimberley to prepare the way for our missioners. It will be a great and important field."[24] Negotiations opened between John Forbes, a White Father who was Bishop Livinhac's interpreter, and Father Chevillion, representing the rector of St Joseph's College, Mill Hill. The plan they agreed on was submitted to the Foreign Office by Herbert Vaughan and approved. According to a decree dated 13 July 1894, Propaganda Fide divided the Nyanza Vicariate, giving the north-eastern area to St Joseph's Society; it became the Vicariate of the Upper Nile.[25]

The missionaries from Mill Hill were invited to Uganda "to help break down the foolish idea of many of the peasantry that Protestantism is English and Catholicism the French religion." H. P. Gale, in his book, *Uganda and the Mill Hill Fathers*, writes that Vaughan's missionaries, who were "at once English and Roman Catholic, came as the mission of peace to heal the breach between the older Christian Missions, and to extend the good work begun by the White Fathers' Mission."[26]

To lead the new mission, Henry Hanlon was recalled from Kashmir in India where he had worked since 1890. He was ordained bishop of Teos in Rome on 25 November at the age of thirty-two and arrived at Mill Hill in December 1894. Thomas Matthews and James Prendergast were appointed to join him. In January two more priests, Gregorius Kestens and Luke Plunkett, were added to the first group, and they all prepared for their new assignment.

On 6 May 1895 the small party prepared to leave Mill Hill for the Vicariate of the Upper Nile. Vaughan was present at the departure ceremony and wrote about it to Mother Mary of Jesus: "A touching scene here—the solemn departure for Uganda, i.e. for martyrdom of one kind or another—of our first bishop and four priests. So we are allowed to spread the faith."[27] Vaughan preached at the ceremony, according to Snead-Cox, a sermon "at once grim and inspiring, typical of the man and the long slow sacrifice of the Vaughan family in the service of the Church, and of his own lifelong haunting wish to ... devote himself body and soul to the work of converting the heathen."[28]

On the evening of 9 May 1895 the missionaries left Mill Hill for St Pancras Station, and from there they took a bus to Holborn. They travelled by train to Dover and took the cross-channel boat at 8 p.m. The party left Marseilles on 12 May and Zanzibar on 31 May. After a long arduous journey, first to Mombasa, and then by caravan inland, the party reached Kampala on 6 September 1895.

As soon as they arrived, there was a dispute over the extent of the Upper Nile vicariate. The disagreement was settled in Bishop Hanlon's favour on

15 June 1896. In September, King Mwanga proposed to give Nsambya hill to the Mill Hill Mission. The King prepared a deed for the land on 16 November 1895. Two of the priests, Prendergast and Kestens, lived in a small grass and reed house at the base of the hill from early October while mission buildings were being put up. There was a house for the bishop, four small houses for the other men, a small church and a catechumenate.

According to Gale, the years 1895-6 witnessed "great quickening of religious life in Uganda." He thought this was due to three things: the Protectorate had suppressed much that was evil in Baganda politics; there were more missionaries; the religious spheres of influence were "officially" ended.[29]

Although, as Gale writes, "the Mill Hill Mission was to bring an additional force working for order and civilization among the native peoples," these achievements were "incidental to the true religious work of the Mission." In 1896 the two stations of Nsambya and Nagalama baptised 1062 persons. By 1914 there would be a Catholic population in the vicariate of 26,095 with 13,872 schoolchildren. In all the centres staffed by Mill Hill missionaries children were taught, the sick cared for, the sacraments administered and the dead buried "in the knowledge of the Resurrection and the Life." "Inadequate food, constant illness, heavy and incessant work under great physical strain, pressed heavily on the missionaries, while blackwater fever decimated their ranks. Over all hung the dead weight of paganism."[30]

Bishop Hanlon wrote to Herbert Vaughan from St Peter's, Nsambya, Mengo, Uganda, on 7 July 1899. The letter went by a monthly mail from Uganda that left on 10 July. Hanlon suggested that a new area be entrusted to his missionaries and commented on a man Vaughan had proposed to be its vicar. He mentioned that a nephew of Archbishop Stonor, Captain Pereira, had been in Uganda and was by then back in England. "Thus, though this Vicariate has extensive uninhabited places, the tribes roused by the inrush of European occupation are more hostile than ever to the white man (a fact however disappointing we must take into account) there are many extensive fields of labour that are peopled and accessible, there is ample room for all the missionaries for whose journeys and support we can get sufficient funds." Hanlon was pleased to hear that Vaughan had recovered from illness—a heart attack in 1897—and felt that he had been spared for the special interests of the foreign missions: "The Catholics of England have to thank Foreign Missions to a greater extent than they may suppose for this new lease of life so much of which will necessarily be devoted to the pressing wants of England. One more proof that what are called home interests will never lose but always gain by what is done for Foreign Missions."[31]

Henry Hanlon worked in the Upper Nile vicariate until 1911, when he was succeeded by John Biermans. During his years, mission stations were established throughout the vicariate; in East Buganda, Busoga, Kavirondo (Kenya), Tororo, and Mbale. Hanlon was also instrumental in bringing Sisters of St

Mary's Abbey at Mill Hill to work in Uganda. They arrived in 1902 with Mother Kevin and were soon fully occupied with the sick on Nsambya Hill. In 1902 Hanlon started a school for catechists and the sons of chiefs at Namilyango. Near the end of his tenure in Uganda, while trekking from Luo land to Nsambya, Hanlon "knew he was finished." He wrote to Francis Henry at Mill Hill asking him to explain to the Pope that "he could not handle the job any longer," and was allowed to retire. In England his health improved and he lived to 1937. "But his heart remained in Uganda—as leading Ugandans from the Kabaka down well knew. They did not go to England without visiting Bishop Hanlon."[32]

4. St Joseph's Missionary Society: A Spirit of Evil and Dissension

Not long after Henry Hanlon and the first band of missionaries left for Uganda, Vaughan faced internal problems with his missionary society. There was an effort by some members to divide the society into two parts "using the specious pretext for this division, the spirit of nationality." A private circular had been sent to every member suggesting that a division take place. This followed, of course, the separation from the American province in 1893 in order to form the Josephites in the United States under John Slattery.

On 6 July 1895, Vaughan wrote to each member about "the latest instance of the efforts made by the spirit of evil and of dissension." The constitutions of the society were written, he continued, not to "accentuate narrow rivalries and national pretensions but to unite in one common purpose and under one rule and spirit, all men who desire to place themselves under St Joseph's care in labouring among foreign races for their conversion." Success in the mission, and strength and happiness among the missionaries would be in proportion to the "charity and good will reigning amongst them and their obedience to the superior whom God had placed over them." Vaughan reminded the members that they should be entirely devoted to the mission work assigned to them. "You leave home and everything in Europe for the souls to whom you are sent; and anything that withdraws you from them is a hindrance to sanctification." Vaughan had acted quickly, writing to Rome that a petition to divide the society should not be accepted.[33]

5. Financial Support

How to finance the work of the missionary society was another matter that troubled Vaughan. In 1896 the Congregation Propaganda Fide wrote to the rector of Mill Hill urging him to collect money for the maintenance of the five missions undertaken by the Society. Vaughan replied, explaining the difficulties faced, but agreeing to "make what effort is possible to collect something in England for the support of our missions abroad. At the same time for the above reasons and those given in the preceding letter the prospects are extremely poor."[34]

He then went on to make a statement as to the condition of each of the missions so that their poverty might be realized and the "impossibility of increasing the number of missioners in them upon their actual income." The Maori Mission in New Zealand had nine missioners and a community of three sisters. In 1895 they received 9200 lire from Propaganda Fide and a 2500 lire grant from Cardinal Moran in Australia. The Borneo Mission had sixteen missioners, two lay Brothers and fourteen Sisters. The annual grant from Propaganda and Holy Childhood worked out to "531 lire for board, lodging, clothes, travelling and church and school expenses." The Catholics on the island numbered over 1200. The "Kafiristan and Cashmere" mission had thirteen missioners, one Brother and an uncertain number of Sisters. Propaganda gave 3000 lire a year supplemented by the income from five military chaplaincies.

The report of the Madras mission, Vaughan wrote, had already been sent to Rome. Vaughan added that "the best work of our missioners in this diocese is that done in the Guntour District among the natives. Our priests are in exclusive charge of these natives. Eighteen years ago, when they first took charge, the number of Christians was about five thousand; now they number over twelve thousand. More priests are urgently needed; but means are needed for their maintenance."

Of Uganda, Vaughan wrote that Hanlon had asked for ten more missioners before the end of the year. "The Protestants are occupying the ground and it is most important that the Catholic missioners should take possession as quickly as possible." He asked Propaganda for 25,000 lire for the new men assigned to Uganda: "How they are to live when they arrive I know not, the Bishop and his four priests are in great need of proper food and money to build chapels." He concluded that if he only had enough money from Propaganda Fide to care for the five missions already entrusted to the society, he had no desire for any other one. "Five mission fields, only poorly cultivated, are more than enough for our little society. I would rather receive help to send out and maintain more priests in them than receive another mission to be poorly worked from want of means."[35]

6. *Missionary Morale*

Vaughan often addressed the morale of missionaries in personal correspondence and circular letters. In 1917 the Madras mission reprinted three letters from Vaughan to his missionaries. One was addressed to Madras on 30 March 1883 and was aimed at a spirit of opposition that had arisen, to the "authorities which as Superior General I have invested the Province." A spirit of "criticism and contention" had led some, he wrote, to question the authority of the Provincial. In another letter addressed to the whole society and dated 6 January 1889, he asked members not to "fail to make the consideration of your own soul your first consideration." It was a "delusion that piety can be dispensed with, provided you say your office and your Mass." He reminded them to use their manual of prayers and make a monthly day of recollection. The third letter encouraged men on the missions to be careful of their use of time. There was a "great and serious danger" that time would be wasted in "sleep, in sloth, in frivolous and useless occupations." In conclusion, he recommended their rule of life to them: "Cherish, respect and obey your local superior, be often with him, tell him your trials and follow his direction. He who is chosen to be provincial has the grace of his state and represents the authority of God speaking to each one of you."[36]

7. St Joseph's Society Council Report

The council that supported St Joseph's Missionary Society held a meeting on 16 May 1902, as it did every six months. On this occasion it was at Archbishop's House, Westminster. The Marquis of Ripon, president of the council, was chairman. The report, and a short history by Elizabeth Herbert written in 1901, document the progress of Vaughan's initiative in 1866. The meeting heard that contributions had totalled "866 pounds 2s 4d for the last six months of 1901." In addition fourteen new missionaries had been sent out. During 1901, 4599 persons had been baptised in the five missions; "Upper Nile, Uganda, 2656; Districts of Madras, 1383; Borneo, 210; Kashmir and Kafiristan, 41; Maori, New Zealand, 309."[37]

By 1901 there were eighty-six priests and three lay Brothers on the missions; twenty-seven priests in the seminaries in Europe and eight lay Brothers caring for 117 students. A place for sick and retired missionaries had also been opened in the south of France at Biarritz.[38]

On 19 November 1902 another meeting was held. Herbert Vaughan was ill and wrote from Derwent Hall: "I shall be with you in spirit ... God bless you and all who attend the meeting." It was held at Herbert House in Belgrave Square. Bishop Hanlon of Uganda attended. At the close of the meeting a matter of "gravest importance" was introduced. There was a danger that in the near future there would be missionaries ready at Mill Hill but no outlet for them because of the poverty of the missions. "In the last two years we have sent out upwards of thirty priests to our various missions. This large increase has taxed to the utmost the small financial resources of these poor missions, and from each mission comes the same cry. 'We are at the end of our means! We cannot support more Fathers.'"

To seek help from the United States and Canada, Vaughan sent Fr Terence Joseph Cullen with a letter addressed to the "Archbishops and Bishops, to the clergy and laity in the United States and in Canada," appealing for help. At the end of the meeting it was decided that "nothing should be done to restrict the number of vocations, it being felt that Providence would provide an outlet for all the vocations that offered themselves."[39]

Crusade of Rescue

Vaughan's work on behalf of poor Catholic children and the rescue organization at Salford did not end when he went to Westminster to succeed Manning
in 1892. In Snead-Cox's opinion there was nothing that Cardinal Manning
had been more successful at in Westminster than providing the diocese with a
network of certified Poor Law Schools.[40] But the Catholic Homes were still
not able to cope with the numbers of Catholic children needing help. It was a
heavy burden, Canon Edward St John wrote, which Manning, the great
"Father of the poor," passed on to Vaughan. Manning's last pastoral was
concerned with children: "The care of children is the first duty and even with
the salvation of our own soul. This is the work to which we are called today."
In Vaughan, St John continued, his hopes were realized: a man who utilized
"all the developments made possible by enlightened public opinion and
legislation."[41]

After the religious census of 1894, and when the facts were grasped,
Vaughan appointed a commission of inquiry. Once the causes of the continued loss of Catholic children were exposed, he took action. The main problem, he wrote in an 1899 pastoral letter, and not a new one, was "leakage"; in
addition, there was the workhouse system, the police courts, certain non-
Catholic "Homes," and destitution.[42]

The committee had employed an officer to attend police courts and report
on the placement of Catholic children who came up before the magistrates.
The officer attended nineteen different police courts and followed 130 cases.
Each time, a Protestant missionary was present, and because there was no
Catholic agency represented, children, including Catholics, were given over
to the care of the non-Catholics. The failure was that there was no Catholic
representative present in the police courts. Vaughan was not blaming the
Protestants but saw it rather to be the fault of Catholics that their interests
were not defended when cases came before the courts. To remedy this, he
wrote, Catholic agents must be employed who would attend the police courts
and claim the custody of Catholic children.

To attack the poverty that was the cause of many of the problems, he first
insisted on the importance of family life, no matter how humble, but but he
also questioned what was to be done when the children were orphans. The
State helped, but "in a large number of cases the State and public opinion
expect us ... to take up the cause of our own destitute and orphan children
ourselves.... To do this, even at a cost, ought not to be reckoned by a Catholic
a burden, but a privilege, inasmuch as 'What ye do to the least of these little
ones, ye do it unto Me.'"[43]

The other cause, the activities of Protestant benevolent societies, was
addressed more gently than would have been the case in earlier years. "We
must hesitate before we reproach our Protestant fellow countrymen for these
losses. Many of them have spoken to us with sufficient plainness, if not with

sufficient satisfaction." It was not their intention to proselytize, Vaughan wrote, but if the Catholic Church made no adequate arrangement to take in Catholic children, they, at least, must open their doors to them.[44] Vaughan had come to this understanding mainly due to his dispute with Dr Barnardo.

According to Snead-Cox, when Vaughan first came into contact with Barnardo, the Doctor's Homes admitted the children of Roman Catholic parents, or of mixed marriages, but with the clear understanding that it was a Protestant institution and that the child would be brought up Protestant. Catholics who were in need of help were quoted as saying, "Anything is better than the life we are now leading and any place better than the place we are stopping in. Do take the child, for God's sake."[45] Canon Edward St John was active in Southwark Diocese on behalf of children. Once he spoke with Dr Barnardo at Stepney and remembers his saying "not unpleasantly that he hated the Catholic religion and everything to do with it, but owing to his inability to deal with the vast numbers of children and youths that were applying to him for assistance, he would rather see Catholic children go to Catholic homes than they should be left in degraded surroundings." When the newspapers were full of speculation about the possibility of Vaughan becoming Manning's successor at Westminster, St John told Barnardo that if Vaughan came to London, he was sure he would be willing to come to some arrangement about the poor Catholic children "as he had already accomplished a great work in Salford for children and working boys."[46]

In 1899 an amicable arrangement was worked out with Dr Barnardo. Snead-Cox credits Mr Richard Huth with bringing about a settlement at a meeting on 22nd October 1899: "Happily, good will and good faith have prevailed on both sides, and no serious difficulty has arisen." In the future, Catholic children applying for admission to one of Dr Barnardo's Homes would be offered to the Catholic authorities.[47]

Manning had made great efforts to care for all of the Catholic children referred to the Church, but there was no machinery in the diocese equal to the tremendous task of dealing with every case of child destitution that might come forward.[48] That machinery was supplied in 1899 as a result of Vaughan's pastoral appeal. The Crusade of Rescue was organized to take care of every destitute Catholic child in London. In 1901 the Crusade was joined with an older society, the "Homes for Destitute Catholic Children" and placed under the administration of Fr E. Bans. Vaughan gave a motto to the Society: "No Catholic child who is really destitute, or whose faith is in danger, and who cannot be otherwise provided for, is ever refused." At the end of 1901 there were 721 boys and girls placed in diocesan institutions; they were all the children who were not provided for by "Poor Law, industrial, or reformatory schools, or by other agencies, and deprived of their natural guardians."[49]

After his death, a small booklet gave thanks to Vaughan as "a lover of children" and acknowledged that "this beautiful side of his character" was a side that was not fully appreciated "even by his intimate friends." The title of the pamphlet was "The Children's Cardinal." It was written by Mrs Katherine Parr.[50]

Education and Voluntary Schools—continued

According to Snead-Cox, Vaughan considered the struggle on behalf of the voluntary schools begun at Salford and continued at Westminster "as the most important work of his life."[51] Just before leaving Salford he wrote an editorial for the *Dublin Review*, "How to save the Voluntary Schools." Vaughan wrote: "Our hope of the future is in our schools, and our schools can never become self-supporting. The idea that we in England could ever venture to throw off State aid and maintain effective schools, such as the Government would recognise as efficient, out of our own private means, is a mere chimera." He outlined a defence of the Voluntary schools: this involved a system of local control and Catholics trained to "fight to the last for the rights and independence of the Voluntary schools."[52]

Before he was installed as Archbishop of Westminster, on 19 June 1892, the Feast of the Sacred Heart, he published a pastoral letter: "The Claims of the Catholic School Committee to Catholic Support." It was to be read on the same day a collection was taken up in every Catholic church in Great Britain to support the committee financially.

The work of the committee included sponsoring three teacher-training colleges; one for men at Hammersmith and two for women in Liverpool and Roehampton. The men's college, St Mary's, was the oldest; founded in Brook Green, Hammersmith in 1850. The two colleges for women were Our Lady's College, Mount Pleasant, Liverpool, staffed by the Sisters of Notre Dame de Namur, and Digby Stuart College, in Roehampton, run by nuns of the Society of the Sacred Heart.[53] Vaughan saw it as a "question of life or death," of the continued existence of Catholic elementary schools or "their speedy extinction." Money was also needed to employ diocesan inspectors of education to make sure that religion was not subordinated to the "necessity of passing a successful secular exam." The final remarks of the pastoral were concerning parliamentary elections: "No matter who may be the candidate of your choice, press upon him your desire to maintain Christianity as the basis and form of Public Elementary Education. Send no man to Parliament without having distinctly informed him of the desire."

Vaughan sought to protect the Catholic voluntary schools by working out a common defence of denominational education with the Anglicans. He also fought to modify the Education Act of 1870 in order to allow a more equitable allocation of funds from the local education rate for the Catholic schools. Board schools and voluntary schools both drew income from Government Exchequer grants and fees. In 1891 the fees largely disappeared and from that time the Board schools received money from the rates and the voluntary schools from subscriptions. "It was here that the main discrepancy in funding arose."[54]

Herbert Vaughan, though active and influential, was representing the Catholic Church, a minority school-proprietor in England and Wales. He was one participant, although an important one, in an effort waged by the Church of England and others on behalf of denominational education.

Over the years pressure grew for the Education Department to set higher standards; curriculum extensions, more teachers, better school buildings and improved equipment. Part of the pressure on the voluntary schools came from the improved condition of board schools. At the same time, the Department, under sympathetic Conservative governments, had to show an understanding of the position of the voluntary schools. The poverty of the Churches made it impossible to comply. It was clear by the 1890s that only large-scale help could save them. The Catholics had favoured a share in rate aid. Vaughan, like Manning, wanted aid and was willing to concede the rate-payers the right of inspection and oversight. "Many Anglicans, too, longed for a more definite policy and in 1893 the *Guardian*, referring wistfully to Roman Catholic solidarity, appealed to the Bishops to give a clear lead instead of leaving the individual priest to take his own line and fight his own battles." However, the Anglicans feared any form of control connected with the use of rate aid.[55]

On 30 September 1895 Vaughan wrote to *The Times*: "Has not the time come to deal with the education problem, not by a tinkering legislation as heretofore, but by the adoption of a comprehensive policy, which shall place the whole of the elementary education of the country upon a common basis which shall as far as possible end or minimise all grievances?"[56]

The Times responded that the Catholics were not "a minority pleading for their life," but, with their supporters, were "a majority, and as such were entitled to demand a full measure of justice."[57]

In November 1895 he wrote to Lord Salisbury: "We ask for no palliatives, but for a substantial remedy to a great English wrong that has sprung up and covered the land within the last twenty-five years."[58]

A disagreement arose with the Anglicans over the approach they should take, especially about rate aid, but Vaughan made up his mind that there should be no ambiguity about the Catholic position. He demanded in "justice and equity" for the Catholic schools that the law "declare that the same payment shall be made for secular instruction given in their public Elementary schools as for that given in Board schools."[59] It was not till November 1896 that for the Anglicans, "after years of wavering and indecision, rate aid had become the accepted policy of the Established Church; at last, therefore, denominationalists could speak with one voice."[60]

An Act in 1897, which freed voluntary school buildings from payment of rates and increased the grant to them, was a disappointment to Catholics and considered by them as no more than a temporary measure. And so, Vaughan continued to work, confident that sooner or later the English public would come to understand the Catholic viewpoint. "He meant never to cease his efforts until the goal of equality was reached."[61]

In the general election of 1900, the school question was raised. Concerning the October election, *The Tablet* commented: "The single thing we want is equality of educational opportunity for all parents, whether they value definite religious instruction or not."[62]

Marjorie Cruickshank gives the national school statistics for 1900. It helps to place the Catholic Church and Herbert Vaughan in context. Of a total of 14,359 voluntary schools with and average daily total attendance of 2,486,597 children, 11,777 were Anglican schools with 1,885,802 children, and 1,045 were Roman Catholic with 255,036 children in average daily attendance.[63]

At the beginning of the twentieth century it was clear that there was a need for educational reform. Unlike Britain's rivals, the United States and Germany, little had been done to improve the educational system; the rivals had acted on the belief that "commercial and industrial success was founded on educational efficiency." According to Marjorie Cruickshank: "Responsible opinion had at last awakened to the realisation that Britain's destiny depended as much on 'school power' as on 'sea power.'" In her opinion, the most controversial problem was in elementary education and the voluntary schools, which were educating more than half the nation's children. They were in urgent need of improvement. At the same time her conclusion that poor voluntary schools dragged down the general level of education seems too sweeping.[64] The higher income of the board schools in this period certainly led to higher salaries for the teachers—a matter of justice—and better buildings, but not necessarily to better education.

Herbert Vaughan, representing the Catholic position, held firmly to a claim for rate aid for the existing schools and those that might be built in the future. The Education Department, through the efforts of Robert Morant, Secretary to the Vice-President, Sir John Gorst, began to prepare for large-scale reforms. On 24 March 1902 the Education Bill was introduced to the House of Commons by Balfour. The emphasis in the Bill was "on the welding of secular education into an organic whole." He denied the suggestion that voluntary schools would be swept away as absurd. "Voluntary schools must remain and, that being the case, they must be invigorated." The Nonconformist opposition was given new life as its anger focused on the Education Bill. The Baptist Dr Clifford came forward as the champion of nonconformity. His picturesque expression "Rome on the rates" was a rallying call for agitators, even though it was the Church of England that had the most to gain from the Bill and not the Catholics.[65]

The Education Bill was introduced to Parliament and discussed in the House of Commons till December. It was before the Commons for longer than any previous Bill in history—a total of fifty-seven days. There was anger among Nonconformists and many others who saw the proposals to give rate aid to denominational schools "as ensuring the permanent subsidization of the Established and Roman Catholic Churches."[66]

Vaughan was often in the Commons following the debate with "painful interest"; he was in the last stages of his final illness. Snead-Cox remembered him as "indefatigable in his representations to all who were in a position to influence votes in however indirect a way. Every clause of the Bill was considered and discussed week by week with a special emergency committee of the Catholic Education Council which had been appointed for the purpose."[67] In October 1902 Vaughan wrote to John Richmond asking him to try to maintain the continued presence of Irish members of Parliament at Westminster during the autumn. The Education Act of 1902 passed and received the Royal Assent on 18 December 1902.[68]

Vaughan reported the passage of the Education Act to Propaganda, saying that it was "favourable to Christianity," and was secured only because the Conservative administration had won such a large electoral majority on the South African War policy. "The general effect of the new law is to make Christian and Catholic Education a part of the law and constitution of England. In principle we have made a large and important advance.[69]

The Tablet of 20 December reported that, "Before these lines are in print the Education Bill will have received the Royal Assent and taken its place in the Statute Book as part of the law of England." The new law was not all that Catholics had hoped it would be, but was "vastly better than it might have been expected...." On 27 December the editor looked back "for the last time upon the old system which has oppressed us for so long, and from which we have at length finally escaped."[70]

According to Cruickshank, while Anglicans and Catholics were on the whole satisfied with assurances of an automatically adjusted form of aid, the gain for the nation was "indisputable." Not only was money available for all schools but "National education was at last to be in the hands of experts instead of amateurs."[71]

At the same time, discussion and passage of the 1902 Act left much bitterness. For example: there was a great Nonconformist demonstration outside Leeds; an Anglican clergyman declared that the Kenyon-Slaney Amendment concerning religious instruction was the "greatest betrayal since the Crucifixion"; and many Nonconformists, especially in Wales, refused to pay rates for denominational schools.[72]

The Act also provoked the last great outburst of public controversy between Anglicans and Free Churchmen. It continued at least into the early years of the Liberal government, that is, after 1905. Successive attempts by the government to legislate on voluntary schools eventually came to nothing. Slowly the controversy died down, and Nonconformity never recovered its old influence. "And the growing secularisation of English life continued to sap its strength until public opinion became deaf to the old war cries."[73]

Snead-Cox visited Vaughan at Archbishop's House in 1903, shortly before he left it for the last time: "The talk turned on the fight for schools, and as in slow retrospect he went back to this phase or that from the earliest stage of the struggle, there was an exultant tone in his words as he spoke which was in odd contrast to his physical weakness ... one by one the claims formulated by the old Voluntary Schools Association had been admitted and the bedrock principle of equality had been reached."[74]

Nearing the End

Wilfrid Ward tried to sum up Vaughan's ten years as Archbishop of Westminster in his 1910 review of Snead-Cox's biography. According to Ward, to a considerable number of Englishmen, Vaughan's "red Biretta and *ferrajinolo* were the proverbial red rag to the bull." Ward thought of many, especially Anglicans, recalling Vaughan "flourishing the unwelcome claims of Rome" in their faces and "treading ruthlessly on the toes of his compatriots, constantly offending their national feelings." His "phrases ... which were perhaps wanting in literary tact were repeated mouth to mouth and exaggerated."

The annoyance he caused was doubled because of his physical presence, family and social connections, and the fact that he was a prince of the Roman Church. For a time, according to Ward, he, like Wiseman before him, became the "embodiment of 'papal aggression.'" To those who took offence at Herbert Vaughan, he had the audacity to dedicate England to St Peter, to "laugh at Anglican orders and called the Anglo-Catholics a sect of the Church of England which posed as Catholics."

Ward wrote that even Queen Victoria was not spared. On her death, as a "heretic," she was afforded no religious rites in the Catholic Church. Vaughan had written a letter from Rome on 23 January 1901, the day after the Queen's death, to be read in all Catholic churches of his diocese. The letter was referred to later by the *Evening News* as Vaughan's "unwise letter on the occasion of the late Queen's death." Vaughan wrote that the Catholic Church has no public religious services for the dead except those "instituted for the souls of her own children." On behalf of the late Queen "no one would feel it to be right that ... to appear to claim her as a member of our Church which we should be doing were we to perform in her behalf religious rites that are exclusively applicable to deceased Catholics. What can we do?"[75]

Snead-Cox devotes a chapter to a controversy over Vaughan's use of the term "Roman Catholic" in an address to Queen Victoria on her Diamond Jubilee in 1897. Vaughan spoke on behalf of the bishops and Catholics of England. There was also a controversy over the language of the royal declaration made by each new monarch. In this instance it was King Edward. About

"Roman Catholic," he asked, at a meeting in Newcastle in September 1901, that Catholics use the term "Roman" and "be proud of it in the true and Catholic sense." But, like those on the Continent and their "English forefathers," and "especially when the word 'Roman' is misunderstood 'they should call themselves simply Catholics.'"[76]

When he met King Edward VII, Vaughan came under more criticism. Following the court ceremony, he genuflected before kissing the new King's hand. The London correspondent of the *Freeman's Journal* commented that there was "natural amazement" when Vaughan presented an address "on his knees yesterday to the King." The same King who "declared the Catholic Church to be idolatrous and superstitious" and "who holds his throne by virtue of that offensive declaration."[77] In Snead-Cox's view, Vaughan later regretted that, at a time he was doing everything possible to be gracious towards the Court, he wrote a letter to the Home Office stating "that neither the address to the King, nor the deputation, was to be taken as in any way condoning the language of the Royal Declaration."[78] Vaughan followed the official discussions that set out to modify the wording of the declaration, and believed that someday it would be changed. "He thought it too offensive to be endured, and believed that some day the country would grant liberty of conscience to the King, or else be content with some simple subscription to the Protestant creed."[79]

A month before his seventy-first birthday in 1903, a weekly magazine wrote of Herbert Vaughan as "a man of benevolent disposition and extreme simplicity of character," who was nevertheless "scarcely popular."[80] Snead-Cox considers it was Vaughan's point of view which chilled people, and not, as the article remarks, a certain coldness of manner, which, he thought, really came from shyness. Vaughan considered the interests of the individual soul and the wider interests of the Church to be priorities and "the rest were nowhere."[81]

However, annoyance with Vaughan was not always due to his spiritual motives. More than once, the word "haughtiness" is used when referring to him. Snead-Cox remembered Vaughan, the "bold and brazen beggar," causing great disappointment when he met again a person who had donated generously to one of his appeals and he did not recognize the donor. He could not remember faces and would ask someone at a social gathering whom he should have recognized: "What is your name?" Some who had given him a great deal of money were treated as strangers. "The light would die" in the person's face as "she knew he had not even recognized her." His "inconvenient candour," as Snead-Cox calls it, could not be covered up because Vaughan "had no art to pretend to know people, or by putting a leading question to try to find out to whom he was speaking."[82]

Even some of his own priests felt he did not know them. When he came to Westminster, his poor health and many projects left him little opportunity for the day-to-day administration of the diocese. He left most of it to his vicar general and his auxiliary bishops; first to Bishop Robert Brindle and later to Bishop Charles Stanley, Brindle's successor. When Vaughan failed to recognize his own priests they thought, "Is this all the interest he takes?"[83]

Despite his public mistakes, Snead-Cox and many others were attracted to the very simplicity and sincerity that got him into difficulties, and seemed to support the opinion of some that he was a zealous, but blundering romantic.[84]

To his friends Vaughan had many lovable qualities "but sincerity was at the root of them all. Certainly few men have had friends more loyal and devoted than he had, and very few have known so well how to make others share in their own high and holy enthusiasms."[85] When he died in 1903, he left many of them a legacy of love inspired by his kindness and loyalty. He also left his Church a cathedral and numerous organizations.[86]

Notes

1. WDA. Vaughan, Archbishop's House, Westminster, 14 January 1894, General Simultaneous Mission: I. Religious condition of the people; II. Labour to be undertaken; III. Four points requiring special attention; IV. General directions for the mission.
2. About mixed marriages: Vaughan wrote to Archbishop Corrigan on 18 September 1897, that in Westminster mixed marriages were always performed in church, but without the marriage blessing. "In this diocese, no music or solemnity is allowed. I have had great difficulty in keeping this rule, which was made by my predecessor. It irritated both Catholic and Protestant parties, because they always want music and a joyful celebration. The rule is not universal in England.... I should regard it as most unwise and as leading to apostasy to refuse the use of the church for a 'mixed marriage.' In this diocese alone we have over 1000 mixed marriages in a year. If we refuse dispensation they go to the protestant Church or the Registrar.... (Corrigan had interpreted the Latin of a regulation to mean that mixed marriages required a special dispensation directly from Rome).... But I cannot bring myself to sympathise with the method you pursue and which seems to reduce the sacrament in the public estimate to the rank of a civil contract. I would at least use the church though without music and festivity. Good Protestants are alienated from the Church by much severity which being faithful, they think they do not deserve." NYAA. No 21, G 25-28.
3. WDA. General Simultaneous Mission.
4. Leslie, *Vaughan Letters*, pp.414-5.
5. CANH.
6. McCormack, pp.275-80; WDA. Lenten Pastoral on Five Current Topics, 1894, p.8: "The dangers of this London life were always great; but they are far greater to-day than they ever were. The sharpening of the intellect by schooling and popular literature, and the growth of rationalism, communism, and atheism by the decay of religion, have rendered the dangers to Catholic youth far more subtle, far more penetrating, far more formidable than they were in the days of greater ignorance and poverty. The Church must arm and defend her children against their spiritual enemies. This must now be done by raising up good Catholic social influences to counteract the influences of materialism, immorality, and unbelief. These Catholic influences must be brought into personal contact with the young. As we need Catholic schools for one-sixth of our population, so we need Continuation schools, or social and recreative Clubs for the care of that other sixth of the population which is between the ages of 13 and 20." According to

an appendix, Austin Oates was honorary secretary of the "Catholic Social Union for the Commonweal." It was "a Society to raise the social, moral and material condition of our people, by educating our young men in habits of sobriety, thrift, self-respect, self-reliance, and independence of character in temporal matters, and in fidelity to the Church in spirituals; and our young women in the knowledge and habits which will help to make them good Catholic wives and mothers;" In 1894 two branches were opened in Sheffield—two clubs for girls in St Marie's and St Vincent's. Thanks to Lady Edmund Talbot there were five clubs in 1897. See: Jennifer F. Supple, "The Role of the Catholic Laity in Yorkshire, 1850-1900," *Recusant History*, pp.304-17, 18, 3, May 1987; "The Catholic Social Union," *The Tablet*, 4 June 1898, p.897: Vaughan wrote the annual report of the Catholic Social Union: "The present workers are in touch with something under 2,000 members, i.e., young people who have left school, and are in their age of first peril. But their influence affects directly or indirectly a much larger number, viz., many of the parents, friends, and companions of the members; indeed it may be said to be felt throughout the mission in which they work...." He appealed for more volunteer workers to give two nights each week. They also needed more settlements and he appealed for anyone to devote 300 pounds a year to such a work.

7. CANH. Rome, 2 March 1895; The Catholic Social Union and its "Social Union Work" involved in more than running clubs. Herbert Vaughan recruited women of the upper classes, in Lady Herbert's words, to "look after the teeming populations" in East End parishes, and "to break down the barriers between rich and poor by the upper classes giving personal service to their less favoured brothers and sisters." She told the story in one of her "Wayside Tales" of one who was asked by Sisters in the district to visit a dying man. Lady Herbert, "What a Crucifix can do," *Wayside Tales*, London, Catholic Truth Society, 1909, p.49, CTS Archive; Vaughan also was instrumental in bringing communities of nuns to work among the poor of the East End. He invited Mother Mary Potter, of The Little Company of Mary, to send her Sisters to help Canon Akkers at St Mary's and St Michael's in Commercial Road. Patrick Dougherty, in his biography of Mother Mary, tells the story of Vaughan visiting the new community. Mother Catherine and Mother de Sales were using a tiny kitchen as a refectory and empty boxes as seats. "One afternoon while the pioneer sisters were transforming one of the rooms into a chapel, the bell rang and to their embarrassment, the Cardinal Archbishop of Westminster was announced. He put the dismayed nuns at their ease, accepted a cup of tea, insisted that he have it in their improvised refectory, and before leaving, granted them the privilege of having Mass celebrated and the Blessed Sacrament reserved in the house." Patrick Dougherty, *Mother Mary Potter*, London, Sands, 1961, p.196.

8. "Establishment of the Polish Catholic Mission in London" trans. from the Polish by a Sister of the Holy Family of Nazareth; Leslie, *Vaughan Letters*, p.417, 7 June 1894; *ibid.*, 14 June: When the Sisters first visited in 1894, Vaughan wrote to Elizabeth Herbert that he could only "give her the Poles and Lithuanians. I have no house, no money and no school. All has to be begun. The Poles must exert themselves and work out, as they say, their own salvation."

9. "Sto lat!," *The Tablet*, 12 November 1994, p.1492: "The celebrations this weekend will be attended by the Primate of Poland, Cardinal Jozef Glemp. This afternoon, in the presence of Cardinal Hume and the pronuncio, Archbishop Barbarito, he will preside at a Solemn Mass of Thanksgiving in Westminster Cathedral for this evolution of Polish life and hope."

10. "Et Caetera," *The Tablet*, 9 April 1932, p.479; For example, see: *The Tablet*, 15 April 1899, p.595: "Secondary Schools in Mediaeval England." The monthly lecture of the Historical Research Society at Archbishop's House was given on Monday evening last by Mr.J.B. Milburn on the subject of 'Edward VI. and Mediaeval Grammar Schools.' The chair was taken by his Eminence the Cardinal Archbishop, and there were also present the Bishop of Clifton, the Right Rev. Mgr. Moyes, the Rev. Father Sydney Smith, SJ., and the Rev. F. Poyer."

11. WDA. Forward, *Catholic Missionary Society*, 1993.

12. McCormack, pp.285-7; The school where Chase studied in Rome is also connected with

Herbert Vaughan. The Beda College had its beginnings in the efforts of Nicholas Wiseman. He persuaded Pius IX to found the Collegio Ecclesiastico as a house of studies for Anglicans wishing to become priests. In 1897, Vaughan asked Leo XIII to take an interest and this led to an order, a *moto proprio*, in 1898, "by which the constitution and rules were sanctioned, the College founded anew, re-named in memory of the Venerable Bede and moved from its first small home to the English College in the Via Monserrato, although retaining its distinctive character." Peter Lane, *The Catenian Association*, 1908-1983, London, 1982, p.73; When Cardinal Vaughan's nephew Herbert became superior, he went to the United States to see the methods used by the Paulists. "Father Vaughan and his associates used a chapel motor car and always featured a Question Box in connection with their lectures, helps to missionary work which he had learned in this country." The Paulists remembered him when he died in February 1936. *The Catholic World*, April 1936, 853, 143, p.108.

13. CANH. 13 March 1895.

14. WDA. "The Pope's Collection for the Evangelization of Africa, and Our New Obligations," by Herbert Cardinal Vaughan, Feast of St Thomas of Canterbury, 1898; And *The Tablet*, 7 January 1899; Letter to the Clergy by Herbert Vaughan: p.8: "Fifteen years ago Leo XIII took up the grand work of the regeneration of Africa. He needs men and means. He appeals for them to Christendom;" The Catholic Truth Society published a lecture given by Cardinal Moran in 1895: "The Mission Field of the 19th Century," CTS archive. Moran countered charges that the Catholic missions in the nineteenth century were a complete failure; that Protestant results far surpassed that of Catholics; and that Catholics entered areas only after Protestant missionaries had prepared the way.

15. MHA. Christmas Message, 1899, by Cardinal Vaughan.

16. McCormack, pp.243-4.

17. SDA. Vaughan to Lewis Casartelli—Vaughan spelled his name Lewis and not Louis in correspondence—from Hotel de Flandre Spa, 25 June.

18. Herbert, Bishop of Salford, "The Evangelization of Africa," *Dublin Review*, 3rd series, January-April 1879, London , Burns & Oates, pp.182-208: Among the books he cited: *The Heart of Africa* by George Schweinfurth, 1878; *The Flooding of the Sahara* by Donald Mackenzie, 1877; *Un Rapport... sur la Mission des Chotts*, by Roudaire, 1878; *L'Evangile au Dahomey* by Abbé Desribes, 1877; and *Les Missions Catholiques*, Lyons; Louis Casartelli, "Our Diamond Jubilee," *Dublin Review*, 4th series, April 1896, no 18, pp.268-9: Cuthbert Hedley remained editor till 1884, when Vaughan combined the work of owner and editor. He was assisted by his sub-editor, Fr Driffield. Another name associated with the *Review*, who sometimes helped to prepare the often unsigned articles, was Miss E. M. Clerke; There were other articles, unsigned, on Africa: "Catholic Missions in Central Africa," *Dublin Review*, 3rd series, 5, April 1881, pp.394-422; "Catholic Missions in Equatorial Africa" 6, July 1881, pp.144-175; A. Hillyard Atteridge, SJ, "The "Encylopaedia Britannica" on Missions," *Dublin Review*, July 1884, pp.109-144.

19. Ronald Robinson and John Gallagher, *Africa and the Victorians*, New York, St Martin's Press, 1961, pp.2-3: "Although doubts grew as the century wore on, most Victorians clung to the gospels of restricted government and free trade. That moral improvement and intellectual enlightenment attended the growth of prosperity, that all three depended upon political and economic freedom, remained their characteristic and passionate beliefs ... Expansion in all its modes seemed not only natural and necessary but inevitable; it was pre-ordained and irreproachably right. It was the spontaneous expression of an inherently dynamic society"; Also see: Philip Curtin *et al*, *African History*, Boston, Little, Brown, 1978, p.376: Some Africans and African-Europeans "saw the appropriate future for Africa in the direction labelled 'Christianity and civilization,' and they were generally proud to have a part in leading Africa to that salvation. Few suspected at mid-century that a colonial period lay ahead (writing of West Africa).... By the 1870s, however, a certain disillusionment began to set in.... Their disillusionment was

muted at first, but deepened in the 1890s. By that time, it was abundantly clear that 'Christianity and civilization' meant European rule, and European rule by Europeans from Europe."

20. Vaughan, "Evangelization," *Dublin Review*, p.208: Vaughan had the attitudes of a Victorian Englishman but often rose above cultural and economic imperialism in seeing the Empire, commerce and science as ways to bring the gospel to the most isolated and slave-trade-strangled areas of Africa. Where it failed to do so it became useless boasting. He also saw that his plan to organize bands of Catholic African-American missionaries for settlement in Africa, after the example of Protestants in Liberia, might not be practical. "Large funds are required, hard heads and generous hearts to direct and carry out such an enterprise; but genuine Faith, Hope, and Charity are divine and creative forces; and we must look for great results where they exist and are brought into energetic action."

21. MHA. *St Joseph's Advocate*, vol II, no 16, Autumn, 1892, pp.259-62: Benoit had been ill for about two years. Very early in the morning, Fr Stotter, the vice-rector, gave the final blessing and Benoit died. At 10 a.m. the following Saturday morning a requiem Mass was celebrated by his successor, Fr Henry. Louis Casartelli, rector of St Bede's, Manchester, was the sub-deacon. After the clergy had left the altar at the end of Mass, Archbishop Vaughan came forward to speak. He concluded his homily: "And while we pray for him, we need not fear to also pray that he may help us by his prayers to our Divine Lord. He is to be looked upon as the true founder of this house; for that man is the true founder— not who lays the bricks and mortar—but who has consolidated the spirit." At the conclusion of his panegyric, Vaughan blessed the coffin and then it was carried by six lay Brothers, preceded by the choir and Casartelli bearing the cross, to the cemetery; the plot is called Calvary. "Slight showers had fallen during the morning, but the sun was shining beautifully as the coffin was lowered."

22. MHA. Francis Henry was born in Liverpool on 11 April 1851. Before he came to Mill Hill in 1876 he was a cashier in Liverpool for a few years. His father, Michael Henry, was born in Ireland and his mother in Wales. Francis Henry was ordained in 1881 and his first appointment was as rector of the apostolic school at Kelvedon in Essex. In 1884 he transferred with the school to Freshfield. In 1892 he was appointed rector of St Joseph's College, Mill Hill. After Vaughan's death in 1903 he was elected superior general. He remained in that position from 1904 until 1924. He died at Mill Hill on 11 July 1930.

23. Jedin, History,9, pp.550-2; In 1892 Cardinal Vaughan's brother Kenelm visited South Africa and then the headquarters of the White Fathers at Maison-Carrie in Algiers. He wrote to *The Tablet* on 17 September 1892, p.456, about reports of Captain Frederick Lugard's killing of Baganda between 23 and 30 January 1892. Fr Kenelm disputed Lugard's account and supported that of Mgr Hirth.

24. Leslie, *Vaughan Letters*, p.414. 7 and 15 April 1894; MHA. Herbert, *A Short History of St Joseph's Society*; Lady Elizabeth Herbert was present at an anti-slavery meeting in London on 31 July 1888 presided over by Lord Granville and addressed by Cardinal Lavigerie. It inspired her to write a Catholic Truth Society pamphlet, "The African Slave Trade," CTS Archive, 1888, chapter 13, pp.137-49: "In the midst of the moral turpitude and the self-indulgence which reign in this nineteenth century, would it not be a great and glorious sight to see men come forward generously to devote their lives to this object; and for them to feel, when they came to die, that they had done a great work for Christ and for the souls He expired on the Cross to save."

25. H. P. Gale, *Uganda and the Mill Hill Fathers*, London, Macmillan, 1959, p.87; also: Yves Tourigny, *So Abundant a Harvest: The Catholic Church in Uganda, 1879-1979*, London, Darton, Longman & Todd, 1979.

26. *ibid.*, p.viii; See also: François Renault, *Cardinal Lavigerie*, London, Athlone Press, 1994, pp.229-247, 265-279.

27. CANH. Vaughan to Mother Mary, 6 May 1895.

28. Gale, *Uganda*, p.88. The Snead-Cox reference is not found in his two-volume work; MHA.

Miss E., 8 Ashley Rise, Walton on Thames, Surrey, 16 September 1957: "In 1900 we lived in the house just below St Joseph's and my father, a very good Catholic, used to go there for 6 a.m. Mass and I went too, tho' not too willingly in deep snow time! And we always went to the station to see young missioners go off.... My father has been dead many years and I am now in my 76th year—but often think of the Mill Hill days and what wonderful work you all do."

29. Gale, *Uganda*, p.138.

30. *ibid.*, pp.316-7.

31. WDA. Hanlon to Vaughan, 7 July 1899: "There are many thousands of our Catholics in England who from their sincere patriotism are much devoted to Imperial interests. For the furtherance of these interests they use their faculties, gifts and influence to have large sums voted in Parliament and are not only willing but happy to devote their sons to this Foreign service. Yet what of the Empire of God's church? What the British Empire is to their patriotism that our foreign missions should be to their faith and loyalty as Catholics"; Vaughan wrote to Casartelli that he had spoken to the Sirdar of Sudan (Sirdar was originally an Indian title and used for the commander-in-chief of the army in Sudan). Vaughan repeated that the Sirdar did not want French missionaries in Sudan: "He does want our Uganda people to come down the Nile ... and will give them help everywhere." Vaughan concluded that "our hope is among the people that have not become Mahomatans and these are south of Khartoum." Mill Hill missionaries did not go to Sudan until years after Vaughan's death.

32. *Tororo Diocesan Centenary Celebration*, 1979, Mbale, pp.23-5; Also: St Mary's Abbey Archive, Logbook: "Sister Mary Paul Murphy of the Incarnation, choir sister, *Et Verbum caro factum est*, age 28," took the habit 30 August 1885, professed 3 September 1887. She was sent to the American missions in 1887 and recalled to take charge of the mission in Uganda, British East Africa.

33. MHA. Mill Hill, 6 July 1895, Vaughan to members.

34. WDA. Rough copy of letter, undated, but probably early in 1896: Vaughan listed the problems of collecting money for the society at home and for the missions overseas. He reminded Rome that "The missions of Missions Etrangères of Paris in Rue du Bac never undertake to find money for the Foreign Missions. It is no more a part of their rule than it is of ours to do so; and the Society of St Joseph's of Mill Hill occupies in England a similar place and relation to the Church in England as that occupied by the Société des Missions Etrangères does to the Church in France;" An advertisement in *The Tablet*, 18 November 1893, p.830: "900,000,000 Heathens!!!, 50,000 pass every day before the dread tribunal of the Sovereign Judge, Without Faith—Without Sacraments, Destitute of all Spiritual Aid!!! Help us send Priests to them. If you cannot give much send Half-a-Crown to the Father Rector and be enrolled as a member of St. Joseph's Society of the Sacred Heart for Foreign Missions."

35. WDA. Letter,1896..

36. MHA. "Three Letters of Herbert Cardinal Vaughan to his Missionaries," reprinted 1917, Madras, Good Pastor Press.

37. MHA. *Catholic Times*, 16 May 1902: From Uganda they heard that Fr Proctor had been asked to meet a party of eight new arrivals at the coast: "The only incident worthy of note was the discovery we made at the end of a day's journey that in the luggage van which we occupied we had been sitting—quite unconsciously of course—upon some nine cases of dynamite. If the train had got into a collision ... more, certainly, might have been heard from us."

38. Herbert, History: 1 January 1901: Missions: Madras, 20; Borneo, 17; Maori, 13; Kashmir, 14; Upper Nile, 22. Colleges: students: Mill Hill, 44; Roozendaal, 35; Freshfield, 26; Brixen, 4; MHA. In 1897 Miss Greene of Guéthary bequeathed St Joseph's Society a home, Villa Liberena, for retired missionaries, in the south of France. It is unclear what became of her gift. In 1901 a benefactor gave £100, and a house near Biarritz was rented; one invalid missionary took up residence. It was a "humble, poor beginning." The first missionary recorded to have died there, on 8 March, was Fr van den Broeck who "died at our sanatorium in the south of

454   CARDINAL HERBERT VAUGHAN

France." He had taught at Freshfield and worked in Borneo between 1891 and 1899.

39. *The Tablet*, 29 November 1902, pp.849-50.
40. Snead-Cox, 2, p.261: Vaughan wrote in 1899 that Manning's zeal and perseverance and an enlightened sense of justice which inspired the Guardians of the Poor led to the creation of Catholic certified poor law schools serving fifty-eight different parishes and unions.
41. Edward St John, *Manning's Work for Children*, London, Sheed and Ward, p.319; See also: Newsome, *Convert Cardinals*, p.319.
42. Snead-Cox, 2, pp.267ff; Edward St John, "The After Care of our Boys from Institutions," *The Tablet*, 3 September 1898, pp.381-2: "Our present Cardinal has the matter much at heart, and has several times invited Catholics to make some attempt to stop the fearful leakage which goes on among our youths when they are sent from their Catholic homes out into an unbelieving world to earn their daily bread."
43. Snead-Cox, 2, pp.269-70.
44. *ibid.*, p.269.
45. *ibid.*, p.262.
46. St John, Children, pp.133-4.
47. Snead-Cox, 2, p.276.
48. *ibid.*, p.265; N. Waugh, editor, *These My Little Ones*, London, Sands, 1911, p.118ff.
49. *ibid.*, p.271; *The Tablet*, "Rescue Work and the Housing of Destitute Children," 14th Annual Report, 1901.
50. Olive Katherine Parr, *The Children's Cardinal*, London, Burns & Oates, 1905; Mrs Parr wrote an article, "The Future of Workhouse Girls," in *The Tablet*, 3 September 1898, pp.382-3.
51. Snead-Cox, 2, p.87; Mr Richard Cunningham, a former Secretary (1960-91) of the Catholic Education Council for England and Wales, advised the author about Vaughan's role on behalf of denominational schools and the passage of the Education Act of 1902.
52. Editorial, *Dublin Review*, Oct 1891, 52, pp.395-411.
53. McClelland, "Teachers' Training," *Paedagogia*, p.18; Correspondence, Richard Cunningham, 9 November 1994: "Vaughan supported the Committee—which in 1905 became the Catholic Education Council—more whole-heartedly than Manning, who would have liked to confine them largely to their work in teacher training, or Bourne, who was less at ease with them." The leading lights of the Committee were lay people of wealth and high social position "from the Duke of Norfolk downwards."
54. For a useful study of events leading up to the Education Act of 1902, see: Marjorie Cruickshank, *Church and State in English Education*, London, Macmillan, 1963, p.52: "Roman Catholics, though few in number compared with the Anglicans, had a much more coherent policy," at least in the Catholic response to the 1870 Act, which she calls "remarkable." The absence of a coherent policy continued until 1896 when Dr Temple succeeded Benson as Archbishop of Canterbury; See also: Gillian Sutherland, *Policy-Making in Elementary Education, 1870-1895*, Oxford, Oxford University Press, 1975, pp.356-60: Graphs and tables illustrate the disparity between expenditure, income, fees paid etc. "per child in average attendance" in board and voluntary schools; Correspondence, Cunningham.
55. *ibid.*, p.62.
56. Snead-Cox, 2, pp.111-140. See p.115.
57. *ibid.*, p.117.
58. *ibid.*
59. *ibid.*, pp.119-20.
60. Cruickshank, *Education*, p.67.
61. *ibid.*, p.66; Snead-Cox, 2, p.124.
62. Snead-Cox, 2, p.127.
63. Cruickshank, *Education*, Appendix C, School Statistics, p.192.

64. *ibid.*, p.69; Correspondence, Cunningham.
65. *ibid.*, pp.69; and pp.79-81: "Nevertheless it was the Roman Catholic community which gave it the most enthusiastic reception ... Cardinal Vaughan welcomed the proposals as a distinct step in the right direction."
66. James Murphy, *Church, State and Schools in Britain*, 1800-1970, London, Routledge and Kegan Paul, n.d., p.90.
67. Snead-Cox, 2, p.134.
68. *ibid.*, p.136; Correspondence, Cunningham: "The main amendments to the Act were from the Government back benches; maintenance of voluntary schools to be obligatory for local authorities; the Kenyon-Slaney amendment vesting control of religious education in a voluntary school in the managers as a whole, not just clergymen—a rather anti-clerical move against High Churchmen"
69. Norman, *Catholic Church*, p.368.
70. "How the Bill became Law," *The Tablet*, 20 December 1902, p.961; "Looking Back," *The Tablet*, 27 December 1902, p.1001.
71. Cruickshank, *Education*, p.86.
72. Murphy, *Schools in Britain*, p.94.
73. Cruickshank, *Education*, p.89; On the Education crisis and Nonconformist pressure after 1902, see: G. I. T. Machin, *Politics and the Churches in Great Britain, 1869-1921*, Oxford, Clarendon, p.260ff; And: Correspondence, Cunningham.
74. Snead-Cox, 2, p.139.
75. Wilfrid Ward, Review of Snead-Cox's *Cardinal Vaughan*, *Dublin Review*, July 1910, 47, p.6.
76. VFA. Scrapbook. *Evening News.* Vaughan obituary; MHA. Queen Victoria dies, 22 January 1901. English College, Rome, Herbert Vaughan, 23 January 1901.
77. Snead-Cox, *vol* 2, p.240.
78. *ibid.*, pp.250-1: Royal Declaration: "I do solemnly and sincerely, in the presence of God, profess, testify and declare, that I do believe in the Sacrament of the Lord's Supper there is not any transubstantiation of the elements of Bread and Wine into the Body and Blood of Christ, at or after the consecration thereof by any person whatsoever; and that the invocation or the adoration of the Virgin Mary or any other Saint and the Sacrifice of the Mass, as they are now used in the Church of Rome, are superstitious and idolatrous...."
79. *ibid.*, p.260.
80. VFA. Scrapbook.
81. Snead-Cox, 2, pp.365-6.
82. *ibid.*, pp.382-3.
83. *ibid.*, pp.384-5.
84. *ibid.*, pp.295-300: Snead-Cox recalls an incident at Salford when Vaughan refused the sacraments to a man who had written to *The Times* a letter he judged incompatible with full acceptance of Papal Infallibility. (This may have been Mr Henry Petre of Dukinfield. See: *Evening News*, 26 March 1885. WDA.) "Herbert Vaughan had done only what seemed his plain duty; but many tongues were let loose against him." What disturbed some was that in Westminster Manning had not punished the first Lord Acton who had written in *The Times* of "the follies and crimes of the Popes." "People asked in perplexity why Herbert Vaughan had struck when Manning held his hand.... Then the facile answer came that the Bishop was young and inexperienced, and narrow-minded, and a bigot; and in certain circles it was common to contrast his blundering zeal with the large charity of the convert Cardinal." Only after the death of all three did it come out that Manning had asked Acton for a declaration of faith in the decrees of the Vatican Council, which he had made, unlike the "obscure" person from Lancashire whom Vaughan had disciplined. In 1895 Acton and Vaughan corresponded. Acton wrote on 30 April in reply to Vaughan: "I was down with congestion of the lungs when I received from your Eminence the kindest and most touching letter that it has ever been my happy fortune to

possess." Acton had recently been appointed Regius Professor of History at Cambridge and Vaughan wrote to congratulate him. Vaughan wrote evidently after seeing a critical article about Acton in the *Irish Catholic* "which ... infuriated" Vaughan. Lord Acton was Vaughan's special guest at the laying of the foundation-stone of Westminster Cathedral.

85. *ibid.*, p.383.

86. WDA. *Directory*, 1904. The 1904 publication uses 1903 statistics: there were also 27 religious orders and congregations of men and 59 of women in Westminster diocese along with 166 public churches and chapels, and 321 secular and 147 regular priests.

PART SIX

THE END

CHAPTER XVIII

Final Illness and Death

Heart Failure

Herbert Vaughan's health began to deteriorate in November 1897.[1] He was travelling through Essex "on a kind of missionary tour, lecturing at Town Halls and in out-of-the-way villages and elsewhere on Catholic subjects and explaining Catholic doctrine," when he had a sharp pain in his heart and found it difficult to breathe. It was, he said, similar to what he experienced at St Edmund's College, Ware, forty years before.[2] To recover his strength, he went for a rest at Grasse on the Riviera for two months in the beginning of January 1898; he stayed with Harman Grisewood and his wife. From Grasse he wrote to a close relative: "It is a very full and a very sweet preparation for the last stage of life—or for death—whichever God wills. I could not wish for a better time. I have had nothing so good for over thirty years. The weather is brighter than the best English summer weather, the air clear as can be, the site 1,000 feet above the sea, and the Isle of Lérins is visible in part."[3] He confided to a friend that the weeks he spent at Grasse helped him to feel better but, more importantly, were of "the greatest advantage to my soul. I have been face to face with death." At the same time he felt that there was no improvement in his heart condition, and so, with his doctor's permission, he decided to return home. "I am therefore returning to work at a lower level of activity and a higher level of communion with God."[3]

In April 1898 he returned to Westminster "depressed in mind and body," according to Fr Bernard Ward.[4] Cardinal Vaughan wrote to Mary Elizabeth Herbert on 27 April that his health had improved considerably since returning to England, enough for the 26th of April to have been a "test day" for his recovery. On that day he attended a synod that lasted "three hours with an Allocution of ¾ of an hour, and I was well heard throughout the Church. This morning has been spent in visiting officially the great London Hospital, the largest hospital in the world. I am only a little tired." The week following Easter was demanding but he got through it successfully although he reported that his "walking powers, though improved, are still those of a tortoise."[5]

During his travels to the Continent, he had spent some days in France during October 1897 when the Archconfraternity of Our Lady of Compassion, the League of Prayer, was inaugurated in the Church of Saint-Sulpice in Paris. It was the final event of a triduum that began in Arles in honour of the thirteenth centenary of the consecration of St Augustine. The aim of the confraternity was "nothing less than the return of Great Britain to the See of Peter, and the eventual gathering of all nations into the one Fold under the one Shepherd." Despite his poor health Vaughan was able to assist the Archbishop of Paris in the long ceremony, from ten o'clock in the morning until half-past five in the evening. There were a thousand priests and six thousand laity present.[6]

He visited Paris again in March or early April, 1898, and spent three mornings praying in Notre Dame des Victoires, "with the usual advantages derived from Our Lady's intercession." One result of his visits to the basilica was a resolution to make "the study of the life and character of Our Lord the special work of the remainder of my life."[7]

In spite of his illness, Vaughan kept working and travelling. For example, he hosted a meeting of the Historical Research Society at Archbishop's House on 2 May. He presided over the meeting, at which Dom Cuthbert Butler lectured on the "Modern School of Historical Criticism." After the lecture the cardinal thanked Butler for a "noble and judicious exposition of the principles of critical investigation," and was happy to know that the Church was taking her place in the field. "The school was not large, but was select and powerful, and in a few years' time would increase and be strengthened."[8]

A few weeks later the *Inverness Courier* reported that he was in the north of Scotland on 25 May to perform the marriage ceremony of the eldest daughter of Lord Lovat, Mary Fraser, to Viscount Encombe. The marriage took place in Eskadale church. Vaughan was related to her mother, his cousin, Lady Alice, who was the daughter of his aunt and uncle, the Weld-Blundells of Ince Blundell, and had baptised the bride. After the wedding breakfast in Beaufort Castle, he planted a memorial tree, a copper beech, in the grounds.[9]

On 7 June 1898 he was at Arundel Castle, the home of the Duke of Norfolk, to see Lady Margaret, who was seriously ill.[10] From Arundel he wrote again to Elizabeth Herbert that he was improving thanks to a diet he had been put on: "The object of it is to reduce weight by reducing fat and to increase strength. The 'food of energy' is the diet prescribed! and so far it is answering." He wrote on 10 July that he was back in Westminster, felt better and had lost fourteen pounds. He was already working and had preached at the Golden Jubilee celebration of the opening of St George's Cathedral, Southwark, on 3 July. Fifty years earlier he had been among the serving boys when Bishop Wiseman solemnly opened the church.[11]

Deaths

On Friday 5 August, Frances Mary Ward, widow of the late William George Ward, died at her home, Clifton Lodge, Hampstead Heath. She was in her eighty-second year. Her son, Monsignor Bernard Ward, was on a retreat given for diocesan clergy at St Edmund's, Ware. He and Cardinal Vaughan went together to Clifton Lodge and arrived around midday on Friday. Mrs Ward was unconscious and died in the evening.

The following Wednesday her body was taken to the Isle of Wight and the church at Weston Manor. Herbert Vaughan arrived the next day. On Friday morning her son celebrated a Mass for her, and after the Mass, the Cardinal spoke: "The widow lady whose remains we have met to carry to their last resting-place, by the side of her husband, was born some 82 years ago, and bred and early trained under the shadow of the old Catholic Cathedral of Worcester, and I have often heard her say how much her soul owed to the old memories that still cling to those ancient walls...." Vaughan recalled her great love for the service of God and "His Church in England." The love was shown all through her life: She helped Vaughan establish the church at Hertford when he was a priest at St Edmund's; helped found the College for Foreign Missions, and "all her life through there was the same interest and desire to promote the welfare of souls and to help poor priests and poor bishops." Mrs Ward was buried in the same vault with her husband, who had died in 1882, while her son Bernard read the final prayers.[12]

At the beginning of October he celebrated a Requiem Mass at the pro-cathedral for Fr Seddon, who had died just before landing in Canada on one of his periodic trips with emigrant children. There were among the people present several Sisters and between two and three hundred children from Nazareth House, Hammersmith. Before the blessing of the catafalque, Vaughan spoke of Seddon: "For thirty-two years he had consecrated his life to the salvation of poor little abandoned children. He had been the right hand of the late Cardinal in carrying out the work for which he would be longest remembered. Tens of thousands of children have been saved to the Catholic religion through the zeal and love shewn by Father Seddon.... His love for the souls of the little children was as tender and earnest at the end of his life as in the beginning."[13]

During November Vaughan rested at Mill Hill, still weak, but by 3 December he was feeling better and had returned to Westminster.[14]

Auxiliary Bishop

In the autumn of 1898 Vaughan was promised an auxiliary bishop to help with his duties at Westminster. An American paper reported an "item of Catholic interest" in February 1899: Cardinal Vaughan, "nearing his sixty-seventh year," who "has not enjoyed the best of health lately," was ordered some time ago "not to do any active work." Even if his health was very good, the article continued, "he would be fully justified in asking for an auxiliary, so large and difficult must be the responsibilities which devolve upon him as the head of England's most important diocese."[15]

The name of his brother John had been suggested,[16] but Rome chose Fr Brindle, an army chaplain on duty in Egypt, where he had been on a military campaign to the Sudan. Brindle resigned his chaplaincy and was ordained bishop in Rome. His task was to help Cardinal Vaughan and Canon Barry, the vicar general, care for the archdiocese. With both Vaughan and Barry ill, Brindle began to "administer the diocese singlehanded" after his arrival near the end of March 1899, and by July he "was active and everywhere."[17]

In 1899 Canon Barry died and Mgr Fenton became the vicar general. Unfortunately for Vaughan, Brindle was appointed to be bishop of Nottingham.[18]

Richard Vaughan, S.J.

On 19 March 1899, Herbert Vaughan's uncle, the Jesuit Richard Joseph Vaughan, died at St Francis Xavier's in Liverpool. After becoming a priest he had served as Minister and Prefect of Philosophers at Stonyhurst. *The Tablet* obituary called him "an attractive man" who made many friends. "His conversation was remarkably interesting, especially when the conversation turned on to engineering questions, ship building and the like." He often took long walks on the Liverpool wharves to see the great ships. There is no mention of the Cardinal being at the funeral.[19]

Herbert Vaughan's general health gradually weakened despite his retreats at Llandrindod Wells in Wales, his rest periods with the Edmund Talbots at Derwent Hall in Derbyshire, and at St Joseph's College, Mill Hill.

The Young Priest and *Humility of Heart*

In April 1902, Vaughan went to the Visitation Convent, Harrow. He rested in between "professions and instructions" for the community. From Harrow he wrote thanking Mother Mary of Jesus and the Carmel Sisters for their Mass and prayers on his seventieth birthday: "It is a long retrospect. I feel that I ought to be overwhelmed by the thought of my sins and ingratitude— especially sins of omission, which always seem to me to be more awful, because the least visible and tangible." Vaughan recalled how he became a member of the Sodality of Our Lady at Stonyhurst when he was thirteen, and now he could look back and see "her hand in all the past: using one, with very poor talents and natural gifts and a very small supply of supernatural virtue, to be an instrument to promote her honour and that of her Divine Son, Our Lord." Since "the end is drawing near" he wanted to spend his remaining time reflecting on "the apostolic life in myself and particularly in the young priests who are entering upon the ministry." He hoped to have time to finish a book he had started years before, titled *Conferences on the Apostolic Life*.[20] He had opportunity to complete a manuscript, along with a translation of an

Italian devotional book he had been using for many years, in the months of declining health before his death in 1903.

He completed *The Young Priest, Conferences on the Apostolic Life*, and after his death his youngest brother, John, edited it and arranged for its publication by Burns & Oates. In the preface John Vaughan reminded readers that, although his brother, Herbert, had written several small booklets on devotional topics, "he never found time, amid his incessant occupations, to undertake any prolonged literary work. It was only when, at last, he was stricken down by disease, and compelled to give up his active life altogether, that he instinctively took to his pen." Herbert Vaughan continued to work on the book "almost to the very end."[21]

One of his successors as superior general of the Mill Hill Missionaries, Noel Hanrahan, used *The Young Priest* in 1957 as a source for his doctoral thesis, "The Apostolic Spirit of Herbert Cardinal Vaughan."[22] Vaughan considered his conferences as suggestions offered "to the Priests whom I have ordained at Mill Hill during the last thirty years and sent forth for life into the midst of the heathen populations of the world" and also to those he had ordained "*ad titulum missionis* for the work of the conversion of England."[23] One reviewer thought the book to have a special meaning for it came "from the deathbed of a venerable and wise guide of the clergy."[24]

The other manuscript completed in his final months was a translation from the Italian of Cajetan Mary Da Bergamo's *Humility of Heart*. Herbert Vaughan added an introduction titled "Thoughts and sentiments on humility" and his brother, Bernard, wrote a preface when it was published in 1905. Bernard Vaughan wrote that his brother had used the Italian version for more than thirty years, and that during the last fourteen years of his life it was "his constant companion, his *vade mecum*." The book was dedicated to the priests ordained by Vaughan for Salford, Westminster and the foreign missions, and for the Ladies of Charity, a group of lay women he had founded at Salford and Westminster. He dated the text 23 April 1903, less than two months before he died.[25]

Vaughan owned a number of volumes in a series written by the Capuchin Da Bergamo, but for many years it was only the first volume of the Monza edition, the one he translated, that he used frequently.[26] He recalled one night he was in the chapel of St Bede's College in Manchester when he thought about God in the Old and New Testament naming people "after their personal characteristics." He then began to apply to himself the seven capital sins and five other "characteristics of my soul, viz.: Weakness, Ignorance, Poverty, Theft and Cruelty." All of them seemed to be "home truths" which might be "valuable for private use."[27] Vaughan was convinced that if the "little flock" in England was to serve the Lord, by some great development of religious activity among the laity, in cooperation with and guided by the clergy, and did not have humility "which our Lord told all of us to learn of

Him," they would be "rejected by God and man." Therefore he dedicated Da Bergamo's book, "written by a most holy and learned missionary, many times commended by zealous popes and bishops, to the Ladies of Charity as well as to the Priests for whose ordination I have been responsible."[28]

Ladies of Charity

Herbert Vaughan established the Association of the Ladies of Charity in 1900. It was modelled on a similar association in France founded by St Vincent de Paul in 1617. Lady Edmund Talbot was the Honorary Organizing Secretary.

Many ladies had undertaken charity work with the Catholic Social Union, others regularly visited the sick in hospitals and supported the activities of groups like the Sisters of Charity, Carlisle Place.[29]

In the second annual report of July 1902, Lady Talbot gave some statistics of work accomplished between October 1901, and July 1902. In addition to other information, she wrote that there were two hundred active members who had made 21,360 visits to those in need of help over ten months. She appealed for more members, and for those who were able to do so, to make the Ladies of Charity their almoners.[30]

Another Collapse

According to a letter at Notting Hill, Vaughan thought: "If Cardinal Manning's last words to me were prophetic I shall have ten years more: but if he was not a prophet it may be as many months, weeks, or days only."[31] Manning was not prophetic in this instance; Vaughan was not to live until he was eighty. His remaining time was measured in months.

In June 1902 he suddenly collapsed again and was forced to give up his work and take a complete rest. He went first to Mill Hill. On 16 June he wrote to his nephew Fr Herbert Vaughan: "My day is ending; new vigour and activity are needed to carry on the campaign against the busy and sleepless enemies of the Church—*et Deus providebit*."[32] On 19 June he was still at Mill Hill. It was the Feast of the Sacred Heart and during the day he had walked across the fields to St Mary's Abbey to receive Lady Edmund Talbot into the Third Order of St Francis. In the Abbey logbook a Sister noted: "The Cardinal walked up from the College and was taken quite ill in our visitors' room from the exertion of the walk up the hill. After a time he became better, but still had to be assisted in the sacristy for the ceremony."[33]

The college at Mill Hill was too near to London for Vaughan to rest. "Herbert Vaughan had its sounds forever in his ears, and they seemed always to be calling him back to his place at Archbishop's House." He tried to return to Westminster but became so weak that his doctor, Lauder Brunton, ordered him out of England to Bad Nauheim in Germany; "the alternative was to stay at home and die of dropsy."³⁴ He left London on 20 June with Mgr Moyes. From Germany he wrote to Elizabeth Herbert that "Dr. Groebal says he is very satisfied with me, which is more than I can say of myself."³⁵ To his nephew, Herbert: "The treatment is kill or cure—I am said to be emerging from the first operation. Before the end of the month we shall see what kind of a cure it is to be."³⁶ Vaughan stayed in Germany until the second week in August and then returned to England "weaker than when he had left and knowing that the end was near." His doctor insisted that it was useless to stay in London and so he accepted an invitation to be a guest with Lord and Lady Edmund Talbot at Derwent Hall. When he arrived at Derwent, he entered the house leaning on another priest's arm, while those who welcomed him thought he was so weak that he had come there to die. At first he could hardly sit in the chapel for twenty minutes a day before having to lie down. His doctors had even forbidden him to offer Mass.³⁷ Fr F. M. Hayward met Vaughan at Derwent Hall and wrote to Mill Hill about the Cardinal many years later. His health was so poor that Fr Hayward gave him the last sacraments: "His stay at Derwent Hall gave me many insights into his matured and holy life," Hayward wrote.³⁸

Lady May Talbot wrote to Elizabeth Herbert on 24 September that it was "essential for him to climb no stairs, to remain quiet, to be dieted, to drive in the open air."³⁹ Vaughan's health began to improve and by 27 October he could write that he was quietly getting better and might even live to "finish two or three matters" he was working on.⁴⁰ During his convalescence at Derwent he followed anxiously the parliamentary debate on the Education Bill of 1902, the completion of Westminster Cathedral, and many others matters.⁴¹ Although he was cared for very well in the seclusion of Derwent Hall, and thought he had become better, he never recovered his former health. He knew that his active life was over.

Bishop William Vaughan; Edmund Vaughan, C.SS.R

While Cardinal Vaughan was at Derwent, at the end of October, his uncle, Bishop William Joseph Vaughan of Plymouth, died in retirement at Newton Abbot. He was eighty-eight years old. Another uncle, Fr Edmund Vaughan, a Redemptorist, outlived the Cardinal. He was eighty-one years old when he died in 1908. Edmund had worked at Clapham and Liverpool, and given missions all over the country. He founded the community at Perth in Scotland, was for a time provincial and spent three years in Australia.⁴²

Herbert Vaughan's Final Months

On 30 November 1902 he wrote a long letter to Mgr Moyes to thank him for accepting "the office of Vice Rector under me at Archbishop's House. My absences are so long and so frequent that it is quite needful for the order and import of the house that someone should be there." He went on to advise him about the common life at the house and the problems to avoid: "if there be a house in the Diocese which ought to give the example of a high tone and of Priestly habits, it is the house."[43]

Early in December he left the Talbots at Sheffield and returned to Westminster. "The winter wore away and the spring-time came," writes Snead-Cox, and Vaughan was "still working and directing all the affairs of the diocese. But the hand was failing from the sceptre, and to those of us who saw him constantly he seemed to grow more feeble from week to week."[44]

Back in London, he divided his time between Mill Hill and Archbishop's House. He wrote to Elizabeth Herbert that he was spending time at Mill Hill each week to gather his strength: "The place is very quiet and restful and the room is everything I could wish, and so is the care they give me. Four or five days here enable me without effort to spend two or three days in London, and there transact a little business."[45] In a very feeble hand he wrote to Mother Mary of Jesus from Archbishop's House on 2 March: "I am in bed and in solitude—so cannot write at length." He advised her about a woman who wished to join their community—to give her a "good chance"—and also asked for prayers for the "catechism movement—which is as important for the whole of England as for London." He accepted his poor health: "Illness and March are always blessed things for me."[46] Vaughan thought he was going to die in March, on the Feast of St Joseph. On 16 March he wrote out instructions to his brother John about his funeral and the disposal of some of his personal things.[47] Vaughan had begun to prepare his last instructions more than three years before, on 31 December 1899. The last entry was to be on 16 June 1903, three days before his death.[48]

On 19 March, St Joseph's Day, his condition worsened and he received the last sacraments, but the attack was not fatal. He was certain that St Joseph was going to take him that day, but "he saw I was not ready then," he wrote to Elizabeth Herbert. He concluded the 22 March letter: "You may be sure if I get home before you, I will do more for you there than I ever could on earth."[49] On 25 March he wrote to Bishop Hedley that he was enjoying his "usual broken health" and feeling "rather reduced at the latter end of my life to the conditions of its beginning, at least in some respects. I believe I may end suddenly or go on indefinitely."[50]

On the same day that he wrote to the Bishop of Newport, the Feast of the Annunciation, 25 March 1903, he left Archbishop's House for the last time and travelled to St Joseph's Missionary College at Mill Hill to await death. He prepared to leave early in the morning and when he came down from his room, helped by Mgr Johnson, the hall was filled with people. News that he was leaving brought priests, students, household staff and friends to see him off. "As the Cardinal came forward all that little crowd ... went on its knees, and the stricken man, as he passed along through the lines of people, paused every few paces and raised his hand to bless."[51] He was suffering from dropsy, his body filling with fluids, brought about by his weakened heart, and was leaving Archbishop's House for the last time.

Of Vaughan's peripatetic final years, Edward Norman wrote that as the century of "Catholic revival moved towards its end, the life of Vaughan, too, was running out. Illness closed in with ever greater frequency; the life of dedicated attention to the stewardship of the English Church, and of faithful preservation of Catholic truth, became increasingly exhausting." By 1902 the "burden of existence was a terrible trial" for Herbert Vaughan. During his final restless months "he moved from place to place seeking somewhere to die in seclusion and repose." Finally he went to "his beloved College in Mill Hill."[52]

After he arrived at Mill Hill his strength slowly slipped away. He was taken each day in a wheelchair around the corridors, outside on the terrace in good weather, and to the cemetery at Calvary and the spot he had chosen for his grave. Often Vaughan was pushed in his chair by Brother Bernard van Berkel, who was to die in 1965 at the age of ninety-seven. In the grove of trees surrounding Calvary there was a large wood-carved crucifix he had found years before in the Tyrol. It had fallen down, abandoned by the the local village, and was covered by brush at the roadside. The village had replaced it and so the local people gave the old one to Vaughan and he brought it to Mill Hill. In the last days of his life he spent hours below the crucifix and near to the place below where he was to be buried. The few visitors that Vaughan saw during this time often met him sitting in his wheelchair on the terrace in front of the college. Sometimes he called for the Mother Superior at St Mary's Abbey. She remembered that he loved to talk with her of the old times when he was beginning the missionary college.

He wrote to Mother Mary of Jesus on Easter Sunday that he had improved enough to attend the 5.30 Mass that morning and receive Holy Communion. He continued: "I thought I was going during March and was a little surprised and disappointed that I was still left behind." He compared his illness to "so many noviciates, in which something unknown and unpractised before has to be learnt." His thoughts turned to the virtue of humility—he was to complete the translation of *Humility of Heart* on 23 April—and continued: "It never appeared so clearly to me before that humility is the first condition required by God in his service." Vaughan concluded by asking Mother Mary to "help me by prayers to begin this late in life to learn something of the first principles."[53]

While he was at Mill Hill awaiting death, Cardinal Vaughan was always available to his vicar general, Mgr Fenton, and canons of the archdiocese. Friends also came to see him during the final months. Among them were John Snead-Cox, Wilfrid Ward and Herbert's brother, Frank.

John Snead-Cox visited Herbert Vaughan twice at Mill Hill during his final illness. The first time was on 22 May: "He was sitting in a little bare room, in a big armchair, propped up with pillows and looking dreadfully changed. His eyes were half closed as I entered, and he was breathing with great difficulty."[54] Maisie Ward also wrote of Snead-Cox's visit in her book about her father, Wilfrid. For her, what happened during Snead-Cox's conversation was "deeply illuminating" not just of Vaughan's own character but "of much in the outlook and action of authority that bewilders the outside world and is at times a trial to Catholics."[55] Vaughan wanted a book by one of his diocesan priests, Fr Carson, to be condemned. Snead-Cox argued that it was unwise to take action against an obscure book by such a young man. "The Cardinal listened in silence, and then, with a gentleness that was poignant, said simply, 'I am too weak to argue. All I know is that one of my priests is teaching false doctrine.'" Vaughan thought he might take action himself but thought people would "say I am senile; you must condemn it in *The Tablet*." After some time, the conversation left Vaughan short of breath "and he lay back panting for some minutes."

Before Snead-Cox could call the nurse, Vaughan smiled and started slowly to reminisce about his trip down the Sacramento River aboard a paddle-steamer in 1864. He described how the paddle wheels sometimes stranded a salmon on the mud "panting and gasping for breath." Vaughan added, "I am just like one of those fish—gasping for life." When Snead-Cox was leaving, Vaughan gave him a photograph of himself for his wife. He wrote on it slowly and painfully: "My Dear Mary, God bless you. And bring up your vigorous little family in fidelity and service to the law of God. Your affectionate cousin, Herbert Cardinal Vaughan."

About ten days later Snead-Cox returned and was shocked by the change in Cardinal Vaughan: "he seemed so tired and distressed, and as though almost too weak to whisper." He was glad nothing had been done about Father Carson's book for he heard that he too was dying. Then came the last words Snead-Cox heard from Vaughan's lips: "You see, I have a fellow-feeling for the dying." The next time John Snead-Cox came to St Joseph's was to stand by Herbert Vaughan's open grave.[56]

On Saturday 23 May, a letter written by Mgr Fenton on behalf of Cardinal Vaughan was published in the Catholic papers asking for the prayers of the clergy, religious communities and faithful. On 24 May Archbishop Francis Bourne of Southwark had a letter read in all the churches of his diocese asking for prayers for the failing Herbert Vaughan.[57]

One of the Cardinal's visitors was Wilfrid Ward. For some minutes Ward could not recognize in the worn features of the dying man the "radiant presence of the old friend who in boyhood had inspired him to great deeds for the Church." Herbert Vaughan talked in a faint voice of Wilfrid's parents and hoped that Wilfrid "should walk in my father's footsteps." Ward wrote:

"'Radiant' was the word which Aubrey de Vere used to describe his face as a youth at Rome, and that adjective best expressed the impression made by his presence all through his life. But now this shrunken form, this worn, sad, tear-stained face was all that remained on earth to represent the noble soul and aspect of Herbert Vaughan."[58]

On 10 June, in a very shaky hand, he wrote to his personal secretary Austin Oates asking him to come to Mill Hill the following Sunday afternoon: "I am on my cross and am looking for Our Lord's mercy and the prayers of friends."[59]

Ten days before his death Vaughan wrote to Mother Mary of Jesus:

A thousand thanks for your note. In a few days I may not be able to answer it with my own hand. I have been for months on the Cross, making my preparations for eternity. I thank you and the [?] whose prayers have been offered for me. They help me much—not to recover but to prepare. How seldom does our Lord wish any one to live and finish his work! When He did not even finish His own, especially in the dogmatic sense. I thank God that I have never turned my attention to the prolongation of this my poor and defective life. To accomplish His will, to die in union with Mary and Joseph—this is enough indeed to satisfy the most enlarging religious ambition. Impress this on your daughters also. This will probably be my last communication to you by letter; but we can pray together in the spirit. Of course I may recover but I do not contemplate [?] so unlikely an eventuality. I must conclude by gratefully thanking you for the help and encouragement—[?]— when God was beginning to draw me closer to Himself. You then pointed out that He might finish in a short time with Himself in sickness what He had delayed through our faults and external activities. Let one hope something of this has been accomplished, the cross and suffering are intended for our salvation. I trust to the prayer and help of Carmel till the last. God bless you all … Herbert Cardinal Vaughan, June 9, 1903, Mill Hill."[60]

Early in June, according to Snead-Cox, Herbert Vaughan said his final Mass and after that he was only able to receive Communion. The rector, Francis Henry, gave him the "Last Blessing" on 6 June and Vaughan in turn gave Henry a message for his missionaries. It was his blessing and he offered them *The Young Priest* as "the last words of a loving father."[61] On 10 June Vaughan and Henry spoke again and the Cardinal said "how strange it was to feel so weak and unable to do anything, simply dying" and that God had "put him as it were on a retreat.[62] During his final days Vaughan suffered from sleeplessness and he could no longer concentrate, not even enough to pray the rosary. He asked for some pictures for his room to help him: "I don't want high art, but just something that will remind me of what to think about." When the pictures were brought, he directed Henry: "Now please hang them up—the Crucifixion at the top, Our Lady at the right, and St. Joseph on the left and St.

Peter below—yes, put St. Peter in his proper place at the feet of Our Lord."
Henry thought it was a pathetic effort to help Vaughan, but it was successful.[63]

On Thursday 11 June 1903, Vaughan wrote some final instructions for his executors.[64] The last letter he seems to have written was to Mgr Fenton on 16 June. Much of it is illegible but it shows Vaughan's concern for others to the last. He praised Mgr Fenton: "You have been an excellent administrator of the Catholic S[??]. I hope your appointments will be [?] and that you will strengthen hands by adding a consultative of scientific men—lay and religious."[65] In the note quoted by Snead-Cox, Vaughan writes: "I do not know who may follow me, but earnestly pray that he may gather all, lay and clergy, by union and consultation, in common action."[66]

1. Public Profession of Faith

On Thursday 18 June, Vaughan felt much weaker and asked to make a public profession of faith in the chapel that afternoon. His vicar general, Mgr Fenton, and three canons—Johnson, Moyes and Dunn—were called from Westminster. His brothers, Frank and Reginald, were also present along with a number of priests, college staff and students. Vaughan was wheeled out of his room by Mr Young, one of his nurses: "he looked around in a dazed, wondering way, but recognised each one of us in turn," recalled Mgr Moyes. Moyes thought it was more like a funeral procession for the dead than one for the dying. Before they reached the chapel he stopped and asked his nurse if Caroline Hanmer had been informed. She had not, and so they waited until she was called from her Rosary Cottage near the road. The four canons "robed in papal purple" awaited Vaughan at the high altar as he was finally wheeled into the church. Mgr Johnson, the senior canon of the chapter, recited the long profession in Latin for the tired Vaughan.[67] After some words from Canon Moyes, Vaughan began to speak in a "strangely weird" voice. "It seemed to be the voice of a man who was already half in the other world."[68] After encouraging the people present to live lives true to their faith, Vaughan gave all his blessing.

Caroline Hanmer wrote to Elizabeth Herbert after Vaughan's death that Canon Johnson had read the profession of faith and "our dear father signed it." He also spoke briefly to Miss Hanmer. She had been away from Mill Hill, and when she was sent for by Vaughan she had just returned home. Miss Hanmer had seen him twice on the terrace of the college, but noticed how much weaker and weaker he was becoming.[69] Once the ceremony was over Vaughan was "visibly weaker." Back in his room he asked the nurse to remove his cardinal's robes: "Take away this finery. I shall not need it again." By evening he told others that he was confident that "Our Lord would take him soon."[70]

2. Other Visitors

The last family member to see Herbert Vaughan alive was his brother, Frank. The account of his visit was given by a cousin in a letter to Elizabeth Herbert on 23 June. When Frank went to his dying brother he spoke with him about the arrival of the Douai monks in London, "but cousin Herbert only said God bless them and appeared too tired to talk much."[71] The letter continues:

> 'Frank, you had better go and have dinner with the students, they are going to have extra fish as it is the Feast of the Sacred Heart.' He seemed pleased at the thought of their having a little treat though the nurse told Frank (that the Cardinal was) trying to mortify himself by taking his disgusting medicine in tiny sips.... After dinner Frank came back to the Cardinal, it was almost two o'clock—and he said to him 'I feel very weak, I think I must send for Canon Johnson.' Then he looked out of the window and saw the rain coming down in torrents, so he said 'Perhaps it is too damp and cold for him, I will have Fr. Considine instead.' Fr. Considine used to hear his confession [Herbert Vaughan says he never did. *Author*] if Canon Johnson was not ... so Fr. Considine came about 3:30.... In the meantime cousin Herbert said to Frank, 'Leave me now, to prepare for death, for I think Our Lord will soon take me.' ... As Frank got up to go, he pulled his head down and kissed him most affectionately as though he knew he should never see him again on earth.[72]

3. Daniel Considine

Only near the end of his life did Herbert Vaughan have a spiritual director in addition to his confessor. According to Snead-Cox, whenever he was in Rome he used to consult a Redemptorist priest, but not until 1901 did he have a regular spiritual advisor. For this task he asked the Jesuit, Father Daniel Considine. At least once a month, when Vaughan was healthy, he would travel to the Jesuit House at Roehampton and at other times Father Considine would come to Archbishop's House.[73]

Daniel Heffernan Considine was born on 1 January 1849 at Derk House in Old Pallas, Co. Limerick. His father was a Protestant and his mother a Catholic. Up until his tenth year, he and his brother, Sir Heffernan Considine, stayed at home on Sunday mornings for prayers with their father while their mother and sister went to Mass. When Mr Considine became a Catholic, he sent his two sons to school at Stonyhurst. Daniel became a Jesuit, and, almost from the beginning of his career, he was "sought after as a spiritual director, and entered on that arduous apostolate of the confessional and of the parlour, and the ceaseless labour of letter writing, that was to be his chief preoccupation in life." Vaughan's clergy knew of Considine's work from retreats he directed, and from monthly meetings of the Apostolic Union held at Manresa retreat house. "His humble, unworldly manner, and anxious care for their comfort, encouraged them to seek for a closer acquaintance with him and then to ask for spiritual advice and help."[74]

On 5 June 1903 Vaughan acknowledged his indebtedness to Considine. "My habit has been to take direction generally by submitting my aspirations and devotions to the best priests in authority round about me—to go to a fixed confessor in any place where I was living. This I did till the end— Mgr. Johnson, confessor in London; Fr. Henry, while I was ill at Mill Hill. In the last one or two years in London I chose Fr. Considine, S.J., to submit to him my personal projects in the spiritual way. He guided me much in work of intercourse with God, and in generosity and liberty of spirit; but I never had occasion to make him my confessor. I derived much encouragement from his wise enlightenment."[75] Considine visited Herbert Vaughan twice during his final days at Mill Hill. The last time was the day of Vaughan's death.

After the Cardinal's death, Considine wrote that near the end Vaughan suffered an "interior trial by which God was pleased to purify his soul at the last." Considine found Herbert Vaughan in a deep depression. Vaughan's eyes, he wrote, "waxed dim as though in sympathy with the bodily senses," and the darkness into which they peered seemed to be haunted by ghostly presences, strange and terrifying. "What if Faith after all were but a dream, and all its gracious truths mere pious imaginings? ... The horror, the cruelty of the temptation lay in its whisper that 'nothing was true, all beliefs were false together, there was no God, no hereafter.'" Vaughan remained mentally clear but "a bewilderment and terror seized him for which he could not account, and which caused him the keenest distress." Calm finally returned and "he knew that God was with him even if hidden behind a veil."

When Considine started to leave, Vaughan insisted on walking him to the door of his room. The Jesuit opened the main door to the college veranda "overlooking a glorious view when lit up by the sun of June, but now swathed in hurrying clouds and rain. In fact, torrents had been falling all day long, and for days before, so that the floods were everywhere and I splashed through pools of water on overflowed roads as I made my way to the station." The next day, "which was calm and beautiful," Considine heard that Herbert Vaughan had died the previous night, 19 June 1903.[76]

Death

Caroline Hanmer spoke to Colonel Frank Vaughan after he had seen his dying brother. The Colonel told Miss Hanmer that he planned to return to the college the following Tuesday. She asked: "Do you really expect to find him? And had not the heart to add: "The Feast of the Sacred Heart is not over," for I felt so strongly that on the Feast, the Sacred Heart would claim him."[77]

After Considine's departure a "great calm came over the dying man." He was certain that he was to die before the Feast of the Sacred Heart was over. He insisted throughout the afternoon that he not be given any more drugs or "sleeping-draughts." "Don't let my thoughts get entangled tonight by stimulants and drugs. I want only to be with Jesus and the Holy Family." A Dr Martin cared for Vaughan during his final illness.

When the summer evening was ending, he was with the nurse and asked him to say the rosary. He had been growing weaker during the day and was having difficulty breathing as he remained seated in an armchair.[78] Later he asked that the nurse, Mr Christie Young, who had cared for him for four months, excuse him for the trouble he had given: "You must try to bear with an impatient and irritable old man." The nurse left at about 11 p.m. and the night nurse, Mr Keating, came on duty.

At about 11.30 p.m. the Cardinal grew worse and Young was called back. According to Caroline Hanmer, Keating returned with Fr Christian van den Biesen, an Old Testament Scripture professor on the college staff, at twenty minutes to twelve and found Vaughan "conscious but rapidly sinking. Vaughan whispered: 'I have had a bad attack—the worst I have had.' A short time passed and he was calm again in his chair, praying 'Jesus, Mary, Joseph.' Minutes went by, and then the words came more slowly and faintly, until an ashen veil seemed to close over his face." Fr Henry was called and he noted the time as he ran to the Cardinal's room: it was ten minutes before midnight. By the time he and another priest reached the sickroom Herbert Vaughan had died quietly, in the presence of van der Biesen and the two nurses, "his lips still trying to shape themselves to the words "Jesus, Mary, Joseph.""[79] Christian van den Biesen had given the final absolution and on this Cardinal Vaughan opened his eyes, "gazed for a moment at the priest's face, and in the next moment expired."[80] One account[81] says that Christie Young, the nurse, held Vaughan in his arms "as he drew his last breath and passed quietly away. His dying words had been uttered a few moments earlier, 'Yes, I am better now.'"[82]

Edward Norman wrote of Vaughan's death: "With a lucid mind and great fortitude, impressed by the frailty of human faith, tired in spirit and yet attaining an ultimate serenity, Vaughan was delivered into eternity. It was the Feast of the Sacred Heart."[83]

The next morning, Caroline Hanmer, on her way to Mass before 6 a.m., passed Herbert Vaughan's window. She later said that she knew something had happened. When she entered the church, "three black Masses were beginning!!!." Vaughan's body was laid out that Saturday morning in St Joseph's College chapel. Again Caroline Hanmer describes the scene: "Saturday I watched by him looking quite himself (could I say more) tho without smile or colour, there he was. This morning (Sunday, 21st June) I watched from 7:30 to 8:45—that was between the Masses—and again for some time before and after dinner. At seven this evening he will be taken to the Cathedral where preparations for the reception are going on all day—to return on Thursday evening and be laid where he wished on Friday."[84]

According to Snead-Cox, the day after his death, when the news was out, "many wanted to have an imposing funeral ceremony," but Mgr Fenton knew Herbert Vaughan's instructions to be otherwise. A year previously, on 27 June 1902, he had instructed his executors that his funeral might be in the cathedral but his body was "to be buried at Mill Hill near Calvary." Vaughan's instructions continued: "After giving my name and title on the tombstone add this most precious title *Servus perpetuus Beatae Mariae Virgini* (*sic*)." This recalled the title of "perpetual slave" he had used when he became a member of the Sodality at Stonyhurst when he was thirteen. Herbert Vaughan added that those arranging his funeral should: "Beware of useless expense in my funeral. Let Hussey provide a cheap coffin without brasses, let no hangings be got to drape the cathedral and only a pair of horses to the hearse that will carry my remains to St.Joseph's College. No flowers."[85]

On Saturday 20 June, the "Death of Cardinal Vaughan" was placarded in London and the following day, Sunday 21 June, a letter from Canon W. A. Johnson was read throughout the diocese describing Vaughan's final days and peaceful end. The letter was read immediately after the Gospel of the Sunday: this told, "appropriately enough," about the "shepherd who went out into the wilderness after the lost sheep."[86]

The Standard newspaper reported in its edition of Monday, 22 June: "We regret to record the death of Cardinal Vaughan, which took place at ten minutes to twelve on Friday night, at St. Joseph's College, Mill Hill, where he had been staying since March 25th.... By the Cardinal's wish, he will be buried from the new and as yet unfinished Cathedral. The solemn Dirge, Presente (*sic*) Corpore, will be sung there at six o'clock on Wednesday evening, and the Requiem at eleven o'clock on Thursday morning. The Right Rev. Dr. Stanley will be the celebrant."[87]

In the Sunday evening twilight the great west door of Vaughan's and Bentley's unfinished cathedral was thrown open for the first solemn religious ceremony to be held within its walls. That night the coffin containing the body of Herbert Vaughan was brought from Mill Hill and received at the cathedral doors by Johnson, Fenton, Moyes, Dunn and the brothers of the dead Cardinal. The heavy rains of the previous week had stopped and "a thin mist hung round the domes and turrets in the chill night air." Outside the cathedral doors, groups of lay people had been waiting for some hours already. At twenty minutes to eleven an open hearse, "of the simplest character, and drawn by two black horses," arrived. The hearse was followed by a coach carrying those who were to bear the coffin into the cathedral. A cathedral bell tolled and the lay people uncovered their heads.

The leaden coffin was then escorted in procession to a black-draped catafalque beneath the dome of the cathedral. *The Tablet* of 27 June thought the scene was "strangely pathetic" when Vaughan's remains "were brought to dwell for a while within its unfinished walls." De l'Hôpital wrote that once the doors were closed and the body placed on the catafalque, prayers were said by the clergy and "the deep mysterious shadows of the mighty pile closed round the body as in the tomb." Vaughan would not give thanks at the cathedral's consecration but "a solemn dirge for his faithful soul was to signalize its sacred dedication and as he lay there in the silence of the night and the stillness of death, up in the domes the echoes seemed to linger of Newman's deathless dream 'Praise to the Holiest in the height and in the depth be praised.'"[88]

The public was not admitted to the cathedral for the blessing of the body. During the first night a wake was kept by clergy and Sisters of Charity. On the Monday night it was kept by the Sisters of Nazareth House, Hammersmith, and on subsequent nights by other congregations. During the day the watch was taken up by members of four religious orders.

Beginning on Monday, the cathedral was open to the public and people began to file in. Each day at 9 a.m. a solemn High Mass of Requiem was celebrated, except on Wednesday, which was the feast of St John the Baptist. The cathedral was closed on Wednesday from 10 a.m. to 6 p.m., when the solemn dirge was to be chanted. On Sunday, Monday, Tuesday and Wednesday nights, a vigil was kept around the body. Vespers and the Office of the Dead were said at 8 p.m. on Monday and Tuesday. Canon Dunn announced in a newspaper interview that tickets for the one thousand reserved seats for the Requiem Mass on Thursday had already been taken, but that there would be "plenty of room for the general public who have no tickets."[89] According to De l'Hôpital twenty-seven thousand people were counted on one of the days. He added that Vaughan's "express wish that not a single unnecessary sixpence should be spent upon his funeral was faithfully observed, and all was characterized by the severest simplicity and plainness."[90]

It was originally intended that the funeral should take place on the Friday of the week, but the King's birthday was to be celebrated that day, and so, the solemn dirge, *Praesente Corpore*, was sung on Wednesday evening in the Cathedral at 6, and the solemn requiem Mass on Thursday at 11 a.m.

From the Saturday after Herbert Vaughan's death, announcements and tributes had come from many quarters:

At the Protestant cathedral in Manchester, Dean Maclure referred to Vaughan as one who was for many years one of the most highly respected citizens of the community, and one who took an active interest in its public life and welfare. More than once the Dean discussed the subject of religious education in elementary schools with Vaughan. Though they differed theologically, the Dean recognized "the fidelity with which he discharged what he conceived to be his duties as a distinguished ecclesiastic. He was constant in season and out of season in advancing whatever cause he had at heart."

At Sidmouth, South Devon, a Requiem was sung on behalf of Vaughan, and Fr Jones preached from the words, "God is not unjust and will not forget your work and labour of love which you have shown towards His cause and how you ministered to the saints (Heb vi, v 10)." Jones said: "Not only the Catholic Church in England but throughout the world mourns today the death of the Cardinal whose life will be recorded in history as that of a faithful priest, a noble prince of the Roman Church, and a worthy ruler of the Catholic Church in England."

The Onlooker said of Vaughan: "An aristocrat by right of birth and temperament, there was a large humanity in his work as a priest which he evidenced alike in the terrible epidemic of smallpox in Panama as in the slums of Salford."

Not all the comments were flattering: One unnamed paper wrote that Vaughan, unlike the convert Manning, came with "antecedents historically unassailable. Sprung from an ancient Roman Catholic stock, allied with all the great Catholic families, an essentially Transmontane, both in instinct and by conviction, Vaughan was enthusiastically welcomed by the old Catholic remnant in England, and as their special representative he became a persona grata at the Vatican." The writer continued that Vaughan always bore himself "with stately dignity, but it is undeniable that to the large working-class section of English Romanists he failed to appeal. An aristocrat, saturated with the ecclesiasticism of the most conservative Church in the world, he proved so often to be out of touch with the poor and middle-class members of that Church that now the immediate and most pressing matter before English Roman Catholics will be to secure in his successor one who will hold the balance between the extremes and be ruler and pastor in one."[91]

The Times ran an article headed: "Death of Cardinal Vaughan." After quoting the announcement of his death by Canon Johnson, it concluded: "The late Cardinal was the third of the eminent ecclesiastics of the Roman Church who claimed to exercise direct spiritual jurisdiction, territorially allotted, over the members of that Church in this country. The half century which has elapsed since the Ecclesiastical Titles Act, 1851, has witnessed an enormous change in the attitude of the English people towards the Roman Catholic Church, and in his measure each of three Archbishops contributed largely to that result."[92]

Another writer could not speak "too highly" of all his good work and concluded: "The staunchness of his Catholicism was unbending; his triumphant paean over the Pope's Encyclical disposing of the Unity question, for instance, though not inexcusable, was a little too loud. He would work fraternally with men of other creeds in social matters, but he drew the line most firmly as soon as the shadow of the religious element came in. 'Winning' or 'conciliatory' indeed were the last epithets that one would have applied to Cardinal Vaughan. He attracted no general personal affections, but he was a great worker, a great organizer, and a strong devout Catholic, and no unworthy, if a very dissimilar, successor to Manning." [93]

The *Daily Graphic*, an illustrated morning newspaper, recalled that when

Herbert Vaughan was made Bishop of Salford in 1872, one of the London papers mistakenly confused him with his father, Colonel John Vaughan, and remarked on the militant spirit of a Church "which could turn good soldiers into Bishops." The *Graphic* article continued: "If Cardinal Vaughan was not a fighter in the ordinary sense of the expression, he was, at any rate, a very strenuous and zealous worker for his Church, and his task in succeeding Cardinal Manning was one of the most critical difficulty. But he solved its problems as he had solved other problems of his life, by going straight on with the work at hand, and during his ten years' tenure of the highest office of the Roman Catholic hierarchy in England, his Church has had a career of unbroken prosperity, and, as many think, of increasing power and influence."[94]

Another paper published a report "from a Roman Catholic correspondent":

> If he had not been Archbishop of Westminster, he would have been Colonel of a crack regiment, and a martinet at that.... Herbert Vaughan was a soldier all his life, a disciplinarian as strict to himself as to others. A courtly gentleman, noble in presence and courteous in expression, of simple life and single in aim.... But as he was dealing with ordinary men and women, and not drilled soldiers with the fear of a Drum-head Court-martial ever before them, it is little to be wondered at that this zealous and saintly gentleman, even aided by all the charm and geniality of the Vaughans of Courtfield, found his troops at times inclined to mutiny. Not in great essentials, but in small things, there was a friction which it would be senseless flattery to ignore. At times the zeal of the great fighting Prelate obscured the claims—the possibly unreasonable and presumptuous claims—of John Bull, and the Englishman under the black coat grumbled and growled but in the end, as a rule, obeyed.

Another side of Herbert Vaughan should not be forgotten, the article continued, "because it is so utterly genuine." Those who disagreed with Vaughan "felt, on coming into close contact with him, the deep sincerity of his religious life. The man was in dead earnest, and religion with him was truly the light behind all his actions. This Prince of the Church, with all his many undertakings, affairs, organisations, and social duties, found time to spend two silent hours of every twenty-four in quiet lonely prayer before the altar in his private chapel."[95]

In *The Littlewoman*, a tribute quoted a saying of the Welsh Borders: "The Vaughans of Courtfield were never aught else but priests or soldiers."[96]

One paper thought that Vaughan "had no vanities, and he had hardly any strong personal desires. He was an official before all, a headpiece; and the man was kept resolutely under. 'I have not prayed to live,' he said to a friend towards the end of his long and trying illness; and that saying meant, to all who knew him, that he thought the duties of his office would be more efficiently discharged by someone else. He was essentially a just man, and though anything but a sentimentalist, he took active steps by his foundation of the Catholic Social Union and other organisations to relieve all sorts of temporal distress. This he did, just as he had renounced the family estate in favour of a younger brother, not out of any natural enthusiasm, but because he found it laid down for him as a duty by the Gospel. He was no respecter of persons; and if he had individual preferences, no man gave them less play than he if any official selection was to be made."[97]

The Rome correspondent of another paper reported that in Rome the clerical papers published long, sympathetic obituaries of Herbert Vaughan. Leo XIII, "who now dislikes to hear of the death of any of his cardinals," when he was told, said: "My contemporaries are all gone, and now the younger men are leaving me behind." But the secular press in Rome was not sympathetic: "Cardinal Vaughan being disliked, as he did not hesitate to proclaim, even in the Eternal City itself, his hopes for the re-establishment of the temporal power" of the Pope and Papal States.[98]

For another Rome correspondent, news of Vaughan's death was received with "profound regret." He was esteemed for "his loyalty to the cause of the Holy See and for his personal piety." The report continued: "His career as Metropolitan of the Catholic Church in England has been subject in Curial circles to fluctuating judgements during its several stages. Pope Leo had come to view the Archbishop of Westminster as carried away by enthusiasms, particularly after having been doomed to bitter disappointment in connection with the grandiose hopes which the Cardinal had led him to entertain concerning the imminent reconversion of the English people to Roman Catholicism. In recent years the disciplinary department of the Roman Curia has been kept unusually busy owing to what were here regarded as grave indiscretions in the Cardinal's diocesan administration and his general ecclesiastical policy."[99] Vaughan was the second of Leo XIII's Cardinals to die in 1903 and the 146th during his rule.

In France the *Petit Parisian* described Vaughan as one of the loyal pioneers of an "entente cordiale" between France and England. The article quoted passages from his speeches given in French at Arles for the commemoration of St Augustine. "It may be added that Cardinal Vaughan was a strong believer in the innocence of Captain Dreyfus and that the Latin appeal of Mme Dreyfus to Leo XIII, drawn up by an English journalist in Paris, reached the Vatican through the medium of the deceased Cardinal." The same article said that in France Vaughan was remembered for having assisted by special invitation at the celebrations in 1896 at Orleans in honour of Joan of Arc. On that occasion, he stated that "England owed much of her national impress to the mission of the French heroine."[100]

In another obituary: He seemed to have acquired "something of the Lancashire accent and speech" during his twenty years at Salford. "He was very popular amongst the men of Lancashire, being a hard, earnest worker, and a plain, forceful speaker, whilst his tall, handsome presence gave emphasis to his utterances."

In a column titled "The Passing Hour" in *Black and White*, an illustrated weekly review: "Cardinal Vaughan was in every way a worker. His point of view may be deemed a limited one by many; the strong convictions that led him often into heated public argument may be deplored by some; but no one can deny his strenuous endeavour and its results. The Cardinal needs no memorial. The results of his work speak far too eloquently of him."

In the opinion of the *Evening News*, a Conservative paper, Vaughan was not a success: "well-meaning, but tactless and quite un-intellectual." His "mistakes" were more obvious "when they were compared, as they inevitably were, with the statesmanlike conduct of his predecessor, Manning."

Bishop Hedley wrote to a friend a few days after Herbert Vaughan's death: "It is sickening to see the newspapers saying he was not an intellectual."[101] It was a statement repeated often when comparing Vaughan especially to Manning and some contemporaries, and even to Hedley himself.

An estimate of Vaughan in *The Observer* concluded: "Whatever may be thought of his views, for sincerity, earnestness, and devotion to his Church his record stands high and clear."

Yet another paper wrote: "In spite of the suavity of his manner, Cardinal Vaughan knew perfectly well how to rule, and when the occasion called for it he could administer discipline with effective severity." Vaughan's "views were, as might be expected, nothing if not definite.... The Cardinal was astute, and a Welshman."

And another: "If one wished to describe Cardinal Vaughan in a sentence one might do so by saying that he was a curious mixture of an English country gentleman and an Italian monsignor. Had not circumstances led him into an ecclesiastical career he would have made an excellent country squire."

The Anglican Bishop of Stepney referred to Vaughan in his sermon on Sunday afternoon at St Paul's Cathedral. He called the attention of the congregation to the work of the "Church of Rome, which exhibited such courage and devotion in dealing with its poor and rough children and keeping them within the obligations of the Church," and gave a tribute to Vaughan "as he passed to that region where voices of their divisions were forever stilled."

The *Saturday Review*, Conservative and Tory, wrote: "Despite the Ultramontanism of his theology, Cardinal Vaughan was no reactionary bigot as an administrator. He studied and urged upon his clergy the duty of co-operating loyally and cordially with the civil authorities in philanthropic and especially in educational work. It may be said of him that he most recalled the great prelates of the Anglican Church of pre-Reformation days, men of noble birth, little tolerance of opposition, strong rulers of the Church, builders of stately cathedrals, founders of chantries and withal of schools and loyal in all singleness of heart to the English Crown and the laws of the State."

Another paper reported the "Death of Cardinal Vaughan, a staunch, unbending Catholic":

The stock thing to say of the late Cardinal was, "What a contrast between him and his predecessor!"

> Manning had taken firm hold upon the sympathies even of non-Catholic England, and the suggested comparison was not usually intended to redound to the glory of his successor.... That Vaughan was as great a man or prelate as Manning it would be idle to pretend; but if he lacked his predecessor's fire and sentiment, he certainly outstripped him in, perhaps, more commonplace qualities, half philosophy, half business instinct, which made him the genius at organization and at distinctly English-like work that he was."

The evening before the funeral Mass, the dirge was sung in the Cathedral. A few minutes after the Cathedral doors had been opened, the nave was filled to capacity. More than five hundred secular and religious clergy were seated on each side of the coffin, while the bishops were in the sanctuary.

The next morning the Cathedral was already crowded an hour before the Requiem Mass was to begin at eleven. Partitions of black bordered the bare unplastered and unpainted walls of the unfinished church. The *Daily Telegraph* reported that "against the darkness of the reredos the six candles that stood upon the altar shone like faint far-away stars."[102] The seats under the dome were set aside for members of the various religious orders and the professors and students of St Joseph's Missionary College of Mill Hill. The clergy sat in six rows of seats on both side of the coffin. The masters of ceremonies were Prebendary Wallis, and Frs David Dunford and Conway. There was a choir of fifty priests drawn from the dioceses of Westminster, Southwark and Portsmouth, directed by Fr Charles Cox, to supplement the Cathedral Boys' Choir.

Vaughan's coffin was covered with a black velvet pall with gold edgings, while his Cardinal's hat rested at the foot. The coffin rested on the catafalque surrounded by a border of lighted candles while four large candles were placed at the corners.[103] What impressed the *Daily Telegraph* reporter at the beginning of the liturgy "was the gradual gathering of an immense congregation, and especially the incoming of clergy and sisters of all ranks and orders." When the Mass was about to begin, the bishops came in and took their places in the sanctuary. "Last of all came Cardinal Logue, Primate of Ireland"—who arrived unexpectedly—"whose scarlet attire gave the dimness of the Cathedral its brightest touch of colour." Among the mourners were the Duke of Norfolk, the American Ambassador, representatives of the Spanish and French embassies, the Portuguese Minister, the Austro-Hungarian Chargé d'Affaires, the Chilean Minister, Lord and Lady Llangattock of the Rolls family, and many others.

A reporter from the *Pall Mall Gazette*, a unionist paper, described the scene: "It was impossible to distinguish well-known faces with any certainty, and untitled guests were stowed away in countless rows of Windsor chairs, a frail accommodation, in marked contrast with the relentless concrete floor and uncovered walls. Up in the many-arched clerestory galleries sat a thousand or so of 'women religious,' their nun's black being varied by forehead-bands of spotless white, and the strange peaked caps of some of the French orders." The reporter continued: "Whether one had a care for ritual or not, the hushed conviction seemed to come home to us that the Roman faith is peculiarly the religion of the dead. It has mapped out the after-world with a synthetical exactness, and half its energies are devoted to rescuing departed souls from the penal fires of Purgatory."

The Mass began with Bishop Stanley, Vaughan's auxiliary, as celebrant, and Charles Cox directing the choir. Each priest held a lighted candle during the service. At the end, before the incensing of the coffin, Bishop John Cuthbert Hedley of Newport ascended the pulpit and gave the homily. According to the *Daily Telegraph* reporter, Hedley said that "the Cardinal had been said on occasion to be harsh and even uncharitable where matters of religious controversy were concerned. But those who really knew the man appreciated how foreign to his character was the least thought of unkindness. He had laboured long and well, and it behoved those who survived him to see that the causes he had ever at heart were not allowed to fall to the ground." Hedley had also spoken at Henry Manning's funeral eleven years before. The catafalque and coffin were then incensed.

Cardinal Logue gave the final absolution: "Once again intimately associated with the history of that cathedral whose first stone he had helped to lay almost to the day eight years before."[104]

Winifred Cary-Elwes wrote to Lady Elizabeth Herbert on 26 June about the funeral: "We all went to the requiem yesterday. It was very impressive and very beautiful indeed. Such a vast concourse of clergy. I never saw anything the like of it and the music beautiful—two choirs, one of the clergy downstairs and in the gallery, the Cathedral Boys' Choir...."[105]

The congregation dispersed after the ceremony, but the coffin remained in the cathedral. One eyewitness remembered that the service was orderly until the end of the Mass and before Hedley's eulogy. At that moment many tried to leave but were kept back by ushers while the ceremony continued; the noise and sounds of "indignation" prevented many from hearing Hedley's words.[106]

It was late afternoon before the final mourners passed by the catafalque. Religious Sisters kept watch over the coffin until Friday morning when it was removed to St Joseph's College at Mill Hill.

Burial at Mill Hill

At 6 a.m. on Friday, 26 June, a hearse carrying the coffin containing the body of Herbert Vaughan left for St Joseph's College, Mill Hill. It was followed by a carriage bringing Johnson, Moyes, Poyer and a Fr Brown. They arrived at the college shortly after 8 a.m. and were met at the door by the rector, representatives from Salford diocese, Sisters, college staff and students. The coffin was carried through the corridor to the church while everyone sang the *Miserere*. In the church it was placed on a catafalque. At 9.30 a.m. a solemn Requiem Mass began. Francis Henry was the main celebrant and the rectors of Roosendaal and Freshfield, Frs Peter Oud and Edmund Farmer, were assistants. The plain chant of the Mass was sung by the students of the college.

Herbert Vaughan's brother, Bernard, gave the panegyric, addressing it to the "Fathers and Brothers of St. Joseph's Society for the Foreign Missions.... The preacher, who throughout was visibly affected, and is understood to have spoken with little opportunity for preparation, then told the story of his brother's life...."

Bernard Vaughan thought that the secret of "your Father's spiritual success in life and in death" could be found in the motto he chose when made Archbishop of Westminster: *Amare et Servire*, "to love and to serve." It became a "sort of rallying cry to the forces of his great and energetic soul, because it seemed to put before his eyes, simply, tersely ... contemplation and action, of prayer and labour, which it is the business of every apostle to make his own if he is to become an efficient instrument in the hands of Jesus Christ for the salvation of souls."[107]

Herbert Vaughan was not buried in his cathedral or in the Church of St Joseph as some had thought he would, but in a "simple earth grave ... on Calvary, a spot to the north of St. Joseph's, which is approached by a rose-bordered walk and is shaded by a small plantation," wrote a reporter from the *Daily Graphic* in Paris. Nearby was the grave of Peter Benoit.

After the final blessing by the Bishop of Emmaus, students carried the coffin to Calvary where Vaughan was to be buried below the crucifix he had brought from the Tyrol. A small crowd of neighbours and school children awaited the procession at the graveside. Mgr Johnson read the committal. Present were many of Vaughan's old friends, collaborators and supporters; Louis Casartelli, who was soon to become Bishop of Salford, the Dowager Duchess of Newcastle, the Talbots, and John Snead-Cox among them. When the ceremony was finished, the mourners walked in procession back to the college singing the *De Profundis*.[108]

Mass at Salford

Louis Charles Casartelli had written an appeal to Vaughan during his final illness. He asked that he intervene on his behalf with the Vatican, withdrawing his name as a candidate to succeed John Bilsborrow as Bishop of Salford.[109] Casartelli's appeal was unsuccessful and it was he who preached at a Requiem Mass for Vaughan at St John's Cathedral in Salford, on Friday 3 July 1903.

Speaking about Herbert Vaughan's career was difficult, Casartelli said, because Vaughan was "bound up with so many varied activities" that a preacher was at a loss to know whether to picture him as a zealous missionary, a bishop, an educator, a spiritual and devotional writer, a social worker, a patron of Christian art or in the mission of the press. "No matter in which particular one studied the character of Herbert Vaughan, [they] would have material for a whole discourse."

For Casartelli the guiding principle behind Vaughan's "life of extraordinary manifold energy" could be found in the motto the cardinal chose when he came to Salford in 1872: "Thy Kingdom come." Vaughan was a "missionary in His Master's vineyard." He began as a missioner and ended as one. Casartelli recalled Herbert Vaughan telling him that he wanted to be a missionary to Wales, but Bishop Brown was not in favour of the idea, and then traced his career from that day. Louis Casartelli had lived with Vaughan for fourteen years at St Bede's and he spoke of the kindness he showed to others residing at the college. Not only did Vaughan spend his energies for the Church but also for the citizens of Salford and Manchester. His work with the Manchester Chamber of Commerce helped lead to the development in 1903 of a Faculty of Commerce at the University of Manchester. He was also one of the founders of the Geographical Society. Through such efforts Vaughan tried to bring "the Kingdom of God to the hearts of men."

However, the preacher continued, the most important part of Vaughan was not seen and this was his "hidden source of power." Although his whole day seemed to be filled with activity, "yet he found a few hours each day for prayer. Every night he would be found in St Bede's College chapel in silent prayer." Casartelli asked the clergy at the Mass "to remember often the beautiful allocutions he addressed to them in synod—those wonderful synods in which he chided or encouraged them, and sent them away with renewed vigour and determination." In conclusion, the new bishop asked that all pray for Herbert Vaughan: "One to whom they all owed so much."[110]

Mass at Courtfield

On Wednesday, 8 July, at 10 a.m., another Requiem Mass for Herbert Vaughan was celebrated at his family home at Courtfield. It was there that the child, Herbert, had, under his mother's hand, been consecrated as a faithful slave *servus fidelius* of the Blessed Virgin Mary, according to Bernard Vaughan in his homily at St Joseph's. At the Courtfield Mass, Herbert's brother John was celebrant, assisted by his nephews Herbert and Francis Vaughan. Bishop Hedley blessed the catafalque. A choir of Benedictine monks from Belmont sang. In addition to many family members and friends, J. Hobson Matthews attended with his wife. There was also "a large gathering of the Courtfield tenantry." As he had in Westminster Cathedral, Bishop Hedley of Newport gave the homily. Speaking of Herbert Vaughan's childhood in the Wye Valley: "The thoughts of the child are wider, more full of imagination and enthusiasm than those of the man, even if they are vague and impracticable; and there are few men who live up to the ideals of their childhood. No one can doubt that the generous ardour which distinguished the life of Herbert Vaughan burned warmly in its obscurity in his young heart in the quiet chapel at Courtfield, and amid those scenes of his childhood."

Hedley went on to speak of the "pastoral speech" of Herbert Vaughan and the question of the late Cardinal's intellectual capacity: "Nothing would do such adequate justice to Cardinal Vaughan's qualities of mind and heart as a complete collection of his writings. For thirty years he had never omitted, like a watchman on the walls of Jerusalem, to lift up his voice whenever there was need of information, of united counsel, of courage, or of sacrifice. Let his friends and the clergy of this country never forget him."[111]

Last Will

Herbert Vaughan left instructions for his executors. The entries begin on 31 December 1899. He wished Mgr Dunn, Father Francis Henry and Joseph Weld to follow his wishes concerning his property and monies. The *Dublin Review* belonged to the archdiocese and the *Illustrated Catholic Missions* to the Propagation of the Faith at Lyons. *The Tablet*, however, was Vaughan's. Executors were to divide its net income between "Mill Hill to be spent on foreign missions to the heathen and not on the education of missioners" and Westminster Archdiocese "for the time being to use if needed to carry on the full liturgical daily service of the Cathedral." According to Michael Walsh, Mill Hill benefited by at least £1,000 a year from *The Tablet*. In 1914, £1,100 went to "the foreign missions of the Upper Nile, Borneo and Maori."[112]

There were also provisions to help pay off the deficit on the new Archbishop's House, vestments and books to be returned to Salford, prayers to be sung every evening at the cathedral "for the conversion of England," a fund for Masses promised for his father, "Dean Newton and Mrs. John Polding," who had given money for the education of priests, to be said by teachers at St Bede's. He gave small token amounts to his confessor, Mgr Johnson, "for his kindnesses and corrections," his three executors, and "15 pounds to Thomas Moyneaux, and 10 pounds to Morris the Coachman." His watch went to Mgr Fenton, the vicar general, and mementos to others "to whom I am under obligation for their zeal and work, or who should be remembered by me on such an occasion." The manuscript of his Conferences on the Apostolic Life were to go to his brother, John S. Vaughan, who was asked to edit and complete them. It was later published as *The Young Priest*. The other manuscript, his translation of *Humility of Heart*, was given to Lady Edmund Talbot. Later, Bernard Vaughan prepared it for publication. "I hope no foolish person," Vaughan wrote, "will write exaggerated accounts of me—and that my MS be not used for such purpose."[113]

Vaughan had a private account at "69 Pall Mall" co-signed by himself, Mgr Dunn and one other. That money, along with £1,000 held by his brother, Frank, was to be used to meet his "bequests and debts." Whatever remained he wished to be used to free Archbishop's House from debt. Any money in the Archbishop's House account, along with money from an Oregon investment of £2,000, was to be paid by Fr Francis Henry, and another £6,000 invested elsewhere, was for the same fund.

About eighty thousand copies of a booklet titled, "What is the Mass?," which he wrote, were to be shared between Salford and Westminster.

According to their logbook, the Sisters of St Mary's Abbey received a gift of the "Cardinal's old white horse." On 4 November 1903 Herbert Vaughan's old coachman, who had served Manning as well, stopped at the Abbey to inform the Sisters that the groom was bringing down one of the cardinal's old horses, "which the Mother was to have!" Vaughan had left instructions that one of a pair should go to the Sisters of Nazareth and the other to the Abbey. "The horse arrived in due time. It was a huge white horse and we had to arrange a stable for it—having then our own little pony for the laundry van." The nuns tried to make the horse pull the van but "the poor beast utterly refused to draw it up the many hills in the neighbourhood and seemed to feel the indignity of being placed in shafts other than those of a gentleman's carriage." After keeping it for a few months, the abbess gave it to a farmer at Totteridge.[114]

In May 1903 he directed that the inscription over his gravestone should be modified, "instead of Servus perpetuus B.V.M. put Servulus perpetuus (poor little slave) Gloriosae et Beatae Mariae Virginis et Sti Josephi." He preferred "a plain granite slab and not a monument, quite unfit a [?] that is in the missionary life of the Church."

In his desk there was a small tin box containing his will. There were also "several sums of money—which I have never considered my own but had the use of": seventy or eighty pounds which had been given to him by the Mother General of the Nazareth Sisters[115] was to be given back to her. "She was always too generous." Fifty pounds was to go to Miss Hanmer.[116]

Caroline Hanmer died at The Rosary Cottage on Friday, 4 September 1908. She was buried not far from Herbert Vaughan, behind the Calvary crucifix at Mill Hill. She was ninety years of age. Mary Elizabeth Herbert,

Lady Herbert of Lea, followed her on 31 October 1911, aged eighty-nine. She died at Herbert House, Belgrave Square. A Solemn Requiem Mass was offered at Westminster Cathedral and her corpse was then carried to St Joseph's College Church, where, after a short service, it was carried to Calvary by the students. She was buried near to Miss Hanmer and not far from her friend Herbert Vaughan.[117]

A niece and godchild of Herbert Vaughan, Julia, a daughter of Herbert's brother, Reginald, was one family member who was influenced by Herbert Vaughan and the family commitment to their Church. She went to see her uncle at Westminster several years before he died and asked his blessing on her intention to become a Poor Clare nun. Vaughan smiled at her and said: "They'll soon choke you off, you long-haired girl. I'll give you two months." In 1961 Julia celebrated over sixty years as Sister Mary Felix Clare at the Poor Clares, Notting Hill. For thirty-seven years she was abbess. She was the "last of her generation," according to the 1961 *Universe* article.[118] Of Reginald's ten children three became religious. Before he died, her uncle, Cardinal Vaughan, "received her vows." Like her grandmother Eliza, according to nuns who knew her when she was young, "her love for the Blessed Sacrament was stronger than her weakness."[119]

Others, outside the family, found encouragement in Vaughan's life. A Carmelite sister wrote to Mill Hill in 1966 that she had "always had a great love and veneration for your holy founder. He was such a help and inspiration to me in my early years of Religious life—that total giving of himself to God without reserve—his whole character and holiness was so inspiring."[120] Another wrote in 1967: "I was struck by the high ideals and the entirely supernatural outlook of Herbert Vaughan—God mattered and nothing else."[121]

In 1932, on the centenary of Herbert Vaughan's birth, a memorial observance was held at Mill Hill. One of the speakers, Archbishop Goodier, said that for him Vaughan's life had three characteristics: a tremendous vision that built for the future, establishing works which reached many parts of the world and were not "confined to the sphere of his own limited field," a perseverance and courage that were "founded on an absolute confidence in the supernatural, and a willingness to learn, to change his mind, showing "how little he lived for himself."[122]

The Tablet, on 13 February 1932, printed a pastoral letter from the Archbishop of Westminster which announced that three events of that year would "furnish much matter for thought, thanksgiving, and the awakening of fresh earnestness." One was a Eucharistic Congress, and the others were celebrations remembering the births of Cardinal William Allen, who founded the English Seminary at Douai in 1568, and "Herbert Vaughan, destined by God to be for twenty years Bishop of Salford, and for eleven years Archbishop of Westminster."

The article continued: "For more than thirty years, during ten of which he was a member of the Sacred College of Cardinals, he was an outstanding figure in the Hierarchy. The services which Cardinal Vaughan rendered to the Church are, for the most part, well known to all; but this is not the place to recall them in detail. There are two indeed which should ever keep alive our lasting gratitude to his memory: the foundation of the great Missionary College at Mill Hill, whereby England was rendered capable of taking an ever-growing part in the evangelization of the non-Christian world; and the building of the Metropolitan Cathedral of Westminster which has given to the Church, not only in London, but throughout England, a position of dignity unknown in the past. These are two achievements for which undying thanks are due to God and to the great prelate whom he raised up to accomplish them."[123]

On 18 June 1903, the day before he died, Herbert Vaughan sent a message to the "Peter Boys" who were students at St Peter's Apostolic School at Freshfield. Until the old building was sold, a marble tablet preserved the Cardinal's message. The inscription carried the following advice: "Tell all your boys to remember the great object of their lives is to discover in all things the Holy Will of God and having discovered it, to use all their efforts to accomplish it. One of the chief characteristics of the members of St. Joseph's Society must be a great and marked devotion to the Holy Will of God." The message continued: "They should desire neither a long life nor an easy life but rather a long life and a hard-working life. Trials and privations will be their lot."[124] The words described a life not unlike Vaughan's own. Once he thought he had discerned the will of God, he spent his lifetime with all its energy and resources in pursuit.

A community of nuns in Hammersmith blessed a memorial to Herbert Vaughan in March 1904. It read *Ecce Sacerdos Magnus*, "Behold a Great Priest." A *Tablet* article said, of The Nazareth House Sisters as of many other communities: "To the Sisters at home and abroad he was a devoted Father and Protector."[125]

A note in Vaughan's final instructions to his executors stated: "I beg pardon for all the scandal and bad example and for much neglect of God. But I die in peace in the arms of the Blessed Virgin Mary, my Mother—professing all that the Church professes and teaches."[126]

Notes

1. MHA. "Cardinal Vaughan By The President," *The Edmundian*, NS, 5, 31, July 1903, p.160ff. The President of St Edmund's was Bernard Ward, the third son and seventh child of William George Ward. He was ordained in 1882. In 1886 he began a new mission at Willesden in North London. In 1888 he went to teach at Oscott and in 1890 to St Edmund's as Vice President and Prefect of Studies. In 1893 Vaughan appointed him President of St Edmund's and he remained in that position for twenty-three years. See: Stewart Foster, OSM, "A Bishop for Essex:

Bernard Ward and the Diocese of Brentwood," *Recusant History*, 21, 4, October 1993, p.561.

2. Cf Chapter V; WDA. Vaughan diaries.

3. MHA. Vaughan, *Edmundian*; Snead-Cox, 2, pp.456-7.

4. MHA. Vaughan, *Edmundian*.

5. Leslie, *Vaughan Letters*, p.433: Vaughan left London sometime after 9 January 1898.

6. WDA. "A Letter on the Confraternity of Our Lady of Compassion by Herbert Cardinal Vaughan," London, Burns & Oates, 1897, pp.4-6.

7. Snead-Cox, 2, pp.457-8.

8. *The Tablet*, 7 May 1898, p.738.

9. *The Tablet*, 4 June 1898, pp.898-9.

10. Leslie, *Vaughan Letters*, p.434.

11. *ibid.*, pp.434-6; Bogan, *History of St George's*, pp.304-5: "Then with a cry of reproach, he addressed the Catholic people. He pointed to their drunkenness and self-indulgence, their worldly views and judgements, their worldliness in labour and expectations, and asked if they had made the service of God visible in their lives."

12. *The Tablet*, 13 August 1898, p.265; *The Tablet*, 20 August 1898, pp.313-5.

13. *The Tablet*, 15 October 1898, p.624.

14. Leslie, *Vaughan Letters*, pp.434-6.

15 "The Cardinal asks for a Coadjutor," *Catholic Transcript*, Hartford, Connecticut, Friday, 3 February 1899.

16. CANH. Mill Hill, 7 November 1898, Vaughan to Mother Mary of Jesus: "I am a good deal occupied with the Lord as to the future bishop auxiliary. My brother is very delicate in health and quite likely to have to leave England during the winter months. It would be fatal to take for auxiliary a man whose health may be—is—almost as uncertain as my own. With many estimable qualities and possessing my confidence in so far that he would do what I tell him, health permitting—he has no initiative of a practical kind, and would have but little authority over the clergy. Another person, not of the Diocese, and possessing many valuable qualities, will be subject to authority, and who would command respect by his post as well as by his practical character and energy, presents himself to my mind—and he is not connected with me by flesh and blood! The Lord will give light."

17. Leslie, *Vaughan Letters*, pp. 438-9; *The Tablet*, 8 October 1898, p.566: Brindle had been a chaplain since 1874 and was with the Egyptian expeditionary force in 1882. He was senior chaplain of the Nile Expedition of 1884-5 and the following year with the frontier force. In 1896 he served with Kitchener's expedition to Dongola.

18. Brindle was replaced by Stanley; According to Friedrich von Hügel, Vaughan counted Merry del Val in place of Brindle: "It is true with the best of intentions," he wrote to Tyrrell—[Vaughan] had been (I know it beyond the shadow of a doubt) working for weeks and months in Rome—and working for all he was worth to get Mgr Merry del Val appointed his co-adjutor, in place of Brindle, with Rights of succession of course." See: Bédoyère, *Von Hügel*, p.152.

19. *The Tablet*, 15 April 1899, p.595.

20. CANH. April 1902, The Lodge, Visitation Convent, Harrow, to Carmel, Notting Hill.

21. Herbert Vaughan, *The Young Priest*, London, Burns & Oates, 1908, Preface by John S. Vaughan, January 1904: On Herbert Vaughan's finishing the book before he died: "The exertion this entailed was a considerable tax upon his diminished strength, and nothing but an indomitable energy, courage, and zeal could have enabled him to continue working at it as he did, almost up to the very last."

22. Hanrahan, *Apostolic Spirit*, p.1: "My aim has been to present 'the particular truths and practices' Herbert Vaughan made 'in a special way his own' in his own priestly life."

23. Vaughan, *Young Priest*, p.2.

24. Book review: "The Young Priest," *American Ecclesiastical Review*, vol xxxi, July 1904, p.95: The reviewer commented: "nor does he in giving advice deal with them as the optimist who

mistakes the greatness of the vocation for the greatness of those who profess it."

25. Cajetan Mary Da Bergamo, *Humility of Heart*, translated by Herbert Cardinal Vaughan, Rockford, TAN , 1978. TAN reprinted a 1944 edition by the Newman Bookshop, Westminster, Maryland, p.xvff: Bergamo was an Italian missionary of the eighteenth century. He was born in 1672, became a Capuchin in 1692, and died in 1753."He was," Vaughan wrote, "one of the reformers of the Italian pulpit, substituting for the vapid, empty rhetoric which prevailed, a solid, learned and instructive style, animated by zeal and real devotion."

26. *L'Umilta Del Cuore, Del Padre Gaetano Maria Da Bergamo*, Monza, Corbetta, 1846.

27. Vaughan, *Da Bergamo*, p.xvi ff.

28. *ibid.*, p.xxiii–iv.

29. Lady Mary Elizabeth Herbert used *The Tablet* to appeal for various causes: On 24 December 1898, she asked for help for the parish priest of Canton Street, Poplar. He was trying to provide breakfast for his school children and to feed "the multitude of starving sick and suffering cases in his parish; In the 3 December issue she appealed for the Sisters of Charity and their work to help the poor and operate a soup kitchen: "Subscriptions in money, food, coal, and bread tickets, and clothes of every kind will be most gratefully received by the Superior of the Sisters of Charity, Carlisle Place"; In December of 1902 she thanked *The Tablet* for allowing her to insert an appeal each Christmas for twenty-two years. Again she listed the needs of the Sisters of Charity and inclosed seven of the most needy cases.

30. "The Association of the Ladies of Charity," *The Tablet*, 19 July 1902, p.113.

31. CANH. Harrow, Vaughan to Mother Mary, April 1902.

32. Snead-Cox, 2, p.460.

33. St Mary's Abbey Archive, Mill Hill, 19 June 1902. The "Lady Edmund" who had been on a short retreat at the Abbey, and been received as a tertiary by Vaughan, was probably May, Lady Edmund, Talbot.

34. Snead-Cox, 2, p.461.

35. Leslie, *Vaughan Letters*, p.447.

36. Snead-Cox, 2, p.461.

37. *ibid.*, pp.462-3.

38. MHA. Box 45, file b, Fr F. M. Hayward, St Mary's Park St, Worksop (no date), to Fr Ireland.

39. VFA. May Talbot to Lady Herbert, 24 September 1902. Fr John Norris of the Oratory had been at Derwent during one of Vaughan's stays. "Those summer days at Derwent were a great privilege." A layman wrote to Norris about Vaughan's stay at another home: "When he came here all he seemed to wish was to be left alone in the chapel before the Blessed Sacrament and this he did literally for hours!" Norris also "knew he did the same at Derwent and that is the secret of the things he has done for God." VFA. Fr John Norris of the Oratory, to the Bishop of Hexham and Newcastle (n.d.).

40. Leslie, *Vaughan Letters*, p.449.

41. Snead-Cox, 2, pp.464-5: Quoting Lady Edmund Talbot: "What struck me always was his humility, gentleness, and detachment from all earthly things. He did a great deal of hard brain work during these months. The Education Bill of 1902 involved his seeing a great many people; then he was engrossed in the Cathedral, and, I think, in drawing up the Constitutions, etc.; then he was finishing his book for Young Priests. He did all this work under the greatest physical difficulty. He suffered from constant exhaustion, and weariness, and heart failures. At this time he remained in his room altogether, even for his meals, and he constantly sat in the Chapel before the Blessed Sacrament. He prayed over all this work."; One of the other matters he took an interest in was the annual Catholic Truth Society Conference at Newport. Although he could not attend, he wrote a letter which was read by the secretary of the Catholic Truth Society, Mr Britten; It was dated Derwent Hall, Sheffield, 17 September 1902: "But far off, in the background, I see a great multitude of eager faces; I hear their voices like the sound of the waves

of the sea. Who are these? They are the boys and girls in our public elementary schools—they are the strength, the hope, the population of the future—they form the young democracy that is going to rule the country, to make or mar the future of Christianity in this land." He encouraged Father James Nicholson, SJ, at Newport, to become associated with the society and to bring it into the schools. *The Tablet*, 27 September 1902, pp.500-1.

42. "Death of the Bishop of Plymouth," *The Tablet*, 1 November 1902, pp.699-700; "Fr Edmund Vaughan, CSSR," *The Tablet*, 4 July 1908, p.29; On Bishop William Vaughan, see: Christopher Smith, *200 Years of Catholicism in Plymouth*, Plymouth, 1994, p.8: "But by the end of his 47 years as bishop, there were 60 churches, 100 priests, 13 houses of male religious and 28 of nuns, 4 orphanages, 27 elementary schools and 5 for other children. He can certainly be called the founding father of the Plymouth diocese."

43. WDA. Vaughan, Derwent Hall, November 30,1902, to Moyes.

44. Snead-Cox, 2, p.468.

45. Leslie, *Vaughan Letters*, Mill Hill, 12 January 1903, p.451.

46. CANH. Archbishop's House, 2 March 1903.

47. Snead-Cox, 2, p.469

48. WDA. "Instructions left by H.E. Cardinal Vaughan." Copy sent to the author by Michael Walsh.

49. Snead-Cox, 2, pp.470-1. Snead-Cox quotes the letter as 21 March 1903 "to a near relative;" See: Leslie, *Vaughan letters*, p.453, 22 March 1903: "Precious letter.—Lady H.." It is the last letter quoted by Shane Leslie.

50. Snead-Cox, 2, pp. 471-2.

51. *ibid.*, pp.472-3; VFA. Scrapbooks. *The Universe*: The same day he left for Mill Hill, 25 March, 1903, two churches opened for public worship in London; St Mary's Moorfields, and the Guardian Angels, Mile End. A letter was read at each of the churches on Vaughan's behalf. "The letter read by Father Keating, the preacher at Mile End, contained one of the most striking tributes ever written to the great personal sanctity of the late Lady Margaret Howard, through whose charity the Church of the Guardian Angels had been built."

52. Norman, *Catholic Church*, p.372. See also: *The Tablet*, Saturday 4 July 1903, p.15: "It was to this college, built by his own wandering footsteps in many lands, that Cardinal Vaughan went to die. Here he found friends, sympathisers, everything that can cheer the dying priest. He was wheeled around the grounds before the day of his death; and doubtless in these promenades he went over as the dying do, the scenes of his past life which these grounds recalled. It was such a death as was appropriate to his life, with its external splendour of position and power, and its inner heart of self-sacrifice and devotion;" And: St Mary's Abbey Archives, Logbook, 25 February 1903: Feast of the Annunciation. "The Cardinal was removed from London to the College by the advice of his doctors. Whenever returned to Westminster, he saw few visitors, but sometimes sent for our dear Mother to come over and talk to him."

53. CANH. Easter Sunday, 1903, Mill Hill to Mother Mary of Jesus.

54. Snead-Cox, 2, pp.474-477.

55. Ward, *Insurrection*, pp.146-7.

56. Snead-Cox, 2, pp.474-77.

57. VFA. Scrapbooks. *The Universe*, tribute, no date; And: *The Tablet*, 23 May 1903.

58. Snead-Cox, 2, p.477; Ward, *Insurrection*, p.147.

59. WDA. 10 June 1903, to Austin Oates; Also: Snead-Cox, 2, p.482.

60. CANH. Vaughan to Mother Mary, Carmel, 9 June 1903: On the envelope is written: "Letter written by Cardinal Vaughan ten days before he went home to God."

61. Snead-Cox, 2, p.479.

62. *ibid.*, p.481.

63. *ibid.*, p.482.

64. WDA. Instructions left by H. E. Cardinal Vaughan, Entry: 11 June 1903; St Mary's Abbey

Archives, Logbook: June 11 was also the Feast of Corpus Christi. "The weather was so wet that the Procession at the College had to be indoors. The Cardinal had himself wheeled in his chair to behind the altar for the Vespers."

65. *ibid.*, 16 June 1903. There are two scribbled letters at WDA along with the copied out "Instructions." One note addressed to Mgr Fenton has a comment written on the back by Mgr Fenton's executor, Henry Grosch of St John's, Duncan Terrace, N.1: "The enclosed letter written by Cardinal Vaughan on June 16th 1903 is stated by Snead-Cox ... to be the last the Cardinal ever wrote. It is fortunate in having the date, as very few of his letters to Mgr Fenton are dated. It came into my possession as Executor of Bishop Fenton, V.G., and I give it to the Right Rev. Thomas Dunn, Bishop of Nottingham, as the most suitable person to possess it."

66. Snead-Cox, 2, p.483.

67. VFA. Scrapbooks. Newspaper clippings concerning Herbert Vaughan and other family members. Many with no references to origin. *The Tablet* for 27 June and 4 July also quoted references to Vaughan's death found in various papers. The issue of 27 June was black-bordered and had a full page photograph of Cardinal Vaughan.

68. Snead-Cox, 2, pp.487-8.

69. VFA. 21 June 1903 to Elizabeth Herbert.

70. Snead-Cox, vol 2, p.489.

71. VFA. 23 June 1903 to Elizabeth Herbert; Scrapbook. *Ross Gazette*; Concerning Frank Vaughan's reference to the arrival of Douai Benedictines: VFA. Scrapbook, "Homecoming of the Benedictines, Presentation at Charing Cross": "Thursday afternoon at Charing Cross...: Benedictines of Douai returned to England to seek freedom from the persecution of the French Government.... Herbert Vaughan, D.D. (his nephew) and many other clergy were there. Colonel Vaughan, Reginald Vaughan ... were present." *The Ross Gazette*, "Death of Cardinal Vaughan": "A pathetic incident in the close of the Cardinal's long and painful illness was his endeavour to send a greeting to the Benedictine monks from Douay, an English foundation, who have been expelled from France under the association's law. Cardinal Vaughan wrote the Abbot a letter in pencil which, however, owing to his weakness he was unable to finish, and which was read on the arrival of the monks in England."

72. VFA. Sr Hilda, OSB, East Bergholt, 23 June, to Elizabeth Herbert; July 14, Clare Lindsay to Elizabeth Herbert.

73. Snead-Cox, 2, pp.408ff; See also: WDA. Last Instructions.

74. F. C. Devas, SJ, "Introductory Memoir," in Daniel Considine, SJ, *The Virtues of the Divine Child*, London, Manresa, 1929.

75. Snead-Cox, 2, p.422 fn.1.

76. *ibid.*, pp.483-6.

77. VFA. Caroline Hanmer to Elizabeth Herbert: "... as was proved, for twenty minutes to twelve, the night nurse seeing a change called ? who came on the instant with Fr. Van de Brissen [*sic*: van den Biesen] found him conscious but rapidly sinking and at exactly ten minutes to twelve, therefore on the Feast breath stopped!!!"

78. VFA. Scrapbooks.

79. VFA. Hanmer to Herbert; Snead-Cox, 2, pp.489-90; MHA. The "van den Brissen" of Hanmer was Christian van den Biesen. He was ordained in 1887 and was the first priest of the Society sent for advanced studies, first in Rome and then at Louvain. He began teaching theology at Mill Hill in 1890. In 1909 he was dismissed along with all major seminary teachers around the world in the purge that followed the condemnation of modernism. He went to a parish in Stow-on-the-Wold where he remained till the 1930s; According to Lawrence Barmann, van den Biesen was a professor of scripture, perhaps the most competent Old Testament scholar in England. His only crime during the modernist purge was his competence as a scholar and being a critic familiar with contemporary historical method. The letter from van den Biesen to Moyes of 29 June 1903 describing the last moments of Vaughan's life is no longer found in the

Moyes papers in the WDA. He was a friend of von Hügel and others. After he retired he took up residence in Liverpool, where he died at eighty-seven, on 17 November 1951. Lawrence Barmann, *Baron Friedrich von Hügel and the Modernist Crisis in England*, Cambridge, CUP, 1972, pp.103-4, 215.

80. VFA. Scrapbooks. *Daily Telegraph*.

81. *ibid.*

82. *ibid.*

83. Norman, *Catholic Church*, p.373.

84. VFA. Hanmer to Herbert.

85. WDA. Instructions.

86. Parr, *Children's Cardinal*: At Stepney there were between 700 and 800 children in the homes. "This then is the noble work conceived by the loving heart of one brave man, who is in very truth known as the children's Cardinal."

87. VFA. Scrapbooks.

88. De l'Hôpital, *Westminster Cathedral*, p.316.

89. VFA. Scrapbooks.

90. De l'Hôpital, *Westminster Cathedral*, p.316

91. VFA. The collection of Press commentary on Vaughan's death is from scrapbooks at the Vaughan Family Archives. Many are undated; some not identified; *The Newspaper Press Directory for 1903*, Public Records Office, Colindale, identifies most of the publications: E.g.: *Daily Chronicle*, Liberal, established 1855; *Daily Express*, Independent, 1900; *Daily Graphic*, "... only illustrated morning newspaper in the world," 1890; *The Times*, "... for the Church of England ... free trade in mercantile and commercial transactions" 1788; *Westminster Gazette*, "... reputation for fairness and impartiality" 1893; *Critic*, "Independent critic of everything pertaining to finance," 1895; *Monitor*, Roman Catholic, official organ of the Guild of Our Lady of Ransom, 1893; *Spectator*, Liberal Unionist, 1828.

92. *ibid.*, *The Times*.

93. VFA. Scrapbooks.

94. *ibid.*

95. *ibid.*

96. *ibid.*, *Littlewoman*.

97. VFA. Scrapbooks.

98. *ibid.*

99. *ibid.*

100. *ibid.*; Alan Riding, "100 Years Later, Dreyfus Affair Still Festers," *New York Times*, 9 February 1994.

101. Snead-Cox, 2, p.398.

102. VFA. Scrapbooks, *Daily Telegraph*.

103. *ibid.*, *Sketch*.

104. De l'Hôpital, *Westminster Cathedral*, p.316.

105. VFA. W. C. Elwes, Mayfair, 26 June, to Elizabeth Herbert.

106. VFA. Scrapbooks.

107. McCormack, p.330.

108. St Mary's Abbey Archives, Logbook, 19 June 1903: "Cardinal Vaughan died—R.I.P.... On the 26th Solemn Requiem in the College. Fr. Bernard Vaughan preached—Fr. Henry sang the Requiem.... Many of the Sisters, Mother Abbess and a good number of the children went over for the burial."

109. WDA. Casartelli wrote to Vaughan on St Patrick's Day 1903 from Louvain in Belgium: "I find to my great dismay the rumours are flying about connecting my name with the succession to the vacant see of Salford. I appeal ... because you have known me so long and followed my career ... my whole character, tastes, experience, career, entirely unfit me for a bishopric in

modern England.... I appeal to your conscience to ... save me from misfortune and Salford from disaster....Please God there is little or no chance, but one never knows what may happen.... I trust in your Eminence as in a father and friend."

110. Rgt Rev Dr Casartelli, "The Late Cardinal Vaughan," *The Harvest*, no 192, September 1903, vol xvi, pp.206-7.

111. *The Tablet*, 11 July 1903: Hedley: "In all these different sorts of address his words were clear, dignified, and appropriate; his sentences well formed and finished, and his whole expression, whilst it had singular power of demonstrating personal conviction, was not wanting in picturesque touches and striking phrases. Was he an intellectual man? An expression for a well-known thinker had been quoted in the negative. But there were various sides of the intellectual character. There was the man whose strength lay in reasoning on abstract principles, in spheres high above practical life. Again there was the man who illuminated ethics, literature, and art by new combinations of thought and fresh illustrations. But there was also the man who used his intelligence, not to find a foothold for metaphysics or to analyse the abstract, but to body forth and to touch with colour and fire the convictions of spiritual insight. This was a work most certainly intellectual. Considered as intellectual, it was not always on the highest plane of intellect—though it might be. But considered absolutely, it was higher than intellect because it was wisdom, understanding, counsel, knowledge. It was to be hoped that a complete collection of his pastorals and addresses would be published without delay by those who loved him. They all breathed the spirit of wisdom and of judgement, the spirit of a pastor who was never satisfied until he knew enough about his flock to speak with intimate conviction. But there were some that, from the point of view of statesmanship and of literature, were striking in a very high degree. His pastorals on 'The Indian Famine,' on 'Spiritual Reading,' on the 'Rescue Society,' and on the 'Sanctification of Lent,' were only examples of many. His 'Manual of Catholic Politics' was a telling exposition of views which, if carried out, would give us a Catholic union in every centre of population. His addresses at such meetings as the Catholic Truth Society Conferences were full of fervour, spirit, and suggestion. So were his too rare papers in *The Dublin Review*."

112. Walsh, *The Tablet*, p.29 fn.34; *The Tablet* on 13 June 1903, was large in size: 39 foolscap pages. The weekly cost 5d per copy and 24s per year in the UK and 26s overseas. There were ninety-two advertisements for products like "Carter's Little Liver Pills," "Alliance Insurance, "Force Cereal," and "Red, White and Blue Coffee;" and convents, schools, and colleges. On one page there were twenty-eight "situations." It was a profitable newspaper.

113. WDA. Instructions.

114. St Mary's Abbey Archives, Logbook: "The Cardinal's old white horse and its disposal."

115. Snead-Cox, 2, p.492; WDA. Instructions.

116. WDA. Instructions; MHA.

117. MHA. Box 25, HCV, and Box 45, copies of death certificates; And: St Mary's Abbey Archives, Logbook, 4 September, 1908: "Miss Hanmer, who had been ailing and confined to bed for some days, died this morning at 7 a.m. She was one of the oldest friends of the Mothers from 1868, and though for a period when the Mothers had to assert their independence in the management of the Industrial School, the friendship had cooled somewhat, she had responded well when the meetings for Tertiaries were organized by Mother Abbess in February 1889 and her heart had been quite won over again when Mother accepted the Uganda Missions (1902)"; 8 September: Feast of Our Lady's Nativity: "Miss Hanmer's funeral took place today. Our dear Mother and several of the Sisters attended it. A few days after, Miss Hanmer's brother, who was seeing to her affairs, asked dear Mother to come down and advise him as to the disposal of some of her religious objects! He is a Protestant. Miss Hanmer left dear Mother a legacy of 5 pounds. During the Retreat our dear Mother had been down to 'The Rosary' herself and had sent some of the sisters."

118. MHA. *The Universe*, 20 October 1961.

119. *ibid.*

120. MHA. Carmelite Convent, Chichester, 26 November 1966, to Fr General.

121. MHA. Sr Miriam Teresa, 16 April 1967, to Fr Thonnen.

122. MHA. HCV. Box 45; Another article places Goodier's speech at the close of celebrations remembering Vaughan's initiation of the work in 1863 that led to the founding of the missionary college. It took place at Mill Hill on 12 June 1933: "a striking feature of the celebrations being a play depicting various incidents of the Cardinal's life which was written and produced by the students of the College." See: Francis J. Bowen, "Cardinal Vaughan," *Catholic World*, 1933, vol 136, p.540.

123. Lenten Pastoral, Westminster, in *The Tablet*, 13 February 1932.

124. "The Cardinal's last message to the Peter Boys," 18 June 1903. The original marble tablet is preserved in the entrance of St Peter's House, Freshfield.

125. "Memorial to Cardinal Vaughan," *The Tablet*, 5 March 1904, p.394.

126. WDA. Instructions. John Snead-Cox continued to be editor of *The Tablet* until his retirement in 1920. During the First World War he and his wife lost their two eldest sons, killed within a few days of each other at Ypres in 1914, and the third at the battle of Jutland. After his retirement he kept an active interest in world affairs and *The Tablet* despite failing eyesight. On his death in Leominster, Hereford, on 30 December 1939, *The Tablet* reported that his Life of Herbert Vaughan remained a "first-rate piece of work" largely because of the self-effacing role of the biographer; it was a role which came without difficulty to a man who had for so long been completely content to be the lieutenant, in one of his enterprises, of the man whose life he was uniquely well-fitted to write. "Catholic journalism has had many men who have been more widely-known in their day, but it has no man to point to who, for a longer period, set and maintained a higher standard of disinterested work for the Church." *The Tablet*, 6 January 1940, p.21.

Epilogue

There is no simple story of Herbert Vaughan. Anyone who ventures an opinion of him needs to consider how he faced matters of life and death. He expressed his views often in the prayers he left behind. One is found in the old prayer book used by his missionaries: "I offer Him all, I ask to be allowed to surrender every fibre, He alone being the Master of every string and note belonging to me. He may take away my health and capacity, send me failure and public dishonour—dry up my soul like the dust, if only He will support me, and let me love Him and serve Him." In another place—a reflection on the shortness of life—he pictures himself "standing with Jesus and Mary on the shore of eternity, looking back over the journey of life just completed." He prays for the wisdom to grasp "each elusive moment and mak[e] it count in terms of eternal merit." How Herbert Vaughan translated his theology into experience was a success that was out of the ordinary. His legacies reflect his greatness. They were his great projects, his qualities of spirit, his loyal friends and supporters, and his world-wide vision.

The often-heard criticism that he was a medieval lord-prelate is refuted by his genuine humility and simplicity. Protestant opponents, men such as Lord Halifax, as well as Catholics such as von Hügel and Snead-Cox, could describe raising disagreements with Vaughan personally and rousing his anger, when he would end up hearing them out and even changing his mind. Vaughan's humility and simplicity were such, one wrote, that a person might not fear to speak bluntly to him. There is a great strength here and an example for any of us. I found no vindictiveness in Herbert Vaughan, nor conceit about his position in English society and the Church. And where he recognized the less than noble in himself he tried to root it out. This struggle contributed to the grimness about Vaughan commented on by Manning and others.

His unpopularity with fellow Catholics originated more in issues than in appearances; for example, his experiences at St Edmund's College in the 1850s, when he championed Rome and Manning and antagonized others with his youthful arrogance. The struggle with the Old Catholics continued during the 1860s, especially in *The Tablet*, and throughout his career. One need only compare the battle between Nicholas Wiseman and his coadjutor and chapter in the 1850s and 1860s with Westminster diocese in the 1890s to see the outcome of that struggle as success for the Roman Church. His country was unfriendly to the restoration of the Roman Catholic hierarchy and he missed no opportunity to remind people that he was a leader of the Church of St Peter, Augustine and the Pope.

His position on the Fenians at Salford and Ireland's struggle for Home Rule did not endear him to others. A look at population statistics for the Catholic Church when they included Ireland and her more than seventy-three members of Parliament suggests a forceful reason for Vaughan to object to Home Rule, a turn of events that would emphasize the true minority status of the Catholic Church in the British Isles.

The weakness of Vaughan's leadership was his need to be active, not always with the mundane, but with the great schemes he knew might be realized if only he applied himself, so much so that he could not remain long at a task at hand. He had energy and wanderlust—in noble causes—but had difficulty in applying himself to any one task for long.

The Downside Benedictines recognized this when he enquired about joining them. They told him that he would need more "elbow room" than they could offer. At Rome he may have attended classes but there is no record of his doing so in his diaries. The entries describe people he met, places he visited and events he witnessed. At one place he complains of illness and inability to pursue the regimen of study. He was ordained early, possibly near death. At St Edmund's there are hints that there was more to Vaughan's unpopularity among staff and older students than his status as an Oblate and "espionage" on behalf of Manning. He was very often away. Yet he was vice-president at a boarding school and responsible for the students' infirmary among other duties. He also regularly visited his family who were then living in London, founded and built the small mission in Hereford and assisted on week-ends at various missions in the area. He also found time to visit the Continent, continuing to add to his information about seminary training, and was part of the Oblate community at Bayswater.

Despite his ill health, he travelled to Rome and Spain where he completed his grand scheme to have the Catholic Church in England take a part in the evangelization of the world. His travels to the Americas speak for his energy, vision and courage. But even the great project of his life, St Joseph's Missionary College, was not enough. He was an initiator, a fund raiser and recruiter. He found caring for a missionary college was too confining, especially when he did not have the help he hoped for from the Oblates. He was very soon searching for others to take it over, starting with his model, the Paris Foreign Missionary Society. Even while he was rector of the college he was often away. Often he was at Archbishop Manning's residence, where he had a room. His health failed due to his austerities at Mill Hill and he was drawn to other activities. He bought the Catholic news journal, *The Tablet*, and is described during the first weeks as sleeping at his desk. But that did not continue; he was soon off to Rome to fight battles for Manning or on behalf of his missionary college, and a sub-editor was employed.

When he went to Salford he seemed to be doing several major works at the same time. He was away from Mill Hill but visited the American mission and paid regular visits to the college. His letters to Lady Elizabeth Herbert describe him recruiting on the Continent or visiting the Pope and Propaganda Fide in Rome. During the dispute with the religious orders he was absent from his diocese for one and a half years. Problems experienced by his missionaries in America and elsewhere can be laid in part at his feet. Poor communication and failure to work out the details of their commitments were often attributable to Herbert Vaughan. Even during his years at Westminster he was often travelling or ill, and the administration of the diocese was left in the hands of others. Snead-Cox notes that this contributed to his not knowing his own clergy.

Any weaknesses in Vaughan's work can often be traced to his temperament and health problems and a consequent inability to take on the everyday tasks of his office as a seminarian, Church leader or founder.

But Herbert Vaughan had a grand vision of what might be accomplished by hard work and prayer and in this he was enthusiastic; it was a contagious enthusiasm. He questioned the bright and the wise, and recorded their ideas and experiences He added information—sometimes from unlikely sources—uncovered by his inquisitiveness during his travels. He was a very effective recruiter and fund raiser. To enable his projects to function he gathered around him loyal and hardworking people, clergy and lay, who shared his vision, or wished they could. Lay people were the first members of St Joseph's Missionary Society of the Sacred Heart. The Rescue Society had over two thousand volunteers when he left Salford. The work on Westminster Cathedral was never interrupted by lack of funds from subscribers. The contributions of Herbert, Ward, Benoit, Gadd, Moyes, Fenton, Johnson and Oates are, with many others, very much part of the successes of Herbert Vaughan and the endurance of his foundations.

He had a vision of the Church as the Rock of St Peter, providing stability in a time of revolution, the papacy standing firm for unity after three hundred years of reformation in his country. As unpalatable as his views about authority and modern philosophy and liberalism may seem today, they were part of his vision.

One of his grandest visions was the missionary training college and society he founded at Mill Hill. His thoughts, and his correspondence, reached many parts of the world. Jesus' instruction to teach all nations motivated him to dream of Wales and Japan, guided him to the Americas and the gold mines of California, to a plan for African-Americans to join the "Back to Africa" movement for the evangelization of that continent, to India, Borneo, New Zealand and East Africa. He was admired for his missionary enthusiasm, knowledge and commitment, not only in England but by the bishops of the United States. The expanding British Empire, seen on the coloured maps of his day, beckoned and challenged him to action.

Another of his grand visions was Westminster Cathedral. It was not to be primarily the bishop's church or, as some have described it, a symbol of Catholic triumphalism. Not only did he want a place where the official liturgy could be performed, as a centre for the worship and prayer of the English Church, but he dreamed of a cathedral that was alive, the head and heart of the Roman Catholic community. He saw it as a "Catholic arsenal" that sent out lecturers and missionaries and within its walls had a library and meeting places to inspire the laity. And its ceremonies and music would be models for all to follow. He wanted to have it ready for the fiftieth anniversary of the restoration of the hierarchy but failed by three years. It was to be a cathedral set up at the centre of the British Empire, in the very heart of London, near to Westminster Abbey, "the ancient shrine of the old religion of the land." Peter Doyle vindicates Vaughan's vision in his recently published book, *Westminster Cathedral, 1895-1995*. Vaughan may sound "worthy but pedestrian," he writes, but such an image is incomplete for one needs to look at what he was able to accomplish with his skills and his limitations.

Herbert Vaughan's lifelong habit of regular prayer was what enabled him to accomplish so much. Prayer put the activities and relationships of his life in a perspective that looked at everything in terms of eternity rather than time.

There used to be a motto over the cloister entrance to the library at St Joseph's College, Mill Hill. "It doesn't matter who does the work," it read, "as long as the work is done." They were Vaughan's words. The work was to be done, in spite of every obstacle, by apostles in God's service. His words can often chill with their impersonal severity and spirit of self-sacrifice, but the accomplishments they led to, and their legacy, cannot be denied.

The Times of Friday December 1 1995 reported that Queen Elizabeth II had attended Vespers at Westminster Cathedral on St Andrew's Day to mark the end of the centenary celebrations. "It was held to mark the 100th anniversary of this 'Christian-Byzantine style' building, which Cardinal Vaughan began to construct in 1895. But the service is more likely to be remembered for a different reason. By her presence in the cathedral yesterday, Her Majesty the Queen became the first British monarch since the Elizabethan Settlement to attend a Roman Catholic service in this country."

The *Daily Telegraph* called her presence "an unprecedented gesture of friendship and recognition to Britain's Catholic community by the head of the Church of England. "

The Queen sat alone below the altar and listened to a welcome by Cardinal Basil Hume: "In 1982, Your Majesty received Pope John Paul into your London home. That was, for us, the healing of many ancient wounds. We were so grateful. The presence of Your Majesty in this cathedral is for us a further affirmation of the place that we Catholics have in the nation."

One of the 1500 Catholics present commented: "There is a very great burden of history in this country and the Queen's presence has gone some way to dealing with that."

Selected Bibliography

Note

The following is a selection of the more important sources. Full bibliographical references are found at the end of each chapter. Herbert Vaughan left little of his correspondence for posterity. The Westminster archive holds the Vaughan material on a few shelves. Salford, where he spent twenty years, has hardly anything but the ACTA. However, his diaries, quoted by Snead-Cox, have reappeared at Westminster. At the same time a diary at Mill Hill referred to by McCormack has disappeared. An important source is the Carmelite Archives at Notting Hill, where the community preserves approximately one hundred letters written by Cardinal Vaughan to the foundress, Mother Mary of Jesus.

Archives and Repositories

Archdiocese of Lucca Archive
Archdiocese of New York Archives
Archives of Propaganda Fide
Carmelite Archives, Notting Hill
Catholic Truth Society
Clwyd County Council Archives
Courtfield, Mill Hill, Archives
Downside Abbey Archives
Daughters of Charity, British Province, Archives
Franciscan Missionary Sisters' Archives
General Theological Seminary Library, New York
Greater London Records Office
Gwent County Records Office
Jesuit Archives: Pamploma, Grenada, Valladolid
Josephite Archives
London Records Office, Colindale
Maryknoll Archives
Mill Hill Archives
Mount St Bernard's Abbey Archives
Notre Dame University Archives
Paulist Archives, Washington

Presentation Sisters Archives, San Francisco
St Beuno's Archives
St Mary's Abbey Archives
Salford Diocesan Archives
Scottish Catholic Archives
Society of the Divine Word Archives
Society of Jesus, English Province, Department of Historiography
    and Archives
Stonyhurst College Archives
Surrey Archives
Vaughan Family Archives
Visitation Sisters, Waldron
Westminster Diocesan Archives
Yuba County Library, Marysville

Printed

Appleby, R. Scott,"Church and Age Unite!" *The Modernist Impulse in Ameri-can Catholicism*, Notre Dame, University of Notre Dame Press, 1992.
Beck, George, editor, *The English Catholics, 1850-1950*, London, Burns & Oates, 1950.
Bence-Jones, Mark, *The Catholic Families*, London, Constable, 1992.
Birt, Henry Norbert, *Benedictine Pioneers in Australia*, 2 vols, London, Herbert and Daniel, 1911.
Bolton, Charles, *Salford Diocese and its Catholic Past*, London, Hollis & Carter, 1950.
Bossey, *The English Catholic Community, 1570-1850*, London, Darton, Longman & Todd, 1976.
Breffy, G. *Notre Dame des Victoires*, Paris, Librairie Letouzey et Ané, 1925.
Bruce, Gordon, *Charlie Rolls*, Derby, Rolls-Royce Heritage Trust, 1990.
Callahan, William, *Church, Politics and Society in Spain, 1750-1874*, London, Harvard, 1984.
Carmelite Sister, A, *In the Silence of Mary, The Life of Mother Mary of Jesus, Carmelite Prioress and Foundress, 1851-1942*, London, Notting Hill, 1964.
Chadwick, Owen, *The Victorian Church*, 2 vols, London, Adam and Charles Black, 1972.
Clifton, Michael, *The Quiet Negotiator*, Formby, Print originata.
Condon, Kevin, *The Missionary College of All Hallows*, Dublin, All Hallows, 1986.
Cruickshank, *Church and State in English Education*, London, Macmillan, 1963
Curry, Ann, *Mother Teresa Comerford*, San Francisco, 1980.
De l'Hôpital, Winifride, *Westminster Cathedral and its Architect*, 2 vols, London, Hutchinson, 1919.

Davies, John, *A History of Wales*, London, Penguin, 1994.

Considine, Daniel, *The Virtues of the Divine Child*, London, Manresa, 1929.

Doyle, Peter, *Westminster Cathedral, 1895-1995*, London, Chapman, 1995.

Dwyer, John, *Condemned to the Mines, The Life of Eugene O'Connell, 1815-1891*, New York, Vantage, 1976.

Evans, Gwynfor, *Land of My Fathers*, Talybont, Y Lolfa Cyf, 1992.

Fielding, Stephen, *Class and ethnicity, Irish Catholics in England, 1880-1939*, Buckingham, Open University, 1993.

Gale, H. P., *Uganda and the Mill Hill Fathers*, London, Macmillan, 1959.

Germaine, Sister, *The Franciscan Missionaries of St Joseph*, Glasgow, Burns and Sons, 1983.

Gray, Robert, *Cardinal Manning*, London, Weidenfeld, 1985.

Gribbin, W. T., *St Edmund's College Bicentenary Book,1793-1993*, Old Hall, 1993.

Guilday, Peter, *The English Catholic Refugees on the Continent, 1558-1795*, London, Longmans, 1914.

Herbert, Elizabeth, *A Short History of the origin of St Joseph's Society of the Sacred Heart for Foreign Missions and of the Foreign Missionary College at Mill Hill*, London, 1901.

Hewitson, A., *Stonyhurst College, Past and Present*, Preston, Chronicle, 1878.

Hogan, Edmund, *The Irish Missionary Movement*, Dublin, Gill and Macmillan, 1990.

Holmes, Derek, *More Roman than Rome*, London, Burns & Oates, 1978.

Hughes, John Jay, *Absolutely Null and Utterly Void*, London, Sheed and Ward, 1968.

James, D'Ambrose, *A History of the Church in Wales*, Carmarthen, Spurrell, 1926.

Jedin, Hubert, ed., *History of the Church*, 10 vols, London, Burns & Oates; New York, Crossroad, 1980-81.

Kelly, Bernard, *English Catholic Missions*, London, Kegan Paul, 1907.

Kelly, Bernard W., "The Life of the Very Rev. Daniel Rock," in *The Church of Our Fathers* by Daniel Rock, vol 1, London, John Murray, 1905.

Kidd, Alan, *Manchester*, Keele, Keele University, 1993.

Klaiber, Jeffrey, *The Catholic Church in Peru, 1821-1985*, Washington, Catholic University, 1988.

Klught, James v d, and Conroy, Michael, *The Opening Door, Mill Hill Mission to Afghanistan: 1879-92*, Rawalpindi, 1979.

Kollar, René, *Westminster Cathedral, from dream to reality*, Edinburgh, Faith and Life, 1987.

———, *The Return of the English Benedictines to London, Ealing Abbey, 1896 to Independence*, Tunbridge Wells, Burns & Oates, 1889.

Leslie, Shane, *The Letters of Herbert Cardinal Vaughan to Lady Herbert of Lea, 1867-1903*, London, Burns & Oates, 1942.

————, *Henry Edward Manning*, London, Burns, Oates & Washbourne, 1921.

Lovat, Lady, *Clare Vaughan*, London, Burns & Oates, 1887.

MacCaffrey, James, *History of the Catholic Church in the Nineteenth Century*, vol 2, Dublin, Gill, 1909.

Martindale, C. C., *Bernard Vaughan, SJ*, London, Longmans, 1924.

Mathew, David, *Catholicism in England*, London, Eyre and Spottiswoode, 1936.

Matthews, John Hobson, *The Hundred of Wormlow*, Hereford, 1915

————, *The Vaughans of Courtfield*, London, Sands, 1912.

McCormack, Arthur, *Cardinal Vaughan*, London, Burns & Oates, 1966.

McClelland, V. A., *English Roman Catholics and Higher Education, 1830-1903*, Oxford, Clarendon, 1973.

————, *Cardinal Manning: His Public Life and Influence, 1865-1892*, London. Oxford Univ. Press, 1962.

McGloin, John, *California's First Archbishop: The Life of Joseph Sadoc Alemany, OP, 1814-1888*, New York, Herder & Herder, 1966.

Mill Hill Father, A, *Remembered in Blessing*, Glasgow, Sands, 1955.

Mill Hill Sister, A, *Light after Darkness*, Glasgow, Burns and Sons, 1962.

Muir, T. E., *Stonyhurst College, 1593-1993*, London, James & James, 1992.

Mulheran, Thomas, *Catholic Children's Rescue Centenary, 1886-1986*, Glasgow, John Burns, 1986.

Murphy, James, *Church State and Schools in Britain, 1800-1970*, London, Routledge and Kegan Paul.

Murphy, John Nicholas, *Terra Incognita or Convents of the United Kingdom*, London, Longmans, 1873.

Nemer, Lawrence, *Anglican and Roman Catholic Attitudes on Missions*, St Augustin, Steyer, 1981.

Newman, John Henry, *St Stephen Harding, The Cistercian Saints of England*, London, Toovey, 1844.

Newsome, David, *The Convert Cardinals*, London, John Murray, 1993.

————, *The Parting of Friends*, London, John Murray, 1966.

Nitti, Francesco, *Catholic Socialism*, London, Swan, 1895.

Norman, Edward, *The English Catholic Church in the 19th Century*, Oxford, Clarendon Press, 1984.

O'Brien, David, *Isaac Hecker*, New York, Paulist Press, 1992.

Ochs, Stephen, *Desegregating the Altar, Baton Rouge*, Louisiana State University, 1990.

Purcell, Edmund, *The Life of Cardinal Manning*, London, Macmillan, 1896.

Ralls, Christopher, *The Catholic Truth Society, a New History*, London, CTS, 1993.

Renault, Francois, *Cardinal Lavigerie*, London, Athlone Press, 1994.

Rooney, John, *Struggling to the Prophets*, St Louis, Mill Hill, 1991.

————, *On the Heels of Battle*, Rawalpindi, 1986.

————, *Khabar Gembira*, Tunbridge Wells, Burns & Oates, 1981.

Ros, F. U., *Mill Hill, 100 Jaar in Nederland 1890-1990*, Roosedaal, Bijeen, 1990.

St John, Edward, *Manning's Work for Children*, London, Sheed and Ward.

Seaman, L. C. B., *Victorian England*, London, Routledge,1973

Snead-Cox, John, *The Life of Cardinal Vaughan*, 2 vols, London, Burns & Oates, 1911.

Schiefen, Richard, *Nicholas Wiseman and the Transformation of English Catholicism*, Shepherdstown, Patmos, 1984.

Ullathorne, Bishop, *History of the Restoration of the Catholic Hierarchy in England*, London, Burns & Oates, 1871.

Schultenover, David, *George Tyrrell—In Search of Catholicism*, Shepherdstown, Patmos, 1981.

————, *A View From Rome, On the Eve of the Modernist Crisis*, Fordham, 1993.

Simmons, E. R., *Pompallier, Prince of Bishops, Auckland*, Catholic Publications Centre, 1984.

Sutherland, Gillian, *Policy-Making in Elementary Education, 1870-1895*, Oxford, Oxford University Press, 1975.

Swift, Roger, and Gilley, Sheridan, *The Irish in the Victorian City*, London, Croom Helm, 1985.

Tavard, George, *A Review of Anglican Orders*, Collegeville, Glazier, 1990.

Vaughan, Herbert, *The Young Priest*, London, Burns & Oates, 1904.

Vaughan, Herbert, trans., *Humility of Heart*, by Cajetan Mary da Bergamo, Rockford, TAN, 1978.

Vaughan, Joseph, *A Monastic Autobiography of Twenty-five Years*, Salford, Roberts, 1894.

Vaughan, Mary, *Courtfield and the Vaughans*, London, Quiller, 1989.

Walsh, Henry, *Hallowed Were the Gold Dust Trails*, Santa Clara, 1946.

Walsh, Michael, *The Tablet, 1840-1990*, London, 1990.

Ward, Bernard, *The Sequel to Catholic Emancipation*, 2 vols, New York, Longmans, 1915.

————, *A History of St Edmund's College*, Old Hall, London, Kegan Paul, 1893.

Ward, Maisie, *The Wilfrid Wards and the Transition*, London, Sheed and Ward, 1934.

————, *Insurrection versus Resurrection*, London, Sheed and Ward, 1937.

Ward, Wilfrid, *William George Ward and the Oxford Movement*, London, Macmillan, 1889.

————, *The Life and Times of Cardinal Wiseman*, London, Longmans, 1897.

Webb, R. K., *Modern England*, New York, Harper and Row, 1968.

Weightman, Gavin, and Humphries, *The Making of Modern London, 1815-1914*, London, Sidgwick and Jackson, 1983.

Wiest, Jean-Paul, *Maryknoll in China*, New York, Sharpe, 1988.
Williams, Michael, *St Alban's College, Valladolid*, London, Hurot, 1986.
Wilson, J. Anselm, *The Life of Bishop Hedley*, London, Burns & Oates, 1929.

Articles

Throughout the text frequent references are made to *The Tablet*, *Dublin Review*, *The Edmundian*, *Baeda*, *The Harvest*, *Recusant History*, *Journal of Ecclesiastical History*, and *Millhilliana*, among others. The following are a few of the more important.

Arx, Jeffrey von, "Manning's Ultramontanism,' *Recusant History*, vol 19, May 1988.
Bolton, C. A., "Cardinal Vaughan as Educator," *Clergy Review*, October 1947, vol xxviii, no 4, pp.237-245.
Bray, John, "The Roman Catholic Mission to Ladakh, 1888-1898, *Millhilliana*, no 4, 1993, pp.124-30.
Britten, James, "The Catholic Truth Society," *Dublin Review*, no 34, April 1887, pp.408-414.
Casartelli, Louis, "The Late Cardinal Vaughan," *The Harvest*, no 192, September 1903, vol xvi, pp.206-7.
Connolly, Gerard, "The Transubstantiation of Myth: towards a new popular history of 19th century Catholicism in England," *JEH*, Jan 1984, vol 35, no 1, p.78ff.
De Muelenaere, J., "Canon Pieter Benoit," *Overdruk uit Handellingen van het Genootschap*, 'Société d'Emulation' te Brugge, deel cvii, 1970.
Dickie, Ian, "Herbert Cardinal Vaughan and His Cathedral," in *Westminster Cathedral, 1895-1995*, pp.11-21, Westminster, 1995.
Doyle, Peter, "The Education and Training of Roman Catholic priests in 19th-Century England," *JEH*, vol 35, no 2, April 1984.
Duffy, C. J., "An Aristocrat in an Unaristocratic Community," *Footprints*, March 1979, vol 3, no 8, pp.23-4.
Ellis, John Tracey, "A Challenge to the American Church on its One Hundredth Birthday," *Catholic Historical Review*, vol xxx, October 1944, pp.290-98.
Gilley, Sheridan, "The Roman Catholic Church and the Nineteenth-Century Irish Diaspora," *JEH*, vol 35, April 1984.
———, "Loss and Gain: Conversions to Catholicism in Britain, 1800-1994," *Friends of Cardinal Newman Newsletter*, Christmas 1994, pp.4-8.
Greene, Gwendolen Plunket, "Recollections of Lady Herbert of Lea," *Pax*, Prinknash, Spring 1943, vol xxxi, no 226, pp.5-13.
Gwynn, Denis, "England and the Foreign Missions," *Clergy Review*, vol xxvi, no 2, February 1946, pp.46-65.

Hedley, Bishop, "Loyal in Life and Death," London, Burns & Oates, 1881.

Herbert, Lady, "Some Further notes on Cardinal Vaughan's work when beginning the Foreign Missionary College," London, Wyman, no date.

———, "How I came Home," London, Catholic Truth Society, 1893.

Hogan, Peter, "Josephite History," *Josephite Harvest*, vol 95, 1995.

Kollar, René, "Bishops and Benedictines: The Case of Father Richard O'Halloran," *JEH*, vol 38, no 3, July 1987, pp.362-85.

Lilly, W. S., "Cardinal Vaughan," *Nineteenth Century*, August 1910, p.284ff.

Leslie, Shane, "Missing Letters of Cardinal Vaughan to Lady Herbert of Lea, 1867-1903," *Dublin Review*, Autumn 1947, vol 220, pp.97-115.

Matthews, John Hobson, "The Catholic Mission of Monmouth," Catholic Record Society, vol ix, London, 1911, p.131ff.

McClelland, V. A., "The Making of Young Imperialists: Rev. Thomas Seddon, Lord Archibald Douglas and the Resettling of British Catholic Orphans in Canada," *Recusant History*, vol 19, 1989.

———,"O Felix Roma! Henry Manning, Cutts Robinson and Sacerdotal Formation, 1862-1872," *Recusant History*, vol 21, no 2, October 1992, pp.180-217.

———, "Herbert Vaughan, The Cambridge Teachers' Training Syndicate, and the Public Schools, 1894-1899," *Paedagogia Historica*, xvi, 1975, pp.16-38.

Meynell, Sebastian, "Lady Herbert of Lea," *Catholic World*, vol xciv, January 1912, p.305ff.

Mullins, Daniel, "The Welsh Harvest: Where are the Labourers?," *Millhilliana*, no 1,1987, pp.19-22.

Newsome, David, "Cardinal Manning and his influence on the Church and Nation," *Recusant History*, vol 21, no 2, October 1992, pp.136-51.

Pereiro, James, "'Truth Before Peace': Manning and Infallibility," *Recusant History*, vol 21, no 2, October 1992, pp.218-253.

Portier, William, "John R. Slattery's Vision for the Evangelization of American Blacks," *US Catholic Historian*, 1986.

Rafferty, Oliver, "The Jesuit College, Manchester, 1875," *Recusant History*, vol 20, no 2, October 1990.

———, "Nicholas Wiseman, Ecclesiastical Politics and Anglo-Irish Relations in the Mid-Nineteenth Century," *Recusant History*, vol 21, no 3, May 1993.

Richards, J. W., "Cardinal Vaughan and Downside," correspondence, *Downside Review*, no 88, vol xxx, March 21, 1911, pp.133-36.

Schiefen, Richard, "Some aspects of the Controversy between Cardinal Wiseman and the Westminster Chapter," *JEH*, vol xxi, no 2, April 1970.

Scully, E., "May Vaughan: 1845-1884," *The Month*, vol clxvii, April 1936, pp.354-357.

Smith, Sydney, "The Life of Cardinal Vaughan," *The Month*, vol 116, July 1910.

Vaughan, Herbert, "California and the Church, a Report by Herbert Vaughan," *Dublin Review*, January 1866, pp.14-35.

————, ed, "Our Duty to the Heathen: A Sermon by the Archbishop of Westminster with Speeches and Letters by Clergy and Laity," London, Burns & Oates, 1896.

————, "The Evangelization of Africa," *Dublin Review*, January–April 1879, pp.182-208.

————, "Three Letters of Herbert Cardinal Vaughan to his Missionaries," Madras, Good Pastor, 1917.

————, "A Letter on the Confraternity of Our Lady of Compassion by Herbert Cardinal Vaughan," London, Burns & Oates, 1897.

Vaughan, John, "Reminiscences of the Late Bishop Hedley," *Ampleforth Journal*, vol 22, no 3, May 1916, pp.291-3.

Walsh, James, "The Catholic Church and Popular Feeling in South America," *Records of the American Catholic Historical Society of Philadelphia*, vol xv 1904, p.173ff.

Ward, Bernard, "Cardinal Vaughan," *The Edmundian*, vol v, no 31, July 1903, p.103ff.

Some unpublished Sources

Hanrahan, Noel, "The Apostolic Spirit of Herbert Cardinal Vaughan," Rome, Ph.D. thesis, no 2876, 1957.

Lannon, David, "Bishop Turner and Educational Provision within the Salford Diocesan area, 1840-1970," M. Phil. thesis, University of Hull, Sept 1994.

McInally, Mary P., "Edward Ilsley, Man of the People," unpublished MS, 1995.

Index

GENERAL THEOLOGICAL SEMINARY
NEW YORK

DATE DUE

Printed
in USA

HIGHSMITH #45230